CRICK... 3

ED...

All...

FOREWORD

What a difference a year makes! A few days ago, England fell an agonising two runs short of recording a unique winter clean sweep of five Test victories out of five, losing to New Zealand in Wellington by one run. The combination of head coach Brendon McCullum and captain Ben Stokes has utterly transformed the England men's Test side after the nadir of last winter's efforts against Australia and West Indies. So-called 'Bazball' – fearless, positive cricket played with a smile (even from Jimmy Anderson) – has made the team one of the most compelling to watch in generations. Run-rates of more than five an over and successful run chases of 300-plus have become commonplace, rather than the statistical outliers they truly are. Like the team of a decade ago, newcomers settle in and perform well immediately: Harry Brook, Matty Potts and record-breaking youngster Rehan Ahmed have all looked at home from the start.

Two big challenges await England this summer. Unlike his all-rounder predecessors, Ian Botham and Andrew Flintoff, Stokes has thrived and grown as a player with the captaincy, revealing astute tactical awareness and a remarkable ability to inspire those around him; he also has developed a habit of giving his best performances when the pressure is most intense. To my mind, the debate about England's greatest all-rounder in my lifetime is now settled in his favour. But the knee problem that hobbled him in the Wellington run-chase is a long-running issue, and there is no obvious replacement for him as player or captain. He will need to be at his best in both roles if England are to regain the Ashes this summer. It is set to be a titanic and entertaining battle, with Australia looking a formidable outfit with few weaknesses. England still have their frailties, especially at the top of the order, but their character is not in question.

At the domestic level, most readers of the *Annual* will have welcomed the retention of the 14-match County Championship season, which is the bedrock of our game and which continues to attract some of the world's best cricketers. It is the importance of the counties as *clubs* that struck me when Northamptonshire's long-serving scorer Tony Kingston decided to step down over the winter. In his resignation letter, he noted how between 1990 and 2018 he had not missed a single full day's play in all that time. An injury and a family funeral meant he missed one session of play in each case, and a further two overs were lost to pick up an award; in total, he missed just 66 overs in almost 30 years. It is hard to imagine anyone displaying such enduring support and loyalty to a franchise. Tony has been a great help and supporter of *Playfair*, so I want to both acknowledge his largely unsung work here and to wish him a long and happy retirement. At all levels of the game, cricket really does rely on such people to ensure it functions as well as it does.

This year's cover star is Sam Curran, of Surrey and England, and the first to be shown bowling left-arm over (an omission I'm personally delighted to rectify!). He played a relatively brief part in his side's County Championship success, but was central to England's ICC T20 World Cup triumph, earning both the Man of the Match award in the final against Pakistan and the Man of the Series prize. The paymasters at the IPL duly took note, and the Punjab Kings recruited him for a record £1.85 million contract for 2023. His performances in Bangladesh this month show how he can set the subcontinent alight, not just in the IPL but also in the World Cup in India this autumn, when he will need to play a key role if England are to defend their title. That England hold both white-ball world titles shows how far they have come in the shorter formats; their progress in the red-ball format is about to face the acid test in the Ashes. It should be a special summer. I hope this year's *Playfair Cricket Annual* keeps you company throughout.

Ian Marshall
Eastbourne, 13 March 2023

ACKNOWLEDGEMENTS AND THANKS

This book could not have been compiled without the assistance of many people giving so generously of their time and expertise, so I must thank the following for all they have done to help ensure this edition of *Playfair Cricket Annual* could be written:

At the counties, I would like to thank the following for their help over the last year: Derbyshire – Stephen Martin and John Brown; Durham – Sam Blacklock and William Dobson; Essex – Ashley Neave and Tony Choat; Glamorgan – Andrew Hignell; Gloucestershire – Lizzie Allen and Adrian Bull; Hampshire – Tim Tremlett and Alan Mills; Kent – Freddie Young and Lorne Hart; Lancashire – Diana Lloyd; Leicestershire – Dan Nice and Paul Rogers; Middlesex – Steven Fletcher and Don Shelley; Northamptonshire – Tony Kingston and Terry Owen; Nottinghamshire – Mick Newell, Matthew Freeman and Roger Marshall; Somerset – Polly Rhodes; Surrey – Steve Howes and Debbie Beesley; Sussex – Colin Bowley and Graham Irwin; Warwickshire – Keith Cook and Mel Smith; Worcestershire – Carrie Lloyd and Sue Drinkwater; Yorkshire – Cecilia Allen and John Potter.

Thanks to Alan Fordham for the Principal Fixtures, Andy Smith for the Second XI Fixtures, Richard Logan for the National County Fixtures. I am hugely grateful as always to Philip Bailey for providing the first-class, List A and T20 career records.

At Headline, my thanks as ever go to Jonathan Taylor for his unwavering support throughout the year; Louise Rothwell keeps me on schedule and ensures the Annual is printed at great speed; Zoe Giles was so helpful with the *Playfair* website last summer, ensuring it provided all the latest information on newcomers. Helen Trotter took over from John Skermer as the proof reader this year, and I hope she found the experience an enlightening one, as it's certainly a different challenge to most proofing jobs. At Letterpart, Chris Leggett and Caroline Leggett undertook their thirtieth edition as the typesetters – I know how much I would struggle to make it all work without them.

As always, thanks to my daughters, Kiri and Sophia, for keeping a low profile at the end (it's shocking to realise that when I took over the *Annual* in February 2009 they hadn't yet started school – and now they're both doing A levels; and to my wife, Sugra, for her patience and understanding. Thank you all.

TOURING TEAMS REGISTER 2023

Neither Ireland nor Australia had selected their 2023 touring teams at the time of going to press. The following players, who had represented those teams in Test matches since 20 November 2021, were still available for selection:

AUSTRALIA

Full Names	Birthdate	Birthplace	Team	Type	F-C Debut
AGAR, Ashton Charles	14.10.93	Melbourne	W Australia	LHB/SLA	2012-13
BOLAND, Scott Michael	11.04.89	Melbourne	Victoria	RHB/RFM	2011-12
CAREY, Alex Tyson	27.08.91	Loxton	S Australia	LHB/WK	2012-13
CUMMINS, Patrick James	08.05.93	Sydney	NSW	RHB/RF	2010-11
GREEN, Cameron David	03.06.99	Subiaco	W Australia	RHB/RFM	2016-17
HANDSCOMB, Peter Stephen Patrick	26.04.91	Box Hill	Victoria	RHB/OB	2011-12
HAZLEWOOD, Josh Reginald	08.01.91	Tamworth	NSW	LHB/RFM	2008-09
HEAD, Travis Michael	29.12.93	Adelaide	S Australia	LHB/OB	2011-12
KHAWAJA, Usman Tariq	18.12.86	Islamabad, Pak	Queensland	LHB/RM	2007-08
KUHNEMANN, Matthew Paul	20.09.96	Brisbane	Queensland	LHB/SLA	2020-21
LABUSCHAGNE, Marnus	22.06.94	Klerksdorp, SA	Queensland	RHB/LB	2014-15
LYON, Nathan Michael	20.11.87	Young	NSW	RHB/OB	2010-11
MURPHY, Todd R.	15.11.00	Echuca	Victoria	RHB/OB	2020-21
NESER, Michael Gertges	29.03.90	Pretoria, SA	Queensland	RHB/RMF	2010-11
RENSHAW, Matthew Thomas	28.03.96	Middlesbrough, Eng	Queensland	LHB/OB	2014-15
SMITH, Steven Peter Devereux	02.06.89	Sydney	NSW	RHB/LB	2007-08
SWEPSON, Mitchell Joseph	04.10.93	Brisbane	Queensland	RHB/LB	2015-16
WARNER, David Andrew	27.10.86	Paddington	NSW	LHB/LB	2008-09

For the Ireland register, go to page 319 for further details.

ENGLAND v AUSTRALIA

SERIES RECORDS
1876-77 to 2021-22

HIGHEST INNINGS TOTALS

England	in England	903-7d	The Oval	1938
	in Australia	644	Sydney	2010-11
Australia	in England	729-6d	Lord's	1930
	in Australia	662-9d	Perth	2017-18

LOWEST INNINGS TOTALS

England	in England	52	The Oval	1948
	in Australia	45	Sydney	1886-87
Australia	in England	36	Birmingham	1902
	in Australia	42	Sydney	1887-88
HIGHEST MATCH AGGREGATE	1753 for 40 wickets		Adelaide	1920-21
LOWEST MATCH AGGREGATE	291 for 40 wickets		Lord's	1888

HIGHEST INDIVIDUAL INNINGS

England	in England	364	L.Hutton	The Oval	1938
	in Australia	287	R.E.Foster	Sydney	1903-04
Australia	in England	334	D.G.Bradman	Leeds	1930
	in Australia	307	R.M.Cowper	Melbourne	1965-66

HIGHEST AGGREGATE OF RUNS IN A SERIES

England	in England	732	(av 81.33)	D.I.Gower (6 Tests)	1985
	in Australia	905	(av 113.12)	W.R.Hammond	1928-29
Australia	in England	974	(av 139.14)	D.G.Bradman	1930
	in Australia	810	(av 90.00)	D.G.Bradman	1936-37

RECORD WICKET PARTNERSHIPS – ENGLAND

1st	323	J.B.Hobbs (178)/W.Rhodes (179)	Melbourne	1911-12
2nd	382	L.Hutton (364)/M.Leyland (187)	The Oval	1938
3rd	262	W.R.Hammond (177)/D.R.Jardine (98)	Adelaide	1928-29
4th	310	P.D.Collingwood (206)/K.P.Pietersen (158)	Adelaide	2006-07
5th	237	D.J.Malan (140)/J.M.Bairstow (119)	Perth	2017-18
6th	215	L.Hutton (364)/J.Hardstaff jr (169*)	The Oval	1938
	215	G.Boycott (107)/A.P.E.Knott (135)	Nottingham	1977
7th	143	F.E.Woolley (133*)/J.Vine (36)	Sydney	1911-12
8th	124	E.H.Hendren (169)/H.Larwood (70)	Brisbane	1928-29
9th	151	W.H.Scotton (90)/W.W.Read (117)	The Oval	1884
10th	130	R.E.Foster (287)/W.Rhodes (40*)	Sydney	1903-04

RECORD WICKET PARTNERSHIPS – AUSTRALIA

1st	329	G.R.Marsh (138)/M.A.Taylor (219)	Nottingham	1989
2nd	451	W.H.Ponsford (266)/D.G.Bradman (244)	The Oval	1934
3rd	276	D.G.Bradman (187)/A.L.Hassett (128)	Brisbane	1946-47
4th	388	W.H.Ponsford (181)/D.G.Bradman (304)	Leeds	1934
5th	405	S.G.Barnes (234)/D.G.Bradman (234)	Sydney	1946-47
6th	346	J.H.W.Fingleton (136)/D.G.Bradman (270)	Melbourne	1936-37
7th	165	C.Hill (188)/H.Trumble (46)	Melbourne	1897-98
8th	243	R.J.Hartigan (116)/C.Hill (160)	Adelaide	1907-08
9th	154	S.E.Gregory (201)/J.M.Blackham (74)	Sydney	1894-95
10th	163	P.J.Hughes (81*)/A.C.Agar (98)	Nottingham	2013

BEST INNINGS BOWLING ANALYSIS

England	in England	10- 53	J.C.Laker	Manchester	1956
	in Australia	8- 35	G.A.Lohmann	Sydney	1886-87
Australia	in England	8- 31	F.Laver	Manchester	1909
	in Australia	9-121	A.A.Mailey	Melbourne	1920-21

BEST MATCH BOWLING ANALYSIS

England	in England	19- 90	J.C.Laker	Manchester	1956
	in Australia	15-124	W.Rhodes	Melbourne	1903-04
Australia	in England	16-137	R.A.L.Massie	Lord's	1972
	in Australia	13- 77	M.A.Noble	Melbourne	1901-02

HIGHEST AGGREGATE OF WICKETS IN A SERIES

England	in England	46	(av 9.60)	J.C.Laker	1956
	in Australia	38	(av 23.18)	M.W.Tate	1924-25
Australia	in England	42	(av 21.26)	T.M.Alderman (6 Tests)	1981
	in Australia	41	(av 12.85)	R.M.Hogg (6 Tests)	1978-79

RESULTS SUMMARY
ENGLAND v AUSTRALIA – IN ENGLAND

	Tests	Series			The Oval			Manchester			Lord's			Nottingham			Leeds			Birmingham			Sheffield			Cardiff		
		E	A	D	E	A	D	E	A	D	E	A	D	E	A	D	E	A	D	E	A	D	E	A	D	E	A	D
1880	1	1	-	-	1	-	-																					
1882	1	-	1	-	-	1	-																					
1884	3	1	-	2	-	-	1	-	-	1	1	-	-															
1886	3	3	-	-	1	-	-	1	-	-	1	-	-															
1888	3	2	1	-	1	-	-	1	-	-	-	1	-															
1890	2	2	-	-	1	-	-				1	-	-															
1893	3	1	-	2	1	-	-	-	-	1	-	-	1															
1896	3	2	1	-	1	-	-	-	1	-	1	-	-															
1899	5	-	1	4	-	-	1	-	-	1	-	1	-	-	-	1	-	-	1									
1902	5	1	2	2	1	-	-	-	1	-	-	-	1							-	-	1	-	1	-			
1905	5	2	-	3	-	-	1	1	-	-	-	-	1	1	-	-	-	-	1									
1909	5	1	2	2	-	-	1	-	-	1	-	1	-				-	1	-	1	-	-						
1912	3	1	-	2	1	-	-	-	-	1	-	-	1															
1921	5	-	3	2	-	-	1	-	-	1	-	1	-	-	1	-	-	1	-									
1926	5	1	-	4	1	-	-	-	-	1	-	-	1	-	-	1	-	-	1									
1930	5	1	2	2	-	1	-	-	-	1	-	1	-	1	-	-	-	-	1									
1934	5	1	2	2	-	1	-	-	-	1	1	-	-	-	1	-	-	-	1									
1938	4	1	1	2	1	-	-				-	-	1	-	-	1	-	1	-									
1948	5	-	4	1	-	1	-	-	-	1	-	1	-	-	1	-	-	1	-									
1953	5	1	-	4	1	-	-	-	-	1	-	-	1	-	-	1	-	-	1									
1956	5	2	1	2	-	-	1	1	-	-	-	1	-	-	-	1	1	-	-									
1961	5	1	2	2	-	-	1	-	1	-	-	1	-				1	-	-	-	-	1						
1964	5	-	1	4	-	-	1	-	-	1	-	-	1	-	-	1	-	1	-									
1968	5	1	1	3	1	-	-	-	1	-	-	-	1				-	-	1	-	-	1						
1972	5	2	2	1	-	1	-	1	-	-	-	1	-	-	-	1	1	-	-									
1975	4	-	1	3	-	-	1	-	-	1	-	-	1							-	1	-						
1977	5	3	-	2	-	-	1	1	-	-	-	-	1	1	-	-	1	-	-									
1980	1	-	-	1							-	-	1															
1981	6	3	1	2	-	-	1	1	-	-	-	-	1	-	1	-	1	-	-	1	-	-						
1985	6	3	1	2	1	-	-	-	-	1	-	1	-	-	-	1	1	-	-	1	-	-						
1989	6	-	4	2	-	-	1	-	1	-	-	1	-	-	1	-	-	1	-	-	-	1						
1993	6	1	4	1	1	-	-	-	1	-	-	1	-	-	-	1	-	1	-	-	1	-						
1997	6	2	3	1	1	-	-	-	1	-	-	-	1	-	1	-	-	1	-	1	-	-						
2001	5	1	4	-	-	1	-				-	1	-	-	1	-	1	-	-	-	1	-						
2005	5	2	1	2	-	-	1	-	-	1	-	1	-	1	-	-				1	-	-						
2009	5	2	1	2	1	-	-				1	-	-				-	1	-	-	-	1	Chester-le-St			-	-	1
2013	5	3	-	2	-	-	1	-	-	1	1	-	-	1	-	-							1	-	-			
2015	5	3	2	-	-	1	-				-	1	-	1	-	-				1	-	-				1	-	-
2019	5	2	2	1	1	-	-	-	1	-	-	-	1				1	-	-	-	1	-						
	171	53	51	67	17	7	14	7	8	15	7	15	15	6	7	9	8	9	8	6	4	5	1	1	-	1	-	1

5

ENGLAND v AUSTRALIA – IN AUSTRALIA

	Tests	Series			Melbourne			Sydney			Adelaide			Brisbane			Perth			Hobart		
		E	A	D	E	A	D	E	A	D	E	A	D	E	A	D	E	A	D	E	A	D
1876-77	2	1	1	–	1	1	–															
1878-79	1	–	1	–	–	1	–															
1881-82	4	–	2	2	–	–	2	–	2	–												
1882-83	4	2	2	–	1	1	–	1	1	–												
1884-85	5	3	2	–	2	–	–	–	2	–	1	–	–									
1886-87	2	2	–	–				2	–	–												
1887-88	1	1	–	–				1	–	–												
1891-92	3	1	2	–	–	1	–	–	1	–	1	–	–									
1894-95	5	3	2	–	2	–	–	1	1	–	–	1	–									
1897-98	5	1	4	–	–	2	–	1	1	–	–	1	–									
1901-02	5	1	4	–	–	2	–	1	1	–	–	1	–									
1903-04	5	3	2	–	1	1	–	2	–	–	–	1	–									
1907-08	5	1	4	–	1	1	–	–	2	–	–	1	–									
1911-12	5	4	1	–	2	–	–	1	1	–	1	–	–									
1920-21	5	–	5	–	–	2	–	–	2	–	–	1	–									
1924-25	5	1	4	–	1	1	–	–	2	–	–	1	–									
1928-29	5	4	1	–	1	1	–	1	–	–	1	–	–	1	–	–						
1932-33	5	4	1	–	–	1	–	2	–	–	1	–	–	1	–	–						
1936-37	5	2	3	–	–	2	–	1	–	–	–	1	–	1	–	–						
1946-47	5	–	3	2	–	–	1	–	2	–	–	–	1	–	1	–						
1950-51	5	1	4	–	1	1	–	–	1	–	–	1	–	–	1	–						
1954-55	5	3	1	1	1	–	–	1	–	1	1	–	–	–	1	–						
1958-59	5	–	4	1	–	2	–	–	–	1	–	1	–	–	1	–						
1962-63	5	1	1	3	1	–	–	–	1	1	–	–	1	–	–	1						
1965-66	5	1	1	3	–	–	2	1	–	–	–	1	–	–	–	1						
1970-71	6	2	–	4	–	–	1	2	–	–	–	–	1	–	–	1	–	–	1			
1974-75	6	1	4	1	1	–	1	–	1	–	–	1	–	–	1	–	–	1	–			
1976-77	1	–	1	–	–	1	–															
1978-79	6	5	1	–	–	1	–	2	–	–	1	–	–	1	–	–	1	–	–			
1979-80	3	–	3	–	–	1	–	–	1	–							–	1	–			
1982-83	5	1	2	2	1	–	–	–	–	1	–	1	–	–	1	–	–	–	1			
1986-87	5	2	1	2	1	–	–	–	1	–	–	–	1	1	–	–	–	–	1			
1987-88	1	–	–	1				–	–	1												
1990-91	5	–	3	2	–	1	–	–	–	1	–	–	1	–	1	–	–	1	–			
1994-95	5	1	3	1	–	1	–	–	–	1	1	–	–	–	1	–	–	1	–			
1998-99	5	1	3	1	1	–	–	–	1	–	–	1	–	–	–	1	–	1	–			
2002-03	5	1	4	–	–	1	–	1	–	–	–	1	–	–	1	–	–	1	–			
2006-07	5	–	5	–	–	1	–	–	1	–	–	1	–	–	1	–	–	1	–			
2010-11	5	3	1	1	1	–	–	1	–	–	1	–	–	–	–	1	–	1	–			
2013-14	5	–	5	–	–	1	–	–	1	–	–	1	–	–	1	–	–	1	–			
2017-18	5	–	4	1	–	–	1	–	1	–	–	1	–	–	1	–	–	1	–			
2021-22	5	–	4	1	–	1	–	–	–	1	–	1	–	–	1	–				–	1	–
	185	57	99	29	20	29	8	22	27	8	9	19	5	5	13	5	1	10	3	–	1	–
Totals	356	110	150	96																		

Matches abandoned without a ball bowled (Manchester 1890 and 1938, Melbourne 1970-71) are excluded from these tables.

2000 RUNS

	Tests	I	NO	HS	Runs	Avge	100	50
D.G.Bradman (A)	37	63	7	334	5028	89.78	19	12
J.B.Hobbs (E)	41	71	4	187	3636	54.26	12	15
A.R.Border (A)	47	82	19	200*	3548	56.31	8	21
D.I.Gower (E)	42	77	4	215	3269	44.78	9	12
S.R.Waugh (A)	46	73	18	177*	3200	58.18	10	14
S.P.D.Smith (A)	32	56	5	239	3044	59.68	11	11
G.Boycott (E)	38	71	9	191	2945	47.50	7	14
W.R.Hammond (E)	33	58	3	251	2852	51.85	9	7
H.Sutcliffe (E)	27	46	5	194	2741	66.85	8	16

	Tests	I	NO	HS	Runs	Avge	100	50
C.Hill (A)	41	76	1	188	2660	35.46	4	16
J.H.Edrich (E)	32	57	3	175	2644	48.96	7	13
G.A.Gooch (E)	42	79	0	196	2632	33.31	4	16
G.S.Chappell (A)	35	65	8	144	2619	45.94	9	12
M.A.Taylor (A)	33	61	2	219	2496	42.30	6	15
A.N.Cook (E)	35	64	2	244*	2493	40.20	5	11
R.T.Ponting (A)	35	58	2	196	2476	44.21	8	9
M.C.Cowdrey (E)	43	75	4	113	2433	34.26	5	11
L.Hutton (E)	27	49	6	364	2428	56.46	5	14
R.N.Harvey (A)	37	68	5	167	2416	38.34	6	12
V.T.Trumper (A)	40	74	5	185*	2263	32.79	6	9
M.J.Clarke (A)	35	62	7	187	2241	40.74	7	7
D.C.Boon (A)	31	57	8	184*	2237	45.65	7	8
W.M.Lawry (A)	29	51	5	166	2233	48.54	7	13
M.E.Waugh (A)	29	51	7	140	2204	50.09	6	11
S.E.Gregory (A)	52	92	7	201	2193	25.80	4	8
W.W.Armstrong (A)	42	71	9	158	2172	35.03	4	6
K.P.Pietersen (E)	27	50	2	227	2158	44.95	4	13
I.M.Chappell (A)	30	56	4	192	2138	41.11	4	16
K.F.Barrington (E)	23	39	6	256	2111	63.96	5	13
A.R.Morris (A)	24	43	2	206	2080	50.73	8	8
J.E.Root (E)	29	56	4	180	2016	38.76	3	16

D.G.Bradman holds the unique record of scoring 2000 runs in both countries in this series (2674 runs in England and 2354 in Australia); J.B.Hobbs is the only other batsman to score 2000 runs in either country (2493 runs in Australia).

100 WICKETS

	Tests	Balls	Runs	Wkts	Avge	Best	5wI	10wM
S.K.Warne (A)	36	10757	4535	195	23.25	8- 71	11	4
D.K.Lillee (A)	29	8516	3507	167	21.00	7- 89	11	4
G.D.McGrath (A)	30	7280	3286	157	20.92	8- 38	10	–
I.T.Botham (E)	36	8479	4093	148	27.65	6- 78	9	2
H.Trumble (A)	31	7895	2945	141	20.88	8- 65	9	3
S.C.J.Broad (E)	35	7224	3806	131	29.05	8- 15	8	1
R.G.D.Willis (E)	35	7294	3346	128	26.14	8- 43	7	–
M.A.Noble (A)	39	6845	2860	115	24.86	7- 17	9	2
R.R.Lindwall (A)	29	6728	2559	114	22.44	7- 63	6	–
J.M.Anderson (E)	35	7675	3782	112	33.76	6- 47	5	1
W.Rhodes (E)	41	5791	2616	109	24.00	8- 68	6	1
S.F.Barnes (E)	20	5749	2288	106	21.58	7- 60	12	1
C.V.Grimmett (A)	22	9224	3439	106	32.44	6- 37	11	2
D.L.Underwood (E)	29	8000	2770	105	26.38	7- 50	4	2
A.V.Bedser (E)	21	7065	2859	104	27.49	7- 44	7	2
G.Giffen (A)	31	6457	2791	103	27.09	7-117	7	1
W.J.O'Reilly (A)	19	7864	2587	102	25.36	7- 54	8	3
R.Peel (E)	20	5216	1715	101	16.98	7- 31	5	1
C.T.B.Turner (A)	17	5195	1670	101	16.53	7- 43	11	2
N.M.Lyon (A)	28	6585	2972	101	29.42	6- 49	2	–
T.M.Alderman (A)	17	4717	2117	100	21.17	6- 47	11	1
J.R.Thomson (A)	21	4951	2418	100	24.18	6- 46	5	–

100 WICKET-KEEPING DISMISSALS

	Tests	Ct	St	Total
R.W.Marsh (A)	42	141	7	148
I.A.Healy (A)	33	123	12	135
A.P.E.Knott (E)	34	97	8	105

R.W.Marsh (141 catches) and W.A.S.Oldfield (A) (31 stumpings) hold the respective individual records in Anglo-Australian Tests

STATISTICAL HIGHLIGHTS IN 2022 TESTS

Including Tests from No. 2442 (Australia v England, 3rd Test) and No. 2445 (South Africa v India, 2nd Test) to No. 2484 (Australia v South Africa, 2nd Test) and No. 2486 (Pakistan v New Zealand, 1st Test).

† = National record

TEAM HIGHLIGHTS
HIGHEST INNINGS TOTALS

657	England v Pakistan	Rawalpindi
612-9d	New Zealand v Pakistan	Karachi
598-4d	Australia v West Indies	Perth
579	Pakistan v England	Rawalpindi
575-8d	Australia v South Africa	Melbourne

HIGHEST FOURTH INNINGS TOTAL

443-7	Pakistan (set 506) v Australia	Karachi
378-3	England (set 378) v India	Birmingham

LOWEST INNINGS TOTALS

53	Bangladesh v South Africa	Durban
77	West Indies v Australia	Adelaide
80	Bangladesh v South Africa	Gqeberha
95	South Africa v New Zealand	Christchurch
99	South Africa v Australia	Brisbane

HIGHEST MATCH AGGREGATES

1768-37	England (657 & 264-7d) v Pakistan (579 & 268)	Rawalpindi

The highest match aggregate since before the Second World War.

1675-35	New Zealand (553 & 284) v England (539 & 299-5)	Nottingham

BATSMEN'S MATCH (Qualification: 1150 runs, average 60 per wicket)

84.78 (1187-14)	Pakistan (476-4d & 252-0) v Australia (459)	Rawalpindi

LOWEST MATCH AGGREGATE

504-34	South Africa (152 & 99) v Australia (218 & 35-4)	Brisbane

LARGE MARGINS OF VICTORY

Inns & 276 runs	New Zealand (482) beat South Africa (95 & 111)	Christchurch
Inns & 222 runs	India (574-8d) beat Sri Lanka (174 & 178)	Mohali
419 runs	Australia (511-7d & 199-6d) beat West Indies (214 & 77)	Adelaide
332 runs	South Africa (453 & 176-6d) beat Bangladesh (217 & 80)	Gqeberha

NARROW MARGINS OF VICTORY

26 runs	England (281 & 275) beat Pakistan (202 & 328)	Multan
3 wkts	India (314 & 145-7) beat Bangladesh (227 & 231)	Mirpur

FOUR HUNDREDS IN AN INNINGS

England (657) v Pakistan	Rawalpindi

MOST EXTRAS IN AN INNINGS

	B	LB	W	NB		
40	4	17	5	14	India (416) v England	Birmingham

BATTING HIGHLIGHTS
DOUBLE HUNDREDS

L.D.Chandimal	206*	Sri Lanka v Australia (*2nd Test*)	Galle
M.Labuschagne	204	Australia v West Indies	Perth
T.W.M.Latham	252	New Zealand v Bangladesh	Christchurch
S.P.D.Smith	200*	Australia v West Indies	Perth

8

| D.A.Warner | 200* | Australia v South Africa | Melbourne |
| K.S.Williamson | 200* | New Zealand v Pakistan | Karachi |

HUNDREDS IN THREE CONSECUTIVE INNINGS

| M.Labuschagne | 204 | 104* | Australia v West Indies | Perth |
| | 163 | | Australia v West Indies | Adelaide |

HUNDRED IN EACH INNINGS OF A MATCH

J.M.Bairstow	106	114*	England v India	Birmingham
Imam-ul-Haq	157	111*	Pakistan v Australia	Rawalpindi
U.T.Khawaja	137	101*	Australia v England	Sydney
M.Labuschagne	204	104*	Australia v West Indies	Perth

FASTEST HUNDRED AGAINST GENUINE BOWLING

| J.M.Bairstow (136) | 77balls | England v New Zealand | Nottingham |

MOST SIXES IN AN INNINGS

| 7 | J.M.Bairstow (136) | England v New Zealand | Nottingham |

MOST RUNS FROM BOUNDARIES IN AN INNINGS

Runs 6s 4s
| 148 | 2 | 34 | T.W.M.Latham | New Zealand v Bangladesh | Christchurch |

MOST RUNS OFF ONE OVER

| 27† | H.C.Brook (644463) | England v Pakistan | Rawalpindi |

He also hit all six deliveries of another over for consecutive boundaries.

HUNDRED ON DEBUT

| Zakir Hasan | 100 | Bangladesh v India | Chittagong |

LONG INNINGS (Qualification: 600 mins and/or 400 balls)

Min Balls
524	408	Abdullah Shafiq (160*)	Pakistan v Sri Lanka (*1st Test*)	Galle
603	425	Babar Azam (196)	Pakistan v Australia	Karachi
710	489	K.C.Brathwaite (160)	West Indies v England	Bridgetown

FIRST-WICKET PARTNERSHIP OF 100 IN EACH INNINGS

| 105/252* | Abdullah Shafiq/Imam-ul-Haq | Pakistan v Australia | Rawalpindi |

OTHER NOTABLE PARTNERSHIPS

Qualifications: 1st-4th wkts: 225 runs; 5th-6th: 200; 7th: 175; 8th: 150; 9th: 125; 10th: 100.

First Wicket
252*	Abdullah Shafiq/Imam-ul-Haq	Pakistan v Australia	Rawalpindi
233	Z.Crawley/B.M.Duckett	England v Pakistan	Rawalpindi
225	Abdullah Shafiq/Imam-ul-Haq	Pakistan v England	Rawalpindi

Third Wicket
251	M.Labuschagne/S.P.D.Smith	Australia v West Indies	Perth
239	D.A.Warner/S.P.D.Smith	Australia v South Africa	Melbourne
228	Abdullah Shafiq/Babar Azam	Pakistan v Australia	Karachi

Fourth Wicket
| 297 | M.Labuschagne/T.M.Head | Australia v West Indies | Adelaide |
| 269* | J.E.Root/J.M.Bairstow | England v India | Birmingham |

Fifth Wicket
| 236 | D.J.Mitchell/T.A.Blundell | New Zealand v England | Nottingham |

Sixth Wicket
| 272† | Mushfiqur Rahim/Liton Das | Bangladesh v Sri Lanka | Mirpur |
| 222 | R.R.Pant/R.A.Jadeja | India v England | Birmingham |

Seventh Wicket
| 241† | J.M.Bairstow/J.Overton | England v New Zealand | Leeds |

BOWLING HIGHLIGHTS
BEST FIGURES IN AN INNINGS

| M.J.Henry | 7-23 | New Zealand v South Africa | Christchurch |

TEN WICKETS IN A MATCH

Abrar Ahmed	11-234	Pakistan v England	Multan
On debut.			
A.M.Fernando	10-144	Sri Lanka v Bangladesh	Mirpur
N.G.R.P.Jayasuriya	12-177	Sri Lanka v Australia (*2nd Test*)	Galle
On debut.			
M.J.Leach	10-166	England v New Zealand	Leeds

FIVE WICKETS IN AN INNINGS ON DEBUT

Abrar Ahmed	7-114	Pakistan v England	Multan
R.Ahmed	5- 48	England v Pakistan	Karachi
W.G.Jacks	6-161	England v Pakistan	Rawalpindi
N.G.R.P.Jayasuriya	6-118	Sri Lanka v Australia (*2nd Test*)	Galle
	6- 59	Sri Lanka v Australia (*2nd Test*)	Galle

BOWLING UNCHANGED THROUGHOUT A COMPLETED INNINGS

| K.A.Maharaj (10-0-32-7)/S.R.Harmer (9-3-21-3) | South Africa v Bangladesh | Durban |
| K.A.Maharaj (12-3-40-7)/S.R.Harmer (11.3-1-34-3) | South Africa v Bangladesh | Gqeberha |

60 OVERS IN AN INNINGS

Abrar Ahmed	67·5-8-205-5	Pakistan v New Zealand	Karachi
M.J.Leach	69·5-27-118-3	England v West Indies	Bridgetown
N.M.Lyon	64-5-194-2	Australia v Sri Lanka (*2nd Test*)	Galle
Nauman Ali	63-8-185-3	Pakistan v New Zealand	Karachi

200 RUNS CONCEDED IN AN INNINGS

| Abrar Ahmed | 67·5-8-205-5 | Pakistan v New Zealand | Karachi |
| Zahid Mahmood | 33-1-235-4 | Pakistan v England | Rawalpindi |

WICKET-KEEPING HIGHLIGHTS
SIX WICKET-KEEPING DISMISSALS IN AN INNINGS

| A.T.Carey | 6ct | Australia v West Indies | Adelaide |

NINE WICKET-KEEPING DISMISSALS IN A MATCH

| A.T.Carey | 9ct | Australia v West Indies | Adelaide |

FIELDING HIGHLIGHTS
FOUR CATCHES IN AN INNINGS IN THE FIELD

Z.Crawley	4ct	England v Australia	Hobart
T.W.M.Latham	4ct	New Zealand v Bangladesh	Christchurch
Shadman Islam	4ct	Bangladesh v New Zealand	Mount Maunganui

SIX CATCHES IN A MATCH IN THE FIELD

| Z.Crawley | 6ct | England v India | Birmingham |
| T.W.M.Latham | 6ct | New Zealand v Bangladesh | Christchurch |

ALL-ROUND HIGHLIGHTS
HUNDRED AND FIVE WICKETS IN AN INNINGS

| R.A.Jadeja | 175* | 5-41 | India v Sri Lanka | Mohali |

LEADING TEST AGGREGATES IN 2022
1000 RUNS IN 2022

	M	I	NO	HS	Runs	Avge	100	50
Babar Azam (P)	9	17	–	196	**1184**	69.64	4	7
J.E.Root (E)	15	27	3	176	**1098**	45.75	5	2
U.T.Khawaja (A)	11	20	4	160	**1080**	67.50	4	5
J.M.Bairstow (E)	10	19	3	162	**1061**	66.31	6	1

RECORD CALENDAR YEAR RUNS AGGREGATE

	M	I	NO	HS	Runs	Avge	100	50
M.Yousuf (P) (2006)	11	19	1	202	**1788**	99.33	9	3

RECORD CALENDAR YEAR RUNS AVERAGE

	M	I	NO	HS	Runs	Avge	100	50
G.St A.Sobers (WI) (1958)	7	12	3	365*	1193	**132.55**	5	3

1000 RUNS IN DEBUT CALENDAR YEAR

	M	I	NO	HS	Runs	Avge	100	50
M.A.Taylor (A) (1989)	11	20	1	219	**1219**	64.15	4	5
A.C.Voges (A) (2015)	12	18	6	269*	**1028**	85.66	4	3
A.N.Cook (E) (2006)	13	24	2	127	**1013**	46.04	4	3

40 WICKETS IN 2022

	M	O	R	W	Avge	Best	5wI	10wM
K.Rabada (SA)	9	267.4	1046	**47**	22.25	5- 52	2	–
N.M.Lyon (A)	11	500.5	1366	**47**	29.06	6-128	3	–
M.J.Leach (E)	14	609.0	1761	**46**	38.28	5- 66	2	1
S.C.J.Broad (E)	9	317.1	1030	**40**	25.75	5-101	1	–

RECORD CALENDAR YEAR WICKETS AGGREGATE

	M	O	R	W	Avge	Best	5wI	10wM
M.Muralitharan (SL) (2006)	11	588.4	1521	**90**	16.90	8-70	9	5
S.K.Warne (A) (2005)	14	691.4	2043	**90**	22.70	6-46	6	2

MOST WICKET-KEEPING DISMISSALS IN 2022

	M	Dis	Ct	St
K.Verreynne (SA)	11	**39**	36	3

RECORD CALENDAR YEAR DISMISSALS AGGREGATE

	M	Dis	Ct	St
J.M.Bairstow (E) (2016)	17	**70**	66	4

20 CATCHES BY FIELDERS IN 2022

	M	Ct
Z.Crawley (E)	15	22
J.E.Root (E)	15	21

RECORD CALENDAR YEAR FIELDER'S AGGREGATE

	M	Ct
G.C.Smith (SA) (2008)	15	**30**

TEST MATCH SCORES
INDIA v SRI LANKA (1st Test)

At Punjab CA I.S.Bindra Stadium, Mohali, on 4, 5, 6 March 2022.
Toss: India. Result: **INDIA** won by an innings and 222 runs.
Debuts: None.

INDIA

M.A.Agarwal	lbw b Ambuldeniya	33
*R.G.Sharma	c Lakmal b Kumara	29
G.H.Vihari	b Fernando	58
V.Kohli	b Ambuldeniya	45
†R.R.Pant	b Lakmal	96
S.S.Iyer	lbw b de Silva	27
R.A.Jadeja	not out	175
R.Ashwin	c Dickwella b Lakmal	61
J.Yadav	c Thirimanne b Fernando	2
Mohammed Shami	not out	20
J.J.Bumrah		
Extras	(B 4, LB 12, NB 12)	28
Total	**(8 wkts dec; 129.2 overs)**	**574**

SRI LANKA

*F.D.M.Karunaratne	lbw b Jadeja	28	(2) c Pant b Shami		27
H.D.R.L.Thirimanne	lbw b Ashwin	17	(1) c Sharma b Ashwin		0
P.N.Silva	not out	61	c Pant b Ashwin		6
A.D.Mathews	lbw b Bumrah	22	lbw b Jadeja		28
D.M.de Silva	lbw b Ashwin	1	c Iyer b Jadeja		30
K.I.C.Asalanka	lbw b Bumrah	29	c Kohli b Ashwin		20
†D.P.D.N.Dickwella	c Iyer b Jadeja	2	not out		51
R.A.S.Lakmal	c Ashwin b Jadeja	0	c Yadav b Jadeja		0
L.Ambuldeniya	c Agarwal b Shami	0	c Pant b Jadeja		2
M.V.T.Fernando	c Sharma b Jadeja	0	lbw b Shami		0
C.B.R.L.S.Kumara	b Jadeja	0	c Shami b Ashwin		4
Extras	(LB 6, NB 8)	14	(B 4, LB 5, NB 1)		10
Total	**(65 overs)**	**174**	**(60 overs)**		**178**

SRI LANKA	O	M	R	W	O	M	R	W
Lakmal	25	1	90	2				
Fernando	26	1	135	2				
Kumara	10.5	1	52	1				
Ambuldeniya	46	3	188	2				
De Silva	18.2	1	79	1				
Asalanka	3.1	0	14	0				
INDIA								
Mohammed Shami	12	5	27	1	(2) 8	1	48	2
Bumrah	14	3	36	2	(5) 4	1	7	0
Ashwin	20	7	49	2	(1) 21	5	47	4
Yadav	6	2	15	0	11	3	21	0
Jadeja	13	4	41	5	(3) 16	5	46	4

FALL OF WICKETS			
	I	SL	SL
Wkt	1st	1st	2nd
1st	52	48	9
2nd	80	59	19
3rd	170	96	45
4th	175	103	94
5th	228	161	121
6th	332	164	121
7th	462	164	121
8th	471	173	153
9th	–	174	170
10th	–	174	178

Umpires: N.N.Menon (*India*) (10) and V.K.Sharma (*India*) (4).
Referee: J.Srinath (*India*) (60).   Test No. 2451/45 (1561/SL300)

INDIA v SRI LANKA (2nd Test)

At M.Chinnaswamy Stadium, Bengaluru, on 12, 13, 14 March 2022 (day/night).
Toss: India. Result: **INDIA** won by 238 runs.
Debuts: None.

INDIA

M.A.Agarwal	run out	4	c de Silva b Ambuldeniya		22
*R.G.Sharma	c de Silva b Ambuldeniya	15	c Mathews b de Silva		46
G.H.Vihari	c Dickwella b Jayawickrama	31	b Jayawickrama		35
V.Kohli	lbw b de Silva	23	lbw b Jayawickrama		13
†R.R.Pant	b Ambuldeniya	39	c and b Jayawickrama		50
S.S.Iyer	st Dickwella b Jayawickrama	92	lbw b Ambuldeniya		67
R.A.Jadeja	c Thirimanne b Ambuldeniya	4	b Fernando		22
R.Ashwin	c Dickwella b de Silva	13	c Dickwella b Jayawickrama		13
A.R.Patel	b Lakmal	9	b Ambuldeniya		9
Mohammed Shami	c de Silva b Jayawickrama	5	not out		16
J.J.Bumrah	not out	0			
Extras	(B 7, LB 8, NB 2)	17	(B 8, LB 1, NB 1)		10
Total	**(59.1 overs)**	**252**	**(9 wkts dec; 68.5 overs)**		**303**

SRI LANKA

B.K.G.Mendis	c Iyer b Bumrah	2	(3) st Pant b Ashwin		54
*F.D.M.Karunaratne	b Shami	4	b Bumrah		107
H.D.R.L.Thirimanne	c Iyer b Bumrah	8	(1) lbw b Bumrah		0
A.D.Mathews	c Sharma b Bumrah	43	b Jadeja		1
D.M.de Silva	lbw b Shami	10	c Vihari b Ashwin		4
K.I.C.Asalanka	c Ashwin b Patel	5	(7) c Sharma b Patel		5
†D.P.D.N.Dickwella	c Pant b Bumrah	21	(6) st Pant b Patel		12
L.Ambuldeniya	c Pant b Bumrah	1	lbw b Ashwin		2
R.A.S.Lakmal	b Ashwin	5	b Bumrah		2
P.A.K.P.Jayawickrama	not out	1	(11) not out		0
M.V.T.Fernando	st Pant b Ashwin	8	(10) c Shami b Ashwin		2
Extras	(B 1)	1	(B 16, LB 3, NB 1)		20
Total	**(35.5 overs)**	**109**	**(59.3 overs)**		**208**

SRI LANKA	O	M	R	W	O	M	R	W
Lakmal	8	3	12	1	10	2	34	0
Fernando	3	0	18	0	(3) 10	2	48	1
Ambuldeniya	24	6	94	3	(2) 20.5	1	87	3
Jayawickrama	17.1	3	81	3	(5) 19	2	78	4
De Silva	7	1	32	2	(4) 9	0	47	1

INDIA	O	M	R	W	O	M	R	W
Bumrah	10	4	24	5	9	4	23	3
Ashwin	8.5	1	30	2	(3) 19.3	3	55	4
Mohammed Shami	6	1	18	2	(2) 6	0	26	0
Jadeja	6	1	15	0	14	2	48	1
Patel	5	1	21	1	11	1	37	2

FALL OF WICKETS

	I	SL	I	SL
Wkt	1st	1st	2nd	2nd
1st	10	2	42	0
2nd	29	14	98	97
3rd	76	14	116	98
4th	86	28	139	105
5th	126	50	184	160
6th	148	85	247	180
7th	183	95	278	204
8th	215	100	278	206
9th	229	100	303	208
10th	252	109	–	208

Umpires: A.K.Chaudhary (*India*) (4) and N.N.Menon (*India*) (11).
Referee: J.Srinath (*India*) (61).   **Test No. 2452/46 (I562/SL301)**

PAKISTAN v AUSTRALIA (1st Test)

At Rawalpindi Cricket Stadium, on 4, 5, 6, 7, 8 March 2022.
Toss: Pakistan. Result: **MATCH DRAWN**.
Debuts: None.

PAKISTAN

Abdullah Shafiq	c Cummins b Lyon	44	not out	136
Imam-ul-Haq	lbw b Cummins	157	not out	111
Azhar Ali	c Green b Labuschagne	185		
*Babar Azam	run out	36		
†Mohammad Rizwan	not out	29		
Iftikhar Ahmed	not out	13		
Fawad Alam				
Nauman Ali				
Sajid Khan				
Shaheen Shah Afridi				
Naseem Shah				
Extras	(B 4, LB 7, NB 1)	12	(LB 2, NB 3)	5
Total	**(4 wkts dec; 162 overs)**	**476**	**(0 wkts dec; 77 overs)**	**252**

AUSTRALIA

U.T.Khawaja	c Imam b Nauman	97
D.A.Warner	b Khan	68
M.Labuschagne	c Shafiq b Afridi	90
S.P.D.Smith	c Rizwan b Nauman	78
T.M.Head	c Rizwan b Nauman	8
C.D.Green	c Ahmed b Nauman	48
†A.T.Carey	b Nauman	19
M.A.Starc	lbw b Afridi	13
*P.J.Cummins	c Imam b Nauman	8
N.M.Lyon	lbw b Nauman	3
J.R.Hazlewood	not out	0
Extras	(B 6, LB 13, NB 8)	27
Total	**(140.1 overs)**	**459**

AUSTRALIA	O	M	R	W		O	M	R	W
Starc	24	5	71	0		7	1	29	0
Hazlewood	26	6	53	0		5	0	8	0
Lyon	52	5	161	1		26	5	75	0
Cummins	28	5	62	1		4	0	15	0
Head	3	0	13	0	(6)	13	1	35	0
Green	15	3	47	0	(8)	4	0	14	0
Labuschagne	12	0	53	1	(5)	15	0	56	0
Smith	2	0	5	0	(7)	2	0	15	0
Khawaja						1	0	3	0

PAKISTAN	O	M	R	W
Sajid Khan	45	9	122	1
Naseem Shah	21	2	89	1
Shaheen Shah Afridi	30	5	88	2
Nauman Ali	38.1	9	107	6
Iftikhar Ahmed	3	0	20	0
Imam-ul-Haq	2	0	9	0
Babar Azam	1	0	5	0

FALL OF WICKETS

	P	A	P
Wkt	1st	1st	2nd
1st	105	156	–
2nd	313	203	–
3rd	414	311	–
4th	442	326	–
5th	–	407	–
6th	–	422	–
7th	–	444	–
8th	–	455	–
9th	–	459	–
10th	–	459	–

Umpires: Ahsan Raza (*Pakistan*) (3) and Alim Dar (*Pakistan*) (137).
Referee: R.S.Madugalle (*Sri Lanka*) (202).   **Test No. 2453/67 (P442/A840)**

PAKISTAN v AUSTRALIA (2nd Test)

At National Stadium, Karachi, on 12, 13, 14, 15, 16 March 2022.
Toss: Australia. Result: **MATCH DRAWN**.
Debut: Australia – M.J.Swepson.

AUSTRALIA

D.A.Warner	c Rizwan b Ashraf	36	(2) c Alam b Hasan		7
U.T.Khawaja	b Khan	160	(1) not out		44
M.Labuschagne	run out	0	b Afridi		44
S.P.D.Smith	c Ashraf b Hasan	72			
N.M.Lyon	b Ashraf	38			
T.M.Head	lbw b Khan	23			
C.D.Green	b Nauman	28			
†A.T.Carey	b Azam	93			
M.A.Starc	c Azhar b Afridi	28			
*P.J.Cummins	not out	34			
M.J.Swepson	not out	15			
Extras	(B 10, LB 7, NB 7, W 5)	29	(LB 2)		2
Total	**(9 wkts dec; 189 overs)**	**556**	**(2 wkts dec; 22.3 overs)**		**97**

PAKISTAN

Abdullah Shafiq	run out	13	c Smith b Cummins		96
Imam-ul-Haq	c Cummins b Lyon	20	lbw b Lyon		1
Azhar Ali	c Green b Starc	14	lbw b Green		6
*Babar Azam	c Khawaja b Swepson	36	c Labuschagne b Lyon		196
Fawad Alam	lbw b Starc	0	c Carey b Cummins		9
†Mohammad Rizwan	c Carey b Cummins	6	not out		104
Faheem Ashraf	lbw b Green	4	c Smith b Lyon		0
Sajid Khan	c Carey b Starc	5	c Smith b Lyon		9
Hasan Ali	run out	0			
Nauman Ali	not out	20	(9) not out		0
Shaheen Shah Afridi	lbw b Swepson	19			
Extras	(B 6, LB 2, NB 3)	11	(B 8, LB 2, NB 5, W 7)		22
Total	**(53 overs)**	**148**	**(7 wkts; 171.4 overs)**		**443**

PAKISTAN	O	M	R	W		O	M	R	W
Shaheen Shah Afridi	32	8	95	1		6.3	0	21	1
Hasan Ali	25	7	71	1		7	0	23	1
Faheem Ashraf	21	4	55	2	(4)	3	0	13	0
Sajid Khan	57	10	167	2	(3)	5	0	31	0
Nauman Ali	48	6	134	1		1	0	7	0
Babar Azam	4	0	7	1					
Azhar Ali	2	0	10	0					

AUSTRALIA	O	M	R	W		O	M	R	W
Starc	13	5	29	3		21	6	58	0
Cummins	13	2	39	1		26	6	75	2
Lyon	9	5	13	1	(4)	55	20	112	4
Swepson	9	1	32	2	(3)	53.4	8	156	0
Green	8	1	23	1		15	4	32	1
Labuschagne	1	0	4	0		1	1	0	0

FALL OF WICKETS

	A	P	A	P
Wkt	1st	1st	2nd	2nd
1st	82	26	20	2
2nd	91	45	97	21
3rd	250	60	–	249
4th	304	60	–	277
5th	347	76	–	392
6th	360	81	–	392
7th	405	97	–	414
8th	503	102	–	–
9th	505	118	–	–
10th	–	148	–	–

Umpires: Ahsan Raza (*Pakistan*) (4) and Alim Dar (*Pakistan*) (138).
Referee: R.S.Madugalle (*Sri Lanka*) (203).   Test No. 2454/68 (P443/A841)

PAKISTAN v AUSTRALIA (3rd Test)

At Gaddafi Stadium, Lahore, on 21, 22, 23, 24, 25 March 2022.
Toss: Australia. Result: **AUSTRALIA** won by 115 runs.
Debuts: None.

AUSTRALIA

D.A.Warner	lbw b Afridi	7	(2)	b Afridi	51
U.T.Khawaja	c Azam b Khan	91	(1)	not out	104
M.Labuschagne	c Rizwan b Afridi	0		c Sajid b Nauman	36
S.P.D.Smith	lbw b Naseem	59		c Rizwan b Naseem	17
T.M.Head	c Rizwan b Naseem	26		not out	11
C.D.Green	b Naseem	79			
†A.T.Carey	lbw b Nauman	67			
M.A.Starc	c Nauman b Afridi	13			
*P.J.Cummins	not out	11			
N.M.Lyon	b Naseem	4			
M.J.Swepson	b Afridi	9			
Extras	(B 13, LB 4, NB 8)	25		(B 5, LB 2, NB 1)	8
Total	**(133.3 overs)**	**391**		**(3 wkts dec; 60 overs)**	**227**

PAKISTAN

Abdullah Shafiq	c Carey b Lyon	81		c Carey b Green	27
Imam-ul-Haq	lbw b Cummins	11		c Labuschagne b Lyon	70
Azhar Ali	c and b Cummins	78		c Smith b Lyon	17
*Babar Azam	lbw b Starc	67		c Smith b Lyon	55
Fawad Alam	b Starc	13		lbw b Cummins	11
†Mohammad Rizwan	b Starc	1		lbw b Cummins	0
Sajid Khan	b Cummins	6		c Khawaja b Starc	21
Nauman Ali	lbw b Cummins	0		not out	1
Hasan Ali	c Smith b Cummins	0		b Lyon	13
Shaheen Shah Afridi	not out	0		c Swepson b Lyon	5
Naseem Shah	b Starc	0		b Cummins	1
Extras	(B 5, NB 6)	11		(B 8, LB 4, NB 1, W 1)	14
Total	**(116.4 overs)**	**268**		**(92.1 overs)**	**235**

PAKISTAN	O	M	R	W	O	M	R	W
Shaheen Shah Afridi	24.3	3	79	4	11	2	45	1
Hasan Ali	20	5	61	0	(3) 11	3	37	0
Naseem Shah	31	13	58	4	(2) 12	3	23	1
Nauman Ali	24	4	77	1	(5) 10	0	55	1
Sajid Khan	33	4	97	1	(4) 16	1	60	0
Babar Azam	1	0	2	0				

AUSTRALIA	O	M	R	W	O	M	R	W
Starc	20.4	6	33	4	17	6	53	1
Cummins	24	8	56	5	15.1	6	23	3
Green	14	4	37	0	(5) 11	4	18	1
Lyon	40	10	95	1	(3) 37	8	83	5
Swepson	18	2	42	0	(4) 10	1	36	0
Labuschagne					2	0	10	0

FALL OF WICKETS

	A	P	A	P
Wkt	1st	1st	2nd	2nd
1st	8	20	96	77
2nd	8	170	161	105
3rd	146	214	216	142
4th	187	248	–	165
5th	206	256	–	167
6th	341	264	–	213
7th	353	268	–	213
8th	369	268	–	226
9th	374	268	–	232
10th	391	268	–	235

Umpires: Ahsan Raza (*Pakistan*) (5) and Alim Dar (*Pakistan*) (139).
Referee: R.S.Madugalle (*Sri Lanka*) (204). **Test No. 2455/69 (P444/A842)**

WEST INDIES v ENGLAND (1st Test)

At Sir Vivian Richards Stadium, North Sound, on 8, 9, 10, 11, 12 March 2022.
Toss: England. Result: **MATCH DRAWN**.
Debut: England – A.Z.Lees.

ENGLAND

A.Z.Lees	lbw b Roach	4	lbw b Roach		6
Z.Crawley	c Da Silva b Seales	8	b Holder		121
*J.E.Root	b Roach	13	b Joseph		109
D.W.Lawrence	c Blackwood b Holder	20	c Permaul b Joseph		37
B.A.Stokes	b Seales	36	c Brooks b Roach		13
J.M.Bairstow	c Holder b Joseph	140	not out		15
†B.T.Foakes	lbw b Holder	42	b Joseph		1
C.R.Woakes	c Da Silva b Seales	28	not out		18
C.Overton	c Bonner b Seales	0			
M.A.Wood	c Permaul b Joseph	1			
M.J.Leach	not out	4			
Extras	(B 1, LB 9, NB 5)	15	(B 15, LB 4, NB 8, W 2)		29
Total	**(100.3 overs)**	**311**	**(6 wkts dec; 88.2 overs)**		**349**

WEST INDIES

*K.C.Brathwaite	c Overton b Wood	55	lbw b Stokes		33
J.D.Campbell	c Foakes b Overton	35	c Overton b Leach		22
S.S.J.Brooks	c Root b Stokes	18	c Crawley b Leach		5
N.E.Bonner	c Foakes b Lawrence	123	not out		38
J.Blackwood	c Overton b Woakes	11	lbw b Leach		2
J.O.Holder	c Foakes b Stokes	45	not out		37
†J.M.Da Silva	lbw b Leach	32			
A.S.Joseph	c sub (O.J.D.Pope) b Overton	2			
K.A.J.Roach	run out	15			
V.Permaul	not out	26			
J.N.T.Seales	lbw b Leach	0			
Extras	(B 3, LB 3, NB 3, W 4)	13	(B 4, LB 4, NB 2)		10
Total	**(157.3 overs)**	**375**	**(4 wkts; 70.1 overs)**		**147**

WEST INDIES	O	M	R	W	O	M	R	W		FALL OF WICKETS			
											E	WI	E	WI
Roach	21	3	86	2	19	2	53	2	Wkt	1st	1st	2nd	2nd
Seales	22	6	79	4	13	2	57	0	1st	12	83	24	59
Holder	21	11	24	2	16	2	56	1	2nd	17	101	225	59
Joseph	20.3	2	70	2	23.2	3	78	3	3rd	27	111	295	65
Permaul	13	4	35	0	12	0	64	0	4th	48	127	310	67
Brathwaite	3	1	7	0	4	0	14	0	5th	115	206	312	—
Bonner					1	0	8	0	6th	214	279	314	—
									7th	285	282	—	—
ENGLAND									8th	285	326	—	—
Woakes	30	6	88	1	9	1	22	0	9th	305	372	—	—
Overton	32	7	85	2	(3) 10	2	23	0	10th	311	375	—	—
Wood	17	4	45	1									
Leach	43.3	20	79	2	(2) 30.1	14	57	3					
Stokes	28	7	42	2	13	3	24	1					
Root	5	0	30	0	(4) 2	0	6	0					
Lawrence	2	2	0	1	(6) 6	3	7	0					

Umpires: G.O.Brathwaite (*West Indies*) (7) and J.S.Wilson (*West Indies*) (26).
Referee: Sir R.B.Richardson (*West Indies*) (36). **Test No. 2456/161 (WI561/E1046)**

WEST INDIES v ENGLAND (2nd Test)

At Kensington Oval, Barbados, on 16, 17, 18, 19, 20 March 2022.
Toss: England. Result: **MATCH DRAWN**.
Debuts: England – M.D.Fisher, S.Mahmood.

ENGLAND

A.Z.Lees	lbw b Permaul	30	c Joseph b Permaul	24
Z.Crawley	c Da Silva b Seales	0	c Seales b Joseph	40
*J.E.Root	lbw b Roach	153	c Campbell b Permaul	9
D.W.Lawrence	c Brathwaite b Holder	91	c Joseph b Seales	41
B.A.Stokes	c Brooks b Brathwaite	120	c Brathwaite b Roach	19
J.M.Bairstow	c Bonner b Joseph	20	c Roach b Seales	29
†B.T.Foakes	st Da Silva b Permaul	33	not out	11
C.R.Woakes	c Seales b Roach	41	not out	9
M.D.Fisher	not out	0		
M.J.Leach	st Da Silva b Permaul	4		
S.Mahmood				
Extras	(B 5, LB 6, NB 3, W 1)	15	(B 1, NB 1, W 1)	3
Total	**(9 wkts dec; 150.5 overs)**	**507**	**(6 wkts dec; 39.5 overs)**	**185**

WEST INDIES

*K.C.Brathwaite	b Leach	160	not out	56
J.D.Campbell	c Foakes b Fisher	4	c Lees b Leach	10
S.S.J.Brooks	c Woakes b Leach	39	c Root b Mahmood	4
N.E.Bonner	lbw b Stokes	9	c Root b Mahmood	3
J.Blackwood	lbw b Lawrence	102	c Bairstow b Leach	27
A.S.Joseph	c Lawrence b Stokes	19		
J.O.Holder	c Fisher b Mahmood	12	(6) c Lawrence b Leach	0
†J.M.Da Silva	lbw b Leach	33	(7) not out	30
K.A.J.Roach	lbw b Woakes	1		
V.Permaul	lbw b Mahmood	5		
J.N.T.Seales	not out	5		
Extras	(B 10, LB 4, NB 8)	22	(B 1, LB 2, NB 2)	5
Total	**(187.5 overs)**	**411**	**(5 wkts; 65 overs)**	**135**

WEST INDIES	O	M	R	W		O	M	R	W
Roach	27	5	68	2		8	3	31	1
Seales	24	4	55	1	(3)	6	0	34	2
Joseph	23	1	109	1	(6)	6	0	45	1
Permaul	35.5	1	126	3	(2)	10	0	29	2
Holder	28	4	76	1		8.5	1	40	0
Bonner	1	0	3	0					
Brathwaite	12	0	59	1	(4)	6	0	5	0
ENGLAND									
Woakes	23	10	51	1		4	0	11	0
Fisher	25	5	67	1		2	1	4	0
Leach	69.5	27	118	3		25	13	36	3
Stokes	29	10	65	2	(6)	7	2	9	0
Mahmood	27	6	58	2	(4)	8	2	21	2
Lawrence	8	2	21	1	(7)	13	4	36	0
Root	6	1	17	0	(5)	6	3	15	0

FALL OF WICKETS

	E	WI	E	WI
Wkt	1st	1st	2nd	2nd
1st	4	14	51	14
2nd	80	83	67	23
3rd	244	101	74	39
4th	373	284	110	89
5th	410	336	161	93
6th	424	351	167	–
7th	499	385	–	–
8th	503	392	–	–
9th	507	403	–	–
10th	–	411	–	–

Umpires: N.Duguid (*West Indies*) (1) and J.S.Wilson (*West Indies*) (27).
Referee: Sir R.B.Richardson (*West Indies*) (37). **Test No. 2457/162 (WI562/E1047)**

WEST INDIES v ENGLAND (3rd Test)

At Queen's Park, St George's, on 24, 25, 26, 27 March 2022.
Toss: West Indies. Result: **WEST INDIES** won by ten wickets.
Debuts: None.

ENGLAND

A.Z.Lees	c Da Silva b Roach	31	b Mayers		31
Z.Crawley	c Brathwaite b Mayers	7	c Holder b Seales		8
*J.E.Root	c Da Silva b Mayers	0	c Campbell b Mayers		5
D.W.Lawrence	lbw b Seales	8	b Mayers		0
B.A.Stokes	c and b Joseph	2	c Brooks b Mayers		4
J.M.Bairstow	c Da Silva b Joseph	0	c Da Silva b Joseph		22
†B.T.Foakes	b Seales	7	run out		2
C.R.Woakes	b Seales	25	c Holder b Roach		19
C.Overton	b Roach	14	c Holder b Mayers		1
M.J.Leach	not out	41	c Da Silva b Roach		4
S.Mahmood	b Blackwood	49	not out		3
Extras	(B 18, LB 2)	20	(B 13, LB 7, W 1)		21
Total	**(89.4 overs)**	**204**	**(64.2 overs)**		**120**

WEST INDIES

*K.C.Brathwaite	lbw b Stokes	17	not out	20
J.D.Campbell	c Foakes b Overton	35	not out	6
S.S.J.Brooks	lbw b Mahmood	13		
N.E.Bonner	c Foakes b Woakes	4		
J.Blackwood	lbw b Woakes	18		
J.O.Holder	c Bairstow b Woakes	0		
K.R.Mayers	c Mahmood b Stokes	28		
†J.M.Da Silva	not out	100		
A.S.Joseph	c Foakes b Overton	28		
K.A.J.Roach	c Foakes b Mahmood	25		
J.N.T.Seales	c and b Root	13		
Extras	(B 1, LB 13, W 2)	16	(B 1, LB 1)	2
Total	**(116.3 overs)**	**297**	**(0 wkts; 4.5 overs)**	**28**

WEST INDIES	O	M	R	W		O	M	R	W
Roach	18	4	41	2		9.2	4	10	2
Seales	17	4	40	3		12	2	26	1
Holder	15	6	34	0	(4)	8	5	6	0
Mayers	10	7	13	2	(3)	17	9	18	5
Joseph	18	6	33	2		16	3	38	1
Bonner	5	1	10	0					
Blackwood	1.4	1	4	1	(6)	2	1	2	0
Brathwaite	5	2	9	0					

ENGLAND	O	M	R	W		O	M	R	W
Woakes	25	7	59	3		2.5	0	13	0
Overton	23	3	81	2					
Mahmood	24	9	45	2	(2)	2	0	13	0
Stokes	22	4	48	2					
Leach	21	6	49	0					
Root	1.3	0	1	1					

FALL OF WICKETS

	E	WI	E	WI
Wkt	1st	1st	2nd	2nd
1st	23	50	14	–
2nd	29	68	27	–
3rd	46	69	27	–
4th	53	82	39	–
5th	53	82	80	–
6th	53	95	83	–
7th	67	128	97	–
8th	90	177	101	–
9th	114	245	116	–
10th	204	297	120	–

Umpires: G.O.Brathwaite (*West Indies*) (8) and J.S.Wilson (*West Indies*) (28).
Referee: Sir R.B.Richardson (*West Indies*) (38).   **Test No. 2458/163 (WI563/E1048)**

SOUTH AFRICA v BANGLADESH (1st Test)

At Kingsmead, Durban, on 31 March, 1, 2, 3, 4 April 2022.
Toss: Bangladesh. Result: **SOUTH AFRICA** won by 220 runs.
Debuts: South Africa – R.D.Rickelton, L.B.Williams.

SOUTH AFRICA

*D.Elgar	c Liton b Khaled	67	(2) lbw b Taskin		64
S.J.Erwee	b Mehedi	41	(1) lbw b Ebadat		8
K.D.Petersen	run out	19	c Mahmudul b Mehedi		36
T.Bavuma	b Mehedi	93	c Yasir b Ebadat		4
R.D.Rickelton	c Mominul b Ebadat	21	not out		39
†K.Verreynne	lbw b Khaled	28	c Shadman b Mehedi		6
P.W.A.Mulder	c Mahmudul b Khaled	0	c Yasir b Mehedi		11
K.A.Maharaj	b Ebadat	19	lbw b Taskin		5
S.R.Harmer	not out	38	run out		11
L.B.Williams	c Mahmudul b Khaled	12	run out		0
D.Olivier	lbw b Mehedi	12	lbw b Ebadat		0
Extras	(B 6, LB 3, NB 3, W 5)	17	(B 12, LB 7, W 1)		20
Total	**(121 overs)**	**367**	**(74 overs)**		**204**

BANGLADESH

Mahmudul Hasan	c Harmer b Williams	137	b Maharaj		4
Shadman Islam	b Harmer	9	c Petersen b Harmer		0
Nazmul Hossain	b Harmer	38	st Verreynne b Harmer		26
*Mominul Haque	c Petersen b Harmer	2	lbw b Maharaj		2
Mushfiqur Rahim	c Verreynne b Harmer	7	lbw b Maharaj		0
Taskin Ahmed	c Mulder b Williams	1	(9) c Mulder b Maharaj		14
†Liton Das	b Williams	41	(6) c Harmer b Maharaj		2
Yasir Ali	run out	22	(7) b Maharaj		5
Mehedi Hasan	c Harmer b Mulder	29	(8) c Petersen b Harmer		0
Khaled Ahmed	c Verreynne b Olivier	0	c Williams b Maharaj		0
Ebadat Hossain	not out	0	not out		0
Extras	(B 5, LB 4, NB 5)	14	–		
Total	**(115.5 overs)**	**298**	**(19 overs)**		**53**

BANGLADESH	O	M	R	W		O	M	R	W
Taskin Ahmed	23	4	69	0	(6)	11	1	24	2
Ebadat Hossain	29	10	86	2	(4)	13	1	40	3
Khaled Ahmed	25	3	92	4	(1)	13	1	33	0
Mehedi Hasan	40	8	94	3	(2)	35	6	85	3
Mominul Haque	4	0	17	0		1	1	0	0
Nazmul Hossain					(3)	1	0	3	0

SOUTH AFRICA	O	M	R	W		O	M	R	W
Olivier	15	5	36	1					
Williams	18.5	3	54	3					
Harmer	40	12	103	4	(2)	9	3	21	3
Maharaj	37	15	65	0	(1)	10	2	32	7
Elgar	1	0	8	0					
Mulder	4	1	23	1					

FALL OF WICKETS

Wkt	SA 1st	B 1st	SA 2nd	B 2nd
1st	113	25	48	4
2nd	117	80	116	6
3rd	146	80	126	8
4th	180	94	126	12
5th	245	101	148	16
6th	245	183	168	26
7th	298	216	183	33
8th	298	267	202	50
9th	332	294	204	51
10th	367	298	204	53

Umpires: M.Erasmus (*South Africa*) (71) and A.T.Holdstock (*South Africa*) (5).
Referee: A.J.Pycroft (*Zimbabwe*) (85).

Test No. 2459/13 (SA451/B129)

SOUTH AFRICA v BANGLADESH (2nd Test)

At St George's Park, Gqeberha (formerly Port Elizabeth), on 8, 9, 10, 11 April 2022.
Toss: South Africa. Result: **SOUTH AFRICA** won by 332 runs.
Debut: South Africa – K.Zondo.

SOUTH AFRICA

*D.Elgar	c Liton b Taijul	70	(2) b Taijul		26
S.J.Erwee	c Liton b Khaled	24	(1) c Mominul b Khaled		41
K.D.Petersen	lbw b Taijul	64	lbw b Taijul		14
T.Bavuma	c Nazmul b Khaled	67	lbw b Mehedi		30
R.D.Rickelton	c Yasir b Taijul	42	c Mominul b Taijul		12
†K.Verreynne	b Khaled	22	not out		39
P.W.A.Mulder	b Taijul	33	b Mehedi		6
K.A.Maharaj	b Taijul	84			
S.R.Harmer	st Liton b Taijul	29			
L.B.Williams	lbw b Mehedi	13			
D.Olivier	not out	0			
Extras	(LB 3, NB 1, W 1)	5	(B 4, LB 4)		8
Total	**(136.2 overs)**	**453**	**(6 wkts dec; 39.5 overs)**		**176**

BANGLADESH

Tamim Iqbal	lbw b Mulder	47	c Mulder b Harmer		13
Mahmudul Hasan	c Erwee b Olivier	0	c Mulder b Maharaj		0
Nazmul Hossain	lbw b Mulder	33	lbw b Maharaj		7
*Mominul Haque	lbw b Mulder	6	c Rickelton b Maharaj		5
Mushfiqur Rahim	b Harmer	51	c Elgar b Maharaj		1
†Liton Das	b Olivier	11	st Verreynne b Maharaj		27
Yasir Ali	c and b Maharaj	46	c Williams b Harmer		0
Mehedi Hasan	c Olivier b Maharaj	11	c Verreynne b Maharaj		20
Taijul Islam	c Williams b Harmer	5	lbw b Harmer		0
Khaled Ahmed	not out	0	lbw b Maharaj		0
Ebadat Hossain	c Williams b Harmer	0	not out		0
Extras	(B 4, LB 2, W 1)	7	(B 6, NB 1)		7
Total	**(74.2 overs)**	**217**	**(23.3 overs)**		**80**

BANGLADESH	O	M	R	W		O	M	R	W
Khaled Ahmed	29	6	100	3	(2)	10	2	38	1
Mehedi Hasan	26.2	4	85	1	(4)	9.5	3	34	2
Ebadat Hossain	28	3	121	0	(1)	5	0	29	0
Taijul Islam	50	10	135	6	(3)	15	2	67	3
Nazmul Hossain	3	0	9	0					

SOUTH AFRICA	O	M	R	W		O	M	R	W
Olivier	15	4	39	2					
Williams	12	2	51	0					
Harmer	10.2	1	39	3	(2)	11.3	1	34	3
Maharaj	24	6	57	2	(1)	12	3	40	7
Mulder	13	7	25	3					

FALL OF WICKETS

	SA	B	SA	B
Wkt	1st	1st	2nd	2nd
1st	52	3	60	1
2nd	133	82	84	11
3rd	184	85	90	27
4th	267	100	119	33
5th	271	122	154	38
6th	300	192	176	44
7th	380	210	–	69
8th	418	216	–	80
9th	453	217	–	80
10th	453	217	–	80

Umpires: M.Erasmus (*South Africa*) (72) and A.Paleker (*South Africa*) (2).
Referee: A.J.Pycroft (*Zimbabwe*) (86).   Test No. 2460/14 (SA452/B130)

G.A.Stuurman and K.Zondo replaced P.W.A.Mulder and S.J.Erwee at the start of Day Four (Covid replacements).

BANGLADESH v SRI LANKA (1st Test)

At Zohur Ahmed Chowdhury Stadium, Chittagong, on 15, 16, 17, 18, 19 May 2022.
Toss: Sri Lanka. Result: **MATCH DRAWN**.
Debuts: None.

‡ (C Karunaratne)

SRI LANKA

B.O.P.Fernando	c Liton b Nayeem	36	run out		19
*F.D.M.Karunaratne	lbw b Nayeem	9	c Mominul b Taijul		52
B.K.G.Mendis	c Nayeem b Taijul	54	(4) b Taijul		48
A.D.Mathews	c Shakib b Nayeem	199	(5) c and b Taijul		0
D.M.de Silva	c Mahmudul b Shakib	34	(6) c Mushfiqur b Shakib		33
L.D.Chandimal	lbw b Nayeem	66	(7) not out		39
†D.P.D.N.Dickwella	b Nayeem	3	(8) not out		61
R.T.M.Wanigamuni	b Shakib	1			
L.Ambuldeniya	lbw b Shakib	0	(3) b Taijul		2
M.V.T.Fernando	not out	17			
A.M.Fernando	b Nayeem	1			
C.A.K.Rajitha					
Extras	(B 4, NB 1)	5	(LB 2, NB 4)		6
Total	**(153 overs)**	**397**	**(6 wkts; 90.1 overs)**		**260**

BANGLADESH

Mahmudul Hasan	c Dickwella b A.M.Fernando	58
Tamim Iqbal	b Rajitha	133
Nazmul Hossain	c Dickwella b Rajitha	1
*Mominul Haque	b Rajitha	2
Mushfiqur Rahim	b Ambuldeniya	105
†Liton Das	c Dickwella b Rajitha	88
Shakib Al Hasan	c Dickwella b A.M.Fernando	26
Nayeem Hasan	c Mendis b de Silva	9
Taijul Islam	c sub‡ b A.M.Fernando	20
Shoriful Islam	retired hurt	3
Khaled Ahmed	not out	0
Extras	(B 4, LB 8, NB 8)	20
Total	**(170.1 overs)**	**465**

BANGLADESH	O	M	R	W		O	M	R	W
Shoriful Islam	20	3	55	0					
Khaled Ahmed	16	1	66	0		7	2	37	0
Nayeem Hasan	30	4	105	6	(1)	23	5	79	0
Taijul Islam	48	12	107	1		34	9	82	4
Shakib Al Hasan	39	12	60	3	(3)	25	5	58	1
Nazmul Hossain					(5)	1	0	2	0
Mahmudul Hasan					(6)	0.1	0	1	0

SRI LANKA	O	M	R	W
M.V.T.Fernando	8	0	42	0
A.M.Fernando	26	4	72	3
Wanigamuni	45	10	119	0
Ambuldeniya	47	9	104	1
De Silva	19	2	48	1
Rajitha	24.1	6	60	4
Mendis	1	0	8	0

FALL OF WICKETS

	SL	B	SL
Wkt	1st	1st	2nd
1st	23	162	36
2nd	66	172	39
3rd	158	184	106
4th	183	385	110
5th	319	385	143
6th	323	421	161
7th	328	439	–
8th	328	450	–
9th	390	465	–
10th	397	–	–

Umpires: R.A.Kettleborough (*England*) (73) and Sharfuddoula (*Bangladesh*) (5).
Referee: B.C.Broad (*England*) (114).   **Test No. 2461/23 (B131/SL302)**

C.A.J.Rajitha replaced M.V.T.Fernando at the start of Day Three (concussion).

BANGLADESH v SRI LANKA (2nd Test)

At Shere Bangla National Stadium, Mirpur, on 23, 24, 25, 26, 27 May 2022.
Toss: Bangladesh. Result: **SRI LANKA** won by ten wickets.
Debuts: None.

BANGLADESH

Mahmudul Hasan	b Rajitha	0		c Mendis b A.M.Fernando	15
Tamim Iqbal	c Jayawickrama b A.M.Fernando	0		c Mendis b A.M.Fernando	0
Nazmul Hossain	b Rajitha	8		run out	2
*Mominul Haque	c Dickwella b A.M.Fernando	9		c Dickwella b Rajitha	0
Mushfiqur Rahim	not out	175		b Rajitha	23
Shakib Al Hasan	lbw b Rajitha	0	(7)	c Dickwella b A.M.Fernando	58
†Liton Das	c Mendis b Rajitha	141	(6)	c and b A.M.Fernando	52
Mosaddek Hossain	c Dickwella b Rajitha	0		lbw b Wanigamuni	9
Taijul Islam	c Dickwella b A.M.Fernando	15		lbw b A.M.Fernando	1
Khaled Ahmed	c Dickwella b A.M.Fernando	0	(11)	b A.M.Fernando	0
Ebadat Hossain	run out	0	(10)	not out	0
Extras	(B 7, LB 5, NB 2, W 3)	17		(LB 1, NB 2, W 6)	9
Total	**(116.2 overs)**	**365**		**(55.3 overs)**	**169**

SRI LANKA

B.O.P.Fernando	c Nazmul b Ebadat	57		not out	21
*F.D.M.Karunaratne	b Shakib	80		not out	7
B.K.G.Mendis	lbw b Shakib	11			
C.A.K.Rajitha	b Ebadat	0			
A.D.Mathews	not out	145			
D.M.de Silva	c Liton b Shakib	58			
L.D.Chandimal	c Tamim b Ebadat	124			
†D.P.D.N.Dickwella	c Liton b Shakib	9			
R.T.M.Wanigamuni	lbw b Ebadat	10			
P.A.K.P.Jayawickrama	c Liton b Shakib	0			
A.M.Fernando	run out	2			
Extras	(LB 8, NB 2)	10		(B 1)	1
Total	**(165.1 overs)**	**506**		**(0 wkts; 3 overs)**	**29**

SRI LANKA	O	M	R	W	O	M	R	W	FALL OF WICKETS				
Rajitha	28.2	7	64	5	12	5	40	2		B	SL	B	SL
A.M.Fernando	26	3	93	4	17.3	5	51	6	Wkt	1st	1st	2nd	2nd
Jayawickrama	38	9	108	0	13	0	47	0	1st	0	95	15	–
Wanigamuni	14	0	53	0	11	2	20	1	2nd	6	139	19	–
De Silva	6	0	27	0	2	0	10	0	3rd	16	144	19	–
Karunaratne	4	1	8	0					4th	24	164	23	–
									5th	24	266	53	–
BANGLADESH									6th	296	465	156	–
Khaled Ahmed	23	3	85	0					7th	296	482	163	–
Ebadat Hossain	38	4	148	4	(3)	1	0	5	0	8th	345	501	169	–
Shakib Al Hasan	40.1	11	96	5	(2)	1	0	7	0	9th	349	502	169	–
Mosaddek Hossain	12	1	38	0					10th	365	506	169	–
Taijul Islam	49	10	124	0	(1)	1	0	16	0					
Mominul Haque	3	0	7	0									

Umpires: Sharfuddoula (*Bangladesh*) (6) and J.S.Wilson (*West Indies*) (29).
Referee: B.C.Broad (*England*) (115).   **Test No. 2462/24 (B132/SL303)**

ENGLAND v NEW ZEALAND (1st Test)

At Lord's London, on 2, 3, 4, 5 June 2022.
Toss: New Zealand. Result: **ENGLAND** won by five wickets.
Debuts: England – M.W.Parkinson, M.J.Potts.

NEW ZEALAND

T.W.M.Latham	c Bairstow b Anderson	1	c Foakes b Potts	14
W.A.Young	c Bairstow b Anderson	1	c Foakes b Anderson	1
*K.S.Williamson	c Foakes b Potts	2	c Bairstow b Potts	15
D.P.Conway	c Bairstow b Broad	3	c Foakes b Broad	13
D.J.Mitchell	b Potts	13	c Foakes b Broad	108
†T.A.Blundell	b Potts	14	lbw b Anderson	96
C.de Grandhomme	not out	42	run out	0
K.A.Jamieson	c Potts b Anderson	6	b Broad	0
T.G.Southee	c Potts b Anderson	26	c Root b Parkinson	21
A.Y.Patel	lbw b Potts	7	lbw b Potts	4
T.A.Boult	c Pope b Stokes	14	not out	4
Extras	(LB 3)	3	(B 1, LB 4, NB 3, W 1)	9
Total	**(40 overs)**	**132**	**(91.3 overs)**	**285**

ENGLAND

A.Z.Lees	lbw b Southee	25	b Jamieson	20
Z.Crawley	c Blundell b Jamieson	43	c Southee b Jamieson	9
O.J.D.Pope	c Blundell b Jamieson	7	b Boult	10
J.E.Root	c Southee b de Grandhomme	11	not out	115
J.M.Bairstow	b Boult	1	b Jamieson	16
*B.A.Stokes	c Blundell b Southee	1	c Blundell b Jamieson	54
†B.T.Foakes	c Mitchell b Southee	7	not out	32
M.J.Potts	c Mitchell b Boult	0		
S.C.J.Broad	b Southee	9		
J.M.Anderson	not out	7		
M.W.Parkinson	c Mitchell b Boult	8		
M.J.Leach				
Extras	(B 14, LB 7, NB 1)	22	(B 6, LB 9, NB 2, W 6)	23
Total	**(42.5 overs)**	**141**	**(5 wkts; 78.5 overs)**	**279**

ENGLAND	O	M	R	W	O	M	R	W	FALL OF WICKETS			
Anderson	16	6	66	4	21	7	57	2		NZ	E	NZ	E
Broad	13	0	45	1	26	7	76	3	Wkt	1st	1st	2nd	2nd
Potts	9.2	4	13	4	20	3	55	3	1st	1	59	5	31
Stokes	1.4	0	5	1	8	1	43	0	2nd	2	75	30	32
Parkinson					15.3	0	47	1	3rd	7	92	35	46
Root					1	0	2	0	4th	12	96	56	69
									5th	27	98	251	159
NEW ZEALAND									6th	36	100	251	–
Southee	14	3	55	4	23.5	5	87	0	7th	45	100	251	–
Boult	13.5	4	21	3	24	3	73	1	8th	86	125	265	–
De Grandhomme	8	2	24	1	(4) 3.5	1	3	0	9th	102	130	281	–
Jamieson	7	3	20	2	(3) 25	4	79	4	10th	132	141	285	–
Mitchell					0.1	0	0	0					
Patel					2	0	22	0					

Umpires: M.A.Gough (*England*) (25) and R.J.Tucker (*Australia*) (76).
Referee: Sir R.B.Richardson (*West Indies*) (39).   **Test No. 2463/108 (E1049/NZ456)**

M.W.Parkinson replaced M.J.Leach after 23 overs NZ (1) (concussion).

ENGLAND v NEW ZEALAND (2nd Test)

At Trent Bridge, Nottingham, on 10, 11, 12, 13, 14 June 2022.
Toss: England. Result: **ENGLAND** won by five wickets.
Debut: New Zealand – M.G.Bracewell.

NEW ZEALAND

*T.W.M.Latham	c Potts b Anderson	26	b Anderson		4
W.A.Young	c Crawley b Stokes	47	run out		56
D.P.Conway	c Foakes b Anderson	46	c Bairstow b Leach		52
H.M.Nicholls	c Foakes b Stokes	30	c Lees b Potts		3
D.J.Mitchell	c Foakes b Potts	190	not out		62
†T.A.Blundell	c Stokes b Leach	106	c Stokes b Broad		24
M.G.Bracewell	c Root b Anderson	49	c Broad b Potts		25
K.A.Jamieson	c Foakes b Broad	14	(10) c Foakes b Broad		1
T.G.Southee	c Root b Broad	4	(8) run out		0
M.J.Henry	c Crawley b Leach	0	(9) c Foakes b Broad		18
T.A.Boult	not out	16	c Stokes b Anderson		17
Extras	(B 1, LB 16, NB 8)	25	(B 9, LB 5, NB 6, W 2)		22
Total	**(145.3 overs)**	**553**	**(84.4 overs)**		**284**

ENGLAND

A.Z.Lees	c Mitchell b Henry	67	c Blundell b Southee		44
Z.Crawley	c Blundell b Boult	4	c Southee b Boult		0
O.J.D.Pope	c Henry b Boult	145	c Blundell b Henry		18
J.E.Root	c Southee b Boult	176	c and b Boult		3
J.M.Bairstow	c Blundell b Boult	8	c Blundell b Boult		136
*B.A.Stokes	c Boult b Bracewell	46	not out		75
†B.T.Foakes	run out	56	not out		12
S.C.J.Broad	c Mitchell b Bracewell	9			
M.J.Potts	b Boult	0			
M.J.Leach	not out	3			
J.M.Anderson	st Blundell b Bracewell	9			
Extras	(B 12, LB 3, W 1)	16	(B 5, LB 6)		11
Total	**(128.2 overs)**	**539**	**(5 wkts; 50 overs)**		**299**

ENGLAND	O	M	R	W		O	M	R	W	FALL OF WICKETS				
Anderson	27	9	62	3		8.4	1	20	2		NZ	E	NZ	E
Broad	26	4	107	2		20	4	70	3	Wkt	1st	1st	2nd	2nd
Potts	30.3	6	126	1		15	6	32	2	1st	84	6	4	12
Stokes	23	2	85	2	(5)	17	3	62	0	2nd	84	147	104	53
Leach	35	6	140	2	(4)	24	5	86	1	3rd	161	334	115	56
Root	4	0	16	0						4th	169	344	131	93
										5th	405	405	176	272
NEW ZEALAND										6th	496	516	204	–
Southee	32	1	154	0		11	0	67	1	7th	513	527	213	–
Boult	33.3	8	106	5		16	1	94	3	8th	517	527	245	–
Henry	27	5	128	1		15	3	67	1	9th	520	530	249	–
Jamieson	16.3	3	66	0						10th	553	539	284	–
Bracewell	17.2	2	62	3	(4)	8	0	60	0					
Mitchell	2	0	8	0										

Umpires: M.A.Gough (*England*) (26) and P.R.Reiffel (*Australia*) (55).
Referee: Sir R.B.Richardson (*West Indies*) (40).   **Test No. 2464/109 (E1050/NZ457)**

ENGLAND v NEW ZEALAND (3rd Test)

At Headingley, Leeds, on 23, 24, 25, 26, 27 June 2022.
Toss: New Zealand. Result: **ENGLAND** won by seven wickets.
Debut: England – J.Overton.

NEW ZEALAND

T.W.M.Latham	c Root b Broad	0	c Bairstow b Overton		76
W.A.Young	lbw b Leach	20	c Pope b Potts		8
*K.S.Williamson	c Foakes b Broad	31	c Bairstow b Potts		48
D.P.Conway	b Overton	26	c Pope b Root		11
H.M.Nicholls	c Lees b Leach	19	c and b Leach		7
D.J.Mitchell	c Stokes b Leach	109	lbw b Potts		56
†T.A.Blundell	lbw b Potts	55	not out		88
M.G.Bracewell	c Crawley b Broad	13	c Crawley b Leach		9
T.G.Southee	c Stokes b Leach	33	b Leach		2
N.Wagner	c Bairstow b Leach	4	c Billings b Leach		0
T.A.Boult	not out	0	b Leach		4
Extras	(B 4, LB 14, NB 1)	19	(B 9, LB 2, NB 2, W 4)		17
Total	**(117.3 overs)**	**329**	**(105.2 overs)**		**326**

ENGLAND

A.Z.Lees	b Boult	4	run out		9
Z.Crawley	b Boult	6	c Williamson b Bracewell		25
O.J.D.Pope	b Boult	5	b Southee		82
J.E.Root	c Blundell b Southee	5	not out		86
J.M.Bairstow	c Boult b Bracewell	162	not out		71
*B.A.Stokes	c Williamson b Wagner	18			
†B.T.Foakes	lbw b Wagner	5			
J.Overton	c Mitchell b Boult	97			
S.C.J.Broad	b Southee	42			
M.J.Potts	not out	1			
M.J.Leach	lbw b Southee	8			
S.W.Billings					
Extras	(LB 11, W 1)	12	(B 9, LB 12, NB 2)		23
Total	**(67 overs)**	**360**	**(3 wkts; 54.2 overs)**		**296**

ENGLAND	O	M	R	W		O	M	R	W
Broad	23	8	62	3		24	7	63	0
Potts	26	11	34	4	(3)	25	5	66	3
Overton	23	2	85	1	(4)	14	2	61	1
Leach	38.3	8	100	5	(2)	32.2	12	66	5
Root	7	0	30	0	(6)	6	0	29	1
Stokes					(5)	4	0	30	0
NEW ZEALAND									
Boult	22	4	104	4		12	2	65	0
Southee	23	2	100	3		19	5	68	1
Wagner	12	1	75	2	(4)	8	2	33	0
Bracewell	7	0	54	1	(3)	15.2	0	109	1
Mitchell	3	0	16	0					

	FALL OF WICKETS			
	NZ	E	NZ	E
Wkt	1st	1st	2nd	2nd
1st	0	4	28	17
2nd	35	14	125	51
3rd	62	17	152	185
4th	83	21	153	–
5th	123	55	161	–
6th	243	55	274	–
7th	265	296	291	–
8th	325	351	305	–
9th	329	351	305	–
10th	329	360	326	–

Umpires: M.Erasmus (*South Africa*) (73) and R.A.Kettleborough (*England*) (74).
Referee: D.C.Boon (*Australia*) (66).   **Test No. 2465/110 (E1051/NZ458)**

S.W.Billings replaced B.T.Foakes at the start of Day Four (Covid replacement).

WEST INDIES v BANGLADESH (1st Test)

At Sir Vivian Richards Stadium, North Sound, on 16, 17, 18, 19 June 2022.
Toss: West Indies. Result: **WEST INDIES** won by seven wickets.
Debut: West Indies – G.Motie.

BANGLADESH

Tamim Iqbal	c Da Silva b Joseph	29		c Da Silva b Joseph	22
Mahmudul Hasan	c Bonner b Roach	0		c Da Silva b Roach	42
Nazmul Hossain	b Roach	0	(4)	c Campbell b Mayers	17
Mominul Haque	c Blackwood b Seales	0	(5)	lbw b Mayers	4
Liton Das	c Da Silva b Mayers	12	(6)	c Mayers b Roach	17
*Shakib Al Hasan	c Roach b Joseph	51	(7)	c Brathwaite b Roach	63
†Nurul Hasan	lbw b Mayers	0	(8)	c Da Silva b Roach	64
Mehedi Hasan	c Da Silva b Seales	2	(3)	c Mayers b Joseph	2
Mustafizur Rahman	c Da Silva b Seales	0	(10)	b Joseph	7
Ebadat Hossain	not out	3	(9)	b Roach	1
Khaled Ahmed	c Bonner b Joseph	0		not out	0
Extras	(B 1, LB 4, W 1)	6		(B 2, LB 1, NB 1, W 2)	6
Total	**(32.5 overs)**	**103**		**(90.5 overs)**	**245**

WEST INDIES

*K.C.Brathwaite	lbw b Khaled	94		c Nurul b Khaled	1
J.D.Campbell	b Mustafizur	24		not out	58
R.A.Reifer	c Nurul b Ebadat	11		c Nurul b Khaled	2
N.E.Bonner	b Shakib	33		b Khaled	0
J.Blackwood	c Mehedi b Khaled	63		not out	26
K.R.Mayers	lbw b Mehedi	7			
†J.M.Da Silva	c Nurul b Mehedi	1			
A.S.Joseph	c Nurul b Mehedi	0			
K.A.J.Roach	c Liton b Ebadat	0			
G.Motie	not out	23			
J.N.T.Seales	lbw b Mehedi	1			
Extras	(LB 4, NB 2, W 2)	8		(LB 1)	1
Total	**(112.5 overs)**	**265**		**(3 wkts; 22 overs)**	**88**

WEST INDIES	O	M	R	W	O	M	R	W	FALL OF WICKETS				
										B	WI	B	WI
Roach	8	2	21	2	24.5	10	53	5	Wkt	1st	1st	2nd	2nd
Seales	10	2	33	3	14	1	45	0	1st	1	44	33	1
Joseph	8.5	2	33	3	19	6	55	3	2nd	3	72	35	3
Mayers	5	2	10	2	13	3	30	2	3rd	16	134	64	9
Motie	2	0	1	0	15	2	42	0	4th	41	197	75	
Reifer					5	1	17	0	5th	41	224	100	
									6th	45	230	109	
BANGLADESH									7th	77	238	232	
Mustafizur Rahman	18	7	30	1	4	1	7	0	8th	81	239	238	
Khaled Ahmed	22	4	59	2	8	0	27	3	9th	103	258	245	
Ebadat Hossain	28	8	65	2	(4)	4	0	30	0	10th	103	265	245	
Shakib Al Hasan	21	5	48	1	(5)	2	0	3	0					
Mehedi Hasan	22.5	6	59	4	(3)	3	2	10	0					
Nazmul Hossain	1	1	0	0		1	0	10	0					

Umpires: C.B.Gaffaney (*New Zealand*) (41) and J.S.Wilson (*West Indies*) (30).
Referee: J.J.Crowe (*New Zealand*) (108). **Test No. 2466/19 (WI564/B133)**

WEST INDIES v BANGLADESH (2nd Test)

At Darren Sammy National Cricket Stadium, Gros Islet, on 24, 25, 26, 27 June 2022.
Toss: West Indies. Result: **WEST INDIES** won by ten wickets.
Debut: West Indies – A.Phillip.

BANGLADESH

Tamim Iqbal	c Blackwood b Joseph	46	c Da Silva b Roach		4
Mahmudul Hasan	b Phillip	10	c Blackwood b Roach		13
Nazmul Hossain	lbw b Mayers	26	c Da Silva b Joseph		42
Anamul Haque	lbw b Phillip	23	lbw b Roach		4
Liton Das	c Brathwaite b Joseph	53	lbw b Seales		19
*Shakib Al Hasan	b Seales	8	c Campbell b Joseph		16
†Nurul Hasan	c Da Silva b Joseph	7	not out		60
Mehedi Hasan	c sub (D.C.Thomas) b Mayers	9	c Da Silva b Joseph		4
Ebadat Hossain	not out	21	c Reifer b Seales		0
Shoriful Islam	c Blackwood b Mayers	26	lbw b Seales		0
Khaled Ahmed	c Bonner b Seales	1	run out		0
Extras	(LB 3, NB 1)	4	(B 9, LB 1, NB 3, W 11)		24
Total	**(64.2 overs)**	**234**	**(45 overs)**		**186**

WEST INDIES

*K.C.Brathwaite	b Mehedi	51	not out		4
J.D.Campbell	c Nurul b Shoriful	45	not out		9
R.A.Reifer	b Khaled	22			
N.E.Bonner	b Khaled	0			
J.Blackwood	lbw b Mehedi	40			
K.R.Mayers	c Shoriful b Khaled	146			
†J.M.Da Silva	lbw b Mehedi	29			
A.S.Joseph	c Liton b Khaled	6			
K.A.J.Roach	not out	18			
A.Phillip	c Nurul b Shoriful	9			
J.N.T.Seales	c Nurul b Khaled	5			
Extras	(B 9, LB 24, NB 4)	37			
Total	**(126.3 overs)**	**408**	**(0 wkts; 2.5 overs)**		**13**

WEST INDIES	O	M	R	W		O	M	R	W		FALL OF WICKETS			
												B WI	B WI	
Roach	15	3	57	0		13	1	54	3	*Wkt*	*1st*	*1st*	*2nd*	*2nd*
Seales	14.2	4	53	3	(4)	8	2	21	3	1st	41	100	4	–
Joseph	15	1	50	3	(2)	14	2	57	3	2nd	68	131	22	–
Phillip	9	1	30	2	(3)	5	1	23	0	3rd	105	131	32	–
Reifer	3	1	6	0						4th	105	132	57	–
Mayers	8	0	35	2	(5)	5	1	21	0	5th	125	248	104	–
										6th	138	344	118	–
BANGLADESH										7th	165	363	148	–
Shoriful Islam	19	6	76	2						8th	191	384	169	–
Khaled Ahmed	31.3	3	106	5		1	0	4	0	9th	227	403	174	–
Shakib Al Hasan	18	5	46	0						10th	234	408	186	–
Ebadat Hossain	19	6	56	0	(1)	1.5	0	9	0					
Mehedi Hasan	39	8	91	3										

Umpires: R.K.Illingworth (*England*) (58) and J.S.Wilson (*West Indies*) (31).
Referee: J.J.Crowe (*New Zealand*) (109).   **Test No. 2467/20 (WI565/B134)**

SRI LANKA v AUSTRALIA (1st Test)

At Galle International Stadium, on 29, 30 June, 1 July 2022.
Toss: Sri Lanka. Result: **AUSTRALIA** won by ten wickets.
Debut: Sri Lanka – J.D.F.Vandersay.

SRI LANKA

P.N.Silva	c Carey b Cummins	23	lbw b Swepson		14
*F.D.M.Karunaratne	c Warner b Lyon	28	c Carey b Lyon		23
B.K.G.Mendis	c Carey b Starc	3	c Swepson b Lyon		8
A.D.Mathews	c Warner b Lyon	39			
D.M.de Silva	c Carey b Swepson	14	lbw b Head		11
L.D.Chandimal	c Warner b Swepson	0	b Head		13
†D.P.D.N.Dickwella	c Carey b Lyon	58	c Labuschagne b Lyon		3
R.T.M.Wanigamuni	lbw b Lyon	22	c Khawaja b Lyon		0
J.D.F.Vandersay	c Starc b Swepson	6	b Head		8
L.Ambuldeniya	c Khawaja b Lyon	6	lbw b Head		0
A.M.Fernando	not out	2	not out		5
B.O.P.Fernando			(4) c Smith b Swepson		12
Extras	(B 5, LB 6)	11	(B 14, LB 1, NB 1)		16
Total	**(59 overs)**	**212**	**(22.5 overs)**		**113**

AUSTRALIA

U.T.Khawaja	c P.N.Silva b Vandersay	71	(2) not out	0
D.A.Warner	lbw b Wanigamuni	25	(1) not out	10
M.Labuschagne	c A.M.Fernando b Wanigamuni	13		
S.P.D.Smith	run out	6		
T.M.Head	c and b de Silva	6		
C.D.Green	lbw b Wanigamuni	77		
†A.T.Carey	c Chandimal b Wanigamuni	45		
M.A.Starc	c and b Vandersay	10		
*P.J.Cummins	b A.M.Fernando	26		
N.M.Lyon	not out	15		
M.J.Swepson	b A.M.Fernando	1		
Extras	(B 20, LB 3, NB 1, W 2)	26		
Total	**(70.5 overs)**	**321**	**(0 wkts; 0.4 overs)**	**10**

AUSTRALIA	O	M	R	W		O	M	R	W
Starc	9	0	31	1		2	0	23	0
Cummins	12	4	25	1					
Lyon	25	2	90	5	(2)	11	1	31	4
Swepson	13	0	55	3	(3)	7	0	34	2
Head					(4)	2.5	0	10	4

SRI LANKA	O	M	R	W		O	M	R	W
A.M.Fernando	8.5	1	37	2					
De Silva	5	0	8	1					
Ambuldeniya	15	0	73	0					
Wanigamuni	32	0	112	4	(1)	0.4	0	10	0
Vandersay	10	0	68	2					

FALL OF WICKETS

Wkt	1st	1st	2nd	2nd
	SL	A	SL	A
1st	38	47	37	–
2nd	42	75	39	–
3rd	74	83	59	–
4th	97	100	63	–
5th	97	157	95	–
6th	139	241	96	–
7th	193	278	97	–
8th	198	278	108	–
9th	206	319	108	–
10th	212	321	113	–

Umpires: H.D.P.K.Dharmasena (*Sri Lanka*) (72) and N.N.Menon (*India*) (12).
Referee: J.Srinath (*India*) (62). **Test No. 2468/32 (SL304/A843)**

B.O.P.Fernando replaced A.D.Mathews from the start of Day Three (Covid replacement).

SRI LANKA v AUSTRALIA (2nd Test)

At Galle International Stadium, on 8, 9, 10, 11 July 2022.
Toss: Australia. Result: **SRI LANKA** won by an innings and 39 runs.
Debuts: Sri Lanka – N.G.R.P.Jayasuriya, P.H.K.D.Mendis, M.M.Theekshana.

AUSTRALIA

U.T.Khawaja	b Wanigamuni	37	(2)	c Fernando b Jayasuriya	29
D.A.Warner	b Rajitha	5	(1)	lbw b Wanigamuni	24
M.Labuschagne	st Dickwella b Jayasuriya	104		lbw b Jayasuriya	32
S.P.D.Smith	not out	145		lbw b Jayasuriya	0
T.M.Head	b Jayasuriya	12		b Wanigamuni	5
C.D.Green	lbw b Jayasuriya	4		st Dickwella b Jayasuriya	23
†A.T.Carey	c Wanigamuni b Jayasuriya	28		not out	16
M.A.Starc	c B.K.G.Mendis b Jayasuriya	1		c B.K.G.Mendis b Jayasuriya	0
*P.J.Cummins	lbw b Rajitha	5		lbw b Theekshana	16
N.M.Lyon	lbw b Jayasuriya	5		lbw b Theekshana	5
M.J.Swepson	lbw b Theekshana	3		b Jayasuriya	0
Extras	(B 5, LB 6, NB 3, W 1)	15		(B 1)	1
Total	**(110 overs)**	**364**		**(41 overs)**	**151**

SRI LANKA

P.N.Silva	c Green b Starc	6
*F.D.M.Karunaratne	lbw b Swepson	86
B.K.G.Mendis	lbw b Lyon	85
A.D.Mathews	c Labuschagne b Starc	52
L.D.Chandimal	not out	206
P.H.K.D.Mendis	b Swepson	61
†D.P.D.N.Dickwella	c Cummins b Lyon	5
R.T.M.Wanigamuni	lbw b Starc	29
M.M.Theekshana	b Cummins	10
N.G.R.P.Jayasuriya	b Starc	0
C.A.K.Rajitha	lbw b Swepson	0
B.O.P.Fernando		
Extras	(B 4, LB 6, NB 1, W 3)	14
Total	**(181 overs)**	**554**

SRI LANKA	O	M	R	W		O	M	R	W
Rajitha	25	4	70	2		5	1	16	0
Wanigamuni	33	1	117	1	(3)	15	2	47	2
Theekshana	16	2	48	1	(2)	5	0	28	2
Jayasuriya	36	3	118	6		16	2	59	6

AUSTRALIA	O	M	R	W
Starc	29	3	89	4
Cummins	30	5	95	1
Lyon	64	5	194	2
Green	6	0	20	0
Swepson	38	2	103	3
Head	8	0	27	0
Labuschagne	6	0	16	0

FALL OF WICKETS			
	A	SL	A
Wkt	1st	1st	2nd
1st	15	12	49
2nd	70	164	59
3rd	204	186	59
4th	238	269	74
5th	252	402	112
6th	329	409	117
7th	333	477	117
8th	338	498	144
9th	345	505	150
10th	364	554	151

Umpires: H.D.P.K.Dharmasena (*Sri Lanka*) (73) and M.A.Gough (*England*) (27).
Referee: J.Srinath (*India*) (63).   Test No. 2469/33 (SL305/A844)

B.O.P.Fernando replaced P.N.Silva from the start of Day Four (Covid replacement).

ENGLAND v INDIA (5th Test)

At Edgbaston, Birmingham, on 1, 2, 3, 4, 5 July 2022.
Toss: England. Result: **ENGLAND** won by seven wickets.
Debuts: None.

INDIA

S.Gill	c Crawley b Anderson	17	c Crawley b Anderson		4
C.A.Pujara	c Crawley b Anderson	13	c Lees b Broad		66
G.H.Vihari	lbw b Potts	20	c Bairstow b Broad		11
V.Kohli	b Potts	11	c Root b Stokes		20
†R.R.Pant	c Crawley b Root	146	c Root b Leach		57
S.S.Iyer	c Billings b Anderson	15	c Anderson b Potts		19
R.A.Jadeja	b Anderson	104	b Stokes		23
S.N.Thakur	c Billings b Stokes	1	c Crawley b Potts		4
Mohammed Shami	c Leach b Broad	16	c Lees b Stokes		13
*J.J.Bumrah	not out	31	c Crawley b Stokes		7
M.Siraj	c Broad b Anderson	2	not out		2
Extras	(B 4, LB 17, NB 14, W 5)	40	(B 6, LB 7, NB 3, W 3)		19
Total	**(84.5 overs)**	**416**	**(81.5 overs)**		**245**

ENGLAND

A.Z.Lees	b Bumrah	6	run out		56
Z.Crawley	c Gill b Bumrah	9	b Bumrah		46
O.J.D.Pope	c Iyer b Bumrah	10	c Pant b Bumrah		0
J.E.Root	c Pant b Siraj	31	not out		142
J.M.Bairstow	c Kohli b Shami	106	not out		114
M.J.Leach	c Pant b Shami	0			
*B.A.Stokes	c Bumrah b Thakur	25			
†S.W.Billings	b Siraj	36			
S.C.J.Broad	c Pant b Siraj	1			
M.J.Potts	c Iyer b Siraj	19			
J.M.Anderson	not out	6			
Extras	(B 16, LB 5, NB 13, W 1)	35	(B 8, LB 7, NB 2, W 3)		20
Total	**(61.3 overs)**	**284**	**(3 wkts; 76.4 overs)**		**378**

ENGLAND	O	M	R	W	O	M	R	W
Anderson	21.5	4	60	5	19	5	46	1
Broad	18	3	89	1	16	1	58	2
Potts	20	1	105	2	17	3	50	2
Leach	9	0	71	0	12	1	28	1
Stokes	13	0	47	1	11.5	0	33	4
Root	3	0	23	1	6	1	17	0

INDIA	O	M	R	W		O	M	R	W
Bumrah	19	3	68	3		17	1	74	2
Mohammed Shami	22	4	78	2		15	2	64	0
Siraj	11.3	2	66	4	(4)	15	0	98	0
Thakur	7	0	48	1	(5)	11	0	65	0
Jadeja	2	0	3	0	(3)	18.4	3	62	0

FALL OF WICKETS				
	I	E	I	E
Wkt	1st	1st	2nd	2nd
1st	27	16	4	107
2nd	46	27	43	107
3rd	64	44	75	109
4th	71	78	153	–
5th	98	83	190	–
6th	320	149	198	–
7th	323	241	207	–
8th	371	248	230	–
9th	375	267	236	–
10th	416	284	245	–

Umpires: Alim Dar (*Pakistan*) (140) and R.A.Kettleborough (*England*) (75).
Referee: D.C.Boon (*Australia*) (67). **Test No. 2470/131 (E1052/I563)**

This Test concluded the interrupted 2021 series, see *Playfair Cricket Annual 2022* pp28-31.

SRI LANKA v PAKISTAN (1st Test)

At Galle International Stadium, on 16, 17, 18, 19, 20 July 2022.
Toss: Sri Lanka. Result: **PAKISTAN** won by four wickets.
Debut: Pakistan – Agha Salman.

SRI LANKA

B.O.P.Fernando	c Rizwan b Hasan	35		c Babar b Yasir	64
*F.D.M.Karunaratne	b Afridi	1		lbw b Nawaz	16
B.K.G.Mendis	c Rizwan b Yasir	21	(4)	b Yasir	76
A.D.Mathews	c Naseem b Yasir	0	(5)	c Babar b Nawaz	9
L.D.Chandimal	c Yasir b Hasan	76	(6)	not out	94
D.M.de Silva	b Afridi	14	(7)	b Yasir	20
†D.P.D.N.Dickwella	c Salman b Afridi	4	(8)	b Nawaz	12
R.T.M.Wanigamuni	c Rizwan b Naseem	11	(9)	b Nawaz	22
N.G.R.P.Jayasuriya	lbw b Nawaz	3	(11)	b Naseem	4
M.M.Theekshana	c Rizwan b Afridi	38		c Rizwan b Hasan	11
C.A.K.Rajitha	not out	12	(3)	lbw b Nawaz	7
Extras	(B 1, LB 3, NB 3)	7		(B 1, NB 1)	2
Total	**(66.1 overs)**	**222**		**(100 overs)**	**337**

PAKISTAN

Abdullah Shafiq	lbw b Jayasuriya	13		not out	160
Imam-ul-Haq	lbw b Rajitha	2		st Dickwella b Wanigamuni	35
Azhar Ali	lbw b Jayasuriya	3		c de Silva b Jayasuriya	6
*Babar Azam	lbw b Theekshana	119		b Jayasuriya	55
†Mohammad Rizwan	c Dickwella b Wanigamuni	4		lbw b Jayasuriya	40
Agha Salman	lbw b Jayasuriya	5		c Dickwella b Jayasuriya	12
Mohammad Nawaz	c Fernando b Jayasuriya	5	(8)	not out	19
Shaheen Shah Afridi	lbw b Jayasuriya	0			
Yasir Shah	c de Silva b Theekshana	17			
Hasan Ali	c Chandimal b Wanigamuni	18	(7)	c Theekshana b de Silva	5
Naseem Shah	not out	5			
Extras	(B 5, LB 1, NB 1, W 5)	12		(B 5, LB 7)	12
Total	**(90.5 overs)**	**218**		**(6 wkts; 127.2 overs)**	**344**

PAKISTAN	O	M	R	W		O	M	R	W
Shaheen Shah Afridi	14.1	3	58	4		7	2	21	0
Hasan Ali	12	2	23	2	(5)	12	3	19	1
Naseem Shah	13	0	53	1	(7)	7	0	24	1
Yasir Shah	21	4	66	2		29	2	122	3
Mohammad Nawaz	6	2	18	1	(2)	28	2	88	5
Agha Salman					(3)	16	1	53	0
Babar Azam					(6)	1	0	9	0
SRI LANKA									
Rajitha	11	2	42	1		9	2	18	0
Theekshana	25.5	6	68	2	(4)	14	2	44	0
Jayasuriya	39	10	82	5	(2)	56.2	10	135	4
Wanigamuni	13	2	18	2	(3)	33	0	102	1
De Silva	2	0	2	0		15	1	33	1

FALL OF WICKETS				
	SL	P	SL	P
Wkt	1st	1st	2nd	2nd
1st	11	12	33	87
2nd	60	21	41	104
3rd	60	24	132	205
4th	68	64	164	276
5th	99	73	178	298
6th	103	85	218	303
7th	130	85	235	–
8th	133	112	267	–
9th	177	148	308	–
10th	222	218	337	–

Umpires: H.D.P.K.Dharmasena (*Sri Lanka*) (74) and M.Erasmus (*South Africa*) (74).
Referee: J.J.Crowe (*New Zealand*) (110).　　**Test No. 2471/56 (SL306/P445)**

SRI LANKA v PAKISTAN (2nd Test)

At Galle International Stadium, on 24, 25, 26, 27, 28 July 2022.
Toss: Sri Lanka. Result: **SRI LANKA** won by 246 runs.
Debut: Sri Lanka – D.N.Wellalage.

SRI LANKA

B.O.P.Fernando	c Rizwan b Nawaz	50	(2)	lbw b Yasir	19
*F.D.M.Karunaratne	c Naseem b Yasir	40	(6)	c Shafiq b Nauman	61
B.K.G.Mendis	run out	3		lbw b Nawaz	15
A.D.Mathews	c Rizwan b Nauman	42		c Babar b Salman	35
L.D.Chandimal	c Alam b Nawaz	80		c Rizwan b Nauman	21
D.M.de Silva	b Naseem	33	(7)	run out	109
†D.P.D.N.Dickwella	c Rizwan b Naseem	51	(1)	c Rizwan b Naseem	15
D.N.Wellalage	c Babar b Naseem	11		c Rizwan b Nawaz	18
R.T.M.Wanigamuni	b Yasir	35		not out	45
N.G.R.P.Jayasuriya	lbw b Yasir	8			
A.M.Fernando	not out	4			
Extras	(B 4, LB 5, NB 12)	21		(B 13, LB 3, NB 5, W 1)	22
Total	**(103 overs)**	**378**		**(8 wkts dec; 91.5 overs)**	**360**

PAKISTAN

Abdullah Shafiq	b A.M.Fernando	0	c Wellalage b Jayasuriya	16
Imam-ul-Haq	b de Silva	32	c Dickwella b Wanigamuni	49
*Babar Azam	b Jayasuriya	16	lbw b Jayasuriya	81
†Mohammad Rizwan	lbw b Wanigamuni	24	b Jayasuriya	37
Fawad Alam	lbw b Wanigamuni	24	run out	1
Agha Salman	c de Silva b Jayasuriya	62	c Mendis b Jayasuriya	4
Mohammad Nawaz	c Dickwella b Wanigamuni	12	c Chandimal b Wanigamuni	12
Yasir Shah	lbw b Wanigamuni	26	c Mendis b Jayasuriya	27
Hasan Ali	b Jayasuriya	21	b Wanigamuni	11
Nauman Ali	c Dickwella b Wanigamuni	1	not out	0
Naseem Shah	not out	4	c Wellalage b Wanigamuni	18
Extras	(B 8, LB 1)	9	(B 2, NB 3)	5
Total	**(88.1 overs)**	**231**	**(77 overs)**	**261**

PAKISTAN	O	M	R	W		O	M	R	W
Hasan Ali	17	3	59	0		10	1	44	0
Naseem Shah	18	3	58	3		12.5	1	44	2
Nauman Ali	21	2	64	1	(5)	14	0	54	1
Agha Salman	6	0	25	0	(6)	12	2	41	1
Mohammad Nawaz	19	3	80	2	(4)	21	4	75	2
Yasir Shah	22	2	83	3	(3)	21	2	80	1
Babar Azam						1	0	6	0

SRI LANKA	O	M	R	W		O	M	R	W
A.M.Fernando	20	2	62	1		6	1	20	0
Jayasuriya	37	10	80	3		32	5	117	5
Wanigamuni	21.1	6	47	5		30	7	101	4
De Silva	4	0	15	1		4	0	40	0
Wellalage	6	1	18	0		7	0	17	0

FALL OF WICKETS

	SL	P	SL	P
Wkt	1st	1st	2nd	2nd
1st	92	0	27	42
2nd	96	35	47	97
3rd	120	65	59	176
4th	195	88	100	181
5th	258	119	117	188
6th	290	145	243	205
7th	327	191	278	205
8th	333	223	360	243
9th	353	226	–	243
10th	378	231	–	261

Umpires: H.D.P.K.Dharmasena (*Sri Lanka*) (75) and R.J.Tucker (*Australia*) (77).
Referee: J.J.Crowe (*New Zealand*) (111). **Test No. 2472/57 (SL307/P446)**

33

ENGLAND v SOUTH AFRICA (1st Test)

At Lord's, London, on 17, 18, 19 August 2022.
Toss: South Africa. Result: **SOUTH AFRICA** won by an innings and 12 runs.
Debuts: None.

ENGLAND

A.Z.Lees	c Verreynne b Rabada	5	c Verreynne b Nortje		35
Z.Crawley	c Markram b Rabada	9	lbw b Maharaj		13
O.J.D.Pope	b Rabada	73	lbw b Maharaj		5
J.E.Root	lbw b Jansen	8	c Markram b Ngidi		6
J.M.Bairstow	b Nortje	0	c Verreynne b Nortje		18
*B.A.Stokes	c Petersen b Nortje	20	c Maharaj b Rabada		20
†B.T.Foakes	b Nortje	6	c Verreynne b Nortje		0
S.C.J.Broad	c Elgar b Rabada	15	c Elgar b Rabada		35
M.J.Potts	not out	6	b Jansen		1
M.J.Leach	b Jansen	15	not out		0
J.M.Anderson	lbw b Rabada	0	b Jansen		1
Extras	(B 1, LB 7)	8	(B 5, LB 7, NB 3)		15
Total	**(45 overs)**	**165**	**(37.4 overs)**		**149**

SOUTH AFRICA

*D.Elgar	b Anderson	47
S.J.Erwee	c Foakes b Stokes	73
K.D.Petersen	c Bairstow b Potts	24
A.K.Markram	c Foakes b Leach	16
H.E.van der Dussen	lbw b Stokes	19
M.Jansen	c Crawley b Broad	48
†K.Verreynne	c Foakes b Broad	11
K.A.Maharaj	c Potts b Stokes	41
K.Rabada	c Broad b Potts	3
A.A.Nortje	not out	28
L.T.Ngidi	c Bairstow b Broad	0
Extras	(B 1, LB 11, NB 3, W 1)	16
Total	**(89.1 overs)**	**326**

SOUTH AFRICA	O	M	R	W		O	M	R	W		FALL OF WICKETS		
Rabada	19	3	52	5		8	2	27	2			E	SA	E
Ngidi	5	1	12	0		7	2	15	1		Wkt	1st	1st	2nd
Jansen	8	1	30	2	(5)	3.4	0	13	2		1st	6	85	20
Nortje	13	2	63	3		7	1	47	3		2nd	25	138	38
Maharaj					(3)	12	0	35	2		3rd	42	160	57
											4th	55	187	81
ENGLAND											5th	100	192	86
Anderson	18	3	51	1							6th	116	210	86
Broad	19.1	3	71	3							7th	134	282	141
Potts	20	2	79	2							8th	145	289	146
Stokes	18	3	71	3							9th	164	318	146
Leach	14	3	42	1							10th	165	326	149

Umpires: R.K.Illingworth (*England*) (59) and N.N.Menon (*India*) (13).
Referee: R.S.Madugalle (*Sri Lanka*) (205). **Test No. 2473/154 (E1053/SA453)**

ENGLAND v SOUTH AFRICA (2nd Test)

At Old Trafford, Manchester, on 25, 26, 27 August 2022.
Toss: South Africa. Result: **ENGLAND** won by an innings and 85 runs.
Debuts: None.

SOUTH AFRICA

*D.Elgar	c Bairstow b Broad	12	(2)	b Anderson	11
S.J.Erwee	c Foakes b Anderson	3	(1)	c Foakes b Robinson	25
K.D.Petersen	c Root b Broad	21		c Foakes b Stokes	42
A.K.Markram	c Foakes b Stokes	14		c Crawley b Broad	6
H.E.van der Dussen	lbw b Stokes	16		c Foakes b Stokes	41
†K.Verreynne	c Foakes b Broad	21		not out	17
S.R.Harmer	lbw b Anderson	2		b Anderson	16
K.A.Maharaj	lbw b Anderson	0		c Pope b Robinson	2
K.Rabada	c Root b Leach	36		c Root b Anderson	2
A.A.Nortje	lbw b Robinson	10		c Foakes b Robinson	0
L.T.Ngidi	not out	4		b Robinson	0
Extras	(B 2, LB 4, NB 6)	12		(B 8, LB 2, NB 7)	17
Total	**(53.2 overs)**	**151**		**(85.1 overs)**	**179**

ENGLAND

A.Z.Lees	c Verreynne b Ngidi	4
Z.Crawley	c Verreynne b Nortje	38
O.J.D.Pope	b Nortje	23
J.E.Root	c Erwee b Rabada	9
J.M.Bairstow	c Erwee b Nortje	49
*B.A.Stokes	c Elgar b Rabada	103
†B.T.Foakes	not out	113
S.C.J.Broad	st Verreynne b Harmer	21
O.E.Robinson	c Markram b Maharaj	17
M.J.Leach	b Maharaj	11
J.M.Anderson		
Extras	(B 5, LB 6, NB 6, W 10)	27
Total	**(9 wkts dec; 106.4 overs)**	**415**

ENGLAND	O	M	R	W		O	M	R	W		FALL OF WICKETS			
												SA	E	SA
Anderson	15	4	32	3		15	4	30	3		*Wkt*	*1st*	*1st*	*2nd*
Robinson	14	0	48	1		15.1	3	43	4		1st	3	5	33
Broad	11	1	37	3	(5)	13	5	24	1		2nd	35	34	39
Stokes	7	0	17	2	(6)	14	3	30	2		3rd	41	43	54
Leach	6.2	1	11	1	(3)	23	13	26	0		4th	68	134	141
Root					(4)	5	2	16	0		5th	76	147	151
											6th	92	320	172
SOUTH AFRICA											7th	92	361	175
Rabada	23	2	110	2							8th	108	395	178
Ngidi	18	3	61	1							9th	143	415	179
Nortje	20	1	82	3							10th	151	–	179
Maharaj	22.4	4	78	2										
Harmer	23	4	73	1										

Umpires: C.B.Gaffaney (*New Zealand*) (42) and R.K.Illingworth (*England*) (60).
Referee: R.S.Madugalle (*Sri Lanka*) (206). Test No. 2474/155 (E1054/SA454)

ENGLAND v SOUTH AFRICA (3rd Test)

At The Oval, London, on 8 (*no play*), 9 (*no play*), 10, 11, 12 September 2022.
Toss: England. Result: **ENGLAND** won by nine wickets.
Debut: England – H.C.Brook.

SOUTH AFRICA

*D.Elgar	b Robinson	1	(2)	lbw b Broad	36
S.J.Erwee	c Foakes b Anderson	0	(1)	c Root b Stokes	26
K.D.Petersen	b Robinson	12		c Pope b Anderson	23
R.D.Rickelton	c Foakes b Broad	11		lbw b Broad	8
K.Zondo	c Lees b Broad	23		lbw b Robinson	16
†K.Verreynne	c Foakes b Robinson	0	(7)	c and b Anderson	12
P.W.A.Mulder	c Foakes b Robinson	3	(6)	b Robinson	14
M.Jansen	c Root b Robinson	30		b Stokes	4
K.A.Maharaj	b Broad	18	(10)	c Brook b Stokes	0
K.Rabada	not out	7	(9)	c Brook b Stokes	0
A.A.Nortje	c Stokes b Broad	7		not out	0
Extras	(LB 2, NB 4)	6		(B 4, LB 4, NB 4)	12
Total	**(36.2 overs)**	**118**		**(56.2 overs)**	**169**

ENGLAND

A.Z.Lees	b Jansen	13		lbw b Rabada	39
Z.Crawley	lbw b Jansen	5		not out	69
O.J.D.Pope	c Verreynne b Rabada	67		not out	11
J.E.Root	c Petersen b Jansen	23			
H.C.Brook	c Rabada b Jansen	12			
*B.A.Stokes	c Erwee b Nortje	6			
†B.T.Foakes	c Petersen b Jansen	14			
S.C.J.Broad	c Verreynne b Rabada	6			
O.E.Robinson	c Elgar b Rabada	3			
M.J.Leach	b Rabada	0			
J.M.Anderson	not out	0			
Extras	(B 1, LB 1, NB 7)	9		(LB 6, NB 5)	11
Total	**(36.2 overs)**	**158**		**(1 wkt; 22.3 overs)**	**130**

ENGLAND	O	M	R	W	O	M	R	W
Anderson	8	2	16	1	15.2	4	37	2
Robinson	14	3	49	5	15	5	40	2
Broad	12.2	1	41	4	13	2	45	3
Leach	2	1	10	0				
Stokes					(4) 13	2	39	3
SOUTH AFRICA								
Rabada	13	1	81	5	11	1	57	1
Jansen	12.2	2	35	5	7.3	0	40	0
Mulder	2	0	11	0				
Nortje	9	0	29	1	(3) 4	0	27	0

FALL OF WICKETS				
	SA	E	SA	E
Wkt	1st	1st	2nd	2nd
1st	2	17	58	108
2nd	7	43	83	–
3rd	21	84	91	–
4th	31	107	95	–
5th	32	129	120	–
6th	36	133	133	–
7th	72	151	146	–
8th	99	155	146	–
9th	118	158	169	–
10th	118	158	169	

Umpires: R.A.Kettleborough (*England*) (76) and N.N.Menon (*India*) (14).
Referee: R.S.Madugalle (*Sri Lanka*) (207). **Test No. 2475/156 (E1055/SA455)**

Play abandoned on Day 1 due to rain; on Day 2 following the death of HM The Queen.

AUSTRALIA v WEST INDIES (1st Test)

At Perth Stadium, on 30 November, 1, 2, 3, 4 December 2022.
Toss: Australia. Result: **AUSTRALIA** won by 164 runs.
Debut: West Indies – T.Chanderpaul.

AUSTRALIA

D.A.Warner	b Seales	5	(2)	c Brooks b Chase	48
U.T.Khawaja	c Da Silva b Mayers	65	(1)	c Da Silva b Roach	6
M.Labuschagne	c Da Silva b Brathwaite	204		not out	104
S.P.D.Smith	not out	200		not out	20
T.M.Head	b Brathwaite	99			
C.D.Green					
†A.T.Carey					
*P.J.Cummins					
M.A.Starc					
N.M.Lyon					
J.R.Hazlewood					
Extras	(B 13, LB 2, NB 5, W 5)	25		(LB 2, NB 1, W 1)	4
Total	**(4 wkts dec; 152.4 overs)**	**598**		**(2 wkts dec; 37 overs)**	**182**

WEST INDIES

*K.C.Brathwaite	b Cummins	64		b Lyon	110
T.Chanderpaul	c Warner b Hazlewood	51		b Starc	45
N.E.Bonner	retired hurt	16			
J.Blackwood	lbw b Starc	36		c Labuschagne b Lyon	24
K.R.Mayers	b Starc	1		c Smith b Lyon	10
J.O.Holder	c Warner b Lyon	27		c Smith b Head	3
S.S.J.Brooks	c Carey b Green	33	(3)	c Smith b Lyon	11
†J.M.Da Silva	b Starc	0	(7)	c Khawaja b Hazlewood	12
R.L.Chase	lbw b Cummins	13	(8)	c Starc b Lyon	55
A.S.Joseph	c Warner b Cummins	4	(9)	b Head	43
K.A.J.Roach	c Smith b Lyon	0		b Lyon	0
J.N.T.Seales	not out	0	(10)	not out	5
Extras	(B 4, LB 27, NB 7)	38		(B 2, LB 7, NB 6)	15
Total	**(98.2 overs)**	**283**		**(110.5 overs)**	**333**

WEST INDIES	O	M	R	W	O	M	R	W
Roach	26	3	91	0	7	2	30	1
Seales	21	3	95	1	(5)	3	0	18	0
Joseph	24	4	83	0	(2)	10	1	42	0
Mayers	15	2	39	1				
Holder	23	6	70	0	(3)	8	1	39	0
Chase	31	2	140	0	(4)	6	0	31	1
Brathwaite	12.4	0	65	2	(6)	3	0	20	0

AUSTRALIA	O	M	R	W	O	M	R	W
Starc	22	7	51	0	23	4	65	1
Hazlewood	21	5	53	1	22	8	52	1
Cummins	20.2	7	34	3				
Lyon	22	3	61	2	(3)	42.5	10	128	6
Green	10	0	35	1	(4)	13	2	45	0
Labuschagne	2	0	14	0	(5)	2	0	9	0
Head	1	0	4	0	(6)	8	1	25	2

		FALL OF WICKETS			
		A	WI	A	WI
Wkt	1st	1st	2nd	2nd	
1st	9	78	20	116	
2nd	151	159	101	133	
3rd	402	166	–	191	
4th	598	209	–	207	
5th	–	245	–	216	
6th	–	245	–	216	
7th	–	266	–	233	
8th	–	282	–	315	
9th	–	283	–	333	
10th	–	283	–	333	

Umpires: R.K.Illingworth (*England*) (61) and R.J.Tucker (*Australia*) (78).
Referee: B.C.Broad (*England*) (116).   **Test No. 2476/117 (A845/WI566)**
S.S.J.Brooks replaced N.E.Bonner, who retired hurt (concussion) at 106-1.

AUSTRALIA v WEST INDIES (2nd Test)

At Adelaide Oval, on 8, 9, 10, 11 December 2022 (day/night).
Toss: Australia. Result: **AUSTRALIA** won by 419 runs.
Debuts: West Indies – M.J.Mindley, D.C.Thomas.

AUSTRALIA

D.A.Warner	c Da Silva b Joseph	21	(2)	b Chase	28
U.T.Khawaja	lbw b Thomas	62	(1)	c Da Silva b Chase	45
M.Labuschagne	c Da Silva b Thomas	163		c Chase b Phillip	31
*S.P.D.Smith	c and b Holder	0		c Thomas b Joseph	35
T.M.Head	run out	175		not out	38
C.D.Green	b Joseph	9		c Brathwaite b Joseph	5
†A.T.Carey	not out	41		b Joseph	8
M.G.Neser	lbw b Brathwaite	18			
M.A.Starc	not out	5			
N.M.Lyon					
S.M.Boland					
Extras	(B 1, LB 4, NB 6, W 6)	17		(LB 6, NB 1, W 2)	9
Total	**(7 wkts dec; 137 overs)**	**511**		**(6 wkts dec; 31 overs)**	**199**

WEST INDIES

*K.C.Brathwaite	c Carey b Neser	19		c Carey b Boland	3
T.Chanderpaul	run out	47		c Carey b Starc	17
S.S.J.Brooks	c Carey b Neser	8		lbw b Boland	0
J.Blackwood	c and b Lyon	3		c Green b Boland	0
D.C.Thomas	b Green	19		c Carey b Starc	12
A.Phillip	run out	43	(10)	not out	1
J.O.Holder	c Carey b Starc	0	(6)	b Starc	11
†J.M.Da Silva	lbw b Lyon	23	(7)	c Carey b Neser	15
R.L.Chase	c Lyon b Starc	34	(8)	c Carey b Neser	13
A.S.Joseph	lbw b Lyon	0	(9)	b Lyon	3
M.J.Mindley	not out	11		c Carey b Neser	0
Extras	(B 1, LB 1, NB 5)	7		(LB 2)	2
Total	**(69.3 overs)**	**214**		**(40.5 overs)**	**77**

WEST INDIES	O	M	R	W		O	M	R	W
Joseph	31	4	107	2		7	0	33	3
Holder	26	6	68	1		8	0	46	0
Chase	30	1	117	0	(6)	4	0	25	2
Mindley	2	0	11	0					
Phillip	26	2	115	0	(3)	6	0	44	1
Brathwaite	8	0	35	1	(5)	4	0	32	0
Thomas	14	1	53	2	(4)	2	0	13	0

AUSTRALIA	O	M	R	W		O	M	R	W
Starc	15.3	4	48	2		10	4	29	3
Boland	16	4	29	0	(3)	10	5	16	3
Neser	12	3	34	2	(2)	10.5	3	22	3
Lyon	20	4	57	3		10	7	8	1
Green	6	0	44	1					

FALL OF WICKETS

	A	WI	A	WI
Wkt	1st	1st	2nd	2nd
1st	34	35	77	15
2nd	129	45	78	15
3rd	131	50	136	15
4th	428	90	156	21
5th	442	102	162	42
6th	452	102	199	49
7th	489	162	–	69
8th	–	170	–	76
9th	–	171	–	76
10th	–	214	–	77

Umpires: H.D.P.K.Dharmasena (*Sri Lanka*) (76) and R.J.Tucker (*Australia*) (79).
Referee: B.C.Broad (*England*) (117).   **Test No. 2477/118 (A846/WI567)**

PAKISTAN v ENGLAND (1st Test)

At Rawalpindi Cricket Stadium, on 1, 2, 3, 4, 5 December 2022.
Toss: England. Result: **ENGLAND** won by 74 runs.
Debuts: Pakistan – Haris Rauf, Mohammad Ali, Saud Shakil, Zahid Mahmood; England – W.G.Jacks, L.S.Livingstone.

ENGLAND

Z.Crawley	b Rauf	122	c Rizwan b Mohammad Ali	50
B.M.Duckett	lbw b Mahmood	107	c Salman b Shah	0
†O.J.D.Pope	lbw b Mohammad Ali	108	c Shah b Mohammad Ali	15
J.E.Root	lbw b Mahmood	23	c Imam b Mahmood	73
H.C.Brook	c Shakil b Shah	153	b Shah	87
*B.A.Stokes	b Shah	41	c Shakil b Mahmood	0
L.S.Livingstone	c Shakil b Shah	9	(8) not out	7
W.G.Jacks	c Shah b Mohammad Ali	30	(7) c Imam b Salman	24
O.E.Robinson	lbw b Mahmood	37		
M.J.Leach	not out	6		
J.M.Anderson	c Imam b Mahmood	6		
Extras	(B 2, LB 10, NB 2, W 1)	15	(LB 3, NB 5)	8
Total	**(101 overs)**	**657**	**(7 wkts dec; 35.5 overs)**	**264**

PAKISTAN

Abdullah Shafiq	c Pope b Jacks	114	c Brook b Robinson	6
Imam-ul-Haq	c Robinson b Leach	121	c Pope b Anderson	48
Azhar Ali	lbw b Leach	27	c Root b Robinson	40
*Babar Azam	c Leach b Jacks	136	c Pope b Stokes	4
Saud Shakil	c Pope b Robinson	37	c sub (K.K.Jennings) b Robinson	76
†Mohammad Rizwan	c Stokes b Anderson	29	c Pope b Anderson	46
Agha Salman	c Crawley b Jacks	53	lbw b Robinson	30
Naseem Shah	c Leach b Jacks	15	lbw b Leach	6
Zahid Mahmood	st Pope b Jacks	17	c Pope b Anderson	1
Haris Rauf	c Root b Jacks	12	lbw b Anderson	0
Mohammad Ali	not out	0	not out	0
Extras	(B 15, NB 3)	18	(LB 3, NB 8)	11
Total	**(155.3 overs)**	**579**	**(96.3 overs)**	**268**

PAKISTAN	O	M	R	W		O	M	R	W		FALL OF WICKETS			
												E	P	E	P
Naseem Shah	24	0	140	3		9.5	0	66	2		Wkt	1st	1st	2nd	2nd
Mohammad Ali	24	1	124	2		10	0	64	2		1st	233	225	1	20
Haris Rauf	13	1	78	1							2nd	235	245	36	25
Zahid Mahmood	33	1	235	4	(3)	11	1	84	2		3rd	286	290	96	89
Agha Salman	5	0	38	0	(4)	5	0	47	1		4th	462	413	192	176
Saud Shakil	2	0	30	0							5th	515	473	192	198
ENGLAND											6th	539	475	248	259
Anderson	22	4	52	1	(3)	24	12	36	4		7th	576	497	264	260
Robinson	21	2	72	1	(1)	22	6	50	4		8th	641	554	–	264
Leach	49	7	190	2	(4)	18.3	6	56	1		9th	649	576	–	264
Jacks	40.3	5	161	6	(5)	6	0	38	0		10th	657	579	–	268
Root	16	3	54	0	(6)	6	0	16	0						
Stokes	7	0	35	0	(2)	20	4	69	1						

Umpires: Ahsan Raza (*Pakistan*) (6) and J.S.Wilson (*West Indies*) (32).
Referee: A.J.Pycroft (*Zimbabwe*) (87).　　　　**Test No. 2478/87 (P447/E1056)**
Azhar Ali retired hurt at 20-1 (2) and resumed at 176-4.

PAKISTAN v ENGLAND (2nd Test)

At Multan Cricket Stadium, on 9, 10, 11, 12 December 2022.
Toss: England. Result: **ENGLAND** won by 26 runs.
Debut: Pakistan – Abrar Ahmed.

ENGLAND

Z.Crawley	b Ahmed	19		run out	3
B.M.Duckett	lbw b Ahmed	63		b Ahmed	79
†O.J.D.Pope	c Shafiq b Ahmed	60	(6)	run out	4
J.E.Root	lbw b Ahmed	8		c Shafiq b Ahmed	21
H.C.Brook	c Nawaz b Ahmed	9		c Shakil b Mahmood	108
*B.A.Stokes	b Ahmed	30	(7)	c Mohammad Ali b Nawaz	41
W.G.Jacks	lbw b Ahmed	31	(3)	b Ahmed	4
O.E.Robinson	c Nawaz b Mahmood	5		b Ahmed	3
M.A.Wood	not out	36		c Azam b Mahmood	6
M.J.Leach	b Mahmood	0		not out	0
J.M.Anderson	b Mahmood	7		lbw b Mahmood	4
Extras	(B 1, LB 12)	13		(NB 2)	2
Total	**(51.4 overs)**	**281**		**(64.5 overs)**	**275**

PAKISTAN

Abdullah Shafiq	c Pope b Leach	14		b Wood	45
Imam-ul-Haq	c Pope b Anderson	0	(5)	c Root b Leach	60
*Babar Azam	c Robinson	75		b Robinson	1
Saud Shakil	c Anderson b Leach	63		c Pope b Wood	94
†Mohammad Rizwan	b Leach	10	(2)	b Anderson	30
Agha Salman	c Stokes b Root	4	(8)	not out	20
Mohammad Nawaz	c Robinson b Leach	1		c Pope b Wood	45
Faheem Ashraf	c Duckett b Wood	22	(6)	c Crawley b Root	10
Mohammad Ali	c Crawley b Root	0	(11)	c Pope b Robinson	0
Zahid Mahmood	lbw b Wood	0		b Wood	0
Abrar Ahmed	not out	7	(9)	c Duckett b Anderson	17
Extras	(B 4, LB 1, NB 1)	6		(LB 3, NB 3)	6
Total	**(62.5 overs)**	**202**		**(102.1 overs)**	**328**

PAKISTAN	O	M	R	W		O	M	R	W
Faheem Ashraf	4	1	16	0	(2)	5	2	12	0
Mohammad Ali	6	1	29	0	(1)	9	0	44	0
Abrar Ahmed	22	1	114	0		29	3	120	4
Zahid Mahmood	7.4	0	63	3	(5)	10.5	1	52	3
Mohammad Nawaz	12	0	46	0	(4)	10	0	42	1
Agha Salman						1	0	5	0

ENGLAND	O	M	R	W		O	M	R	W
Anderson	5	0	16	1	(5)	16	1	44	2
Leach	27	7	98	4		26	0	113	1
Wood	11.5	1	40	2	(4)	21	2	65	4
Root	10	3	23	2	(3)	21	3	65	1
Jacks	4	0	18	0	(6)	4	0	15	0
Robinson	5	3	2	1	(1)	14.1	3	23	2

FALL OF WICKETS

	E	P	E	P
Wkt	1st	1st	2nd	2nd
1st	38	5	11	66
2nd	117	51	25	67
3rd	145	142	79	83
4th	164	158	147	191
5th	167	165	155	210
6th	228	169	256	290
7th	231	169	259	291
8th	245	169	270	310
9th	245	179	271	319
10th	281	202	275	328

Umpires: Alim Dar (*Pakistan*) (141) and M.Erasmus (*South Africa*) (75).
Referee: A.J.Pycroft (*Zimbabwe*) (88).　　　　Test No. 2479/88 (P448/E1057)

PAKISTAN v ENGLAND (3rd Test)

At National Stadium, Karachi, on 17, 18, 19, 20 December 2022.
Toss: Pakistan. Result: **ENGLAND** won by eight wickets.
Debuts: Pakistan – Mohammad Wasim; England – R.Ahmed.

PAKISTAN

Abdullah Shafiq	lbw b Leach	8	lbw b Leach		26
Shan Masood	c Leach b Wood	30	b Leach		24
Azhar Ali	c Foakes b Robinson	45	b Leach		0
*Babar Azam	run out	78	c Pope b Ahmed		54
Saud Shakil	c Pope b Ahmed	23	c Leach b Ahmed		53
†Mohammad Rizwan	c Stokes b Root	19	c Foakes b Ahmed		7
Agha Salman	st Foakes b Leach	56	c Brook b Ahmed		21
Faheem Ashraf	lbw b Ahmed	4	c Foakes b Root		1
Nauman Ali	c Stokes b Leach	20	lbw b Wood		15
Mohammad Wasim	not out	8	c Robinson b Ahmed		2
Abrar Ahmed	b Leach	4	not out		1
Extras	(B 2, LB 2, NB 4, W 1)	9	(B 4, LB 3, NB 5)		12
Total	**(79 overs)**	**304**	**(74.5 overs)**		**216**

ENGLAND

Z.Crawley	lbw b Ahmed	0	lbw b Ahmed		41
B.M.Duckett	lbw b Nauman	26	not out		82
O.J.D.Pope	b Ahmed	51			
J.E.Root	c Salman b Nauman	0			
H.C.Brook	lbw b Wasim	111			
*B.A.Stokes	run out	26	(4) not out		35
†B.T.Foakes	c Shafiq b Nauman	64			
R.Ahmed	c Shakil b Nauman	1	(3) b Ahmed		10
M.A.Wood	c Shafiq b Ahmed	35			
O.E.Robinson	b Ahmed	29			
M.J.Leach	not out	9			
Extras	(NB 1, W 1)	2	(LB 1, NB 1)		2
Total	**(81.4 overs)**	**354**	**(2 wkts; 28.1 overs)**		**170**

ENGLAND	O	M	R	W		O	M	R	W
Robinson	8	1	31	1	(5)	7	1	13	0
Leach	31	2	140	4	(1)	26	6	72	3
Wood	15	2	33	1	(4)	12	3	25	1
Ahmed	22	2	89	2	(3)	14.5	1	48	5
Root	3	0	7	1	(2)	7	1	31	1
Stokes						8	3	20	2
PAKISTAN									
Abrar Ahmed	34.4	5	150	4		12	0	78	2
Nauman Ali	30	1	126	4		5	0	38	0
Mohammad Wasim	15	0	71	1		9.1	1	40	0
Faheem Ashraf	1	0	2	0		2	0	13	0
Agha Salman	1	0	5	0					

FALL OF WICKETS				
	P	E	P	E
Wkt	1st	1st	2nd	2nd
1st	18	0	53	87
2nd	46	58	53	97
3rd	117	58	54	–
4th	162	98	164	
5th	196	145	176	
6th	219	262	177	
7th	237	265	178	
8th	285	316	208	
9th	300	324	211	
10th	304	354	216	

Umpires: Ahsan Raza (*Pakistan*) (7) and J.S.Wilson (*West Indies*) (33).
Referee: A.J.Pycroft (*Zimbabwe*) (89). **Test No. 2480/89 (P449/E1058)**

BANGLADESH v INDIA (1st Test)

At Zohur Ahmed Chowdhury Stadium, Chittagong, on 14, 15, 16, 17, 18 December 2022.
Toss: India. Result: **INDIA** won by 188 runs.
Debut: Bangladesh – Zakir Hasan.

INDIA

*K.L.Rahul	b Khaled	22	c Taijul b Khaled	23
S.Gill	c Yasir b Taijul	20	c sub (Mahmudul Hasan) b Mehedi	110
C.A.Pujara	b Taijul	90	not out	102
V.Kohli	lbw b Taijul	1	not out	19
†R.R.Pant	b Mehedi	46		
S.S.Iyer	b Ebadat	86		
A.R.Patel	lbw b Mehedi	14		
R.Ashwin	st Nurul b Mehedi	58		
K.Yadav	lbw b Taijul	40		
U.T.Yadav	not out	15		
M.Siraj	c Mushfiqur b Mehedi	4		
Extras	(LB 1, NB 2, Pen 5)	8	(LB 1, NB 3)	4
Total	**(133.5 overs)**	**404**	**(2 wkts dec; 61.4 overs)**	**258**

BANGLADESH

Nazmul Hossain	c Pant b Siraj	0	c Pant b U.T.Yadav	67
Zakir Hasan	c Pant b Siraj	20	c Kohli b Ashwin	100
Yasir Ali	b U.T.Yadav	4	b Patel	5
Liton Das	b Siraj	24	c U.T.Yadav b K.Yadav	19
Mushfiqur Rahim	lbw b K.Yadav	28	b Patel	23
*Shakib Al Hasan	c Kohli b K.Yadav	3	b K.Yadav	84
†Nurul Hasan	c Gill b K.Yadav	16	st Pant b Patel	3
Mehedi Hasan	st Pant b Patel	25	c U.T.Yadav b Siraj	13
Taijul Islam	b K.Yadav	0	b Patel	4
Ebadat Hossain	c Pant b K.Yadav	17	c Iyer b K.Yadav	0
Khaled Ahmed	not out	0	not out	0
Extras	(B 6, LB 7)	13	(B 4, LB 1, NB 1)	6
Total	**(55.5 overs)**	**150**	**(113.2 overs)**	**324**

BANGLADESH	O	M	R	W		O	M	R	W	FALL OF WICKETS				
Ebadat Hossain	21	2	70	1							I	B	I	B
Khaled Ahmed	20	3	43	1	(1)	13	0	51	1	Wkt	1st	1st	2nd	2nd
Shakib Al Hasan	12	4	26	0						1st	41	0	70	124
Taijul Islam	46	10	133	4	(2)	23.4	3	71	0	2nd	45	5	183	131
Mehedi Hasan	31.5	6	112	4	(3)	14	1	82	1	3rd	48	39	–	173
Yasir Ali	1	0	7	0	(4)	6	0	28	0	4th	112	56	–	208
Nazmul Hossain	2	0	7	0	(6)	3	0	12	0	5th	261	75	–	234
Liton Das					(5)	2	0	13	0	6th	278	97	–	238
										7th	293	102	–	283
INDIA										8th	385	102	–	320
Siraj	13	2	20	3		19	4	67	1	9th	393	144	–	324
U.T.Yadav	8	1	33	1		15	3	27	1	10th	404	150	–	324
Ashwin	10	1	34	0		27	3	75	1					
K.Yadav	16	6	40	5	(5)	20	3	73	3					
Patel	8.5	4	10	1	(4)	32.2	10	77	4					

Umpires: M.A.Gough (*England*) (28) and Sharfuddoula (*Bangladesh*) (7).
Referee: R.S.Madugalle (*Sri Lanka*) (208).   **Test No. 2481/12 (B135/I564)**

BANGLADESH v INDIA (2nd Test)

At Shere Bangla National Stadium, Mirpur, on 22, 23, 24, 25 December 2022.
Toss: Bangladesh. Result: **INDIA** won by three wickets.
Debuts: None.

BANGLADESH

Nazmul Hossain	lbw b Ashwin	24	lbw b Ashwin		5
Zakir Hasan	c Rahul b Unadkat	15	c Siraj b Yadav		51
Mominul Haque	c Pant b Ashwin	84	c Pant b Siraj		5
*Shakib Al Hasan	c Pujara b Yadav	16	c Gill b Unadkat		13
Mushfiqur Rahim	c Pant b Unadkat	26	lbw b Patel		9
Liton Das	c Rahul b Ashwin	25	b Siraj		73
Mehedi Hasan	c Pant b Yadav	15	lbw b Patel		0
†Nurul Hasan	lbw b Yadav	6	st Pant b Patel		31
Taskin Ahmed	c Siraj b Yadav	1	not out		31
Taijul Islam	not out	4	lbw b Ashwin		1
Khaled Ahmed	c Unadkat b Ashwin	0	run out		4
Extras	(B 3, LB 7, W 1)	11	(B 1, LB 6, W 1)		8
Total	**(73.5 overs)**	**227**	**(70.2 overs)**		**231**

INDIA

*K.L.Rahul	lbw b Taijul	10	(2) c Nurul b Shakib		2
S.Gill	lbw b Taijul	20	(1) st Nurul b Mehedi		7
C.A.Pujara	c Mominul b Taijul	24	st Nurul b Mehedi		6
V.Kohli	c Nurul b Taskin	24	(5) c Mominul b Mehedi		1
†R.R.Pant	c Nurul b Mehedi	93	(7) lbw b Mehedi		9
S.S.Iyer	lbw b Shakib	87	(3) not out		29
A.R.Patel	c Nazmul b Shakib	4	(4) b Mehedi		34
R.Ashwin	lbw b Shakib	12	(9) not out		42
J.D.Unadkat	not out	14	(6) lbw b Shakib		13
U.T.Yadav	c Liton b Taijul	14			
M.Siraj	st Nurul b Shakib	7			
Extras	(LB 1, NB 3, W 1)	5	(B 1, LB 1)		2
Total	**(86.3 overs)**	**314**	**(7 wkts; 47 overs)**		**145**

INDIA	O	M	R	W		O	M	R	W	FALL OF WICKETS				
Siraj	9	1	39	0	(4)	11	0	41	2		**B**	**I**	**B**	**I**
Yadav	15	4	25	4	(1)	9	1	32	1	*Wkt*	*1st*	*1st*	*2nd*	*2nd*
Unadkat	16	2	50	2		9	3	17	1	1st	39	27	13	3
Ashwin	21.5	3	71	4	(2)	22	2	66	2	2nd	39	38	26	12
Patel	12	3	32	0		19.2	1	68	3	3rd	82	72	51	29
BANGLADESH										4th	130	94	70	37
Taskin Ahmed	15	2	58	1	(4)	1	0	4	0	5th	172	253	102	56
Shakib Al Hasan	19.3	3	79	4	(1)	14	0	50	2	6th	213	264	113	71
Khaled Ahmed	10	1	41	0	(5)	2	0	12	0	7th	219	271	159	74
Taijul Islam	25	3	74	4	(2)	11	4	14	0	8th	223	286	219	
Mehedi Hasan	17	2	61	1	(3)	19	4	63	5	9th	227	305	220	
										10th	227	314	231	

Umpires: C.M.Brown (*New Zealand*) (6) and Sharfuddoula (*Bangladesh*) (8).
Referee: R.S.Madugalle (*Sri Lanka*) (209).   Test No. 2482/13 (B136/I565)

AUSTRALIA v SOUTH AFRICA (1st Test)

At Woolloongabba, Brisbane, on 17, 18 December 2022.
Toss: Australia. Result: **AUSTRALIA** won by six wickets.
Debuts: None.

SOUTH AFRICA

*D.Elgar	c Carey b Starc	3	(2) lbw b Cummins		2
S.J.Erwee	c Green b Boland	10	(1) c Green b Cummins		3
H.E.van der Dussen	c Carey b Cummins	5	b Starc		0
T.Bavuma	b Starc	38	lbw b Lyon		29
K.Zondo	lbw b Boland	0	not out		36
†K.Verreynne	c Smith b Lyon	64	c Smith b Boland		0
M.Jansen	c Green b Lyon	2	b Boland		0
K.A.Maharaj	c Smith b Starc	2	c Carey b Starc		16
K.Rabada	not out	10	c Carey b Cummins		3
A.A.Nortje	c Head b Lyon	0	c Green b Cummins		0
L.T.Ngidi	c Green b Cummins	3	c Warner b Cummins		9
Extras	(B 4, LB 10, W 1)	15	(NB 1)		1
Total	**(48.2 overs)**	**152**	**(37.4 overs)**		**99**

AUSTRALIA

D.A.Warner	c Zondo b Rabada	0	(2) c Erwee b Rabada		3
U.T.Khawaja	c sub (S.R.Harmer) b Nortje	11	(1) c Maharaj b Rabada		2
M.Labuschagne	c Elgar b Jansen	11	not out		5
S.P.D.Smith	b Nortje	36	c Verreynne b Rabada		6
T.M.Head	c Verreynne b Jansen	92	c Verreynne b Rabada		0
S.M.Boland	c Verreynne b Rabada	1			
C.D.Green	c Erwee b Jansen	18	(6) not out		0
†A.T.Carey	not out	22			
M.A.Starc	c and b Ngidi	14			
*P.J.Cummins	c Nortje b Rabada	0			
N.M.Lyon	c van der Dussen b Rabada	0			
Extras	(B 1, LB 5, NB 2, W 5)	13	(B 4, W 15)		19
Total	**(50.3 overs)**	**218**	**(4 wkts; 7.5 overs)**		**35**

AUSTRALIA	O	M	R	W		O	M	R	W	FALL OF WICKETS				
Starc	14	1	41	3		11	3	26	2		SA	A	SA	A
Cummins	12.2	3	35	2		12.4	3	42	5	Wkt	1st	1st	2nd	2nd
Boland	11	2	28	2		8	2	14	2	1st	12	0	2	8
Green	3	0	20	0						2nd	27	18	3	9
Lyon	8	2	14	3	(4)	6	0	17	1	3rd	27	27	5	19
										4th	27	144	47	23
SOUTH AFRICA										5th	125	145	48	–
Rabada	17.3	1	76	4		4	1	13	4	6th	132	181	48	–
Ngidi	9	1	35	1						7th	135	182	64	–
Jansen	9	1	32	3						8th	139	213	69	–
Nortje	13	2	52	2	(2)	3.5	0	18	0	9th	145	214	69	–
Maharaj	2	0	17	0						10th	152	218	99	–

Umpires: C.B.Gaffaney (*New Zealand*) (43) and R.J.Tucker (*Australia*) (80).
Referee: Sir R.B.Richardson (*West Indies*) (41). **Test No. 2483/99 (A847/SA456)**

AUSTRALIA v SOUTH AFRICA (2nd Test)

At Melbourne Cricket Ground, on 26, 27, 28, 29 December 2022.
Toss: Australia. Result: **AUSTRALIA** won by an innings and 182 runs.
Debuts: None.

SOUTH AFRICA

*D.Elgar	run out	26	(2) c Carey b Cummins		0
S.J.Erwee	c Khawaja b Boland	18	(1) lbw b Starc		21
T.B.de Bruyn	c Carey b Green	12	c Smith b Boland		28
T.Bavuma	c Carey b Starc	1	c sub (M.S.Harris) b Lyon		65
K.Zondo	c Labuschagne b Starc	5	run out		1
†K.Verreynne	c Smith b Green	52	lbw b Boland		33
M.Jansen	c Carey b Green	59	lbw b Lyon		5
K.A.Maharaj	c Cummins b Lyon	2	run out		13
K.Rabada	b Green	4	c Cummins b Lyon		3
A.A.Nortje	not out	1	not out		8
L.T.Ngidi	b Green	2	b Smith		19
Extras	(B 3, LB 3, NB 1)	7	(B 1, LB 5, NB 2)		8
Total	**(68.4 overs)**	**189**	**(68.5 overs)**		**204**

AUSTRALIA

D.A.Warner	b Nortje	200
U.T.Khawaja	c Verreynne b Rabada	1
M.Labuschagne	run out	14
S.P.D.Smith	c de Bruyne b Nortje	85
T.M.Head	b Nortje	51
C.D.Green	not out	51
†A.T.Carey	c and b Jansen	111
*P.J.Cummins	c Verreynne b Rabada	4
N.M.Lyon	c Zondo b Ngidi	25
M.A.Starc	not out	10
S.M.Boland		
Extras	(B 5, LB 12, NB 5, W 1)	23
Total	**(8 wkts dec; 145 overs)**	**575**

AUSTRALIA	O	M	R	W		O	M	R	W		FALL OF WICKETS		
Starc	13	2	39	2		18	4	62	1			SA	A	SA
Cummins	14	4	30	0		16	8	20	1		Wkt	1st	1st	2nd
Boland	14	2	34	1		15	2	49	2		1st	29	21	0
Lyon	17	3	53	1		17	1	58	3		2nd	56	75	47
Green	10.4	3	27	5							3rd	58	314	57
Smith						(5) 2.5	0	9	1		4th	58	395	65
											5th	67	395	128
SOUTH AFRICA											6th	179	400	144
Rabada	28	1	144	2							7th	182	440	174
Ngidi	22.1	2	98	1							8th	186	557	176
Jansen	28	1	89	1							9th	186	–	177
Nortje	25	1	92	3							10th	189	–	204
Maharaj	41.5	3	135	0										

Umpires: R.A.Kettleborough (*England*) (77) and P.R.Reiffel (*Australia*) (56).
Referee: Sir R.B.Richardson (*West Indies*) (42).   **Test No. 2484/100 (A848/SA457)**
D.A.Warner retired hurt from 329-3 to 395-4; C.D.Green retired hurt from 363-3 to 440-7.

AUSTRALIA v SOUTH AFRICA (3rd Test)

At Sydney Cricket Ground, on 4, 5, 6 (*no play*), 7, 8 January 2023.
Toss: Australia. Result: **MATCH DRAWN**.
Debuts: None.

‡ (H.E.van der Dussen)

AUSTRALIA

U.T.Khawaja	not out		195
D.A.Warner	c Jansen b Nortje		10
M.Labuschagne	c Verreynne b Nortje		79
S.P.D.Smith	c and b Maharaj		104
T.M.Head	c sub‡ b Rabada		70
M.T.Renshaw	not out		5
†A.T.Carey			
*P.J.Cummins			
N.M.Lyon			
J.R.Hazlewood			
Extras	(LB 5, NB 6, W 1)		12
Total	**(4 wkts dec; 131 overs)**		**475**

SOUTH AFRICA

*D.Elgar	c Carey b Hazlewood	15	(2) c Carey b Cummins		10
S.J.Erwee	b Lyon	18	(1) not out		42
H.Klaasen	c Carey b Cummins	2	b Hazlewood		35
T.Bavuma	c Carey b Hazlewood	35	not out		17
K.Zondo	lbw b Cummins	39			
†K.Verreynne	c Smith b Cummins	19			
M.Jansen	c Carey b Head	11			
S.R.Harmer	b Hazlewood	47			
K.A.Maharaj	lbw b Hazlewood	53			
K.Rabada	c and b Lyon	3			
A.A.Nortje	not out	0			
Extras	(B 2, LB 1, NB 5, Pen 5)	13	(NB 2)		2
Total	**(108 overs)**	**255**	**(2 wkts; 41.5 overs)**		**106**

SOUTH AFRICA	O	M	R	W	O	M	R	W		FALL OF WICKETS		
Rabada	28	3	119	1							A	SA	SA
Nortje	22	5	55	2						Wkt	1st	1st	2nd
Jansen	25	4	79	0						1st	12	22	27
Maharaj	25	1	108	1						2nd	147	37	75
Harmer	31	3	109	0						3rd	356	37	–
										4th	468	85	–
AUSTRALIA										5th	–	130	–
Hazlewood	23	7	48	4	5	2	9	1		6th	–	137	–
Cummins	23	7	60	3	(3) 8	1	16	1		7th	–	167	–
Lyon	40	16	88	2	(4) 15	5	32	0		8th	–	252	–
Agar	14	3	30	0	(2) 8	2	28	0		9th	–	255	–
Head	7	1	21	1	2	0	4	0		10th	–	255	–
Smith	1	1	0	0	1	0	8	0					
Labuschagne					2.5	1	9	0					

Umpires: C.B.Gaffaney (*New Zealand*) (44) and P.R.Reiffel (*Australia*) (57).
Referee: Sir R.B.Richardson (*West Indies*) (43).   **Test No. 2485/101 (A849/SA458)**

PAKISTAN v NEW ZEALAND (1st Test)

At National Stadium, Karachi, on 26, 27, 28, 29, 30 December 2022.
Toss: Pakistan. Result: **MATCH DRAWN**.
Debuts: None.

PAKISTAN

Batsman	1st innings		2nd innings	
Abdullah Shafiq	st Blundell b Patel	7	c sub (G.D.Phillips) b Bracewell	17
Imam-ul-Haq	c Southee b Bracewell	24	st Blundell b Sodhi	96
Shan Masood	c Blundell b Bracewell	3	lbw b Sodhi	10
*Babar Azam	c Blundell b Southee	161	(5) lbw b Sodhi	14
Saud Shakil	c Nicholls b Southee	22	(8) not out	55
†Sarfraz Ahmed	c Mitchell b Patel	86	c Blundell b Sodhi	53
Agha Salman	lbw b Southee	103	b Sodhi	6
Nauman Ali	c Bracewell b Wagner	7	(4) lbw b Bracewell	4
Mohammad Wasim	c Blundell b Sodhi	2	lbw b Sodhi	43
Mir Hamza	lbw b Sodhi	1	not out	3
Abrar Ahmed	not out	6		
Extras	(B 3, LB 10, NB 2, W 1)	16	(B 8, NB 2)	10
Total	**(130.5 overs)**	**438**	**(8 wkts dec; 103.5 overs)**	**311**

NEW ZEALAND

Batsman	1st innings		2nd innings	
T.W.M.Latham	c sub (Kamran Ghulam) b Abrar	113	(3) not out	35
D.P.Conway	lbw b Nauman	92	not out	18
K.S.Williamson	not out	200		
H.M.Nicholls	b Nauman	22		
D.J.Mitchell	c Sarfraz b Abrar	42		
†T.A.Blundell	lbw b Wasim	47		
M.G.Bracewell	c Wasim b Abrar	5	(1) b Abrar	3
I.S.Sodhi	c Babar b Abrar	65		
*T.G.Southee	c Masood b Nauman	0		
N.Wagner	c Agha b Abrar	0		
A.Y.Patel	not out	0		
Extras	(B 7, LB 11, NB 1, W 2, Pen 5)	26	(Pen 5)	5
Total	**(9 wkts dec; 194.5 overs)**	**612**	**(1 wkt; 7.3 overs)**	**61**

NEW ZEALAND	O	M	R	W		O	M	R	W
Southee	25.5	4	69	3		5	1	39	0
Wagner	21	2	66	1	(5)	3	0	7	0
Patel	36	6	112	2	(2)	24	2	89	0
Bracewell	24	6	72	2	(3)	25	5	82	2
Sodhi	21	0	87	2	(4)	36.5	11	86	6
Mitchell	3	0	19	0					

PAKISTAN	O	M	R	W		O	M	R	W
Mir Hamza	26	3	83	0	(4)	1	0	4	0
Mohammad Wasim	34	6	105	1	(3)	1.3	0	15	0
Abrar Ahmed	67.5	8	205	5		3	0	23	1
Nauman Ali	63	5	185	3					
Babar Azam	4	1	11	0					
Agha Salman					(2)	2	0	14	0

FALL OF WICKETS

	P	NZ	P	NZ
Wkt	1st	1st	2nd	2nd
1st	12	183	47	4
2nd	19	231	71	—
3rd	48	272	82	—
4th	110	337	100	—
5th	306	427	185	—
6th	318	436	205	—
7th	372	595	206	—
8th	398	596	277	—
9th	414	597	—	—
10th	438	—	—	—

Umpires: Alim Dar (*Pakistan*) (142) and A.G.Wharf (*England*) (3).
Referee: Mohammad Javed (*Pakistan*) (3).

Test No. 2486/61 (P450/NZ459)

PAKISTAN v NEW ZEALAND (2nd Test)

At National Stadium, Karachi, on 2, 3, 4, 5, 6 January 2023.
Toss: New Zealand. Result: **MATCH DRAWN**.
Debuts: None.

NEW ZEALAND

T.W.M.Latham	lbw b Shah	71	c Abrar b Shah		62
D.P.Conway	c Sarfraz b Agha	122	b Hamza		0
K.S.Williamson	c Sarfraz b Shah	36	lbw b Abrar		41
H.M.Nicholls	c Sarfraz b Agha	26	c Babar b Hasan		5
D.J.Mitchell	b Agha	3	(7) not out		6
†T.A.Blundell	b Abrar	51	(5) c Imam b Agha		74
M.G.Bracewell	lbw b Abrar	0	(6) not out		74
I.S.Sodhi	b Shah	11			
*T.G.Southee	st Sarfraz b Abrar	10			
M.J.Henry	not out	68			
A.Y.Patel	c Agha b Abrar	35			
Extras	(B 5, LB 5, NB 5, W 1)	16	(B 4, LB 8, NB 2, W 1)		15
Total	**(131 overs)**	**449**	**(5 wkts dec; 82 overs)**		**277**

PAKISTAN

Abdullah Shafiq	c Patel b Henry	19	b Southee		0
Imam-ul-Haq	c Blundell b Southee	83	b Sodhi		12
Shan Masood	c Conway b Patel	20	(4) c Williamson b Bracewell		35
*Babar Azam	run out	24	(5) c Latham b Bracewell		27
Saud Shakil	not out	125	(7) c Mitchell b Bracewell		32
†Sarfraz Ahmed	st Blundell b Mitchell	78	c Williamson b Bracewell		118
Agha Salman	c Bracewell b Patel	41	(8) b Henry		30
Hasan Ali	c Conway b Patel	4	(9) lbw b Southee		5
Naseem Shah	b Sodhi	4	(10) not out		15
Mir Hamza	b Sodhi	0	(3) b Sodhi		0
Abrar Ahmed	lbw b Sodhi	0	not out		7
Extras	(LB 7, NB 3)	10	(B 16, LB 5, W 2)		23
Total	**(133 overs)**	**408**	**(9 wkts; 90 overs)**		**304**

PAKISTAN	O	M	R	W		O	M	R	W		FALL OF WICKETS				
Mir Hamza	21	3	72	0	(2)	11	2	38	1			NZ	P	NZ	P
Naseem Shah	24	7	71	3	(1)	13	3	43	1		*Wkt*	*1st*	*1st*	*2nd*	*2nd*
Hasan Ali	23	4	72	0	(4)	11	1	39	1		1st	134	27	5	0
Abrar Ahmed	37	5	149	4	(3)	33	6	103	1		2nd	234	56	114	0
Agha Salman	26	3	75	3		14	3	42	1		3rd	240	99	114	35
											4th	255	182	128	77
NEW ZEALAND											5th	278	332	255	80
Southee	25	7	62	1		20	7	43	2		6th	279	385	–	203
Henry	28	9	58	1		21	3	69	1		7th	309	393	–	273
Patel	17	2	88	3	(5)	7	1	32	0		8th	340	397	–	282
Bracewell	26	3	87	0		20	2	75	4		9th	345	397	–	287
Sodhi	27	3	95	3	(3)	18	2	59	2		10th	449	408	–	–
Mitchell	10	6	11	1		4	2	5	0						

Umpires: Alim Dar (*Pakistan*) (143) and A.G.Wharf (*England*) (4).
Referee: D.C.Boon (*Australia*) (68).   Test No. 2487/62 (P451/NZ460)

ZIMBABWE v WEST INDIES (1st Test)

At Queens Sports Club, Bulawayo, on 4, 5, 6, 7, 8 February 2023.
Toss: West Indies. Result: **MATCH DRAWN**.
Debuts: Zimbabwe – B.N.Evans, I.Kaia, T.Makoni, T.E.Tsiga.

WEST INDIES

*K.C.Brathwaite	lbw b Masakadza	182	lbw b Masakadza		25
T.Chanderpaul	not out	207	b Evans		15
K.R.Mayers	b Mavuta	20	(6) not out		17
R.A.Reifer	c Kaia b Mavuta	2	(3) c and b Masakadza		58
J.Blackwood	c Tsiga b Mavuta	5	(4) c Tsiga b Masakadza		57
R.L.Chase	c Ervine b Mavuta	7	(5) c Tsiga b Evans		14
J.O.Holder	c Tsiga b Mavuta	11			
†J.M.Da Silva		3	(7) not out		9
A.S.Joseph					
G.Motie					
K.A.J.Roach					
Extras	(B 6, NB 3, W 1)	10	(B 3, LB 1, NB 4)		8
Total	**(6 wkts dec; 143 overs)**	**447**	**(5 wkts dec; 60 overs)**		**203**

ZIMBABWE

I.Kaia	lbw b Joseph	67	c Brathwaite b Motie		24
T.Makoni	c Mayers b Joseph	33	c Da Silva b Motie		9
C.J.Chibhabha	c Da Silva b Motie	9	c Blackwood b Chase		31
*C.R.Ervine	b Brathwaite	13	c Da Silva b Motie		17
G.S.Ballance	not out	137	c Da Silva b Chase		18
†T.E.Tsiga	lbw b Joseph	2	not out		24
B.N.Evans	c Da Silva b Roach	7	lbw b Motie		0
W.P.Masakadza	c Mayers b Motie	15	not out		0
B.A.Mavuta	b Holder	56			
V.M.Nyauchi	c Da Silva b Holder	13			
R.Ngarava	not out	19			
Extras	(B 2, LB 5, NB 1)	8	(B 8, LB 3)		11
Total	**(9 wkts dec; 125 overs)**	**379**	**(6 wkts; 54 overs)**		**134**

ZIMBABWE	O	M	R	W		O	M	R	W		FALL OF WICKETS			
Ngarava	20	4	69	0	(5)	3	0	19	0			WI	Z	WI	Z
Nyauchi	27	6	73	0	(1)	16	5	38	0		Wkt	1st	1st	2nd	2nd
Evans	24	3	74	0		12	2	41	2		1st	336	63	32	14
Masakadza	31	8	85	1	(2)	23	5	71	3		2nd	373	84	50	61
Mavuta	41	5	140	5	(4)	6	0	30	0		3rd	383	114	157	83
											4th	389	128	174	83
WEST INDIES											5th	413	132	180	119
Roach	15	4	35	1		3	0	16	0		6th	435	147	–	120
Joseph	26	2	75	3	(3)	5	0	19	0		7th	–	192	–	–
Mayers	10	4	22	0	(7)	1	0	6	0		8th	–	327	–	–
Motie	33	10	110	2	(2)	24	6	50	4		9th	–	341	–	–
Holder	17	2	55	2	(4)	5	1	13	0		10th	–	–	–	–
Chase	14	1	45	0		12	6	9	2						
Brathwaite	5	1	12	1	(5)	4	0	10	0						
Reifer	3	0	7	0											
Blackwood	2	0	11	0											

Umpires: P.R.Reiffel (*Australia*) (58) and L.Rusere (*Zimbabwe*) (4).
Referee: J.J.Crowe (*New Zealand*) (112).   **Test No. 2488/11 (Z116/WI568)**

ZIMBABWE v WEST INDIES (2nd Test)

At Queens Sports Club, Bulawayo, on 12, 13, 14 February 2023.
Toss: Zimbabwe. Result: **WEST INDIES** won by an innings and 4 runs.
Debut: Zimbabwe – L.T.Chivanga.

ZIMBABWE

T.Makoni	c Da Silva b Joseph	0	(2) c Da Silva b Joseph		1
I.Kaia	c Mayers b Motie	38	(1) c Da Silva b Motie		43
C.J.Chibhabha	c Chanderpaul b Holder	10	b Holder		1
*C.R.Ervine	lbw b Motie	22	lbw b Motie		72
M.Shumba	c Reifer b Motie	3	b Motie		7
†T.E.Tsiga	c Chanderpaul b Motie	0	b Motie		2
D.T.Tiripano	not out	23	b Gabriel		0
W.P.Masakadza	c Chase b Motie	1	c Reifer b Motie		7
B.A.Mavuta	c Blackwood b Motie	1	c Reifer b Chase		16
V.M.Nyauchi	b Motie	2	st Da Silva b Motie		2
L.T.Chivanga	b Motie	6	not out		3
Extras	(B 4, LB 4, W 1)	9	(B 18, LB 1)		19
Total	**(40.5 overs)**	**115**	**(47.3 overs)**		**173**

WEST INDIES

*K.C.Brathwaite	lbw b Masakadza	7
T.Chanderpaul	c Tiripano b Mavuta	36
R.A.Reifer	run out	53
J.Blackwood	c Nyauchi b Mavuta	22
K.R.Mayers	c Masakadza b Mavuta	30
R.L.Chase	b Nyauchi	70
†J.M.Da Silva	b Nyauchi	44
J.O.Holder	c Tsiga b Nyauchi	3
A.S.Joseph	c Makoni b Nyauchi	4
G.Motie	c Mavuta b Nyauchi	12
S.T.Gabriel	not out	0
Extras	(B 3, NB 6, W 2)	11
Total	**(92.3 overs)**	**292**

WEST INDIES	O	M	R	W	O	M	R	W	FALL OF WICKETS			
										Z	WI	Z
Joseph	9	1	29	1	7	1	23	1	*Wkt*	*1st*	*1st*	*2nd*
Gabriel	8	2	19	0	7	1	20	1	1st	16	13	13
Holder	7	2	18	2	4	1	16	1	2nd	48	86	15
Motie	14.5	4	37	7	17.3	1	62	6	3rd	49	117	56
Chase	2	0	4	0	11	2	30	1	4th	64	124	86
Brathwaite					1	0	3	0	5th	68	184	102
									6th	75	269	103
ZIMBABWE									7th	81	270	132
Nyauchi	17.3	1	56	5					8th	87	274	166
Masakadza	20	5	58	1					9th	89	290	170
Chivanga	14	0	59	0					10th	115	292	173
Tiripano	13	2	26	0								
Mavuta	24	3	73	3								
Shumba	4	0	17	0								

Umpires: P.R.Reiffel (*Australia*) (59) and L.Rusere (*Zimbabwe*) (5).
Referee: J.J.Crowe (*New Zealand*) (113).　　　　　　　Test No. 2489/12 (Z117/WI569)

NEW ZEALAND v ENGLAND (1st Test)

At Bay Oval, Mount Maunganui, on 16, 17, 18, 19 February 2023 (day/night).
Toss: New Zealand. Result: **ENGLAND** won by 267 runs.
Debuts: New Zealand – S.C.Kuggeleijn, B.M.Tickner.

ENGLAND

Z.Crawley	c Bracewell b Southee	4	c Blundell b Kuggeleijn	28
B.M.Duckett	c Bracewell b Tickner	84	c Latham b Tickner	25
O.J.D.Pope	c Latham b Southee	42	c Blundell b Wagner	49
J.E.Root	c Mitchell b Wagner	14	(5) c Mitchell b Bracewell	57
H.C.Brook	b Wagner	89	(6) c Mitchell b Tickner	54
*B.A.Stokes	c Latham b Kuggeleijn	19	(8) st Blundell b Bracewell	31
†B.T.Foakes	c Williamson b Wagner	38	c Blundell b Tickner	51
S.C.J.Broad	c Conway b Kuggeleijn	2	(4) c Nicholls b Wagner	7
O.E.Robinson	not out	15	c Nicholls b Kuggeleijn	39
M.J.Leach	c Latham b Wagner	1	st Blundell b Bracewell	12
J.M.Anderson			not out	6
Extras	(LB 7, NB 6, W 4)	17	(B 5, LB 6, NB 2, W 2)	15
Total	**(9 wkts dec; 58.2 overs)**	**325**	**(73.5 overs)**	**374**

NEW ZEALAND

T.W.M.Latham	c Pope b Robinson	1	b Broad	15
D.P.Conway	c Pope b Stokes	77	b Broad	2
K.S.Williamson	lbw b Anderson	6	b Broad	0
H.M.Nicholls	c Crawley b Anderson	4	c Foakes b Robinson	7
N.Wagner	c Robinson b Broad	27	(10) c Foakes b Anderson	9
D.J.Mitchell	lbw b Robinson	0	(5) not out	57
†T.A.Blundell	c and b Anderson	138	(6) b Broad	1
M.G.Bracewell	c Stokes b Leach	7	(7) c Brook b Leach	25
S.C.Kuggeleijn	b Robinson	20	(8) lbw b Anderson	0
*T.G.Southee	c Duckett b Robinson	10	(9) c Root b Anderson	0
B.M.Tickner	not out	3	b Anderson	8
Extras	(B 4, LB 3, NB 5, W 1)	13		
Total	**(82.5 overs)**	**306**	**(45.3 overs)**	**126**

NEW ZEALAND	O	M	R	W	O	M	R	W		FALL OF WICKETS			
											E	NZ	E	NZ
Southee	13	1	71	2	15	2	49	0						
Wagner	16.2	0	82	4	13	0	110	2		Wkt	1st	1st	2nd	2nd
Tickner	13	0	72	1	12	0	55	3		1st	18	10	52	14
Kuggeleijn	13	0	80	2	14	1	81	2		2nd	117	23	68	14
Bracewell	3	0	13	0	19.5	2	68	3		3rd	152	31	82	19
										4th	154	82	144	27
ENGLAND										5th	209	83	225	28
Anderson	16.5	5	36	3	10.3	3	18	4		6th	298	158	237	68
Broad	17	2	72	1	15	5	49	4		7th	305	182	293	71
Robinson	19	2	54	4	8	0	34	1		8th	319	235	335	71
Leach	18	3	84	1	11	4	25	1		9th	325	247	358	91
Root	5	2	15	0	1	1	0	0		10th	–	306	374	126
Stokes	7	0	38	1										

Umpires: Alim Dar (*Pakistan*) (144) and C.B.Gaffaney (*New Zealand*) (45).
Referee: D.C.Boon (*Australia*) (69).   **Test No. 2494/111 (NZ461/E1059)**

NEW ZEALAND v ENGLAND (2nd Test)

At Basin Reserve, Wellington, on 24, 25, 26, 27, 28 February 2023.
Toss: New Zealand. Result: **NEW ZEALAND** won by 1 run.
Debuts: None.

‡ (S.C.Kuggeleijn)

ENGLAND

Z.Crawley	c Blundell b Henry	2		b Southee	24
B.M.Duckett	c Bracewell b Southee	9		c Blundell b Henry	33
O.J.D.Pope	c Bracewell b Henry	10	(4)	c Latham b Wagner	14
J.E.Root	not out	153	(5)	c Bracewell b Wagner	95
H.C.Brook	c and b Henry	186	(6)	run out	0
*B.A.Stokes	c sub‡ b Wagner	27	(7)	c Latham b Wagner	33
†B.T.Foakes	st Blundell b Bracewell		(8)	c Wagner b Southee	35
S.C.J.Broad	lbw b Bracewell	14	(9)	c Wagner b Henry	11
O.E.Robinson	c Southee b Henry	18	(3)	c Bracewell b Southee	2
M.J.Leach	not out	6		not out	1
J.M.Anderson				c Blundell b Wagner	4
Extras	(LB 8, W 2)	10		(LB 1, NB 1, W 2)	4
Total	**(8 wkts dec; 87.1 overs)**	**435**		**(74.2 overs)**	**256**

NEW ZEALAND

T.W.M.Latham	c Root b Leach	35	lbw b Root	83
D.P.Conway	c Foakes b Anderson	0	c Pope b Leach	61
K.S.Williamson	c Foakes b Anderson	4	c Foakes b Brook	132
W.A.Young	c Foakes b Anderson	2	b Leach	8
H.M.Nicholls	c Pope b Leach	30	c Brook b Robinson	29
D.J.Mitchell	c Pope b Leach	13	c Root b Broad	54
†T.A.Blundell	c Leach b Broad	38	c Root b Leach	90
M.G.Bracewell	c and b Broad	6	run out	8
*T.G.Southee	c Crawley b Broad	73	c sub (M.J.Potts) b Leach	2
M.J.Henry	c Anderson b Broad	6	c Root b Leach	0
N.Wagner	not out	0	not out	0
Extras	(NB 2)	2	(B 1, B 5, NB 8, W 2)	16
Total	**(53.2 overs)**	**209**	**(162.3 overs)**	**483**

NEW ZEALAND	O	M	R	W		O	M	R	W
Southee	24	5	93	1		20.1	5	45	3
Henry	22.1	3	100	4		21.5	3	75	2
Mitchell	9	1	61	0					
Wagner	21	1	119	1		15.2	0	62	4
Bracewell	11	0	54	2	(3)	17	2	73	0

ENGLAND	O	M	R	W		O	M	R	W
Anderson	10	1	37	3		27	7	77	0
Broad	14.2	2	61	4	(3)	24	3	79	1
Robinson	12	4	31	0	(2)	28	6	84	1
Leach	17	1	80	3		61.3	12	157	5
Root						12	0	39	1
Stokes						2	0	16	0
Brook						8	0	25	1

FALL OF WICKETS				
	E	NZ	NZ	E
Wkt	1st	1st	2nd	2nd
1st	5	1	149	39
2nd	21	7	155	53
3rd	21	21	167	59
4th	323	60	222	80
5th	362	77	297	80
6th	363	96	455	201
7th	389	103	478	202
8th	424	201	482	215
9th	–	208	482	251
10th	–	209	483	256

Umpires: C.B.Gaffaney (*New Zealand*) (46) and R.J.Tucker (*Australia*) 81.
Referee: D.C.Boon (*Australia*) (70).   **Test No. 2495/112 (NZ462/E1060)**

INTERNATIONAL UMPIRES AND REFEREES 2023

ELITE PANEL OF UMPIRES 2023

The Elite Panel of ICC Umpires and Referees was introduced in April 2002 to raise standards and guarantee impartial adjudication. Two umpires from this panel stand in Test matches while one officiates with a home umpire from the Supplementary International Panel in limited-overs internationals.

Full Names	Birthdate	Birthplace	Tests	Debut	LOI	Debut
ALIM Sarwar DAR	06.06.68	Jhang, Pakistan	144	2003-04	222	1999-00
DHARMASENA, H.D.P.Kumar	24.04.71	Colombo, Sri Lanka	77	2010-11	118	2008-09
ERASMUS, Marais	27.02.64	George, South Africa	76	2009-10	111	2007-08
GAFFANEY, Christopher Blair	30.11.75	Dunedin, New Zealand	46	2014	77	2010
GOUGH, Michael Andrew	18.12.79	Hartlepool, England	29	2016	74	2013
ILLINGWORTH, Richard Keith	23.08.63	Bradford, England	62	2012-13	77	2010
KETTLEBOROUGH, Richard Allan	15.03.73	Sheffield, England	77	2010-11	95	2009
MENON, Nitin Narendra	02.11.83	Indore, India	17	2019-20	39	2016-17
REIFFEL, Paul Ronald	19.04.66	Box Hill, Australia	59	2012	79	2008-09
TUCKER, Rodney James	28.08.64	Sydney, Australia	81	2009-10	89	2008-09
WILSON, Joel Sheldon	30.12.66	Trinidad, West Indies	34	2015	84	2011

ELITE PANEL OF REFEREES 2023

Full Names	Birthdate	Birthplace	Tests	Debut	LOI	Debut
BOON, David Clarence	29.12.60	Launceston, Australia	70	2011	161	2011
BROAD, Brian Christopher	29.09.57	Bristol, England	118	2003-04	344	2003-04
CROWE, Jeffrey John	14.09.58	Auckland, New Zealand	123	2004-05	310	2003-04
MADUGALLE, Ranjan Senerath	22.04.59	Kandy, Sri Lanka	210	1993-94	383	1993-94
PYCROFT, Andrew John	06.06.56	Harare, Zimbabwe	91	2009	203	2009
RICHARDSON, Sir Richard Benjamin	12.01.62	Five Islands, Antigua	43	2016	74	2016
SRINATH, Javagal	31.08.69	Mysore, India	63	2006	239	2006-07

INTERNATIONAL UMPIRES PANEL 2023

Nominated by their respective cricket boards, members from this panel officiate in home LOIs and supplement the Elite panel for Test matches. The number of Test matches/LOI in which they have stood is shown in brackets.

Afghanistan	Ahmed Shah Pakteen (2/30)	Ahmed Shah Durrani (-/7)	Bismillah Jan Shinwari (-/15)
			Izatullah Safi (-/4)
Australia	D.M.Koch (-/5)	P.Wilson (7/36)	S.J.Nogajski (-/10)
			P.J.Gillespie (-/-)
Bangladesh	Tanvir Ahmed (-/6)	Sharfuddoula (8/49)	Masudur Rahman (-/16)
			Gazi Sohel (-/6)
England	A.G.Wharf (4/11)	D.J.Millns (-/6)	M.Burns (-/6)
			M.J.Saggers (-/3)
India	J.Madanagopal (-/4)	A.K.Chaudhary (4/26)	V.K.Sharma (4/5)
			K.N.Ananthapadmanabhan (-/5)
Ireland	M.Hawthorne (-/33)	R.E.Black (-/20)	J.McCready (-/-)
			P.A.Reynolds (-/6)
New Zealand	W.R.Knights (4/19)	C.M.Brown (6/21)	S.B.Haig (-/7)
Pakistan	Faisal Afridi (-/-)	Ahsan Raza (7/41)	Asif Yaqoob (-/5)
			Rashid Riaz (-/13)
South Africa	A.T.Holdstock (5/42)	S.George (-/60)	B.P.Jele (-/9)
			A.Paleker (2/6)
Sri Lanka	R.M.P.J.Rambukwella (-/2)	R.S.A.Palliyaguruge (9/88)	R.R.Wimalasiri (-/25)
			L.E.Hannibal (-/17)
West Indies	G.O.Brathwaite (8/50)	L.S.Reifer (-/18)	P.A.Gustard (-/7)
			N.Duguid (1/13)
Zimbabwe	L.Rusere (5/23)	I.Chabi (1/7)	C.Phiri (-/1)
			F.Mutizwa (-/2)

Test Match and LOI statistics to 7 March 2023.

TEST MATCH CAREER RECORDS

These records, complete to 7 March 2023, contain all players registered for county cricket in 2023 at the time of going to press, plus those who have played Test cricket since 20 November 2021 (Test No. 2432). Some players who may return to Test action have also been listed, even if their most recent game was earlier than this date.

ENGLAND – BATTING AND FIELDING

	M	I	NO	HS	Runs	Avge	100	50	Ct/tSt
R.Ahmed	1	2	–	10	11	5.50	–	–	–
M.M.Ali	64	111	8	155*	2914	28.29	5	14	40
J.M.Anderson	179	250	107	81	1312	9.17	–	1	104
J.C.Archer	13	20	–	30	155	7.75	–	–	2
J.M.Bairstow	89	159	11	167*	5482	37.04	12	23	210/13
J.T.Ball	4	8	–	31	67	8.37	–	–	1
D.M.Bess	14	19	5	57	319	22.78	–	1	3
S.W.Billings	3	3	–	36	66	22.00	–	–	8
R.S.Bopara	13	19	1	143	575	31.94	3	–	6
S.G.Borthwick	1	2	–	4	5	2.50	–	–	2
J.R.Bracey	2	3	–	8	8	2.66	–	–	6
S.C.J.Broad	161	236	39	169	3584	18.19	1	13	55
H.C.Brook	6	10	–	186	809	80.90	4	3	5
R.J.Burns	32	59	–	133	1789	30.32	3	11	24
J.C.Buttler	57	100	9	152	2907	31.94	2	18	153/1
A.N.Cook	161	291	16	294	12472	45.35	33	57	175
M.S.Crane	1	2	–	4	4	3.00	–	–	–
Z.Crawley	33	61	1	267	1656	27.60	3	7	39
S.M.Curran	24	38	5	78	815	24.69	–	3	5
T.K.Curran	2	3	1	39	66	33.00	–	–	–
L.A.Dawson	3	6	2	66*	84	21.00	–	1	2
J.L.Denly	15	28	–	94	827	29.53	–	6	7
B.M.Duckett	9	17	1	107	618	38.62	1	5	4
S.T.Finn	36	47	22	56	279	11.16	–	1	8
M.D.Fisher	1	1	1	0*	0	–	–	–	–
B.T.Foakes	20	36	7	113*	934	32.20	2	4	57/6
A.D.Hales	11	21	–	94	573	27.28	–	5	8
H.Hameed	10	19	1	82	439	24.38	–	4	7
W.G.Jacks	2	4	–	31	89	22.25	–	–	–
K.K.Jennings	17	32	1	146*	781	25.19	2	1	17
C.J.Jordan	8	11	1	35	180	18.00	–	–	14
D.W.Lawrence	11	21	2	91	551	29.00	–	4	3
M.J.Leach	34	53	19	92	446	13.11	–	1	16
A.Z.Lees	10	19	–	67	453	23.84	–	2	6
L.S.Livingstone	1	2	1	9	16	16.00	–	–	–
A.Lyth	7	13	–	107	265	20.38	1	–	8
S.Mahmood	2	2	1	49	52	52.00	–	–	–
D.J.Malan	22	39	–	140	1074	27.53	1	9	13
C.Overton	8	14	2	41*	182	15.16	–	–	7
J.Overton	1	1	–	97	97	97.00	–	1	–
M.W.Parkinson	1	1	–	8	8	8.00	–	–	–
S.R.Patel	6	9	–	42	151	16.77	–	–	3
O.J.D.Pope	35	62	5	145	1841	32.29	3	11	47/1
M.J.Potts	5	6	2	19	30	7.50	–	–	4
A.U.Rashid	19	33	5	61	540	19.28	–	2	4
O.E.Robinson	16	26	3	42	293	12.73	–	–	8
S.D.Robson	7	11	–	127	336	30.54	1	1	5
T.S.Roland-Jones	4	6	2	25	82	20.50	–	–	–
J.E.Root	129	237	19	254	10948	50.22	29	57	171
J.J.Roy	5	10	–	72	187	18.70	–	1	1
D.P.Sibley	22	39	3	133*	1042	28.94	2	5	12
B.A.Stokes	91	166	7	258	5712	35.92	12	28	95

	M	I	NO	HS	Runs	Avge	100	50	Ct/St
O.P.Stone	3	6	–	20	55	9.16	–	–	1
M.D.Stoneman	11	20	1	60	526	27.68	–	5	1
J.M.Vince	13	22	–	83	548	24.90	–	3	8
T.Westley	5	9	1	59	193	24.12	–	1	1
C.R.Woakes	45	74	14	137*	1675	27.91	1	6	19
M.A.Wood	28	47	8	52	641	16.43	–	1	8

ENGLAND – BOWLING

	O	M	R	W	Avge	Best	5wI	10wM
R.Ahmed	36.5	3	137	7	19.57	5- 48	1	–
M.M.Ali	1975.4	278	7149	195	36.66	6- 53	5	1
J.M.Anderson	6382.1	1663	17807	685	25.99	7- 42	32	3
J.C.Archer	434.5	95	1304	42	31.04	6- 45	3	–
J.T.Ball	102	23	343	3	114.33	1- 47	–	–
D.M.Bess	417	82	1223	36	33.97	5- 30	2	–
R.S.Bopara	72.2	10	290	1	290.00	1- 39	–	–
S.G.Borthwick	13	0	82	4	20.50	3- 33	–	–
S.C.J.Broad	5400.4	1264	15981	576	27.74	8- 15	19	3
H.C.Brook	8	0	25	1	25.00	1- 25	–	–
A.N.Cook	3	0	7	1	7.00	1- 6	–	–
M.S.Crane	48	3	193	1	193.00	1-193	–	–
S.M.Curran	515.1	96	1669	47	35.51	4- 58	–	–
T.K.Curran	66	14	200	2	100.00	1- 65	–	–
L.A.Dawson	87.4	12	298	7	42.57	4-101	–	–
J.L.Denly	65	11	219	2	109.50	2- 42	–	–
S.T.Finn	1068.4	190	3800	125	30.40	6- 79	5	–
M.D.Fisher	27	6	71	1	71.00	1- 67	–	–
A.D.Hales	3	1	2	0	–	–	–	–
W.G.Jacks	54.3	5	232	6	38.66	6-161	1	–
K.K.Jennings	12.1	1	55	0	–	–	–	–
C.J.Jordan	255	74	752	21	35.80	4- 18	–	–
D.W.Lawrence	35	11	97	3	32.33	1- 0	–	–
M.J.Leach	1361.4	282	4114	120	34.28	5- 66	5	1
A.Lyth	1	1	0	0	–	–	–	–
S.Mahmood	61	17	137	6	22.83	2- 21	–	–
D.J.Malan	37	4	131	2	65.50	2- 33	–	–
C.Overton	245.2	43	760	21	36.19	3- 14	–	–
J.Overton	37	4	146	2	73.00	1- 61	–	–
M.W.Parkinson	15.3	0	47	1	47.00	1- 47	–	–
S.R.Patel	143	23	421	7	60.14	2- 27	–	–
M.J.Potts	182.5	41	560	20	28.00	4- 13	–	–
A.U.Rashid	636	50	2390	60	39.83	5- 49	2	–
O.E.Robinson	517	131	1404	66	21.27	5- 49	3	–
T.S.Roland-Jones	89.2	23	334	17	19.64	5- 57	1	–
J.E.Root	753.2	133	2429	53	45.83	5- 8	1	–
D.P.Sibley	1	0	7	0	–	–	–	–
B.A.Stokes	1882.5	339	6229	194	32.10	6- 22	4	–
O.P.Stone	59.4	14	194	10	19.40	3- 29	–	–
J.M.Vince	4	1	13	0	–	–	–	–
T.Westley	4	0	12	0	–	–	–	–
C.R.Woakes	1314.5	300	3996	130	30.73	6- 17	4	1
M.A.Wood	848.5	166	2780	90	30.88	6- 37	3	–

TESTS

AUSTRALIA – BATTING AND FIELDING

	M	I	NO	HS	Runs	Avge	100	50	Ct/tSt
A.C.Agar	5	7	1	98	195	32.50	–	1	–
S.M.Boland	7	6	1	10*	26	5.20	–	–	5
A.T.Carey	18	24	3	111	689	32.80	1	3	60/2
P.J.Cummins	49	67	9	63	924	15.93	–	2	25
C.D.Green	19	27	3	114	827	34.45	–	6	19
P.S.P.Handscomb	19	34	6	110	1062	37.92	2	5	29
M.S.Harris	14	26	2	79	607	25.29	–	3	8
J.R.Hazlewood	59	70	33	39	445	12.02	–	–	21
T.M.Head	35	55	5	175	2239	44.78	5	12	16
U.T.Khawaja	59	104	11	195*	4315	46.39	13	21	44
M.P.Kuhnemann	2	3	1	6	6	3.00	–	–	1
M.Labuschagne	36	62	4	215	3328	57.37	10	14	26
N.M.Lyon	118	147	43	47	1303	12.52	–	–	57
G.J.Maxwell	7	14	1	104	339	26.07	1	–	5
T.R.Murphy	3	5	1	3*	5	1.25	–	–	2
M.G.Neser	2	3	–	35	56	18.66	–	–	–
M.T.Renshaw	14	24	2	184	645	29.31	1	3	9
J.A.Richardson	3	3	–	9	18	6.00	–	–	–
P.M.Siddle	67	94	15	51	1164	14.73	–	2	19
S.P.D.Smith	95	167	21	239	8774	59.89	30	37	154
M.A.Starc	76	108	24	99	1846	21.97	–	10	34
M.J.Swepson	4	5	1	15*	28	7.00	–	–	2
D.A.Warner	103	187	8	335*	8158	45.57	25	34	81

AUSTRALIA – BOWLING

	O	M	R	W	Avge	Best	5wI	10wM
A.C.Agar	167.4	36	468	9	52.00	3- 46	–	–
S.M.Boland	172.1	52	376	28	13.42	6- 7	1	–
P.J.Cummins	1707.4	423	4667	217	21.50	6- 23	8	1
C.D.Green	242.2	50	699	23	30.39	5- 27	1	–
J.R.Hazlewood	2110.1	553	5735	222	25.83	6- 67	9	–
T.M.Head	69.5	8	234	7	33.42	4- 10	–	–
U.T.Khawaja	3	0	0	0	–	–	–	–
M.P.Kuhnemann	53.3	8	186	8	23.25	5- 16	1	–
M.Labuschagne	197.5	18	735	13	56.53	3- 45	–	–
N.M.Lyon	5086.3	998	14904	479	31.11	8- 50	23	4
G.J.Maxwell	77	4	341	8	42.62	4-127	–	–
T.R.Murphy	91.4	23	240	11	21.81	7-124	1	–
M.G.Neser	46.5	11	117	7	16.71	3- 22	–	–
M.T.Renshaw	5	0	20	0	–	–	–	–
J.A.Richardson	89.1	28	243	11	22.09	5- 42	1	–
P.M.Siddle	2317.5	615	6777	221	30.66	6- 54	8	–
S.P.D.Smith	244	28	1007	19	53.00	3- 18	–	–
M.A.Starc	2529.1	509	8325	305	27.29	6- 50	13	2
M.J.Swepson	148.4	14	458	10	45.80	3- 55	–	–
D.A.Warner	57	1	269	4	67.25	2- 45	–	–

SOUTH AFRICA – BATTING AND FIELDING

	M	I	NO	HS	Runs	Avge	100	50	Ct/tSt
K.J.Abbott	11	14	–	17	95	6.78	–	–	4
T.Bavuma	55	95	12	102*	2797	33.69	1	20	26
G.W.Coetzee	1	2	–	20	37	18.50	–	–	–
T.B.de Bruyn	13	25	1	101	468	19.50	1	–	12
Q.de Kock	54	91	6	141*	3300	38.82	6	22	221/11
T.de Zorzi	1	2	–	28	28	14.00	–	–	–
M.de Lange	2	2	–	9	9	4.50	–	–	1
D.Elgar	83	147	11	199	5099	37.49	13	23	87

	M	I	NO	HS	Runs	Avge	100	50	Ct/St
S.J.Erwee	10	19	1	108	479	26.61	1	1	8
M.Z.Hamza	6	12	–	62	212	17.66	–	1	5
S.R.Harmer	9	12	2	47	201	20.10	–	–	4
M.Jansen	11	18	3	59	306	20.40	–	1	9
H.Klaasen	3	6	–	35	73	12.16	–	–	8/1
G.F.Linde	3	6	–	37	135	22.50	–	–	–
K.A.Maharaj	48	76	6	84	1118	15.97	–	5	16
P.J.Malan	3	6	–	84	156	26.00	–	1	3
A.K.Markram	34	62	1	152	2171	35.59	6	9	34
P.W.A.Mulder	11	19	–	36	272	14.31	–	–	17
S.Muthusamy	3	6	2	49*	105	26.25	–	–	3
L.T.Ngidi	17	27	9	19	89	4.94	–	–	7
A.A.Nortje	19	33	9	40	187	7.79	–	–	6
D.Olivier	15	19	9	12	50	5.00	–	–	3
D.Paterson	2	4	3	39*	43	43.00	–	–	1
K.D.Petersen	11	20	–	82	596	29.80	–	4	18
K.Rabada	59	91	16	47	875	11.66	–	–	29
R.D.Rickelton	3	6	1	42	133	26.60	–	–	1
L.L.Sipamla	3	4	1	10*	15	5.00	–	–	2
G.A.Stuurman	2	2	–	11	11	5.50	–	–	–
H.E.van der Dussen	18	32	2	98	905	30.16	–	6	23
K.Verreynne	14	23	3	136*	572	28.60	1	2	39/3
D.J.Vilas	6	9	–	26	94	10.44	–	–	13
L.B.Williams	2	3	–	13	25	8.33	–	–	4
K.Zondo	5	7	1	39	120	20.00	–	–	2

SOUTH AFRICA – BOWLING

	O	M	R	W	Avge	Best	5wI	10wM
K.J.Abbott	346.5	95	886	39	22.71	7- 29	3	–
T.Bavuma	16	1	61	1	61.00	1- 29	–	–
G.W.Coetzee	18	1	65	3	21.66	2- 45	–	–
T.B.de Bruyn	17	1	74	0	–	–	–	–
M.de Lange	74.4	10	277	9	30.77	7- 81	1	–
D.Elgar	172.4	12	673	15	44.86	4- 22	–	–
S.R.Harmer	316.1	58	967	34	28.44	4- 61	–	–
M.Jansen	295.5	54	985	44	22.38	5- 35	1	–
G.F.Linde	78.5	17	252	9	28.00	5- 64	1	–
K.A.Maharaj	1572	294	4974	155	32.09	9-129	9	1
P.J.Malan	2	0	5	0	–	–	–	–
A.K.Markram	41.2	5	130	2	65.00	2- 27	–	–
P.W.A.Mulder	160	45	475	18	26.38	3- 1	–	–
S.Muthusamy	45.3	4	190	2	95.00	1- 63	–	–
L.T.Ngidi	385.5	93	1192	51	23.37	6- 39	3	–
A.A.Nortje	509.3	81	1870	70	26.71	6- 56	4	–
D.Olivier	348	61	1294	59	21.93	6- 37	3	1
D.Paterson	57.5	11	166	4	41.50	2- 86	–	–
K.Rabada	1833.5	363	6219	276	22.53	7-112	13	4
L.L.Sipamla	69.5	14	245	11	22.27	4- 76	–	–
G.A.Stuurman	29	5	124	1	124.00	1-124	–	–
L.B.Williams	30.5	5	105	3	35.00	3- 54	–	–

WEST INDIES – BATTING AND FIELDING

	M	I	NO	HS	Runs	Avge	100	50	Ct/St
J.Blackwood	53	96	5	112*	2829	31.08	3	18	43
N.E.Bonner	15	25	4	123	803	38.23	2	3	14
K.C.Brathwaite	84	161	10	212	5314	35.19	12	28	41

	M	I	NO	HS	Runs	Avge	100	50	Ct/tSt
S.S.J.Brooks	13	24	–	111	553	23.04	1	3	12
J.D.Campbell	20	40	6	68	888	26.11	–	3	12
T.Chanderpaul	5	9	1	207*	450	56.25	1	1	3
R.L.Chase	48	88	4	137*	2237	26.63	5	11	21
R.R.S.Cornwall	9	15	2	73	238	18.30	–	2	15
J.Da Silva	21	36	7	100*	797	27.48	1	3	79/5
S.T.Gabriel	58	87	34	20*	229	4.32	–	–	16
J.O.Holder	61	108	16	202*	2644	28.73	3	11	61
S.D.Hope	38	72	3	147	1726	25.01	2	5	53/1
A.S.Joseph	27	40	–	86	511	12.77	–	2	12
K.R.Mayers	17	30	3	210*	913	33.81	2	2	10
M.J.Mindley	1	2	1	11*	11	11.00	–	–	–
G.Motie	3	2	1	23*	35	35.00	–	–	–
S.P.Narine	6	7	2	22*	40	8.00	–	–	2
V.Permaul	9	13	2	26*	145	13.18	–	–	4
A.Phillip	2	3	1	43	53	26.50	–	–	–
R.A.Reifer	6	10	1	62	270	30.00	–	3	5
K.A.J.Roach	76	120	25	41	1117	11.75	–	–	20
J.N.T.Seales	10	15	8	13	41	5.85	–	–	3
J.L.Solozano	1	1	–	–	–	–	–	–	–
D.C.Thomas	1	2	–	19	31	15.50	–	–	1
J.A.Warrican	13	23	9	41	163	11.64	–	–	5

WEST INDIES – BOWLING

	O	M	R	W	Avge	Best	5wI	10wM
J.Blackwood	72.4	12	257	4	64.25	2-14	–	–
N.E.Bonner	19	2	82	1	82.00	1-16	–	–
K.C.Brathwaite	445	34	1498	29	51.65	6-29	1	–
J.D.Campbell	10.1	0	30	0	–	–	–	–
R.L.Chase	1104.1	126	3811	85	44.83	8-60	4	–
R.R.S.Cornwall	444.1	79	1284	34	37.76	7-75	2	1
S.T.Gabriel	1539.1	269	5241	164	31.95	8-62	6	1
J.O.Holder	1703.3	451	4377	151	28.98	6-42	8	1
A.S.Joseph	778.4	135	2688	79	34.02	5-81	1	–
K.R.Mayers	228	72	544	28	19.42	5-18	1	–
M.J.Mindley	2	0	11	0	–	–	–	–
G.Motie	105.2	23	302	19	15.89	7-37	2	1
S.P.Narine	275	60	851	21	40.52	6-91	2	–
V.Permaul	352.2	46	1183	31	38.16	5-35	1	–
A.Phillip	46	4	212	3	70.66	2-30	–	–
R.A.Reifer	41	11	118	2	59.00	1-36	–	–
K.A.J.Roach	2291.3	507	7053	260	27.12	6-48	11	1
J.N.T.Seales	265	53	897	37	24.24	5-55	1	–
D.C.Thomas	16	1	66	2	33.00	2-53	–	–
J.A.Warrican	449.3	64	1444	41	35.21	4-50	–	–

NEW ZEALAND – BATTING AND FIELDING

	M	I	NO	HS	Runs	Avge	100	50	Ct/tSt
T.A.Blundell	24	40	4	138	1631	45.30	4	10	59/9
T.A.Boult	78	94	46	52*	759	15.81	–	1	43
M.G.Bracewell	6	12	1	74*	224	20.36	–	1	8
D.P.Conway	14	26	1	200	1290	51.60	4	7	4
C.de Grandhomme	29	44	7	120*	1432	38.70	2	8	19
M.J.Henry	19	25	6	68*	386	20.31	–	3	8
K.A.Jamieson	16	22	3	51*	372	19.57	–	1	5
S.C.Kuggeleijn	1	2	–	20	22	11.00	–	–	–

	M	I	NO	HS	Runs	Avge	100	50	Ct/tSt
T.W.M.Latham	72	127	6	264*	5038	41.63	13	26	83
D.J.Mitchell	16	24	4	190	1116	55.80	4	7	22
C.Munro	1	2	–	15	16	8.00	–	–	–
H.M.Nicholls	52	80	6	174	2726	36.83	8	12	32
A.Y.Patel	14	19	8	35	126	11.45	–	–	7
R.Ravindra	3	6	1	18*	73	14.60	–	–	2
M.J.Santner	24	32	1	126	766	24.70	1	2	16
I.S.Sodhi	19	27	4	65	524	22.78	–	4	11
W.E.R.Somerville	6	10	2	40*	115	14.37	–	–	6
T.G.Southee	92	132	11	77*	1950	16.11	–	6	71
L.R.P.L.Taylor	112	196	24	290	7683	44.66	19	35	163
B.M.Tickner	1	2	1	8	11	11.00	–	–	–
N.Wagner	62	81	23	66*	815	14.05	–	1	17
K.S.Williamson	92	161	15	251	7787	53.33	26	33	77
W.A.Young	13	22	–	89	582	26.45	–	6	6

NEW ZEALAND – BOWLING

	O	M	R	W	Avge	Best	5wI	10wM
T.A.Blundell	3	0	13	0	–	–	–	–
T.A.Boult	2902.5	656	8717	317	27.49	6- 30	10	1
M.G.Bracewell	193.3	22	809	18	44.94	4- 75	–	–
C.de Grandhomme	675.4	163	1615	49	32.95	6- 41	1	–
M.J.Henry	750.1	147	2435	61	39.91	7- 23	1	–
K.A.Jamieson	527	168	1401	72	19.45	6- 48	5	1
S.C.Kuggeleijn	27	1	161	4	40.25	2- 80	–	–
D.J.Mitchell	89.1	22	280	3	93.33	1- 7	–	–
C.Munro	18	4	40	2	20.00	2- 40	–	–
A.Y.Patel	499.5	100	1510	48	31.45	10-119	3	1
R.Ravindra	61	11	188	3	62.66	3- 56	–	–
M.J.Santner	672.5	140	1871	41	45.63	3- 53	–	–
I.S.Sodhi	633.5	88	2319	54	42.94	6- 86	1	–
W.E.R.Somerville	244.2	34	724	15	48.26	4- 75	–	–
T.G.Southee	3506.1	794	10532	359	29.33	7- 64	14	1
L.R.P.L.Taylor	16.3	3	48	3	16.00	2- 4	–	–
B.M.Tickner	25	0	127	4	31.75	3- 55	–	–
N.Wagner	2250.3	465	7018	258	27.20	7- 39	9	–
K.S.Williamson	358.3	48	1207	30	40.23	4- 44	–	–

INDIA – BATTING AND FIELDING

	M	I	NO	HS	Runs	Avge	100	50	Ct/tSt
M.A.Agarwal	21	36	–	243	1488	41.33	4	6	14
R.Ashwin	91	130	15	124	3122	27.14	5	13	31
J.J.Bumrah	30	46	17	34*	212	7.31	–	–	8
S.Gill	14	27	2	110	762	30.48	1	4	10
S.S.Iyer	9	16	1	105	666	44.40	1	5	11
R.A.Jadeja	63	93	209	175*	2630	36.02	3	18	39
V.Kohli	107	182	11	254*	8230	48.12	27	28	108
Kuldeep Yadav	8	9	–	40	94	10.44	–	–	3
Mohammed Shami	62	86	25	56*	724	11.86	–	2	16
R.R.Pant	33	56	4	159*	2271	43.67	5	11	119/14
A.R.Patel	11	17	4	84	434	33.38	–	3	2
C.A.Pujara	101	173	11	206*	7112	43.90	19	35	65
A.M.Rahane	82	140	12	188	4931	38.52	12	25	99
K.L.Rahul	47	81	2	199	2642	33.44	7	13	54
W.P.Saha	40	56	10	117	1353	29.41	3	6	92/12
I.Sharma	105	142	47	57	785	8.26	–	1	23

TESTS   **INDIA – BATTING AND FIELDING (continued)**

	M	I	NO	HS	Runs	Avge	100	50	Ct/St
R.G.Sharma	48	82	9	212	3344	45.80	9	14	50
M.Siraj	18	25	10	16*	79	5.26	–	–	9
K.Srikar Bharat	3	5	1	23*	57	14.25	–	–	6/1
S.N.Thakur	8	14	1	67	254	19.53	–	3	2
J.D.Unadkat	2	4	2	14*	29	14.50	–	–	1
G.H.Vihari	16	28	3	111	839	33.56	1	5	4
J.Yadav	6	9	1	104	248	31.00	1	1	3
S.A.Yadav	1	1	–	8	8	8.00	–	–	–
U.T.Yadav	55	65	27	31	454	11.94	–	–	19

INDIA – BOWLING

	O	M	R	W	Avge	Best	5wI	10wM
R.Ashwin	4024.1	822	11195	467	23.97	7-59	31	7
J.J.Bumrah	1044.4	254	2815	128	21.99	6-27	8	–
R.A.Jadeja	2564.4	641	6272	263	23.84	7-42	12	2
V.Kohli	29.1	2	84	0	–	–	–	–
Kuldeep Yadav	213.1	33	733	34	21.55	5-40	3	–
Mohammed Shami	1834.4	350	6032	223	27.04	6-56	6	–
A.R.Patel	329.2	76	775	48	16.14	6-38	5	1
C.A.Pujara	1	0	2	0	–	–	–	–
I.Sharma	3193.2	640	10078	311	32.40	7-74	11	1
R.G.Sharma	63.5	5	224	2	112.00	1-26	–	–
M.Siraj	447.4	89	1471	47	31.29	5-73	1	–
S.N.Thakur	184.3	26	660	27	24.44	7-61	1	–
J.D.Unadkat	51	9	168	3	56.00	2-50	–	–
G.H.Vihari	57.3	10	180	5	36.00	3-37	–	–
J.Yadav	137.3	28	465	16	29.06	4-49	–	–
U.T.Yadav	1426.3	237	5006	168	29.79	6-88	3	1

PAKISTAN – BATTING AND FIELDING

	M	I	NO	HS	Runs	Avge	100	50	Ct/St
Abdullah Shafiq	12	23	2	160*	992	47.23	3	4	9
Abid Ali	16	26	2	215*	1180	49.16	4	3	6
Abrar Ahmed	4	7	4	17	42	14.00	–	–	1
Agha Salman	7	14	1	103	447	34.38	1	3	5
Azhar Ali	97	180	11	302*	7142	42.26	19	35	66
Babar Azam	47	85	9	196	3696	48.63	9	26	33
Faheem Ashraf	16	25	1	91	673	28.04	–	4	5
Fawad Alam	19	30	4	168	1011	38.88	5	2	13
Haris Rauf	1	2	–	12	12	6.00	–	–	–
Hasan Ali	22	34	5	30	375	12.93	–	–	6
Iftikhar Ahmed	4	6	1	27	61	12.20	–	–	2
Imam-ul-Haq	20	39	3	157	1417	39.36	3	7	13
Mir Hamza	3	6	3	4*	8	2.66	–	–	–
Mohammad Abbas	25	36	16	29	110	5.50	–	–	7
Mohammad Ali	2	4	2	0*	0	0.00	–	–	1
Mohammad Nawaz	6	10	1	45	144	16.00	–	–	4
Mohammad Rizwan	27	43	7	115*	1373	38.13	2	7	70/2
Mohammad Wasim	2	4	1	43	55	18.33	–	–	1
Naseem Shah	15	21	8	18	96	7.38	–	–	5
Nauman Ali	13	17	4	97	250	19.23	–	1	1
Sajid Khan	7	7	–	21	73	10.42	–	–	4
Sarfraz Ahmed	51	90	13	118	2992	38.85	4	21	150/22
Saud Shakil	5	10	2	125*	580	72.50	1	5	5
Shadab Khan	6	11	2	56	300	33.33	–	3	3
Shaheen Shah Afridi	25	32	8	19	145	6.04	–	–	2

	M	I	NO	HS	Runs	Avge	100	50	Ct/tSt
Shan Masood	28	53	–	156	1500	28.30	4	6	17
Yasir Shah	48	72	7	113	918	14.12	1	–	24
Zafar Gohar	1	2	–	37	71	35.50	–	–	–
Zahid Mahmood	2	4	–	17	18	4.50	–	–	–

PAKISTAN – BOWLING

	O	M	R	W	Avge	Best	5wI	10wM
Abrar Ahmed	238.3	28	942	28	33.64	7-114	2	1
Agha Salman	88	9	345	6	57.50	3- 75	–	–
Azhar Ali	144.3	8	621	8	77.62	2- 35	–	–
Babar Azam	15	2	42	2	21.00	1- 1	–	–
Faheem Ashraf	294	78	861	24	35.87	3- 42	–	–
Fawad Alam	16	1	54	2	27.00	2- 46	–	–
Haris Rauf	13	1	78	1	78.00	1- 78	–	–
Hasan Ali	650	149	2003	78	25.67	5- 27	6	1
Iftikhar Ahmed	34.2	1	161	1	161.00	1- 1	–	–
Imam-ul-Haq	2	0	9	0	–	–	–	–
Mir Hamza	74	10	264	2	132.00	1- 38	–	–
Mohammad Abbas	855.4	261	2072	90	23.02	5- 33	4	1
Mohammad Ali	49	2	261	4	65.25	2- 64	–	–
Mohammad Nawaz	159.5	23	496	16	31.00	5- 88	1	–
Mohammad Wasim	59.4	8	231	2	115.50	1- 71	–	–
Naseem Shah	410.2	65	1518	42	36.14	5- 31	1	–
Nauman Ali	470.4	85	1376	37	37.18	6-107	3	–
Sajid Khan	277.4	50	832	22	37.81	8- 42	1	1
Saud Shakil	2	0	30	0	–	–	–	–
Shadab Khan	159	19	513	14	36.64	3- 31	–	–
Shaheen Shah Afridi	809.4	173	2462	99	24.86	6- 51	4	1
Shan Masood	24	6	92	2	46.00	1- 6	–	–
Yasir Shah	2375.5	359	7657	244	31.38	8- 41	16	3
Zafar Gohar	32	0	159	0	–	–	–	–
Zahid Mahmood	62.3	3	434	12	36.16	4-235	–	–

SRI LANKA – BATTING AND FIELDING

	M	I	NO	HS	Runs	Avge	100	50	Ct/tSt
L.Ambuldeniya	17	27	1	40	191	7.34	–	–	2
K.I.C.Asalanka	3	6	–	29	88	14.66	–	–	1
P.V.D.Chameera	12	21	2	22	104	5.47	–	–	5
L.D.Chandimal	70	127	13	206*	4936	43.29	13	24	82/10
D.M.de Silva	45	81	6	173	2815	37.53	9	10	53
D.P.D.N.Dickwella	53	94	7	96	2750	31.60	–	22	131/27
A.M.Fernando	7	11	6	5*	18	3.60	–	–	2
B.O.P.Fernando	19	33	4	102	1039	35.82	1	7	14
M.V.T.Fernando	17	25	12	38	85	6.53	–	–	3
N.G.R.P.Jayasuriya	3	4	–	8	15	3.75	–	–	–
P.A.K.P.Jayawickrama	5	6	5	8*	12	12.00	–	–	2
F.D.M.Karunaratne	82	158	6	244	6023	39.62	14	31	55
C.B.R.L.S.Kumara	24	32	15	10	56	3.29	–	–	6
R.A.S.Lakmal	70	109	25	42	934	11.11	–	–	22
A.D.Mathews	100	178	24	200*	6953	45.14	13	38	70
B.K.G.Mendis	54	103	4	196	3402	34.36	7	15	79
P.H.K.D.Mendis	1	1	–	61	61	61.00	–	1	–
C.A.K.Rajitha	13	16	3	12*	54	4.15	–	–	4
P.N.Silva	9	15	1	103	537	38.35	1	5	3
M.M.Theekshana	2	3	–	38	59	19.66	–	–	1
H.D.R.L.Thirimanne	44	85	6	155*	2088	26.43	3	10	36

SRI LANKA – BATTING AND FIELDING (continued)

	M	I	NO	HS	Runs	Avge	100	50	Ct/St
J.D.F.Vandersay	1	2	–	8	14	7.00	–	–	1
R.T.M.Wanigamuni	10	16	1	45*	275	18.33	–	–	2
D.N.Wellalage	1	2	–	18	29	14.50	–	–	2

SRI LANKA – BOWLING

	O	M	R	W	Avge	Best	5wI	10wM
L.Ambuldeniya	807.3	141	2611	71	36.77	7-137	5	1
K.I.C.Asalanka	4.1	0	16	0	–	–	–	–
P.V.D.Chameera	337	28	1321	32	41.28	5- 47	1	–
D.M.de Silva	528.3	60	1770	33	53.63	3- 25	–	–
A.M.Fernando	151.2	25	491	20	24.55	6- 51	1	1
B.O.P.Fernando	3	0	19	0	–	–	–	–
M.V.T.Fernando	444	54	1646	43	38.27	5-101	1	–
N.G.R.P.Jayasuriya	216.2	40	591	29	20.37	6- 59	4	1
P.A.K.P.Jayawickrama	220	50	642	25	25.68	6- 92	2	1
F.D.M.Karunaratne	51.2	5	199	2	99.50	1- 12	–	–
C.B.R.L.S.Kumara	710.5	98	2694	70	38.48	6-122	1	–
R.A.S.Lakmal	2073.5	439	6232	171	36.44	5- 47	4	–
A.D.Mathews	655	159	1766	33	53.51	4- 44	–	–
B.K.G.Mendis	22	1	118	1	118.00	1- 10	–	–
C.A.K.Rajitha	350.2	71	1089	39	27.92	5- 64	1	–
M.M.Theekshana	60.5	10	188	5	37.60	2- 28	–	–
H.D.R.L.Thirimanne	14	1	51	0	–	–	–	–
J.D.F.Vandersay	10	0	68	2	34.00	2- 68	–	–
R.T.M.Wanigamuni	440.1	60	1306	46	28.39	6- 70	3	1
D.N.Wellalage	13	1	35	0	–	–	–	–

P.N.Silva is also known as P.Nissanka; R.T.M.Wanigamuni is also known as W.R.T.Mendis.

ZIMBABWE – BATTING AND FIELDING

	M	I	NO	HS	Runs	Avge	100	50	Ct/St
G.S.Ballance †	1	2	1	137*	155	155.00	1	–	1
C.J.Chibhabha	5	10	–	60	175	17.50	–	1	–
T.L.Chivanga	1	2	1	6	9	9.00	–	–	–
C.R.Ervine	20	40	2	160	1332	35.05	3	5	17
B.N.Evans	1	2	–	7	7	3.50	–	–	–
I.Kaia	2	4	–	67	172	43.00	–	1	1
T.Makoni	2	4	–	33	43	10.75	–	–	1
W.P.Masakadza	3	6	1	17	44	8.80	–	–	3
B.A.Mavuta	4	7	–	56	82	11.71	–	1	4
R.Ngarava	4	7	2	19*	50	10.00	–	–	1
V.M.Nyauchi	8	13	4	13	57	6.33	–	–	3
M.Shumba	4	8	–	41	111	13.87	–	–	1
D.T.Tiripano	16	31	7	95	531	22.12	–	2	5
T.E.Tsiga	2	4	1	24*	28	9.33	–	–	5

† G.S.Ballance's batting and fielding record for England was as follows:

	23	42	2	156	1498	37.45	4	7	22

ZIMBABWE – BOWLING

	O	M	R	W	Avge	Best	5wI	10wM
C.J.Chibhabha	41	4	162	1	162.00	1- 44	–	–
T.L.Chivanga	14	0	59	0	–	–	–	–
B.N.Evans	36	5	115	2	57.50	2- 41	–	–
W.P.Masakadza	87.1	20	268	7	38.28	3- 71	–	–
B.A.Mavuta	127	11	480	12	40.00	5-140	1	–
R.Ngarava	108	18	369	5	73.80	2-104	–	–

	O	M	R	W	Avge	Best	5wI	10wM
V.M.Nyauchi	229.2	41	734	20	36.70	5-56	1	–
M.Shumba	61.4	8	250	1	250.00	1-64	–	–
D.T.Tiripano	448.5	99	1273	26	48.96	3-23	–	–

BANGLADESH – BATTING AND FIELDING

	M	I	NO	HS	Runs	Avge	100	50	Ct/tSt
Abu Jayed	13	22	8	8	36	2.57	–	–	1
Anamul Haque	5	10	–	23	100	10.00	–	–	2
Ebadat Hossain	18	30	15	21*	50	3.33	–	–	1
Khaled Ahmed	11	19	6	4*	9	0.69	–	–	2
Liton Das	37	64	1	141	2253	35.76	3	15	63/6
Mahmudul Hasan	8	14	–	137	363	25.92	1	2	4
Mehedi Hasan	37	69	7	103	1142	18.41	1	3	22
Mohammad Naim	1	2	–	24	24	12.00	–	–	1
Mominul Haque	55	102	6	181	3618	37.68	11	16	36
Mosaddek Hossain	4	8	2	75	173	28.83	–	1	2
Mushfiqur Rahim	84	155	13	219*	5321	37.47	9	25	109/15
Mustafizur Rahman	15	22	7	16	66	4.40	–	–	1
Nayeem Hasan	8	11	3	26	118	14.75	–	–	5
Nazmul Hossain	21	40	1	163	1009	25.87	2	3	14
Nurul Hasan	9	17	1	64	394	24.62	–	3	18/7
Saif Hasan	6	11	–	43	159	14.45	–	–	–
Shadman Islam	13	25	1	115*	559	23.29	1	2	10
Shakib Al Hasan	65	120	7	217	4367	38.64	5	30	26
Shoriful Islam	5	8	2	26	38	6.33	–	–	4
Taijul Islam	40	68	9	39*	533	9.03	–	–	20
Tamim Iqbal	69	132	2	206	5082	39.09	10	31	19
Taskin Ahmed	12	21	3	75	219	12.16	–	1	1
Yasir Ali	6	11	1	55	205	20.50	–	1	5
Zakir Hasan	2	4	–	100	186	46.50	1	1	–

BANGLADESH – BOWLING

	O	M	R	W	Avge	Best	5wI	10wM
Abu Jayed	327.2	64	1118	30	37.26	4- 71	–	–
Ebadat Hossain	508.5	98	1820	32	56.87	6- 46	1	–
Khaled Ahmed	308	49	1085	21	51.66	5-106	1	–
Liton Das	2	0	13	0	–	–	–	–
Mehedi Hasan	1560	239	4929	146	33.76	7- 58	9	2
Mominul Haque	127.2	9	480	7	68.57	3- 27	–	–
Mosaddek Hossain	27	2	87	0	–	–	–	–
Mustafizur Rahman	357.3	76	1139	31	36.74	4- 37	–	–
Nayeem Hasan	273.2	44	840	31	27.09	6-105	3	–
Nazmul Hossain	18.4	1	81	0	–	–	–	–
Saif Hasan	6	0	27	1	27.00	1- 22	–	–
Shakib Al Hasan	2446.3	465	7204	231	31.18	7- 36	19	2
Shoriful Islam	135	33	408	8	51.00	3- 69	–	–
Taijul Islam	1822.5	314	5520	166	33.25	8- 39	10	1
Tamim Iqbal	5	0	20	0	–	–	–	–
Taskin Ahmed	394.1	65	1460	26	56.15	4- 82	–	–
Yasir Ali	7	0	35	0	–	–	–	–

IRELAND – BATTING AND FIELDING

	M	I	NO	HS	Runs	Avge	100	50	Ct/tSt
M.R.Adair	1	2	–	8	11	5.50	–	–	1
A.Balbirnie	3	6	–	82	146	24.33	–	2	3
G.H.Dockrell	1	2	–	39	64	32.00	–	–	–

	M	I	NO	HS	Runs	Avge	100	50	Ct/St
A.R.McBrine	2	4	–	11	18	4.50	–	–	–
T.J.Murtagh	3	6	2	54*	109	27.25	–	1	–
W.T.S.Porterfield	3	6	–	32	58	9.66	–	–	2
P.R.Stirling	3	6	–	36	104	17.33	–	–	4

IRELAND – BOWLING

	O	M	R	W	Avge	Best	5wI	10wM
M.R.Adair	27.4	8	98	6	16.33	3-32	–	–
A.Balbirnie	1	0	8	0	–	–	–	–
G.H.Dockrell	40	11	121	2	60.50	2-63	–	–
A.R.McBrine	50	10	159	3	53.00	2-77	–	–
T.J.Murtagh	95	25	213	13	16.38	5-13	1	–
P.R.Stirling	2	0	11	0	–	–	–	–

Ireland did not play a Test match between 26 July 2019 and 4 April 2023. The players listed above include all those featured in the Ireland players' register (see page 319).

AFGHANISTAN – BATTING AND FIELDING

	M	I	NO	HS	Runs	Avge	100	50	Ct/St
Abdul Malik	1	2	–	0	0	0.00	–	–	2
Abdul Wasi	1	2	–	9	12	6.00	–	–	–
Afsar Zazai	5	8	1	48*	172	24.57	–	–	9/1
Hashmatullah Shahidi	5	10	4	200*	353	58.83	1	1	2
Ibrahim Zadran	4	8	–	87	356	44.50	–	3	6
Mujeeb Zadran	1	2	–	15	18	9.00	–	–	–
Munir Ahmad	1	2	–	12	13	6.50	–	–	–
Nasir Ahmadzai	2	4	2	55*	76	38.00	–	1	2
Qais Ahmad	1	2	–	14	23	11.50	–	–	–
Rahmat Shah	6	12	–	102	385	32.08	1	3	4
Rashid Khan	5	7	–	51	106	15.14	–	1	–
Shahidullah	1	1	–	0	0	0.00	–	–	–
Yamin Ahmadzai	5	9	–	18	32	3.55	–	–	–
Zahir Khan	3	6	3	0*	0	0.00	–	–	–

AFGHANISTAN – BOWLING

	O	M	R	W	Avge	Best	5wI	10wM
Abdul Wasi	8.5	0	23	0	–	–	–	–
Ibrahim Zadran	2	0	13	1	13.00	1- 13	–	–
Mujeeb Zadran	15	1	75	1	75.00	1- 75	–	–
Qais Ahmad	9	2	28	1	28.00	1- 22	–	–
Rahmat Shah	3	0	9	0	–	–	–	–
Rashid Khan	255.4	48	760	30	22.35	7-137	4	2
Shahidullah	5	1	6	0	–	–	–	–
Yamin Ahmadzai	88.3	18	264	11	24.00	3- 41	–	–
Zahir Khan	56	3	239	7	34.14	3- 59	–	–

Afghanistan have not played Test cricket since the March 2021 series with Zimbabwe. Those listed include anyone who has played international cricket for them since 20 November 2021.

INTERNATIONAL TEST MATCH RESULTS

Complete to 7 March 2023.

	Opponents	Tests	E	A	SA	WI	NZ	I	P	SL	Z	B	Ire	Afg	Tied	Drawn
England	Australia	356	110	150	–	–	–	–	–	–	–	–	–	–	–	96
	South Africa	156	66	–	35	–	–	–	–	–	–	–	–	–	–	55
	West Indies	163	51	–	–	59	–	–	–	–	–	–	–	–	–	53
	New Zealand	112	52	–	–	–	13	–	–	–	–	–	–	–	–	47
	India	131	50	–	–	–	–	31	–	–	–	–	–	–	–	50
	Pakistan	89	29	–	–	–	–	–	21	–	–	–	–	–	–	39
	Sri Lanka	36	17	–	–	–	–	–	–	8	–	–	–	–	–	11
	Zimbabwe	6	3	–	–	–	–	–	–	–	0	–	–	–	–	3
	Bangladesh	10	9	–	–	–	–	–	–	–	–	1	–	–	–	0
	Ireland	1	1	–	–	–	–	–	–	–	–	–	0	–	–	0
Australia	South Africa	101	–	54	26	–	–	–	–	–	–	–	–	–	–	21
	West Indies	118	–	60	–	32	–	–	–	–	–	–	–	–	1	25
	New Zealand	60	–	34	–	–	8	–	–	–	–	–	–	–	–	18
	India	105	–	44	–	–	–	32	–	–	–	–	–	–	1	28
	Pakistan	69	–	34	–	–	–	–	15	–	–	–	–	–	–	20
	Sri Lanka	33	–	20	–	–	–	–	–	5	–	–	–	–	–	8
	Zimbabwe	3	–	3	–	–	–	–	–	–	0	–	–	–	–	0
	Bangladesh	6	–	5	–	–	–	–	–	–	–	1	–	–	–	0
S Africa	West Indies	31	–	–	21	3	–	–	–	–	–	–	–	–	–	7
	New Zealand	47	–	–	26	–	5	–	–	–	–	–	–	–	–	16
	India	42	–	–	17	–	–	15	–	–	–	–	–	–	–	10
	Pakistan	28	–	–	15	–	–	–	6	–	–	–	–	–	–	7
	Sri Lanka	31	–	–	16	–	–	–	–	9	–	–	–	–	–	6
	Zimbabwe	9	–	–	8	–	–	–	–	–	0	–	–	–	–	1
	Bangladesh	14	–	–	12	–	–	–	–	–	–	0	–	–	–	2
W Indies	New Zealand	49	–	–	–	13	17	–	–	–	–	–	–	–	–	19
	India	98	–	–	–	30	–	22	–	–	–	–	–	–	–	46
	Pakistan	54	–	–	–	18	–	–	21	–	–	–	–	–	–	15
	Sri Lanka	24	–	–	–	4	–	–	–	11	–	–	–	–	–	9
	Zimbabwe	12	–	–	–	8	–	–	–	–	0	–	–	–	–	4
	Bangladesh	20	–	–	–	14	–	–	–	–	–	4	–	–	–	2
	Afghanistan	1	–	–	–	1	–	–	–	–	–	–	–	–	0	0
N Zealand	India	62	–	–	–	–	13	22	–	–	–	–	–	–	–	27
	Pakistan	62	–	–	–	–	14	–	25	–	–	–	–	–	–	23
	Sri Lanka	36	–	–	–	–	16	–	–	9	–	–	–	–	–	11
	Zimbabwe	17	–	–	–	–	11	–	–	–	0	–	–	–	–	6
	Bangladesh	17	–	–	–	–	13	–	–	–	–	1	–	–	–	3
India	Pakistan	59	–	–	–	–	–	9	12	–	–	–	–	–	–	38
	Sri Lanka	46	–	–	–	–	–	22	–	7	–	–	–	–	–	17
	Zimbabwe	11	–	–	–	–	–	7	–	–	2	–	–	–	–	2
	Bangladesh	13	–	–	–	–	–	11	–	–	–	0	–	–	–	2
	Afghanistan	1	–	–	–	–	–	1	–	–	–	–	–	0	–	0
Pakistan	Sri Lanka	57	–	–	–	–	–	–	21	17	–	–	–	–	–	19
	Zimbabwe	19	–	–	–	–	–	–	12	–	3	–	–	–	–	4
	Bangladesh	13	–	–	–	–	–	–	12	–	–	0	–	–	–	1
	Ireland	1	–	–	–	–	–	–	1	–	–	–	0	–	–	0
Sri Lanka	Zimbabwe	20	–	–	–	–	–	–	–	14	0	–	–	–	–	6
	Bangladesh	24	–	–	–	–	–	–	–	18	–	1	–	–	–	5
Zimbabwe	Bangladesh	18	–	–	–	–	–	–	–	–	7	8	–	–	–	3
	Afghanistan	2	–	–	–	–	–	–	–	–	1	–	–	1	–	0
Bangladesh	Afghanistan	1	–	–	–	–	–	–	–	–	–	0	–	1	–	0
Ireland	Afghanistan	1	–	–	–	–	–	–	–	–	–	–	0	1	–	0
		2495	388	404	176	182	110	172	146	98	13	16	0	3	2	785

	Tests	Won	Lost	Drawn	Tied	Toss Won
England	1060	388	318	354	–	518
Australia	852†	405†	229	216	2	431†
South Africa	459	176	158	125	–	215
West Indies	570	182	207	180	1	299
New Zealand	462	110	182	170	–	230
India	568	172	175	220	1	284
Pakistan	451	146	139	166	–	212
Sri Lanka	307	98	117	92	–	167
Zimbabwe	117	13	75	29	–	65
Bangladesh	136	16	102	18	–	70
Ireland	3	–	3	–	–	2
Afghanistan	6	3	3	–	–	4

† total includes Australia's victory against the ICC World XI.

INTERNATIONAL TEST CRICKET RECORDS

(To 7 March 2023)

TEAM RECORDS
HIGHEST INNINGS TOTALS

952-6d	Sri Lanka v India	Colombo (RPS)	1997-98
903-7d	England v Australia	The Oval	1938
849	England v West Indies	Kingston	1929-30
790-3d	West Indies v Pakistan	Kingston	1957-58
765-6d	Pakistan v Sri Lanka	Karachi	2008-09
760-7d	Sri Lanka v India	Ahmedabad	2009-10
759-7d	India v England	Chennai	2016-17
758-8d	Australia v West Indies	Kingston	1954-55
756-5d	Sri Lanka v South Africa	Colombo (SSC)	2006
751-5d	West Indies v England	St John's	2003-04
749-9d	West Indies v England	Bridgetown	2008-09
747	West Indies v South Africa	St John's	2004-05
735-6d	Australia v Zimbabwe	Perth	2003-04
730-6d	Sri Lanka v Bangladesh	Dhaka	2013-14
729-6d	Australia v England	Lord's	1930
726-9d	India v Sri Lanka	Mumbai	2009-10
715-6d	New Zealand v Bangladesh	Hamilton	2018-19
713-3d	Sri Lanka v Zimbabwe	Bulawayo	2003-04
713-9d	Sri Lanka v Bangladesh	Chittagong	2017-18
710-7d	England v India	Birmingham	2011
708	Pakistan v England	The Oval	1987
707	India v Sri Lanka	Colombo (SSC)	2010
705-7d	India v Australia	Sydney	2003-04
701	Australia v England	The Oval	1934
699-5	Pakistan v India	Lahore	1989-90
695	Australia v England	The Oval	1930
692-8d	West Indies v England	The Oval	1995
690	New Zealand v Pakistan	Sharjah	2014-15
687-8d	West Indies v England	The Oval	1976
687-6d	India v Bangladesh	Hyderabad	2016-17
682-6d	South Africa v England	Lord's	2003
681-8d	West Indies v England	Port-of-Spain	1953-54
680-8d	New Zealand v India	Wellington	2013-14
679-7d	Pakistan v India	Lahore	2005-06

676-7	India v Sri Lanka	Kanpur	1986-87
675-5d	India v Pakistan	Multan	2003-04
674	Australia v India	Adelaide	1947-48
674-6	Pakistan v India	Faisalabad	1984-85
674-6d	Australia v England	Cardiff	2009
671-4	New Zealand v Sri Lanka	Wellington	1990-91
668	Australia v West Indies	Bridgetown	1954-55
664	India v England	The Oval	2007
662-9d	Australia v England	Perth	2017-18
660-5d	West Indies v New Zealand	Wellington	1994-95
659-8d	Australia v England	Sydney	1946-47
659-4d	Australia v India	Sydney	2011-12
659-6d	New Zealand v Pakistan	Christchurch	2020-21
658-8d	England v Australia	Nottingham	1938
658-9d	South Africa v West Indies	Durban	2003-04
657-8d	Pakistan v West Indies	Bridgetown	1957-58
657-7d	India v Australia	Calcutta	2000-01
657	England v Pakistan	Rawalpindi	2022-23
656-8d	Australia v England	Manchester	1964
654-5	England v South Africa	Durban	1938-39
653-4d	England v India	Lord's	1990
653-4d	Australia v England	Leeds	1993
652-8d	West Indies v England	Lord's	1973
652	Pakistan v India	Faisalabad	1982-83
652-7d	England v India	Madras	1984-85
652-7d	Australia v South Africa	Johannesburg	2001-02
651	South Africa v Australia	Cape Town	2008-09
650-6d	Australia v West Indies	Bridgetown	1964-65

The highest for Zimbabwe is 563-9d (v WI, Harare, 2001), and for Bangladesh 638 (v SL, Galle, 2012-13).

LOWEST INNINGS TOTALS
† One batsman absent

26	New Zealand v England	Auckland	1954-55
30	South Africa v England	Port Elizabeth	1895-96
30	South Africa v England	Birmingham	1924
35	South Africa v England	Cape Town	1898-99
36	Australia v England	Birmingham	1902
36	South Africa v Australia	Melbourne	1931-32
36	India v Australia	Adelaide	2020-21
38	Ireland v England	Lord's	2019
42	Australia v England	Sydney	1887-88
42	New Zealand v Australia	Wellington	1945-46
42†	India v England	Lord's	1974
43	South Africa v England	Cape Town	1888-89
43	Bangladesh v West Indies	North Sound	2018
44	Australia v England	The Oval	1896
45	England v Australia	Sydney	1886-87
45	South Africa v Australia	Melbourne	1931-32
45	New Zealand v South Africa	Cape Town	2012-13
46	England v West Indies	Port-of-Spain	1993-94
47	South Africa v England	Cape Town	1888-89
47	New Zealand v England	Lord's	1958
47	West Indies v England	Kingston	2003-04
47	Australia v South Africa	Cape Town	2011-12
49	Pakistan v South Africa	Johannesburg	2012-13

The lowest for Sri Lanka is 71 (v P, Kandy, 1994-95) and for Zimbabwe 51 (v NZ, Napier, 2011-12).

BATTING RECORDS
5000 RUNS IN TESTS

Runs			M	I	NO	HS	Avge	100	50
15921	S.R.Tendulkar	I	200	329	33	248*	53.78	51	68
13378	R.T.Ponting	A	168	287	29	257	51.85	41	62
13289	J.H.Kallis	SA/ICC	166	280	40	224	55.37	45	58
13288	R.S.Dravid	I/ICC	164	286	32	270	52.31	36	63
12472	A.N.Cook	E	161	291	16	294	45.35	33	57
12400	K.C.Sangakkara	SL	134	233	17	319	57.40	38	52
11953	B.C.Lara	WI/ICC	131	232	6	400*	52.88	34	48
11867	S.Chanderpaul	WI	164	280	49	203*	51.37	30	66
11814	D.P.M.D.Jayawardena	SL	149	252	15	374	49.84	34	50
11174	A.R.Border	A	156	265	44	205	50.56	27	63
10948	J.E.Root	E	129	237	19	254	50.22	29	57
10927	S.R.Waugh	A	168	260	46	200	51.06	32	50
10122	S.M.Gavaskar	I	125	214	16	236*	51.12	34	45
10099	Younus Khan	P	118	213	19	313	52.05	34	33
9282	H.M.Amla	SA	124	215	16	311*	46.64	28	41
9265	G.C.Smith	SA/ICC	117	205	13	277	48.25	27	38
8900	G.A.Gooch	E	118	215	6	333	42.58	20	46
8832	Javed Miandad	P	124	189	21	280*	52.57	23	43
8830	Inzamam-ul-Haq	P/ICC	120	200	22	329	49.60	25	46
8781	V.V.S.Laxman	I	134	225	34	281	45.97	17	56
8765	A.B.de Villiers	SA	114	191	18	278*	50.66	22	46
8744	S.P.D.Smith	A	95	167	21	239	59.89	30	37
8643	M.J.Clarke	A	115	198	22	329*	49.10	28	27
8625	M.L.Hayden	A	103	184	14	380	50.73	30	29
8586	V.Sehwag	I/ICC	104	180	6	319	49.34	23	32
8540	I.V.A.Richards	WI	121	182	12	291	50.23	24	45
8463	A.J.Stewart	E	133	235	21	190	39.54	15	45
8231	D.I.Gower	E	117	204	18	215	44.25	18	39
8230	V.Kohli	I	107	182	11	254*	48.12	27	28
8181	K.P.Pietersen	E	104	181	8	227	47.28	23	35
8158	D.A.Warner	A	103	187	8	335*	45.57	25	34
8114	G.Boycott	E	108	193	23	246*	47.72	22	42
8032	G.St A.Sobers	WI	93	160	21	365*	57.78	26	30
8029	M.E.Waugh	A	128	209	17	153*	41.81	20	47
7787	K.S.Williamson	NZ	92	161	15	251	53.33	26	33
7728	M.A.Atherton	E	115	212	7	185*	37.70	16	46
7727	I.R.Bell	E	118	205	24	235	42.69	22	46
7696	J.L.Langer	A	105	182	12	250	45.27	23	30
7683	L.R.P.L.Taylor	NZ	112	196	24	290	44.66	19	35
7624	M.C.Cowdrey	E	114	188	15	182	44.06	22	38
7558	C.G.Greenidge	WI	108	185	16	226	44.72	19	34
7530	Mohammad Yousuf	P	90	156	12	223	52.29	24	33
7525	M.A.Taylor	A	104	186	13	334*	43.49	19	40
7515	C.H.Lloyd	WI	110	175	14	242*	46.67	19	39
7487	D.L.Haynes	WI	116	202	25	184	42.29	18	39
7422	D.C.Boon	A	107	190	20	200	43.65	21	32
7289	G.Kirsten	SA	101	176	15	275	45.27	21	34
7249	W.R.Hammond	E	85	140	16	336*	58.45	22	24
7214	C.H.Gayle	WI	103	182	11	333	42.18	15	37
7212	S.C.Ganguly	I	113	188	17	239	42.17	16	35
7172	S.P.Fleming	NZ	111	189	10	274*	40.06	9	46
7142	Azhar Ali	P	97	180	11	302*	42.26	19	35
7112	C.A.Pujara	I	101	173	11	206*	43.90	19	35

Runs			M	I	NO	HS	Avge	100	50
7110	G.S.Chappell	A	87	151	19	247*	53.86	24	31
7037	A.J.Strauss	E	100	178	6	177	40.91	21	27
6996	D.G.Bradman	A	52	80	10	334	99.94	29	13
6973	S.T.Jayasuriya	SL	110	188	14	340	40.07	14	31
6971	L.Hutton	E	79	138	15	364	56.67	19	33
6953	A.D.Mathews	SL	100	178	24	200*	45.14	13	38
6868	D.B.Vengsarkar	I	116	185	22	166	42.13	17	35
6806	K.F.Barrington	E	82	131	15	256	58.67	20	35
6744	G.P.Thorpe	E	100	179	28	200*	44.66	16	39
6453	B.B.McCullum	NZ	101	176	9	302	38.64	12	31
6361	P.A.de Silva	SL	93	159	11	267	42.97	20	22
6235	M.E.K.Hussey	A	79	137	16	195	51.52	19	29
6227	R.B.Kanhai	WI	79	137	6	256	47.53	15	28
6215	M.Azharuddin	I	99	147	9	199	45.03	22	21
6167	H.H.Gibbs	SA	90	154	7	228	41.95	14	26
6149	R.N.Harvey	A	79	137	10	205	48.41	21	24
6080	G.R.Viswanath	I	91	155	10	222	41.93	14	35
6023	F.D.M.Karunaratne	SL	82	158	6	244	39.62	14	31
5949	R.B.Richardson	WI	86	146	12	194	44.39	16	27
5842	R.R.Sarwan	WI	87	154	8	291	40.01	15	31
5825	M.E.Trescothick	E	76	143	10	219	43.79	14	29
5807	D.C.S.Compton	E	78	131	15	278	50.06	17	28
5768	Salim Malik	P	103	154	22	237	43.69	15	29
5764	N.Hussain	E	96	171	16	207	37.19	14	33
5762	C.L.Hooper	WI	102	173	15	233	36.46	13	27
5719	M.P.Vaughan	E	82	147	9	197	41.44	18	18
5712	B.A.Stokes	E	91	166	7	258	35.92	12	28
5570	A.C.Gilchrist	A	96	137	20	204*	47.60	17	26
5515	M.V.Boucher	SA/ICC	147	206	24	125	30.30	5	35
5502	M.S.Atapattu	SL	90	156	15	249	39.02	16	17
5492	T.M.Dilshan	SL	87	145	11	193	40.98	16	23
5482	J.M.Bairstow	E	89	159	11	167*	37.04	12	23
5462	T.T.Samaraweera	SL	81	132	20	231	48.76	14	30
5444	M.D.Crowe	NZ	77	131	11	299	45.36	17	18
5410	J.B.Hobbs	E	61	102	7	211	56.94	15	28
5357	K.D.Walters	A	74	125	14	250	48.26	15	33
5345	I.M.Chappell	A	75	136	10	196	42.42	14	26
5334	J.G.Wright	NZ	82	148	7	185	37.82	12	23
5321	Mushfiqur Rahim	B	84	144	13	219*	37.47	9	25
5314	K.C.Brathwaite	WI	84	161	10	212	35.19	12	28
5312	M.J.Slater	A	74	131	7	219	42.84	14	21
5248	Kapil Dev	I	131	184	15	163	31.05	8	27
5234	W.M.Lawry	A	67	123	12	210	47.15	13	27
5222	Misbah-ul-Haq	P	75	132	20	161*	46.62	10	39
5200	I.T.Botham	E	102	161	6	208	33.54	14	22
5138	J.H.Edrich	E	77	127	9	310*	43.54	12	24
5105	A.Ranatunga	SL	93	155	12	135*	35.69	4	38
5099	D.Elgar	SA	83	147	11	199	37.49	13	23
5082	Tamim Iqbal	B	69	132	2	206	39.09	10	31
5062	Zaheer Abbas	P	78	124	11	274	44.79	12	20
5038	T.W.M.Latham	NZ	72	127	6	264*	41.63	13	26

The most for Zimbabwe is 4794 by A.Flower (112 innings).

750 RUNS IN A SERIES

Runs			Series	M	I	NO	HS	Avge	100	50
974	D.G.Bradman	A v E	1930	5	7	–	334	139.14	4	–
905	W.R.Hammond	E v A	1928-29	5	9	1	251	113.12	4	–
839	M.A.Taylor	A v E	1989	6	11	1	219	83.90	2	5
834	R.N.Harvey	A v SA	1952-53	5	9	–	205	92.66	4	3
829	I.V.A.Richards	WI v E	1976	4	7	–	291	118.42	3	2
827	C.L.Walcott	WI v A	1954-55	5	10	–	155	82.70	5	2
824	G.St A.Sobers	WI v P	1957-58	5	8	2	365*	137.33	3	3
810	D.G.Bradman	A v E	1936-37	5	9	–	270	90.00	3	1
806	D.G.Bradman	A v SA	1931-32	5	5	1	299*	201.50	4	–
798	B.C.Lara	WI v E	1993-94	5	8	–	375	99.75	2	2
779	E.de C.Weekes	WI v I	1948-49	5	7	–	194	111.28	4	2
774	S.M.Gavaskar	I v WI	1970-71	4	8	3	220	154.80	4	3
774	S.P.D.Smith	A v E	2019	4	7	–	211	110.57	3	3
769	S.P.D.Smith	A v I	2014-15	4	8	2	192	128.16	4	2
766	A.N.Cook	E v A	2010-11	5	7	1	235*	127.66	3	2
765	B.C.Lara	WI v E	1995	6	10	1	179	85.00	3	3
761	Mudassar Nazar	P v I	1982-83	5	8	2	231	126.83	4	1
758	D.G.Bradman	A v E	1934	5	8	–	304	94.75	2	1
753	D.C.S.Compton	E v SA	1947	5	8	–	208	94.12	4	2
752	G.A.Gooch	E v I	1990	3	6	–	333	125.33	3	2

HIGHEST INDIVIDUAL INNINGS

400*	B.C.Lara	WI v E	St John's	2003-04
380	M.L.Hayden	A v Z	Perth	2003-04
375	B.C.Lara	WI v E	St John's	1993-94
374	D.P.M.D.Jayawardena	SL v SA	Colombo (SSC)	2006
365*	G.St A.Sobers	WI v P	Kingston	1957-58
364	L.Hutton	E v A	The Oval	1938
340	S.T.Jayasuriya	SL v I	Colombo (RPS)	1997-98
337	Hanif Mohammed	P v WI	Bridgetown	1957-58
336*	W.R.Hammond	E v NZ	Auckland	1932-33
335*	D.A.Warner	A v P	Adelaide	2019-20
334*	M.A.Taylor	A v P	Peshawar	1998-99
334	D.G.Bradman	A v E	Leeds	1930
333	G.A.Gooch	E v I	Lord's	1990
333	C.H.Gayle	WI v SL	Galle	2010-11
329*	M.J.Clarke	A v I	Sydney	2011-12
329	Inzamam-ul-Haq	P v NZ	Lahore	2001-02
325	A.Sandham	E v WI	Kingston	1929-30
319	V.Sehwag	I v SA	Chennai	2007-08
319	K.C.Sangakkara	SL v B	Chittagong	2013-14
317	C.H.Gayle	WI v SA	St John's	2004-05
313	Younus Khan	P v SL	Karachi	2008-09
311*	H.M.Amla	SA v E	The Oval	2012
311	R.B.Simpson	A v E	Manchester	1964
310*	J.H.Edrich	E v NZ	Leeds	1965
309	V.Sehwag	I v P	Multan	2003-04
307	R.M.Cowper	A v E	Melbourne	1965-66
304	D.G.Bradman	A v E	Leeds	1934
303*	K.K.Nair	I v E	Chennai	2016-17
302*	Azhar Ali	P v WI	Dubai (DSC)	2016-17
302	L.G.Rowe	WI v E	Bridgetown	1973-74
302	B.B.McCullum	NZ v I	Wellington	2013-14
299*	D.G.Bradman	A v SA	Adelaide	1931-32

299	M.D.Crowe	NZ v SL	Wellington	1990-91
294	A.N.Cook	E v I	Birmingham	2011
293	V.Sehwag	I v SL	Mumbai	2009-10
291	I.V.A.Richards	WI v E	The Oval	1976
291	R.R.Sarwan	WI v E	Bridgetown	2008-09
290	L.R.P.L.Taylor	NZ v A	Perth	2015-16
287	R.E.Foster	E v A	Sydney	1903-04
287	K.C.Sangakkara	SL v SA	Colombo (SSC)	2006
285*	P.B.H.May	E v WI	Birmingham	1957
281	V.V.S.Laxman	I v A	Calcutta	2000-01
280*	Javed Miandad	P v I	Hyderabad	1982-83
278*	A.B.de Villiers	SA v P	Abu Dhabi	2010-11
278	D.C.S.Compton	E v P	Nottingham	1954
277	B.C.Lara	WI v A	Sydney	1992-93
277	G.C.Smith	SA v E	Birmingham	2003
275*	D.J.Cullinan	SA v NZ	Auckland	1998-99
275	G.Kirsten	SA v E	Durban	1999-00
275	D.P.M.D.Jayawardena	SL v I	Ahmedabad	2009-10
274*	S.P.Fleming	NZ v SL	Colombo (SSC)	2002-03
274	R.G.Pollock	SA v A	Durban	1969-70
274	Zaheer Abbas	P v E	Birmingham	1971
271	Javed Miandad	P v NZ	Auckland	1988-89
270*	G.A.Headley	WI v E	Kingston	1934-35
270	D.G.Bradman	A v E	Melbourne	1936-37
270	R.S.Dravid	I v P	Rawalpindi	2003-04
270	K.C.Sangakkara	SL v Z	Bulawayo	2004
269*	A.C.Voges	A v WI	Hobart	2015-16
268	G.N.Yallop	A v P	Melbourne	1983-84
267*	B.A.Young	NZ v SL	Dunedin	1996-97
267	P.A.de Silva	SL v NZ	Wellington	1990-91
267	Younus Khan	P v I	Bangalore	2004-05
267	Z.Crawley	E v P	Southampton	2020
266	W.H.Ponsford	A v E	The Oval	1934
266	D.L.Houghton	Z v SL	Bulawayo	1994-95
264*	T.W.M.Latham	NZ v SL	Wellington	2018-19
263	A.N.Cook	E v P	Abu Dhabi	2015-16
262*	D.L.Amiss	E v WI	Kingston	1973-74
262	S.P.Fleming	NZ v SA	Cape Town	2005-06
261*	R.R.Sarwan	WI v B	Kingston	2004
261	F.M.M.Worrell	WI v E	Nottingham	1950
260	C.C.Hunte	WI v P	Kingston	1957-58
260	Javed Miandad	P v E	The Oval	1987
260	M.N.Samuels	WI v B	Khulna	2012-13
259*	M.J.Clarke	A v SA	Brisbane	2012-13
259	G.M.Turner	NZ v WI	Georgetown	1971-72
259	G.C.Smith	SA v E	Lord's	2003
258	T.W.Graveney	E v WI	Nottingham	1957
258	S.M.Nurse	WI v NZ	Christchurch	1968-69
258	B.A.Stokes	E v SA	Cape Town	2015-16
257*	Wasim Akram	P v Z	Sheikhupura	1996-97
257	R.T.Ponting	A v I	Melbourne	2003-04
256	R.B.Kanhai	WI v I	Calcutta	1958-59
256	K.F.Barrington	E v A	Manchester	1964
255*	D.J.McGlew	SA v NZ	Wellington	1952-53
254*	V.Kohli	I v SA	Pune	2019-20
254	D.G.Bradman	A v E	Lord's	1930
254	V.Sehwag	I v P	Lahore	2005-06

				E v P	Manchester	2016

254 J.E.Root E v P Manchester 2016
253* H.M.Amla SA v I Nagpur 2009-10
253 S.T.Jayasuriya SL v P Faisalabad 2004-05
253 D.A.Warner A v NZ Perth 2015-16
252 T.W.M.Latham NZ v B Christchurch 2021-22
251 W.R.Hammond E v A Sydney 1928-29
251 K.S.Williamson NZ v WI Hamilton 2020-21
250 K.D.Walters A v NZ Christchurch 1976-77
250 S.F.A.F.Bacchus WI v I Kanpur 1978-79
250 J.L.Langer A v E Melbourne 2002-03

The highest for Bangladesh is 219* by Mushfiqur Rahim (v Z, Dhaka, 2018-19).

20 HUNDREDS

					Opponents								
			200	Inn	E	A	SA	WI	NZ	I	P	SL	Z	B
51	S.R.Tendulkar	I	6	329	7	11	7	3	4	–	2	9	3	5
45	J.H.Kallis	SA	2	280	8	–	8	6	7	6	1	3	1	
41	R.T.Ponting	A	6	287	8	–	8	7	2	8	5	1	1	1
38	K.C.Sangakkara	SL	11	233	3	1	3	3	4	5	10	–	2	7
36	R.S.Dravid	I	5	286	7	2	2	5	6	–	5	3	3	3
34	Younus Khan	P	6	213	4	4	4	3	2	5	–	8	1	3
34	S.M.Gavaskar	I	4	214	4	8	–	13	2	–	5	2	–	–
34	B.C.Lara	WI	9	232	7	9	4	–	1	2	4	5	1	1
34	D.P.M.D.Jayawardena	SL	7	252	8	2	6	1	3	6	2	–	1	5
33	A.N.Cook	E	5	291	–	5	2	6	3	7	5	3	–	2
32	S.R.Waugh	A	1	260	10	–	2	7	2	2	3	3	1	2
30	S.P.D.Smith	A	4	167	11	–	2	3	2	8	2	2	–	–
30	M.L.Hayden †	A	2	184	5	–	6	5	1	6	1	3	2	–
30	S.Chanderpaul	WI	2	280	5	5	5	–	2	7	1	–	1	4
29	D.G.Bradman	A	12	80	19	–	4	2	–	4	–	–	–	–
29	J.E.Root	E	5	237	–	3	2	5	5	9	1	4	–	–
28	M.J.Clarke	A	4	198	7	–	5	1	4	7	1	3	–	–
28	H.M.Amla	SA	4	215	6	5	–	1	4	5	2	2	–	3
27	V.Kohli	I	7	182	5	7	3	2	3	–	–	5	–	2
27	G.C.Smith	SA	5	205	7	3	–	7	2	–	4	–	1	3
27	A.R.Border	A	2	265	8	–	–	3	5	4	6	1	–	–
26	G.St A.Sobers	WI	2	160	10	4	–	1	8	3	–	–	–	–
26	K.S.Williamson	NZ	5	161	4	2	3	3	–	2	5	3	1	3
25	D.A.Warner	A	3	187	3	–	5	1	5	4	5	2	–	–
25	Inzamam-ul-Haq	P	2	200	5	1	–	4	3	3	–	5	2	2
24	G.S.Chappell	A	4	151	9	–	5	3	1	6	–	–	–	–
24	Mohammad Yousuf	P	4	156	6	1	–	7	1	4	–	1	2	2
24	I.V.A.Richards	WI	3	182	8	5	–	–	1	8	2	–	–	–
23	V.Sehwag	I	6	180	2	3	5	2	2	–	4	5	–	–
23	K.P.Pietersen	E	3	181	–	4	3	3	2	6	2	3	–	–
23	J.L.Langer	A	3	182	5	–	2	3	4	3	4	2	–	–
23	Javed Miandad	P	6	189	2	6	–	2	7	5	–	1	–	–
22	W.R.Hammond	E	7	140	–	9	6	1	4	2	–	–	–	–
22	M.Azharuddin	I	–	147	6	2	4	–	2	–	3	5	–	–
22	M.C.Cowdrey	E	–	188	–	5	3	6	2	3	3	–	–	–
22	A.B.de Villiers	SA	2	191	2	6	–	6	–	3	4	1	–	–
22	G.Boycott	E	1	193	–	7	1	5	2	4	3	–	–	–
22	I.R.Bell	E	1	205	–	4	2	2	1	4	4	2	–	3
22	R.N.Harvey	A	2	137	6	–	8	3	–	4	–	–	–	–
21	G.Kirsten	SA	3	176	5	2	–	3	2	3	2	1	1	2
21	A.J.Strauss	E	–	178	4	3	6	3	3	2	–	–		

									Opponents					
			200	*Inn*	*E*	*A*	*SA*	*WI*	*NZ*	*I*	*P*	*SL*	*Z*	*B*
21	D.C.Boon	A	1	190	7	–	–	3	3	6	1	1	–	–
20	K.F.Barrington	E	1	131	–	5	2	3	3	3	4	–	–	–
20	P.A.de Silva	SL	2	159	2	1	–	–	2	5	8	–	1	1
20	M.E.Waugh	A	–	209	6	–	4	4	1	1	3	1	–	–
20	G.A.Gooch	E	2	215	–	4	–	5	4	5	1	1	–	–

† Includes century scored for Australia v ICC in 2005-06.
The most for Zimbabwe 12 by A.Flower (112), and for Bangladesh 11 by Mominul Haque (102).
The most double hundreds by batsmen not included above are 6 by M.S.Atapattu (16 hundreds for Sri Lanka), 4 by L.Hutton (19 for England), 4 by C.G.Greenidge (19 for West Indies), 4 by Zaheer Abbas (12 for Pakistan), and 4 by B.B.McCullum (12 for New Zealand).

HIGHEST PARTNERSHIP FOR EACH WICKET

1st	415	N.D.McKenzie/G.C.Smith	SA v B	Chittagong	2007-08
2nd	576	S.T.Jayasuriya/R.S.Mahanama	SL v I	Colombo (RPS)	1997-98
3rd	624	K.C.Sangakkara/D.P.M.D.Jayawardena	SL v SA	Colombo (SSC)	2006
4th	449	A.C.Voges/S.E.Marsh	A v WI	Hobart	2015-16
5th	405	S.G.Barnes/D.G.Bradman	A v E	Sydney	1946-47
6th	399	B.A.Stokes/J.M.Bairstow	E v SA	Cape Town	2015-16
7th	347	D.St E.Atkinson/C.C.Depeiza	WI v A	Bridgetown	1954-55
8th	332	I.J.L.Trott/S.C.J.Broad	E v P	Lord's	2010
9th	195	M.V.Boucher/P.L.Symcox	SA v P	Johannesburg	1997-98
10th	198	J.E.Root/J.M.Anderson	E v I	Nottingham	2014

BOWLING RECORDS
200 WICKETS IN TESTS

Wkts			*M*	*Balls*	*Runs*	*Avge*	*5wI*	*10wM*
800	M.Muralitharan	SL/ICC	133	44039	18180	22.72	67	22
708	S.K.Warne	A	145	40705	17995	25.41	37	10
685	J.M.Anderson	E	179	38293	17807	25.99	32	3
619	A.Kumble	I	132	40850	18355	29.65	35	8
576	S.C.J.Broad	E	161	32404	15981	27.74	19	3
563	G.D.McGrath	A	124	29248	12186	21.64	29	3
519	C.A.Walsh	WI	132	30019	12688	24.44	22	3
479	N.M.Lyon	A	118	30519	14904	31.11	23	4
467	R.Ashwin	I	91	24145	11195	23.97	31	7
439	D.W.Steyn	SA	93	18608	10077	22.95	26	5
434	Kapil Dev	I	131	27740	12867	29.64	23	2
433	H.M.R.K.B.Herath	SL	93	25993	12157	28.07	34	9
431	R.J.Hadlee	NZ	86	21918	9612	22.30	36	9
421	S.M.Pollock	SA	108	24453	9733	23.11	16	1
417	Harbhajan Singh	I	103	28580	13537	32.46	25	5
414	Wasim Akram	P	104	22627	9779	23.62	25	5
405	C.E.L.Ambrose	WI	98	22104	8500	20.98	22	3
390	M.Ntini	SA	101	20834	11242	28.82	18	4
383	I.T.Botham	E	102	21815	10878	28.40	27	4
376	M.D.Marshall	WI	81	17584	7876	20.94	22	4
373	Waqar Younis	P	87	16224	8788	23.56	22	5
362	Imran Khan	P	88	19458	8258	22.81	23	6
362	D.L.Vettori	NZ/ICC	113	28814	12441	34.36	20	3
359	T.G.Southee	NZ	92	21037	10532	29.33	14	1
355	D.K.Lillee	A	70	18467	8493	23.92	23	7
355	W.P.J.U.C.Vaas	SL	111	23438	10501	29.58	12	2

Wkts			M	Balls	Runs	Avge	5wI	10wM
330	A.A.Donald	SA	72	15519	7344	22.25	20	3
325	R.G.D.Willis	E	90	17357	8190	25.20	16	–
317	T.A.Boult	NZ	78	17417	8717	27.49	10	1
313	M.G.Johnson	A	73	16001	8891	28.40	12	3
311	I.Sharma	I	105	19160	10078	32.40	11	1
311	Z.Khan	I	92	18785	10247	32.94	11	1
310	B.Lee	A	76	16531	9554	30.81	10	–
309	M.Morkel	SA	86	16498	8550	27.66	8	–
309	L.R.Gibbs	WI	79	27115	8989	29.09	18	2
307	F.S.Trueman	E	67	15178	6625	21.57	17	3
305	M.A.Starc	A	76	15175	8325	27.29	13	2
297	D.L.Underwood	E	86	21862	7674	25.83	17	6
292	J.H.Kallis	SA/ICC	166	20232	9535	32.65	5	–
291	C.J.McDermott	A	71	16586	8332	28.63	14	2
276	K.Rabada	SA	59	11003	6219	22.53	13	4
266	B.S.Bedi	I	67	21364	7637	28.71	14	1
263	R.A.Jadeja	I	63	15388	6272	23.84	12	2
261	Danish Kaneria	P	61	17697	9082	34.79	15	2
260	K.A.J.Roach	WI	76	13749	7053	27.12	11	1
259	J.Garner	WI	58	13169	5433	20.97	7	–
259	J.N.Gillespie	A	71	14234	6770	26.13	8	–
258	N.Wagner	NZ	62	13503	7018	27.20	9	–
255	G.P.Swann	E	60	15349	7642	29.96	17	3
252	J.B.Statham	E	70	16056	6261	24.84	9	1
249	M.A.Holding	WI	60	12680	5898	23.68	13	2
248	R.Benaud	A	63	19108	6704	27.03	16	1
248	M.J.Hoggard	E	67	13909	7564	30.50	7	1
246	G.D.McKenzie	A	60	17681	7328	29.78	16	3
244	Yasir Shah	P	48	14255	7657	31.38	16	3
242	B.S.Chandrasekhar	I	58	15963	7199	29.74	16	2
236	A.V.Bedser	E	51	15918	5876	24.89	15	5
236	J.Srinath	I	67	15104	7196	30.49	10	1
236	Abdul Qadir	P	67	17126	7742	32.80	15	5
235	G.St A.Sobers	WI	93	21599	7999	34.03	6	–
234	A.R.Caddick	E	62	13558	6999	29.91	13	1
233	C.S.Martin	NZ	71	14026	7878	33.81	10	1
231	Shakib Al Hasan	B	65	14679	7204	31.18	19	2
229	D.Gough	E	58	11821	6503	28.39	9	–
228	R.R.Lindwall	A	61	13650	5251	23.03	12	–
226	S.J.Harmison	E/ICC	63	13375	7192	31.82	8	1
226	A.Flintoff	E/ICC	79	14951	7410	32.78	3	–
224	V.D.Philander	SA	64	11391	5000	22.32	13	2
223	Mohammed Shami	I	62	11008	6032	27.04	6	–
222	J.R.Hazlewood	A	59	12661	5735	25.83	9	–
221	P.M.Siddle	A	67	13907	6777	30.66	8	–
218	C.L.Cairns	NZ	62	11698	6410	29.40	13	1
217	P.J.Cummins	A	49	10246	4667	21.50	8	1
216	C.V.Grimmett	A	37	14513	5231	24.21	21	7
216	H.H.Streak	Z	65	13559	6079	28.14	7	–
212	M.G.Hughes	A	53	12285	6017	28.38	7	1
208	S.C.G.MacGill	A	44	11237	6038	29.02	12	2
208	Saqlain Mushtaq	P	49	14070	6206	29.83	13	3
202	A.M.E.Roberts	WI	47	11136	5174	25.61	11	2
202	J.A.Snow	E	49	12021	5387	26.66	8	1
200	J.R.Thomson	A	51	10535	5601	28.00	8	–

35 OR MORE WICKETS IN A SERIES

Wkts			Series	M	Balls	Runs	Avge	5wI	10wM
49	S.F.Barnes	E v SA	1913-14	4	1356	536	10.93	7	3
46	J.C.Laker	E v A	1956	5	1703	442	9.60	4	2
44	C.V.Grimmett	A v SA	1935-36	5	2077	642	14.59	5	3
42	T.M.Alderman	A v E	1981	6	1950	893	21.26	4	–
41	R.M.Hogg	A v E	1978-79	5	1740	527	12.85	5	2
41	T.M.Alderman	A v E	1989	6	1616	712	17.36	6	1
40	Imran Khan	P v I	1982-83	6	1339	558	13.95	4	2
40	S.K.Warne	A v E	2005	5	1517	797	19.92	3	2
39	A.V.Bedser	E v A	1953	5	1591	682	17.48	5	1
39	D.K.Lillee	A v E	1981	6	1870	870	22.30	2	1
38	M.W.Tate	E v A	1924-25	5	2528	881	23.18	5	1
37	W.J.Whitty	A v SA	1910-11	5	1395	632	17.08	2	–
37	H.J.Tayfield	SA v E	1956-57	5	2280	636	17.18	4	1
37	M.G.Johnson	A v E	2013-14	5	1132	517	13.97	3	–
36	A.E.E.Vogler	SA v E	1909-10	5	1349	783	21.75	4	1
36	A.A.Mailey	A v E	1920-21	5	1465	946	26.27	4	2
36	G.D.McGrath	A v E	1997	6	1499	701	19.47	2	–
35	G.A.Lohmann	E v SA	1895-96	3	520	203	5.80	4	2
35	B.S.Chandrasekhar	I v E	1972-73	5	1747	662	18.91	4	1
35	M.D.Marshall	WI v E	1988	5	1219	443	12.65	3	1

The most for New Zealand was 33 by R.J.Hadlee (3 Tests v A, 1985-86), for Sri Lanka 30 by M.Muralitharan (3 Tests v Z, 2001-02), for Zimbabwe 22 by H.H.Streak (3 Tests v P, 1994-95), and for Bangladesh 19 by Mehedi Hasan (2 Tests v E, 2016-17).

15 OR MORE WICKETS IN A TEST († On debut)

19- 90	J.C.Laker	E v A	Manchester	1956
17-159	S.F.Barnes	E v SA	Johannesburg	1913-14
16-136†	N.D.Hirwani	I v WI	Madras	1987-88
16-137†	R.A.L.Massie	A v E	Lord's	1972
16-220	M.Muralitharan	SL v E	The Oval	1998
15- 28	J.Briggs	E v SA	Cape Town	1888-89
15- 45	G.A.Lohmann	E v SA	Port Elizabeth	1895-96
15- 99	C.Blythe	E v SA	Leeds	1907
15-104	H.Verity	E v A	Lord's	1934
15-123	R.J.Hadlee	NZ v A	Brisbane	1985-86
15-124	W.Rhodes	E v A	Melbourne	1903-04
15-217	Harbhajan Singh	I v A	Madras	2000-01

The best analysis for South Africa is 13-132 by M.Ntini (v WI, Port-of-Spain, 2004-05), for West Indies 14-149 by M.A.Holding (v E, The Oval, 1976), for Pakistan 14-116 by Imran Khan (v SL, Lahore, 1981-82), for Zimbabwe 11-257 by A.G.Huckle (v NZ, Bulawayo, 1997-98), and for Bangladesh 12-117 by Mehedi Hasan (v WI, Dhaka, 2018-19).

NINE OR MORE WICKETS IN AN INNINGS

10- 53	J.C.Laker	E v A	Manchester	1956
10- 74	A.Kumble	I v P	Delhi	1998-99
10-119	A.Y.Patel	NZ v I	Mumbai	2021-22
9- 28	G.A.Lohmann	E v SA	Johannesburg	1895-96
9- 37	J.C.Laker	E v A	Manchester	1956
9- 51	M.Muralitharan	SL v Z	Kandy	2001-02
9- 52	R.J.Hadlee	NZ v A	Brisbane	1985-86
9- 56	Abdul Qadir	P v E	Lahore	1987-88
9- 57	D.E.Malcolm	E v SA	The Oval	1994
9- 65	M.Muralitharan	SL v E	The Oval	1998

9- 69	J.M.Patel	I v A	Kanpur	1959-60
9- 83	Kapil Dev	I v WI	Ahmedabad	1983-84
9- 86	Sarfraz Nawaz	P v A	Melbourne	1978-79
9- 95	J.M.Noreiga	WI v I	Port-of-Spain	1970-71
9-102	S.P.Gupte	I v WI	Kanpur	1958-59
9-103	S.F.Barnes	E v SA	Johannesburg	1913-14
9-113	H.J.Tayfield	SA v E	Johannesburg	1956-57
9-121	A.A.Mailey	A v E	Melbourne	1920-21
9-127	H.M.R.K.B.Herath	SL v P	Colombo (SSC)	2014
9-129	K.A.Maharaj	SA v SL	Colombo (SSC)	2018

The best analysis for Zimbabwe is 8-109 by P.A.Strang (v NZ, Bulawayo, 2000-01), and for Bangladesh 8-39 by Taijul Islam (v Z, Dhaka, 2014-15).

HAT-TRICKS

F.R.Spofforth	Australia v England	Melbourne	1878-79
W.Bates	England v Australia	Melbourne	1882-83
J.Briggs[7]	England v Australia	Sydney	1891-92
G.A.Lohmann	England v South Africa	Port Elizabeth	1895-96
J.T.Hearne	England v Australia	Leeds	1899
H.Trumble	Australia v England	Melbourne	1901-02
H.Trumble	Australia v England	Melbourne	1903-04
T.J.Matthews (2)[2]	Australia v South Africa	Manchester	1912
M.J.C.Allom[1]	England v New Zealand	Christchurch	1929-30
T.W.J.Goddard	England v South Africa	Johannesburg	1938-39
P.J.Loader	England v West Indies	Leeds	1957
L.F.Kline	Australia v South Africa	Cape Town	1957-58
W.W.Hall	West Indies v Pakistan	Lahore	1958-59
G.M.Griffin[7]	South Africa v England	Lord's	1960
L.R.Gibbs	West Indies v Australia	Adelaide	1960-61
P.J.Petherick[1/7]	New Zealand v Pakistan	Lahore	1976-77
C.A.Walsh[3]	West Indies v Australia	Brisbane	1988-89
M.G.Hughes[3/7]	Australia v West Indies	Perth	1988-89
D.W.Fleming[1]	Australia v Pakistan	Rawalpindi	1994-95
S.K.Warne	Australia v England	Melbourne	1994-95
D.G.Cork	England v West Indies	Manchester	1995
D.Gough[7]	England v Australia	Sydney	1998-99
Wasim Akram[4]	Pakistan v Sri Lanka	Lahore	1998-99
Wasim Akram[4]	Pakistan v Sri Lanka	Dhaka	1998-99
D.N.T.Zoysa[5]	Sri Lanka v Zimbabwe	Harare	1999-00
Abdul Razzaq	Pakistan v Sri Lanka	Galle	2000-01
G.D.McGrath	Australia v West Indies	Perth	2000-01
Harbhajan Singh	India v Australia	Calcutta	2000-01
Mohammad Sami[7]	Pakistan v Sri Lanka	Lahore	2001-02
J.J.C.Lawson[7]	West Indies v Australia	Bridgetown	2002-03
Alok Kapali[7]	Bangladesh v Pakistan	Peshawar	2003
A.M.Blignaut	Zimbabwe v Bangladesh	Harare	2003-04
M.J.Hoggard	England v West Indies	Bridgetown	2003-04
J.E.C.Franklin	New Zealand v Bangladesh	Dhaka	2004-05
I.K.Pathan[6/7]	India v Pakistan	Karachi	2005-06
R.J.Sidebottom[7]	England v New Zealand	Hamilton	2007-08
P.M.Siddle	Australia v England	Brisbane	2010-11
S.C.J.Broad	England v India	Nottingham	2011
Sohag Gazi	Bangladesh v New Zealand	Chittagong	2013-14
S.C.J.Broad[7]	England v Sri Lanka	Leeds	2014
H.M.R.K.B.Herath	Sri Lanka v Australia	Galle	2016
M.M.Ali	England v South Africa	The Oval	2017

76

J.J.Bumrah	India v West Indies	Kingston		2019
Naseem Shah	Pakistan v Bangladesh	Rawalpindi		2019-20
K.A.Maharaj	South Africa v West Indies	Gros Islet		2021

[1] On debut. [2] Hat-trick in each innings. [3] Involving both innings. [4] In successive Tests. [5] His first 3 balls (second over of the match). [6] The fourth, fifth and sixth balls of the match. [7] On losing side.

WICKET-KEEPING RECORDS
150 DISMISSALS IN TESTS†

Total			Tests	Ct	St
555	M.V.Boucher	South Africa/ICC	147	532	23
416	A.C.Gilchrist	Australia	96	379	37
395	I.A.Healy	Australia	119	366	29
355	R.W.Marsh	Australia	96	343	12
294	M.S.Dhoni	India	90	256	38
270	B.J.Haddin	Australia	66	262	8
270†	P.J.L.Dujon	West Indies	81	265	5
269	A.P.E.Knott	England	95	250	19
265	B.J.Watling	New Zealand	75	257	8
256	M.J.Prior	England	79	243	13
241†	A.J.Stewart	England	133	227	14
232	Q.de Kock	South Africa	54	221	11
228	Wasim Bari	Pakistan	81	201	27
219	R.D.Jacobs	West Indies	65	207	12
219	T.G.Evans	England	91	173	46
217	D.Ramdin	West Indies	74	205	12
206	Kamran Akmal	Pakistan	53	184	22
201†	A.C.Parore	New Zealand	78	194	7
198	S.M.H.Kirmani	India	88	160	38
193†	J.M.Bairstow	England	89	180	13
189	D.L.Murray	West Indies	62	181	8
187	A.T.W.Grout	Australia	51	163	24
179†	B.B.McCullum	New Zealand	101	168	11
176	I.D.S.Smith	New Zealand	63	168	8
174	R.W.Taylor	England	57	167	7
172	Sarfraz Ahmed	Pakistan	51	150	22
165	R.C.Russell	England	54	153	12
157	T.D.Paine	Australia	35	150	7
157	D.P.D.N.Dickwella	Sri Lanka	53	130	27
156	H.A.P.W.Jayawardena	Sri Lanka	58	124	32
152	D.J.Richardson	South Africa	42	150	2
151†	K.C.Sangakkara	Sri Lanka	134	131	20
151†	A.Flower	Zimbabwe	63	142	9

The most for Bangladesh is 113 (98 ct, 15 st) by Mushfiqur Rahim in 84 Tests.
† *Excluding catches taken in the field*

25 OR MORE DISMISSALS IN A SERIES

29	B.J.Haddin	Australia v England	2013
28	R.W.Marsh	Australia v England	1982-83
27 (inc 2st)	R.C.Russell	England v South Africa	1995-96
27 (inc 2st)	I.A.Healy	Australia v England (6 Tests)	1997
26 (inc 3st)	J.H.B.Waite	South Africa v New Zealand	1961-62
26	R.W.Marsh	Australia v West Indies (6 Tests)	1975-76
26 (inc 5st)	I.A.Healy	Australia v England (6 Tests)	1993
26 (inc 1st)	M.V.Boucher	South Africa v England	1998
26 (inc 2st)	A.C.Gilchrist	Australia v England	2001

26 (inc 2st)	A.C.Gilchrist	Australia v England		2006-07
26 (inc 1st)	T.D.Paine	Australia v England		2017-18
25 (inc 2st)	I.A.Healy	Australia v England		1994-95
25 (inc 2st)	A.C.Gilchrist	Australia v England		2002-03
25	A.C.Gilchrist	Australia v India		2007-08

TEN OR MORE DISMISSALS IN A TEST

11	R.C.Russell	England v South Africa	Johannesburg	1995-96
11	A.B.de Villiers	South Africa v Pakistan	Johannesburg	2012-13
11	R.R.Pant	India v Australia	Adelaide	2018-19
10	R.W.Taylor	England v India	Bombay	1979-80
10	A.C.Gilchrist	Australia v New Zealand	Hamilton	1999-00
10	W.P.Saha	India v South Africa	Cape Town	2017-18
10	Sarfraz Ahmed	Pakistan v South Africa	Johannesburg	2018-19

SEVEN DISMISSALS IN AN INNINGS

7	Wasim Bari	Pakistan v New Zealand	Auckland	1978-79
7	R.W.Taylor	England v India	Bombay	1979-80
7	I.D.S.Smith	New Zealand v Sri Lanka	Hamilton	1990-91
7	R.D.Jacobs	West Indies v Australia	Melbourne	2000-01
7	J.Da Silva	West Indies v South Africa	Centurion	2022-23

FIVE STUMPINGS IN AN INNINGS

| 5 | K.S.More | India v West Indies | Madras | 1987-88 |

FIELDING RECORDS
100 CATCHES IN TESTS

Total			Tests	Total			Tests
210	R.S.Dravid	India/ICC	164	122	I.V.A.Richards	West Indies	121
205	D.P.M.D.Jayawardena	Sri Lanka	149	121†	A.B.de Villiers	South Africa	114
200	J.H.Kallis	South Africa/ICC	166	121	A.J.Strauss	England	100
196	R.T.Ponting	Australia	168	120	I.T.Botham	England	102
181	M.E.Waugh	Australia	128	120	M.C.Cowdrey	England	114
175	A.N.Cook	England	161	115	C.L.Hooper	West Indies	102
171	S.P.Fleming	New Zealand	111	115	S.R.Tendulkar	India	200
171	J.E.Root	England	129	112	S.R.Waugh	Australia	168
169	G.C.Smith	South Africa/ICC	117	110	R.B.Simpson	Australia	62
164	B.C.Lara	West Indies/ICC	131	110	W.R.Hammond	England	85
163	L.R.P.L.Taylor	New Zealand	112	109	G.St A.Sobers	West Indies	93
157	M.A.Taylor	Australia	104	108	V.Kohli	India	99
156	A.R.Border	Australia	156	108	H.M.Amla	South Africa	124
154	S.P.D.Smith	Australia	95	108	S.M.Gavaskar	India	125
139	Younus Khan	Pakistan	118	105	I.M.Chappell	Australia	75
135	V.V.S.Laxman	India	134	105	M.Azharuddin	India	99
134	M.J.Clarke	Australia	115	105	G.P.Thorpe	England	100
128	M.L.Hayden	Australia	103	104	J.M.Anderson	England	179
125	S.K.Warne	Australia	145	103	G.A.Gooch	England	118
122	G.S.Chappell	Australia	87	100	I.R.Bell	England	118

The most for Zimbabwe is 60 by A.D.R.Campbell (60) and for Bangladesh 38 by Mahmudullah (50).

† *Excluding catches taken when wicket-keeping.*

15 CATCHES IN A SERIES

| 15 | J.M.Gregory | Australia v England | | 1920-21 |

78

SEVEN OR MORE CATCHES IN A TEST

8	A.M.Rahane	India v Sri Lanka	Galle	2015
7	G.S.Chappell	Australia v England	Perth	1974-75
7	Yajurvindra Singh	India v England	Bangalore	1976-77
7	H.P.Tillekeratne	Sri Lanka v New Zealand	Colombo (SSC)	1992-93
7	S.P.Fleming	New Zealand v Zimbabwe	Harare	1997-98
7	M.L.Hayden	Australia v Sri Lanka	Galle	2003-04
7	K.L.Rahul	India v England	Nottingham	2018

FIVE CATCHES IN AN INNINGS

5	V.Y.Richardson	Australia v South Africa	Durban	1935-36
5	Yajurvindra Singh	India v England	Bangalore	1976-77
5	M.Azharuddin	India v Pakistan	Karachi	1989-90
5	K.Srikkanth	India v Australia	Perth	1991-92
5	S.P.Fleming	New Zealand v Zimbabwe	Harare	1997-98
5	G.C.Smith	South Africa v Australia	Perth	2012-13
5	D.J.G.Sammy	West Indies v India	Mumbai	2013-14
5	D.M.Bravo	West Indies v Bangladesh	Kingstown	2014
5	A.M.Rahane	India v Sri Lanka	Galle	2015
5	J.Blackwood	West Indies v Sri Lanka	Colombo (PSS)	2015-16
5	S.P.D.Smith	Australia v South Africa	Cape Town	2017-18
5	B.A.Stokes	England v South Africa	Cape Town	2019-20
5	H.D.R.L.Thirimanne	Sri Lanka v England	Galle	2020-21

APPEARANCE RECORDS
100 TEST MATCH APPEARANCES

			Opponents									
			E	A	SA	WI	NZ	I	P	SL	Z	B
200	S.R.Tendulkar	India	32	39	25	21	24	–	18	25	9	7
179	J.M.Anderson	England	–	35	29	22	20	35	20	14	2	2
168†	R.T.Ponting	Australia	35	–	26	24	17	29	15	14	3	4
168	S.R.Waugh	Australia	46	–	16	32	23	18	20	8	3	2
166†	J.H.Kallis	South Africa/ICC	31	28	–	24	18	18	19	15	6	6
164	S.Chanderpaul	West Indies	35	20	24	–	21	25	14	7	8	10
164†	R.S.Dravid	India/ICC	21	32	21	23	15	–	15	20	9	7
161*	S.C.J.Broad	England	–	35	25	19	23	24	19	12	–	3
161	A.N.Cook	England	–	35	19	20	15	30	20	16	–	6
156	A.R.Border	Australia	47	–	6	31	23	20	22	7	–	–
149	D.P.M.D.Jayawardena	Sri Lanka	23	16	18	11	13	18	29	–	8	13
147†	M.V.Boucher	South Africa/ICC	25	20	–	24	17	14	15	17	6	8
145†	S.K.Warne	Australia	36	–	24	19	20	14	15	13	1	2
134	V.V.S.Laxman	India	17	29	19	22	10	–	15	13	6	3
134	K.C.Sangakkara	Sri Lanka	22	11	17	12	12	17	23	–	5	15
133†	M.Muralitharan	Sri Lanka/ICC	16	12	15	12	14	22	16	–	14	11
133	A.J.Stewart	England	–	33	23	24	16	9	13	9	6	–
132	A.Kumble	India	19	20	21	17	11	–	15	18	7	4
132	C.A.Walsh	West Indies	36	38	10	–	10	15	18	3	2	–
131	Kapil Dev	India	27	20	4	25	10	–	29	14	2	–
131†	B.C.Lara	West Indies/ICC	30	30	18	–	11	17	12	8	2	2
129*	J.E.Root	England	–	29	15	14	18	25	15	10	–	2
128	M.E.Waugh	Australia	29	–	18	28	14	14	15	9	1	–
125	S.M.Gavaskar	India	38	20	–	27	9	–	24	7	–	–
124	H.M.Amla	South Africa	21	21	–	9	14	21	14	14	2	8
124	Javed Miandad	Pakistan	22	24	–	17	18	28	–	12	3	–
124†	G.D.McGrath	Australia	30	–	17	23	14	11	17	8	1	2

			Opponents									
			E	A	SA	WI	NZ	I	P	SL	Z	B
121	I.V.A.Richards	West Indies	36	34	–	–	7	28	16	–	–	–
120†	Inzamam-ul-Haq	Pakistan/ICC	19	13	13	15	12	10	–	20	11	6
119	I.A.Healy	Australia	33	–	12	28	11	9	14	11	1	–
118	I.R.Bell	England	–	33	11	12	13	20	13	10	–	6
118	G.A.Gooch	England	–	42	3	26	15	19	10	3	–	–
118	N.M.Lyon	Australia	28	–	18	10	10	25	12	13	–	2
118	Younus Khan	Pakistan	17	11	14	15	11	9	–	29	5	7
117	D.I.Gower	England	–	42	–	19	13	24	17	2	–	–
117†	G.C.Smith	South Africa/ICC	21	21	–	14	13	15	16	7	2	8
116	D.L.Haynes	West Indies	36	33	1	–	10	19	16	1	–	–
116	D.B.Vengsarkar	India	26	24	–	25	11	–	22	8	–	–
115	M.A.Atherton	England	–	33	18	27	11	7	11	4	4	–
115†	M.J.Clarke	Australia	35	–	14	12	11	22	10	8	–	2
114	M.C.Cowdrey	England	–	43	14	21	18	8	10	–	–	–
114	A.B.de Villiers	South Africa	20	24	–	13	10	20	12	7	4	4
113	S.C.Ganguly	India	12	24	17	12	8	–	12	14	9	5
113†	D.L.Vettori	New Zealand/ICC	17	18	14	10	–	15	9	11	9	9
112	L.R.P.L.Taylor	New Zealand	19	12	8	14	–	17	15	12	4	11
111	S.P.Fleming	New Zealand	19	14	15	11	–	13	9	13	11	6
111	W.P.J.U.C.Vaas	Sri Lanka	15	12	11	9	10	14	18	–	15	7
110	S.T.Jayasuriya	Sri Lanka	14	13	15	10	13	10	17	–	13	5
110	C.H.Lloyd	West Indies	34	29	–	–	8	28	11	–	–	–
108	G.Boycott	England	–	38	7	29	15	13	6	–	–	–
108	C.G.Greenidge	West Indies	29	32	–	–	10	23	14	–	–	–
108	S.M.Pollock	South Africa	23	13	–	16	11	12	12	13	5	3
107	D.C.Boon	Australia	31	–	6	22	17	11	11	9	–	–
107	V.Kohli	India	28	23	14	14	11	–	–	11	–	6
105†	J.L.Langer	Australia	21	–	11	18	14	14	13	8	3	2
105‡	I.Sharma	India	23	25	15	12	9	–	1	12	–	7
104	K.P.Pietersen	England	–	27	10	14	8	16	14	11	–	4
104†	V.Sehwag	India/ICC	17	23	15	10	12	–	9	11	3	4
104	M.A.Taylor	Australia	33	–	11	20	11	9	12	8	–	–
104	Wasim Akram	Pakistan	18	13	14	17	9	12	–	19	10	2
103	C.H.Gayle	West Indies	20	8	16	–	12	14	8	10	8	7
103	Harbhajan Singh	India	14	18	11	11	13	–	9	16	7	4
103†	M.L.Hayden	Australia	20	–	19	15	11	18	6	7	2	4
103	Salim Malik	Pakistan	19	15	1	7	18	22	–	15	6	–
103	D.A.Warner	Australia	28	–	15	10	10	20	10	8	–	2
102	I.T.Botham	England	–	36	–	20	15	14	14	3	–	–
102	C.L.Hooper	West Indies	24	25	10	–	2	19	14	6	2	–
101	G.Kirsten	South Africa	22	18	–	13	13	10	11	9	3	2
101	B.B.McCullum	New Zealand	16	16	13	13	–	10	8	12	4	9
101	M.Ntini	South Africa	18	15	–	15	11	10	9	12	3	8
101‡	C.A.Pujara	India	27	23	17	9	12	–	–	7	–	5
100	A.D.Mathews	Sri Lanka	11	11	10	8	11	17	21	–	3	8
100	A.J.Strauss	England	–	20	16	18	9	12	13	8	4	–
100	G.P.Thorpe	England	–	16	16	27	13	5	8	9	2	4

† Includes appearance in the Australia v ICC 'Test' in 2005-06; * includes appearance v Ireland in 2019; ‡ includes appearance v Afghanistan in 2018. The most for Zimbabwe is 67 by G.W.Flower, and for Bangladesh 84 by Mushfiqur Rahim.

100 CONSECUTIVE TEST APPEARANCES

159	A.N.Cook	England	May 2006 to September 2018
153	A.R.Border	Australia	March 1979 to March 1994
107	M.E.Waugh	Australia	June 1993 to October 2002
106	S.M.Gavaskar	India	January 1975 to February 1987
101	B.B.McCullum	New Zealand	March 2004 to February 2016

50 TESTS AS CAPTAIN

			Won	Lost	Drawn	Tied
109	G.C.Smith	South Africa	53	29	27	–
93	A.R.Border	Australia	32	22	38	1
80	S.P.Fleming	New Zealand	28	27	25	–
77	R.T.Ponting	Australia	48	16	13	–
74	C.H.Lloyd	West Indies	36	12	26	–
68	V.Kohli	India	40	17	11	–
64	J.E.Root	England	27	26	11	–
60	M.S.Dhoni	India	27	18	15	–
59	A.N.Cook	England	24	22	13	–
57	S.R.Waugh	Australia	41	9	7	–
56	Misbah-ul-Haq	Pakistan	26	19	11	–
56	A.Ranatunga	Sri Lanka	12	19	25	–
54	M.A.Atherton	England	13	21	20	–
53	W.J.Cronje	South Africa	27	11	15	–
51	M.P.Vaughan	England	26	11	14	–
50	I.V.A.Richards	West Indies	27	8	15	–
50	M.A.Taylor	Australia	26	13	11	–
50	A.J.Strauss	England	24	11	15	–

The most for Zimbabwe is 21 by A.D.R.Campbell and H.H.Streak, and for Bangladesh 34 by Mushfiqur Rahim.

70 TEST UMPIRING APPEARANCES

144	Alim Dar	(Pakistan)	21.10.2003 to 19.02.2023
128	S.A.Bucknor	(West Indies)	28.04.1989 to 22.03.2009
108	R.E.Koertzen	(South Africa)	26.12.1992 to 24.07.2010
95	D.J.Harper	(Australia)	28.11.1998 to 23.06.2011
92	D.R.Shepherd	(England)	01.08.1985 to 07.06.2005
84	B.F.Bowden	(New Zealand)	11.03.2000 to 03.05.2015
81	R.J.Tucker	(Australia)	15.02.2010 to 28.02.2023
78	D.B.Hair	(Australia)	25.01.1992 to 08.06.2008
77	H.D.P.K.Dharmasena	(Sri Lanka)	04.11.2010 to 02.03.2023
77	R.A.Kettleborough	(England)	15.11.2010 to 29.12.2022
76	M.Erasmus	(South Africa)	17.01.2010 to 02.03.2023
74	I.J.Gould	(England)	19.11.2008 to 23.02.2019
74	S.J.A.Taufel	(Australia)	26.12.2000 to 20.08.2012
73	S.Venkataraghavan	(India)	29.01.1993 to 20.01.2004

THE FIRST-CLASS COUNTIES
REGISTER, RECORDS AND 2022 AVERAGES

All statistics are to 10 March 2023.

ABBREVIATIONS – General

*	not out/unbroken partnership	IT20	International Twenty20
b	born	l-o	limited-overs
BB	Best innings bowling analysis	LOI	Limited-Overs Internationals
Cap	Awarded 1st XI County Cap	Tests	International Test Matches
f-c	first-class	F-c Tours	Overseas tours involving first-class
HS	Highest Score		appearances

Awards

PCA 2022	Professional Cricketers' Association Player of 2022
Wisden 2021	One of *Wisden Cricketers' Almanack*'s Five Cricketers of 2021
YC 2022	Cricket Writers' Club Young Cricketer of 2022

ECB Competitions

CB40	Clydesdale Bank 40 (2010-12)	EP	Eastern Province
CC	County Championship	FATA	Federally Administered Tribal Areas
FPT	Friends Provident Trophy (2007-09)	FS	Free State
P40	NatWest PRO 40 League (2006-09)	GL	Gujarat Lions
RLC	Royal London One-Day Cup	GT	Gujarat Titans
	(2014-to date)	GW	Griqualand West
T20	Twenty20 Competition	HH	Hobart Hurricanes
Y40	Yorkshire Bank 40 (2013)	KKR	Kolkata Knight Riders

Education

		KRL	Khan Research Laboratories
Ac	Academy	KXIP	Kings XI Punjab
C	College	KZN	KwaZulu-Natal Inland
CS	Comprehensive School	LSG	Lucknow Super Giants
GS	Grammar School	ME	Mashonaland Eagles
HS	High School	MI	Mumbai Indians
S	School	MR	Melbourne Renegades
SFC	Sixth Form College	MS	Melbourne Stars
SS	Secondary School	MT	Matabeleland Tuskers
U	University	MWR	Mid West Rhinos

Playing Categories

		NBP	National Bank of Pakistan
LBG	Bowls right-arm leg-breaks and googlies	ND	Northern Districts
LF	Bowls left-arm fast	NSW	New South Wales
LFM	Bowls left-arm fast-medium	NW	North West
LHB	Bats left-handed	PDSC	Prime Doleshwar Sporting Club
LM	Bowls left-arm medium pace	PK	Punjab Kings
LMF	Bowls left-arm medium fast	PS	Perth Scorchers
OB	Bowls right-arm off-breaks	PW	Pune Warriors
RF	Bowls right-arm fast	Q	Queensland
RFM	Bowls right-arm fast-medium	RCB	Royal Challengers Bangalore
RHB	Bats right-handed	RPS	Rising Pune Supergiant
RM	Bowls right-arm medium pace	RR	Rajasthan Royals
RMF	Bowls right-arm medium-fast	SA	South Australia
SLA	Bowls left-arm leg-breaks	SGR	Speen Ghar Region
SLC	Bowls left-arm 'Chinamen'	SH	Sunrisers Hyderabad
WK	Wicket-keeper	SJD	Sheikh Jamal Dhanmondi
		SNGPL	Sui Northern Gas Pipelines Limited
Teams (see also p 221)		SR	Southern Rocks
AS	Adelaide Strikers	SS	Sydney Sixers
BH	Brisbane Heat	ST	Sydney Thunder
CC&C	Combined Campuses & Colleges	Tas	Tasmania
CD	Central Districts	T&T	Trinidad & Tobago
CSK	Chennai Super Kings	TU	Tamil Union
DC	Deccan Chargers	Vic	Victoria
DCa	Delhi Capitals	WA	Western Australia
DD	Delhi Daredevils	WAPDA	Water & power Developemnt Authority
EL	England Lions	WP	Western Province

DERBYSHIRE

Formation of Present Club: 4 November 1870
Inaugural First-Class Match: 1871
Colours: Chocolate, Amber and Pale Blue
Badge: Rose and Crown
County Champions: (1) 1936
NatWest Trophy Winners: (1) 1981
Benson and Hedges Cup Winners: (1) 1993
Sunday League Winners: (1) 1990
Twenty20 Cup Winners: (0) best – Semi-Finalist 2019

Chief Executive: Ryan Duckett, Derbyshire County Cricket Club, The Incora County Ground, Nottingham Road, Derby, DE21 6DA ● Tel: 01332 388101 ● Email: info@derbyshireccc.com ● Web: www.derbyshireccc.com ● Twitter: @DerbyshireCCC (75,808 followers)

Head of Cricket: Mickey Arthur. **Assistant Coaches**: Ajmal Shahzad (bowling) and Ian Bell (batting). **Captain**: J.L.Du Plooy. **Overseas Players**: Haider Ali and R.A.S.Lakmal. **2023 Testimonial**: None. **Head Groundsman**: Neil Godrich. **Scorer**: Jane Hough. **Blast Team name**: Derbyshire Falcons. ‡ New registration. NQ Not qualified for England.

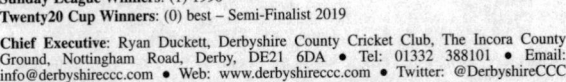

AITCHISON, **Ben**jamin William (Merchant Taylors' S; Ormskirk Range HS), b Southport, Lancs 6 Jul 1999. RHB, RFM. Squad No 11. Debut (Derbyshire) 2020. Lancashire 2nd XI 2019. Cheshire 2018-19. HS 50 v Notts (Derby) 2021. BB 6-28 v Durham (Derby) 2021. LO HS 19 v Surrey (Derby) 2021 (RLC). LO BB 4-39 v Hants (Derby) 2022 (RLC). T20 HS 2. T20 BB 2-30.

CAME, **Harry** Robert Charles (Bradfield C), b Basingstoke, Hants 27 Aug 1998. Son of P.R.C.Came (Hampshire 2nd XI 1986-87); grandson of K.C.Came (Free Foresters 1957); great-grandson of R.W.V.Robins (Middlesex, Cambridge U & England 1925-58). 5'9". RHB, OB. Squad No 4. Hampshire 2019-20. Derbyshire debut 2021. Hampshire 2nd XI 2017-19. Kent 2nd XI 2017-18. HS 78 v Durham (Derby) 2022. BB –. LO HS 57 v Notts (Derby) 2021 (RLC). T20 HS 56.

‡CHAPPELL, Zachariah John ('Zak') (Stamford S), b Grantham, Lincs 21 Aug 1996. 6'4". RHB, RFM. Squad No 32. Leicestershire 2015-18. Nottinghamshire 2019-21. Gloucestershire 2022 (on loan); cap 2022. HS 96 Le v Derbys (Derby) 2015. BB 6-44 Le v Northants (Northampton) 2018. LO HS 59* Le v Durham (Gosforth) 2017 (RLC). LO BB 3-35 Nt v Somerset (Taunton) 2022 (RLC). T20 HS 16. T20 BB 3-19.

CONNERS, **Sam**uel (George Spencer Ac), b Nottingham 13 Feb 1999. 6'0". RHB, RM. Squad No 59. Debut (Derbyshire) 2019; cap 2022. Derbyshire 2nd XI debut 2016. England U19 2018. HS 39 v Kent (Derby) 2021. 50 wkts (1): 50 (2022). BB 5-51 v Durham (Leicester) 2022. LO HS 5 v Glamorgan (Derby) 2022 (RLC). LO BB 5-28 v Yorks (Chesterfield) 2022 (RLC). T20 HS 2*. T20 BB 3-25.

DAL, **Anuj** Kailash (Durban HS; Nottingham HS), b Newcastle-upon-Tyne, Northumb 8 Jul 1996. 5'9". RHB, RM. Squad No 65. Debut (Derbyshire) 2018; cap 2022. HS 146* v Sussex (Hove) 2022. BB 5-40 v Worcs (Worcester) 2022. LO HS 52 v Lancs (Manchester) 2019 (RLC). LO BB 1-16 v Worcs (Worcester) 2022 (RLC). T20 HS 35.

NQDu PLOOY, Jacobus **Leus**, b Pretoria, South Africa 12 Jan 1995. LHB, SLA. Squad No 76. Free State 2014-15 to 2017-18. Knights 2015-16. Northerns 2018-19. Titans 2018-19. Derbyshire debut 2019; cap 2022; captain 2023. SW Districts 2021-22. Welsh Fire 2021 to date. HS 136 SW Districts v Northern Cape (Kimberley) 2021-22. De HS 134 v Durham (Chester-le-St) 2022. BB 3-76 Northerns v WP (Pretoria, TU) 2018-19. De BB 2-24 v Glamorgan (Swansea) 2019. LO HS 155 Northerns v WP (Pretoria, TU) 2018-19. LO BB 3-19 Northerns v KZN (Pretoria, TU) 2018-19. T20 HS 92. T20 BB 4-15.

GODLEMAN, Billy Ashley (Islington Green S), b Islington, London 11 Feb 1989. 6'3". LHB, LB. Squad No 1. Middlesex 2005-09. Essex 2010-12. Derbyshire debut 2013; cap 2015; captain 2016-22. F-c Tour (MCC): Nepal 2019-20. 1000 runs (2); most – 1087 (2019). HS 227 v Glamorgan (Swansea) 2016. BB –. LO HS 137 v Warwks (Birmingham) 2018 (RLC). T20 HS 92.

GUEST, Brooke David (Kent Street Senior HS, Perth, WA; Murdoch U, Perth), b Whitworth Park, Manchester, Lancs 14 May 1997. 5'11". RHB, WK. Squad No 29. Lancashire 2018-19. Derbyshire debut 2020; cap 2022. HS 138 v Glamorgan (Derby) 2022. LO HS 88 v Essex (Chelmsford) 2022 (RLC). T20 HS 54.

‡NO**HAIDER ALI**, b Attock, Punjab, Pakistan 2 Oct 2000. RHB, OB. Northern 2019-20 to date. **LOI** (P): 2 (2020-21); HS 29 v Z (Rawalpindi) 2020-21. **IT20** (P): 33 (2020 to 2022-23); HS 68 v WI (Karachi) 2021-22. HS 206 Northern v Central Punjab (Karachi) 2021-22. BB –. LO HS 118 P U23 v Oman (Cox's Bazar) 2019-20. T20 HS 91*.

HARRISON, Archie (West Park S; Repton S), b Derby 11 Feb 2004. RHB, RMF. Squad No 88. Derbyshire 2nd XI debut 2022. Awaiting f-c debut. LO HS 5 v Worcs (Worcester) 2022 (RLC) – only 1st XI appearance. LO BB –.

NO**LAKMAL**, Ranasinghe Arachchige **Suranga**, b Matara, Sri Lanka 10 Mar 1987. RHB, RMF. Squad No 82. Tamil Union 2007-08 to date. Derbyshire debut 2022. **Tests** (SL): 70 (2010-11 to 2021-22); HS 42 v B (Colombo, PSS) 2016-17; BB 5-47 v WI (North Sound) 2020-21. **LOI** (SL): 86 (2009-10 to 2020-21); HS 26 v P (Cardiff) 2017; BB 4-13 v I (Dharamsala) 2017-18. **IT20** (SL): 11 (2011 to 2018-19); HS 5* v I (Colombo, RPS) 2017-18; BB 2-26 v E (Bristol) 2011. F-c Tours (SL): E 2011, 2016; A 2011-12, 2018-19; SA 2008-09 (SL A), 2016-17, 2018-19; WI 2013 (SL A), 2018, 2020-21; NZ 2014-15, 2015-16, 2018-19; I 2017-18, 2021-22; Z 2016-17, 2019-20; B 2013-14; UAE (v P) 2011-12, 2013-14, 2017-18. HS 58* TU v SL Navy (Welisara) 2012-13. De HS 5 and De BB 5-82 v Glamorgan (Derby) 2022. LO BB 6-68 TU v Nondescripts (Colombo, NCC) 2012-13. LO HS 38* SL A v The Rest (Pallekele) 2013. LO BB 5-31 TU v Nondescripts (Colombo, NCC) 2008-09. T20 HS 33. T20 BB 5-34.

‡**LAMB, Matt**hew James (North Bromsgrove HS; Bromsgrove S), b Wolverhampton, Staffs 19 July 1996. 6'1". RHB, RM. Squad No 7. Warwickshire 2016-22. HS 173 and BB 2-38 Wa v Worcs (Worcester) 2021. LO HS 119* Wa v Leics (Birmingham) 2021 (RLC). LO BB 4-35 Wa v Somerset (Birmingham) 2021 (RLC). T20 HS 39.

McKIERNAN, Matthew Harry ('**Mattie**') (Lowton HS; St John Rigby C, Wigan), b Billinge, Lancs 14 Jun 1994. 6'0". RHB, LB. Squad No 21. Debut (Derbyshire) 2019. Cumberland 2016-17. HS 101 v Leics (Leicester) 2022. BB 2-3 v Notts (Nottingham) 2020. LO HS 72* v Essex (Chelmsford) 2022 (RLC). LO BB 1-14 v Northants (Northampton) 2022 (RLC). T20 HS 26. T20 BB 3-9.

MADSEN, Wayne Lee (Kearsney C, Durban; U of South Africa), b Durban, South Africa 2 Jan 1984. Nephew of M.B.Madsen (Natal 1967-68 to 1978-79), T.R.Madsen (Natal 1976-77 to 1989-90) and H.R.Fotheringham (Natal, Transvaal 1971-72 to 1989-90), cousin of G.S.Fotheringham (KwaZulu-Natal 2008-09 to 2009-10). 5'11". RHB, OB. Squad No 77. KwaZulu-Natal 2003-04 to 2007-08. Dolphins 2006-07 to 2007-08. Derbyshire debut 2009, scoring 170 v Glos (Cheltenham). cap 2011; captain 2012-15; testimonial 2017. Manchester Originals 2022. Qualified for England by residence in February 2015. 1000 runs (6); most – 1292 (2016). HS 231* v Northants (Northampton) 2012. BB 3-45 KZN v EP (Pt Elizabeth) 2007-08. De BB 2-8 v Sussex (Hove) 2021. LO HS 138 v Hants (Derby) 2014 (RLC). LO BB 3-27 v Durham (Derby) 2013 (Y40). T20 HS 100*. T20 BB 2-20.

POTTS, Nicholas James (de Ferrers Ac), b Burton-on-Trent, Staffs 17 Jul 2002. RHB, RFM. Squad No 26. Debut (Derbyshire) 2022. Derbyshire 2nd XI debut 2018. HS 13 v Leics (Derby) 2022. BB 4-50 v Notts (Nottingham) 2022. LO HS 6* and LO BB 2-63 v Worcs (Worcester) 2022 (RLC).

REECE, Luis Michael (St Michael's HS, Chorley; Leeds Met U), b Taunton, Somerset 4 Aug 1990. 6'1". LHB, LM. Squad No 10. Leeds/Bradford MCCU 2012-13. Lancashire 2013-15, no f-c appearances in 2016. Derbyshire debut 2017; cap 2019. MCC 2014. Unicorns 2011-12. London Spirit 2021. HS 184 v Sussex (Derby) 2019. 50 wkts (1): 55 (2019). BB 7-20 v Glos (Derby) 2018. LO HS 136 v Worcs (Worcester) 2022 (RLC). LO BB 4-35 Unicorns v Glos (Exmouth) 2011 (CB40). T20 HS 97*. T20 BB 3-33.

SCRIMSHAW, George Louis Sheridan (John Taylor HS, Burton), b Burton-on-Trent, Staffs 10 Feb 1998. 6'7". RHB, RMF. Squad No 5. Debut (Derbyshire) 2021. Worcestershire 2017 (T20 only). Welsh Fire 2022. HS 8* v Notts (Derby) 2022. BB 2-22 v Worcs (Worcester) 2022. LO HS 13* v Surrey (Derby) 2021 (RLC). LO BB 2-41 v Notts (Derby) 2021 (RLC). T20 HS 5*. T20 BB 3-20.

THOMSON, Alexander Thomas (Kings S, Macclesfield; Denstone C; Cardiff Met U), b Macclesfield, Cheshire 30 Oct 1993. 6'2". RHB, OB. Squad No 15. Cardiff MCCU 2014-16. Warwickshire 2017-20. Derbyshire debut 2021. Staffordshire 2013-16. F-c Tour (MCC): Nepal 2019-20. HS 54 v Worcs (Derby) 2022. BB 6-138 CfU v Hants (Southampton) 2016. De BB 4-103 v Middx (Lord's) 2022. LO HS 68* Wa v Derbys (Derby) 2019 (RLC). LO BB 3-25 v Lancs (Manchester) 2022 (RLC). T20 HS 28. T20 BB 4-35.

WAGSTAFF, Mitchell David (John Port S), b Derby 2 Sep 2003. LHB, LB. Squad No 22. Derbyshire 2nd XI debut 2019. Awaiting f-c debut. LO HS 36 v Surrey (Derby) 2021 (RLC). No 1st XI appearances in 2022.

NQ**WATT, Mark** Robert James, b Edinburgh, Scotland 29 Jul 1996. LHB, SLA. Squad No 51. Scotland 2016 to 2017-18. Lancashire 2018 (T20 only). Derbyshire debut 2022; white-ball debut 2019. **LOI** (Scot): 54 (2016 to 2022-23); HS 37* v Oman (Dubai, DSC) 2022; BB 5-33 v UAE (Aberdeen) 2022. **IT20** (Scot): 52 (2015 to 2022-23); HS 22 v B (Al Amerat) 2021-22; BB 5-27 v Netherlands (Dubai, ICCA) 2015-16. HS 81* Scot v PNG (Port Moresby) 2017-18. De HS 55* v Sussex (Hove) 2022. BB 3-60 Scot v Ire (Dubai, DSC) 2017-18. De BB 2-37 v Durham (Derby) 2022. LO HS 37* (*see LOI*). LO BB 5-33 (*see LOI*). T20 HS 22. T20 BB 5-27.

WOOD, Thomas Anthony (Heanor Gate Science C), b Derby 11 May 1994. 6'3". RHB, RM. Squad No 24. Debut (Derbyshire) 2016. HS 31 v Notts (Derby) 2020. LO HS 109 v Notts (Derby) 2021 (RLC). LO BB 1-13 v Surrey (Derby) 2021 (RLC). T20 HS 67.

RELEASED/RETIRED

(Having made a County 1st XI appearance in 2022, even if not formally contracted. Some may return in 2023.)

NQ**CARTWRIGHT, Hilton** William Raymond, b Harare, Zimbabwe 14 Feb 1992. RHB, RM. W Australia 2012-13 to date. Middlesex 2018. Derbyshire 2022. Big Bash: PS 2012-13 to 2018-19; MS 2019-20 to date. Oval Invincibles 2022. **Tests** (A): 2 (2016-17 to 2017); HS 37 v P (Sydney) 2016-17; BB – . **LOI** (A): 2 (2017-18); HS 1 (twice). F-c Tours (A): NZ 2015-16 (Cricket Aus); B 2017. HS 170* WA v NSW (Perth) 2016-17. CC HS 80 M v Leics (Leicester) 2018. De HS 71* v Durham (Chester-le-St) 2022. BB 4-23 WA v Tas (Perth) 2021-22. CC BB 4-33 M v Glos (Lord's) 2018. LO HS 99 Cricket Aus v Q (Sydney, DO) 2015-16. LO BB 3-26 Aus Nat Perf XI v Aus A (Townsville) 2016. T20 HS 79. T20 BB 2-34.

HUGHES, Alex Lloyd (Ounsdale HS, Wolverhampton), b Wordsley, Staffs 29 Sep 1991. 5'10". RHB, RM. Derbyshire 2013-22; cap 2017. HS 142 v Glos (Bristol) 2017. BB 4-46 v Glamorgan (Derby) 2014. LO HS 96* v Leics (Leicester) 2016 (RLC). LO BB 4-44 v Northants (Derby) 2019 (RLC). T20 HS 43*. T20 BB 4-42.

NQ**KERR, Hayden** Lewis, b Bowral, NSW, Australia 10 Jul 1996. RHB, LFM. New South Wales 2021-22 to date. Derbyshire 2022. Big Bash: SS 2019-20 to date. HS 88 NSW v Tas (Sydney) 2021-22. De HS 16 and BB 3-63 v Sussex (Hove) 2022. LO HS 43 and LO BB 2-16 NSW v Vic (Sydney) 2021-22. T20 HS 98*. T20 BB 4-32.

SHAN MASOOD – *see YORKSHIRE*.

SYLVESTER, Adam Ryan (Barry Boys CS), b Llandough Hospital, Glamorgan 18 May 2000. RHB, RM. Derbyshire 2022. Derbyshire 2nd XI debut 2021. HS 11* v Glamorgan (Cardiff) 2022. BB –.

M.A.R.Cohen and D.R.Melton left the staff without making a County 1st XI appearance in 2022.

DURHAM RELEASED/RETIRED (continued from p 92)

NQ**RAVINDRA, Rachin**, b Wellington, New Zealand 18 Nov 1999. LHB, SLA. Wellington 2018-19 to date. Durham 2022; cap 2022. **Tests** (NZ): 3 (2021-22); HS 18* v I (Kanpur) 2021-22; BB 3-56 v I (Mumbai) 2021-22. **IT20** (NZ): 6 (2021 to 2021-22); HS 20 v B (Mirpur) 2021; BB 3-22 v B (Mirpur) 2021 – separate games. F-c Tours (NZ): I 2021-22; UAE (v PA) 2018-19 (NZA). HS 217 v Worcs (Chester-le-St) 2022 – on UK debut. BB 6-89 NZA v West Indies A (Nelson) 2020-21. LO HS 130 Wellington v Auckland (Lincoln) 2019-20. LO BB 3-52 Wellington v ND (Whangarei) 2019-20. T20 HS 67. T20 BB 3-22.

RUSHWORTH, C. – *see WARWICKSHIRE*.

SALISBURY, M.E.T. – *see LEICESTERSHIRE*.

NQ**TURNER, Ashton** James, b Subiaco, Perth, W Australia 25 Jan 1993. RHB, OB. W Australia 2013-14 to date. Durham 2022 (T20 only). IPL: RR 2019. Big Bash: PS 2013-14 to date. Manchester Originals 2022. **LOI** (A): 9 (2018-19 to 2021); HS 84* v I (Mohali) 2018-19; BB 1-23 v WI (Bridgetown) 2021. **IT20** (A): 18 (2016-17 to 2021); HS 24 v WI (Gros Islet) 2021; BB 2-12 v SL (Melbourne) 2016-17. HS 110 WA v Tas (Perth) 2016-17. BB 6-111 WA v NSW (Perth) 2016-17. LO HS 100 WA v Tas (Perth) 2021-22. LO BB 2-22 WA v SA (Perth) 2022-23. T20 HS 84*. T20 BB 2-3.

TYE, A.J. – *see NORTHAMPTONSHIRE*.

J.O.I.Campbell left the staff without making a County 1st XI appearance in 2022.

COUNTY CAPS AWARDED IN 2022

Derbyshire	S.Conners, A.K.Dal, J.L.Du Plooy, B.D.Guest, Shan Masood
Durham	C.G.Benjamin, J.J.Bushnell, G.S.Drissell, O.J.Gibson, S.J.C.McAlindon, T.S.S.Mackintosh, N.J.Maddinson, K.D.Petersen, R.Ravindra
Essex	S.Snater
Glamorgan	S.A.Northeast, A.G.Salter
Gloucestershire	J.G.Bethell, Z.J.Chappell, A.S.Dale, M.S.Harris, Mohammad Amir, Naseem Shah, B.T.J.Wheal
Hampshire	J.K.Fuller, N.R.T.Gubbins, Mohammad Abbas
Kent	O.G.Robinson
Lancashire	Hasan Ali, L.W.P.Wells
Leicestershire	Naveen-ul-Haq, C.F.Parkinson
Middlesex	E.R.Bamber, M.D.Stoneman
Northamptonshire	–
Nottinghamshire	–
Somerset	M.T.Renshaw, P.M.Siddle
Surrey	J.Clark, W.G.Jacks
Sussex	W.A.T.Beer, S.T.Finn, Mohammad Rizwan, C.A.Pujara
Warwickshire	–
Worcestershire (colours)	Azhar Ali, T.R.Cornall, B.J.Gibbon, Kashif Ali, Mohammad Hasnain, E.J.Pollock, M.J.Waite
Yorkshire	M.D.Fisher, J.A.Tattersall, J.A.Thompson

Durham and Gloucestershire now award caps on first-class debut. Worcestershire award club colours on Championship debut.

DERBYSHIRE 2022

RESULTS SUMMARY

	Place	Won	Lost	Drew	NR
LV= Insurance County Champ (Div 2)	5th	3	3	8	
Royal London One-Day Cup (Group B)	7th	3	4		1
Vitality Blast (North Group)	QF	9	6		

LV= INSURANCE COUNTY CHAMPIONSHIP AVERAGES
BATTING AND FIELDING

Cap		M	I	NO	HS	Runs	Avge	100	50	Ct/St
2022	Shan Masood	8	13	–	239	1074	82.61	3	4	5
2022	A.K.Dal	13	19	6	146*	957	73.61	3	5	7
2011	W.L.Madsen	14	24	3	176	1273	60.61	3	10	22
2022	J.L.du Plooy	14	23	3	134	845	42.25	2	5	6
2022	B.D.Guest	14	24	–	138	923	38.45	4	2	52
	M.H.McKiernan	4	5	–	101	174	34.80	1	1	1
	H.R.C.Came	5	9	–	78	300	33.33	–	3	3
2019	L.M.Reece	12	21	2	116	620	32.63	1	3	3
	H.W.R.Cartwright	3	6	2	71*	96	24.00	–	1	3
2015	B.A.Godleman	12	20	–	158	468	23.40	1	–	3
	M.R.J.Watt	3	4	1	55*	57	19.00	–	1	–
	A.T.Thomson	11	15	2	54	234	18.00	–	2	5
	B.W.Aitchison	6	10	2	25*	119	14.87	–	–	4
	N.J.Potts	5	7	–	13	46	6.57	–	–	2
2022	S.Conners	14	15	3	23	65	5.41	–	–	6

Also batted: A.L.Hughes (1 match – cap 2017) 33, 49 (1 ct); L.J.Hurt (1) 13, 49; H.L.Kerr (1) 16, 8 (1 ct); R.A.S.Lakmal (5) 0*, 1, 5 (1 ct); T.H.S.Pettman (2) 0*, 0; G.L.S.Scrimshaw (2) 8*, 0*, 4; R.N.Sidebottom (3) 0, 0, 31*; A.R.Sylvester (1) 11*, 0*.

BOWLING

	O	M	R	W	Avge	Best	5wI	10wM
A.K.Dal	332.4	62	1016	34	29.88	5- 40	1	–
B.W.Aitchison	194.3	41	599	20	29.95	4- 40	–	–
N.J.Potts	113.5	13	428	12	35.66	4- 50	–	–
S.Conners	453.5	60	1790	50	35.80	5- 51	2	–
R.A.S.Lakmal	213.5	50	605	15	40.33	5- 82	1	–
L.M.Reece	145.3	25	503	10	50.30	3- 26	–	–
A.T.Thomson	375.5	92	1109	22	50.40	4-103	–	–

Also bowled:

T.H.S.Pettman	50.5	15	145	7	20.71	3- 40	–	–
R.N.Sidebottom	55	6	216	7	30.85	4- 50	–	–
M.R.J.Watt	109.1	35	317	9	35.22	2- 37	–	–

H.R.C.Came 8-1-37-0; J.L.du Plooy 44.2-4-170-2; A.L.Hughes 11-0-44-0; L.J.Hurt 20-0-110-0; H.L.Kerr 24.4-2-82-3; M.H.McKiernan 42.1-1-146-4; W.L.Madsen 45-18-102-1; G.L.S.Scrimshaw 31.1-2-116-4; A.R.Sylvester 19-0-95-0.

Derbyshire played no first-class fixtures outside the County Championship in 2022. The First-Class Averages (pp 221–234) give the records of Derbyshire players in all first-class county matches, with the exceptions of T.H.S.Pettman and R.N.Sidebottom, whose first-class figures for Derbyshire are as above.

DERBYSHIRE RECORDS

FIRST-CLASS CRICKET

Highest Total	For 801-8d		v	Somerset	Taunton	2007
	V 677-7d		by	Yorkshire	Leeds	2013
Lowest Total	For 16		v	Notts	Nottingham	1879
	V 23		by	Hampshire	Burton upon T	1958
Highest Innings	For 274	G.A.Davidson	v	Lancashire	Manchester	1896
	V 343*	P.A.Perrin	for	Essex	Chesterfield	1904

Highest Partnership for each Wicket

1st	333	L.M.Reece/B.A.Godleman	v	Northants	Derby	2017
2nd	417	K.J.Barnett/T.A.Tweats	v	Yorkshire	Derby	1997
3rd	316*	A.S.Rollins/K.J.Barnett	v	Leics	Leicester	1997
4th	328	P.Vaulkhard/D.Smith	v	Notts	Nottingham	1946
5th	302*†	J.E.Morris/D.G.Cork	v	Glos	Cheltenham	1993
6th	227	B.D.Guest/A.K.Dal	v	Leics	Derby	2021
7th	258	M.P.Dowman/D.G.Cork	v	Durham	Derby	2000
8th	198	K.M.Krikken/D.G.Cork	v	Lancashire	Manchester	1996
9th	283	A.Warren/J.Chapman	v	Warwicks	Blackwell	1910
10th	132	A.Hill/M.Jean-Jacques	v	Yorkshire	Sheffield	1986

† 346 runs were added for this wicket in two separate partnerships

Best Bowling	For 10- 40	W.Bestwick	v	Glamorgan	Cardiff	1921
(Innings)	V 10- 45	R.L.Johnson	for	Middlesex	Derby	1994
Best Bowling	For 17-103	W.Mycroft	v	Hampshire	Southampton	1876
(Match)	V 16-101	G.Giffen	for	Australians	Derby	1886

Most Runs – Season	2165	D.B.Carr	(av 48.11)		1959
Most Runs – Career	23854	K.J.Barnett	(av 41.12)		1979-98
Most 100s – Season	8	P.N.Kirsten			1982
Most 100s – Career	53	K.J.Barnett			1979-98
Most Wkts – Season	168	T.B.Mitchell	(av 19.55)		1935
Most Wkts – Career	1670	H.L.Jackson	(av 17.11)		1947-63
Most Career W-K Dismissals	1304	R.W.Taylor	(1157 ct; 147 st)		1961-84
Most Career Catches in the Field	563	D.C.Morgan			1950-69

LIMITED-OVERS CRICKET

Highest Total	50ov	366-4		v	Comb Univs	Oxford	1991
	40ov	321-5		v	Essex	Leek	2013
	T20	222-5		v	Yorkshire	Leeds	2010
		222-5		v	Notts	Nottingham	2017
Lowest Total	50ov	73		v	Lancashire	Derby	1993
	40ov	60		v	Kent	Canterbury	2008
	T20	72		v	Leics	Derby	2013
Highest Innings	50ov	173*	M.J.Di Venuto	v	Derbys CB	Derby	2000
	40ov	141*	C.J.Adams	v	Kent	Chesterfield	1992
	T20	111	W.J.Durston	v	Notts	Nottingham	2010
Best Bowling	50ov	8-21	M.A.Holding	v	Sussex	Hove	1988
	40ov	6- 7	M.Hendrick	v	Notts	Nottingham	1972
	T20	5-27	T.Lungley	v	Leics	Leicester	2009

DURHAM

Formation of Present Club: 23 May 1882
Inaugural First-Class Match: 1992
Colours: Navy Blue, Yellow and Maroon
Badge: Coat of Arms of the County of Durham
County Champions: (3) 2008, 2009, 2013
Friends Provident Trophy Winners: (1) 2007
Royal London One-Day Cup Winners: (1) 2014
Twenty20 Cup Winners: (0); best – Finalist 2016

Chief Executive: Tim Bostock, Seat Unique Riverside, Chester-le-Street, Co Durham DH3 3QR ● Tel: 0191 387 1717 ● Email: reception@durhamcricket.co.uk ● Web: www.durhamcricket.co.uk ● Twitter: @DurhamCricket (91,415 followers)

Director of Cricket: Marcus North. **Head Coach**: Ryan Campbell. **Assistant Coaches**: Alan Walker and Will Gidman. **Captain**: S.G.Borthwick. **Overseas Players**: D.G.Bedingham and T.Stubbs. **2023 Testimonial**: None. **Head Groundsman**: Vic Demain. **Scorer**: William Dobson. ‡ New registration. ᴺᴼ Not qualified for England.

Durham revised their capping system in 2020 and now award players with their County Caps when they make their first-class debut.

ᴺᴼ**BEDINGHAM, David** Guy, b George, Cape Province, South Africa 22 Apr 1994. 5'9". RHB, OB, occ WK. Squad No 5. Western Province 2012-13 to 2021-22. Boland 2015-16 to 2018-19. Cape Cobras 2018-19 to 2019-20. Durham debut/cap 2020. Birmingham Phoenix 2021. 1000 runs (1): 1029 (2021). HS 257 v Derbys (Chester-le-St) 2021. BB –. LO HS 104* Boland v Border (East London) 2017-18. LO BB –. T20 HS 73.

BORTHWICK, Scott George (Farringdon Community Sports C, Sunderland), b Sunderland 19 Apr 1990. 5'9". LHB, LBG. Squad No 16. Debut (Durham) 2009; cap 2009; captain 2021 to date. Chilaw Marians 2014-15. Wellington 2015-16 to 2016-17. Surrey 2017-20; cap 2018. **Tests**: 1 (2013-14); HS 4 and BB 3-33 v A (Sydney) 2013-14. **LOI**: 2 (2011 to 2011-12); HS 15 v Ire (Dublin) 2011; BB –. **IT20**: 1 (2011); HS 14 and BB 1-15 v WI (Oval) 2011. F-c Tours: A (2013-14); SL 2013-14 (EL). 1000 runs (5); most – 1390 (2015). HS 216 v Middx (Chester-le-St) 2014, sharing Du record 2nd wkt partnership of 274 with M.D.Stoneman. BB 6-70 v Surrey (Oval) 2013. LO HS 88 v Somerset (Taunton) 2022 (RLC). LO BB 5-38 v Leics (Leicester) 2015 (RLC). T20 HS 62. T20 BB 4-18.

BUSHNELL, Jonathan James (Durham S), b Durham 6 Sep 2001. 6'1". RHB, RM. Squad No 20. Debut (Durham) 2022; cap 2022. Durham 2nd XI debut 2019. HS 66 and BB 1-15 v Worcs (Chester-le-St) 2022. LO HS 25 v Glos (Chester-le-St) 2022 (RLC). T20 HS 25*.

CARSE, Brydon Alexander (Pearson HS, Pt Elizabeth), b Port Elizabeth, South Africa 31 Jul 1995. Son of J.A.Carse (Rhodesia, W Province, E Province, Northants, Border, Griqualand W 1977-78 to 1992-93). 6'1½". RHB, RF. Squad No 99. Debut (Durham) 2016; cap 2016. Northern Superchargers 2021. **ECB Pace Bowling Development Contract 2022-23**. **LOI**: 9 (2021 to 2022); HS 31 v P (Lord's) 2021; BB 5-61 v P (Birmingham) 2021. F-c Tour (EL): A 2019-20. HS 77* v Northants (Chester-le-St) 2019. BB 6-26 v Middx (Lord's) 2019. LO HS 31 (*see LOI*). LO BB 5-61 (*see LOI*). T20 HS 51. T20 BB 3-30.

CLARK, Graham (St Benedict's Catholic HS, Whitehaven), b Whitehaven, Cumbria 16 Mar 1993. Younger brother of J.Clark (*see SURREY*). 6'1". RHB, LB. Squad No 7. Debut (Durham) 2015; cap 2015. HS 109 v Glamorgan (Chester-le-St) 2017. BB 1-10 v Sussex (Arundel) 2018. LO HS 141* v Kent (Beckenham) 2021 (RLC). LO BB 3-18 v Leics (Leicester) 2018 (RLC). T20 HS 91*. T20 BB –.

COUGHLIN, Paul (St Robert of Newminster Catholic CS, Washington), b Sunderland 23 Oct 1992. Elder brother of J.Coughlin (Durham 2016-19); nephew of T.Harland (Durham 1974-78). 6'3". RHB, RM. Squad No 23. Debut (Durham) 2012; cap 2012. Nottinghamshire 2019. Northumberland 2011. F-c Tour (EL): WI 2017-18. HS 100* v Worcs (Chester-le-St) 2022. BB 5-49 (10-133 match) v Northants (Chester-le-St) 2017. LO HS 77 v Glos (Chester-le-St) 2022 (RLC). LO BB 3-36 v Worcs (Worcester) 2017 (RLC). T20 HS 53. T20 BB 5-42.

CRAWSHAW, Harry Michael (Q Ethelberga's Collegiate, York), b Middlesbrough, Yorks 16 Feb 2003. LHB, SLA. Squad No 3. Durham 2nd XI debut 2021. Awaiting f-c debut. T20 HS 5. T20 BB –. No 1st XI appearances in 2022.

‡NODe LEEDE, Bastiaan** Franciscus Wilhelmus (St Maartens C), b Nootdorp, Netherlands 15 Nov 1999. Son of T.B.M.de Leede (Netherlands 1995 to 2006-07). RHB, RMF. Squad No 4. Netherlands 2018. MCC YC 2019. **LOI** (Neth): 23 (2018 to 2022); HS 89 v P (Rotterdam) 2022; BB 3-50 v P (Rotterdam) 2022 – separate matches. **IT20** (Neth): 31 (2018 to 2022-23); HS 91* v USA (Bulawayo) 2022; BB 3-19 v UAE (Geelong) 2022-23. HS 56* Neth v Namibia (Dubai) 2017-18. LO HS 89 (*see LOI*). LO BB 3-50 (*see LOI*). T20 HS 91*. T20 BB 3-19.

DONEATHY, Luke (Prudhoe HS), b Newcastle upon Tyne 26 Jul 2001. RHB, RM. Squad No 24. Durham 2nd XI debut 2019. Awaiting f-c debut. LO HS 69* and LO BB 4-36 v Lancs (Gosforth) 2021 (RLC). T20 HS 5*. T20 BB 1-19.

DRISSELL, George (Bedminster Down SS; Filton C), b Bristol, Glos 20 Jan 1999. 6'1½". RHB, OB. Squad No 8. Gloucestershire 2017-19; cap 2017. Durham debut/cap 2022. Gloucestershire 2nd XI 2016-19. Worcestershire 2nd XI 2021. Somerset 2nd XI 2021. Durham 2nd XI debut 2021. HS 19 Gs v Warwks (Birmingham) 2018. Du HS 16 v Notts (Nottingham) 2022. BB 4-83 Gs v Glamorgan (Newport) 2019. Du BB –. LO HS 37* v Sussex (Chester-le-St) 2022 (RLC). LO BB 1-21 Sm v Glamorgan (Taunton) 2021 (RLC). T20 HS –. T20 BB –.

GIBSON, Oliver James (Q Elizabeth GS, Hexham; Derwentside SFC), b Northallerton, Yorks 7 Jul 2000. 5'11". RHB, RFM. Squad No 73. Debut (Durham) 2022; cap 2022. Durham 2nd XI debut 2018. HS 6 and BB 2-25 v Leics (Leicester) 2022. BB 2-25 v Sussex (Chester-le-St) 2022 (RLC). LO HS 6 v Surrey (Gosforth) 2022 (RLC). LO BB 3-54 v Somerset (Taunton) 2022 (RLC).

‡NOGLOVER, Brandon** Dale (St Stithians C), b Johannesburg, South Africa 3 Apr 1997. 6'2½". RHB, RFM. Squad No 20. Boland 2016-17 to 2018-19. Northamptonshire 2020. **LOI** (Neth): 8 (2019 to 2021-22); HS 18 v Ire (Utrecht) 2021; BB 3-43 v Afg (Doha) 2021-22. **IT20** (Neth): 24 (2019 to 2022-23); HS 1* (twice); BB 4-12 v UAE (Dubai, DSC) 2019-20. HS 12* Boland v Gauteng (Paarl) 2018-19. CC HS 0. BB 4-83 Boland v FS (Bloemfontein) 2017-18. CC BB 2-45 Nh v Somerset (Northampton) 2020. LO HS 27 Boland v Easterns (Benoni) 2017-18. LO BB 3-43 (*see LOI*). T20 HS 15. T20 BB 4-12.

NOJONES, Michael Alexander (Ormskirk S; Myerscough C), b Ormskirk, Lancs 5 Jan 1998. 6'2". RHB, OB. Squad No 10. Debut (Durham) 2018; cap 2018. **LOI** (Scot): 12 (2017-18 to 2022); HS 87 v Ire (Dubai, ICCA) 2017-18. **IT20** (Scot): 4 (2022 to 2022-23); HS 86 v Ire (Hobart) 2022-23. HS 206 v Middx (Chester-le-St) 2020. LO HS 119 v Middx (Chester-le-St) 2022 (RLC). T20 HS 86.

KILLEEN, Mitchell Jack (St Bede's, Lanchester), b Durham 28 Sep 2004. Son of N.Killeen (Durham 1995 to 2008). RHB, RM. Durham 2nd XI debut 2021. Awaiting f-c debut. LO HS 32 v Leics (Leicester) 2022 (RLC). LO BB 1-17 v Notts (Grantham) 2022 (RLC).

LEES, Alexander Zak (Holy Trinity SS, Halifax), b Halifax, Yorks 14 Apr 1993. 6'3". LHB, LB. Squad No 14. Yorkshire 2010-18; cap 2014; captain (l-o) 2016. Durham debut/cap 2018. MCC 2017. YC 2014. **Tests**: 10 (2021-22 to 2022); HS 67 v NZ (Nottingham) 2022. F-c Tours: WI 2021-22; SL 2022-23 (EL). 1000 runs (2); most – 1199 (2016). HS 275* Y v Derbys (Chesterfield) 2013. Du HS 182* v Glamorgan (Cardiff) 2022. BB 2-51 Y v Middx (Lord's) 2016. Du BB 1-12 v Yorks (Chester-le-St) 2022. LO HS 126* v Essex (Chester-le-St) 2021 (RLC). T20 HS 77*.

McALINDON, Stanley James C. (Trinity S), b Carlisle, Cumberland 28 Apr 2004. RHB, RFM. Debut (Durham) 2022; cap 2022. Durham 2nd XI debut 2021. England U19 2022. HS 26* and BB 2-63 v Derbys (Chester-le-St) 2022. LO HS 50 and LO BB 4-29 v Leics (Leicester) 2022 (RLC).

McKINNEY, Ben Stewart (Seaham HS), b Sunderland 4 Oct 2004. 6'7". LHB, OB. Durham 2nd XI debut 2021. England U19 2022 to 2022-23. Awaiting 1st XI debut.

NO**MACKINTOSH, Tom**as Scott Sabater (Merchiston Castle S), b Madrid, Spain 11 Jan 2003. 5'10". RHB, WK. Squad No 14. Debut (Durham) 2022; cap 2022. Durham 2nd XI debut 2021. **LOI** (Scot): 3 (2022-23); HS 34 v Namibia (Kirtipur) 2022-23. HS 51 v Derbys (Chester-le-St) 2022. LO HS 36 v Glos (Chester-le-St) 2022 (RLC).

‡NO**MURPHY, Todd** R., b Echuca, Victoria, Australia 15 Nov 2000. LHB, OB. Victoria 2020-21 to date. Big Bash: SS 2021-22 to date. **Tests** (A): 4 (2022-23); HS 41 v I (Ahmedabad) 2022-23; BB 7-124 v I (Nagpur) 2022-23 – on debut. HS 41 (see Tests). BB 7-124 (see Tests). LO HS 19 Vic v WA (Melbourne, SK) 2022-23. LO BB 2-29 Vic v NSW (Melbourne, SK) 2022-23. T20 HS 0. T20 BB 3-35.

POTTS, Matthew ('Matty') James (St Robert of Newminster Catholic S), b Sunderland 29 Oct 1998. 6'0". RHB, RFM. Squad No 35. Debut (Durham) 2017; cap 2017. Northern Superchargers 2021 to date. Durham 2nd XI debut 2016. England U19 2017. **ECB Increment Contract 2022-23**. **Tests**: 5 (2022); HS 19 v I (Nottingham) 2022; BB 4-13 v NZ (Lord's) 2022, taking the wicket of K.S.Williamson with his fifth delivery in Test cricket. **LOI**: 1 (2022); HS 3* v SA (Chester-le-St) 2022; BB –. HS 81 v Northants (Northampton) 2021. 50 wkts (1): 78 (2022). BB 7-40 (11-101 match) v Glamorgan (Chester-le-St) 2022. LO HS 30 v Yorks (Chester-le-St) 2018 (RLC). LO BB 4-62 v Northants (Chester-le-St) 2019 (RLC). T20 HS 40*. T20 BB 3-8.

RAINE, Benjamin Alexander (St Aidan's RC SS, Sunderland), b Sunderland, 14 Sep 1991. 6'0". LHB, RMF. Squad No 44. Debut (Durham) 2011; cap 2011. Leicestershire 2013-18; cap 2018. HS 103* v Worcs (Chester-le-St) 2022, sharing Du record 8th wkt partnership of 213* with P.Coughlin. 50 wkts (2); most – 61 (2015). BB 6-27 v Sussex (Hove) 2019. LO HS 83 Le v Worcs (Worcester) 2018 (RLC). LO BB 3-31 Le v Northants (Northampton) 2018 (RLC). T20 HS 113. T20 BB 3-7.

‡**ROBINSON, Oliver** Graham (Hurtsmere S, Greenwich), b Sidcup 1 Dec 1998. 5'8". RHB, WK, occ RM. Squad No 21. Kent 2018-22; cap 2022. Kent 2nd XI debut 2015. England U19 2017 to 2018. HS 143 K v Warwks (Birmingham) 2019. LO HS 206* K v Worcs (Worcester) 2022 (RLC) - K record. T20 HS 56.

SOWTER, Nathan Adam (Hill Sport HS, NSW), b Penrith, NSW, Australia 12 Oct 1992. 5'10". RHB, LB. Middlesex 2017-21. Durham debut 2022 (T20 only). Oval Invincibles 2021 to date. HS 57* M v Glamorgan (Cardiff) 2019. BB 3-42 M v Lancs (Manchester) 2017. LO HS 31 M v Surrey (Oval) 2019 (RLC). LO BB 6-62 M v Essex (Chelmsford) 2019 (RLC). T20 HS 37*. T20 BB 4-23.

STOKES, Benjamin Andrew (Cockermouth S), b Christchurch, Canterbury, New Zealand 4 Jun 1991. 6'1". LHB, RFM. Squad No 38. Debut (Durham) 2010; cap 2010. IPL: RPS 2017; RR 2018-21. Big Bash: MR 2014-15. Northern Superchargers 2021. YC 2013. Wisden 2015. PCA 2019. BBC Sports Personality of the Year 2019. OBE 2020. **ECB Central Contract 2022-23**. **Tests**: 91 (2013-14 to 2022-23, 13 as captain); HS 258 v SA (Cape Town) 2015-16, setting E record fastest double century in 163 balls; BB 6-22 v WI (Lord's) 2017. **LOI**: 105 (2011 to 2022, as captain); HS 102* v A (Birmingham) 2017; BB 5-61 v A (Southampton) 2013. **IT20**: 43 (2011 to 2022); HS 52* v P (Melbourne) 2022-23, in World Cup final; BB 3-26 v NZ (Delhi) 2015-16. F-c Tours (C=Captain): A 2013-14, 2021-22; SA 2015-16, 2019-20; WI 2010-11 (EL), 2014-15, 2018-19, 2021-22; NZ 2017-18, 2019-20, 2022-23C; I 2016-17, 2020-21; 2022-23C; SL 2018-19; B 2016-17; UAE 2015-16 (v P). HS 258 (see Tests). Du HS 185 v Lancs (Chester-le-St) 2011, sharing Du record 4th wkt partnership of 331 with D.M.Benkenstein. BB 7-67 (10-121 match) v Sussex (Chester-le-St) 2014. LO HS 164 v Notts (Chester-le-St) 2014 (RLC) – Du record. LO BB 5-61 (see LOI). T20 HS 107*. T20 BB 4-16.

^{NO}**STUBBS, Tristan** (Knysna Primary S), b Johannesburg, South Africa 14 Aug 2000. RHB, WK, occ OB. E Province 2019-20 to date. Joins Durham in 2023 for T20 only. IPL: MI 2022. Manchester Originals 2022. **IT20** (SA): 13 (2022 to 2022-23); HS 72 v E (Bristol) 2022; BB –. HS 132 EP v C Gauteng (Potchefstroom) 2020-21. BB 1-13 EP v WP (Gqeberha) 2021-22. LO HS 144 EP v Gauteng (Gqeberha) 2022-23. LO BB 2-29 EP v KZN (Durban) 2022-23. T20 HS 80*. T20 BB 2-6.

TREVASKIS, Liam (Q Elizabeth GS, Penrith), b Carlisle, Cumberland 18 Apr 1999. 5'8". LHB, SLA. Squad No 80. Debut (Durham) 2017; cap 2017. Durham 2nd XI debut 2015. HS 88 v Sussex (Hove) 2022. BB 5-78 v Glos (Bristol) 2021. LO HS 59* v Notts (Grantham) 2022 (RLC). LO BB 3-38 v Worcs (Worcester) 2021 (RLC). T20 HS 31*. T20 BB 4-16.

WHITFIELD, Ross Gillings (Whickham S), b Gateshead 10 Sep 2004. 6'3". RHB, LB. Durham 2nd XI debut 2022. England U19 2022. Awaiting 1st XI debut.

WOOD, Mark Andrew (Ashington HS; Newcastle C), b Ashington 11 Jan 1990. 5'11". RHB, RF. Squad No 33. Debut (Durham) 2011; cap 2011. IPL: CSK 2018. Northumberland 2008-10. **ECB Central Contract 2022-23. Tests**: 28 (2015 to 2022-23); HS 52 v NZ (Christchurch) 2017-18; BB 6-37 v A (Hobart) 2021-22. **LOI**: 59 (2015 to 2022-23); HS 14 v I (Pune) 2020-21; BB 4-33 v A (Birmingham) 2017. **IT20**: 27 (2015 to 2022-23); HS 5* v A (Hobart) 2017-18 and 5* v NZ (Wellington) 2017-18; BB 3-9 v WI (Basseterre) 2018-19. F-c Tours: A 2021-22; SA 2014-15 (EL), 2019-20; WI 2018-19, 2021-22; NZ 2017-18; P 2022-23; SL 2013-14 (EL), 2020-21; UAE 2015-16 (v P), 2018-19 (EL v P A). HS 72* v Kent (Chester-le-St) 2017. BB 6-46 v Derbys (Derby) 2018. LO HS 24 EL v Pakistan A (Abu Dhabi) 2018-19. LO BB 4-33 (*see LOI*). T20 HS 27*. T20 BB 4-25.

RELEASED/RETIRED

(Having made a County 1st XI appearance in 2022)

DICKSON, S.R. – *see SOMERSET*.

ECKERSLEY, Edmund John Holden ('Ned') (St Benedict's GS, Ealing), b Oxford 9 Aug 1989. 6'0". RHB, WK, occ OB. Leicestershire 2011-18; cap 2013. Mountaineers 2011-12. Durham 2019-22; cap 2019; captain 2020. MCC 2013. 1000 runs (1): 1302 (2013). HS 158 Le v Derbys (Derby) 2017. Du HS 118 v Sussex (Hove) 2019, sharing Du record 6th wkt partnership of 282 with C.T.Bancroft. BB 2-29 Le v Lancs (Manchester) 2013. Du BB –. LO HS 108 Le v Yorks (Leicester) 2013 (Y40). T20 HS 50*.

^{NO}**MADDINSON, Nic**olas James, b Shoalhaven, NSW, Australia 21 Dec 1991. LHB, SLA. New South Wales 2010-11 to 2017-18. Victoria 2018-19 to date. Durham 2022; cap 2022. Surrey 2018 (T20 only). IPL: RCB 2014-15. Big Bash: SS 2011-12 to 2017-18; MS 2018-19 to 2020-21; MR 2021-22 to date. **Tests** (A): 3 (2016-17); HS 22 v P (Melbourne) 2016-17; BB –. **IT20** (A): 6 (2013-14 to 2018); HS 34 v I (Rajkot) 2013-14. F-c Tours (Aus A): E/Ire 2013; SA/Z 2013; I 2015; SL 2022. HS 224 Vic v SA (Melbourne, St K) 2019-20. Scored 181 Aus A v Glos (Bristol) 2013 – on UK debut. Du HS 90 v Sussex (Chester-le-St) 2022. BB 2-10 NSW v SA (Coffs Harbour) 2015-16. LO HS 137 NSW v Tas (Perth) 2017-18. LO BB 4-29 Vic v WA (Melbourne, St K) 2018-19. T20 HS 87. T20 BB 3-20.

^{NO}**PETERSEN, Keegan** Darryl, b Paarl, South Africa 8 Aug 1993. RHB, LB. Boland 2011-12 to 2016-17. Cape Cobras 2014-15 to 2016-17. Knights 2016-17 to 2019-20. Northern Cape 2017-18 to 2019-20. Dolphins 2020-21. KZN-Coastal 2021-22 to date. Durham 2022; cap 2022. **Tests** (SA): 11 (2021 to 2022-23); HS 82 v I (Cape Town) 2021-22. F-c Tours (SA): E 2022; WI 2021. 1000 runs (0+1): 1263 (2018-19). HS 225* Boland v NW (Paarl) 2013-14. Du HS 78 v Glamorgan (Chester-le-St) 2022. BB 3-49 Knights v Dolphins (Durban) 2017-18. LO HS 134* Boland v EP (Pt Elizabeth) 2012-13. LO BB 1-18 Boland v KZN (Pietermaritzburg) 2012-13. T20 HS 73*. T20 BB –.

RELEASED/RETIRED continued on p 86

DURHAM 2022

RESULTS SUMMARY

	Place	Won	Lost	Drew	NR
LV= Insurance County Champ (Div 2)	6th	3	3	8	
Royal London One-Day Cup (Group A)	9th	1	7		
Vitality Blast (North Group)	8th	3	10		1

LV= INSURANCE COUNTY CHAMPIONSHIP AVERAGES
BATTING AND FIELDING

Cap		M	I	NO	HS	Runs	Avge	100	50	Ct/St
2018	A.Z.Lees	7	13	2	182*	651	59.18	2	2	1
2010	B.A.Stokes	3	5	–	161	284	56.80	1	1	–
2018	M.A.Jones	10	18	1	206	878	51.64	2	5	1
2020	S.R.Dickson	10	18	–	186	858	47.66	4	2	5
2020	D.G.Bedingham	12	17	3	191	664	47.42	2	2	9
2022	J.J.Bushnell	4	7	2	66	216	43.20	–	1	–
2012	P.Coughlin	5	6	2	100*	157	39.25	1	–	4
2009	S.G.Borthwick	14	24	3	96	764	34.72	–	7	19
2022	N.J.Maddinson	6	11	1	90	339	33.90	–	2	7
2017	L.Trevaskis	11	15	5	88	337	33.70	–	2	3
2022	K.D.Petersen	6	11	2	78	287	31.88	–	2	1
2011	B.A.Raine	13	18	4	103*	366	26.14	1	1	2
2022	T.S.S.Mackintosh	4	4	–	51	90	22.50	–	1	21
2016	B.A.Carse	4	4	1	28	63	21.00	–	–	–
2018	M.E.T.Salisbury	5	4	–	45	59	14.75	–	–	–
2019	E.J.H.Eckersley	8	11	1	58	143	14.30	–	1	22/1
2022	G.S.Drissell	3	5	1	16	48	12.00	–	–	1
2010	C.Rushworth	11	11	5	33	65	10.83	–	–	3
2017	M.J.Potts	10	11	–	40	119	10.81	–	–	2
2022	O.J.Gibson	7	7	2	6	7	1.40	–	–	1

Also batted: C.G.Benjamin (2 matches – cap 2022) 82*, 0, 33 (4 ct); S.J.C.McAlindon (2 – cap 2022) 26*, 18*; R.Ravindra (1 – cap 2022) 217, 46*.

BOWLING

	O	M	R	W	Avge	Best	5wI	10wM
M.J.Potts	381.1	100	1037	58	17.87	7- 40	6	2
B.A.Raine	464.2	110	1187	47	25.25	5- 43	2	–
C.Rushworth	332.4	85	930	34	27.35	7- 44	1	1
P.Coughlin	135	34	403	12	33.58	3- 33	–	–
L.Trevaskis	262.4	49	842	16	52.62	5-128	1	–

Also bowled: O.J.Gibson 146 22 533 8 66.62 2- 25; M.E.T.Salisbury 147 31 484 6 80.66 2- 71. S.G.Borthwick 116.3-6-441-2; J.J.Bushnell 27.5-0-107-1; B.A.Carse 40-3-212-2; G.S.Drissell 55-3-217-0; M.A.Jones 1-0-1-0; S.J.C.McAlindon 36.1-3-191-4; N.J.Maddinson 12-2-40-0; R.Ravindra 9-0-28-0; B.A.Stokes 63-12-226-4.

Durham played no first-class fixtures outside the County Championship in 2022. The First-Class Averages (pp 221–234) give the records of Durham players in all first-class county matches, with the exception of C.G.Benjamin, A.Z.Lees, K.D.Petersen, M.J.Potts and B.A.Stokes, whose first-class figures for Durham are as above.

DURHAM RECORDS

FIRST-CLASS CRICKET

Highest Total	For 648-5d		v	Notts	Chester-le-St^2	2009
	V 810-4d		by	Warwicks	Birmingham	1994
Lowest Total	For 61		v	Leics	Leicester	2018
	V 18		by	Durham MCCU	Chester-le-St^2	2012
Highest Innings	For 273	M.L.Love	v	Hampshire	Chester-le-St^2	2003
	V 501*	B.C.Lara	for	Warwicks	Birmingham	1994

Highest Partnership for each Wicket

1st	334*	S.Hutton/M.A.Roseberry	v	Oxford U	Oxford	1996
2nd	274	M.D.Stoneman/S.G.Borthwick	v	Middlesex	Chester-le-St^2	2014
3rd	212	M.J.Di Venuto/D.M.Benkenstein	v	Essex	Chester-le-St^2	2010
4th	331	B.A.Stokes/D.M.Benkenstein	v	Lancashire	Chester-le-St^2	2011
5th	254*	D.G.Bedingham/E.J.H.Eckersley	v	Notts	Nottingham	2021
6th	282	C.T.Bancroft/E.J.H.Eckersley	v	Sussex	Hove	2019
7th	315	D.M.Benkenstein/O.D.Gibson	v	Yorkshire	Leeds	2006
8th	213*	B.A.Raine/P.Coughlin	v	Worcs	Chester-le-St^2	2022
9th	150	P.Mustard/P.Coughlin	v	Northants	Chester-le-St^2	2014
10th	103	M.M.Betts/D.M.Cox	v	Sussex	Hove	1996

Best Bowling	For 10- 47	O.D.Gibson	v	Hampshire	Chester-le-St^2	2007
(Innings)	V 9- 34	J.A.R.Harris	for	Middlesex	Lord's	2015
Best Bowling	For 15- 95	C.Rushworth	v	Northants	Chester-le-St^2	2014
(Match)	V 13-103	J.A.R.Harris	for	Middlesex	Lord's	2015

Most Runs – Season	1654	M.J.Di Venuto	(av 78.76)	2009
Most Runs – Career	12030	P.D.Collingwood	(av 33.98)	1996-2018
Most 100s – Season	7	K.K.Jennings		2016
Most 100s – Career	25	P.D.Collingwood		1996-2018
Most Wkts – Season	88	C.Rushworth	(av 20.09)	2015
Most Wkts – Career	598	C.Rushworth	(av 22.51)	2010-22
Most Career W-K Dismissals	638	P.Mustard	(619 ct; 19 st)	2002-16
Most Career Catches in the Field	246	P.D.Collingwood		1996-2018

LIMITED-OVERS CRICKET

Highest Total	50ov	405-4		v	Kent	Beckenham	2021
	40ov	325-9		v	Surrey	The Oval	2011
	T20	225-2		v	Leics	Chester-le-St^2	2010
Lowest Total	50ov	82		v	Worcs	Chester-le-St^1	1968
	40ov	72		v	Warwicks	Birmingham	2002
	T20	78		v	Lancashire	Chester-le-St^2	2018
Highest Innings	50ov	164	B.A.Stokes	v	Notts	Chester-le-St^2	2014
	40ov	150*	B.A.Stokes	v	Warwicks	Birmingham	2011
	T20	108*	P.D.Collingwood	v	Worcs	Worcester	2017
Best Bowling	50ov	7-32	S.P.Davis	v	Lancashire	Chester-le-St^1	1983
	40ov	6-31	N.Killeen	v	Derbyshire	Derby	2000
	T20	5- 6	P.D.Collingwood	v	Northants	Chester-le-St^2	2011

^{1} Chester-le-Street CC (Ropery Lane) ^{2} Emirates Riverside

ESSEX

Formation of Present Club: 14 January 1876
Inaugural First-Class Match: 1894
Colours: Blue, Gold and Red
Badge: Three Seaxes above Scroll bearing 'Essex'
County Champions: (8) 1979, 1983, 1984, 1986, 1991, 1992, 2017, 2019
NatWest/Friends Prov Trophy Winners: (3) 1985, 1997, 2008
Benson and Hedges Cup Winners: (2) 1979, 1998
Pro 40/National League (Div 1) Winners: (2) 2005, 2006
Sunday League Winners: (3) 1981, 1984, 1985
Twenty20 Cup Winners: (1) 2019
Bob Willis Trophy Winners: (1) 2020

Interim Chairman: John Stephenson, The Cloud County Ground, New Writtle Street, Chelmsford CM2 0PG ● Tel: 01245 252420 ● Email: questions@essexcricket.org.uk ● Web: www.essexcricket.org.uk ● Twitter: @EssexCricket (115,071 followers)

Head Coach: Anthony McGrath. **Bowling Coach**: Mick Lewis. **Batting Coach**: Tom Huggins. **Captains**: T.Westley (f-c and 50 ov) and S.R.Harmer (T20). **Overseas Players**: S.R.Harmer and D.R.Sams (T20 only). **2023 Testimonial**: None. **Head Groundsman**: Stuart Kerrison. **Scorer**: Tony Choat. **Blast Team Name**: Essex Eagles. ‡ New registration. NO Not qualified for England.

ALLISON, Benjamin Michael John (New Hall S; Chelmsford C), b Colchester 18 Dec 1999. RHB, RFM. Squad No 65. Gloucestershire 2019; cap 2019. Essex debut 2021. Essex 2nd XI debut 2017. Bedfordshire 2018. Cambridgeshire 2019. HS 69* and BB 5-32 v Northants (Northampton) 2022. LO HS 21* v Essex (Southampton) 2022 (RLC). LO BB 2-33 v Kent (Chelmsford) 2021 (RLC). T20 HS 6*. T20 BB 3-33.

BEARD, Aaron Paul (Boswells S, Chelmsford), b Chelmsford 15 Oct 1997. LHB, RFM. Squad No 14. Debut (Essex) 2016. Sussex 2022 (on loan). HS 58* v Durham MCCU (Chelmsford) 2017. CC HS 41 v Yorks (Chelmsford) 2019. BB 4-21 v Middx (Chelmsford) 2020. LO HS 22* v Kent (Beckenham) 2019 (RLC). LO BB 3-51 v Glos (Chelmsford) 2019 (RLC). T20 HS 13. T20 BB 4-29.

BENKENSTEIN, Luc Martin (Hilton C; Seaford C), b Durban, South Africa 2 Nov 2004. Son of D.M.Benkenstein (Natal, KZN, Dolphins and Durham 1993-94 to 2013); grandson of M.M.Benkenstein (Rhodesia and Natal B 1970-71 to 1980-81); nephew of B.N.Benkenstein (Natal B and Griqualand W 1994-95 to 1996-97) and B.R.Benkenstein (Natal B 1993-94). RHB, LBG. Squad No 99. Sussex 2nd XI 2021. Hampshire 2nd XI 2021. Essex 2nd XI debut 2021. Awaiting f-c debut. LO HS 55 v Worcs (Worcester) 2022 (RLC). LO BB 6-42 v Glamorgan (Chelmsford) 2022 (RLC) – Ex 50 ov record.

BROWNE, Nicholas Lawrence Joseph (Trinity Catholic HS, Woodford Green), b Leytonstone 24 Mar 1991. 6'3½". LHB, LB. Squad No 10. Debut (Essex) 2013; cap 2015. MCC 2016. 1000 runs (3); most – 1262 (2016). HS 255 v Derbys (Chelmsford) 2016. BB –. LO HS 99 v Glamorgan (Chelmsford) 2016 (RLC). T20 HS 38.

BUTTLEMAN, William Edward Lewis (Felsted S), b Chelmsford 20 Apr 2000. Younger brother of J.E.L.Buttleman (Durham UCCE 2007-09). RHB, WK, occ OB. Squad No 9. Debut (Essex) 2019. Essex 2nd XI debut 2017. HS 0 v Yorks (Leeds) 2019. LO HS 23 v Middx (Chelmsford) 2021 (RLC). T20 HS 56*.

COOK, Sir Alastair Nathan (Bedford S), b Gloucester 25 Dec 1984. 6'3". LHB, OB. Squad No 26. Debut (Essex) 2003; cap 2005; benefit 2014. MCC 2004-07, 2015. YC 2005. *Wisden* 2011. Knighted in 2019 New Year's honours list. **Tests**: 161 (2005-06 to 2018, 59 as captain); 1000 runs (5); most – 1364 (2015); HS 294 v I (Birmingham) 2011. Scored 60 and 104* v I (Nagpur) 2005-06 on debut, and 71 and 147 in final Test v I (Oval) 2018. Second, after M.A.Taylor, to score 1000 runs in the calendar year in Tests twice. Finished career after appearing in world record 159 consecutive Tests. BB 1-6 v I (Nottingham) 2014. **LOI**: 92 (2006 to 2014-15, 69 as captain); HS 137 v P (Abu Dhabi) 2011-12. **IT20**: 4 (2007 to 2009-10); HS 26 v SA (Centurion) 2009-10. F-c Tours (C=Captain): A 2006-07, 2010-11, 2013-14C, 2017-18; SA 2009-10, 2015-16C; WI 2005-06 (Eng A), 2008-09, 2014-15C; NZ 2007-08, 2012-13C, 2017-18; I 2005-06, 2008-09, 2012-13C, 2016-17C; SL 2004-05 (Eng A), 2007-08, 2011-12; B 2009-10C, 2016-17C; UAE 2011-12 (v P), 2015-16C (v P). 1000 runs (8+1); most – 1466 (2005). HS 294 (*see Tests*). CC HS 195 v Northants (Northampton) 2005. BB 3-13 v Northants (Chelmsford) 2005. LO HS 137 (*see LOI*). LO BB –. T20 HS 100*.

COOK, Samuel James (Great Baddow HS & SFC; Loughborough U), b Chelmsford 4 Aug 1997. RHB, RFM. Squad No 16. Loughborough MCCU 2016-17. Essex debut 2017; cap 2020. MCC 2019. Trent Rockets 2021 to date. F-c Tour (EL): SL 2022-23. HS 38 v Kent (Canterbury) 2022. 50 wkts (2); most – 58 (2021). BB 7-23 (12-65 match) v Kent (Canterbury) 2019. LO HS 6 v Middx (Chelmsford) 2019 (RLC) and 6 EL v South Africans (Worcester) 2022. LO BB 3-37 v Surrey (Oval) 2019 (RLC). T20 HS 18. T20 BB 4-15.

CRITCHLEY, Matthew James John (St Michael's HS, Chorley), b Preston, Lancs 13 Aug 1996. 6'2". RHB, LB. Squad No 20. Derbyshire 2015-21; cap 2019. Essex debut 2022. Big Bash: MR 2022-23. Welsh Fire 2021 to date. 1000 runs (1): 1060 (2021). HS 137* De v Northants (Derby) 2015. Ex HS 132 and Ex BB 4-114 v Kent (Chelmsford) 2022. BB 6-73 De v Leics (Leicester) 2020. LO HS 64* v Northants (Derby) 2019 (RLC). LO BB 4-48 v Northants (Derby) 2015 (RLC). T20 HS 80*. T20 BB 4-36.

DAS, Robin James (Brentwood S), b Leytonstone 27 Feb 2002. RHB. Squad No 47. Essex 2nd XI debut 2018. Awaiting f-c debut. LO HS 63 v Worcs (Worcester) 2022 (RLC). T20 HS 7.

NO**HARMER, Simon** Ross, b Pretoria, South Africa 10 Feb 1993. RHB, OB. Squad No 11. Eastern Province 2009-10 to 2011-12. Warriors 2010-11 to 2018-19. Essex debut 2017; cap 2018; captain 2020 to date (T20 only). Northerns 2021-22 to date. *Wisden* 2019. **Tests** (SA): 10 (2014-15 to 2022-23); HS 47 v A (Sydney) 2022-23; BB 4-61 v I (Mohali) 2015-16. F-c Tours (SA): E 2022; A 2014 (SA A), 2022-23; I 2015-16; B 2015; Ire 2012 (SA A). HS 102* v Surrey (Oval) 2018. 50 wkts (5+1); most – 86 (2019). BB 9-80 (12-202 match) v Derbys (Chelmsford) 2021. LO HS 44* v Surrey (Oval) 2017 (RLC). LO BB 4-42 Warriors v Lions (Potchefstroom) 2011-12. T20 HS 43. T20 BB 4-19.

KALLEY, Eshun Singh (Barking Abbey S), b Ilford 23 Nov 2001. RHB, RM. Squad No 30. Essex 2nd XI debut 2017. Hertfordshire 2021. Awaiting 1st XI debut.

KHUSHI, Feroze Isa Nazir (Kelmscott S, Walthamstow; Leyton SFC), b Whipps Cross 23 Jun 1999. RHB. OB. Squad No 23. Debut (Essex) 2020. Essex 2nd XI debut 2015. Suffolk 2019-21. HS 164 v Kent (Canterbury) 2022. LO HS 118 v Northants (Northampton) 2022 (RLC). T20 HS 67.

LAWRENCE, Daniel William (Trinity Catholic HS, Woodford Green), b Whipps Cross 12 Jul 1997. 6'2". RHB, LB. Squad No 28. Debut (Essex) 2015; cap 2017. MCC 2019. Big Bash: BH 2020-21. London Spirit 2021 to date. **Tests**: 11 (2020-21 to 2021-22); HS 91 v WI (Bridgetown) 2021-22; BB 1-0 v WI (North Sound) 2021-22. F-c Tours: A 2019-20 (EL); WI 2021-22; I 2020-21; SL 2020-21. 1000 runs (1): 1070 (2016). HS 161 v Surrey (Oval) 2015. RHB 3-98 v Kent (Chelmsford) 2022. LO HS 115 v Kent (Chelmsford) 2018 (RLC). LO BB 3-35 v Middx (Lord's) 2016 (RLC). T20 HS 86. T20 BB 4-20.

NIJJAR, Aron Stuart Singh (Ilford County HS), b Goodmayes 24 Sep 1994. LHB, SLA. Squad No 24. Debut (Essex) 2015. Cardiff MCCU 2017. Suffolk 2014. HS 53 v Northants (Chelmsford) 2015. BB 2-28 v Cambridge MCCU (Cambridge) 2019. CC BB 2-33 v Lancs (Chelmsford) 2015. LO HS 32* v Glos (Bristol) 2021 (RLC). LO BB 2-26 v Yorks (Chelmsford) 2021 (RLC). T20 HS 27*. T20 BB 3-22.

PEPPER, Michael-Kyle Steven (The Perse S), b Harlow 25 Jun 1998. Younger brother of C.A.Pepper (Cambridgeshire 2013-16). RHB, WK. Squad No 19. Debut (Essex) 2018. Northern Superchargers 2022. Essex 2nd XI debut 2017. Cambridgeshire 2014-19. HS 92 v Durham (Chester-le-St) 2021. LO HS 34 v Hants (Southampton) 2021 (RLC). T20 HS 86*.

PORTER, James Alexander (Oak Park HS, Newbury Park; Epping Forest C), b Leytonstone 25 May 1993. 5'11½". RHB, RFM. Squad No 44. Debut (Essex) 2014, taking a wkt with his 5th ball; cap 2015. *Wisden* 2017. F-c Tours (EL): WI 2017-18; I 2018-19; UAE 2018-19 (v P A). HS 34 v Glamorgan (Cardiff) 2015. 50 wkts (5); most – 85 (2017). BB 7-41 (11-98 match) v Worcs (Chelmsford) 2018. LO HS 10* v Derbys (Chelmsford) 2012 (RLC). LO BB 4-29 v Glamorgan (Chelmsford) 2018 (RLC). T20 HS 1*. T20 BB 4-20.

RICHARDS, Jamal Adrian (Norlington S; Waltham Forest C), b Edmonton, Middx 3 Mar 2004. RHB, RFM. Squad No 87. Awaiting f-c debut. Essex 2nd XI debut 2021. LO HS 46 v Derbys (Chelmsford) 2022 (RLC). LO BB 2-37 v Northants (Northampton) 2022 (RLC).

ROSSINGTON, Adam Matthew (Mill Hill S), b Edgware, Middx 5 May 1993. 5'11". RHB, WK, occ RM. Squad No 17. Middlesex 2010-14. Northamptonshire 2014-21; cap 2019; captain 2020-21. Essex debut 2022. London Spirit 2021 to date. HS 138* Nh v Sussex (Arundel) 2016. Ex HS 100 v Surrey (Oval) 2022. Won 2013 Walter Lawrence Trophy with 55-ball century M v Cambridge MCCU (Cambridge). LO HS 97 Nh v Notts (Nottingham) 2016 (RLC). T20 HS 95.

RYMELL, Joshua Sean (Ipswich S; Colchester SFC), b Ipswich, Suffolk 4 Apr 2001. RHB. Squad No 49. Debut (Essex) 2021. Essex 2nd XI debut 2017. Suffolk 2021. HS 14 v Glos (Chelmsford) 2021. LO HS 121 v Yorks (Chelmsford) 2021 (RLC). T20 HS 21.

NO**SAMS, Daniel** Richard, b Milperra, NSW, Australia 27 Oct 1992. RHB, LFM. Squad No 95. Canterbury 2017-18. New South Wales 2018-19 to date. Essex debut 2022 (T20 only). IPL: DC 2020-21; RCB 2021; MI 2022. Big Bash: SS 2017-18; ST 2018-19 to date. Trent Rockets 2022. **IT20** (A): 10 (2020-21 to 2022-23); HS 41 v NZ (Dunedin) 2020-21; BB 2-33 v I (Hyderabad) 2022-23. HS 88 Cant v ND (Rangiora) 2017-18. BB 4-55 Cant v Auckland (Auckland) 2017-18. LO HS 62 NSW v WA (Perth) 2018-19. LO BB 5-46 NSW v Vic (Melbourne) 2019-20. T20 HS 98*. T20 BB 4-14.

NO**SNATER, Shane** (St John's C, Harare), b Harare, Zimbabwe 24 Mar 1996. RHB, RM. Squad No 29. Netherlands 2016 to 2017-18. Southern Rocks 2020-21. Essex debut 2021; cap 2022. **LOI** (Neth): 4 (2018 to 2022); HS 17* v E (Amstelveen) 2022; BB 1-41 v Nepal (Amstelveen) 2018. **IT20** (Neth): 13 (2018 to 2019-20); HS 10 and BB 3-42 v Scotland (Dublin) 2019. HS 79* v Northants (Chelmsford) 2022. BB 7-98 v Notts (Nottingham) 2021. LO HS 64 v Hants (Southampton) 2022 (RLC). LO BB 5-29 v Kent (Chelmsford) 2022 (RLC). T20 HS 16*. T20 BB 3-42.

WALTER, Paul Ian (Billericay S), b Basildon 28 May 1994. LHB, LMF. Squad No 22. Debut (Essex) 2016. Manchester Originals 2022. HS 141 v Yorks (Chelmsford) 2022. BB 3-44 v Derbys (Derby) 2016. LO HS 50 v Glamorgan (Cardiff) 2021 (RLC). LO BB 4-37 v Middx (Chelmsford) 2017 (RLC). T20 HS 76. T20 BB 3-20.

WESTLEY, Thomas (Linton Village C; Hills Road SFC), b Cambridge 13 March 1989. 6'2". RHB, OB. Squad No 21. Debut (Essex) 2007; cap 2013; captain 2020 to date. MCC 2007, 2009, 2016, 2019. Durham MCCU 2009-11. Bloomfield 2014-15. Cambridgeshire 2005. **Tests**: 5 (2017); HS 59 v SA (Oval) 2017. F-c Tours: SL 2016-17 (EL); Nepal 2019-20 (MCC). 1000 runs (1): 1435 (2016). HS 254 v Worcs (Chelmsford) 2016. BB 4-55 DU v Durham (Durham) 2010. LO HS 134 v Surrey (Colchester) 2015. LO HS 134 v Middx (Radlett) 2018 (RLC). LO BB 4-60 v Northants (Northampton) 2014 (RLC). T20 HS 109*. T20 BB 2-27.

RELEASED/RETIRED

(Having made a County 1st XI appearance in 2022)

^{NQ}**ROELOFSEN, Grant** (King Edward VII S, Johannesburg), b Roodepoort, South Africa, 27 Jul 1996. RHB, WK. Gauteng 2016-17. KwaZulu-Natal Inland 2017-18 to 2019-20. Dolphins 2018-19 to 2020-21. KwaZulu-Natal Coastal 2021-22 to date. Essex 2022 (l-o only). HS 224* KZN Inland v Namibia (Pietermaritzburg) 2017-18. LO HS 147* Dolphins v Titans (Centurion) 2019-20. T20 HS 91.

^{NQ}**STEKETEE, Mark** Thomas, b Warwick, Queensland, Australia 17 Jan 1994. RHB, RFM. Queensland 2014-15 to date. Essex 2022. Big Bash: BH 2013-14 to date. HS 53 Q v NSW (Sydney) 2016-17. Ex HS 18 v Northants (Chelmsford) 2022. BB 7-44 (10-92 match) Q v SA (Adelaide) 2021-22. Ex BB 4-130 v Warwks (Birmingham) 2022. LO HS 35* Q v Tas (Brisbane, AB) 2022-23. LO BB 4-25 Q v Vic (Melbourne, St K) 2019-20. T20 HS 33. T20 BB 4-33.

TOOLE, Raymond Lawrence, b Johannesburg, South Africa 30 Oct 1997. LHB, LM. Central Districts 2019-20 to date. Essex 2022 (l-o only). HS 17* CD v Canterbury (Nelson) 2019-20. BB 6-54 CD v ND (Napier) 2021-22. LO HS 14 v Glamorgan (Chelmsford) 2022 (RLC). LO BB 2-19 v Yorks (Chelmsford) 2022 (RLC). T20 HS 0*. T20 BB 3-23.

WHEATER, Adam Jack Aubrey (Millfield S; Anglia Ruskin U), b Whipps Cross 13 Feb 1990. 5'6". RHB, WK. Essex 2008-22; cap 2020. Cambridge MCCU 2010. Matabeleland Tuskers 2010-11 to 2012-13. Badureliya Sports Club 2011-12. Northern Districts 2012-13. Hampshire 2013-16; cap 2016. HS 204* H v Warwks (Birmingham) 2016. Ex HS 164 v Northants (Chelmsford) 2011, sharing Ex record 6th wkt partnership of 253 with J.S.Foster. BB 1-86 v Leics (Leicester) 2012 – in contrived circumstances. LO HS 135 v Essex (Chelmsford) 2014 (RLC). T20 HS 78.

J.H.Plom left the staff without making a County 1st XI appearance in 2022.

ESSEX 2022

RESULTS SUMMARY

	Place	Won	Lost	Drew	NR
LV= Insurance County Champ (Div 1)	4th	7	3	4	
Royal London One-Day Cup (Group B)	6th	3	4		1
Vitality Blast (South Group)	QF	9	5		1

LV= INSURANCE COUNTY CHAMPIONSHIP AVERAGES
BATTING AND FIELDING

Cap		M	I	NO	HS	Runs	Avge	100	50	Ct/St
	B.M.J.Allison	3	5	2	69*	164	54.66	–	2	1
2005	A.N.Cook	14	25	2	145	966	42.00	4	2	20
	P.I.Walter	7	11	1	141	415	41.50	1	2	5
2015	N.L.J.Browne	14	26	3	234*	797	34.65	2	2	10
	A.P.Beard	3	4	2	33	59	29.50	–	–	2
2013	T.Westley	14	25	3	90	641	29.13	–	4	3
2018	S.R.Harmer	11	18	3	75*	396	26.40	–	4	9
	F.I.N.Khushi	6	10	–	164	250	25.00	1	–	2
	A.M.Rossington	12	18	1	100	424	24.94	1	2	28/4
2022	S.Snater	14	22	2	79*	463	23.15	–	4	2
	M.J.J.Critchley	13	20	–	132	446	22.30	1	1	9
2017	D.W.Lawrence	12	19	–	120	420	22.10	1	1	10
2020	A.J.A.Wheater	4	7	1	37	118	19.66	–	–	7
2020	S.J.Cook	12	20	7	38	179	13.76	–	–	5
	M.T.Steketee	5	8	2	18	56	9.33	–	–	–
	M.S.Pepper	2	4	–	7	13	3.25	–	–	6
2015	J.A.Porter	8	10	4	4*	9	1.50	–	–	–

BOWLING

	O	M	R	W	Avge	Best	5wI	10wM
B.M.J.Allison	65.1	18	161	12	13.41	5- 32	1	–
S.J.Cook	375.5	115	828	51	16.23	7- 33	1	1
S.R.Harmer	423	115	1220	59	20.67	8- 46	7	2
S.Snater	316	84	886	36	24.61	6- 10	2	–
J.A.Porter	190.1	37	587	19	30.89	4- 64	–	–
M.J.J.Critchley	198.1	25	749	19	39.42	4-114	–	–
M.T.Steketee	134.2	26	481	10	48.10	4-130	–	–
Also bowled:								
A.P.Beard	43	2	193	5	38.60	3- 52	–	–

A.N.Cook 1-0-8-0; D.W.Lawrence 45.3-4-216-3; P.I.Walter 28-2-97-1; T.Westley 2-0-19-0.

Essex played no first-class fixtures outside the County Championship in 2022. The First-Class Averages (pp 221–234) give the records of Essex players in all first-class county matches, with the exception of A.P.Beard and S.R.Harmer, whose first-class figures for Essex are as above.

ESSEX RECORDS

FIRST-CLASS CRICKET

Highest Total	For 761-6d		v	Leics	Chelmsford	1990
	V 803-4d		by	Kent	Brentwood	1934
Lowest Total	For 20		v	Lancashire	Chelmsford	2013
	V 14		by	Surrey	Chelmsford	1983
Highest Innings	For 343*	P.A.Perrin	v	Derbyshire	Chesterfield	1904
	V 332	W.H.Ashdown	for	Kent	Brentwood	1934

Highest Partnership for each Wicket

1st	373	N.L.J.Browne/A.N.Cook	v	Middlesex	Chelmsford	2017
2nd	403	G.A.Gooch/P.J.Prichard	v	Leics	Chelmsford	1990
3rd	347*	M.E.Waugh/N.Hussain	v	Lancashire	Ilford	1992
4th	314	Salim Malik/N.Hussain	v	Surrey	The Oval	1991
5th	339	J.C.Mickleburgh/J.S.Foster	v	Durham	Chester-le-St[2]	2010
6th	253	A.J.A.Wheater/J.S.Foster	v	Northants	Chelmsford	2011
7th	261	J.W.H.T.Douglas/J.R.Freeman	v	Lancashire	Leyton	1914
8th	263	D.R.Wilcox/R.M.Taylor	v	Warwicks	Southend	1946
9th	251	J.W.H.T.Douglas/S.N.Hare	v	Derbyshire	Leyton	1921
10th	218	F.H.Vigar/T.P.B.Smith	v	Derbyshire	Chesterfield	1947

Best Bowling	For 10- 32	H.Pickett	v	Leics	Leyton	1895
(Innings)	V 10- 40	E.G.Dennett	for	Glos	Bristol	1906
Best Bowling	For 17-119	W.Mead	v	Hampshire	Southampton[1]	1895
(Match)	V 17- 56	C.W.L.Parker	for	Glos	Gloucester	1925

Most Runs – Season	2559	G.A.Gooch	(av 67.34)	1984
Most Runs – Career	30701	G.A.Gooch	(av 51.77)	1973-97
Most 100s – Season	9	J.O'Connor		1929, 1934
	9	D.J.Insole		1955
Most 100s – Career	94	G.A.Gooch		1973-97
Most Wkts – Season	172	T.P.B Smith	(av 27.13)	1947
Most Wkts – Career	1610	T.P.B Smith	(av 26.68)	1929-51
Most Career W-K Dismissals	1231	B.Taylor	(1040 ct; 191 st)	1949-73
Most Career Catches in the Field	519	K.W.R.Fletcher		1962-88

LIMITED-OVERS CRICKET

Highest Total	50ov	391-5	v	Surrey	The Oval	2008
	40ov	368-7	v	Scotland	Chelmsford	2013
	T20	254-5	v	Glamorgan	Chelmsford	2022
Lowest Total	50ov	57	v	Lancashire	Lord's	1996
	40ov	69	v	Derbyshire	Chesterfield	1974
	T20	74	v	Middlesex	Chelmsford	2013
Highest Innings	50ov	201*	R.S.Bopara	v	Leics	Leicester	2008
	40ov	180	R.N.ten Doeschate	v	Scotland	Chelmsford	2013
	T20	152*	G.R.Napier	v	Sussex	Chelmsford	2008
Best Bowling	50ov	6-42	L.M.Benkenstein	v	Glamorgan	Chelmsford	2022
	40ov	8-26	K.D.Boyce	v	Lancashire	Manchester	1971
	T20	6-16	T.G.Southee	v	Glamorgan	Chelmsford	2011

GLAMORGAN

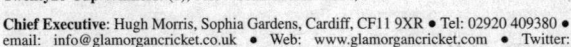

Formation of Present Club: 6 July 1888
Inaugural First-Class Match: 1921
Colours: Blue and Gold
Badge: Gold Daffodil
County Champions: (3) 1948, 1969, 1997
Pro 40/National League (Div 1) Winners: (2) 2002, 2004
Sunday League Winners: (1) 1993
Royal London One-Day Cup Winners: (1) 2021

GLAMORGAN

Twenty20 Cup Winners: (0); best – Semi-Finalist 2004, 2017

Chief Executive: Hugh Morris, Sophia Gardens, Cardiff, CF11 9XR ● Tel: 02920 409380 ● email: info@glamorgancricket.co.uk ● Web: www.glamorgancricket.com ● Twitter: @GlamCricket (81,287 followers)

Director of Cricket: Mark Wallace. **Head Coach**: Matthew Maynard (red ball). **Asst Coaches**: David Harrison, Adrian Shaw and Steve Watkin. **Captain**: D.L.Lloyd. **Overseas Players**: C.A.Ingram, M.Labuschagne and M.G.Neser. **2023 Testimonial**: None. **Head Groundsman**: Robin Saxton. **Scorer**: Andrew K.Hignell. ‡ New registration. ᴺᴼ Not qualified for England.

BEVAN, Thomas Rhys (Millfield S), b Cardiff 9 Sep 1999. RHB, OB. Squad No 13. Debut (Glamorgan) 2022. Glamorgan 2nd XI debut 2018. Wales Minor Cos 2017 to date. HS 48 v Derbys (Cardiff) 2022. LO HS 134 v Hants (Neath) 2022 (RLC). T20 HS 21.

BYROM, Edward James (St John's C, Harare; King's C, Taunton), b Harare, Zimbabwe 17 Jun 1997. 5'11". LHB, OB. Squad No 97. Irish passport. Somerset 2017-21. Rising Stars 2017-18. Glamorgan debut 2021. Mid West Rhinos 2022-23. HS 176 v Sussex (Cardiff) 2022, sharing Gm record 2nd wkt partnership of 328 with C.A.Ingram. BB 2-64 v Surrey (Oval) 2021. LO HS 71* MWR v Tuskers (Bulawayo) 2022-23. T20 HS 54*.

CARLSON, Kiran Shah (Whitchurch HS; Cardiff U), b Cardiff 16 May 1998. 5'8". RHB, OB. Squad No 5. Debut (Glamorgan) 2016; cap 2021; l-o captain 2022. Cardiff MCCU 2019. Mid West Rhinos 2022-23. Glamorgan 2nd XI debut 2015. Wales MC 2014. HS 191 v Glos (Cardiff) 2017. BB 5-28 v Northants (Northampton) 2016 – on debut, aged 18y 119d (also scored hundred in same match). LO HS 82 v Durham (Nottingham) 2021 (RLC). LO BB 4-41 v Northants (Northampton) 2022 (RLC). T20 HS 58.

COOKE, Christopher Barry (Bishops S, Cape Town; U of Cape Town), b Johannesburg, South Africa 30 May 1986. 5'11". RHB, WK, occ RM. Squad No 46. W Province 2009-10. Glamorgan debut 2013; cap 2016; captain 2019-21. Birmingham Phoenix 2021. HS 205* v Surrey (Oval) 2021. LO HS 161 v Glos (Bristol) 2019 (RLC). T20 HS 72.

DOUTHWAITE, Daniel Alexander (Reed's S, Cobham; Cardiff Met U), b Kingston-upon-Thames, Surrey 8 Feb 1997. RHB, RMF. Squad No 88. Cardiff MCCU 2019. Glamorgan debut 2019. Warwickshire 2018 (l-o only). Manchester Originals 2021. HS 100* CfU v Sussex (Hove) 2019. Gm HS 96 v Durham (Chester-le-St) 2021. BB 4-48 v Derbys (Derby) 2019. LO HS 52* v Sussex (Hove) 2019 (RLC). LO BB 3-43 Wa v West Indies A (Birmingham) 2018. T20 HS 53. T20 BB 3-28.

GORVIN, Andrew William (Portsmouth HS; Cardiff Met U), b Winchester, Hants 10 May 1997. RHB, RM. Squad No 11. Wales MC 2019 to date. Debut (Glamorgan) 2022. HS 23 v Leics (Cardiff) 2022. BB 2-35 v Sussex (Cardiff) 2022. LO HS 12* v Somerset (Taunton) 2021 (RLC). LO BB 2-41 v Hants (Neath) 2022 (RLC).

HARRIS, James Alexander Russell (Pontardulais CS; Gorseinon C), b Morriston, Swansea 16 May 1990. 6'0". RHB, RMF. Squad No 9. Debut (Glamorgan) 2007, aged 16y 351d – youngest Gm player to take a f-c wicket; cap 2010. Middlesex 2013-21; cap 2015. Kent 2017 (on loan). MCC 2016. Wales MC 2005-08. F-c Tours (EL): WI 2010-11; SL 2013-14. HS 87* v Notts (Swansea) 2007. 50 wkts (3); most – 73 (2015). BB 9-34 (13-103 match) M v Durham (Lord's) 2015 – record innings and match analysis v Durham. Gm BB 7-66 (12-118 match) v Glos (Bristol) 2007 – youngest (17y 3d) to take 10 wickets in any CC match. LO HS 117 M v Lancs (Lord's) 2019 (RLC). LO BB 4-38 M v Glamorgan (Lord's) 2015 (RLC). T20 HS 18. T20 BB 4-23.

HORTON, Alex Jack (St Edward's, Oxford), b Newport, Monmouths 7 Jan 2004. RHB, WK. Squad No 37. Glamorgan 2nd XI debut 2019. Awaiting f-c debut. T20 HS 1*.

NO**INGRAM, Colin** Alexander, b Port Elizabeth, South Africa 3 Jul 1985. LHB, LB. Squad No 41. Free State 2004-05 to 2005-06. Eastern Province 2005-06 to 2008-09. Warriors 2006-07 to 2016-17. Somerset 2014. Glamorgan debut 2015; cap 2017; captain 2018-19 (T20 only). IPL: DD 2011. Big Bash: AS 2017-18 to 2018-19. HH 2020-21. Oval Invincibles 2021. **LOI** (SA): 31 (2010-11 to 2013-14); HS 124 v Z (Bloemfontein) 2010-11 – on debut; BB –. **IT20** (SA): 9 (2010-11 to 2011-12); HS 78 v I (Johannesburg) 2011-12. HS 190 EP v KZN (Port Elizabeth) 2008-09. Gm HS 178 v Sussex (Cardiff) 2022, sharing Gm record 2nd wkt partnership of 328 with E.J.Byrom. BB 4-16 EP v Boland (Pt Elizabeth) 2005-06. Gm BB 3-90 v Essex (Chelmsford) 2015. LO HS 155 v Kent (Cardiff) 2022 (RLC). LO BB 4-39 v Middx (Radlett) 2017 (RLC). T20 HS 127*. T20 BB 4-32.

KELLAWAY, Benjamin Ian (Chepstow CS; Clifton C; Cardiff U), b Newport 5 Jan 2004. RHB, OB, occ WK. Awaiting 1st XI debut. Glamorgan 2nd XI debut 2021. Wales MC 2019.

NO**LABUSCHAGNE, Marnus** b Klerksdorp, South Africa 22 Jun 1994. RHB, LB. Squad No 99. Queensland 2014-15 to date. Glamorgan debut 2019; cap 2019. Big Bash: BH 2016-17 to date. *Wisden* 2019. **Tests** (A): 36 (2018-19 to 2022-23); 1000 runs (1): 1104 (2019); HS 215 v NZ (Sydney) 2019-20; BB 3-45 v P (Abu Dhabi) 2018-19. **LOI** (A): 27 (2019-20 to 2022-23); HS 108 v SA (Potchefstroom) 2019-20; BB 2-9 v SL (Pallekelle) 2022. F-c Tours (A): E 2019; I 2018-19 (Aus A), 2022-23; P 2021-22; SL 2022; UAE 2018-19 (v P). 1000 runs (1+2); most – 1530 (2019). HS 215 (*see* Tests). Gm HS 182 v Sussex (Hove) 2019. BB 3-35 v Durham (Chester-le-St) 2022. LO HS 135 Q v SA (Brisbane) 2019-20. LO BB 3-46 v Somerset (Cardiff) 2019 (RLC). T20 HS 93*. T20 BB 3-13.

LLOYD, David Liam (Darland HS; Shrewsbury S), b St Asaph, Denbighs 15 May 1992. 5'9". RHB, RM. Squad No 73. Debut (Glamorgan) 2012; cap 2019; captain 2022 to date. Wales MC 2010-11. Welsh Fire 2021. HS 313* v Derbys (Cardiff) 2022. BB 4-11 v Kent (Cardiff) 2021. LO HS 92 v Middx (Cardiff) 2018 (RLC). LO BB 5-53 v Kent (Swansea) 2017 (RLC). T20 HS 97*. T20 BB 2-13.

McILROY, Jamie Peter (Builth Wells HS), b Hereford 19 Jun 1994. RHB, LFM. Squad No 35. Debut (Glamorgan) 2021. HS 0. BB 1-12 v Yorks (Leeds) 2021. LO HS 10* v Yorks (Cardiff) 2022 (RLC). LO BB 2-13 v Derbys (Derby) 2022 (RLC). T20 HS –. T20 BB 3-31.

MORRIS, Benjamin James (King Henry VIII S; Cardiff U) b Abergavenny 4 Nov 2003. RHB, RM. Awaiting 1st XI debut. Glamorgan 2nd XI debut 2021. Wales NC 2021-22.

NO**NESER, Michael** Gertges, b Pretoria, South Africa 29 Mar 1990. 6'0". RHB, RMF. Squad No 30. Queensland 2010-11 to date. Glamorgan debut/cap 2022. IPL: KXIP 2013. Big Bash: BH 2011-12 to date. AS 2012-13 to 2020-21. **Tests** (A): 2 (2021-22 to 2022-23); HS 35 v E (Adelaide); BB 3-22 v WI (Adelaide) 2022-23; took wicket of H.Hameed with 2nd ball in Test cricket. **LOI** (A): 2 (2018); HS 6 and BB 2-46 v E (Oval) 2018. F-c Tours (Aus A): E 2019; I 2018-19; UAE (v P) 2018-19. HS 136 Q v NSW (Sydney, DO) 2022-23. Gm HS 62 v Durham (Chester-le-St) 2022. BB 6-57 Q v Tas (Hobart) 2017-18. Gm BB 5-39 v Yorks (Cardiff) 2021. LO HS 122 Q v WA (Sydney, DO) 2017-18. LO BB 4-41 Q v WA (Perth) 2022-23. T20 HS 48*. T20 BB 4-25.

NORTHEAST, Sam Alexander (Harrow S), b Ashford, Kent 16 Oct 1989. 5'11". RHB, LB. Squad No 16. Kent 2007-17; cap 2012; captain 2016-17. Hampshire 2018-21; cap 2019. Yorkshire 2021 (on loan). Nottinghamshire 2021 (on loan). Glamorgan debut/cap 2022. MCC 2013, 2018. 1000 runs (5); most – 1402 (2016). HS 410* v Leics (Leicester) 2022 – county record score and the 3rd highest in CC history, sharing Gm record 6th wkt partnership of 461* with C.B.Cooke. BB 1-60 K v Glos (Cheltenham) 2013. LO HS 177* v Worcs (Worcester) 2022 (RLC). T20 HS 114.

PHILLIPS, Tegid Daniel Canning (Melingriffith PS; Ysgol Glantaf; Cardiff U), b Cardiff 21 Feb 2002. RHB, OB. Squad No 23. Glamorgan 2nd XI debut 2021. Wales NC 2019-22. Awaiting 1st XI debut.

PODMORE, Harry William (Twyford HS), b Hammersmith, London 23 Jul 1994. 6'3". RHB, RMF. Squad No 1. Debut (Glamorgan) 2016 (on loan). Middlesex 2016 to 2016-17. Derbyshire 2017 (on loan). Kent 2018-22; cap 2019. HS 66* De v Sussex (Hove) 2017. Gm HS 16* v Kent (Canterbury) 2016. 50 wkts (1): 54 (2019). BB 6-36 K v Middx (Canterbury) 2018. Gm BB 3-59 v Glos (Bristol) 2016. LO HS 40 v Hants (Canterbury) 2019 (RLC). LO BB 4-57 v Notts (Nottingham) 2018 (RLC). T20 HS 9. T20 BB 3-13.

ROOT, William ('Billy') Thomas (Worksop C; Leeds Beckett U), b Sheffield, Yorks 5 Aug 1992. Younger brother of J.E.Root (see *YORKSHIRE*). LHB, OB. Squad No 7. Leeds/Bradford MCCU 2015-16. Nottinghamshire 2015-18. Glamorgan debut 2019; cap 2021. Suffolk 2014. HS 229 v Northants (Northampton) 2019. BB 3-29 Nt v Sussex (Hove) 2017. Gm BB 2-63 v Northants (Cardiff) 2019. LO HS 113* v Surrey (Cardiff) 2019 (RLC) and 113* v Worcs (Worcester) 2022 (RLC). LO BB 2-36 v Middx (Lord's) 2019 (RLC). T20 HS 41*. T20 BB –.

SALTER, Andrew Graham (Milford Haven SFC; Cardiff Met U), b Haverfordwest 1 Jun 1993. 5'9". RHB, OB. Squad No 21. Cardiff MCCU 2012-14. Glamorgan debut 2013; cap 2022. Wales MC 2010-11. HS 90 v Durham (Chester-le-St) 2021. BB 7-45 v Durham (Cardiff) 2022. LO HS 51 v Pakistan A (Newport) 2016. LO BB 3-37 v Surrey (Cardiff) 2021 (RLC). T20 HS 39*. T20 BB 4-12.

SISODIYA, Prem (Clifton C; Cardiff Met U), b Cardiff 21 Sep 1998. RHB, SLA. Squad No 32. Debut (Glamorgan) 2018. Cardiff MCCU 2019. Wales MC 2017-19. HS 38 and CC BB 3-54 v Derbys (Swansea) 2018. BB 4-79 CfU v Somerset (Taunton) 2019. LO HS 7 v Lancs (Neath) 2022 (RLC). LO BB 3-76 v Worcs (Worcester) 2022 (RLC). T20 HS 9*. T20 BB 3-26.

TAYLOR, Callum Zinzan (The Southport S), b Newport, Monmouths 19 Jun 1998. RHB, OB. Squad No 4. Debut (Glamorgan) 2020, scoring 106 v Northants (Northampton). Glamorgan 2nd XI debut 2017. Wales MC 2017-19. HS 106 (*see above*). BB 2-16 v Yorks (Leeds) 2020. LO HS 36 v Northants (Northampton) 2021 (RLC). LO BB 1-6 v Somerset (Taunton) 2021 (RLC). T20 HS 23. T20 BB 2-9.

^NO^**van der GUGTEN, Timm**, b Hornsby, Sydney, Australia 25 Feb 1991. 6'1½". RHB, RFM. Squad No 64. New South Wales 2011-12. Netherlands 2012 to date. Glamorgan debut 2016; cap 2018. Big Bash: HH 2014-15. Trent Rockets 2021. Birmingham Phoenix 2022. **LOI** (Neth): 8 (2011-12 to 2021-22); HS 49 v Ire (Utrecht) 2021; BB 5-24 v Canada (King City, NW) 2013. **IT20** (Neth): 42 (2011-12 to 2022-23); HS 40* v PNG (Dubai, ICCA) 2019-20; BB 3-9 v Singapore (Dubai, ICCA) 2019-20. HS 85* v Yorks (Leeds) 2021. 50 wkts (1): 56 (2016). BB 7-42 v Kent (Cardiff) 2018. LO HS 49 (*see LOI*). LO BB 5-24 (*see LOI*). T20 HS 40*. T20 BB 5-21.

ZAIN-UL-HASSAN (Pedmore Tech C, Stourbridge), b Islamabad, Pakistan 28 Oct 2000. LHB, RM. Worcestershire 2nd XI 2017-21. Gloucestershire 2nd XI 2021. Surrey 2nd XI 2022. Northamptonshire 2nd XI 2022. Kent 2nd XI 2022. Glamorgan 2nd XI debut 2022. Herefordshire 2021. Awaiting f-c debut. LO HS 9* Wo v West Indies A (Worcester) 2018. LO BB –.

RELEASED/RETIRED

(Having made a County 1st XI appearance in 2022)

COOKE, Joseph Michael (Durham U), b Hemel Hempstead, Herts 30 May 1997. LHB, RMF. Durham MCCU 2017-18. Glamorgan 2020-21. Hertfordshire 2014-18. HS 68 v Surrey (Oval) 2020. BB 1-26 DU v Warwks (Birmingham) 2018. LO HS 66* and LO BB 5-61 v Essex (Cardiff) 2021 (RLC). T20 HS 10*.

CULLEN, Thomas Nicholas (Aquinas C, Stockport; Cardiff Met U), b Perth, Australia 4 Jan 1992. RHB, WK. Cardiff MCCU 2015-17. Glamorgan 2017-22. HS 63 v Northants (Northampton) 2019. LO HS 80* v Kent (Cardiff) 2022 (RLC). T20 HS 5.

NQ**GILL, Shubman**, b Firozpur, India 8 Sep 1999. RHB, OB. Punjab 2017-18 to date. Glamorgan 2022. IPL: KKR 2018-21; GT 2022. **Tests** (I): 14 (2020-21 to 2022-23); HS 110 v B (Chittagong) 2022-23. **LOI** (I): 21 (2018-19 to 2022-23); HS 208 v NZ (Hyderabad) 2022-23. F-c Tours (I): E 2021, 2022; A 2020-21; WI 2019 (IA); NZ 2018-19 (IA), 2019-20 (IA); B 2022-23. HS 268 Punjab v Tamil Nadu (Mohali) 2018-19. Gm HS 119 v Sussex (Hove) 2022. BB –. LO HS 208 (see *LOI*). LO BB –. T20 HS 126*.

HOGAN, M.G. – see KENT.

NQ**PATEL, Ajaz** Yunus, b Bombay, India 21 Oct 1988. LHB, SLA. Central Districts 2012-13 to date. Yorkshire 2019. Glamorgan 2022. **Tests** (NZ): 14 (2018-19 to 2022-23); HS 35 v P (Karachi) 2022-23; BB 10-119 (14-225 match) v I (Mumbai) 2021-22 – third best analysis in all Test cricket. **IT20** (NZ): 7 (2018-19 to 2021); HS 4 v B (Mirpur) 2021; BB 4-16 v B (Mirpur) 2021 – separate matches. F-c Tours (NZ): E 2021, 2022; I 2021-22; P 2022-23; SL 2019; UAE (v P) 2018-19. HS 52 CD v Wellington (Napier) 2020-21. CC HS 51* v Sussex (Hove) 2022. BB 10-119 (see *Tests*). CC BB 5-68 v Derbys (Cardiff) 2022. LO HS 45 CD v ND (Hamilton) 2020-21. LO BB 3-31 CD v Auckland (New Plymouth) 2022-23. T20 HS 13. T20 BB 4-16.

NQ**SMITH, Ruaidhri** Alexander James (Llandaff Cathedral S; Shrewsbury S; Bristol U), b Glasgow, Scotland 5 Aug 1994. 6'1". RHB, RM. Glamorgan 2013-21. Scotland 2017. Wales MC 2010-16. **LOI** (Scot): 2 (2016); HS 10 and BB 1-34 v Afg (Edinburgh) 2016. **IT20** (Scot): 2 (2018-19); HS 9* v Netherlands (Al Amerat) 2018-19; BB –. HS 57* v Glos (Bristol) 2014. BB 5-87 v Durham (Cardiff) 2018. LO HS 14 v Hants (Swansea) 2018 (RLC). LO BB 4-7 Scot v Oman (Al Amerat) 2018-19. T20 HS 22*. T20 BB 4-6.

WEIGHELL, William James (Stokesley S), b Middlesbrough, Yorks 28 Jan 1994. 6'4". LHB, RMF. Durham 2015-19. Leicestershire 2020. Glamorgan 2021-22. Northumberland 2012-15. HS 84 Du v Kent (Chester-le-St) 2018. Gm HS 45 and Gm BB 2-25 v Notts (Nottingham) 2022. BB 7-32 Du v Leics (Chester-le-St) 2018. LO HS 33 v Yorks (Cardiff) 2022 (RLC). LO BB 5-57 Du v Warwks (Birmingham) 2017 (RLC). T20 HS 51. T20 BB 3-28.

L.J.Carey, S.J.Pearce and S.J.Reingold left the staff without making a County 1st XI appearance in 2022.

GLAMORGAN 2022

RESULTS SUMMARY

	Place	Won	Lost	Drew	NR
LV= Insurance County Champ (Div 2)	3rd	6	3	5	
Royal London One-Day Cup (Group B)	4th	4	4		
Vitality Blast (South Group)	6th	5	7		2

LV= INSURANCE COUNTY CHAMPIONSHIP AVERAGES
BATTING AND FIELDING

Cap		M	I	NO	HS	Runs	Avge	100	50	Ct/St
2017	C.A.Ingram	5	9	–	178	596	66.22	3	1	4
	S.Gill	3	4	–	119	244	61.00	1	1	3
2022	S.A.Northeast	14	24	4	410*	1189	59.45	2	5	13
2016	C.B.Cooke	13	21	6	191*	840	56.00	2	5	51/5
	E.J.Byrom	8	13	1	176	588	49.00	2	2	3
2019	M.Labuschagne	5	10	1	130	377	41.88	1	2	4
2018	T.van der Gugten	9	12	7	62	203	40.60	–	1	1
2019	D.L.Lloyd	14	25	2	313*	899	39.08	1	5	9
	A.Y.Patel	4	4	1	51*	106	35.33	–	1	4
2021	W.T.Root	9	14	1	99*	418	32.15	–	4	3
2021	M.G.Neser	9	12	1	62	277	25.18	–	1	4
	W.J.Weighell	4	4	–	45	95	23.75	–	–	1
2021	K.S.Carlson	12	22	1	91	491	23.38	–	3	6
2022	A.G.Salter	12	17	2	45*	284	18.93	–	1	4
2010	J.A.R.Harris	11	13	3	34	162	16.20	–	–	1
	C.Z.Taylor	3	5	1	23*	57	14.25	–	–	–
	T.N.Cullen	2	4	–	21	47	11.75	–	–	8
2013	M.G.Hogan	14	13	4	19*	91	10.11	–	–	3
	A.W.Gorvin	3	4	–	23	27	6.75	–	–	2

Also batted: T.R.Bevan (1 match) 48.

BOWLING

	O	M	R	W	Avge	Best	5wI	10wM
M.G.Neser	328	64	931	37	25.16	4-50	–	–
M.G.Hogan	418.4	78	1235	45	27.44	4-43	–	–
M.Labuschagne	79.5	8	287	10	28.70	3-35	–	–
T.van der Gugten	241	46	708	24	29.50	4-60	–	–
A.G.Salter	390.3	62	1083	33	32.81	7-45	2	–
A.Y.Patel	169	37	519	14	37.07	5-68	1	–
J.A.R.Harris	317	46	1181	31	38.09	5-90	1	–

Also bowled:

	O	M	R	W	Avge	Best	5wI	10wM
A.W.Gorvin	66	14	187	5	37.40	2-35		
W.J.Weighell	100.5	18	346	6	57.66	2-25		
D.L.Lloyd	184	28	708	9	78.66	2-36		

T.R.Bevan 2-0-6-0; E.J.Byrom 3-1-12-0; K.S.Carlson 21.4-2-65-1; C.B.Cooke 4-0-15-0; C.A.Ingram 38-3-142-4; S.A.Northeast 3-0-10-0; W.T.Root 4-0-26-0; C.Z.Taylor 20-1-71-0.

Glamorgan played no first-class fixtures outside the County Championship in 2022. The First-Class Averages (pp 221–234) give the records of Glamorgan players in all first-class county matches, with the exception of S.Gill and A.Y.Patel, whose first-class figures for Glamorgan are as above.

GLAMORGAN RECORDS

FIRST-CLASS CRICKET

Highest Total	For 795-5d		v	Leics	Leicester	2022
	V 750		by	Northants	Cardiff	2019
Lowest Total	For 22		v	Lancashire	Liverpool	1924
	V 33		by	Leics	Ebbw Vale	1965
Highest Innings	For 410*	S.A.Northeast	v	Leics	Leicester	2022
	V 322*	M.B.Loye	for	Northants	Northampton	1998

Highest Partnership for each Wicket

1st	374	M.T.G.Elliott/S.P.James	v	Sussex	Colwyn Bay	2000
2nd	328	E.J.Byrom/C.A.Ingram	v	Sussex	Cardiff	2022
3rd	313	D.E.Davies/W.E.Jones	v	Essex	Brentwood	1948
4th	425*	A.Dale/I.V.A.Richards	v	Middlesex	Cardiff	1993
5th	307*	K.S.Carlson/C.B.Cooke	v	Northants	Cardiff	2021
6th	461*	S.A.Northeast/C.B.Cooke	v	Leics	Leicester	2022
7th	211	P.A.Cottey/O.D.Gibson	v	Leics	Swansea	1996
8th	202	D.Davies/J.J.Hills	v	Sussex	Eastbourne	1928
9th	203*	J.J.Hills/J.C.Clay	v	Worcs	Swansea	1929
10th	143	T.Davies/S.A.B.Daniels	v	Glos	Swansea	1982

Best Bowling	For 10- 51	J.Mercer	v	Worcs	Worcester	1936
(Innings)	V 10- 18	G.Geary	for	Leics	Pontypridd	1929
Best Bowling	For 17-212	J.C.Clay	v	Worcs	Swansea	1937
(Match)	V 16- 96	G.Geary	for	Leics	Pontypridd	1929

Most Runs – Season	2276	H.Morris	(av 55.51)		1990
Most Runs – Career	34056	A.Jones	(av 33.03)		1957-83
Most 100s – Season	10	H.Morris			1990
Most 100s – Career	54	M.P.Maynard			1985-2005
Most Wkts – Season	176	J.C.Clay	(av 17.34)		1937
Most Wkts – Career	2174	D.J.Shepherd	(av 20.95)		1950-72
Most Career W-K Dismissals	933	E.W.Jones	(840 ct; 93 st)		1961-83
Most Career Catches in the Field	656	P.M.Walker			1956-72

LIMITED-OVERS CRICKET

Highest Total	50ov	429	v	Surrey	The Oval	2002
	40ov	328-4	v	Lancashire	Colwyn Bay	2011
	T20	240-3	v	Surrey	The Oval	2015
Lowest Total	50ov	68	v	Lancashire	Manchester	1973
	40ov	42	v	Derbyshire	Swansea	1979
	T20	44	v	Surrey	The Oval	2019
Highest Innings	50ov	177*	S.A.Northeast	v	Worcs	Worcester	2022
	40ov	155*	J.H.Kallis	v	Surrey	Pontypridd	1999
	T20	116*	I.J.Thomas	v	Somerset	Taunton	2004
Best Bowling	50ov	6-20	S.D.Thomas	v	Comb Univs	Cardiff	1995
	40ov	7-16	S.D.Thomas	v	Surrey	Swansea	1998
	T20	5-14	G.G.Wagg	v	Worcs	Worcester	2013

GLOUCESTERSHIRE

Formation of Present Club: 1871
Inaugural First-Class Match: 1870
Colours: Blue, Gold, Brown, Silver, Green and Red
Badge: Coat of Arms of the City and County of Bristol
County Champions (since 1890): (0); best – 2nd 1930, 1931, 1947, 1959, 1969, 1986
Gillette/NatWest/C&G Trophy Winners: (5) 1973, 1999, 2000, 2003, 2004
Benson and Hedges Cup Winners: (3) 1977, 1999, 2000
Pro 40/National League (Div 1) Winners: (1) 2000
Royal London One-Day Cup Winners: (1) 2015
Twenty20 Cup Winners: (0); best – Finalist 2007

Chief Executive: Will Brown, Seat Unique Stadium, Nevil Road, Bristol BS7 9EJ ● Tel: 0117 910 8000 ● Email: reception@gloscc.co.uk ● Web: www.gloscricket.co.uk ● Twitter: @Gloscricket (79,327 followers)

Head Coach: Dale Benkenstein. **Assistant Coach**: William Porterfield. **Performance Director**: Steve Snell. **Bowling Coach**: Robbie Joseph. **Captain**: G.L.van Buuren (f-c) and J.M.R.Taylor (white ball). **Overseas Players**: M.S.Harris and Zafar Gohar. **2023 Testimonial**: None. **Head Groundsman**: Sean Williams. **Scorer**: Adrian Bull. ‡ New registration. NQ Not qualified for England.

Gloucestershire revised their capping policy in 2004 and now award players with their County Caps when they make their first-class debut.

BRACEY, James Robert (Filton CS), b Bristol 3 May 1997. Younger brother of S.N.Bracey (Cardiff MCCU 2014-15). 6'1". LHB, WK, occ RM. Squad No 25. Debut (Gloucestershire) 2016; cap 2016. Loughborough MCCU 2017-18. **Tests**: 2 (2021): HS 8 v NZ (Birmingham) 2021. F-c Tour (EL): A 2019-20. HS 177 v Yorks (Bristol) 2022. BB –. LO HS 113* and LO BB 1-23 v Essex (Chelmsford) 2019 (RLC). T20 HS 70.

CHARLESWORTH, Ben Geoffrey (St Edward's S), b Oxford 19 Nov 2000. Elder brother of L.A.Charlesworth (*see below*); son of G.M.Charlesworth (Griqualand W and Cambridge U 1989-90 to 1993). 6'2½". LHB, RM/OB. Squad No 64. Debut (Gloucestershire) 2018; cap 2018. Gloucestershire 2nd XI debut 2016. Oxfordshire 2016. England U19 2018 to 2018-19. HS 77* and BB 3-25 v Middx (Bristol) 2018. HS 77* v Northants (Bristol) 2019. LO HS 99* v Northants (Bristol) 2021 (RLC). LO BB –.

CHARLESWORTH, Luke Alexander (St Edward's S; Exeter U), b Oxford 4 Apr 2003. Younger brother of B.G.Charlesworth (*see above*); son of G.M.Charlesworth (Griqualand W and Cambridge U 1989-90 to 1993). 6'2". RHB, RM. Squad No 19. Awaiting f-c debut. Gloucestershire 2nd XI debut 2019. HS 1. T20 BB 1-32.

DALE, Ajeet Singh (Wellington C), b Slough, Berks 3 Jul 2000. 6'1". RHB, RFM. Squad No 39. Hampshire 2020. Gloucestershire debut/cap 2022. Hampshire 2nd XI 2018-21. Gloucestershire 2nd XI debut 2021. HS 36 v Hants (Southampton) 2022. BB 4-72 v Yorks (Bristol) 2022. LO HS –. LO BB 2-42 v Middx (Radlett) 2022 (RLC). T20 HS 0. T20 BB –.

‡De LANGE, Marchant, b Tzaneen, South Africa 13 Oct 1990. RHB, RF. Qualified as a domestic player in 2023. Squad No 90. Easterns 2010-11 to 2015-16. Titans 2010-11 to 2015-16. Knights 2016-17 to 2017-18. Free State 2016-17. Glamorgan 2017-20; cap 2019. Somerset 2021-22. IPL: KKR 2012; MI 2014-15. Trent Rockets 2021. **Tests** (SA): 2 (2011-12); HS 9 and BB 7-81 v SL (Durban) 2011-12 – on debut. **LOI** (SA): 4 (2011-12 to 2015-16); HS – ; BB 4-46 v NZ (Auckland) 2011-12. **IT20** (SA): 6 (2011-12 to 2015-16); HS – ; BB 2-26 v WI (Durban 2014-15. F-c Tours (SA): A 2014 (SA A); NZ 2011-12. HS 113 Gm v Northants (Northampton) 2020. BB 7-23 Knights v Titans (Centurion) 2016-17. CC BB 5-62 Gm v Glos (Bristol) 2018. LO HS 58* Gm v Surrey (Cardiff) 2019 (RLC). LO BB 5-49 Gm v Hants (Southampton) 2017 (RLC). T20 HS 28*. T20 BB 5-20.

DENT, Christopher David James (Backwell CS; Alton C), b Bristol 20 Jan 1991. 5'9". LHB, WK, occ SLA. Squad No 15. Debut (Gloucestershire) 2010; cap 2010; captain 2018-21. 1000 runs (4); most – 1336 (2016). HS 268 v Glamorgan (Bristol) 2015. BB 2-21 v Sussex (Hove) 2016. LO HS 151* v Glamorgan (Cardiff) 2013 (Y40). LO BB 4-43 v Leics (Bristol) 2012 (CB40). T20 HS 87. T20 BB 1-4.

GOODMAN, Dominic Charles (Dr Challenor's GS), b Ashford, Kent 23 Oct 2000. 6'6". RHB, RM. Squad No 83. Debut (Gloucestershire) 2021; cap 2021. Gloucestershire 2nd XI debut 2019. HS 18 v Hants (Southampton) 2022. BB 2-19 v Somerset (Taunton) 2021. LO BB –.

HAMMOND, Miles Arthur Halhead (St Edward's S, Oxford), b Cheltenham 11 Jan 1996. 5'11". LHB, OB. Squad No 88. Debut (Gloucestershire) 2013; cap 2013. Birmingham Phoenix 2021 to date. F-c Tour (MCC): Nepal 2019-20. HS 169 v Hants (Cheltenham) 2022. BB 2-37 v Leics (Leicester) 2021. LO HS 95 v Sussex (Eastbourne) 2019 (RLC). LO BB 2-18 v Northants (Northampton) 2015 (RLC). T20 HS 63. T20 BB –.

NO**HARRIS, Marcus** Sinclair, b Perth, W Australia 21 July 1992. 5'8". LHB, OB. Squad No 21. W Australia 2010-11 to 2015-16. Victoria 2016-17 to date. Leicestershire 2021. Gloucestershire debut/cap 2022. Big Bash: PS 2014-15 to 2015-16; MR 2016-17 to date. **Tests** (A): 14 (2018-19 to 2021-22); HS 79 v I (Sydney) 2018-19. HS 250* Vic v NSW (Melbourne) 2018-19. CC HS 185 Le v Middx (Leicester) 2021. Gs HS 159 v Somerset (Taunton) 2022. BB –. LO HS 142* Vic v Tas (Launceston) 2022-23. T20 HS 85.

LACE, Thomas Cresswell (Millfield S), b Hammersmith, Middx 27 May 1998. 5'8". RHB, WK. Squad No 8. Derbyshire 2018-19 (on loan). Middlesex 2019. Gloucestershire debut/ cap 2020. Middlesex 2nd XI 2015-18. HS 143 De v Glamorgan (Swansea) 2019. Gs HS 118 v Hants (Cheltenham) 2021. LO HS 48 De v Durham (Chester-le-St) 2019 (RLC). T20 HS 5.

NAISH, William Lewis (Wycliffe C; Clifton C), b Guildford, Surrey 19 Jun 2003. 5'11". RHB, RM. Squad No 22. Awaiting f-c debut. Gloucestershire 2nd XI debut 2019. Wiltshire 2021. T20 HS 0.

PAYNE, David Alan (Lytchett Minster S), b Poole, Dorset, 15 Feb 1991. 6'2". RHB, LMF. Squad No 14. Debut (Gloucestershire) 2011; cap 2011. Big Bash: PS 2022-23. Welsh Fire 2021 to date. Dorset 2009. **LOI**: 1 (2022); HS – ; BB 1-38 v Neth (Amstelveen) 2022. HS 67* v Glamorgan (Cardiff) 2016. BB 6-26 v Leics (Bristol) 2011. LO HS 40 EL v South Africans (Worcester) 2022. LO BB 7-29 v Essex (Chelmsford) 2010 (CB40), inc 4 wkts in 4 balls and 6 wkts in 9 balls – Gs record. T20 HS 10. T20 BB 5-24.

PRICE, Oliver James (Magdalen Coll S), b Oxford 12 Jun 2001. Younger brother of T.J.Price (*see below*). 6'3". RHB, OB. Squad No 67. Debut (Gloucestershire) 2021; cap 2021. Gloucestershire 2nd XI debut 2018. Oxfordshire 2018-19. HS 68 v Yorks (Leeds) 2022. BB 1-14 v Hants (Cheltenham) 2022. LO HS 45 and LO BB 2-34 v Surrey (Oval) 2022 (RLC). T20 HS 33. T20 BB –.

PRICE, Thomas James (Magdalen Coll S), b Oxford 2 Jan 2000. Elder brother of O.J.Price (*see above*). 6'1". RHB, RM. Squad No 53. Debut (Gloucestershire) 2020; cap 2020. Gloucestershire 2nd XI debut 2015. Oxfordshire 2018-19. HS 71 v Glamorgan (Cardiff) 2021. BB 8-27 (10-73 match) v Warwks (Bristol) 2022. LO HS 45 v Leics (Bristol) 2022 (RLC). LO BB 4-70 v Durham (Chester-le-St) 2022 (RLC). T20 HS 25. T20 BB –.

SHAW, Joshua (Crofton HS, Wakefield; Skills Exchange C), b Wakefield, Yorks 3 Jan 1996. Son of C.Shaw (Yorkshire 1984-88). 6'1". RHB, RMF. Squad No 5. Debut (Gloucestershire) 2016 (on loan); cap 2016. Yorkshire 2016-19. HS 42 Y v Somerset (Leeds) 2018. Gs HS 41* v Leics (Bristol) 2021. BB 5-79 v Sussex (Bristol) 2016. LO HS 8* v Durham (Chester-le-St) 2022 (RLC). LO BB 4-36 v Lancs (Bristol) 2021 (RLC). T20 HS 4. T20 BB 3-32.

SMITH, Thomas Michael John (Seaford Head Community C; Sussex Downs C), b Eastbourne, Sussex 29 Aug 1987. 5'9". RHB, SLA. Squad No 6. Sussex 2007-09. Surrey 2009 (l-o only). Middlesex 2010-13. Gloucestershire debut/cap 2013. HS 84 v Leics (Cheltenham) 2019. BB 4-35 v Kent (Canterbury) 2014. LO HS 65 Sy v Leics (Leicester) 2009 (P40). LO BB 4-26 v Sussex (Cheltenham) 2016 (RLC). T20 HS 36*. T20 BB 5-16 v Warwks (Birmingham) 2020 – Gs record.

TAYLOR, Jack Martin Robert (Chipping Norton S), b Banbury, Oxfordshire 12 Nov 1991. Elder brother of M.D.Taylor (*see below*). 5'11". RHB, OB. Squad No 10. Debut (Gloucestershire) 2010; cap 2010. Oxfordshire 2009-11. HS 156 v Northants (Cheltenham) 2015. BB 4-16 v Glamorgan (Bristol) 2016. LO HS 95 v Notts (Bristol) 2022 (RLC). LO BB 4-31 v Somerset (Bristol) 2022 (RLC). T20 HS 80. T20 BB 4-16.

TAYLOR, Matthew David (Chipping Norton S), b Banbury, Oxfordshire 8 Jul 1994. Younger brother of J.M.R.Taylor (*see above*). 6'0". RHB, LMF. Squad No 36. Debut (Gloucestershire) 2013; cap 2013. Oxfordshire 2011-12. HS 56 v Somerset (Taunton) 2021. BB 5-15 v Cardiff MCCU (Bristol) 2018. CC BB 5-40 v Middx (Cheltenham) 2021. LO HS 51* v Lancs (Bristol) 2021 (RLC). LO BB 3-39 v Sussex (Eastbourne) 2019 (RLC). T20 HS 18*. T20 BB 3-16.

van BUUREN, Graeme Lourens, b Pretoria, South Africa 22 Aug 1990. 5'6". RHB, SLA. Squad No 12. Northerns 2009-10 to 2015-16. Titans 2012-13 to 2014-15. Gloucestershire debut/cap 2016; captain 2022 to date. Birmingham Phoenix 2022. England resident since May 2019. HS 235 Northerns v EP (Centurion) 2014-15. Gs HS 172* v Worcs (Worcester) 2016. BB 4-12 Northerns v SW Districts (Oudtshoorn) 2012-13. Gs BB 4-18 v Durham MCCU (Bristol) 2017. CC BB 3-15 v Glamorgan (Bristol) 2016. LO HS 119* Northerns v EP (Pt Elizabeth, Grey HS) 2013-14. LO BB 5-35 Northerns v SW Districts (Pretoria) 2011-12. T20 HS 64. T20 BB 5-8.

NQ**VAN MEEKEREN, Paul** Adriaan, b Amsterdam, Netherlands 15 Jan 1993. 6'4". RHB, RMF. Squad No 47. Netherlands 2013 to date. Somerset 2016-18. Durham 2021 (white ball only). Gloucestershire debut 2022 (white ball only). **LOI** (Neth): 8 (2013 to 2022); HS 15* v SA (Amstelveen) 2013; BB 2-28 v Scot (Rotterdam) 2021. **IT20** (Neth): 58 (2013 to 2022-23); HS 24 v B (Hobart) 2022-23; BB 4-11 v Ire (Dharamsala) 2015-16. HS 34 Neth v PNG (Amstelveen) 2015. Gs HS 59 Sm v Lancs (Manchester) 2018. BB 4-60 Sm v Essex (Chelmsford) 2017. LO HS 15* (*see LOI*). LO BB 5-48 v Sussex (Hove) 2022 (RLC). T20 HS 24. T20 BB 4-11.

WARNER, Jared David (Kettleborough Park HS; Silcoates SFC), b Wakefield, Yorks 14 Nov 1996. 6'1". RHB, RFM. Squad No 4. Sussex 2019 (on loan). Yorkshire 2020. Gloucestershire debut 2021; cap 2021. HS 32* v Hants (Southampton) 2022. BB 3-35 Sx v Glamorgan (Hove) 2019. Gs BB 2-54 v Northants (Bristol) 2021. LO HS 0*. LO BB 3-42 v Sussex (Hove) 2021 (RLC). T20 HS 1. T20 BB –.

WELLS, Ben Joseph James (Monkton Combe S), b Bath, Somerset 30 Jul 2000. 5'9". RHB, WK. Squad No 72. Debut (Gloucestershire) 2021. Somerset 2nd XI 2018-21. Warwickshire 2nd XI 2021. Gloucestershire 2nd XI debut 2021. Dorset 2018. HS 40 v Glamorgan (Cardiff) 2021. LO HS 76 v Warwks (Cheltenham) 2022 (RLC). T20 HS 42.

NQ**ZAFAR GOHAR**, b Lahore, Pakistan 1 Feb 1995. 5'11". LHB, SLA. Squad No 77. ZT Bank 2013-14. State Bank 2014-15. SSGC 2015-16 to 2016-17. Lahore Blues 2018-19. Central Punjab 2019-20 to date. Gloucestershire debut 2021. **Tests** (P): 1 (2020-21); HS 37 v NZ (Christchurch) 2020-21; BB –. **LOI** (P): 1 (2015-16); HS 15 and BB 2-54 v E (Sharjah) 2015-16. F-c Tours (P): NZ 2020-21; SL 2015 (PA). HS 100* C Punjab v Baluchistan (Quetta) 2019-20. Gs HS 81 v Essex (Chelmsford) 2022. BB 7-79 (11-133 match) C Punjab v Northern (Faisalabad) 2019-20. Gs BB 6-43 v Glamorgan (Cardiff) 2021. LO HS 62 v Warwks (Cheltenham) 2022 (RLC). LO BB 5-56 ZT v SNGPL (Islamabad) 2013-14. T20 HS 32*. T20 BB 4-14.

(Having made a County 1st XI appearance in 2022)

COCKBAIN, Ian Andrew (Maghull HS), b Bootle, Liverpool 17 Feb 1987. Son of I.Cockbain (Lancs and Minor Cos 1979-94). 6'0". RHB, RM. Gloucestershire 2011-21; cap 2011; testimonial 2019. Big Bash: AS 2021-22. Welsh Fire 2021. Trent Rockets 2022. HS 151* v Surrey (Bristol) 2014. BB 1-23 v Durham MCCU (Bristol) 2016. LO HS 108* v Middx (Lord's) 2017 (RLC). T20 HS 123.

HIGGINS, R.F. – *see MIDDLESEX.*

HOWELL, B.A.C. – *see HAMPSHIRE.*

NQ**MOHAMMAD AMIR**, b Gujar Khan, Punjab, Pakistan 13 Apr 1992. LHB, LF. Federal Areas 2008-09. National Bank 2008-09 to 2009-10. SSGC 2015-16 to 2018-19. Essex 2017-19. Gloucestershire 2022; cap 2022. London Spirit 2021. **Tests** (P): 36 (2009 to 2018-19); HS 48 v A (Brisbane) 2016-17; BB 6-44 v WI (Kingston) 2017. **LOI** (P): 61 (2009 to 2019-20); HS 73* v NZ (Abu Dhabi) 2009-10; BB 5-30 v A (Taunton) 2019. **IT20** (P): 50 (2009 to 2020); HS 21* v A (Birmingham) 2010; BB 4-13 v SL (Lahore) 2017-18. F-c Tours (P): E 2010, 2016, 2018; A 2009-10, 2016-17; SA 2018-19; WI 2017; NZ 2009-10, 2016-17; SL 2009; Ire 2018. HS 66 SSGC v Lahore Blues (Lahore) 2015-16. CC HS 28 Ex v Kent (Canterbury) 2019. Gs HS 18 and Gs BB 3-33 v Hants (Southampton) 2022. 50 wkts (0+1): 56 (2008-09). BB 7-61 (10-97 match) NBP v Lahore Shalimar (Lahore) 2008-09. CC BB 5-18 (10-72 match) Ex v Yorks (Scarborough) 2017. LO HS 73* *(see LOI).* LO BB 5-30 *(see LOI).* T20 HS 21*. T20 BB 6-17.

NQ**NASEEM SHAH**, b Lower Dir, NWFP, Pakistan 15 Feb 2003. 5'8". RHB, RF. ZT Bank 2018-19. Central Punjab 2019-20. Southern Punjab 2021-22. Gloucestershire 2022; cap 2022. **Tests** (P): 15 (2019-20 to 2022-23); HS 18 v SL (Galle) 2022; BB 5-31 v SL (Karachi) 2019-20. **LOI** (P): 5 (2022 to 2022-23); HS 3 and BB 5-33 v Neth (Rotterdam) 2022. **IT20** (P): 16 (2022 to 2022-23); HS 14* v Afg (Sharjah) 2022; BB 2-7 v Hong Kong (Sharjah) 2022. F-c Tours (P): E 2020; A 2019-20; NZ 2020-21; SL 2021-22 (PA), 2022. HS 31 P Shaheens v Sri Lanka A (Pallekele) 2021-22. Gs HS 19 and Gs BB 1-41 v Northants (Northampton) 2022. BB 6-59 ZT v PT (Rawalpindi) 2018-19. LO HS 9 Khyber Pak v Baluchistan (Karachi) 2022-23. LO BB 5-33 *(see LOI).* T20 HS 14*. T20 BB 5-20.

NQ**PHILLIPS, Glenn** Dominic, b East London, South Africa 6 Dec 1996. Elder brother of D.N.Phillips (Otago 2019-20 to date). RHB, WK, OB. Auckland 2016-17 to 2021-22. Gloucestershire 2021-22; cap 2021. Otago 2022-23. IPL: RR 2021. Welsh Fire 2021. **Tests** (NZ): 1 (2019-20); HS 52 v A (Sydney) 2019-20. **LOI** (NZ): 15 (2022 to 2022-23); HS 63* v P (Karachi) 2022-23; BB 1-9 v Ire (Dublin) 2022. **IT20** (NZ): 59 (2016-17 to 2022-23); HS 108 v WI (Mt Maunganui) 2020-21; BB 1-11 v B (Auckland) 2020-21. F-c Tour (NZ): A 2019-20. HS 147 Otago v Canterbury (Dunedin) 2022-23. Gs HS 125 v Kent (Canterbury) 2022. BB 4-70 Auckland v Wellington (Auckland) 2019-20. Gs BB 2-67 v Hants (Cheltenham) 2021. LO HS 156 Auckland v Otago (Lincoln) 2019-20. LO BB 3-40 Auckland v Otago (Auckland) 2019-20. T20 HS 116*. T20 BB 2-11.

SCOTT, George Frederick Buchan (Beechwood Park S; St Albans S; Leeds U), b Hemel Hempstead, Herts 6 Nov 1995. Younger brother of J.E.B.Scott (Hertfordshire 2013-18); elder brother of C.F.B.Scott (Durham MCCU 2019) and P.E.B.Scott (Hertfordshire 2014-17). 6'2". RHB, RM. Leeds/Bradford MCCU 2015-16. Middlesex 2018-19. Gloucestershire 2020-22; cap 2020. Hertfordshire 2011-14. HS 77 v Hants (Southampton) 2022. BB 2-34 v Warwks (Bristol) 2020. LO HS 66* v Surrey (Oval) 2021 (RLC). LO BB 1-65 M v Lancs (Lord's) 2019 (RLC). T20 HS 38*. T20 BB 1-14.

GLOUCESTERSHIRE 2022

RESULTS SUMMARY

	Place	Won	Lost	Drew	NR
LV= Insurance County Champ (Div 1)	10th	2	8	4	
Royal London One-Day Cup (Group A)	5th	5	3		
Vitality Blast (South Group)	5th	6	6		2

LV= INSURANCE COUNTY CHAMPIONSHIP AVERAGES BATTING AND FIELDING

Cap†		M	I	NO	HS	Runs	Avge	100	50	Ct/St
2021	G.D.Phillips	2	4	–	125	212	53.00	1	1	1
2022	M.S.Harris	9	17	–	159	726	42.70	3	2	8
2010	C.D.J.Dent	10	19	1	207*	714	39.66	2	4	6
2013	M.A.H.Hammond	14	27	2	169	836	33.44	1	6	10
2018	R.F.Higgins	11	19	1	139	586	32.55	1	3	5
2010	J.M.R.Taylor	4	6	–	71	172	28.66	–	2	4
2016	G.L.van Buuren	12	20	2	127*	502	27.88	1	1	8
2021	Zafar Gohar	11	21	3	81	493	27.38	–	4	5
2016	J.R.Bracey	14	27	1	177	702	27.00	2	3	47/4
2021	O.J.Price	8	15	–	68	386	25.73	–	5	11
2020	T.C.Lace	5	8	–	73	184	23.00	–	2	–
2018	B.G.Charlesworth	5	10	–	64	208	20.80	–	2	5
2020	G.F.B.Scott	4	8	–	77	160	20.00	–	1	2
2021	J.D.Warner	2	4	1	32*	59	19.66	–	–	–
2020	T.J.Price	8	15	2	39	190	14.61	–	–	–
2016	J.Shaw	5	9	2	29	97	13.85	–	–	–
2022	A.S.Dale	8	14	8	36*	71	11.83	–	–	–
2013	M.D.Taylor	6	9	2	24*	69	9.85	–	–	2
2011	D.A.Payne	6	8	5	17*	25	8.33	–	–	3
2022	Z.J.Chappell	4	8	1	20	51	7.28	–	–	1

Also batted: J.G.Bethell (1 match – cap 2022) 37, 61; D.C.Goodman (1 – cap 2021) 18, 1 (3 ct); Mohammad Amir (2 – cap 2022) 0, 18; Naseem Shah (1 – cap 2022) 19, 7; B.T.J.Wheal (1 – cap 2022) 10, 13* (1 ct).

BOWLING

	O	M	R	W	Avge	Best	5wI	10wM
T.J.Price	195.4	48	643	32	20.09	8-27	3	1
Zafar Gohar	449.1	94	1335	47	28.40	5-40	5	1
D.A.Payne	179.4	29	573	17	33.70	4-51	–	–
A.S.Dale	164.5	25	645	18	35.83	4-72	–	–
R.F.Higgins	348.3	94	1032	28	36.85	4-68	–	–

Also bowled:

	O	M	R	W	Avge	Best	5wI	10wM
Mohammad Amir	67	20	170	6	28.33	3-33		
Z.J.Chappell	106.1	17	340	9	37.77	3-70		
G.L.van Buuren	101.1	10	354	8	44.25	3-53		
M.D.Taylor	143	37	410	8	51.25	3-85		
J.Shaw	84	15	343	6	57.16	2-56		

J.G.Bethell 2-0-15-0; B.G.Charlesworth 19-3-71-2; D.C.Goodman 21-3-65-1; M.A.H.Hammond 54-7-249-1; Naseem Shah 11-1-41-1; G.D.Phillips 29.4-3-123-1; O.J.Price 24-5-85-1; G.F.B.Scott 17-4-77-0; J.M.R.Taylor 18-0-91-1; J.D.Warner 30.2-3-144-1; B.T.J.Wheal 26-5-122-1.

Gloucestershire played no first-class fixtures outside the County Championship in 2022. The First-Class Averages (pp 221–234) give the records of Gloucestershire players in all first-class county matches, with the exception of J.G.Bethell, R.F.Higgins and B.T.J.Wheal, whose first-class figures for Gloucestershire are as above.

† Gloucestershire revised their capping policy in 2004 and now award players with their County Caps when they make their first-class debut.

GLOUCESTERSHIRE RECORDS

FIRST-CLASS CRICKET

Highest Total	For	695-9d		v	Middlesex	Gloucester	2004
	V	774-7d		by	Australians	Bristol	1948
Lowest Total	For	17		v	Australians	Cheltenham	1896
	V	12		by	Northants	Gloucester	1907
Highest Innings	For	341	C.M.Spearman	v	Middlesex	Gloucester	2004
	V	319	J.L.Rogers	for	Northants	Northampton	2006

Highest Partnership for each Wicket

1st	395	D.M.Young/R.B.Nicholls	v	Oxford U	Oxford	1962
2nd	256	C.T.M.Pugh/T.W.Graveney	v	Derbyshire	Chesterfield	1960
3rd	392	G.H.Roderick/A.P.R.Gidman	v	Leics	Bristol	2014
4th	321	W.R.Hammond/W.L.Neale	v	Leics	Gloucester	1937
5th	261	W.G.Grace/W.O.Moberly	v	Yorkshire	Cheltenham	1876
6th	320	G.L.Jessop/J.H.Board	v	Sussex	Hove	1903
7th	248	W.G.Grace/E.L.Thomas	v	Sussex	Hove	1896
8th	239	W.R.Hammond/A.E.Wilson	v	Lancashire	Bristol	1938
9th	193	W.G.Grace/S.A.P.Kitcat	v	Sussex	Bristol	1896
10th	137	C.N.Miles/L.C.Norwell	v	Worcs	Cheltenham	2014

Best Bowling	For	10-40	E.G.Dennett	v	Essex	Bristol	1906
(Innings)	V	10-66	A.A.Mailey	for	Australians	Cheltenham	1921
		10-66	K.Smales	for	Notts	Stroud	1956
Best Bowling	For	17-56	C.W.L.Parker	v	Essex	Gloucester	1925
(Match)	V	15-87	A.J.Conway	for	Worcs	Moreton-in-M	1914

Most Runs – Season	2860	W.R.Hammond	(av 69.75)	1933
Most Runs – Career	33664	W.R.Hammond	(av 57.05)	1920-51
Most 100s – Season	13	W.R.Hammond		1938
Most 100s – Career	113	W.R.Hammond		1920-51
Most Wkts – Season	222	T.W.J.Goddard	(av 16.80)	1937
	222	T.W.J.Goddard	(av 16.37)	1947
Most Wkts – Career	3170	C.W.L.Parker	(av 19.43)	1903-35
Most Career W-K Dismissals	1054	R.C.Russell	(950 ct; 104 st)	1981-2004
Most Career Catches in the Field	719	C.A.Milton		1948-74

LIMITED-OVERS CRICKET

Highest Total	50ov	401-7		v	Bucks	Wing	2003
	40ov	344-6		v	Northants	Cheltenham	2001
	T20	254-3		v	Middlesex	Uxbridge	2011
Lowest Total	50ov	82		v	Notts	Bristol	1987
	40ov	49		v	Middlesex	Bristol	1978
	T20	68		v	Hampshire	Bristol	2010
Highest Innings	50ov	177	A.J.Wright	v	Scotland	Bristol	1997
	40ov	153	C.M.Spearman	v	Warwicks	Gloucester	2003
	T20	126*	M.Klinger	v	Essex	Bristol	2015
Best Bowling	50ov	6-13	M.J.Proctor	v	Hampshire	Southampton[1]	1977
	40ov	7-29	D.A.Payne	v	Essex	Chelmsford	2010
	T20	5-16	T.M.J.Smith	v	Warwicks	Birmingham	2020

HAMPSHIRE

Formation of Present Club: 12 August 1863
Inaugural First-Class Match: 1864
Colours: Blue, Gold and White
Badge: Tudor Rose and Crown
County Champions: (2) 1961, 1973
NatWest/C&G/FP Trophy Winners: (3) 1991, 2005, 2009
Benson and Hedges Cup Winners: (2) 1988, 1992
Sunday League Winners: (3) 1975, 1978, 1986
Clydesdale Bank Winners: (1) 2012
Royal London One-Day Cup: (1) 2018
Twenty20 Cup Winners: (3) 2010, 2012, 2022

HAMPSHIRE
CRICKET

CEO: David Mann, The Ageas Bowl, Botley Road, West End, Southampton SO30 3XH ●
Tel: 023 8047 2002 ● Email: enquiries@ageasbowl.com ● Web: www.ageasbowl.com ●
Twitter: @hantscricket (103,675 followers)

Cricket Operations Manager: Tim Tremlett. **Director of Cricket**: Giles White. **1st XI Manager**: Adrian Birrell. **1st XI Assistant Coach**: Jimmy Adams. **Bowling Lead Coach**: Graeme Welch. **Captain**: J.M.Vince. **Overseas Players**: K.J.Abbott, N.T.Ellis, B.R.McDermott and Mohammad Abbas. **2023 Testimonial**: None. **Head Groundsman**: Simon Lee. **Scorer**: Fiona Newnham. **Blast Team** Name: Hampshire Hawks. ‡ New registration. NQ Not qualified for England.

NO**ABBOTT, Kyle** John (Kearnsey C, KZN), b Empangeni, South Africa 18 Jun 1987. 6'3½". RHB, RFM. Squad No 87. KwaZulu-Natal 2008-09 to 2009-10. Dolphins 2008-09 to 2014-15. Hampshire debut 2014; cap 2017. Worcestershire 2016. Boland 2021-22. IPL: KXIP 2016. Middlesex 2015 (T20 only). **Tests** (SA): 11 (2012-13 to 2016-17); HS 17 v A (Adelaide) 2016-17; BB 7-29 v P (Centurion) 2012-13. **LOI** (SA): 28 (2012-13 to 2016-17); HS 23 v Z (Bulawayo) 2014; BB 4-21 v Ire (Canberra) 2014-15. **IT20** (SA): 21 (2012-13 to 2015-16); HS 9* v NZ (Centurion) 2015; BB 3-20 v B (Dhaka) 2015. F-c Tours (SA): A 2016-17; I 2015-16. HS 97* v Lancs (Manchester) 2017. 50 wkts (4+1): 72 (2019). BB 9-40 (17-86 match) v Somerset (Southampton) 2019 – 4th best match figures in CC history. Hat-tricks (2): v Worcs (Worcester) 2018 and v Glos (Cheltenham) 2022. LO HS 56 v Surrey (Oval) 2017 (RLC). LO BB 5-43 v Worcs (Southampton) 2021 (RLC). T20 HS 30. T20 BB 5-14.

ALBERT, Toby Edward (Park House S), b Basingstoke 12 Nov 2001. 6'1". RHB, WK. Squad No 15. Debut (Hampshire) 2022. Hampshire 2nd XI debut 2021. HS 69* v SL Dev (Southampton) 2022. LO HS 84* v Derbys (Derby) 2022 (RLC). T20 HS 24*.

BARKER, Keith Hubert Douglas (Moorhead HS; Fulwood C, Preston), b Manchester 21 Oct 1986. Son of K.H.Barker (British Guiana 1960-61 to 1963-64). Played football for Blackburn Rovers and Rochdale. 6'3". LHB, LMF. Squad No 13. Warwickshire 2009-18; cap 2013. Hampshire 2019; cap 2021. HS 125 Wa v Surrey (Guildford) 2013. H HS 84 v Middx (Lord's) 2021. 50 wkts (4); most – 62 (2016). BB 7-46 v Notts (Southampton) 2021. LO HS 56 Wa v Scotland (Birmingham) 2011 (CB40). LO BB 4-33 Wa v Scotland (Birmingham) 2010 (CB40). T20 HS 46. T20 BB 4-19.

BROWN, Ben Christopher (Ardingly C); b Crawley, Sussex 23 Nov 1988. 5'8". RHB, WK. Squad No 10. Sussex 2007-21; cap 2014; captain 2017-20. Hampshire debut 2022. 1000 runs (2); most – 1031 (2015, 2018). HS 163 Sx v Durham (Hove) 2014. H HS 157 v Kent (Canterbury) 2022, sharing H record 5th wkt partnership of 273 with L.A.Dawson. BB 1-48 Sx v Essex (Colchester) 2016. LO HS 105 Sx v Middx (Hove) 2021 (RLC). T20 HS 68.

CAMPBELL, Jack Oliver Ian (Churcher's C, Petersfield; Durham U), b Portsmouth, Hants 11 Nov 1999. 6'7". RHB, LMF. Squad No 11. Durham MCCU 2019. Durham 2019; cap 2019. Hampshire debut 2022. Hampshire 2nd XI debut 2017. Kent 2nd XI 2018. Durham 2nd XI 2018-21. HS 2 DU v Durham (Chester-le-St) 2019. CC HS 0* and BB 1-43 Du v Leics (Leicester) 2019. LO HS 1* v Yorks (Scarborough) 2022 (RLC). LO BB 4-44 v Kent (Beckenham) 2022 (RLC). T20 HS 6. T20 BB 1-21.

CRANE, Mason Sidney (Lancing C), b Shoreham-by-Sea, Sussex 18 Feb 1997. 5'10". RHB, LB. Squad No 32. Debut (Hampshire) 2015; cap 2021. NSW 2016-17. Sussex 2022 (on loan). MCC 2017. London Spirit 2021 to date. **Test**: 1 (2017-18); HS 4 and BB 1-193 v A (Sydney) 2017-18. **IT20**: 2 (2017); HS − ; BB 1-38 v SA (Cardiff) 2017. F-c Tours: A 2017-18; WI 2017-18 (EL). HS 29 v Somerset (Taunton) 2017. BB 5-35 v Warwks (Southampton) 2015. LO HS 28* v Somerset (Lord's) 2019 (RLC). LO BB 4-30 v Middx (Southampton) 2015 (RLC). T20 HS 12*. T20 BB 4-24.

CURRIE, Scott William (St Edward's RC & C of E S), b Poole, Dorset 2 May 2001. Younger brother of B.J.Currie (see SUSSEX). 6'5". RHB, RMF. Squad No 44. Debut (Hampshire) 2020. Hampshire 2nd XI debut 2018. Dorset 2019. HS 38 v Kent (Canterbury) 2020. BB 4-109 v Surrey (Oval) 2021. LO HS 43* v Worcs (Southampton) 2022 (RLC). LO BB 3-25 v Lancs (Southampton) 2022 (RLC). T20 HS 3. T20 BB 4-24.

DAWSON, Liam Andrew (John Bentley S, Calne), b Swindon, Wilts 1 Mar 1990. 5'8". RHB, SLA. Squad No 8. Debut (Hampshire) 2007; cap 2013. Mountaineers 2011-12. Essex 2015 (on loan). London Spirit 2022. Wiltshire 2006-07. **Tests**: 3 (2016-17 to 2017); HS 66* v I (Chennai) 2016-17; BB 2-34 v SA (Lord's) 2017. **LOI**: 6 (2016 to 2022-23); HS 20 v A (Sydney) 2022-23; BB 2-70 v P (Cardiff) 2016. **IT20**: 11 (2016 to 2022-23); HS 34 v P (Karachi) 2022-23; BB 3-27 v SL (Southampton) 2016. F-c Tour: I 2016-17. HS 171 v Kent (Canterbury) 2022, sharing H record 5th wkt partnership of 273 with B.C.Brown. BB 7-51 Mountaineers v ME (Mutare) 2011-12 (also scored 110* in same match). H BB 7-68 (10-139 match) v Essex (Chelmsford) 2019. LO HS 113* SJD v Kalabagan (Savar) 2014-15. LO BB 6-47 v Sussex (Southampton) 2015 (RLC). T20 HS 82. T20 BB 5-17.

DONALD, Aneurin Henry Thomas (Pontarddulais CS), b Swansea, Glamorgan 20 Dec 1996. 6'2". RHB, OB. Squad No 12. Glamorgan 2014-18. Hampshire debut 2019. Wales MC 2012. No 1st XI appearances in 2020 and 2021 due to injury. 1000 runs (1): 1088 (2016). HS 234 Gm v Derbys (Colwyn Bay) 2016, in 123 balls, equalling world record for fastest 200, inc 15 sixes, going from 0-127* between lunch and tea, and 127-234 after tea. T20 H HS 173 v Warwks (Southampton) 2019. LO HS 76 v Yorks (Scarborough) 2022 (RLC). T20 HS 76.

ECKLAND, Joseph Robert (Millfield S), b Yeovil, Somerset 22 May 2004. Younger brother of A.J.Eckland (Dorset 2017 to date); nephew of V.J.Marks (Oxford U, Somerset, W Australia & England 1975-89). 6'1". RHB, WK. Hampshire 2nd XI debut 2021. Dorset 2022. Awaiting 1st XI debut.

NO**ELLIS, Nathan** Trevor, b Greenacre, NSW, Australia 22 Sep 1994. 6'0". RHB, RMF. Squad No 72. Tasmania 2019-20 to date. Hampshire debut 2022 (T20 only). IPL: PK 2021 to date. Big Bash: HH 2018-19 to date. London Spirit 2022. **LOI** (A): 3 (2021-22); HS 3* and BB 1-36 v P (Lahore) 2021-22. **IT20** (A): 5 (2021 to 2022-23); HS 1 v b (Mirpur) 2021; BB 4-28 v P (Lahore) 2021-22. HS 41 Tas v WA (Adelaide, P25) 2020-21. BB 6-43 Tas v NSW (Hobart) 2019-20. LO HS 31 Tas v NSW (Hobart) 2020-21. LO BB 5-38 Tas v NSW (Sydney, NS) 2019-20. T20 HS 24. T20 BB 4-27.

FULLER, James Kerr (Otago U, NZ), b Cape Town, South Africa 24 Jan 1990. UK passport. 6'3". RHB, RFM. Squad No 26. Otago 2009-10 to 2012-13. Gloucestershire 2011-15; cap 2011. Middlesex 2016-18. Hampshire debut 2019; cap 2022. HS 93 M v Somerset (Taunton) 2016. H HS 78* v Kent (Southampton) 2022. BB 6-24 (10-79 match) Otago v Wellington (Dunedin) 2012-13. CC BB 6-47 Gs v Surrey (Oval) 2014. H BB 4-17 v Surrey (Arundel) 2020. Hat-tricks (2): Gs v Worcs (Cheltenham) 2013; v Surrey (Arundel) 2020. LO HS 55* v Somerset (Lord's) 2019 (RLC). LO BB 6-35 M v Netherlands (Amstelveen) 2012 (CB40). T20 HS 53*. T20 BB 6-28 M v Hants (Southampton) 2018 – M record.

GUBBINS, Nicholas Richard Trail (Radley C; Leeds U), b Richmond, Surrey 31 Dec 1993. 6'0½". LHB, LB. Squad No 31. Leeds/Bradford MCCU 2013-15. Middlesex 2014-21; cap 2016. Hampshire debut 2021; cap 2022. Matabeleland Tuskers 2021-22. Southern Rocks 2022-23. F-c Tours (EL): WI 2017-18; SL 2016-17; UAE 2016-17 (v Afg), 2018-19 (v PA). 1000 runs (1): 1409 (2016). HS 201* M v Lancs (Lord's) 2016. H HS 137* v Glos (Cheltenham) 2021. BB 4-41 MT v ME (Harare) 2021-22. LO HS 141 M v Sussex (Hove) 2015 (RLC). LO BB 4-38 v Sussex (Southampton) 2021 (RLC). T20 HS 57*. T20 BB 3-27.

HOLLAND, Ian Gabriel (Ringwood Secondary C, Melbourne), b Stevens Point, Wisconsin, USA 3 Oct 1990. 6'0". RHB, RMF. Squad No 22. England qualified at the start of the 2020 season. Victoria 2015-16. Hampshire debut 2017; cap 2021. **LOI** (USA): 15 (2019-20 to 2022-23); HS 75 v Nepal (Kirtipur) 2019-20; BB 3-11 v UAE (Dubai, ICCA) 2019-20. **IT20** (USA): 6 (2021-22); HS 39* v Bahamas (Coolidge) 2021-22; BB 2-3 v Panama (Coolidge) 2021-22. HS 146* v Middx (Southampton) 2021. BB 4-16 v Somerset (Southampton) 2017. LO HS 75 (see LOI). LO BB 4-12 v Kent (Beckenham) 2021 (RLC). T20 HS 65. T20 BB 2-3.

HOWELL, Benny Alexander Cameron (The Oratory S), b Bordeaux, France 5 Oct 1988. Son of J.B.Howell (Warwickshire 2nd XI 1978). 5'11". RHB, RM. Squad No 7. Debut (Hampshire) 2011; rejoined in 2023 with white-ball contract. Gloucestershire 2012-19; cap 2012. Big Bash: MR 2020-21. Birmingham Phoenix 2021 to date. Berkshire 2007. HS 163 Gs v Glamorgan (Cardiff) 2017. H HS 71 v Lancs (Southampton) 2011. BB 5-57 Gs v Leics (Leicester) 2013. LO HS 122 v Surrey (Croydon) 2011 (CB40). LO BB 3-37 Gs v Yorks (Leeds) 2015 (RLC). T20 HS 57. T20 BB 5-18.

KELLY, Dominic Christopher (Millfield S), b Winchester 1 Oct 2005. 6'0". LHB, RM. Debut (Hampshire) 2022, aged 16y 224d. Hampshire 2nd XI debut 2022. England U19 2022 to 2022-23. HS –. BB 2-55 v SL Dev (Southampton) 2022. LO HS 17 v Lancs (Southampton) 2022 (RLC). LO BB –.

ᴺᵠ**McDERMOTT, Ben**jamin Reginald, b Caboolture, Queensland, Australia 12 Dec 1994. Son of C.J.McDermott (Queensland and Australia 1983-84 to 1995-96); younger brother of A.C.McDermott (Queensland 2009-10 to 2014-15). 6'0". RHB, WK, occ RM. Squad No 28. Queensland 2014-15. Tasmania 2015-16 to date. Derbyshire 2021. Hampshire debut 2022 (T20 only). Big Bash: BH 2013-14; MR 2015-16; HH 2016-17 to date. London Spirit 2022. **LOI** (A): 5 (2021 to 2021-22); HS 104 v P (Lahore) 2021-22. **IT20** (A): 23 (2018-19 to 2021-22); HS 53 v SL (Sydney) 2021-22. HS 107* Aus A v Indians (Sydney) 2020-21. CC HS 25 De v Worcs (Worcester) 2021. BB –. LO HS 133 Tas v WA (Hobart) 2021-22. T20 HS 127.

MIDDLETON, Fletcha Scott (Wyvern C), b Winchester 21 Jan 2002. Son of T.C.Middleton (Hampshire 1984-95). 5'8½". RHB, OB. Squad No 19. Debut (Hampshire) 2022. Hampshire 2nd XI debut 2018. HS 64 v SL Dev (Southampton) 2022. LO HS 64 v Derbys (Derby) 2022 (RLC).

ᴺᵠ**MOHAMMAD ABBAS**, b Sialkot, Pakistan 10 Mar 1990. 5'11". RHB, RMF. Squad No 38. Sialkot 2008-09 to 2012-13. KRL 2015-16 to 2016-17. SNGPL 2017-18 to 2018-19. Leicestershire 2018-19; cap 2018. Southern Punjab 2019-20 to date. Hampshire debut 2021; cap 2022. **Tests** (P): 25 (2017 to 2021); HS 29 v A (Adelaide) 2019-20; BB 5-33 v A (Abu Dhabi) 2018-19. **LOI** (P): 3 (2018-19); HS – ; BB 1-44 v A (Sharjah) 2018-19. F-c Tours (P): E 2018, 2020; A 2019-20; SA 2018-19; WI 2017, 2021; NZ 2020-21; Ire 2018. HS 40 and BB 8-46 (14-93 match) KRL v Karachi Whites (Karachi) 2016-17. CC HS 32* Le v Sussex (Hove) 2018. H HS 8 v Kent (Southampton) 2022. 50 wkts (2+2); most – 71 (2016-17). CC BB 6-11 v Middx (Southampton) 2021, inc hat-trick. LO HS 15* KRL v Habib Bank (Karachi) 2016-17. LO BB 4-31 KRL v SNGPL (Karachi) 2016-17. T20 HS 15*. T20 BB 3-22.

MUMFORD, Charles Simon (Bedford S), b Watford, Herts 30 May 2004. 5'9". RHB, WK. Debut (Hampshire) 2022 – did not bat or bowl. Hampshire 2nd XI debut 2021.

ORGAN, Felix Spencer (Canford S), b Sydney, Australia 2 Jun 1999. 5'9". RHB, OB. Squad No 3. Debut (Hampshire) 2017. Hampshire 2nd XI debut 2015. Dorset 2019. HS 100 v Glos (Cheltenham) 2022. BB 5-25 v Surrey (Southampton) 2019. LO HS 79 v Durham (Chester-le-St) 2021 (RLC). LO BB 3-39 v Kent (Beckenham) 2022 (RLC). T20 HS 9. T20 BB 2-21.

PETRIE, Harry William (Wellington C), b Wycombe, Bucks 6 Sep 2002. 6'3". RHB, RFM. Squad No 30. Debut (Hampshire) 2022. Hampshire 2nd XI debut 2021. HS –. BB 3-48 v SL Dev (Southampton) 2022 – only 1st XI appearance.

PREST, Thomas James (Canford S), b Wimborne, Dorset 24 Mar 2003. 5'11". RHB, OB. Squad No 24. Debut (Hampshire) 2021. Hampshire 2nd XI debut 2019. Dorset 2019. HS 35 v SL Dev (Southampton) 2022. CC HS 18 v Glos (Cheltenham) 2021. LO HS 181 v Kent (Beckenham) 2022 (RLC). LO BB 2-28 v Glos (Bristol) 2021 (RLC). T20 HS 64. T20 BB 1-8.

TURNER, John Andrew (Hilton C, Johannesburg), b Johannesburg, South Africa 10 Apr 2001. 6'1". RHB, RFM. Squad No 6. Debut (Hampshire) 2022. Hampshire 2nd XI debut 2021. HS 0 and BB 5-31 v SL Dev (Southampton) 2022. LO HS 12 v Glamorgan (Neath) 2022 (RLC). LO BB 5-25 v Lancs (Southampton) 2022 (RLC).

VINCE, James Michael (Warminster S), b Cuckfield, Sussex 14 Mar 1991. 6'2". RHB, RM. Squad No 14. Debut (Hampshire) 2009; cap 2013; captain 2016 to date. Wiltshire 2007-08. Big Bash: ST 2016-17 to 2017-18; SS 2018-19 to date. Southern Brave 2021 to date. **Tests**: 13 (2016-17 to 2017-18); HS 83 v A (Brisbane) 2017-18; BB –. **LOI**: 25 (2015 to 2022-23); HS 102 v P (Birmingham) 2021; BB 1-18 v Ire (Southampton) 2020. **IT20**: 17 (2015-16 to 2021-22); HS 59 v NZ (Christchurch) 2019-20. F-c Tours: A 2017-18; SA 2014-15 (EL); NZ 2017-18; SL 2013-14 (EL). 1000 runs (2); most – 1525 (2014). HS 240 v Essex (Southampton) 2014. BB 5-41 v Loughborough MCCU (Southampton) 2013. CC BB 2-2 v Lancs (Southport) 2013. LO HS 190 v Glos (Southampton) 2019 (RLC) – H record. LO BB 1-18 EL v Australia A (Sydney) 2012-13 and (*see LOI*). T20 HS 129* v Somerset (Taunton) 2022 – H record. T20 BB 1-5.

WEATHERLEY, Joe James (King Edward VI S, Southampton), b Winchester 19 Jan 1997. 6'1". RHB, OB. Squad No 5. Debut (Hampshire) 2016; cap 2021. Kent 2017 (on loan). HS 168 v Somerset (Southampton) 2022. BB 1-2 v Notts (Southampton) 2018. LO HS 105* v Kent (Southampton) 2018 (RLC). LO BB 4-25 v T&T (Cave Hill) 2017-18. T20 HS 71. T20 BB –.

WHEAL, Bradley Thomas James (Clifton C), b Durban, South Africa 28 Aug 1996. 5'9". RHB, RMF. Squad No 58. Debut (Hampshire) 2015; cap 2021. Gloucestershire 2022 (on loan); cap 2022. Warwickshire 2022 (on loan). London Spirit 2021 to date. **LOI** (Scot): 13 (2015-16 to 2019); HS 14 v Ire (Harare) 2017-18; BB 3-34 v WI (Harare) 2017-18. **IT20** (Scot): 17 (2015-16 to 2022-23); HS 2* (twice); BB 3-20 v Hong Kong (Mong Kok) 2015-16. HS 46* v Warwks (Birmingham) 2021. BB 6-51 v Notts (Nottingham) 2016. LO HS 18* v CC&C (Edgbaston) 2017-18. LO BB 4-38 v Kent (Southampton) 2016 (RLC). T20 HS 16. T20 BB 5-38.

WHITELEY, Ross Andrew (Repton S), b Sheffield, Yorks 13 Sep 1988. 6'2". LHB, LM. Squad No 4. Derbyshire 2008-13. Worcestershire 2013-21; cap 2013. Hampshire debut 2022. Southern Brave 2021 to date. HS 130* De v Kent (Derby) 2011. H HS 55* v SL Dev (Southampton) 2022. BB 2-6 De v Hants (Derby) 2012. LO HS 131 Wo v Leics (Leicester) 2019 (RLC). LO BB 4-58 Wo v West Indies A (Worcester) 2018. T20 HS 91*. T20 BB 2-2.

WOOD, Christopher Philip (Alton C), b Basingstoke 27 June 1990. 6'2". RHB, LM. Squad No 25. Debut (Hampshire) 2010; cap 2018. London Spirit 2021 to date. HS 105* v Leics (Leicester) 2012. BB 5-39 v Kent (Canterbury) 2014. LO HS 41 v Essex (Southampton) 2013 (Y40). LO BB 5-22 v Glamorgan (Cardiff) 2012 (CB40). T20 HS 27. T20 BB 5-32.

RELEASED/RETIRED

(Having made a County 1st XI appearance in 2022)

T.P.Alsop and L.D.McManus left the staff without making a County 1st XI appearance in 2022.

HAMPSHIRE 2022

RESULTS SUMMARY

	Place	Won	Lost	Drew	NR
LV= Insurance County Champ (Div 1)	3rd	9	4	1	
All First-Class Matches		9	4	2	
Royal London One-Day Cup (Group B)	SF	7	2		
Vitality Blast (South Group)	**Winners**	12	5		

LV= INSURANCE COUNTY CHAMPIONSHIP AVERAGES
BATTING AND FIELDING

Cap		M	I	NO	HS	Runs	Avge	100	50	Ct/St
	B.C.Brown	13	20	2	157	696	38.66	1	4	42/1
2013	J.M.Vince	14	24	2	111	839	38.13	1	6	19
2022	N.R.T.Gubbins	14	24	3	130	754	35.90	2	2	4
2013	L.A.Dawson	12	18	1	171	587	34.52	1	3	18
	F.S.Organ	14	25	2	118	726	31.56	2	3	4
2022	J.K.Fuller	13	21	4	78*	527	31.00	–	2	6
2021	J.J.Weatherley	8	13	–	168	396	30.46	1	2	12
2021	K.H.D.Barker	14	22	2	76	595	29.75	–	4	1
	A.H.T.Donald	9	14	–	94	398	28.42	–	3	19
2021	I.G.Holland	14	24	1	99	519	22.56	–	3	13
2017	K.J.Abbott	13	18	3	57*	233	15.53	–	1	–
2021	B.T.J.Wheal	3	5	4	7*	12	12.00	–	–	1
2022	Mohammad Abbas	12	16	9	8	21	3.00	–	–	3

Also played: M.S.Crane (1 match – cap 2021) did not bat.

BOWLING

	O	M	R	W	Avge	Best	5wI	10wM
Mohammad Abbas	374.1	121	881	50	17.62	6-45	1	–
K.J.Abbott	405.1	100	1159	58	19.98	6-36	4	1
B.T.J.Wheal	73.1	11	244	11	22.18	4-59	–	–
K.H.D.Barker	449.3	127	1164	52	22.38	6-27	3	–
I.G.Holland	162.2	40	503	19	26.47	3-85	–	–
L.A.Dawson	261.4	52	680	24	28.33	7-68	1	1
J.K.Fuller	205.2	16	808	28	28.78	4-34	–	–
F.S.Organ	97	13	314	10	31.40	3-57	–	–

Also bowled:
M.S.Crane 23-0-108-0; N.R.T.Gubbins 1-0-4-0.

The First-Class Averages (pp 221–234) give the records of Hampshire players in all first-class county matches (Hampshire's other opponents being the Sri Lanka Cricket Development XI), with the exception of M.S.Crane and B.T.J.Wheal, whose first-class figures for Hampshire are as above.

HAMPSHIRE RECORDS

FIRST-CLASS CRICKET

Highest Total	For 714-5d		v	Notts	Southampton[2]	2005
	V 742		by	Surrey	The Oval	1909
Lowest Total	For 15		v	Warwicks	Birmingham	1922
	V 23		by	Yorkshire	Middlesbrough	1965
Highest Innings	For 316	R.H.Moore	v	Warwicks	Bournemouth	1937
	V 303*	G.A.Hick	for	Worcs	Southampton[1]	1997

Highest Partnership for each Wicket

1st	347	V.P.Terry/C.L.Smith	v	Warwicks	Birmingham	1987
2nd	373	J.H.K.Adams/M.A.Carberry	v	Somerset	Taunton	2011
3rd	523	M.A.Carberry/N.D.McKenzie	v	Yorkshire	Southampton[2]	2011
4th	367	J.H.K.Adams/S.M.Ervine	v	Warwicks	Southampton[2]	2017
5th	273	L.A.Dawson/B.C.Brown	v	Kent	Canterbury	2022
6th	411	R.M.Poore/E.G.Wynyard	v	Somerset	Taunton	1899
7th	325	G.Brown/C.H.Abercrombie	v	Essex	Leyton	1913
8th	257	N.Pothas/A.J.Bichel	v	Glos	Cheltenham	2005
9th	230	D.A.Livingstone/A.T.Castell	v	Surrey	Southampton[1]	1962
10th	192	H.A.W.Bowell/W.H.Livsey	v	Worcs	Bournemouth	1921

Best Bowling	For 9- 25	R.M.H.Cottam	v	Lancashire	Manchester	1965
(Innings)	V 10- 46	W.Hickton	for	Lancashire	Manchester	1870
Best Bowling	For 17- 86	K.J.Abbott	v	Somerset	Southampton[2]	2019
(Match)	V 17-103	W.Mycroft	for	Derbyshire	Southampton	1876

Most Runs – Season	2854	C.P.Mead	(av 79.27)	1928
Most Runs – Career	48892	C.P.Mead	(av 48.84)	1905-36
Most 100s – Season	12	C.P.Mead		1928
Most 100s – Career	138	C.P.Mead		1905-36
Most Wkts – Season	190	A.S.Kennedy	(av 15.61)	1922
Most Wkts – Career	2669	D.Shackleton	(av 18.23)	1948-69
Most Career W-K Dismissals	700	R.J.Parks	(630 ct; 70 st)	1980-92
Most Career Catches in the Field	629	C.P.Mead		1905-36

LIMITED-OVERS CRICKET

Highest Total	50ov	396-5		v	Kent	Beckenham	2022
	40ov	353-8		v	Middlesex	Lord's	2005
	T20	249-8		v	Derbyshire	Derby	2017
Lowest Total	50ov	50		v	Yorkshire	Leeds	1991
	40ov	43		v	Essex	Basingstoke	1972
	T20	85		v	Sussex	Southampton[2]	2008
Highest Innings	50ov	190	J.M.Vince	v	Glos	Southampton[2]	2019
	40ov	172	C.G.Greenidge	v	Surrey	Southampton[1]	1987
	T20	129*	J.M.Vince	v	Somerset	Taunton	2022
Best Bowling	50ov	7-30	P.J.Sainsbury	v	Norfolk	Southampton[1]	1965
	40ov	6-20	T.E.Jesty	v	Glamorgan	Cardiff	1975
	T20	6-19	Shaheen Shah Afridi	v	Middlesex	Southampton[2]	2020

[1] County Ground (Northlands Road) [2] Ageas Bowl

KENT

Formation of Present Club: 1 March 1859
Substantial Reorganisation: 6 December 1870
Inaugural First-Class Match: 1864
Colours: Maroon and White
Badge: White Horse on a Red Ground
County Champions: (6) 1906, 1909, 1910, 1913, 1970, 1978
Joint Champions: (1) 1977
Gillette Cup Winners: (2) 1967, 1974
Benson and Hedges Cup Winners: (3) 1973, 1976, 1978
Pro 40/National League (Div 1) Winners: (1) 2001
Sunday League Winners: (4) 1972, 1973, 1976, 1995
Royal London One-Day Cup Winners: (1) 2022
Twenty20 Cup Winners: (2) 2007, 2021

Cricket Chief Executive: Simon Storey, The Spitfire Ground, Old Dover Road, Canterbury, CT1 3NZ ● Tel: 01227 456886 ● Email: feedback@kentcricket.co.uk ● Web: www.kentcricket.co.uk ● Twitter: @kentcricket (106,347 followers)

Director of Cricket: Paul Downton. **Head Coach**: Matt Walker. **Batting Coach**: Alex Gidman. **Bowling Coach**: Simon Cook. **Captain**: S.W.Billings. **Overseas Players**: G.F.Linde and K.W.Richardson. **2023 Testimonial**: None. **Head Groundsman**: Adrian Llong. **Scorer**: Lorne Hart. **Blast Team Name**: Kent Spitfires. ‡ New registration. ᴺᵠ Not qualified for England.

BELL-DRUMMOND, Daniel James (Millfield S), b Lewisham, London 4 Aug 1993. 5'10". RHB, RMF. Squad No 23. Debut (Kent) 2011; cap 2015. MCC 2014, 2018. Birmingham Phoenix 2021. London Spirit 2022. 1000 runs (1): 1058 (2015). HS 206* v Loughborough MCCU (Canterbury) 2016. CC HS 166 v Warwks (Canterbury) 2019. BB 3-37 v Essex (Canterbury) 2022. LO HS 171* EL v Sri Lanka A (Canterbury) 2016. LO BB 2-22 v Surrey (Oval) 2019 (RLC). T20 HS 112*. T20 BB 2-19.

BILLINGS, Samuel William (Haileybury S; Loughborough U), b Pembury 15 Jun 1991. 5'11". RHB, WK. Squad No 7. Loughborough MCCU 2011, scoring 131 v Northants (Loughborough) on f-c debut. Kent debut 2011; cap 2015; captain 2018 to date. MCC 2015. IPL: DD 2016-17; CSK 2018-19; KKR 2022. Big Bash: SS 2016-17 to 2017-18; ST 2020-21 to 2021-22; BH 2022-23. Oval Invincibles 2021 to date. **Tests**: 3 (2021-22 to 2022); HS 36 v I (Birmingham) 2022. **LOI**: 28 (2015 to 2022-23); HS 118 v A (Manchester) 2020. **IT20**: 37, inc 1 for ICC World XI (2015 to 2021-22); HS 87 v WI (Basseterre) 2018-19 – world record IT20 score by a No 6 batsman. F-c Tours (EL): A 2021-22 (E); I 2018-19; UAE 2018-19 (v P). HS 171 v Glos (Bristol) 2016. LO HS 175 EL v Pakistan A (Canterbury) 2016. T20 HS 95*.

BLAKE, Alexander James (Hayes SS; Leeds Met U), b Farnborough 25 Jan 1989. 6'1". LHB, RMF. Squad No 10. Debut (Kent) 2008; cap 2017. Oval Invincibles 2021. HS 105* v Yorks (Leeds) 2010. BB 2-9 v Pakistanis (Canterbury) 2010. CC BB 1-60 v Hants (Southampton) 2010. LO HS 116 v Somerset (Taunton) 2017 (RLC). LO BB 2-13 v Yorks (Leeds) 2011 (CB40). T20 HS 71*. T20 BB 1-17.

COMPTON, Benjamin Garnet (Clifton C, Durban), b Durban, S Africa 29 Mar 1994. Son of P.M.D.Compton (Natal 1979-80); grandson of D.S.C.Compton (Middlesex and England 1936-58); cousin of N.R.D.Compton (Middlesex, Somerset, ME, Worcs and England 2004-17). 6'1". LHB, OB. Squad No 2. Nottinghamshire 2019-21. Mountaineers 2021-22 to date. Kent debut 2022. Norfolk 2021. 1000 runs (1): 1193 (2022). HS 217 Mountaineers v SR (Harare) 2022-23. CC HS 140 v Northants (Northampton) 2022. LO HS 110 Mountaineers v Eagles (Harare) 2021-22.

COX, Jordan Matthew (Felsted S), b Margate 21 Oct 2000. 5'8". RHB, WK. Squad No 22. Debut (Kent) 2019. Big Bash: HH 2021-22. Oval Invincibles 2022. Kent 2nd XI debut 2017. England U19 2018-19. YC 2022. HS 238* v Sussex (Canterbury) 2020, sharing K record 2nd wkt partnership of 423 with J.A.Leaning. LO HS 46 EL v Sri Lanka A (Colombo, RPS) 2022-23. T20 HS 94.

CRAWLEY, Zak (Tonbridge S), b Bromley 3 Feb 1998. 6'6". RHB, RM. Squad No 16. Debut (Kent) 2017; cap 2019. Big Bash: HH 2022-23. London Spirit 2021 to date. YC 2020. *Wisden* 2020. **ECB Central Contract 2022-23. Tests**: 33 (2019-20 to 2022-23); HS 267 v P (Southampton) 2020. **LOI**: 3 (2021); HS 58* v P (Cardiff) 2021. F-c Tours: A 2021-22; SA 2019-20; WI 2021-22; NZ 2019-20, 2022-23; I 2020-21; P 2022-23; SL 2019-20, 2020-21. HS (*see Tests*). HS 168 v Glamorgan (Canterbury) 2018. LO HS 120 v Middx (Canterbury) 2019 (RLC). T20 HS 108*.

DENLY, Joseph Liam (Chaucer TC), b Canterbury 16 Mar 1986. 6'0". RHB, LB. Squad No 6. Kent debut 2004; cap 2008; testimonial 2019. Middlesex 2012-14; cap 2012. MCC 2013. IPL: KKR 2019. Big Bash: SS 2017-18 to 2018-19; BH 2020-21. London Spirit 2021. PCA 2018. **Tests**: 15 (2018-19 to 2020); HS 94 v A (Oval) 2019; BB 2-42 v SA (Cape Town) 2019-20. **LOI**: 16 (2009 to 2019-20); HS 87 v SA (Cape Town) 2019-20; BB 1-24 v Ire (Dublin) 2019. **IT20**: 13 (2009 to 2020); HS 30 v WI (Gros Islet) 2018-19; BB 4-19 v SL (Colombo, RPS) 2018-19. F-c Tours: SA 2019-20; WI 2018-19; NZ 2008-09 (Eng A), 2019-20; I 2007-08 (Eng A); SL 2019-20. 1000 runs (4); most – 1266 (2017). HS 227 v Worcs (Worcester) 2017. BB 4-36 v Derbys (Derby) 2018. LO HS 150* v Glamorgan (Canterbury) 2018 (RLC). LO BB 4-35 v Jamaica (North Sound) 2017-18. T20 HS 127 v Essex (Chelmsford) 2017 – K record. T20 BB 4-19.

EVISON, Joseph David Michael (Stamford S), b Peterborough, Cambs 14 Nov 2001. Son of G.M.Evison (Lincolnshire 1993-97); younger brother of S.H.G.Evison (Lincolnshire 2017-18). 6'2". RHB, RM. Squad No 33. Nottinghamshire 2020-22. Leicestershire 2022 (on loan). Kent debut 2022. Nottinghamshire 2nd XI debut 2017. HS 109* Nt v Sussex (Hove) 2022. K HS 34 v Hants (Southampton) 2022. BB 5-21 Nt v Durham (Chester-le-St) 2021. K BB 1-19 v Somerset (Canterbury) 2022. LO HS 109 v Glamorgan (Cardiff) 2022 (RLC). LO BB 3-62 v Essex (Chelmsford) 2022 (RLC). T20 BB –.

FINCH, Harry Zachariah (St Richard's Catholic C, Bexhill; Eastbourne C), b Hastings, E.Sussex 10 Feb 1995. 5'8". RHB, RM. Squad No 72. Sussex 2013-20. Kent debut 2021. HS 135* and BB 1-9 Sx v Leeds/Bradford MCCU (Hove) 2016. CC HS 115 v Sussex (Canterbury) 2021. CC BB 1-30 Sx v Northants (Arundel) 2016. LO HS 108 Sx v Hants (Hove) 2018 (RLC). LO BB –. T20 HS 47.

GILCHRIST, Nathan Nicholas (St Stithian's C; King's C, Taunton), b Harare, Zimbabwe 11 Jun 2000. 6'5". RHB, RFM. Squad No 17. Debut (Kent) 2020. Somerset 2nd XI 2016-19. HS 25 v Surrey (Oval) 2020. BB 6-61 v Somerset (Canterbury) 2022. LO HS 33 v Hants (Beckenham) 2022 (RLC). LO BB 5-45 v Middx (Radlett) 2021 (RLC).

HAMIDULLAH QADRI (Derby Moor S; Chellaston Ac), b Kandahar, Afghanistan 5 Dec 2000. 5'9". RHB, OB. Squad No 75. Derbyshire 2017-19, taking 5-60 v Glamorgan (Cardiff), the youngest to take 5 wkts on CC debut, and the first born this century to play f-c cricket in England. Kent debut 2020. Matabeleland Tuskers 2022-23. England U19 2018-19. HS 87 v Somerset (Canterbury) 2022. BB 6-129 v Lancs (Canterbury) 2022. LO HS 42* v Durham (Beckenham) 2021 (RLC). LO BB 4-36 v Northants (Canterbury) 2022 (RLC). T20 BB 1-34. Youngest to play domestic T20 Blast, aged 16y, 223d.

‡**HOGAN, Michael** Garry, b Newcastle, New South Wales, Australia 31 May 1981. British passport. 6'5". RHB, RFM. Squad No 31. W Australia 2009-10 to 2015-16. Glamorgan 2013-22; cap 2013; captain 2018; testimonial 2020-22. Big Bash: HH 2011-12 to 2012-13. Southern Brave 2022. HS 57 Gm v Lancs (Colwyn Bay) 2015. 50 wkts (3); most – 67 (2013). BB 7-92 Gm v Glos (Bristol) 2013. LO HS 27 WA v Vic (Melbourne) 2011-12. LO BB 5-44 WA v Vic (Melbourne) 2010-11. T20 HS 17*. T20 BB 5-17.

KLAASSEN, Frederick Jack (Sacred Heart C, Auckland, NZ), b Haywards Heath, Sussex 13 Nov 1992. 6'4". RHB, LMF. Squad No 18. England-qualified thanks to UK passport. Debut (Kent) 2019. Manchester Originals 2021 to date. **LOI** (Neth): 14 (2018 to 2022); HS 13 v Nepal (Amstelveen) 2018; BB 3-23 v Ire (Utrecht) 2021. **IT20** (Neth): 37 (2018 to 2022-23); HS 13 v Z (Rotterdam) 2019; BB 5-19 v Uganda (Bulawayo) 2022. HS 14* v Loughborough MCCU (Canterbury) 2019. CC HS 13 v Yorks (Canterbury) 2019. BB 4-44 v Middx (Canterbury) 2020. LO HS 13 (*see LOI*). LO BB 3-23 (*see LOI*). T20 HS 13. T20 BB 5-19.

LEANING, Jack Andrew (Archbishop Holgate's S, York; York C), b Bristol, Glos 18 Oct 1993. 5'10". RHB, RMF. Squad No 34. Yorkshire 2013-19; cap 2016. Kent debut 2020; cap 2021. YC 2015. HS 220* v Sussex (Canterbury) 2020, sharing K record 2nd wkt partnership of 423 with J.M.Cox. BB 2-20 Y v Hants (Southampton) 2019. LO HS 131* Y v Leics (Leicester) 2016 (RLC). LO BB 5-22 Y v Unicorns (Leeds) 2013 (Y40). T20 HS 81*. T20 BB 3-15.

NQ**LINDE, George** Fredrik (Pretoria U), b Cape Town, South Africa 4 Dec 1991. 6'2". LHB, SLA. Squad No 27. W Province 2011-12 to date. Cape Cobras 2014-15 to 2020-21. Kent debut 2022. **Tests** (SA): 3 (2019-20 to 2020-21); HS 37 v I (Ranchi) 2019-20; BB 5-64 v P (Rawalpindi) 2020-21. **LOI** (SA): 2 (2021); HS 18 and BB 2-32 v SL (Colombo, RPS) 2021. **IT20** (SA): 14 (2020-21 to 2021); HS 29 v E (Paarl) 2020-21; BB 3-23 v P (Johannesburg) 2020-21. F-c Tours (SA): I 2019-20; P 2020-21. HS 148* Cobras v Titans (Cape Town) 2019-20. K HS 107 SL Dev (Canterbury) 2022. CC HS 31 v Northants (Northampton) 2022. BB 7-29 Cobras v Knights (Cape Town) 2020-21. K BB 3-43 v Northants (Canterbury) 2022. LO HS 93* WP v Northerns (Rondebosch) 2015-16. LO BB 6-47 Cobras v Warriors (Oudtshoorn) 2017-18. T20 HS 63*. T20 BB 4-19.

LOGAN, James Edwin Graham (Normanton Freestone HS; Pontefract New C), b Wakefield, Yorks 12 Oct 1997. 6'1". LHB, SLA. Squad No 11. Yorkshire 2018-19. Kent debut 2021. No 1st XI appearances in 2022. HS 21 and K BB 3-8 v Leics (Leicester) 2021. BB 4-22 Y v Warwks (York) 2019. LO HS 17* v Glos (Beckenham) 2021 (RLC). LO BB 2-45 v Worcs (Worcester) 2021 (RLC). T20 BB 1-4.

NQ**MUYEYE, Tawanda** Sean (Eastbourne C), b Harare, Zimbabwe 5 March 2001. 6'0". RHB, OB. Squad No 14. Wisden Schools Cricketer of the Year 2020. Debut (Kent) 2021. HS 89 v Middx (Canterbury) 2021. BB 2-70 v Hants (Canterbury) 2022. LO HS 40 v Hants (Beckenham) 2022 (RLC). LO BB 1-17 v Northants (Canterbury) 2022 (RLC). T20 HS 41.

O'RIORDAN, Marcus Kevin (Tonbridge S), b Pembury 25 Jan 1998. 5'10". RHB, OB. Squad No 55. Debut (Kent) 2019. HS 102* v SL Dev (Canterbury) 2022. CC HS 52* v Hants (Canterbury) 2020. BB 3-50 v Sussex (Canterbury) 2020. LO HS 60 v Middx (Radlett) 2021 (RLC). LO BB 1-77 v Durham (Beckenham) 2021 (RLC). T20 HS 13*. T20 BB 2-24.

QUINN, Matthew Richard, b Auckland, New Zealand 28 Feb 1993. 6'4". RHB, RMF. Squad No 64. Auckland 2012-13 to 2015-16. Essex 2016-20. Kent debut 2021. UK passport. HS 50 Auckland v Canterbury (Auckland) 2013-14. CC HS 19* v Northants (Northampton) 2022. BB 7-76 (11-163 match) Ex v Glos (Cheltenham) 2016. K BB 6-23 v Hants (Southampton) 2022. LO HS 36 Auckland v CD (Auckland) 2013-14. LO BB 4-71 Ex v Sussex (Hove) 2016 (RLC). T20 HS 8*. T20 BB 4-20.

‡NQ**RICHARDSON, Kane** William, b Eudunda, S Australia 12 Feb 1991. RHB, RMF. Squad No 47. S Australia 2010-11 to 2020-21. Joins Kent in 2023 (T20 only). IPL: PW 2013; RR 2014; RCB 2016 to 2021. Big Bash: AS 2011-12 to 2016-17; MR 2017-18 to date. Birmingham Phoenix 2022. **LOI** (A): 25 (2012-13 to 2019-20); HS 24* v I (Rajkot) 2019-20; BB 5-68 v I (Canberra) 2015-16. **IT20** (A): 35 (2014-15 to 2022-23); HS 9 v I (Adelaide) 2015-16; BB 4-30 v SL (Colombo, RPS) 2022. HS 49 SA v Tas (Adelaide) 2013-14. BB 5-69 SA v WA (Adelaide, GS) 2016-17. LO HS 36 SA v Tas (Sydney, HO) 2016-17. LO BB 6-48 SA v Q (Adelaide) 2012-13. T20 HS 45. T20 BB 4-22.

SINGH, Jaskaran (Wilmington Ac), b Denmark Hill, London 19 Sep 2002. 6'5". RHB, RFM. Squad No 19. Debut (Kent) 2021, dismissing A.G.H.Orr with his fifth ball in f-c cricket. Kent 2nd XI debut 2021. HS 14* v SL Dev (Canterbury) 2022. CC HS 4 v Surrey (Oval) 2022. BB 4-51 v Sussex (Canterbury) 2021. T20 BB –.

STEWART, Grant (All Saints C, Maitland; U of Newcastle) b Kalgoorlie, W Australia 19 Feb 1994. 6'2". RHB, RMF. Squad No 9. England qualified due to Italian mother. Debut (Kent) 2017. Sussex 2022 (on loan). **IT20** (Italy): 10 (2021-22 to 2022-23); HS 76 v Germany (Almeria) 2022-23; BB 2-17 v Denmark (Almeria) 2021-22. HS 103 and BB 6-22 v Middx (Canterbury) 2018. LO HS 49 v Lancs (Canterbury) 2022 (RLC). LO BB 4-42 v Leics (Leicester) 2022 (RLC). T20 HS 76. T20 BB 3-33.

RELEASED/RETIRED

(Having made a County 1st XI appearance in 2022. Some may return in 2023.)

NO**BIRD, Jackson** Munro (St Pius X C, Sydney; St Ignatius C, Riverview), b Paddington, Sydney, Australia 11 Dec 1986. RHB, RFM. Kent 2022. Big Bash: MS 2011-12 to 2018-19; SS 2015-16 to date. **Tests** (A): 9 (2012-13 to 2017-18); HS 19* v P (Brisbane) 2016-17; BB 5-59 v NZ (Christchurch) 2015-16. F-c Tours (A): E 2012 (Aus A), 2013, 2019 (Aus A); NZ 2015-16; I 2016-17 (Aus A), SL 2016. HS 64 Tas v WA (Perth) 2020-21. CC HS 53* and K BB 3-85 v Essex (Chelmsford) 2022. 50 wkts (0+2): most – 53 (2011-12). BB 7-18 Tas v NSW (Hobart) 2020-21. CC BB 4-56 Nt v Surrey (Nottingham) 2016. LO HS 28* Tas v NSW (Hobart) 2020-21. LO BB 6-25 Tas v NSW (Hobart) 2019-20. T20 HS 14*. T20 BB 4-31.

NO**DUFFY, Jacob** Andrew, b Lumsden, New Zealand 2 Aug 1994. Younger brother of R.M.Duffy. Otago 2013-14 to 2016-17. RHB, RFM. Otago 2011-12 to date. Kent 2022. **LOI** (NZ): 3 (2022 to 2022-23); HS 0; BB 3-52 v Scotland (Edinburgh) 2022. **IT20** (NZ): 10 (2020-21 to 2022-23); HS 6* v I (Lucknow) 2022-23; BB 4-33 v P (Auckland) 2020-21. F-c Tours (NZ): E 2015; I 2022-23 (NZA). HS 71 Otago v Auckland (Dunedin) 2018-19. K HS 1. BB 7-89 Otago v Wellington (Wellington) 2019-20. K BB 5-66 v Glos (Canterbury) 2022. LO HS 39 Otago v Auckland (Auckland) 2014-15. LO BB 6-35 Otago v Canterbury (Christchurch) 2018-19. T20 HS 18. T20 BB 5-18.

HENRY, M.J. – *see* SOMERSET.

LUCKETT, Max John (Dartford GS; Loughborough U), b Dartford 18 Nov 2002. RHB, RFM. Kent 2022. Kent 2nd XI debut 2021. Nottinghamshire 2nd XI 2022. Derbyshire 2nd XI 2022. HS –. BB 2-73 v SL Dev (Canterbury) 2022.

MEAD, Sebastian William ('**Billy**') (Marlborough C), b Winchester, Hants 3 Feb 1999. Great-grandson of S.C.Griffith (Cambridge U, Surrey, Sussex and England 1934-54); great-nephew of M.G.Griffith (Sussex and Cambridge U 1962-74). RHB, WK, occ OB. Kent 2022, scoring 106* v SL Dev (Canterbury) 2022 in only 1st XI appearance. Hampshire 2nd XI 2017. MCC YC 2018-19. Surrey 2nd XI 2021. Somerset 2nd XI 2021.

MILNES, M.E. – *see* YORKSHIRE.

PODMORE, H.W. – *see* GLAMORGAN.

NO**QAIS AHMAD** Kamawal, b Nangarhar, Afghanistan 15 Aug 2000. RHB, LB. Squad No 32. Speen Ghar Region 2017-18 to 2018-19. Kent 2021-22 (T20 only). Big Bash: HH 2018-19 to 2019-20; MS 2021-22. Welsh Fire 2021. **Tests** (Afg): 1 (2019); HS 14 and BB 1-22 v B (Chittagong) 2019. **LOI** (Afg): 1 (2021-22); BB 3-32 v Neth (Doha) 2021-22. **IT20** (Afg): 2 (2019-20 to 2021-22); HS 8 v B (Mirpur) 2021-22; BB 3-25 v Ire (Greater Noida) 2019-20. HS 46* Afg A v Bangladesh A (Khulna) 2019. BB 7-41 SGR v Band-e-Amir (Ghazi Amanullah Khan) 2019. LO HS 66 Afg Emerging Players v Oman (Colombo, CCC) 2018-19. LO BB 3-21 SGR v Amo Region (Kandahar) 2020-21. T20 HS 50*. T20 BB 5-18.

RELEASED/RETIRED continued on p 129

KENT 2022
RESULTS SUMMARY

	Place	Won	Lost	Drew	NR
LV= Insurance County Champ (Div 1)	5th	4	5	5	
All First-Class Matches		4	5	6	
Royal London One-Day Cup (Group B)	**Winners**	7	3		1
Vitality Blast (South Group)	9th	3	11		

LV= INSURANCE COUNTY CHAMPIONSHIP AVERAGES BATTING AND FIELDING

Cap		M	I	NO	HS	Runs	Avge	100	50	Ct/St
	B.G.Compton	13	25	3	140	1193	54.22	4	6	7
	Hamidullah Qadri	3	5	1	87	208	52.00	–	2	–
	J.M.Cox	12	20	1	158	917	45.85	2	6	14
2015	D.J.Bell-Drummond	14	25	4	149	923	43.95	4	3	6
2021	J.A.Leaning	11	19	1	128	755	41.94	2	4	15
2008	J.L.Denly	7	11	–	141	448	40.72	1	3	2
	J.M.Bird	3	5	2	53*	85	28.33	–	1	–
2022	O.G.Robinson	12	20	2	85*	497	27.61	–	4	28/1
2019	Z.Crawley	9	17	–	84	467	27.47	–	4	9
	T.S.Muyeye	5	8	–	85	211	26.37	–	2	4
	G.Stewart	6	10	1	90	231	25.66	–	3	1
2005	D.I.Stevens	5	7	1	51	148	24.66	–	1	1
2015	S.W.Billings	5	7	1	44	143	23.83	–	–	25/1
	M.J.Henry	2	4	–	34	79	19.75	–	–	1
2021	M.E.Milnes	10	17	3	67	268	19.14	–	1	1
	G.F.Linde	3	5	–	31	109	15.57	–	–	3
	M.R.Quinn	10	15	9	19*	58	9.66	–	–	1
2019	H.W.Podmore	2	4	–	13	35	8.75	–	–	–
	N.N.Gilchrist	8	13	–	14	57	4.38	–	–	2
	N.Saini	2	4	1	5*	8	2.66	–	–	–

Also batted: J.A.Duffy (2 matches) 0, 1 (2 ct); J.D.M.Evison 34, 1, 21 (1 ct); H.Z.Finch (1) 0, 24 (1 ct); C.McKerr (2) 1, 0, 6 (1 ct); T.H.S.Pettman (1) 3* (1 ct); J.Singh (2) 4.

BOWLING

	O	M	R	W	Avge	Best	5wI	10wM
M.J.Henry	83	15	226	12	18.83	5- 45	1	–
N.Saini	57	8	262	11	23.81	5- 72	1	–
N.N.Gilchrist	224.1	26	892	33	27.03	6- 61	1	–
M.R.Quinn	291.5	62	886	30	29.53	6- 23	1	–
M.E.Milnes	253	43	901	21	42.90	4- 11	–	–
G.Stewart	159.2	22	556	11	50.54	3- 81	–	–
G.F.Linde	208.1	27	733	12	61.08	3- 43	–	–

Also bowled:

D.J.Bell-Drummond	84.1	10	273	9	30.33	3- 37	–	–
H.W.Podmore	55.2	4	164	5	32.80	2- 11	–	–
J.A.Duffy	62	4	320	8	40.00	5- 66	1	–
J.L.Denly	56	5	211	5	42.20	2- 31	–	–
Hamidullah Qadri	80.5	6	345	8	43.12	6-129	1	–
J.A.Leaning	132.3	12	499	7	71.28	2- 36	–	–

J.M.Bird 64-12-226-3; B.G.Compton 3-0-13-0; J.D.M.Evison 15-3-58-1; C.McKerr 25-3-98-2; T.S.Muyeye 49.5-3-192-3; T.H.S.Pettman 22-2-102-2; J.Singh 36.2-4-165-1; D.I.Stevens 126-31-371-4.

The First-Class Averages (pp 221–234) give the records of Kent players in all first-class county matches (Kent's other opponents being the Sri Lanka Cricket Development XI), with the exception of S.W.Billings, Z.Crawley, J.D.M.Evison, M.J.Henry, C.McKerr, T.H.S.Pettman and G.Stewart, whose first-class figures for Kent are as above.

KENT RECORDS

FIRST-CLASS CRICKET

Highest Total	For 803-4d		v	Essex	Brentwood	1934
	V 676		by	Australians	Canterbury	1921
Lowest Total	For 18		v	Sussex	Gravesend	1867
	V 16		by	Warwicks	Tonbridge	1913
Highest Innings	For 332	W.H.Ashdown	v	Essex	Brentwood	1934
	V 344	W.G.Grace	for	MCC	Canterbury	1876

Highest Partnership for each Wicket

1st	300	N.R.Taylor/M.R.Benson	v	Derbyshire	Canterbury	1991
2nd	423*	J.M.Cox/J.A.Leaning	v	Sussex	Canterbury	2020
3rd	323	R.W.T.Key/M.van Jaarsveld	v	Surrey	Tunbridge Wells	2005
4th	368	P.A.de Silva/G.R.Cowdrey	v	Derbyshire	Maidstone	1995
5th	277	F.E.Woolley/L.E.G.Ames	v	N Zealanders	Canterbury	1931
6th	346	S.W.Billings/D.I.Stevens	v	Yorkshire	Leeds	2019
7th	248	A.P.Day/E.Humphreys	v	Somerset	Taunton	1908
8th	222	S.A.Northeast/J.C.Tredwell	v	Essex	Chelmsford	2016
9th	171	M.A.Ealham/P.A.Strang	v	Notts	Nottingham	1997
10th	235	F.E.Woolley/A.Fielder	v	Worcs	Stourbridge	1909

Best Bowling	For	10- 30	C.Blythe	v	Northants	Northampton	1907
(Innings)	V	10- 48	C.H.G.Bland	for	Sussex	Tonbridge	1899
Best Bowling	For	17- 48	C.Blythe	v	Northants	Northampton	1907
(Match)	V	17-106	T.W.J.Goddard	for	Glos	Bristol	1939

Most Runs – Season	2894	F.E.Woolley	(av 59.06)	1928
Most Runs – Career	47868	F.E.Woolley	(av 41.77)	1906-38
Most 100s – Season	10	F.E.Woolley		1928, 1934
Most 100s – Career	122	F.E.Woolley		1906-38
Most Wkts – Season	262	A.P.Freeman	(av 14.74)	1933
Most Wkts – Career	3340	A.P.Freeman	(av 17.64)	1914-36
Most Career W-K Dismissals	1253	F.H.Huish	(901 ct; 352 st)	1895-1914
Most Career Catches in the Field	773	F.E.Woolley		1906-38

LIMITED-OVERS CRICKET

Highest Total	50ov	384-6		v	Berkshire	Finchampstead	1994
		384-8		v	Surrey	Beckenham	2018
	40ov	337-7		v	Sussex	Canterbury	2013
	T20	236-3		v	Essex	Canterbury	2021
Lowest Total	50ov	60		v	Somerset	Taunton	1979
	40ov	83		v	Middlesex	Lord's	1984
	T20	72		v	Hampshire	Southampton[2]	2011
Highest Innings	50ov	206*	O.G.Robinson	v	Worcs	Worcester	2022
	40ov	146	A.Symonds	v	Lancashire	Tunbridge Wells	2004
	T20	127	J.L.Denly	v	Essex	Chelmsford	2017
Best Bowling	50ov	8-31	D.L.Underwood	v	Scotland	Edinburgh	1987
	40ov	6- 9	R.A.Woolmer	v	Derbyshire	Chesterfield	1979
	T20	5-11	A.F.Milne	v	Somerset	Taunton	2017

LANCASHIRE

Formation of Present Club: 12 January 1864
Inaugural First-Class Match: 1865
Colours: Red, Green and Blue
Badge: Red Rose
County Champions (since 1890): (8) 1897, 1904, 1926, 1927, 1928, 1930, 1934, 2011
Joint Champions: (1) 1950
Gillette/NatWest Trophy Winners: (7) 1970, 1971, 1972, 1975, 1990, 1996, 1998
Benson and Hedges Cup Winners: (4) 1984, 1990, 1995, 1996
Pro 40/National League (Div 1) Winners: (1) 1999.
Sunday League Winners: (4) 1969, 1970, 1989, 1998
Twenty20 Cup Winners: (1) 2015

Chief Executive: Daniel Gidney, Emirates Old Trafford, Talbot Road, Manchester M16 0PX • Tel: 0161 282 4000 • Email: enquiries@lancashirecricket.co.uk • Web: www.lancashirecricket.co.uk • Twitter: @lancscricket (147,602 followers)

Head Coach: Glen Chapple. **Assistant Head Coach**: Carl Crowe **Director of Cricket Performance**: Mark Chilton. **Bowling Coach**: Graham Onions. **Captain**: K.K.Jennings. **Overseas Players**: C.de Grandhomme, D.J.Mitchell and D.J.Vilas. **2023 Testimonial**: None. **Head Groundsman**: Matthew Merchant. **Scorer**: Chris Rimmer. **Blast Team Name**: Lancashire Lightning. ‡ New registration. NQ Not qualified for England.

ANDERSON, James Michael (St Theodore RC HS and SFC, Burnley), b Burnley 30 Jul 1982. 6'2". LHB, RFM. Squad No 9. Debut (Lancashire) 2002; cap 2003; benefit 2012. Auckland 2007-08. YC 2003. *Wisden* 2008. OBE 2015. **ECB Central Contract 2022-23.** Tests: 179 (2003 to 2022-23); HS 81 v I (Nottingham) 2014, sharing a world Test record 10th wkt partnership of 198 with J.E.Root; 50 wkts (3); most – 57 (2010); BB 7-42 v WI (Lord's) 2017. LOI: 194 (2002-03 to 2014-15); HS 28 v NZ (Southampton) 2013; BB 5-23 v SA (Port Elizabeth) 2009-10. Hat-trick v P (Oval) 2003. IT20: 19 (2006-07 to 2009-10); HS 1* v A (Sydney) 2006-07; BB 3-23 v Netherlands (Lord's) 2009. F-c Tours: A 2006-07, 2010-11, 2013-14, 2017-18, 2021-22; SA 2004-05, 2009-10, 2015-16, 2019-20; WI 2003-04, 2005-06 (Eng A) (*part*), 2008-09, 2014-15, 2018-19; NZ 2007-08, 2012-13, 2017-18, 2022-23; I 2005-06 (*part*), 2008-09, 2012-13, 2016-17, 2020-21; P 2022-23; SL 2003-04, 2007-08, 2011-12, 2018-19, 2020-21; UAE 2011-12 (v P), 2015-16 (v P). HS 81 (*see Tests*). La HS 42 v Surrey (Manchester) 2015. 50 wkts (4); most – 60 (2005, 2017). BB 7-19 v Kent (Manchester) 2021. Hat-trick v Essex (Manchester) 2003. LO HS 28 (*see LOI*). LO BB 5-23 (*see LOI*). T20 HS 16. T20 BB 3-23.

ASPINWALL, Thomas Henry (Sedbergh S), b Lancaster 13 Mar 2004. 5'10". RHB, RM. Squad No 13. Lancashire 2nd XI debut 2021. England U19 2022 to 2022-23. Awaiting 1st XI debut.

BAILEY, Thomas Ernest (Our Lady's Catholic HS, Preston), b Preston 21 Apr 1991. 6'4". RHB, RMF. Squad No 8. Debut (Lancashire) 2012; cap 2018. F-c Tour (EL): I 2018-19. HS 68 v Northants (Manchester) 2019. 50 wkts (3); most – 65 (2018). BB 7-37 v Hants (Liverpool) 2021. LO HS 45 v Sussex (Sedbergh) 2021 (RLC). LO BB 3-22 v Glamorgan (Neath) 2022 (RLC). T20 HS 10. T20 BB 5-17.

BALDERSON, George Philip (Cheadle Hulme HS), b Manchester 11 Oct 2000. 5'11". LHB, RM. Squad No 10. Debut (Lancashire) 2020. Lancashire 2nd XI debut 2018. England U19 2018-19. HS 97 v Surrey (Manchester) 2022. BB 5-14 v Essex (Chelmsford) 2022. LO HS 106* v Kent (Canterbury) 2022 (RLC). LO BB 3-25 v Hants (Southampton) 2021 (RLC).

BELL, George Joseph (Manchester GS), b Manchester 25 Sep 2002. RHB, WK. Squad No 17. Debut (Lancashire) 2022. Lancashire 2nd XI debut 2021. HS 24 v Essex (Chelmsford) 2022. LO HS 35 v Worcs (Manchester) 2022 (RLC). T20 HS 31.

BLATHERWICK, Jack Morgan (Holgate Ac, Hucknall; Central C, Nottingham), b Nottingham 4 June 1998. 6'2". RHB, RMF. Squad No 4. Nottinghamshire 2019. Lancashire debut 2021. Northamptonshire 2019 (L-o only). England U19 2017. HS 11 v Warwks (Lord's) 2021. BB 4-28 v Somerset (Taunton) 2021. LO HS 5* and LO BB 3-57 v Kent (Canterbury) 2022 (RLC).

BOHANNON, Joshua James (Harper Green HS), b Bolton 9 Apr 1997. 5'8". RHB, RM. Squad No 20. Debut (Lancashire) 2018; cap 2021. F-c Tour (EL): SL 2022-23. HS 231 v Glos (Manchester) 2022. BB 3-46 v Hants (Southampton) 2018. LO HS 75 v Kent (Canterbury) 2022 (RLC). LO BB 1-33 v Notts (Nottingham) 2019. T20 HS 35.

BOYDEN, Joshua Ashton (Parklands HS, Chorley; Runshaw C), b Chorley 16 Apr 2004. LHB, LMF. Squad No 27. Lancashire 2nd XI debut 2021. Awaiting 1st XI debut.

BUTTLER, Joseph Charles (King's C, Taunton), b Taunton, Somerset 8 Sep 1990. 6'0". RHB, WK. Squad No 6. Somerset 2009-13; cap 2013. Lancashire debut 2014; cap 2018. IPL: MI 2016-17; RR 2018 to date. Big Bash: MR 2013-14; ST 2017-18 to 2018-19. Manchester Originals 2021 to date. *Wisden* 2018. MBE 2020. **ECB Central Contract 2022-23. Tests**: 57 (2014 to 2021-22); HS 152 v P (Southampton) 2020. **LOI**: 165 (2011-12 to 2022-23, 23 as captain); HS 162* (in 70 balls) v Neth (Amstelveen) 2022. **IT20**: 103 (2011 to 2022-23, 20 as captain); HS 101* v SL (Sharjah) 2021-22. F-c Tours: A 2021-22; SA 2019-20; WI 2015, 2018-19; NZ 2019-20; I 2016-17, 2020-21; SL 2018-19, 2019-20, 2020-21; UAE 2015-16 (v P). CC HS 144 Sm v Hants (Southampton) 2010. La HS 100* v Durham (Chester-le-St) 2014. BB –. LO HS 162* (*see LOI*). T20 HS 124.

CROFT, Steven John (Highfield HS, Blackpool; Myerscough C), b Blackpool 11 Oct 1984. 5'10". RHB, OB. Squad No 15. Debut (Lancashire) 2005; cap 2010; captain 2017; testimonial 2018. Auckland 2008-09. HS 156 v Northants (Manchester) 2014. BB 6-41 v Worcs (Manchester) 2012. LO HS 127 v Warwks (Birmingham) 2017 (RLC). LO BB 4-24 v Scotland (Manchester) 2008 (FPT). T20 HS 94*. T20 BB 3-6.

‡[NQ]**De GRANDHOMME, Colin**, b Harare, Zimbabwe 22 Jul 1986. Son of L.L.de Grandhomme (Rhodesia B and Zimbabwe 1979-80 to 1987-88). RHB, RMF. Zimbabwe A 2005-06. Auckland 2006-07 to 2017-18. N Districts 2018-19 to date. Hampshire 2021. Surrey 2022. Warwickshire 2017-18 (T20 only). IPL: KKR 2017; RCB 2018-19. Big Bash: AS 2022-23. Southern Brave 2021. **Tests** (NZ): 29 (2016-17 to 2022); HS 120* v SA (Christchurch) 2021-22; BB 6-41 v P (Christchurch) 2016-17 – on debut. **LOI** (NZ): 45 (2011-12 to 2019-20); HS 74* v P (Hamilton) 2017-18; BB 3-26 v I (Hamilton) 2018-19. **IT20** (NZ): 41 (2011-12 to 2021); HS 59 v SL (Pallekele) 2019; BB 2-22 v SA (Auckland) 2016-17. F-c Tours (NZ): E 2014 (NZ A), 2021, 2022; A 2019-20; SA 2005-06 (Z U23); SL 2019; UAE 2018-19 (v P). HS 174* H v Surrey (Southampton) 2021. BB 6-24 Auckland v Wellington (Auckland) 2013-14. CC BB 4-31 H v Glos (Cheltenham) 2021. LO HS 151 NZ A v Northants (Northampton) 2014. LO BB 4-37 Auckland v Wellington (Wellington) 2015-16. T20 HS 86. T20 BB 3-4.

GLEESON, Richard James (Baines HS), b Blackpool, Lancs 2 Dec 1987. 6'3". RHB, RFM. Squad No 11. Northamptonshire 2015-18. Lancashire debut 2019. MCC 2018. Big Bash: MR 2019-20. Manchester Originals 2022. Cumberland 2010-15. **IT20**: 6 (2022 to 2022-23); HS 2 and BB 3-15 v I (Birmingham) 2022. F-c Tour (EL): WI 2017-18. HS 31 Nh v Glos (Bristol) 2016. La HS 11 v Leics (Liverpool) 2019. BB 6-43 v Leics (Leicester) 2019. Hat-trick MCC v Essex (Bridgetown) 2017-18. LO HS 13 EL v West Indies A (Coolidge) 2017-18. LO BB 5-47 Nh v Worcs (Worcester) 2016 (RLC). T20 HS 8. T20 BB 5-33.

HARTLEY, Tom William (Merchant Taylors S), b Ormskirk 3 May 1999. 6'3". LHB, SLA. Squad No 2. Debut (Lancashire) 2020. Manchester Originals 2021 to date. Lancashire 2nd XI debut 2018. HS 25 v Northants (Manchester) 2021. BB 5-52 v Surrey (Manchester) 2022. LO HS 23 v Sri Lanka A (Colombo, RPS) 2022-23. LO BB 1-46 v Sri Lanka A (Colombo, RPS) 2022-23 – separate matches. T20 HS 19*. T20 BB 4-16.

HURST, Matthew ('Matty') Frederick (Byrchall HS, Wigan; Winstanley C), b Billinge, Cheshire 10 Dec 2003. RHB, WK. Squad No 21. Lancashire 2nd XI debut 2021. England U19 2022 to 2022-23. Awaiting 1st XI debut.

JENNINGS, Keaton Kent (King Edward VII S, Johannesburg), b Johannesburg, South Africa 19 Jun 1992. Son of R.V.Jennings (Transvaal 1973-74 to 1992-93), brother of D.Jennings (Gauteng and Easterns 1999 to 2003-04), nephew of K.E.Jennings (Northern Transvaal 1981-82 to 1982-83). 6'4". LHB, RM. Squad No 1. Gauteng 2011-12. Durham 2012-17; captain 2017 (l-o only). Lancashire debut/cap 2018; captain 2023. **Tests**: 17 (2016-17 to 2018-19); HS 146* v SL (Galle) 2018-19; scored 112 v I (Mumbai) on debut; BB –. F-c Tours (C=Captain): A 2019-20 (EL)C; WI 2017-18 (EL)C, 2018-19; I 2016-17; SL 2016-17 (EL), 2018-19. 1000 runs (2); most – 1602 (2016), inc seven hundreds (Du record). HS 318 v Somerset (Southport) 2022. BB 3-37 Du v Sussex (Chester-le-St) 2017. La BB 1-8 v Durham (Sedbergh) 2019. LO HS 139 Du v Warwks (Birmingham) 2017 (RLC). LO BB 2-19 v Worcs (Worcester) 2018 (RLC). T20 HS 108 v Durham (Chester-le-St) 2020 – La record. T20 BB 4-37.

JONES, Robert Peter (Bridgewater HS), b Warrington, Cheshire 3 Nov 1995. 5'10". RHB, LB. Squad No 12. Debut (Lancashire) 2016. Cheshire 2014. HS 122 v Middx (Lord's) 2019. BB 1-4 v Northants (Manchester) 2021. LO HS 85* v Worcs (Manchester) 2022 (RLC). LO BB 1-3 v Leics (Manchester) 2019 (RLC). T20 HS 61*.

LAMB, Daniel John (St Michael's HS, Chorley; Cardinal Newman C, Preston), b Preston 7 Sep 1995. 6'0". RHB, RMF. Squad No 26. Debut (Lancashire) 2018. HS 125 v Kent (Canterbury) 2021, sharing La record 8th wkt partnership of 187 with L.Wood. BB 4-55 v Yorks (Leeds) 2019. LO HS 86* v Sussex (Sedbergh) 2021 (RLC). LO BB 5-30 v Glos (Bristol) 2021 (RLC). T20 HS 29*. T20 BB 3-23.

LAVELLE, George Isaac Davies (Merchant Taylors S), b Ormskirk 24 Mar 2000. 5'8". RHB, WK. Squad No 24. Debut (Lancashire) 2020. Lancashire 2nd XI debut 2017. England U19 2018. HS 32 v Notts (Nottingham) 2021. LO HS 61* v Northants (Blackpool) 2022 (RLC). T20 HS 12.

LIVINGSTONE, Liam Stephen (Chetwynde S, Barrow-in-Furness), b Barrow-in-Furness, Cumberland 4 Aug 1993. 6'1". RHB, LB. Squad No 23. Debut (Lancashire) 2016; cap 2017; captain 2018. IPL: RR 2019 to 2021; PK 2022. Big Bash: PS 2019-20 to 2020-21. Birmingham Phoenix 2021 to date. **ECB Central Contract 2022-23. Tests**: 1 (2022-23); HS 9 v P (Rawalpindi) 2022-23. **LOI**: 12 (2020-21 to 2022); HS 66* (fastest fifty by an England player: 17 balls) v Neth (Amstelveen) 2022; BB 2-30 v SA (Chester-le-St) 2022; took wkt of K.L.Rahul with 2nd delivery in international cricket. **IT20**: 29 (2017 to 2022-23); HS 103 v P (Nottingham) 2021; BB 3-17 v Ire (Melbourne) 2022-23. F-c Tours (EL): WI 2017-18; P 2022-23 (E); SL 2016-17. HS 224 v Warwks (Manchester) 2017. BB 6-52 v Surrey (Manchester) 2017. LO HS 129 EL v South Africa A (Northampton) 2017. LO BB 3-51 v Yorks (Manchester) 2016 (RLC). T20 HS 103. T20 BB 4-17.

MAHMOOD, Saqib (Matthew Moss HS, Rochdale), b Birmingham, Warwks 25 Feb 1997. 6'3". RHB, RFM. Squad No 25. Debut (Lancashire) 2016. Big Bash: ST 2021-22. Oval Invincibles 2021. **ECB Pace Bowling Development Contract 2022-23. Tests**: 2 (2021-22) HS 49 v WI (St George's) 2021-22; BB 2-21 v WI (Bridgetown) 2021-22. **LOI**: 8 (2019-20 to 2022-23); HS 12 v Ire (Southampton) 2020; BB 4-42 v P (Cardiff) 2021. **IT20**: 12 (2019-20 to 2022); HS 7* v WI (Bridgetown) 2021; BB 3-33 v P (Leeds) 2021. F-c Tours (EL): A 2021-22; WI 2017-18, 2022-23 (E). HS 49 (*see* Tests). La HS 34 v Middx (Manchester) 2019. BB 5-47 v Yorks (Manchester) 2021. LO HS 45 v Warwks (Birmingham) 2019 (RLC). LO BB 6-37 v Northants (Manchester) 2019 (RLC). T20 HS 11*. T20 BB 4-14.

‡NQMITCHELL, Daryl Joseph, b Hamilton, New Zealand 20 May 1991. RHB, RM. N Districts 2011-12 to 2019-20. Canterbury debut 2020-21. Middlesex 2021. IPL: RR 2022. **Tests** (NZ): 16 (2019-20 to 2022-23); HS 190 v E (Nottingham) 2022; BB 1-7 v WI (Hamilton) 2020-21. **LOI** (NZ): 19 (2020-21 to 2022-23); HS 100* v B (Wellington) 2020-21; BB 3-25 v I (Christchurch) 2022-23. **IT20** (NZ): 44 (2018-19 to 2022-23); HS 72* v E (Abu Dhabi) 2021-22; BB 2-27 v I (Hamilton) 2018-19. F-c Tours (NZ): E 2021, 2022; I/SL 2013-14 (NZA); I 2021-22; P 2022-23. HS 190 (see Tests). CC HS 73 M v Glos (Cheltenham) 2021. BB 5-44 Cant v Otago (Alexandra) 2020-21. LO HS 126* ND v Wellington (Wellington) 2017-18. LO BB 3-25 (see LOI). T20 HS 88*. T20 BB 4-32.

MORLEY, Jack Peter (Siddal Moor Sports C), b Rochdale 25 Jun 2001. 5'10". LHB, SLA. Squad No 18. Debut (Lancashire) 2020. Lancashire 2nd XI debut 2018. England U19 2018-19. HS 3 v Derbys (Liverpool) 2020. BB 5-69 v Somerset (Southport) 2022. LO HS 6 v Durham (Gosforth) 2021 (RLC). LO BB 2-22 v Glos (Bristol) 2021 (RLC).

PARKINSON, Matthew William (Bolton S), b Bolton 24 Oct 1996. Twin brother of C.F.Parkinson (see LEICESTERSHIRE). 6'0". RHB, LB. Squad No 28. Debut (Lancashire) 2016; cap 2019. Mashonaland Eagles 2022-23. Manchester Originals 2021 to date. Staffordshire 2014. **Tests**: 1 (2022); HS 8 and BB 1-47 v NZ (Lord's) 2022. **LOI**: 5 (2019-20 to 2021); HS 7* v P (Lord's) 2021; BB 2-28 v P (Cardiff) 2021. **IT20**: 6 (2019-20 to 2022); HS 5 v P (Nottingham) 2021; BB 4-47 v NZ (Napier) 2019-20. HS 21* v Northants (Manchester) 2021. BB 7-126 v Kent (Canterbury) 2021. LO HS 15* EL v West Indies A (Coolidge) 2017-18. LO BB 5-51 v Worcs (Manchester) 2019 (RLC). T20 HS 18. T20 BB 4-9.

SALT, Philip Dean (Reed's S, Cobham), b Bodelwyddan, Denbighs 28 Aug 1996. 5'10". RHB, OB. Squad No 7. Sussex 2013-20. Lancashire debut 2022. Big Bash: AS 2019-20 to 2020-21. Manchester Originals 2021 to date. **LOI**: 14 (2021 to 2022). **IT20**: 15 (2021-22 to 2022-23); HS 122 v Neth (Amstelveen) 2022. **IT20**: 13 (2021-22 to 2022-23); HS 88* v P (Lahore) 2022-23. HS 148 Sx v Derbys (Hove) 2018. La HS 97 v Kent (Canterbury) 2022. BB 1-32 Sx v Warwks (Hove) 2018. LO HS 137* Sx v Kent (Beckenham) 2019 (RLC). T20 HS 88*.

SINGH, Harry (Clitheroe RGS), b Blackburn 16 Jun 2004. Son of R.P.Singh (Uttar Pradesh & India 1982-83 to 1995-96). RHB, OB. Squad No 16. Lancashire 2nd XI debut 2021. England U19 2022 to 2022-23. Awaiting 1st XI debut.

NQVILAS, Dane James, b Johannesburg, South Africa 10 Jun 1985. 6'2". RHB, WK. Squad No 33. Gauteng 2006-07 to 2009-10. Lions 2008-09 to 2009-10. W Province 2010-11. Cape Cobras 2011-12 to 2016-17. Lancashire debut 2017; cap 2018; captain 2019-22. Dolphins 2017-18 to 2018-19. Northern Superchargers 2021. **Tests** (SA): 6 (2015 to 2015-16); HS 26 v E (Johannesburg) 2015-16. **IT20** (SA): 1 (2011-12); HS –. F-c Tours (SA): A 2016 (SA A), I 2015 (SA A), I 2015-16; Z 2016 (SA A), B 2015. 1000 runs (1): 1036 (2019). HS 266 v Glamorgan (Colwyn B) 2019. LO HS 166 v Notts (Nottingham) 2019 (RLC). T20 HS 75*.

WELLS, Luke William Peter (St Bede's S, Upper Dicker), b Eastbourne, E Sussex 29 Dec 1990. Son of A.P.Wells (Border, Kent, Sussex and England 1981-2000); elder brother of D.A.C.Wells (Oxford MCCU 2017); nephew of C.M.Wells (Border, Derbyshire, Sussex and WP 1979-96). 6'4". LHB, LB. Squad No 3. Sussex 2010-19; cap 2016. Colombo CC 2011-12. Lancashire debut 2021; cap 2022. 1000 runs (2); most – 1292 (2017). HS 258 Sx v Durham (Hove) 2017. La HS 175* Warwks (Birmingham) 2022. BB 5-63 Sx v Glamorgan (Hove) 2019. La BB 3-8 v Somerset (Taunton) 2021. LO HS 88 v Yorks (York) 2022 (RLC). BB 3-19 Sx v Netherlands (Amstelveen) 2011 (CB40). T20 HS 42. T20 BB 2-26.

NQWILLIAMS, William Salter Austen (Christchurch BHS), b Christchurch, New Zealand 6 Oct 1992. RHB, RMF. Canterbury 2012-13 to 2021-22. Lancashire debut 2022. HS 38 Cant v Wellington (Rangiora) 2019-20. La HS 29* and La BB 5-41 v Northants (Northampton) 2022. BB 5-26 Cant v ND (Rangiora) 2020-21. LO HS 19* Cant v Auckland (Auckland) 2017-18. LO BB 4-20 v Derbys (Manchester) 2022 (RLC). T20 HS 29*. T20 BB 5-12.

WOOD, Luke (Portland CS, Worksop), b Sheffield, Yorks 2 Aug 1995. 5'9". LHB, LFM. Squad No 14. Nottinghamshire 2014-19. Worcestershire 2018 (on loan). Northamptonshire 2019 (on loan). Lancashire debut 2020. Big Bash: MS 2022-23. Trent Rockets 2021 to date. **LOI:** 1 (2022-23); HS 10 v A (Adelaide) 2022-23; BB – . **IT20:** 2 (2022-23); HS – ; BB 3-24 v P (Karachi) 2022-23. HS 119 v Kent (Canterbury) 2021, sharing La record 8th wkt partnership of 187 with D.J.Lamb. BB 5-40 Nt v Cambridge MCCU (Cambridge) 2016. CC BB 5-67 Nt v Yorks (Scarborough) 2019. La BB 3-31 v Northants (Manchester) 2021. LO HS 52 Nt v Leics (Leicester) 2016 (RLC). LO BB 2-36 Nt v Worcs (Worcester) 2019 (RLC). T20 HS 33*. T20 BB 5-50.

RELEASED/RETIRED

(Having made a County 1st XI appearance in 2022)

NODAVID, Tim**othy Hays, b Singapore 16 Mar 1996. Son of R.David (Singapore 1996-97). 6'5". RHB, RMF. Surrey 2021 (white ball only). Lancashire 2022 (T20 only). IPL: RCB 2021; MI 2022. Big Bash: PS 2017-18 to 2019-20; HH 2020-21 to date. Southern Brave 2021 to date. **IT20** (A/Sing): 25 (14 for Singapore 2019 to 2019-20; 11 for Australia 2022-23); HS 92* Sing v Malaysia (Bangkok) 2019-20; BB 1-18 Sing v Namibia (Dubai, DSC) 2019-20 and 1-18 Sing v Hong Kong (Bangkok) 2019-20. LO HS 140* Sy v Warwks (Oval) 2021 (RLC). LO BB 3-26 Sing v Canada (Kuala Lumpur) 2019-20. T20 HS 92*. T20 BB 1-4.

HASAN ALI – *see WARWICKSHIRE.*

HURT, Liam Jack (Balshaw's CE HS, Leyland), b Preston 15 Mar 1994. 6'4". RHB, RMF. Lancashire 2019-20. Derbyshire 2022 (on loan). Leicestershire 2015 (l-o only). HS 49 Le v Notts (Nottingham) 2022. La HS 38 v Leics (Leicester) 2019. BB 4-27 v Durham (Chester-le-St) 2020. LO HS 15* v Yorks (Leeds) 2019 (RLC). LO BB 3-25 v Hants (Southampton) 2022 (RLC). T20 HS 7. T20 BB 3-22.

NOWASHINGTON SUNDAR**, M.S., b Chennai, India 5 Oct 1999. LHB, OB. Tamil Nadu 2016-17 to date. Lancashire 2022. IPL: RPS 2017; RCB 2018-21; SH 2022. **Tests** (I): 4 (2020-21); HS 96* v E (Ahmedabad) 2020-21; BB 3-89 v A (Brisbane) 2020-21. **LOI** (I): 16 (2017-18 to 2022-23); HS 51 v NZ (Christchurch) 2022-23; BB 3-30 v WI (Ahmedabad) 2021-22. **IT20** (I): 35 (2017-18 to 2022-23); HS 50 v NZ (Ranchi) 2022-23; BB 3-22 v B (Colombo, RPS) 2017-18. F-c Tours (I): E 2021; A 2020-21. HS 159 TN v Tripura (Chennai) 2017-18. La HS 34* and La BB 5-76 v Northants (Northampton) 2022. BB 6-87 (11-181) India Red v India Blue (Lucknow) 2017-18. LO HS 70 TN v Saurashtra (Jaipur) 2021-22. LO BB 5-48 TN v Puducherry (Thumba) 2021-22. T20 HS 54*. T20 BB 3-10.

KENT RELEASED/RETIRED (continued from p 122)

ROBINSON, O.G. – *see DURHAM.*

NOSAINI, Navdeep**, b Kamal, Haryana, India 23 Nov 1992. RHB, RFM. Delhi 2013-14 to date. Kent 2022. IPL: RCB 2019-21; RR 2022. **Tests** (I): 2 (2020-21); HS 5 v A (Brisbane) 2020-21; BB 2-54 v A (Sydney) 2020-21. **LOI** (I): 8 (2019-20 to 2021); HS 45 v NZ (Auckland) 2019-20; BB 2-58 v WI (Cuttack) 2019-20. **IT20** (I): 11 (2019 to 2021); HS 11* v NZ (Wellington) 2019-20; BB 3-17 v WI (Lauderhill) 2019. F-c Tours (IA): E 2018; A 2020-21 (I); SA 2017, 2021-22; NZ 2018-19. BB 9-22 v Bangladesh A (Sylhet) 2022-23. K HS 5* and K BB 5-72 v Warwks (Birmingham) 2022. BB 6-32 Delhi v Maharashtra (Delhi) 2015-16. LO HS (*see LOI*). LO BB 5-46 IA v West Indies A (North Sound) 2019. T20 HS 12*. T20 BB 4-17.

STEVENS, Darren Ian (Hinckley C), b Leicester 30 Apr 1976. 5'11". RHB, RM. Leicestershire 1997-2004; cap 2002. Kent 2005-22; cap 2005; benefit 2016. MCC 2002. *Wisden* 2020, the oldest to be given the honour since W.E.Astill in 1933. F-c Tour (ECB Acad): SL 2002-03. 1000 runs (3); most – 1304 (2013). HS 237 v Yorks (Leeds) 2019, sharing K record 6th wkt partnership of 346 with S.W.Billings. 50 wkts (4); most – 63 (2017). BB 8-75 v Leics (Canterbury) 2017. LO HS 147 v Glamorgan (Swansea) 2017 (RLC). LO BB 6-25 v Surrey (Beckenham) 2018 (RLC). T20 HS 90. T20 BB 4-14.

LANCASHIRE 2022

RESULTS SUMMARY

	Place	Won	Lost	Tied	Drew	NR
LV= Insurance County Champ (Div 1)	2nd	7	1		6	
Royal London One-Day Cup (Group B)	Finalist	7	3			1
Vitality Blast (North Group)	Finalist	10	5	1		1

LV= INSURANCE COUNTY CHAMPIONSHIP AVERAGES
BATTING AND FIELDING

Cap		M	I	NO	HS	Runs	Avge	100	50	Ct/St
2018	K.K.Jennings	11	17	–	318	1233	72.52	5	2	12
2022	L.W.P.Wells	14	22	3	175*	991	52.15	3	4	10
2010	S.J.Croft	14	20	1	155	837	44.05	2	3	9
	P.D.Salt	7	8	–	97	349	43.62	–	2	19/1
2021	J.J.Bohannon	14	20	–	231	805	40.25	3	1	6
	R.P.Jones	5	7	1	66	206	34.33	–	2	14
2018	D.J.Vilas	13	18	–	124	567	31.50	2	2	11
	D.J.Lamb	4	5	2	41*	78	26.00	–	–	2
	G.P.Balderson	11	16	3	97	253	19.46	–	1	3
	L.Wood	8	10	–	50	188	18.80	–	1	2
	M.Washington Sundar	2	4	1	34*	52	17.33	–	–	1
	W.S.A.Williams	8	11	6	29*	86	17.20	–	–	4
2018	T.E.Bailey	13	16	2	59	208	14.85	–	1	1
	T.W.Hartley	3	3	–	23	55	13.75	–	–	3
	G.I.D.Lavelle	2	4	–	30	49	12.25	–	–	10/1
	M.W.Parkinson	10	12	3	17*	89	9.88	–	–	1
2022	Hasan Ali	5	6	–	19	39	6.50	–	–	–

Also batted: J.M.Anderson (4 matches – cap 2003) 5*, 0*, 5* (2 ct); G.J.Bell (2) 16, 24, 2 (1 ct); S.Mahmood (1 – cap 2021) 17*; J.P.Morley (3) 1*, 0*, 2* (3 ct).

BOWLING

	O	M	R	W	Avge	Best	5wI	10wM
T.W.Hartley	81.2	31	144	11	13.09	5-52	1	–
W.S.A.Williams	292.4	93	614	36	17.05	5-41	1	–
Hasan Ali	184	42	515	25	20.60	6-47	2	–
T.E.Bailey	461.3	113	1176	52	22.61	6-64	3	1
J.M.Anderson	138	52	274	12	22.83	3-24	–	–
J.P.Morley	117.2	18	355	12	29.58	5-69	1	–
M.W.Parkinson	396.3	74	1012	33	30.66	4-66	–	–
G.P.Balderson	226.2	42	737	22	33.50	5-14	1	–
L.Wood	206.4	37	658	15	43.86	3-34	–	–

Also bowled:

M.Washington Sundar	68	6	198	8	24.75	5-76	1	–
D.J.Lamb	66	8	240	7	34.28	3-43	–	–

S.J.Croft 10-1-33-0; S.Mahmood 45-15-90-4; L.W.P.Wells 98.5-14-271-4.

Lancashire played no first-class fixtures outside the County Championship in 2022. The First-Class Averages (pp 221–234) give the records of Lancashire players first-class county matches, with the exception of J.M.Anderson and M.W.Parkinson, whose first-class figures for Lancashire are as above.

LANCASHIRE RECORDS
FIRST-CLASS CRICKET

Highest Total	For 863		v	Surrey	The Oval	1990
	V 707-9d		by	Surrey	The Oval	1990
Lowest Total	For 25		v	Derbyshire	Manchester	1871
	V 20		by	Essex	Chelmsford	2013
Highest Innings	For 424	A.C.MacLaren	v	Somerset	Taunton	1895
	V 315*	T.W.Hayward	for	Surrey	The Oval	1898

Highest Partnership for each Wicket

1st	368	A.C.MacLaren/R.H.Spooner	v	Glos	Liverpool	1903
2nd	371	F.B.Watson/G.E.Tyldesley	v	Surrey	Manchester	1928
3rd	501	A.N.Petersen/A.G.Prince	v	Glamorgan	Colwyn Bay	2015
4th	358	S.P.Titchard/G.D.Lloyd	v	Essex	Chelmsford	1996
5th	360	S.G.Law/C.L.Hooper	v	Warwicks	Birmingham	2003
6th	278	J.Iddon/H.R.W.Butterworth	v	Sussex	Manchester	1932
7th	248	G.D.Lloyd/I.D.Austin	v	Yorkshire	Leeds	1997
8th	187	L.Wood/D.J.Lamb	v	Kent	Canterbury	2021
9th	142	L.O.S.Poidevin/A.Kermode	v	Sussex	Eastbourne	1907
10th	173	J.Briggs/R.Pilling	v	Surrey	Liverpool	1885

Best Bowling	For 10-46	W.Hickton	v	Hampshire	Manchester	1870
(Innings)	V 10-40	G.O.B.Allen	for	Middlesex	Lord's	1929
Best Bowling	For 17-91	H.Dean	v	Yorkshire	Liverpool	1913
(Match)	V 16-65	G.Giffen	for	Australians	Manchester	1886

Most Runs – Season	2633	J.T.Tyldesley	(av 56.02)	1901
Most Runs – Career	34222	G.E.Tyldesley	(av 45.20)	1909-36
Most 100s – Season	11	C.Hallows		1928
Most 100s – Career	90	G.E.Tyldesley		1909-36
Most Wkts – Season	198	E.A.McDonald	(av 18.55)	1925
Most Wkts – Career	1816	J.B.Statham	(av 15.12)	1950-68
Most Career W-K Dismissals	925	G.Duckworth	(635 ct; 290 st)	1923-38
Most Career Catches in the Field	556	K.J.Grieves		1949-64

LIMITED-OVERS CRICKET

Highest Total	50ov	406-9		v	Notts	Nottingham	2019
	40ov	324-4		v	Worcs	Worcester	2012
	T20	231-4		v	Yorkshire	Manchester	2015
Lowest Total	50ov	59		v	Worcs	Worcester	1963
	40ov	68		v	Yorkshire	Leeds	2000
		68		v	Surrey	The Oval	2002
	T20	83		v	Durham	Manchester	2020
Highest Innings	50ov	166	D.J.Vilas	v	Notts	Nottingham	2019
	40ov	143	A.Flintoff	v	Essex	Chelmsford	1999
	T20	108	K.K.Jennings	v	Durham	Chester-le-St[2]	2020
Best Bowling	50ov	6-10	C.E.H.Croft	v	Scotland	Manchester	1982
	40ov	6-25	G.Chapple	v	Yorkshire	Leeds	1998
	T20	5-13	S.D.Parry	v	Worcs	Manchester	2016

LEICESTERSHIRE

Formation of Present Club: 25 March 1879
Inaugural First-Class Match: 1894
Colours: Dark Green and Scarlet
Badge: Gold Running Fox on Green Ground
County Champions: (3) 1975, 1996, 1998
Benson and Hedges Cup Winners: (3) 1972, 1975, 1985
Sunday League Champions: (2) 1974, 1977
Twenty20 Cup Winners: (3) 2004, 2006, 2011

Chief Executive: Sean Jarvis, Uptonsteel County Ground, Grace Road, Leicester LE2 8EB
● Tel: 0116 283 2128 ● Email: enquiries@leicestershireccc.co.uk ● Web:
www.leicestershireccc.co.uk ● Twitter: @leicsccc (73,463 followers)

Director of Cricket: Claude Henderson. **Head Coach**: Paul Nixon. **Batting Coach**: James
Taylor. **Asst/Bowling Coach**: Alfonso Thomas. **Captains**: L.J.Hill (f-c & 50 ov) and
C.N.Ackermann (T20). **Overseas Players**: P.W.A.Mulder, Naveen-ul-Haq (T20 only) and
A.M.Rahane. **2023 Testimonial**: None. **Head Groundsman**: Andy Ward. **Scorer**: Paul
Rogers. **Blast Team Name**: Leicestershire Foxes. ‡ New registration. ᴺᴼ Not qualified for
England.

ᴺᴼ**ACKERMANN, Colin** Neil (Grey HS, Port Elizabeth; U of SA), b George, South Africa
4 Apr 1991. 6'1". RHB, OB. Squad No 48. Eastern Province 2010-11 to 2015-16. Warriors
2013-14 to 2018-19. Leicestershire debut 2017; cap 2019; captain 2020 to date (T20 only in
2020 and in 2023). **LOI** (Neth); 4 (2021-22); HS 81 v Afg (Doha) 2021-22; BB 1-10 v Afg
(Doha) 2021-22 – separate matches. **IT20** (Neth): 22 (2019-20 to 2022-23); HS 62 v B
(Hobart) 2022-23; BB 1-6 v Bermuda (Dubai, DSC) 2019-20. 1000 runs (0+1): 1200
(2013-14). HS 277* v Sussex (Hove) 2022, sharing Le and CC record 5th wkt partnership of
477* with P.W.A.Mulder. BB 5-69 v Sussex (Hove) 2019. LO HS 152* v Worcs (Leicester)
2019 (RLC). LO BB 4-48 Warriors v Dolphins (Durban) 2017-18. T20 HS 85. T20 BB 7-18
v Warwks (Leicester) 2019 – world record T20 figures.

AHMED, Rehan (Bluecoat Aspley SFC), b Nottingham 13 Aug 2004. 5'9". RHB, LB.
Squad No 16. Debut (Leicestershire) 2022. Southern Brave 2022. Leicestershire 2nd XI
debut 2021. **Tests**: 1 (2022-23); HS 10 and BB 5-48 v P (Karachi) 2022-23 – youngest Test
debutant for England at 18y 126d. **LOI**: 1 (2022-23); HS 2 and BB 1-62 v B (Chittagong)
2022-23 – youngest LOI debutant for England at 18y 205d. HS 122 and Le BB 5-114 v
Derbys (Derby) 2022 – youngest ever to score a century & take five wkts in an innings in f-c
career at 18y 57d. LO HS 40* v Northants (Northampton) 2021 (RLC). LO BB 2-25 v
Surrey (Leicester) 2021 (RLC). T20 HS 33. T20 BB 4-22.

BARNES, Edward (King James S, Knaresborough), b York 26 Nov 1997. 6'0". RHB, RFM.
Squad No 62. Derbyshire 2020. Leicestershire debut 2021. HS 83* v Somerset (Taunton)
2021. BB 5-101 v Derbys (Leicester) 2022. LO HS 33* v Surrey (Leicester) 2021 (RLC).
LO BB 2-32 v Notts (Leicester) 2022 (RLC). T20 HS 7. T20 BB 2-27.

BUDINGER, Soloman George (Southport S, Queensland), b Colchester, Essex 21 Aug
1999. 6'0". LHB, OB, occ WK. Squad No 1. Debut (Leicestershire) 2022. Nottinghamshire
2021-22 (white-ball only). Birmingham Phoenix 2022. Sussex 2nd XI 2016-17.
Nottinghamshire 2nd XI 2018-22. HS 64 v Durham (Leicester) 2022. LO HS 89 Nt v Glos
(Bristol) 2022 (RLC). T20 HS 24. T20 BB 2-21.

DAVIS, William Samuel (Stafford GS), b Stafford 6 Mar 1996. 6'1". RHB, RFM. Squad No
44. Derbyshire 2015-18. Leicestershire debut 2019. HS 42 v Kent (Leicester) 2021. Le BB
7-146 De v Glamorgan (Colwyn Bay) 2016. Le BB 5-66 v Middx (Northwood) 2021. LO
HS 15* v Durham (Chester-le-St) 2019 (RLC) and 15* v Surrey (Leicester) 2021 (RLC).
LO BB 2-40 v Northants (Northampton) 2021 (RLC). T20 HS 5*. T20 BB 3-24.

EVANS, Samuel Thomas (Lancaster S, Leicester; Wyggeston & QE I C; Leicester U), b Leicester 20 Dec 1997. 5'8". RHB, OB. Squad No 21. Loughborough MCCU 2017-18. Leicestershire debut 2017. HS 138 v Surrey (Oval) 2021. BB –. LO HS 20 v India A (Leicester) 2018.

FINAN, Michael George Anthony (Astley Sports C), b Tameside, Lancs 11 Aug 1996. 6'0". RHB, LFM. Squad No 4. Debut (Leicestershire) 2022. Cheshire 2019-22. HS 58 v Notts (Nottingham) 2022. LO HS 0* v Notts (Leicester) 2022 (RLC). LO BB –.

HILL, Lewis John (Hastings HS, Hinckley; John Cleveland C), b Leicester 5 Oct 1990. 5'7½". RHB, WK, occ RM. Squad No 23. Debut (Leicestershire) 2015; cap 2021; captain 2023. Unicorns 2012-13. HS 145 v Sussex (Leicester) 2021. LO HS 118 v Worcs (Leicester) 2019 (RLC). T20 HS 59.

HULL, Joshua Owen (Stamford S), b Huntingdon 20 Aug 2004. 6'7". LHB, LFM. Squad No 12. Leicestershire 2nd XI debut 2022. Awaiting 1st XI debut.

KIMBER, Louis Philip James (William Farr C of E S; Loughborough U), b Lincoln 24 Feb 1997. Elder brother of J.F.Kimber (Lincolnshire 2016-18) and N.J.H.Kimber (*see SURREY*). 6'3". RHB, OB, occ WK. Squad No 17. Loughborough MCCU 2019. Leicestershire debut 2021. Lincolnshire 2015-19. HS 104 v Sussex (Hove) 2022. BB 1-8 v Middx (Leicester) 2022. LO HS 102 v Somerset (Leicester) 2022 (RLC). T20 HS 53.

LILLEY, Arron Mark (Mossley Hollins HS; Ashton SFC), b Tameside, Lancs 1 Apr 1991. 6'1". RHB, OB. Squad No 7. Lancashire 2013-18. Leicestershire debut 2019. White-ball contract in 2021. HS 63 and BB 5-23 La v Derbys (Southport) 2015. Le HS 13 and Le BB 3-21 v Yorks (Leeds) 2020. LO HS 60 v Durham (Leicester) 2022 (RLC). LO BB 4-30 La v Derbys (Manchester) 2013 (Y40). T20 HS 99*. T20 BB 3-26.

NQ**MULDER**, Peter Willem Adriaan ('**Wiaan**'), b Johannesburg, South Africa 19 Feb 1998. 6'0". RHB, RMF. Squad No 24. Lions 2016-17 to 2020-21. Gauteng 2017-18 to date. Kent 2019. Leicestershire debut 2022. **Tests** (SA): 11 (2018-19 to 2022); HS 36 v SL (Centurion) 2020-21; BB 3-1 v WI (Gros Islet) 2021. **LOI** (SA): 12 (2017-18 to 2021); HS 19* v SL (Dambulla) 2018; BB 2-59 v SL (Colombo, RPS) 2018. **IT20** (SA): 5 (2021); HS 36 v Ire (Belfast) 2021; BB 2-10 v Ire (Belfast) 2021 – separate matches. F-c Tours (SA): E 2017 (SA A), 2022; WI 2021; NZ 2021-22; P 2020-21. HS 235* v Sussex (Hove) 2022, sharing Le and CC record 5th wkt partnership of 477* with C.N.Ackermann. BB 7-25 Lions v Dolphins (Potchefstroom) 2016-17. CC BB 4-118 K v Surrey (Beckenham) 2019. Le BB 4-125 v Worcs (Worcester) 2022. LO HS 116* and LO BB 4-47 v Middx (Radlett) 2022 (RLC). T20 HS 63. T20 BB 2-10.

NQ**NAVEEN-UL-HAQ** Murid, b Logar, Afghanistan 23 Sep 1999. 6'1". RHB, RMF. Squad No 78. Kabul Region 2017-18 to 2018-19. Leicestershire debut 2021 (T20 only); cap 2022. Big Bash: SS 2022-23. **LOI** (Afg): 7 (2016 to 2020-21); HS 10* v Ire (Abu Dhabi) 2020-21; BB 4-42 v Ire (Abu Dhabi) 2020-21 – separate matches. **IT20** (Afg): 25 (2019 to 2022-23); HS 10* v Ire (Belfast) 2022; BB 3-21 v Ire (Greater Noida) 2019-20 and 3-21 v A (Adelaide) 2022-23. HS 34 Kabul v Mis Ainak (Asadabad) 2017-18. BB 8-35 Kabul v Mis Ainak (Kabul) 2018. LO HS 30 Kabul v Band-e-Amir (Kabul) 2018. LO BB 5-40 Afg A v Bangladesh A (Savar) 2019. T20 HS 20*. T20 BB 5-11.

PARKINSON, Callum Francis (Bolton S), b Bolton, Lancs 24 Oct 1996. Twin brother of M.W.Parkinson (*see LANCASHIRE*). 5'8". RHB, SLA. Squad No 10. Derbyshire 2016. Leicestershire debut 2017; cap 2022. Northern Superchargers 2021 to date. Staffordshire 2015-16. HS 75 v Kent (Canterbury) 2017. BB 8-148 (10-185 match) v Worcs (Worcester) 2017. LO HS 52* v Notts (Leicester) 2018 (RLC). LO BB 1-34 v Derbys (Derby) 2018 (RLC). T20 HS 27*. T20 BB 4-20.

PATEL, Rishi Ketan (Brentwood S), b Chigwell, Essex 26 Jul 1998. 6'2". RHB, LB. Squad No 26. Cambridge MCCU 2019. Essex 2019. Leicestershire debut 2020. Essex 2nd XI 2015-19. Hertfordshire 2019. HS 99 v Sussex (Hove) 2022. LO HS 118 v Warwks (Birmingham) 2021 (RLC). T20 HS 57.

‡NORAHANE, Ajinkya Madhukar, b Ashwi Khurd, India 6 Jun 1988. RHB, RM. Squad No 3. Mumbai 2007-08 to date. Hampshire 2019. IPL: MI 2007-08 to 2009; RR 2011-19; RPS 2016-17; DCa 2020-21; KKR 2022. Tests (I): 82 (2012-13 to 2021-22); HS 188 v NZ (Indore) 2016-17. LOI (I): 90 (2011 to 2017-18); HS 111 v SL (Cuttack) 2014-15. IT20 (I): 20 (2011 to 2016); HS 61 v E (Manchester) 2011. F-c Tours (I): E 2010 (IA), 2014, 2018, 2021; A 2014-15, 2018-19, 2020-21; SA 2013 (IA), 2013-14, 2017-18, 2021-22; WI 2012 (IA), 2016, 2019; NZ 2013-14, 2018-19 (IA), 2019-20; SL 2015, 2017; B 2015. 1000 runs (0+3); most – 1390 (2008-09). HS 265* Mumbai v Hyderabad (Hyderabad) 2009-10. CC HS 119 H v Notts (Newport, IoW) 2019. BB –. LO HS 187 Mumbai v Maharashtra (Pune) 2007-08. LO BB 2-36 Mumbai v Tamil Nadu (Agartala) 2008-09. T20 HS 105*. T20 BB 1-5.

‡SALISBURY, Matthew Edward Thomas (Shenfield HS; Anglia Ruskin U), b Chelmsford, Essex 18 Apr 1993. 6'0½". RHB, RMF. Squad No 18. Cambridge MCCU 2012-13. Essex 2014-15. Hampshire 2017. Durham 2018-22; cap 2018. Suffolk 2016. HS 45 Du v Middx (Lord's) 2022. BB 6-37 Du v Middx (Chester-le-St) 2018. LO HS 5* Ex v Leics (Chelmsford) 2014 (RLC). LO BB 4-55 Ex v Lancs (Chelmsford) 2014 (RLC). T20 HS 1*. T20 BB 2-19.

SCRIVEN, Thomas Antony Rhys (Magdalen Coll S), b Oxford 18 Nov 1998. 6'0½". RHB, RMF. Squad No 88. Hampshire 2020. Leicestershire debut 2022. Hampshire 2nd XI 2016-21. Berkshire 2022. HS 68 and BB 2-24 H v Kent (Canterbury) 2020. Le HS 65 and Le BB 2-44 v Middx (Leicester) 2022. LO HS 42 H v Durham (Chester-le-S) 2021 (RLC). LO BB 2-46 v Surrey (Guildford) 2022 (RLC). T20 HS 2. T20 BB –.

STEEL, Scott (Belmont Community S), b Durham 20 Apr 1999. 6'0". RHB, OB. Squad No 55. Durham 2019. Leicestershire debut 2022. Durham 2nd XI 2016-19. Northumberland 2017. HS 39 Du v Middx (Lord's) 2019. Le HS 18 and BB 1-20 v Glamorgan (Cardiff) 2022. LO HS 68 Du v Northants (Chester-le-St) 2019 (RLC) and 68 Du v Yorks (Leeds) 2019 (RLC). LO BB 1-31 v Durham (Leicester) 2022 (RLC). T20 HS 72. T20 BB 3-20.

SWINDELLS, Harry John (Brockington C; Lutterworth C), b Leicester 21 Feb 1999. 5'7". RHB, WK. Squad No 28. Debut (Leicestershire) 2019. Leicestershire 2nd XI debut 2015. England U19 2017. HS 171* v Somerset (Taunton) 2021. LO HS 75 v Surrey (Leicester) 2021 (RLC). T20 HS 63.

WALKER, Roman Isaac (Ysgol Bryn Alyn), b Wrexham, Denbighs 6 Aug 2000. 6'4". RHB, RFM. Squad No 49. Debut (Leicestershire) 2022. Glamorgan 2019-21 (white ball only). Glamorgan 2nd XI 2016-21. Wales MC 2018. HS 64 v Glamorgan (Leicester) 2022. BB 3-84 v Derbys (Derby) 2022. LO HS 23 v Sussex (Hove) 2022 (RLC). LO BB 2-51 v Somerset (Leicester) 2022 (RLC). T20 HS 19*. T20 BB 3-15.

WELCH, Nicholas Roy (St John's C, Harare; Loughborough U), b Harare, Zimbabwe 5 Feb 1998. 5'11". RHB, LBG. Squad No 67. Mashonaland Eagles 2013-14 to date. Loughborough MCCU 2019. Leicestershire debut 2022. HS 100 ME v MWR (Harare) 2022-23. Le HS 3 v Notts (Leicester) 2022. LO HS 127* v Surrey (Guildford) 2022 (RLC). T20 HS 68.

WRIGHT, Christopher Julian Clement (Eggars S, Alton; Anglia Ruskin U), b Chipping Norton, Oxon 14 Jul 1985. 6'3". RHB, RFM. Squad No 31. Cambridge UCCE 2004-05. Middlesex 2004-07. Tamil Union 2005-06. Essex 2008-11. Warwickshire 2011-18; cap 2013. Leicestershire debut 2019; cap 2021. F-c Tour (MCC): Nepal 2019-20. HS 87 v Derbys (Derby) 2021. 50 wkts (2); most – 67 (2012). BB 7-53 v Glos (Bristol) 2021. LO HS 42 Ex v Glos (Cheltenham) 2011 (CB40). LO BB 6-35 v Notts (Leicester) 2022 (RLC). T20 HS 6*. T20 BB 4-24.

RELEASED/RETIRED

(Having made a County 1st XI appearance in 2022)

AZAD, Mohammad **Hasan** (Fernwood S, Nottingham; Bilborough SFC; Loughborough U), b Quetta, Pakistan 7 Jan 1994. Son of Imran Azad (Public Works 1986-87). LHB, OB. Loughborough MCCU 2015-19. Leicestershire 2019-22, scoring 139 v Loughborough MCCU (Leicester) on debut. 1000 runs (1): 1189 (2019). HS 152 v Sussex (Leicester) 2021. BB 1-15 v Durham (Leicester) 2020.

BOWLEY, Nathan John (Woodvale S, Loughborough; Loughborough C), b Nottingham 3 Aug 2001. LHB, OB. Leicestershire 2nd XI 2018-22. LO HS 50 v Middx (Radlett) 2022 (RLC). LO BB –.

^{NO}**HENDRICKS, Beuran** Eric, b Cape Town, South Africa 8 Jun 1990. LHB, LFM. W Province 2009-10 to date. Cape Cobras 2010-11 to 2016-17. Lions 2016-17 to 2020-21. Leicestershire 2022. IPL: KXIP 2014-15. **Tests** (SA): 1 (2019-20); HS 5* and BB 5-64 v E (Johannesburg) 2019-20. **LOI** (SA): 8 (2018-19 to 2020-21); HS 3 and BB 3-59 v E (Johannesburg) 2019-20. **IT20** (SA): 19 (2013-14 to 2021); HS 12* v A (Centurion) 2013-14; BB 4-14 v P (Centurion) 2018-19. F-c Tours (SAA): E 2017; I 2015, 2018. HS 68 Lions v Dolphins (Johannesburg) 2017-18. LE HS 22 v Middx (Lord's) 2022. 50 wkts (0+1): 60 (2012-13). BB 7-29 (10-83 match) Lions v Cobras (Johannesburg) 2020-21. Le BB 2-97 v Durham (Chester-le-St) 2022. LO HS 24 SA A v Australia A (Darwin) 2014. LO BB 5-31 Cobras v Titans (Benoni) 2015-16. T20 HS 17*. T20 BB 6-29.

MIKE, B.W.M. – *see YORKSHIRE.*

RHODES, George Harry (Chase HS & SFC, Malvern), b Birmingham 26 Oct 1993. Son of S.J.Rhodes (Yorkshire, Worcestershire & England 1981-2004) and grandson of W.E.Rhodes (Nottinghamshire 1961-64). 6'0". RHB, OB. Worcestershire 2016-19. Leicestershire 2019-22. HS 90 v Worcs (Worcester) 2021. BB 2-83 Wo v Kent (Canterbury) 2016. Le BB 1-64 v Durham (Chester-le-St) 2022. LO HS 106 Wo v Yorks (Worcester) 2019 (RLC). LO BB 3-44 v Glamorgan (Leicester) 2021 (RLC). T20 HS 30*. T20 BB 4-13.

^{NO}**RUTHERFORD, Hamish** Duncan, b Dunedin, New Zealand 27 Apr 1989. Son of K.R.Rutherford (Gauteng, Otago, Transvaal & New Zealand 1982-83 to 1999-00). Nephew of I.A.Rutherford (C Districts, Otago & Worcestershire 1974-75 to 1983-84). 5'10". LHB, SLA. Otago 2008-09 to date. Essex 2013. Derbyshire 2015-16. Worcestershire 2019. Glamorgan 2021. Leicestershire 2022 (T20 only). **Tests** (NZ): 16 (2012-13 to 2014-15); HS 171 v E (Dunedin) 2012-13 – on debut. **LOI** (NZ): 4 (2012-13 to 2013-14); HS 11 v E (Napier) 2012-13. **IT20** (NZ): 8 (2012-13 to 2019); HS 62 v E (Oval) 2013. F-c Tours (NZ): E 2013, 2014 (NZ A); WI 2014; B 2013-14. 1000 runs (0+1): 1077 (2012-13). HS 239 Otago v Wellington (Dunedin) 2011-12. CC HS 123 Wo v Leics (Leicester) 2019 – on Wo debut. BB 1-26 Gm v Surrey (Oval) 2021. LO HS 155 Otago v CD (Dunedin) 2019-20. LO BB 1-4 Otago v Wellington (Dunedin) 2017-18. T20 HS 106. T20 BB 1-6.

S.D.Bates, H.A.Evans, G.T.Griffiths and A.Sakande left the staff without making a County 1st XI appearance in 2022.

LEICESTERSHIRE 2022

RESULTS SUMMARY

	Place	Won	Lost	Drew	NR
LV= Insurance County Champ (Div 2)	8th		9	5	
Royal London One-Day Cup (Group A)	QF	6	3		
Vitality Blast (North Group)	6th	8	6		

LV= INSURANCE COUNTY CHAMPIONSHIP AVERAGES
BATTING AND FIELDING

Cap		M	I	NO	HS	Runs	Avge	100	50	Ct/St
	P.W.A.Mulder	8	15	1	235*	689	49.21	2	2	2
2021	L.J.Hill	7	13	–	104	503	38.69	1	4	1
2019	C.N.Ackermann	12	23	2	277*	744	35.42	2	2	16
	R.Ahmed	3	6	–	122	195	32.50	1	–	2
	B.W.M.Mike	8	14	1	99*	415	31.92	–	4	3
	T.A.R.Scriven	3	6	–	65	178	29.66	–	2	–
	M.H.Azad	11	21	1	104*	579	28.95	1	4	3
	S.T.Evans	9	18	2	77*	457	28.56	–	4	1
	R.K.Patel	8	15	–	99	418	27.86	–	3	5
	L.P.J.Kimber	11	19	–	104	503	26.47	1	3	6
	M.G.A.Finan	3	6	2	58	102	25.50	–	1	1
2022	C.F.Parkinson	13	23	6	49	397	23.35	–	–	2
	S.G.Budinger	3	6	–	64	126	21.00	–	1	3
	R.I.Walker	3	6	1	64	103	20.60	–	1	1
	B.E.Hendricks	6	11	5	22	118	19.66	–	–	1
2021	C.J.C.Wright	13	22	7	36*	279	18.60	–	–	5
	H.J.Swindells	14	25	–	67	454	18.16	–	3	25/1
	E.Barnes	10	17	2	46	260	17.33	–	–	4
	W.S.Davis	3	5	2	32*	52	17.33	–	–	1
	G.H.Rhodes	3	6	–	23	48	8.00	–	–	2

Also batted: J.D.M.Evison (1 match) 12, 0; S.Steel (1) 0, 18 (1 ct); N.R.Welch (2) 2, 3.

BOWLING

	O	M	R	W	Avge	Best	5wI	10wM
M.G.A.Finan	75.2	8	362	13	27.84	5- 58	1	–
B.W.M.Mike	134	10	709	16	44.31	4- 15	–	–
E.Barnes	201.1	18	868	19	45.68	5-101	1	–
C.J.C.Wright	374.4	60	1234	27	45.70	3- 26	–	–
C.F.Parkinson	442.4	62	1487	30	49.56	5-128	1	–
P.W.A.Mulder	181	27	716	14	51.14	4-125	–	–
Also bowled:								
R.Ahmed	74.2	5	271	9	30.11	5-114	1	–
R.I.Walker	73	13	285	7	40.71	3- 84	–	–
C.N.Ackermann	135.3	10	460	5	92.00	2- 69	–	–

M.H.Azad 1-0-6-0; W.S.Davis 81-12-361-4; J.D.M.Evison 20-2-103-0; B.E.Hendricks 148-15-563-4; L.J.Hill 2-0-15-0; L.P.J.Kimber 22-4-69-2; G.H.Rhodes 19-1-78-1; T.A.R.Scriven 50-6-168-4; S.Steel 6.4-0-33-1; H.J.Swindells 1-0-3-0.

Leicestershire played no first-class fixtures outside the County Championship in 2022. The First-Class Averages (pp 221–234) give the records of Leicestershire players in all first-class county matches, with the exception of J.D.M.Evison, B.W.M.Mike and P.W.A.Mulder, whose first-class figures for Leicestershire are as above.

LEICESTERSHIRE RECORDS

FIRST-CLASS CRICKET

Highest Total	For	756-4d		v	Sussex	Hove	2022
	V	795-5d		by	Glamorgan	Leicester	2022
Lowest Total	For	25		v	Kent	Leicester	1912
	V	24		by	Glamorgan	Leicester	1971
		24		by	Oxford U	Oxford	1985
Highest Innings	For	309*	H.D.Ackerman	v	Glamorgan	Cardiff	2006
	V	410*	S.A.Northeast	for	Glamorgan	Leicester	2022

Highest Partnership for each Wicket

1st	390	B.Dudleston/J.F.Steele	v	Derbyshire	Leicester	1979
2nd	320	M.H.Azad/N.J.Dexter	v	Glos	Leicester	2019
3rd	436*	D.L.Maddy/B.J.Hodge	v	L'boro UCCE	Leicester	2003
4th	360*	J.W.A.Taylor/A.B.McDonald	v	Middlesex	Leicester	2010
5th	477*	C.N.Ackermann/P.W.A.Mulder	v	Sussex	Hove	2022
6th	284	P.V.Simmons/P.A.Nixon	v	Durham	Chester-le-St[2]	1996
7th	219*	J.D.R.Benson/P.Whitticase	v	Hampshire	Bournemouth	1991
8th	203*	H.J.Swindells/E.Barnes	v	Somerset	Taunton	2021
9th	160	R.T.Crawford/W.W.Odell	v	Worcs	Leicester	1902
10th	228	R.Illingworth/K.Higgs	v	Northants	Leicester	1977

Best Bowling	For	10- 18	G.Geary	v	Glamorgan	Pontypridd	1929
(Innings)	V	10- 32	H.Pickett	for	Essex	Leyton	1895
Best Bowling	For	16- 96	G.Geary	v	Glamorgan	Pontypridd	1929
(Match)	V	16-102	C.Blythe	for	Kent	Leicester	1909

Most Runs – Season		2446	L.G.Berry	(av 52.04)	1937
Most Runs – Career		30143	L.G.Berry	(av 30.32)	1924-51
Most 100s – Season		7	L.G.Berry		1937
		7	W.Watson		1959
		7	B.F.Davison		1982
Most 100s – Career		45	L.G.Berry		1924-51
Most Wkts – Season		170	J.E.Walsh	(av 18.96)	1948
Most Wkts – Career		2131	W.E.Astill	(av 23.18)	1906-39
Most Career W-K Dismissals		905	R.W.Tolchard	(794 ct; 111 st)	1965-83
Most Career Catches in the Field		426	M.R.Hallam		1950-70

LIMITED-OVERS CRICKET

Highest Total	50ov	406-5		v	Berkshire	Leicester	1996
	40ov	344-4		v	Durham	Chester-le-St[2]	1996
	T20	229-5		v	Warwicks	Birmingham	2018
Lowest Total	50ov	56		v	Northants	Leicester	1964
		56		v	Minor Cos	Wellington	1982
	40ov	36		v	Sussex	Leicester	1973
	T20	89		v	Derbyshire	Leicester	2022
Highest Innings	50ov	201	V.J.Wells	v	Berkshire	Leicester	1996
	40ov	154*	B.J.Hodge	v	Sussex	Horsham	2004
	T20	118*	J.P.Inglis	v	Worcs	Leicester	2021
Best Bowling	50ov	6-16	C.M.Willoughby	v	Somerset	Leicester	2005
	40ov	6-17	K.Higgs	v	Glamorgan	Leicester	1973
	T20	7-18	C.N.Ackermann	v	Warwicks	Leicester	2019

MIDDLESEX

Formation of Present Club: 2 February 1864
Inaugural First-Class Match: 1864
Colours: Blue
Badge: Three Seaxes
County Champions (since 1890): (11) 1903, 1920, 1921, 1947, 1976, 1980, 1982, 1985, 1990, 1993, 2016
Joint Champions: (2) 1949, 1977
Gillette/NatWest Trophy Winners: (4) 1977, 1980, 1984, 1988
Benson and Hedges Cup Winners: (2) 1983, 1986
Sunday League Winners: (1) 1992
Twenty20 Cup Winners: (1) 2008

Chief Executive: Andrew Cornish, Lord's Cricket Ground, London NW8 8QN ● Tel: 020 7289 1300 ● Email: enquiries@middlesexccc.com ● Web: www.middlesexccc.com ● Twitter: @Middlesex_CCC (98,429 followers)

Head of Men's Cricket: Alan Coleman. **1st Team Coach**: Richard Johnson. **Club Coach**: Rory Coutts. **Coaching Consultants**: Mark Ramprakash and Ian Salisbury. **Captains**: T.S.Roland-Jones (f-c) and S.S.Eskinazi (white ball). **Overseas Players**: K.A.Maharaj and P.J.Malan. **2023 Testimonial**: J.A.Simpson. **Head Groundsman**: Karl McDermott. **Scorer**: Don Shelley. ‡ New registration. NQ Not qualified for England.

ANDERSSON, Martin Kristoffer (Reading Blue Coat S), b Reading, Berks 6 Sep 1996. 6'1". RHB, RM. Squad No 24. Debut (Leeds/Bradford MCCU) 2017. Derbyshire 2018 (on loan). Middlesex debut 2018. Berkshire 2015-16. HS 92 v Hants (Radlett) 2020. BB 4-25 De v Glamorgan (Derby) 2018. M BB 4-27 v Leics (Leicester) 2021. LO HS 44* v Sussex (Hove) 2021 (RLC). LO BB 2-48 v Surrey (Radlett) 2022 (RLC). T20 HS 25*. T20 BB 3-32.

BAMBER, Ethan Read (Mill Hill S), b Westminster 17 Dec 1998. 5'11". RHB, RMF. Squad No 54. Debut (Middlesex) 2018; cap 2022. Gloucestershire 2019 (on loan). Middlesex 2nd XI debut 2015. Berkshire 2017. HS 37* v Derbys (Chesterfield) 2022. 50 wkts (1): 52 (2021). BB 5-41 v Derbys (Lord's) 2021. LO HS 21 and LO BB 3-41 v Kent (Radlett) 2021 (RLC). T20 HS 3*. T20 BB –.

CRACKNELL, Joseph Benjamin (London Oratory S), b Enfield 16 Mar 2000. 5'9". RHB, WK. Squad No 48. Debut (Middlesex) 2021. London Spirit 2021. Middlesex 2nd XI debut 2017. Berkshire 2018. HS 13 v Leics (Northwood) 2021. LO HS 71 v Sussex (Hove) 2022 (RLC). T20 HS 77.

CULLEN, Blake Carlton (Hampton S), b Hounslow 19 Feb 2002. 6'1". RHB, RMF. Squad No 19. Debut (Middlesex) 2020. London Spirit 2021. Middlesex 2nd XI debut 2017, aged 15y 142d. HS 34 v Sussex (Radlett) 2020. BB 3-30 v Surrey (Oval) 2021. T20 HS 20*. T20 BB 4-32.

DAVIES, Jack Leo Benjamin (Wellington C), b Reading, Berks 30 Mar 2000. Son of A.G.Davies (Cambridge U 1982-89). 5'10". LHB, WK. Squad No 17. Debut (Middlesex) 2020. Middlesex 2nd XI debut 2017. Berkshire 2017-19. England U19 2018. HS 25 v Derbys (Lord's) 2022. LO HS 70 v Essex (Chelmsford) 2021 (RLC). T20 HS 47.

De CAIRES, Joshua Michael (St Albans S; Leeds U), b Paddington 25 Apr 2002. Son of M.A.Atherton (Lancashire, Cambridge U & England 1987-2001); great-grandson of F.I.de Caires (British Guiana & West Indies 1928/29-1938). 6'0". RHB, RM. Squad No 25. Middlesex 2nd XI debut 2017. HS 80 and BB 1-49 v Derbys (Lord's) 2022. LO HS 43 and LO BB 1-13 v Kent (Radlett) 2021 (RLC). T20 HS 24.

ESKINAZI, Stephen Sean (Christ Church GS, Claremont; U of WA), b Johannesburg, South Africa 28 Mar 1994. 6'2". RHB, WK. Squad No 28. Debut (Middlesex) 2015; cap 2018; captain 2020 and 2023 (white-ball only). Big Bash: PS 2022-23. UK passport. HS 179 v Warwks (Birmingham) 2017. LO HS 182 v Surrey (Radlett) 2022 (RLC) – M record. T20 HS 102*.

FERNANDES, Nathan Shane (St Gregory's Catholic Science C), b Margao, Goa, India 26 Apr 2004. 5'9". LHB, SLA. Squad No 18. Middlesex 2nd XI debut 2021. Awaiting 1st XI debut.

GREATWOOD, Toby Louie (Reading Blue Coats S), b High Wycombe, Bucks 21 Oct 2001. 6'1". RHB, RMF. Squad No 31. Middlesex 2nd XI debut 2019. Berkshire 2018-21. Awaiting f-c debut. LO HS 7* and LO BB 2-30 v Kent (Radlett) 2021 (RLC). T20 HS –. T20 BB 1-35.

HARRIS, Max Benjamin (Alexandra Park S), b Muswell Hill, London 17 Aug 2001. 5'10". RHB, RFM. Squad No 44. Middlesex 2nd XI debut 2019. Awaiting f-c debut. LO HS 12 v Glos (Radlett) 2022 (RLC). LO BB 3-98 v Sussex (Hove) 2022 (RLC). T20 HS 7*. T20 BB 2-26.

HELM, Thomas George (Misbourne S, Gt Missenden), b Stoke Mandeville Hospital, Bucks 7 May 1994. 6'4". RHB, RMF. Squad No 7. Debut (Middlesex) 2013; cap 2019. Glamorgan 2014 (on loan). Birmingham Phoenix 2021 to date. Buckinghamshire 2011. F-c Tour (EL): SL 2016-17. HS 52 v Derbys (Derby) 2018. BB 5-36 v Worcs (Worcester) 2019. LO HS 30 v Surrey (Lord's) 2018 (RLC). LO BB 5-33 EL v Sri Lanka A (Colombo, CCC) 2016-17. T20 HS 28*. T20 BB 5-11.

HIGGINS, Ryan Francis (Bradfield C), b Harare, Zimbabwe 6 Jan 1995. 5'10". RHB, RM. Squad No 29. Debut (Middlesex) 2017. Gloucestershire 2018-22; cap 2018. Welsh Fire 2021 to date. HS 199 v Leics (Leicester) 2019. M HS 53 v Leics (Leicester) 2022. 50 wkts (2); most – 51 (2021). BB 7-42 (11-96 match) Gs v Warwks (Bristol) 2020. M BB 4-59 v Glamorgan (Lord's) 2022. LO HS 81* Gs v Surrey (Oval) 2018 (RLC). LO BB 4-50 ECB XI v India A (Leeds) 2018. T20 HS 77*. T20 BB 5-13.

HOLDEN, Max David Edward (Sawston Village C; Hills Road SFC, Cambridge), b Cambridge 18 Dec 1997. 5'11". LHB, OB. Squad No 4. Northamptonshire 2017 (on loan). Middlesex debut 2017. F-c Tour (EL): I 2018-19. HS 153 and BB 2-59 Nh v Kent (Beckenham) 2017. M HS 119* v Derbys (Lord's) 2018. M BB 1-15 v Leics (Leicester) 2018. LO HS 166 v Kent (Canterbury) 2019 (RLC). LO BB 1-29 v Australians (Lord's) 2018. T20 HS 102*. T20 BB –.

HOLLMAN, Luke Barnaby Kurt (Acland Burghley S), b Islington 16 Sep 2000. 6'2". LHB, LB. Squad No 56. Debut (Middlesex) 2021. Middlesex 2nd XI debut 2017. Berkshire 2019. England U19 2018 to 2018-19. HS 82 v Sussex (Hove) 2022. BB 5-65 v Sussex (Hove) 2021. LO HS 20 v Sussex (Hove) 2022 (RLC). LO BB 4-34 v Warwks (Radlett) 2022 (RLC). T20 HS 51. T20 BB 3-18.

KAUSHAL, Ishaan (Dovay Martyrs S; Brunel U), b Hillingdon 9 Feb 2002. 6'1". RHB, RM. Squad No 22. Middlesex 2nd XI debut 2021. Awaiting 1st XI debut.

‡NOMAHARAJ, Keshav** Athmanand, b Durban, South Africa 7 Feb 1990. 5'10". RHB, SLA. Squad No 16. KwaZulu-Natal 2006-07 to 2014-15. Dolphins 2009-10 to 2020-21. Lancashire 2018. Yorkshire 2019. KZN Coastal 2022-23. **Tests** (SA): 48 (2016-17 to 2022-23); HS 84 v B (Gqeberha) 2021-22; BB 9-129 (match 12-283) v SL (Colombo, SSC) 2018 – 2nd best innings analysis for SA. **LOI** (SA): 27 (2017 to 2022-23); HS 28 v B (Centurion) 2021-22; BB 3-25 v E (Lord's) 2017. **IT20** (SA): 25 (2021 to 2022-23); HS 41 v I (Thiruvananthapuram) 2022-23; BB 2-21 v E (Southampton) 2022. F-c Tours (SA): E 2017, 2022; A 2016-17, 2022-23; WI 2021; NZ 2016-17, 2021; I 2015 (SAA), 2019-20; P 2020-21; SL 2018; Z 2016 (SAA). HS 114* KZN v Northerns (Pretoria) 2012-13. CC HS 85 Y v Essex (Chelmsford) 2019. BB 9-129 (see Tests). CC BB 7-37 (11-102 match) La v Somerset (Taunton) 2018. LO HS 50* Dolphins v Cobras (Cape Town) 2019-20. LO BB 5-34 KZN v Border (Durban) 2014-15. T20 HS 45*. T20 BB 4-15.

^{NQ}**MALAN, Pieter** Jacobus (Waterkloof Hoer S), b Nelspruit, South Africa 13 Aug 1989. Elder brother of J.N.Malan (North West, Cape Cobras, Boland & South Africa 2015-16 to date) and A.J.Malan (Northerns, North West, W Province, Cape Cobras & SW Districts 2010-11 to date). RHB, RMF. Squad No 13. Northerns 2006-07 to 2012-13. Titans 2008-09 to 2012-13. W Province 2013-14 to 2019-20. Cape Cobras 2014-15 to 2020-21. Warwickshire 2021. Boland 2021-22 to date. Middlesex debut 2022. Tests (SA): 3 (2019-20); HS 84 v E (Cape Town) 2019-20; BB – . F-c Tours (SA A): 1 2018, 2019. 1000 runs (0+2); most – 1114 (2017-18). HS 264 Cobras v Knights (Cape Town) 2020-21. CC HS 141 Wa v Worcs (Worcester) 2021. M HS 93 v Worcs (Worcester) 2022. BB 5-35 WP v EP (Pt Elizabeth) 2017-18. LO HS 169* Northerns v WP (Pretoria) 2008-09. LO BB 1-28 v Leics (Radlett) 2022 (RLC). T20 HS 140*. T20 BB 2-30.

^{NQ}**MURTAGH, Tim**othy James (John Fisher S, St Mary's C), b Lambeth, London 2 Aug 1981. Elder brother of C.P.Murtagh (Loughborough UCCE and Surrey 2005-09), nephew of A.J.Murtagh (Hampshire and EP 1973-77). 6'0". LHB, RMF. Squad No 34. British U 2000-03. Surrey 2001-06. Middlesex debut 2007; cap 2008; benefit 2015; captain 2022. Ireland 2012-13 to 2019. MCC 2010. Tests (Ire): 3 (2018 to 2019); HS 54* v Afg (Dehradun) 2018-19; BB 5-13 v E (Lord's) 2019. LOI (Ire): 58 (2012 to 2019); HS 23* v Scotland (Belfast) 2013; BB 5-21 v Z (Belfast) 2019. IT20 (Ire): 14 (2012 to 2015-16); HS 12* v UAE (Abu Dhabi) 2015-16; BB 3-23 v PNG (Townsville) 2015-16. HS 74* Sy v Middx (Oval) 2004 and 74* Sy v Warwks (Croydon) 2005. M HS 55 v Leics (Leicester) 2011, sharing M record 9th wkt partnership of 172 with G.K.Berg. 50 wkts (9); most – 85 (2011). BB 7-82 v Derbys (Derby) 2009. LO HS 35* v Surrey (Lord's) 2008 (FPT). LO BB 5-21 (see LOI). T20 HS 40*. T20 BB 6-24 Sy v Middx (Lord's) 2005 – Sy record.

O'DRISCOLL, Daniel Mark (Ruislip HS), b Hillingdon 10 Oct 2002. 5'9". RHB, WK. Squad No 2. Middlesex 2nd XI debut 2019. Awaiting 1st XI debut.

ROBSON, Sam David (Marcellin C, Randwick), b Paddington, Sydney, Australia 1 Jul 1989. Elder brother of A.J.Robson Leicestershire, Sussex and Durham 2013-19). 6'0". RHB, LB. Squad No 12. Qualified for England in April 2013. Debut (Middlesex) 2009; cap 2013-14. Tests: 7 (2014); HS 127 v SL (Leeds) 2014. F-c Tours (EL): SA 2014-15; SL 2013-14. 1000 runs (2); most – 1180 (2013). HS 253 v Sussex (Hove) 2012, sharing M record 1st wkt partnership of 376 with M.D.Stoneman. BB 2-0 v Surrey (Oval) 2020. LO HS 111 v Warwks (Radlett) 2022 (RLC). LO BB 2-23 v Notts (Grantham) 2022 (RLC). T20 HS 60.

ROLAND-JONES, Tobias Skelton ('**Toby**') (Hampton S; Leeds U), b Ashford 29 Jan 1988. 6'4". RHB, RFM. Squad No 21. Debut (Middlesex) 2010; cap 2012; captain 2023. MCC 2011. Wisden 2016. Leeds/Bradford UCCE 2009 (not f-c). Tests: 4 (2017); HS 25 and BB 5-57 v SA (Oval) 2017. LOI: 1 (2017); HS 37* and BB 1-34 v SA (Lord's) 2017. F-c Tours (EL): WI 2017-18; SL 2016-17; UAE 2016-17 (v Afg). HS 103* v Yorks (Lord's) 2015. 50 wkts (3); most – 67 (2022). BB 7-52 (10-79 match) v Glos (Northwood) 2019. Hat-tricks (2): v Derbys (Lord's) 2013, and v Yorks (Lord's) 2016 – at end of match to secure the Championship. LO HS 65 v Glos (Lord's) 2017 (RLC). LO BB 4-10 v Hants (Southampton) 2017 (RLC). T20 HS 40. T20 BB 5-21.

SIMPSON, John Andrew (St Gabriel's RC HS), b Bury, Lancs 13 Jul 1988. 5'10". LHB, WK. Squad No 20. Debut (Middlesex) 2009; cap 2011. MCC 2018. Northern Superchargers 2021 to date. Cumberland 2007. LOI: 3 (2021); HS 17 v P (Lord's) 2021. 1000 runs (1): 1039 (2022). HS 167* v Lancs (Manchester) 2019. LO HS 82* v Sussex (Lord's) 2017 (RLC). T20 HS 84*.

STONEMAN, Mark Daniel (Whickham CS), b Newcastle upon Tyne, Northumb 26 Jun 1987. 5'10". LHB, OB. Squad No 11. Durham 2007-16; captain (l-o only) 2015-16. Surrey 2017-21; cap 2018. Middlesex debut 2022; cap 2022. Yorkshire 2021 (T20 only). Tests: 11 (2017 to 2018); HS 60 v NZ (Christchurch) 2017-18. F-c Tour: A 2017-18; NZ 2017-18. 1000 runs (6); most – 1481 (2017). HS 197 Sy v Essex (Guildford) 2017. M HS 174 v Sussex (Hove) 2021, sharing M record 1st wkt partnership of 376 with S.D.Robson. BB 1-34 v Sussex (Hove) 2022. LO HS 144* v Notts (Lord's) 2017 (RLC). LO BB 1-8 Du v Derbys (Derby) 2016 (RLC). T20 HS 89*.

WALALLAWITA, Thilan Nipuna (Oaklands S), b Colombo, Sri Lanka 23 Jun 1998. 5'9". LHB, SLA. Squad No 32. Moved to UK in 2004; granted citizenship in March 2022. Debut (Middlesex) 2020. Pandura 2022-23. Middlesex 2nd XI debut 2015. HS 20* v Derbys (Lord's) 2021. BB 3-28 v Hants (Radlett) 2020. LO HS 29 v Lancs (Manchester) 2021 (RLC). LO BB 2-54 v Worcs (Worcester) 2021 (RLC). T20 HS 10. T20 BB 3-18.

WHITE, Robert George (Harrow S; Loughborough U), b Ealing 15 Sep 1995. 5'9". RHB, WK, occ RM. Squad No 14. Loughborough MCCU 2015-17. Middlesex debut 2018. Essex 2019 (on loan). HS 120 v Derbys (Lord's) 2021. LO HS 55 v Durham (Radlett) 2021 (RLC). T20 HS 11*.

RELEASED/RETIRED

(Having made a County 1st XI appearance in 2022)

NQ**BEHRENDORFF, Jason** Paul (Alfred Deakin HS; Canberra C), b Camden, NSW, Australia 20 Apr 1990. RHB, LFM. W Australia 2011-12 to date. Sussex 2019 (T20 only). Middlesex 2022 (T20 only). IPL: MI 2019. Big Bash: PS 2012-13 to date. **LOI** (A): 12 (2018-19 to 2021-22); HS 11* v SA (Manchester) 2019; BB 5-44 v E (Lord's) 2019. **IT20** (A): 9 (2017-18 to 2021); HS 5 v WI (Gros Islet) 2021; BB 4-21 v I (Guwahati) 2017-18. HS 39* WA v Q (Perth) 2017-18. BB 9-37 (14-89 match) WA v Vic (Perth) 2016-17. LO HS 35* WA v Tas (Perth) 2020-21. LO BB 5-27 WA v NSW (Sydney) 2014-15. T20 HS 26. T20 BB 4-21.

NQ**GREEN, Chris**topher James (Knox GS, Wahroonga), b Durban, South Africa 1 Oct 1993. RHB, OB. Debut (New South Wales) 2022-23; white-ball debut 2014-15. Warwickshire 2019 (T20 only). Middlesex 2021-22 (T20 only). IPL: KKR 2020-21. Big Bash: ST 2014-15 to date. HS 59* NSW v Tas (Sydney) 2022-23. BB 5-41 NSW v WA (Sydney) 2022-23 – on debut. LO HS 24 NSW v Tas (Sydney, NS) 2018-19. LO BB 5-53 NSW v Q (Sydney, DO) 2018-19. T20 HS 50. T20 BB 5-32.

NQ**HANDSCOMB, Peter** Stephen Patrick (Mt Waverley SC; Deakin U, Melbourne), b Melbourne, Australia 26 Apr 1991. RHB, WK. British passport (English parents). Victoria 2011-12 to date. Gloucestershire 2015; cap 2015. Yorkshire 2017. Durham 2019. Middlesex 2021-22; captain 2022. IPL: RPS 2016. Big Bash: MS 2012-13 to 2019-20; HH 2020-21 to 2021-22; MR 2022-23. **Tests** (A): 19 (2016-17 to 2022-23); HS 110 v P (Sydney) 2016-17. **LOI** (A): 22 (2016-17 to 2019); HS 117 v I (Mohali) 2018-19. **IT20** (A): 2 (2018-19); HS 20* v I (Bengaluru) 2018-19. F-c Tours (A): SA 2017-18; I 2015 (Aus A), 2016-17, 2018-19, 2022-23; B 2017. HS 281* Vic v WA (Melbourne, SK) 2022-23. CC HS 101* Y v Lancs (Manchester) 2017. M HS 79 v Sussex (Hove) 2022. LO HS 140 Y v Derbys (Leeds) 2017 (RLC). T20 HS 103*.

MORGAN, Eoin Joseph Gerard (Catholic University S), b Dublin, Ireland 10 Sep 1986. 6'0". LHB, RM. UK passport. Ireland 2004 to 2007-08. Middlesex 2006-19; cap 2008; testimonial 2022; l-o captain 2014-15; T20 captain 2020-22. IPL: RCB 2009-10; KKR 2011-21; SH 2015-16; KXIP 2017. Big Bash: ST 2013-14 to 2016-17. London Spirit 2021 to date. **Wisden** 2010. CBE 2020. **Tests**: 16 (2010 to 2011-12); HS 130 v P (Nottingham) 2010. **LOI** (E/Ire): 248 (23 for Ire 2006 to 2008-09; 225 for E 2009 to 2022, 126 as captain); HS 148 v Afg (Manchester) 2019, inc world record 17 sixes. **IT20**: 115 (2009 to 2021-22, 72 as captain); HS 91 v NZ (Napier) 2019-20. F-c Tours (Ire): A 2010-11 (E); NZ 2008-09 (Eng A); Namibia 2005-06; UAE 2006-07, 2007-08, 2011-12 (v P). 1000 runs (1): 1085 (2008). HS 209* Ire v UAE (Abu Dhabi) 2006-07. M HS 191 v Notts (Nottingham) 2014. BB 2-24 v Notts (Lord's) 2007. LO HS 161 v Kent (Canterbury) 2009 (FPT). LO BB –. T20 HS 91.

RELEASED/RETIRED continued on p 154

MIDDLESEX 2022

RESULTS SUMMARY

	Place	Won	Lost	Drew	NR
LV= Insurance County Champ (Div 2)	2nd	6	2	6	
Royal London One-Day Cup (Group A)	4th	5	3		
Vitality Blast (South Group)	8th	4	10		

LV= INSURANCE COUNTY CHAMPIONSHIP AVERAGES
BATTING AND FIELDING

Cap		M	I	NO	HS	Runs	Avge	100	50	Ct/St
2011	J.A.Simpson	14	19	3	132	1039	64.93	3	6	46/2
2019	T.G.Helm	7	8	4	51	207	51.75	–	2	1
2022	M.D.Stoneman	14	24	3	128	1025	48.80	3	4	6
	M.K.Andersson	5	6	1	62	234	46.80	–	2	–
	U.T.Yadav	3	4	2	44*	85	42.50	–	–	1
2018	S.S.Eskinazi	8	12	1	118	437	39.72	2	1	9
	M.D.E.Holden	14	21	2	91	749	39.42	–	6	4
2013	S.D.Robson	13	22	3	149	708	37.26	3	2	18
	L.B.K.Hollman	12	15	–	82	518	34.53	–	4	11
	P.J.Malan	5	6	–	93	200	33.33	–	2	1
	P.S.P.Handscomb	5	8	1	79	220	31.42	–	1	9
2012	T.S.Roland-Jones	13	17	5	85	354	29.50	–	3	4
	R.G.White	6	9	–	81	263	29.22	–	2	7
	R.F.Higgins	3	4	–	53	106	26.50	–	1	–
	J.M.De Caires	3	6	–	80	101	16.83	–	1	1
2022	E.R.Bamber	10	12	3	37*	109	12.11	–	–	3
	J.L.B.Davies	3	4	–	25	39	9.75	–	–	3
2008	T.J.Murtagh	10	13	3	15	48	4.80	–	–	1

Also batted: B.C.Cullen (1 match) 1 (1 ct); Shaheen Shah Afridi (3) 29, 29, 18 (2 ct);
T.N.Walallawita (2) 1, 1, 3 (1 ct).

BOWLING

	O	M	R	W	Avge	Best	5wI	10wM
T.S.Roland-Jones	475.5	111	1260	67	18.80	6- 35	4	1
T.G.Helm	200.5	43	637	29	21.96	5-109	1	–
Shaheen Shah Afridi	101.5	16	356	14	25.42	3- 35	–	–
T.J.Murtagh	334.1	83	920	30	30.66	3- 40	–	–
E.R.Bamber	324.4	79	958	25	38.32	3- 18	–	–
M.K.Andersson	132.2	8	560	11	50.90	3- 87	–	–
L.B.K.Hollman	229	18	993	19	52.26	4-122	–	–

Also bowled:
R.F.Higgins 65.1 8 236 8 29.50 4- 59
B.C.Cullen 28-3-145-1; J.M.De Caires 43-4-153-1; S.S.Eskinazi 1-1-0-0; P.J.Malan
8-0-26-0; S.D.Robson 23.3-4-96-3; M.D.Stoneman 31-1-123-1; T.N.Walallawita
18-1-76-1; U.T.Yadav 105-24-286-4.

Middlesex played no first-class fixtures outside the County Championship in 2022. The
First-Class Averages (pp 221–234) give the records of Middlesex players in all first-class
county matches, with the exception of R.F.Higgins, whose first-class figures for Middlesex
are as above.

MIDDLESEX RECORDS

FIRST-CLASS CRICKET

Highest Total	For 676-5d		v	Sussex	Hove	2021
	V 850-7d		by	Somerset	Taunton	2007
Lowest Total	For 20		v	MCC	Lord's	1864
	V 31		by	Glos	Bristol	1924
Highest Innings	For 331*	J.D.B.Robertson	v	Worcs	Worcester	1949
	V 341	C.M.Spearman	for	Glos	Gloucester	2004

Highest Partnership for each Wicket

1st	376	S.D.Robson/M.D.Stoneman	v	Sussex	Hove	2021
2nd	380	F.A.Tarrant/J.W.Hearne	v	Lancashire	Lord's	1914
3rd	424*	W.J.Edrich/D.C.S.Compton	v	Somerset	Lord's	1948
4th	325	J.W.Hearne/E.H.Hendren	v	Hampshire	Lord's	1919
5th	338	R.S.Lucas/T.C.O'Brien	v	Sussex	Hove	1895
6th	270	J.D.Carr/P.N.Weekes	v	Glos	Lord's	1994
7th	271*	E.H.Hendren/F.T.Mann	v	Notts	Nottingham	1925
8th	182*	M.H.C.Doll/H.R.Murrell	v	Notts	Lord's	1913
9th	172	G.K.Berg/T.J.Murtagh	v	Leics	Leicester	2011
10th	230	R.W.Nicholls/W.Roche	v	Kent	Lord's	1899

Best Bowling	For 10- 40	G.O.B.Allen	v	Lancashire	Lord's	1929
(Innings)	V 9- 38	R.C.R.Glasgow†	for	Somerset	Lord's	1924
Best Bowling	For 16-114	G.Burton	v	Yorkshire	Sheffield	1888
(Match)	16-114	J.T.Hearne	v	Lancashire	Manchester	1898
	V 16-100	J.E.B.B.P.Q.C.Dwyer	for	Sussex	Hove	1906

Most Runs – Season	2669	E.H.Hendren	(av 83.41)	1923
Most Runs – Career	40302	E.H.Hendren	(av 48.81)	1907-37
Most 100s – Season	13	D.C.S.Compton		1947
Most 100s – Career	119	E.H.Hendren		1907-37
Most Wkts – Season	158	F.J.Titmus	(av 14.63)	1955
Most Wkts – Career	2361	F.J.Titmus	(av 21.27)	1949-82
Most Career W-K Dismissals	1223	J.T.Murray	(1024 ct; 199 st)	1952-75
Most Career Catches in the Field	561	E.H.Hendren		1907-37

LIMITED-OVERS CRICKET

Highest Total	50ov	380-5	v	Kent	Canterbury	2019
	40ov	350-6	v	Lancashire	Lord's	2012
	T20	229-9	v	Glos	Radlett	2022
Lowest Total	50ov	41	v	Essex	Westcliff	1972
	40ov	23	v	Yorkshire	Leeds	1974
	T20	80	v	Kent	Lord's	2021
Highest Innings	50ov	182	S.S.Eskinazi	v	Surrey	Radlett	2022
	40ov	147*	M.R.Ramprakash	v	Worcs	Lord's	1990
	T20	129	D.T.Christian	v	Kent	Canterbury	2014
Best Bowling	50ov	7-12	W.W.Daniel	v	Minor Cos E	Ipswich	1978
	40ov	6- 6	R.W.Hooker	v	Surrey	Lord's	1969
	T20	6-28	J.K.Fuller	v	Hampshire	Southampton[2]	2018

† R.C.Robertson-Glasgow

143

NORTHAMPTONSHIRE

Formation of Present Club: 31 July 1878
Inaugural First-Class Match: 1905
Colours: Maroon
Badge: Tudor Rose
County Champions: (0); best – 2nd 1912, 1957, 1965, 1976
Gillette/NatWest/C&G/FP Trophy Winners: (2) 1976, 1992
Benson and Hedges Cup Winners: (1) 1980
Twenty20 Cup Winners: (2) 2013, 2016

est. 1878
NORTHAMPTONSHIRE
COUNTY CRICKET CLUB

Chief Executive: Ray Payne, County Ground, Abington Avenue, Northampton, NN1 4PR • Tel: 01604 514455 • Email: info@nccc.co.uk • Web: www.nccc.co.uk • Twitter: @NorthantsCCC (71,113 followers)

Head Coach: John Sadler. **Batting Coach**: Ben Smith. **Assistant Coach/Bowling Lead**: Chris Liddle. **Captains**: L.A.Procter (f-c) and J.J.Cobb (white ball). **Overseas Players**: C.A.Lynn, A.J.Tye (both T20 only) and S.M.Whiteman. **2023 Testimonial**: None. **Head Groundsman**: Craig Harvey. **Scorer**: Terry Owen. **Blast Team Name**: Northamptonshire Steelbacks. ‡ New registration. ᴺQ Not qualified for England.

BERG, Gareth Kyle (South African College S), b Cape Town, South Africa 18 Jan 1981. 6'0". RHB, RMF. Squad No 13. England qualified through residency. Middlesex 2008-14; cap 2010. Hampshire 2015-19; cap 2016. Northamptonshire debut 2019. Italy 2011-12 to date (l-o and T20 only). **IT20** (Italy): 10 (2021-22 to 2022); HS 39* v Finland (Kerava) 2022; BB 2-9 v Sweden (Vantaa) 2022. HS 130* M v Leics (Leicester) 2011, sharing M record 9th wkt partnership of 172 with T.J.Murtagh. Nh HS 75 v Essex (Chelmsford) 2022. BB 6-56 H v Yorks (Southampton) 2016. Nh BB 5-18 v Sussex (Northampton) 2021. LO HS 75 M v Glamorgan (Lord's) 2013 (Y40). LO BB 5-26 H v Lancs (Southampton) 2019 (RLC). T20 HS 90. T20 BB 4-20.

COBB, Joshua James (Oakham S), b Leicester 17 Aug 1990. Son of R.A.Cobb (Leics and N Transvaal 1980-89). 5'11½". RHB, OB. Squad No 4. Leicestershire 2007-14; l-o captain 2014. Northamptonshire debut 2015; cap 2018; captain 2020 to date (white ball only). Welsh Fire 2021 to date. HS 148* Le v Middx (Lord's) 2008. Nh HS 139 v Durham MCCU (Northampton) 2019. BB 2-11 Le v Glos (Leicester) 2008. Nh BB 2-44 v Loughborough MCCU (Northampton) 2017. LO HS 146* v Pakistanis (Northampton) 2019. LO BB 3-34 Le v Glos (Leicester) 2013 (Y40). T20 HS 103. T20 BB 5-25.

GAY, Emilio Nico (Bedford S), b Bedford 14 Apr 2000. 6'2". LHB, RM. Squad No 19. Debut (Northamptonshire) 2019. Northamptonshire 2nd XI debut 2018. HS 145 v Surrey (Northampton) 2022. BB 1-8 v Kent (Northampton) 2021. LO HS 131 v Lancs (Blackpool) 2022 (RLC). LO BB –. T20 HS 30. T20 BB –.

GOULDSTONE, Harry Oliver Michael (Bedford S), b Kettering 26 Mar 2001. 5'11". RHB, WK. Squad No 62. Debut (Northamptonshire) 2020. Northamptonshire 2nd XI debut 2019. HS 67* v Glamorgan (Cardiff) 2021. No 1st XI appearances in 2022.

GOWLER, George Edward (Wisbech GS), b Huntingdon 21 Oct 2003. 6'3½". RHB, RM. Northamptonshire 2nd XI debut 2021. Awaiting 1st XI debut.

HELDREICH, Frederick James (Framlingham C), b Ipswich, Suffolk 12 Sep 2001. 6'3". RHB, SLC. Squad No 80. Northamptonshire 2nd XI debut 2021. Awaiting f-c debut. LO HS 5 and LO BB 2-69 v Glamorgan (Northampton) 2021 (RLC). T20 HS 4. T20 BB 3-22.

KEOGH, Robert Ian (Queensbury S; Dunstable C), b Luton, Beds 21 Oct 1991. 5'11". RHB, OB. Squad No 21. Debut (Northamptonshire) 2012; cap 2019. Bedfordshire 2009-10. HS 221 v Hants (Southampton) 2013. BB 9-52 (13-125 match) v Glamorgan (Northampton) 2016. LO HS 134 v Durham (Northampton) 2016 (RLC). LO BB 3-32 v Hants (Newport) 2022 (RLC). T20 HS 59*. T20 BB 3-30.

KERRIGAN, Simon Christopher (Corpus Christi RC HS, Preston), b Preston, Lancs 10 May 1989. 5'9". RHB, SLA. Squad No 10. Lancashire 2010-17; cap 2013. Northamptonshire debut 2017. MCC 2013. **Tests**: 1 (2013); HS 1* and BB – v A (Oval) 2013. F-c Tour (EL): SL 2013-14. HS 62* La v Hants (Southport) 2013. Nh HS 62 v Glamorgan (Cardiff) 2017. 50 wkts (2); most – 58 (2013). BB 9-51 (12-192 match) La v Hants (Liverpool) 2011. Nh BB 5-39 v Yorks (Northampton) 2021. LO HS 10 La v Middx (Lord's) 2012 (CB40). LO BB 4-48 v Somerset (Northampton) 2021 (RLC). T20 HS 4*. T20 BB 3-17.

NQ**LYNN, Chris**topher Austin, b Herston, Brisbane, Australia 10 Apr 1990. 5'11". RHB, SLA. Squad No 90. Queensland 2009-10 to 2016-17. Northamptonshire debut 2022 (T20 only). IPL: DC 2012; KKR 2014-19; MI 2021. Big Bash: BH 2011-12 to 2021-22; AS 2022-23. Northern Superchargers 2021. **LOI** (A): 4 (2016-17 to 2018-19); HS 44 v SA (Adelaide) 2018-19. **IT20** (A): 18 (2013-14 to 2018-19); HS 44 v NZ (Sydney) 2017-18. HS 250 Q v Vic (Brisbane) 2014-15. BB –. LO HS 135 Q v NSW (Sydney, DO) 2018-19. LO BB 1-3 Q v WA (Sydney, BO) 2013-14. T20 HS 113* v Worcs (Northampton) 2022 – Nh record. T20 BB 2-15.

McMANUS, Lewis David (Clayesmore S, Bournemouth; Exeter U), b Poole, Dorset 9 Oct 1994. 5'10". RHB, WK. Squad No 15. Hampshire 2015-21; cap 2021. Northamptonshire debut 2022. Dorset 2011-19. HS 132* H v Surrey (Southampton) 2016. Nh HS 62 v Yorks (Northampton) 2022. LO HS 107 v Derbys (Northampton) 2022 (RLC). T20 HS 60*.

MILLER, Augustus ('Gus') Horatio (Bedford S), b Oxford 8 Jan 2002. 6'1". RHB, RFM. Squad No 24. Awaiting f-c debut. Northamptonshire 2nd XI debut 2021. Bedfordshire 2018-21. LO HS 31 v Hants (Newport) 2022 (RLC). T20 HS 5.

PROCTER, Luke Anthony (Counthill S, Oldham), b Oldham, Lancs 24 June 1988. 5'11". LHB, RM. Squad No 2. Lancashire 2010-17. Northamptonshire debut 2017; cap 2020; captain 2023. Cumberland 2007. HS 144 v Warwks (Northampton) 2022. BB 7-71 La v Surrey (Liverpool) 2012. Nh BB 5-33 v Durham (Chester-le-St) 2017. LO HS 97 La v West Indies A (Manchester) 2010. LO BB 3-29 La v Unicorns (Colwyn Bay) 2010 (CB40). T20 HS 25*. T20 BB 3-22.

RUSSELL, Alexander Kian (Chosen Hill S; Hartpury C), b Newport, Monmouths 17 Apr 2002. 5'10". RHB, LB. Squad No 61. Awaiting f-c debut. Gloucestershire 2nd XI 2018-21. Essex 2nd XI 2021. Northamptonshire 2nd XI debut 2022. Herefordshire 2018-21. LO HS 3* v Kent (Canterbury) 2022 (RLC). LO BB 2-69 v Essex (Northampton) 2022 (RLC). T20 HS 1*. T20 BB 1-27.

‡**SALE, Oliver** Richard Trethowan (Sherborne S), b Newcastle-under-Lyme, Staffs 30 Sep 1995. 6'1". RHB, RMF. Squad No 82. Awaiting f-c debut. Somerset 2016-22 (white ball only). LO HS 13 Sm v Leics (Leicester) 2022 (RLC). LO BB 3-80 Sm v Middx (Taunton) 2022 (RLC). T20 HS 14*. T20 BB 3-32.

SALES, James John Grimwood (Wellingborough S), b Northampton 11 Feb 2003. Son of D.J.G.Sales (Northamptonshire and Wellington 1996-2014). 6'0". RHB, RM. Squad No 5. Debut (Northamptonshire) 2021. Northamptonshire 2nd XI debut 2021. England U19 2022. HS 71 and BB 2-52 v Glos (Cheltenham) 2022. LO HS 34* v Essex (Northampton) 2022 (RLC). LO BB 2-65 v Lancs (Blackpool) 2022 (RLC). T20 HS 12. T20 BB –.

SANDERSON, Ben William (Ecclesfield CS; Sheffield C), b Sheffield, Yorks 3 Jan 1989. 6'0". RHB, RMF. Squad No 26. Yorkshire 2008-10. Northamptonshire debut 2015; cap 2018. Shropshire 2013-15. HS 42 v Kent (Canterbury) 2015. 50 wkts (3); most – 61 (2019). BB 8-73 v Glos (Northampton) 2016. LO HS 31 v Derbys (Derby) 2019 (RLC). LO BB 3-17 v Glamorgan (Northampton) 2022 (RLC). T20 HS 12*. T20 BB 4-21.

TAYLOR, Thomas Alex Ian (Trentham HS, Stoke-on-Trent), b Stoke-on-Trent, Staffs 21 Dec 1994. Elder brother of J.P.A.Taylor (see SURREY). 6'2". RHB, RMF. Squad No 12. Derbyshire 2014-17. Leicestershire 2018-20. Northamptonshire debut 2021. HS 80 De v Kent (Derby) 2016. Nh HS 60* v Somerset (Taunton) 2022. BB 6-47 (10-122 match) Le v Sussex (Hove) 2019. Nh BB 5-41 v Surrey (Northampton) 2021. LO HS 98* Le v Warwks (Leicester) 2019 (RLC). LO BB 5-49 v Notts (Grantham) 2021 (RLC). T20 HS 50*. T20 BB 4-27.

^{NQ}**TYE, Andrew** James (Padbury Senior HS, WA), b Perth, Australia 12 Dec 1986. 6'4". RHB, RMF. W Australia 2014-15 to date. Gloucestershire 2016-19 (T20 only). Durham 2022 (T20 only). Joins Northamptonshire in 2023 (T20 only). IPL: GL 2017; KXIP 2018-19; RR 2020-21; LSG 2022. Big Bash: ST 2013-14; PS 2014-15 to date. **LOI** (A): 7 (2017-18 to 2018); HS 19 v E (Oval) 2018; BB 5-46 v E (Perth) 2017-18. **IT20** (A): 32 (2015-16 to 2021); HS 20 v E (Birmingham) 2018; BB 4-23 v NZ (Sydney) 2017-18. HS 10 WA v Tas (Hobart) 2014-15. BB 3-47 WA v Q (Brisbane) 2014-15. LO HS 44 WA v Tas (Perth) 2021-22. LO BB 6-46 WA v Q (Sydney, NO) 2018-19. T20 HS 44. T20 BB 5-17.

^{NQ}**VASCONCELOS, Ricardo** Surrador (St Stithians C), b. Johannesburg, South Africa 27 Oct 1997. 5'5". LHB, WK, occ OB. Squad No 27. Boland 2016-17 to 2017-18. Northamptonshire debut 2018; cap 2021. Portuguese passport. No 185* v Glamorgan (Northampton) 2021. BB –. LO HS 112 v Yorks (Northampton) 2019 (RLC). T20 HS 78*.

WELDON, George Peter le Huray (Eton C), b 17 May 2004. 6'0". RHB, RFM. Northamptonshire 2nd XI debut 2022. Awaiting 1st XI debut.

WHITE, Curtley-Jack (Ullswater Comm C; Queen Elizabeth GS, Penrith), b Kendal, Cumberland 19 Feb 1992. 6'2". LHB, RFM. Squad No 9. Debut (Northamptonshire) 2020. Cumberland 2013. Cheshire 2016-17. HS 15* v Glos (Bristol) 2021. BB 6-38 v Essex (Northampton) 2022. LO HS 10* v Leics (Northampton) 2021 (RLC). LO BB 4-20 v Derbys (Northampton) 2021 (RLC).

WHITE, Graeme Geoffrey (Stowe S), b Milton Keynes, Bucks 18 Apr 1987. 5'11". RHB, SLA. Squad No 87. Debut (Northamptonshire) 2006; cap 2021. Nottinghamshire 2010-13. Welsh Fire 2021. HS 65 v Glamorgan (Colwyn Bay) 2007. BB 6-44 v Glamorgan (Northampton) 2016. LO HS 41* v Yorks (Leeds) 2018 (RLC). LO BB 6-37 v Lancs (Northampton) 2016 (RLC). T20 HS 37*. T20 BB 5-22 Nt v Lancs (Nottingham) 2013 – Nt record.

‡^{NQ}**WHITEMAN, Sam** McFarlane, b Doncaster, Yorks 19 Mar 1992. LHB, WK. W Australia 2012-13 to date. Big Bash: PS 2013-14 to 2019-20; ST 2021-22 to date. F-c Tour (Aus A): NZ 2015-16. HS 193 WA v SA (Perth) 2022-23. LO HS 79 WA v Tas (Hobart) 2021-22. T20 HS 68.

WILLEY, David Jonathan (Northampton S), b Northampton 28 Feb 1990. Son of P.Willey (Northants, Leics and England 1966-91). 6'1". LHB, LMF. Squad No 15. Debut (Northamptonshire) 2009; cap 2013. Yorkshire 2016-21; cap 2016; captain 2020 (T20 only). Bedfordshire 2008. IPL: CSK 2018; RCB 2022. Big Bash: PS 2015-16 to 2018-19. Northern Superchargers 2021 to date. **ECB Increment Contract 2022-23. LOI**: 64 (2015 to 2022-23); HS 51 v Ire (Southampton) 2020; BB 5-30 v Ire (Southampton) 2020 – separate matches. **IT20**: 43 (2015 to 2022-23); HS 33* v I (Birmingham) 2022; BB 4-7 v WI (Basseterre) 2018-19. HS 104* v Glos (Northampton) 2015. BB 5-29 (10-75 match) v Glos (Northampton) 2011. LO HS 167 v Warwks (Birmingham) 2013 (Y40). LO BB 5-30 (*see LOI*). T20 HS 118. T20 BB 4-7.

ZAIB, Saif Ali (RGS High Wycombe), b High Wycombe, Bucks 22 May 1998. 5'7½". LHB, SLA. Squad No 18. Debut (Northamptonshire) 2015. Northamptonshire 2nd XI debut 2013, aged 15y 90d. HS 135 v Sussex (Northampton) 2021. BB 6-115 v Loughborough MCCU (Northampton) 2017. CC BB 5-148 v Leics (Northampton) 2016. LO HS 136 v Essex (Northampton) 2022 (RLC). LO BB 4-23 v Glamorgan (Northampton) 2022 (RLC). T20 HS 92. T20 BB 1-20.

RELEASED/RETIRED

(Having made a County 1st XI appearance in 2022)

BUCK, Nathan Liam (Newbridge HS; Ashby S), b Leicester 26 Apr 1991. 6'2". RHB, RMF. Leicestershire 2009-14; cap 2011. Lancashire 2015-16. Northamptonshire 2017-22. F-c Tour (EL): WI 2010-11. HS 53 v Glamorgan (Cardiff) 2019. BB 6-34 v Durham (Chester-le-St) 2017. LO HS 21 Le v Glamorgan (Leicester) 2009 (P40). LO BB 5-59 v Essex (Northampton) 2022 (RLC). T20 HS 26*. T20 BB 4-26.

CURRAN, Benjamin Jack (Wellington C), b Northampton 7 Jun 1996. Son of K.M.Curran (Glos, Natal, Northants, Boland and Zimbabwe 1980-81 to 1999); grandson of K.P.Curran (Rhodesia 1947-48 to 1954-55); younger brother of T.K.Curran (*see SURREY*) and elder brother of S.M.Curran (*see SURREY*). 5'8". LHB, OB. Northamptonshire 2018-22. Southern Rocks 2020-21 to date. HS 134* SR v MT (Bulawayo) 2022-23. Nh HS 83* v Sussex (Northampton) 2018. BB 1-31 v Kent (Northampton) 2022. LO HS 94 v Somerset (Northampton) 2021 (RLC). T20 HS 71.

GLOVER, B.D. – *see DURHAM*.

NQ**KELLY, Matt**hew Liam, b Durban, South Africa 7 Dec 1994. RHB, RMF. W Australia 2017-18 to date. Northamptonshire 2022. Big Bash: PS 2017-18 to date. HS 89 WA v NSW (Adelaide P25) 2020-21. Nh HS 42 v Yorks (Northampton) 2022. BB 6-67 WA v SA (Perth) 2018-19. Nh BB 2-50 v Essex (Chelmsford) 2022. LO HS 33 WA v Q (Perth) 2022-23. LO BB 4-25 WA v Q (Sydney, DO) 2017-18. T20 HS 23*. T20 BB 4-25.

NQ**NEESHAM, James** Douglas Sheahan, b Auckland, New Zealand 17 Sep 1990. LHB, RM. Auckland 2009-10 to 2010-11. Otago 2011-12 to 2017-18. Wellington 2018-19 to 2021-22. Essex 2021. Northamptonshire 2022. Derbyshire 2016 (white ball only). Kent 2017 (T20 only). IPL: DD 2014; KXIP 2020-21; MI 2021; RR 2022. Big Bash: HH 2022-23. Welsh Fire 2021. **Tests** (NZ): 12 (2013-14 to 2016-17); HS 137* v I (Wellington) 2013-14; BB 3-42 v SL (Wellington) 2014-15. **LOI** (NZ): 71 (2012-13 to 2022); HS 97* v P (Birmingham) 2019; BB 5-27 v B (Wellington) 2020-21. **IT20** (NZ): 60 (2012-13 to 2022-23); HS 48* v WI (Auckland) 2020-21; BB 3-16 v WI (Auckland) 2013-14. F-c Tours (NZ): A 2015-16; WI 2014; I 2013-14 (NZ A), 2016-17; UAE (v P) 2014-15. HS 147 Otago v CD (Nelson) 2013-14. Nh HS 91 and Nh BB 1-43 v Kent (Canterbury) 2022. BB 5-65 Otago v ND (Whangarei) 2013-14. LO HS 120* Wellington v Auckland (Auckland) 2018-19. LO BB 5-27 (*see LOI*). T20 HS 75*. T20 BB 4-24.

NQ**RICKELTON, Ryan** David (St Stithians C), b Johannesburg, South Africa 11 Jul 1996. LHB, WK, occ SLA. Gauteng 2015-16 to date. Lions 2019-20 to 2020-21. Central Gauteng 2019-20. Northamptonshire 2022. **Tests** (SA): 3 (2021-22 to 2022); HS 42 v B (Gqeberha) 2021-22. F-c Tours (SA): E 2022; Z 2021 (SAA). HS 202* C Gauteng v FS (Johannesburg) 2019-20. Nh HS 133 v Kent (Canterbury) 2022. BB – . Nh HS 169 SAA v Zimbabwe A (Harare) 2021. LO BB 1-7 Gauteng v FS (Johannesburg) 2017-18. T20 HS 91. T20 BB 1-14.

NQ**WILLIAMS, Lizaad** Buyron, b Vredenburg, South Africa 1 Oct 1993. LHB, RMF. Boland 2012-13 to 2019-20. Cape Cobras 2012-13 to 2019-20. W Province 2014-15 to 2015-16. Titans 2020-21. Northerns 2021-22 to date. Northamptonshire 2022. **Tests** (SA): 2 (2021-22); HS 13 v B (Gqeberha) 2021-22; BB 3-54 v B (Durban) 2021-22. **LOI** (SA): 1 (2021); BB 1-62 v Ire (Dublin) 2021. **IT20** (SA): 6 (2020-21 to 2021); HS 2* (twice); BB 3-35 v P (Johannesburg) 2020-21. HS 83* Cobras v Warriors (East London) 2019-20. Nh HS 30 and Nh BB 2-114 v Surrey (Northampton) 2022. BB 7-75 (11-106 match) WP v Boland (Cape Town) 2015-16. LO HS 20 Boland v SW Districts (Paarl) 2018-19. LO BB 4-74 Cobras v Titans (Cape Town) 2016-17. T20 HS 17*. T20 BB 4-13.

NQ**YOUNG, Will**iam Alexander, New Plymouth, New Zealand 22 Nov 1992. RHB, OB. Central Districts 2011-12 to date. Durham 2021; cap 2021. Northamptonshire 2022. **Tests** (NZ): 13 (2020-21 to 2022-23); HS 89 v I (Kanpur) 2021-22. **LOI** (NZ): 8 (2020-21 to 2022); HS 120 v Neth (Hamilton) 2021-22. **IT20** (NZ): 5 (2020-21 to 2021); HS 53 v B (Hamilton) 2020-21. F-c Tours (NZ): E 2021, 2022; I 2017-18 (NZA), 2021-22; UAE 2018-19 (v P A). HS 162 CD v Auckland (Auckland) 2017-18. CC HS 134 v Warwks (Birmingham) 2022. LO HS 136 NZ A v Pakistan A (Abu Dhabi) 2018-19. T20 HS 101.

A.M.Rossington and C.O.Thurston left the staff without making a County 1st XI appearance in 2022.

NORTHAMPTONSHIRE 2022

RESULTS SUMMARY

	Place	Won	Lost	Drew	NR
LV= Insurance County Champ (Div 1)	6th	2	5	7	
Royal London One-Day Cup (Group B)	8th	2	6		
Vitality Blast (North Group)	7th	6	6		2

LV= INSURANCE COUNTY CHAMPIONSHIP AVERAGES
BATTING AND FIELDING

Cap		M	I	NO	HS	Runs	Avge	100	50	Ct/St
	R.D.Rickelton	4	8	–	133	539	77.00	2	4	2
2020	L.A.Procter	13	23	5	144*	961	53.38	3	4	4
	W.A.Young	10	18	–	134	672	37.33	1	4	13
	E.N.Gay	14	25	–	145	825	33.00	2	4	20
2019	R.I.Keogh	14	25	–	130	804	32.16	3	2	3
	G.K.Berg	6	8	1	75	207	29.57	–	2	1
	L.D.McManus	10	16	2	62*	410	29.28	–	4	27
	M.L.Kelly	5	7	1	42	151	25.16	–	–	2
2018	J.J.Cobb	8	14	1	88	327	25.15	–	2	3
	S.A.Zaib	7	13	1	124	301	25.08	1	1	3
2021	R.S.Vasconcelos	13	23	–	156	576	25.04	1	2	18/1
	J.J.G.Sales	4	8	–	71	159	19.87	–	1	1
	S.C.Kerrigan	7	10	2	43	140	17.50	–	–	5
	T.A.I.Taylor	10	17	3	60*	221	15.78	–	1	6
2018	B.W.Sanderson	13	20	6	38	209	14.92	–	–	4
	L.B.Williams	3	6	1	30	69	13.80	–	–	1
	C.J.White	9	14	6	14*	55	6.87	–	–	3

Also batted: N.L.Buck (1 match) 13, 1*; B.J.Curran (2) 9, 18, 1 (3 ct); J.D.S.Neesham (1) 33, 91 (3 ct).

BOWLING

	O	M	R	W	Avge	Best	5wI	10wM
C.J.White	296	83	786	37	21.24	6-38	2	–
B.W.Sanderson	449	127	1164	41	28.39	5-66	1	–
R.I.Keogh	334	56	1028	34	30.23	5-31	1	–
T.A.I.Taylor	258.5	61	800	25	32.00	5-49	1	–
G.K.Berg	181.3	48	505	13	38.84	5-58	1	–
L.A.Procter	169.1	49	528	12	44.00	3-68	–	–
S.C.Kerrigan	244	37	822	10	82.20	5-43	1	–

Also bowled:
M.L.Kelly 142 24 500 8 62.50 2-50 – –
N.L.Buck 37.4-3-153-3; J.J.Cobb 19.4-5-78-2; B.J.Curran 8-1-31-1; E.N.Gay 21-0-73-1; J.D.S.Neesham 19-3-83-1; J.J.G.Sales 22-1-138-2; L.B.Williams 69-7-343-2; R.S.Vasconcelos 6-0-34-0; S.A.Zaib 22-3-94-1.

Northamptonshire played no first-class fixtures outside the County Championship in 2022. The First-Class Averages (pp 221–234) give the records of Northamptonshire players in all first-class county matches, with the exception of R.D.Rickelton and W.A.Young, whose first-class figures for Northamptonshire are as above.

NORTHAMPTONSHIRE RECORDS

FIRST-CLASS CRICKET

Highest Total	For 781-7d		v	Notts	Northampton	1995
	V 701-7d		by	Kent	Beckenham	2017
Lowest Total	For 12		v	Glos	Gloucester	1907
	V 33		by	Lancashire	Northampton	1977
Highest Innings	For 331*	M.E.K.Hussey	v	Somerset	Taunton	2003
	V 333	K.S.Duleepsinhji	for	Sussex	Hove	1930

Highest Partnership for each Wicket

1st	375	R.A.White/M.J.Powell	v	Glos	Northampton	2002
2nd	344	G.Cook/R.J.Boyd-Moss	v	Lancashire	Northampton	1986
3rd	393	A.Fordham/A.J.Lamb	v	Yorkshire	Leeds	1990
4th	370	R.T.Virgin/P.Willey	v	Somerset	Northampton	1976
5th	401	M.B.Loye/D.Ripley	v	Glamorgan	Northampton	1998
6th	376	R.Subba Row/A.Lightfoot	v	Surrey	The Oval	1958
7th	293	D.J.G.Sales/D.Ripley	v	Essex	Northampton	1999
8th	179	A.J.Hall/J.D.Middlebrook	v	Surrey	The Oval	2011
9th	156	R.Subba Row/S.Starkie	v	Lancashire	Northampton	1955
10th	148	B.W.Bellamy/J.V.Murdin	v	Glamorgan	Northampton	1925

Best Bowling	For 10-127	V.W.C.Jupp	v	Kent	Tunbridge W	1932
(Innings)	V 10- 30	C.Blythe	for	Kent	Northampton	1907
Best Bowling	For 15- 31	G.E.Tribe	v	Yorkshire	Northampton	1958
(Match)	V 17- 48	C.Blythe	for	Kent	Northampton	1907

Most Runs – Season	2198	D.Brookes	(av 51.11)	1952
Most Runs – Career	28980	D.Brookes	(av 36.13)	1934-59
Most 100s – Season	8	R.A.Haywood		1921
Most 100s – Career	67	D.Brookes		1934-59
Most Wkts – Season	175	G.E.Tribe	(av 18.70)	1955
Most Wkts – Career	1102	E.W.Clark	(av 21.26)	1922-47
Most Career W-K Dismissals	810	K.V.Andrew	(653 ct; 157 st)	1953-66
Most Career Catches in the Field	469	D.S.Steele		1963-84

LIMITED-OVERS CRICKET

Highest Total	50ov	425		v	Notts	Nottingham	2016
	40ov	324-6		v	Warwicks	Birmingham	2013
	T20	231-5		v	Warwicks	Birmingham	2018
Lowest Total	50ov	62		v	Leics	Leicester	1974
	40ov	41		v	Middlesex	Northampton	1972
	T20	47		v	Durham	Chester-le-St[2]	2011
Highest Innings	50ov	161	D.J.G.Sales	v	Yorkshire	Northampton	2006
	40ov	172*	W.Larkins	v	Warwicks	Luton	1983
	T20	113*	C.A.Lynn	v	Worcs	Northampton	2022
Best Bowling	50ov	7-10	C.Pietersen	v	Denmark	Brondby	2005
	40ov	7-39	A.Hodgson	v	Somerset	Northampton	1976
	T20	6-21	A.J.Hall	v	Worcs	Northampton	2008

NOTTINGHAMSHIRE

Formation of Present Club: March/April 1841
Substantial Reorganisation: 11 December 1866
Inaugural First-Class Match: 1864
Colours: Green and Gold
County Champions (since 1890): (6) 1907, 1929, 1981, 1987, 2005, 2010
NatWest Trophy Winners: (1) 1987
Benson and Hedges Cup Winners: (1) 1989
Sunday League Winners: (1) 1991
Yorkshire Bank 40 Winners: (1) 2013
Royal London Cup Winners: (1) 2017
Twenty20 Cup Winners: (2) 2017, 2020

Chief Executive: Lisa Pursehouse, Trent Bridge, West Bridgford, Nottingham NG2 6AG ● Tel: 0115 982 3000 ● Email: questions@nottsccc.co.uk ● Web: www.trentbridge.co.uk ● Twitter: @TrentBridge (99,031 followers)

Director of Cricket: Mick Newell. **Head Coach**: Peter Moores. **Assistant Head Coach**: Paul Franks. **Assistant Coach**: Kevin Shine. **Captains**: S.J.Mullaney (f-c), H.Hameed (l-o). **Vice-captain**: H.Hameed. **Overseas Players**: C.Munro (T20 only) and D.Paterson. **2023 Testimonial**: L.J.Fletcher. **Head Groundsman**: Steve Birks. **Scorer**: Roger Marshall and Anne Cusworth. **Blast Team Name**: Nottinghamshire Outlaws. ‡ New registration. NQ Not qualified for England.

BALL, Jacob Timothy ('Jake') (Meden CS), b Mansfield 14 Mar 1991. Nephew of B.N.French (Notts and England 1976-95). 6'0". RHB, RFM. Squad No 28. Debut (Nottinghamshire) 2011; cap 2016. MCC 2016. Big Bash: SS 2020-21. Welsh Fire 2021 to date. **Tests**: 4 (2016 to 2017-18); HS 31 and BB 1-47 v I (Mumbai) 2016-17. **LOI**: 18 (2016-17 to 2018); HS 28 v B (Dhaka) 2016-17; BB 5-51 v B (Dhaka) 2016-17 – separate matches. **IT20**: 2 (2018); HS – ; BB 1-39 v I (Bristol) 2018. F-c Tours: A 2017-18; I 2016-17. HS 49* v Warwks (Nottingham) 2015. 50 wkts (1): 54 (2015). BB 6-49 v Sussex (Nottingham) 2015. Hat-trick v Middx (Nottingham) 2016. LO HS 28 (*see LOI*). BB 5-51 (*see LOI*). T20 HS 18*. T20 BB 4-11.

BROAD, Stuart Christopher John (Oakham S), b Nottingham 24 Jun 1986. Son of B.C.Broad (Glos, Notts, OFS and England 1979-94). 6'6". LHB, RFM. Squad No 8. Debut (Leicestershire) 2005; cap 2007. Nottinghamshire debut/cap 2008; testimonial 2019. MCC 2019. Big Bash: HH 2016-17. YC 2006. *Wisden* 2009. **ECB Central Contract 2022-23**. **Tests**: 161 (2007-08 to 2022-23); HS 169 v P (Lord's) 2010, sharing in record Test and UK f-c 8th wkt partnership of 332 with I.J.L.Trott; 50 wkts (2); most – 62 (2013); BB 8-15 v A (Nottingham) 2015. Hat-tricks (2): v I (Nottingham) 2011, and v SL (Leeds) 2014. **LOI**: 121 (2006 to 2015-16, 3 as captain); HS 45* v I (Manchester) 2007; BB 5-23 v SA (Nottingham) 2008. **IT20**: 56 (2006 to 2013-14, 27 as captain); HS 18* v SA (Chester-le-St) 2012 and 18* v A (Melbourne) 2013-14; BB 4-24 v NZ (Auckland) 2012-13. F-c Tours: A 2010-11, 2013-14, 2017-18, 2021-22; SA 2009-10, 2015-16, 2019-20; WI 2005-06 (Eng A), 2008-09, 2014-15, 2018-19; NZ 2007-08, 2012-13, 2017-18, 2019-20, 2022-23; I 2008-09, 2012-13, 2016-17, 2020-21; SL 2007-08, 2011-12, 2018-19, 2020-21; B 2006-07 (Eng A), 2009-10, 2016-17; UAE 2011-12 (v P), 2015-16 (v P). HS 169 (*see Tests*). CC HS 91* Le v Derbys (Leicester) 2007. Nt HS 60 v Worcs (Nottingham) 2009. BB 8-15 (*see Tests*). CC BB 8-52 (11-131 match) v Warwks (Birmingham) 2010. LO HS 45* (*see LOI*). LO BB 5-23 (*see LOI*). T20 HS 18*. T20 BB 4-24.

CARTER, Matthew (Branston S), b Lincoln 26 May 1996. Younger brother of A.Carter (Nottinghamshire, Essex, Glamorgan, Derbyshire, Hampshire & Northamptonshire 2009-17). RHB, OB. Squad No 20. Debut (Nottinghamshire) 2015, taking 7-56 v Somerset (Taunton) – the best debut figures for Nt since 1914. Trent Rockets 2021 to date. Lincolnshire 2013-17. IS 33 v Sussex (Hove) 2017. BB 7-56 (10-195 match) (*see above*). LO HS 21* v Warwks (Birmingham) 2019 (RLC). LO BB 4-40 v Warwks (Nottingham) 2018 (RLC). T20 HS 23*. T20 BB 3-14.

CLARKE, Joe Michael (Llanfyllin HS), b Shrewsbury, Shrops 26 May 1996. 5'11". RHB, WK, occ RM. Squad No 33. Worcestershire 2015-18. Nottinghamshire debut 2019. MCC 2017. Big Bash: PS 2020-21; MS 2021-22 to date. Manchester Originals 2021. Welsh Fire 2022. Shropshire 2012-13. F-c Tours (EL): WI 2017-18; UAE 2016-17 (v Afg). 1000 runs (1): 1325 (2016). HS 194 Wo v Derbys (Worcester) 2016. Nt HS 133 v Durham (Nottingham) 2020. BB –. LO HS 139 v Lancs (Nottingham) 2019 (RLC). T20 HS 136 v Northants (Northampton) 2021 – Nt record.

DUCKETT, Ben Matthew (Stowe S), b Farnborough, Kent 17 Oct 1994. 5'7". LHB, WK, occ OB. Squad No 17. Northamptonshire 2013-18; cap 2016. Nottinghamshire debut 2018; cap 2019. MCC 2017. Big Bash: HH 2018-19; BH 2021-22. Welsh Fire 2021 to date. PCA 2016. YC 2016. *Wisden* 2016. **Tests**: 9 (2016-17 to 2022-23); HS 107 v P (Rawalpindi) 2022-23. **LOI**: 6 (2016-17 to 2022-23); HS 63 v B (Chittagong) 2016-17. **IT20**: 9 (2019 to 2022-23); HS 70* v P (Karachi) 2022-23. F-c Tours: NZ 2022-23; I 2016-17; P 2022-23; B 2016-17. 1000 runs (3); most – 1338 (2016). HS 282* Nh v Sussex (Northampton) 2016. Nt HS 241 v Derbys (Derby) 2022, sharing in Nt record 2nd wkt partnership of 402 with H.Hameed. BB 1-15 v Middx (Nottingham) 2022. LO HS 220* EL v Sri Lanka A (Canterbury) 2016. T20 HS 96.

FLETCHER, Luke Jack (Henry Mellish S, Nottingham), b Nottingham 18 Sep 1988. 6'6". RHB, RMF. Squad No 19. Debut (Nottinghamshire) 2008; cap 2014; testimonial 2023. Surrey 2015 (on loan). Derbyshire 2016 (on loan). Welsh Fire 2021. Trent Rockets 2022. HS 92 v Hants (Nottingham) 2009 and 92 v Durham (Chester-le-St) 2017. 50 wkts (1): 66 (2021). BB 7-37 (10-57 match) v Worcs (Nottingham) 2021. LO HS 53* v Kent (Nottingham) 2018 (RLC). LO BB 5-56 v Derbys (Derby) 2019 (RLC). T20 HS 27. T20 BB 5-32.

HALES, Alexander Daniel (Chesham HS), b Hillingdon, Middx 3 Jan 1989. 6'5". RHB, OB, occ WK. Squad No 10. Debut (Nottinghamshire) 2008; cap 2011. White-ball contract since 2018. Worcestershire 2014 (on loan). Buckinghamshire 2006-07. IPL: SH 2018. Big Bash: MR 2012-13; AS 2013-14; HH 2014-15; ST 2019-20 to date. Trent Rockets 2021 to date. **Tests**: 11 (2015-16 to 2016); HS 94 v SL (Lord's) 2016; BB –. **LOI**: 70 (2014 to 2018-19); HS 171 v P (Nottingham) 2018. **IT20**: 75 (2011 to 2022-23); HS 116* v SL (Chittagong) 2013-14 – E record. 1000 runs (3); most – 1127 (2011). HS 236 v Yorks (Nottingham) 2015. BB 2-63 v Yorks (Nottingham) 2009. LO HS 187* v Surrey (Lord's) 2017 (RLC) – Nt record. T20 HS 116*.

HAMEED, Haseeb (Bolton S), b Bolton, Lancs 17 Jan 1997. 6'2". RHB, LB. Squad No 99. Lancashire 2015-19; cap 2016. Nottinghamshire debut/cap 2020. **Tests**: 10 (2016-17 to 2021-22); HS 82 v I (Rajkot) 2016-17 – on debut. F-c Tours: A 2021-22; WI 2017-18 (EL); I 2016-17; SL 2016-17 (EL), 2022-23 (EL). 1000 runs (2): most – 1235 (2022). HS 196 v Derbys (Derby) 2022, sharing in Nt record 2nd wkt partnership of 402 with B.M.Duckett. BB –. LO HS 114 v Middx (Grantham) 2022 (RLC).

HARRISON, Calvin Grant (King's C, Taunton; Oxford Brookes U), b Durban, S Africa 29 Apr 1998. 6'4". RHB, LBG. Squad No 31. Oxford MCCU 2019. Hampshire 2020 (T20 only). Nottinghamshire debut 2021 (T20 only). Manchester Originals 2021. HS 37* and BB 1-30 OU v Middx (Northwood) 2019. T20 HS 23. T20 BB 4-17.

HAYES, James Philip Henry (King's C, Taunton; Richard Huish C), b Haywards Heath, Sussex 27 Jun 2001. RHB, RFM. Squad No 35. Awaiting f-c debut. Nottinghamshire 2nd XI debut 2021. LO HS 1* and LO BB 2-58 v Middx (Grantham) 2022 (RLC).

HUTTON, Brett Alan (Worksop C), b Doncaster, Yorks 6 Feb 1993. 6'2". RHB, RM. Squad No 16. Debut (Nottinghamshire) 2011. Northamptonshire 2018-20. Surrey 2022 (on loan). HS 74 v Durham (Nottingham) 2016. BB 8-57 Nh v Glos (Northampton) 2018. Nt BB 5-29 v Durham (Nottingham) 2015. LO HS 46 v Derbys (Derby) 2021 (RLC). LO BB 7-26 v Leics (Leicester) 2022 (RLC) – Nt record. T20 HS 18*. T20 BB 2-28.

JAMES, Lyndon Wallace (Oakham S), b Worksop 27 Dec 1998. RHB, RMF. Squad No 45. Debut (Nottinghamshire) 2018. Nottinghamshire 2nd XI debut 2017. HS 164* v Durham (Nottingham) 2022. BB 4-51 v Essex (Nottingham) 2022. LO HS 54 v Surrey (Mansfield) 2022 (RLC). LO BB 5-48 v Warwks (Birmingham) 2021 (RLC). T20 HS 20. T20 BB 1-23.

KING, Samuel Isaac Michael (Nottingham HS; Nottingham U), b Nottingham 12 Jan 2003. RHB, RM. Squad No 94. Awaiting f-c debut. Nottinghamshire 2nd XI debut 2021. LO HS 11 v Glamorgan (Cardiff) 2021 (RLC) – only 1st XI appearance.

‡**LOTEN, Thomas** William (Pocklington S), b York 8 Jan 1999. 6'5". RHB, RMF. Squad No 24. Yorkshire 2019-22. Yorkshire 2nd XI 2018-22. HS 58 Y v Warwks (Birmingham) 2019. BB 2-31 Y v Warwks (Leeds) 2022. LO HS 43* Y v Hants (Scarborough) 2022 (RLC). LO BB 2-37 Y v Northants (York) 2022 (RLC).

MARTINDALE, Benjamin John Richardson (Nottingham HS), b Nottingham 12 Dec 2002. Son of D.J.R.Martindale (Nottinghamshire 1985-91). LHB, RMF. Squad No 95. Awaiting f-c debut. Nottinghamshire 2nd XI debut 2021. LO HS 1 v Glos (Bristol) 2022 (RLC). LO BB –.

MONTGOMERY, Matthew (Clifton C; Loughborough U), b Johannesburg, South Africa 10 May 2000. RHB, OB. Squad No 14. KwaZulu-Natal 2018-19. Nottinghamshire debut 2022. Nottinghamshire 2nd XI debut 2021. S Africa U19 2018-19. HS 178 v Durham (Nottingham) 2022. HS LO 104 KZN v WP (Chatsworth) 2018-19 – on debut. LO BB 2-48 v Glos (Bristol) 2022 (RLC). T20 HS 30*.

MOORES, Thomas James (Loughborough GS), b Brighton, Sussex 4 Sep 1996. Son of P.Moores (Worcestershire, Sussex & OFS 1983-98); nephew of S.Moores (Cheshire 1995). LHB, WK, occ RM. Squad No 23. Lancashire 2016 (on loan). Nottinghamshire debut 2016; cap 2021. Trent Rockets 2021 to date. HS 106 v Yorks (Nottingham) 2020. LO HS 76 v Leics (Leicester) 2018 (RLC). T20 HS 80*.

MULLANEY, Steven John (St Mary's RC S, Astley), b Warrington, Cheshire 19 Nov 1986. 5'9". RHB, RM. Squad No 5. Lancashire 2006-08. Nottinghamshire debut 2010, scoring 100* v Hants (Southampton); cap 2013; captain 2018 to date. Trent Rockets 2021. F-c Tour (EL): I 2018-19. 1000 runs (1): 1148 (2016). HS 192 v Sussex (Hove) 2022. BB 5-32 v Glos (Nottingham) 2017. LO HS 124 v Durham (Chester-le-St) 2018 (RLC). LO BB 4-29 v Kent (Nottingham) 2013 (Y40). T20 HS 79. T20 BB 4-19.

‡NQ**MUNRO, Colin** (Pakuranga C, Auckland), b Durban, South Africa 11 Mar 1987. LHB, RM. Auckland 2006-07 to 2017-18. Worcestershire 2015. Hampshire 2018. Notts (only). Joins Nottinghamshire in 2023 (T20 only). IPL: KKR 2016; DD 2018; DC 2019. Big Bash: SS 2016-17; PS 2020-21 to 2021-22; BH 2022-23. Manchester Originals 2021. Trent Rockets 2022. **Tests** (NZ): 1 (2012-13); HS 15 and BB 2-40 v SA (Pt Elizabeth) 2012-13. **LOI** (NZ): 57 (2012-13 to 2019); HS 87 v B (Christchurch) 2016-17 and 87 v SL (Mt Maunganui) 2018-19; BB 2-10 v P (Dunedin) 2017-18. **IT20** (NZ): 65 (2012-13 to 2019-20); HS 109* v I (Rajkot) 2017-18; BB 1-12 v P (Wellington) 2017-18. F-c Tours (NZ): SA 2012-13; SL 2013-14. HS 281 Auckland v CD (Napier) 2014-15, inc world record 23 sixes. CC HS 34 Wo v Hants (Southampton) 2015. BB 4-36 Auckland v CD (Auckland) 2010-11. LO HS 174* Auckland v Canterbury (Auckland) 2017-18. LO BB 3-45 Auckland v Otago (Oamaru) 2010-11. T20 HS 114*. T20 BB 4-15.

PATEL, Samit Rohit (Worksop C), b Leicester 30 Nov 1984. Elder brother of A.Patel (Derbyshire and Notts 2007-11). 5'8". RHB, SLA. Squad No 21. Debut (Nottinghamshire) 2002; cap 2008; testimonial 2017. Glamorgan (2019 on loan). Big Bash: MR 2019-20. Trent Rockets 2021 to date. MCC 2014, 2016. PCA 2017. **Tests**: 6 (2011-12 to 2015-16); HS 42 v P (Sharjah) 2015-16; BB 2-27 v SL (Galle) 2011-12. **LOI**: 36 (2008 to 2012-13); HS 70* v I (Mohali) 2011-12; BB 5-41 v SA (Oval) 2008. **IT20**: 18 (2011 to 2012-13); HS 67 v SL (Pallekele) 2012-13; BB 2-6 v Afg (Colombo, RPS) 2012-13. F-c Tours: NZ 2008-09 (Eng A); I 2012-13; SL 2011-12; UAE 2015-16 (v P). 1000 runs (2); most – 1125 (2014). HS 257* v Glos (Bristol) 2017. BB 7-68 (11-111 match) v Hants (Southampton) 2011. LO HS 136* v Northants (Northampton) 2019 (RLC). LO BB 6-13 v Ireland (Dublin) 2009 (FPT). T20 HS 90*. T20 BB 4-5.

NQ**PATERSON, Dane**, b Cape Town, South Africa 4 Apr 1989. RHB, RFM. Squad No 2. Western Province 2009-10 to date. Dolphins 2010-11 to 2012-13. KwaZulu-Natal 2011-12 to 2012-13. Cape Cobras 2013-14 to 2019-20. Nottinghamshire debut/cap 2021. Eastern Province 2021-22. **Tests** (SA): 2 (2019-20); HS 39* v E (Pt Elizabeth) 2019-20; BB 2-86 v E (Johannesburg) 2019-20. **LOI** (SA): 4 (2017-18 to 2018-19); HS – ; BB 3-44 v B (East London) 2017-18. **IT20** (SA): 8 (2016-17 to 2018-19); HS 4* v E (Taunton) 2017; BB 4-32 v E (Cardiff) 2017. F-c Tour (SA A): E 2017. HS 59 KZN v FS (Bloemfontein) 2012-13. Nt HS 22 v Warwks (Nottingham) 2021. 50 wkts (2+2); most – 67 (2013-14). BB 8-52 (10-117 match) v Worcs (Nottingham) 2022. LO HS 29 Cape Cobras v Dolphins (Cape Town) 2017-18. LO BB 5-19 SA A v India A (Bangalore) 2018. T20 HS 24*. T20 BB 4-24.

PATTERSON-WHITE, Liam Anthony (Worksop C), b Sunderland, Co Durham 8 Nov 1998. LHB, SLA. Squad No 22. Debut (Nottinghamshire) 2019, taking 5-73 v Somerset (Taunton). Nottinghamshire 2nd XI debut 2016. England U19 2016-17. F-c Tour (EL): SL 2022-23. HS 101 v Somerset (Taunton) 2021. BB 5-41 v Hants (Southampton) 2021. LO HS 62* v Sussex (Nottingham) 2022 (RLC). LO BB 5-19 v Northants (Grantham) 2021 (RLC).

PETTMAN, Toby Henry Somerville (Tonbridge S; Jesus C, Oxford), b Kingston-upon-Thames, Surrey 11 May 1998. 6'7". RHB, RFM. Squad No 15. Oxford University 2017-20. Derbyshire 2022 (on loan). Kent 2022 (on loan). HS 54* OU v Cambridge U (Oxford) 2018. CC HS 3* K v Surrey (Oval) 2022. BB 5-19 OU v Cambridge U (Cambridge) 2019. CC BB 3-40 De v Middx (Chesterfield) 2022 and 3-40 De v Durham (Chester-le-St) 2022. LO HS 5* v Leics (Leicester) 2022 (RLC). LO BB 4-44 v Surrey (Mansfield) 2022 (RLC).

NQ**SCHADENDORF, Dane** J., b Harare, Zimbabwe 31 Jul 2002. RHB, WK. Squad No 89. Debut (Nottinghamshire) 2021. Zimbabwe U19 2019-20. HS 24 v Derbys (Nottingham) 2021. LO HS 44* v Surrey (Guildford) 2021.

SINGH, Fateh (Trent C), b Nottingham 20 Apr 2004. LHB, SLA. Squad No 11. Awaiting f-c debut. Nottinghamshire 2nd XI debut 2021. LO HS 45 v Middx (Grantham) 2022 (RL). LO BB 2-7 v Leics (Leicester) 2022 (RLC).

SLATER, Benjamin Thomas (Netherthorpe S; Leeds Met U), b Chesterfield, Derbys 26 Aug 1991. 5'10". LHB, OB. Squad No 26. Debut (Leeds/Bradford MCCU) 2012. Southern Rocks 2012-13. Derbyshire 2013-18. Nottinghamshire debut 2018; cap 2021. Leicestershire 2020 (on loan). HS 225* v Durham (Chester-le-St) 2022. BB 1-1 v Middx (Nottingham) 2022. LO HS 148* De v Northants (Northampton) 2016 (RLC). T20 HS 57.

‡**STONE, Oli**ver Peter (Thorpe St Andrew HS), b Norwich, Norfolk 9 Oct 1993. 6'1". RHB, RF. Squad No 9. Northamptonshire 2012-16. Warwickshire 2017-21; cap 2020. Norfolk 2011. **ECB Pace Bowling Development Contract 2022-23. Tests**: 3 (2019 to 2021); HS 20 v NZ (Birmingham) 2021; BB 3-29 v Ire (Lord's) 2019. **LOI**: 8 (2018-19 to 2022-23); HS 9* v SL (Dambulla) 2018-19; BB 4-85 v A (Melbourne) 2022-23. **IT20**: 1 (2022-23); HS 0; BB –. HS 60 Nh v Kent (Northampton) 2016. BB 8-80 Wa v Sussex (Birmingham) 2018. LO HS 24* Nh v Derbys (Derby) 2015 (RLC). LO BB 4-71 Wa v Worcs (Birmingham) 2018 (RLC). T20 HS 22*. T20 BB 4-21.

(Having made a County 1st XI appearance in 2022)

BUDINGER, S.G. – *see LEICESTERSHIRE.*

CHAPPELL, Z.J. – *see DERBYSHIRE.*

NQ**CHRISTIAN, Dan**iel Trevor, b Camperdown, NSW, Australia 4 May 1983. RHB, RFM. S Australia 2007-08 to 2012-13. Hampshire 2010. Gloucestershire 2013; cap 2013. Victoria 2013-14 to 2017-18. Nottinghamshire 2016; cap 2015; captain 2016-22 (T20 only). IPL: DC 2011-12; RCB 2013-21; RPS 2017; DD 2018. Big Bash: BH 2011-12 to 2014-15; HH 2015-16 to 2017-18; MR 2018-19 to 2019-20; SS 2020-21 to date. **LOI** (A): 20 (2011-12 to 2021); HS 39 v I (Adelaide) 2011-12; BB 5-31 v SL (Melbourne) 2011-12. **IT20** (A): 23 (2009-10 to 2021); HS 39 v B (Mirpur) 2021; BB 3-27 v WI (Gros Islet) 2011-12. HS 131* SA v NSW (Adelaide) 2011-12. CC HS 36 and CC BB 2-115 H v Somerset (Taunton) 2010. Nt HS 31 v Hants (Southampton) 2016. BB 5-24 SA v WA (Perth) (2009-10). Nt BB 1-22 v Warwks (Birmingham) 2016. LO HS 117 Vic v NSW (Sydney) 2013-14. LO BB 6-48 SA v Vic (Geelong) 2010-11. T20 HS 129 M v Kent (Canterbury) 2014 – M record. T20 BB 5-14.

EVISON, J.D.M. – *see KENT.*

NQ**PATTINSON, James** Lee, b Melbourne, Australia 3 May 1990. Younger brother of D.J.Pattinson (Victoria, Nottinghamshire and England 2006-07 to 2011-12). RHB, RFM. Victoria 2009-09 to 2021-22. Nottinghamshire 2017-22; cap 2017. IPL: MI 2020-21. Big Bash: MR 2013-14 to 2021-22; BH 2018-19 to 2019-20. **Tests** (A): 21 (2011-12 to 2019-20); HS 47* v E (Birmingham) 2019; BB 5-27 v NZ (Brisbane) 2011-12 and 5-27 v WI (Hobart) 2015-16. **LOI** (A): 15 (2011 to 2015); HS 13 v E (Manchester) 2012; BB 4-51 v SL (Melbourne) 2011-12. **IT20** (A): 4 (2011-12); HS 5* and BB 2-17 v SA (Johannesburg) 2011-12. F-c Tours (A): E 2013, 2019; SA 2013-14; WI 2011-12; NZ 2015-16; I 2012-13. HS 89* v Leics (Leicester) 2017. BB 6-32 Vic v Q (Brisbane) 2012-13. Nt BB 6-73 v Kent (Tunbridge W) 2019. LO HS 54 Vic v NSW (N Sydney) 2020-21. LO BB 6-48 Vic v NSW (Sydney) 2009-10. T20 HS 27*. T20 BB 5-33.

MIDDLESEX RELEASED/RETIRED (continued from p 141)

NQ**SHAHEEN** Shah **AFRIDI**, b Khyber Agency, Pakistan 6 Apr 2000. 6'4½". LHB, LFM. Khan Research Laboratories 2017-18. Northern Areas 2019-20. Middlesex 2022. Hampshire 2020 (T20 only). **Tests** (P): 25 (2018-19 to 2022); HS 19 and BB 6-51 v WI (Kingston) 2021; and 19 v A (Karachi) 2021-22. **LOI** (P): 32 (2018-19 to 2022); HS 19* v E (Leeds) 2019; BB 6-35 v B (Lord's) 2019. **IT20** (P): 47 (2017-18 to 2022-23); HS 16 v I (Melbourne) 2022-23; BB 4-22 v B (Adelaide) 2022-23. F-c Tours (P): E 2020; A 2019-20; SA 2018-19; WI 2021; NZ 2020-21; SL 2022; B 2021-22. HS 29 v Glamorgan (Cardiff) 2022 and 29 v Leics (Lord's) 2022. BB 8-39 KRL v Rawalpindi (Rawalpindi) 2017-18 – on f-c debut, aged 17y 174d. LO HS 19* (*see LOI*). LO BB 6-35 (*see LOI*). T20 HS 52. T20 BB 6-19 v Middx (Southampton) 2020 – H record.

SOWTER, N.A. – *see DURHAM.*

NQ**YADAV, Umesh**kumar Tilak, b Nagpur, India 25 Oct 1987. RHB, RFM. Vidarbha 2008-09 to date. Central Zone 2008-09 to 2013-14. Middlesex 2022. IPL: DD 2009-10 to 2013; KKR 2014 to date; RCB 2018 to 2020-21. **Tests** (I): 55 (2011-12 to 2022-23); HS 31 v SA (Ranchi) 2019-20; BB 6-88 v WI (Hyderabad) 2018-19. **LOI** (I): 75 (2010 to 2018-19); HS 18* v NZ (Delhi) 2016-17; BB 4-31 v B (Melbourne) 2014-15. **IT20** (I): 9 (2012 to 2022-23); HS 20* v SA (Indore) 2022-23; BB 2-19 v Ire (Dublin) 2018. F-c Tours (I): E 2018, 2021; A 2011-12, 2014-15, 2018-19, 2020-21; SA 2021-22; WI 2016, 2019 (I A); NZ 2019-20; SL 2015, 2017; B 2015, 2022-23. HS 128* Vidarbha v Orissa (Nagpur) 2015-16. M HS 44* and M BB 1-25 v Worcs (Northwood) 2022. BB 7-48 (12-79 match) Vidarbha v Kerala (Wayanad) 2018-19. LO HS 30 C Zone v West Zone (Visakhapatnam) 2013-14. LO BB 5-26 Vidarbha v Rajasthan (Jaipur) 2013-14. T20 HS 26. T20 BB 5-18.

NOTTINGHAMSHIRE 2022

RESULTS SUMMARY

	Place	Won	Lost	Drew	NR
LV= Insurance County Champ (Div 2)	1st	8	2	4	
Royal London One-Day Cup (Group A)	QF	5	4		
Vitality Blast (North Group)	5th	7	6		1

LV= INSURANCE COUNTY CHAMPIONSHIP AVERAGES
BATTING AND FIELDING

Cap		M	I	NO	HS	Runs	Avge	100	50	Ct/St
2019	B.M.Duckett	10	14	–	241	1012	72.28	3	5	8
2020	H.Hameed	14	24	3	196	1235	58.80	4	7	6
	L.W.James	13	19	2	164*	890	52.35	3	5	9
2013	S.J.Mullaney	14	21	2	192	993	52.26	3	4	15
	J.D.M.Evison	3	4	1	109*	148	49.33	1	–	1
	M.Montgomery	4	8	–	178	369	46.12	1	1	8
2021	J.M.Clarke	14	22	3	95	682	35.89	–	5	13
2021	B.T.Slater	14	24	3	225*	703	33.47	1	2	6
2017	J.L.Pattinson	8	10	2	45*	239	29.87	–	–	1
2021	T.J.Moores	13	17	2	81*	385	25.66	–	1	38/1
	L.A.Patterson-White	17	17	1	54	379	23.68	–	2	8
2014	L.J.Fletcher	10	9	3	51	132	22.00	–	2	2
2021	B.A.Hutton	6	8	2	20*	87	14.50	–	–	3
2021	D.Paterson	12	12	7	16	50	10.00	–	–	1

Also batted: J.T.Ball (1 match – cap 2016) 0, 20; S.C.J.Broad (4 – cap 2008) 45*, 11*, 3 (2 ct).

BOWLING

	O	M	R	W	Avge	Best	5wI	10wM
S.C.J.Broad	123.1	30	333	16	20.81	4-72	–	–
D.Paterson	404	89	1252	56	22.35	8-52	2	1
S.J.Mullaney	151.3	26	393	15	26.20	3-29	–	–
B.A.Hutton	197.3	37	631	24	26.29	4-76	–	–
L.J.Fletcher	284.5	74	801	29	27.62	4-23	–	–
L.A.Patterson-White	452.1	106	1146	41	27.95	5-54	2	–
J.L.Pattinson	261.1	43	964	33	29.21	5-56	1	–

Also bowled:

	O	M	R	W	Avge	Best		
L.W.James	125	17	381	6	63.50	3-49		

J.T.Ball 21-7-60-3; J.M.Clarke 6-0-26-0; B.M.Duckett 7-0-15-1; J.D.M.Evison 48-4-175-3; H.Hameed 12-2-39-0; M.Montgomery 1-0-4-0; T.J.Moores 1-0-5-0; B.T.Slater 40-12-82-3.

Nottinghamshire played no first-class fixtures outside the County Championship in 2022. The First-Class Averages (pp 221–234) give the records of Nottinghamshire players in all first-class county matches, with the exception of S.C.J.Broad, J.D.M.Evison and B.A.Hutton, whose first-class figures for Nottinghamshire are as above.

NOTTINGHAMSHIRE RECORDS

FIRST-CLASS CRICKET

Highest Total	For 791		v	Essex	Chelmsford	2007
	V 781-7d		by	Northants	Northampton	1995
Lowest Total	For 13		v	Yorkshire	Nottingham	1901
	V 16		by	Derbyshire	Nottingham	1879
	16		by	Surrey	The Oval	1880
Highest Innings	For 312*	W.W.Keeton	v	Middlesex	The Oval	1939
	V 345	C.G.Macartney	for	Australians	Nottingham	1921

Highest Partnership for each Wicket

1st	406*	D.J.Bicknell/G.E.Welton	v	Warwicks	Birmingham	2000
2nd	402	H.Hameed/B.M.Duckett	v	Derbyshire	Derby	2022
3rd	367	W.Gunn/J.R.Gunn	v	Leics	Nottingham	1903
4th	361	A.O.Jones/J.R.Gunn	v	Essex	Leyton	1905
5th	359	D.J.Hussey/C.M.W.Read	v	Essex	Nottingham	2007
6th	372*	K.P.Pietersen/J.E.Morris	v	Derbyshire	Derby	2001
7th	301	C.C.Lewis/B.N.French	v	Durham	Chester-le-St[2]	1993
8th	220	G.F.H.Heane/R.Winrow	v	Somerset	Nottingham	1935
9th	170	J.C.Adams/K.P.Evans	v	Somerset	Taunton	1994
10th	152	E.B.Alletson/W.Riley	v	Sussex	Hove	1911
	152	U.Afzaal/A.J.Harris	v	Worcs	Nottingham	2000

Best Bowling	For 10-66	K.Smales	v	Glos	Stroud	1956
(Innings)	V 10-10	H.Verity	for	Yorkshire	Leeds	1932
Best Bowling	For 17-89	F.C.L.Matthews	v	Northants	Nottingham	1923
(Match)	V 17-89	W.G.Grace	for	Glos	Cheltenham	1877

Most Runs – Season	2620	W.W.Whysall	(av 53.46)		1929
Most Runs – Career	31592	G.Gunn	(av 35.69)		1902-32
Most 100s – Season	9	W.W.Whysall			1928
	9	M.J.Harris			1971
	9	B.C.Broad			1990
Most 100s – Career	65	J.Hardstaff jr			1930-55
Most Wkts – Season	181	B.Dooland	(av 14.96)		1954
Most Wkts – Career	1653	T.G.Wass	(av 20.34)		1896-1920
Most Career W-K Dismissals	983	C.M.W.Read	(939 ct; 44 st)		1998-2017
Most Career Catches in the Field	466	A.O.Jones			1892-1914

LIMITED-OVERS CRICKET

Highest Total	50ov	445-8	v	Northants	Nottingham	2016
	40ov	296-7	v	Somerset	Taunton	2002
	T20	247-6	v	Derbyshire	Nottingham	2022
Lowest Total	50ov	74	v	Leics	Leicester	1987
	40ov	57	v	Glos	Nottingham	2009
	T20	91	v	Lancashire	Manchester	2006
		91	v	Lancashire	Nottingham	2022
Highest Innings	50ov	187*	A.D.Hales	v	Surrey	Lord's	2017
	40ov	150*	A.D.Hales	v	Worcs	Nottingham	2009
	T20	136	J.M.Clarke	v	Northants	Northampton	2021
Best Bowling	50ov	7-26	B.A.Hutton	v	Leics	Leicester	2022
	40ov	6-12	R.J.Hadlee	v	Lancashire	Nottingham	1980
	T20	5-22	G.G.White	v	Lancashire	Nottingham	2013

SOMERSET

Formation of Present Club: 18 August 1875
Inaugural First-Class Match: 1882
Colours: Black, White and Maroon
Badge: Somerset Dragon
County Champions: (0); best – 2nd (Div 1) 2001, 2010, 2012, 2016, 2018, 2019
Gillette/NatWest/C&G Trophy Winners: (3) 1979, 1983, 2001
Benson and Hedges Cup Winners: (2) 1981, 1982
Sunday League Winners: (1) 1979
Royal London One-Day Cup Winners: (1) 2019
Twenty20 Cup Winners: (1) 2005

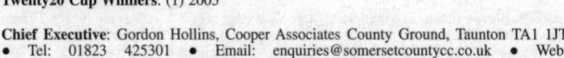

Chief Executive: Gordon Hollins, Cooper Associates County Ground, Taunton TA1 1JT
• Tel: 01823 425301 • Email: enquiries@somersetcountycc.co.uk • Web: www.somersetcountycc.co.uk • Twitter: @SomersetCCC (169,867 followers)

Director of Cricket: Andy Hurry. **Head Coach**: Jason Kerr. **Assistant Coaches**: Steve Kirby, Lachlan Stevens and Paul Tweddle. **Captain**: T.B.Abell. **Overseas Players**: M.J.Henry and P.M.Siddle. **2023 Testimonial**: M.T.C.Waller. **Groundsman**: Scott Hawkins. **Scorer**: Polly Rhodes. ‡ New registration. NQ Not qualified for England.

ABELL, Thomas Benjamin (Taunton S; Exeter U), b Taunton 5 Mar 1994. 5'10". RHB, RM. Squad No 28. Debut (Somerset) 2014; captain 2017 to date; cap 2018. MCC 2019. Big Bash: BH 2021-22. Birmingham Phoenix 2021. Wisden Schools Cricketer of the Year 2012. F-c Tours (EL): A 2019-20; SL 2022-23. HS 150* v Surrey (Oval) 202. BB 4-39 v Warwks (Birmingham) 2019. Hat-trick v Notts (Nottingham) 2018. LO HS 106 v Sussex (Taunton) 2016 (RLC). LO BB 2-19 v Hants (Lord's) 2019 (RLC). T20 HS 101*. T20 BB 1-11.

ALDRIDGE, Kasey Luke (Millfield S), b Bristol 24 Dec 2000. RHB, RM. Squad No 5. Debut (Somerset) 2021. Somerset 2nd XI debut 2019. Devon 2019. England U19 2018-19. HS 41 v Yorks (Taunton) 2022. BB 6-110 v Kent (Canterbury) 2022. LO HS 12 v Surrey (Oval) 2021 (RLC). LO BB 5-50 v Surrey (Oval) 2022 (RLC).

BAKER, Sonny (Torquay Boys' GS; King's C, Taunton), b Torbay 13 Mar 2003. Nephew of A.K.Hele (Devon 1998-2001). RHB, RM. Squad No 16. Southern Brave 2022. Somerset 2nd XI debut 2019. Awaiting f-c debut. LO HS 7* v Surrey (Oval) 2021 (RLC). LO BB 6-46 v Durham (Taunton) 2022 (RLC). T20 HS 0. T20 BB 2-28.

BANTON, Thomas (Bromsgrove S; King's C, Taunton), b Chiltern, Bucks 11 Nov 1998. Son of C.Banton (Nottinghamshire 1995); elder brother of J.Banton (*see WORCESTERSHIRE*). 6'2". RHB, WK. Squad No 18. Debut (Somerset) 2018. Big Bash: BH 2019-20. Welsh Fire 2021 to date. Warwickshire 2nd XI 2015. Somerset 2nd XI debut 2016. England U19 2018. **LOI**: 6 (2019-20 to 2020); HS 58 v Ire (Southampton) 2020. **IT20**: 14 (2019-20 to 2021-22); HS 73 v WI (Bridgetown) 2021-22. HS 126 v Essex (Chelmsford) 2022. LO HS 112 v Worcs (Worcester) 2019 (RLC). T20 HS 107*.

BARTLETT, George Anthony (Millfield S), b Frimley, Surrey 14 Mar 1998. 6'0". RHB, OB. Squad No 14. Debut (Somerset) 2017. HS 137 v Surrey (Guildford) 2019. BB –. LO HS 108 v Leics (Taunton) 2021 (RLC). T20 HS 82*.

BASHIR, Shoaib (Fulbrook S; Woking C), b Chertsey, Surrey 13 Oct 2003. RHB, OB. Squad No 13. Somerset 2nd XI debut 2022. Awaiting 1st XI debut.

BROOKS, Jack Alexander (Wheatley Park S), b Oxford 4 Jun 1984. 6'2". RHB, RFM. Squad No 70. Northamptonshire 2009-12; cap 2012. Yorkshire 2013-18; cap 2013. Somerset debut 2019. Sussex 2022 (on loan). Oxfordshire 2004-09. F-c Tour (EL): SA 2014-15. HS 109* Y v Lancs (Manchester) 2017. Sm HS 72 v Glamorgan (Taunton) 2020. 50 wkts (4); most – 71 (2014). BB 6-65 Y v Middx (Lord's) 2016. Sm BB 5-33 v Surrey (Guildford) 2019. LO HS 28 v Sussex (Taunton) 2022 (RLC). LO BB 4-38 v Warwks (Birmingham) 2022 (RLC). T20 HS 33*. T20 BB 5-21.

NQDAVEY, Joshua Henry (Culford S), b Aberdeen, Scotland 3 Aug 1990. 5'11". RHB, RMF. Squad No 38. Middlesex 2010-12. Scotland 2011-12 to 2016. Somerset debut 2019; cap 2021. Suffolk 2014. **LOI** (Scot): 31 (2010 to 2019-20); HS 64 v Afg (Sharjah) 2012-13; BB 6-28 v Afg (Abu Dhabi) 2014-15 – Scot record. **IT20** (Scot): 31 (2012 to 2022-23); HS 24 v Z (Nagpur) 2015-16; BB 4-18 v PNG (Al Amerat) 2021-22. HS 75* v Leics (Taunton) 2021. BB 5-21 v Yorks (Taunton) 2019. LO HS 91 Scot v Warwks (Birmingham) 2011 (CB40). LO BB 6-28 (*see LOI*). T20 HS 24. T20 BB 4-18.

DAVIES, Steven Michael (King Charles I S, Kidderminster), b Bromsgrove, Worcs 17 Jun 1986. 5'10". LHB, WK. Squad No 11. Worcestershire 2005-09. Surrey 2010-16; cap 2011. Somerset debut/cap 2017. MCC 2006-07, 2011. F-c Tours: A 2010-11; B 2006-07 (Eng A); UAE 2011-12 (v P). 1000 runs (6); most – 1147 (2016). HS 200* Sy v Glamorgan (Cardiff) 2015. Sm HS 142 v Surrey (Taunton) 2017. LO HS 127* Sy v Hants (Oval) 2013 (Y40). T20 HS 99*.

‡DICKSON, Sean Robert, b Johannesburg, South Africa 2 Sep 1991. 5'10". RHB, RM. Squad No 58. Northerns 2013-14 to 2014-15. Kent 2015-19. Durham 2020-22; cap 2020. UK passport holder; England qualified. HS 318 K v Northants (Beckenham) 2017, 2nd highest score in K history. BB 1-15 Northerns v GW (Centurion) 2014-15. CC BB –. LO HS 103* Du v Lancs (Gosforth) 2021 (RLC). T20 HS 53. T20 BB 1-9.

GOLDSWORTHY, Lewis Peter (Cambourne Science & Int Ac), b Truro, Cornwall 8 Jan 2001. RHB, SLA. Squad No 44. Debut (Somerset) 2021. Somerset 2nd XI debut 2017. Cornwall 2017-19. England U19 2018-19. HS 130 v Lancs (Southport) 2022. BB –. LO HS 111 and LO BB 2-58 v Warwks (Birmingham) 2022 (RLC). T20 HS 48. T20 BB 3-14.

GREEN, Benjamin George Frederick (Exeter S), b Exeter, Devon 28 Sep 1997. 6'2". RHB, RFM. Squad No 54. Debut (Somerset) 2018. Devon 2014-18. HS 54 v Glamorgan (Taunton) 2020. BB 3-31 v Hants (Southampton) 2022. LO HS 157 (in 84 balls) v Durham (Taunton) 2022 (RLC). LO BB 3-64 v Derbys (Taunton) 2021 (RLC). T20 HS 43*. T20 BB 5-29.

GREGORY, Lewis (Hele's S, Plympton), b Plymouth, Devon 24 May 1992. 6'0". RHB, RMF. Squad No 24. Debut (Somerset) 2011; cap 2015; T20 captain 2018-21. MCC 2017. Devon 2008. Big Bash: BH 2020-21. Trent Rockets 2021 to date. **LOI**: 3 (2021); HS 77 v P (Birmingham) 2021; BB 3-44 v P (Lord's) 2021. **IT20**: 9 (2019-20 to 2021); HS 15 and BB 1-10 v NZ (Wellington) 2019-20. Sm HS 137 v Middx (Lord's) 2017. 50 wkts (1): 59 (2019). BB 6-32 (11-53 match) v Kent (Canterbury) 2019. LO HS 105* v Durham (Taunton) 2014 (RLC). LO BB 4-23 v Essex (Chelmsford) 2016 (RLC). T20 HS 76*. T20 BB 5-24.

‡NQHENRY, Matthew James (St Bede's C), b Christchurch, New Zealand 14 Dec 1991. RHB, RFM. Canterbury 2010-11 to date. Worcestershire 2016. Kent 2018-22; cap 2018. Derbyshire 2017 (T20 only). IPL: KXIP 2017. **Tests** (NZ): 20 (2015 to 2022-23); HS 72 v SL (Christchurch) 2022-23; BB 7-23 v SA (Christchurch) 2021-22. **LOI** (NZ): 65 (2013-14 to 2022-23); HS 48* v P (Wellington) 2015-16; BB 5-30 v P (Abu Dhabi) 2014-15. **IT20** (NZ): 6 (2014-15 to 2022-23); HS 10 v P (Auckland) 2015-16; BB 3-44 v SL (Mt Maunganui) 2015-16. F-c Tours (NZ): E 2014 (NZA), 2015, 2021, 2022; A 2015-16, 2019-20; I 2016-17, 2017-18 (NZA); P 2022-23; SL 2013-14 (NZA). HS 81 K v Derbys (Derby) 2018. 50 wkts (1): 75 (2018). BB 7-23 (*see Tests*). CC BB 7-42 (11-114 match) K v Northants (Canterbury) 2018. LO HS 48* (*see LOI*). LO BB 6-45 Canterbury v Auckland (Auckland) 2012-13. T20 HS 44. T20 BB 4-43.

‡**KOHLER-CADMORE, Tom** (Malvern C), b Chatham, Kent 19 Aug 1994. 6'2". RHB, OB. Squad No 32. Worcestershire 2014-17. Yorkshire 2017-22; cap 2019. Northern Superchargers 2021. Trent Rockets 2022. 1000 runs (1): 1004 (2019). HS 176 Y v Leeds/Brad MCCU (Leeds) 2019. CC HS 169 Wo v Glos (Worcester) 2016. LO HS 164 Y v Durham (Chester-le-St) 2018 (RLC). T20 HS 127 Wo v Durham (Worcester) 2016 – Wo record.

LAMMONBY, Thomas Alexander (Exeter S), b Exeter, Devon 2 Jun 2000. LHB, LM. Squad No 15. Debut (Somerset) 2020. Big Bash: HH 2021-22. Manchester Originals 2021 to date. Somerset 2nd XI debut 2015. Devon 2016-18. England U19 2018-19. HS 116 v Essex (Lord's) 2020. BB 3-35 v Essex (Chelmsford) 2022. LO HS 6 EL v Sri Lanka A (Colombo, RPS) 2022-23. T20 HS 90. T20 BB 2-32.

LEACH, Matthew Jack (Bishop Fox's Community S, Taunton; Richard Huish C; UWIC), b Taunton 22 Jun 1991. 6'0". LHB, SLA. Squad No 17. Cardiff MCCU 2012. Somerset debut 2012; cap 2017. MCC 2017. Dorset 2011. **ECB Central Contract 2022-23. Tests:** 34 (2017-18 to 2022-23); HS 92 v Ire (Lord's) 2019; BB 5-66 (10-166 match) v NZ (Leeds) 2022. F-c Tours: A 2021-22; WI 2017-18 (EL); 2021-22; NZ 2017-18, 2019-20, 2022-23; I 2020-21; P 2022-23; SL 2016-17 (EL), 2018-19, 2019-20, 2020-21; UAE (v Afg)(EL). HS 92 (*see Tests*). Sm HS 66 v Lancs (Manchester) 2018. 50 wkts (2); most – 68 (2016). BB 8-85 (10-112 match) v Essex (Taunton) 2018. LO HS 18 v Surrey (Oval) 2014 (RLC). LO BB 3-7 EL v UAE (Dubai, DSC) 2016-17. T20 BB 3-28.

LEONARD, Edward Owen ('Ned') (Millfield S), b Hammersmith, Middx 15 Aug 2002. RHB, RMF. Squad No 19. Debut (Somerset) 2021. Somerset 2nd XI debut 2018. HS 8 v Hants (Southampton) 2022. BB 1-68 v Lancs (Taunton) 2021. LO HS 1* v Warwks (Birmingham) 2021 (RLC). LO BB 2-84 v Leics (Taunton) 2021 (RLC). T20 BB 1-8.

OGBORNE, Alfie Richard James (Ansford Ac; Richard Huish C), b Yeovil 15 Jul 2003. RHB, LFM. Squad No 3. Awaiting f-c debut. Somerset 2nd XI debut 2021. LO HS 27* v Sussex (Taunton) 2022 (RLC). LO BB 3-49 v Leics (Leicester) 2022 (RLC).

OVERTON, Craig (West Buckland S), b Barnstaple, Devon 10 Apr 1994. Twin brother of Jamie Overton (*see SURREY*). 6'5". RHB, RMF. Squad No 7. Debut (Somerset) 2012; cap 2016. MCC 2017. Southern Brave 2021 to date. Devon 2010-11. **ECB Pace Bowling Development Contract 2022-23. Tests:** 8 (2017-18 to 2021-22); HS 41* v A (Adelaide) 2017-18; BB 3-14 v I (Leeds) 2021. **LOI:** 7 (2018 to 2022); HS 32 v I (Manchester) 2022; BB 2-23 v P (Cardiff) 2021. F-c Tours: A 2017-18, 2019-20 (EL); WI 2021-22; NZ 2017-18. HS 138 v Hants (Taunton) 2016. BB 7-57 (13-87 match) v Essex (Taunton) 2022. LO HS 66* and LO BB 5-18 v Kent (Taunton) 2019 (RLC). T20 HS 35*. T20 BB 4-25.

REW, James Edward Kenneth (King's C, Taunton), b Lambeth, London 11 Jan 2004. LHB, WK. Squad No 55. County Select XI 2021. Somerset 2nd XI debut 2019. HS 101* v Essex (Chelmsford) 2022. LO HS 114 v Middx (Taunton) 2022 (RLC). T20 HS 47.

ᴺᵠ**SIDDLE, Peter** Matthew, b Traralgon, Victoria, Australia 25 Nov 1984. 6'1½". RHB, RFM. Victoria 2005-06 to 2019-20. Nottinghamshire 2014; cap 2014. Lancashire 2015. Essex 2018-21; cap 2021. Tasmania 2020-21 to date. Somerset debut/cap 2022. Big Bash: MR 2013-14 to 2014-15; AS 2017-18 to date. **Tests** (A): 67 (2008-09 to 2019); HS 51 v I (Delhi) 2012-13; BB 6-54 v E (Brisbane) 2010-11. **LOI** (A): 20 (2008-09 to 2018-19); HS 10* v I (Melbourne) 2018-19; BB 3-55 v E (Centurion) 2009-10. **IT20** (A): 2 (2008-09 to 2010-11); HS 1* and BB 2-24 v NZ (Sydney) 2008-09. F-c Tours: E 2009, 2013, 2015, 2019; SA 2008-09, 2011-12, 2013-14; WI 2011-12; NZ 2015-16; I 2008-09 (Aus A), 2008-09, 2012-13; SL 2011; Z 2011 (Aus A); UAE 2014-15 (v P), 2018-19 (v P). HS 103* Aus A v Scotland (Edinburgh) 2013. CC HS 89 La v Northants (Northampton) 2015. Sm HS 42 v Surrey (Taunton) 2022. 50 wkts (0+1): 54 (2011-12). BB 8-54 Vic v SA (Adelaide) 2014-15. CC BB 6-38 Ex v Warwks (Chelmsford) 2021. Sm BB 6-51 v Surrey (Oval) 2022. LO HS 62 Vic v Q (N Sydney) 2017-18. LO BB 4-22 Tas v Vic (Hobart) 2021-22. T20 HS 11*. T20 BB 5-16.

SMEED, William Conrad Francis (King's C, Taunton), b Cambridge 26 Oct 2001. RHB, OB. Squad No 23. Birmingham Phoenix 2021 to date. Somerset 2nd XI debut 2017. Awaiting f-c debut. LO HS 0 EL v South Africans (Worcester) 2022. T20 HS 101*.

THOMAS, George William (King's C, Taunton), b Musgrove, Taunton 14 Nov 2003. RHB, RM. Squad No 46. Somerset 2nd XI debut 2021. Awaiting f-c debut. LO HS 75 v Leics (Taunton) 2021 (RLC). LO BB –. No 1st XI appearances in 2022.

NO**VAN DER MERWE**, Roelof Erasmus (Pretoria HS), b Johannesburg, South Africa 31 Dec 1984. RHB, SLA. Squad No 52. Northerns 2006-07 to 2013-14. Titans 2007-08 to 2014-15. Netherlands 2015 to 2017-18. Somerset debut 2016; cap 2018. IPL: RCB 2009 to 2009-10; DD 2011-13. Big Bash: BH 2011-12. London Spirit 2021. Northern Superchargers 2022. **LOI** (SA/Neth): 16 (13 for SA 2008-09 to 2010; 3 for Neth 2019 to 2021-22); HS 57 v Z (Deventer) 2019; BB 3-27 v Z (Centurion) 2009-10. **IT20** (SA/Neth): 52 (13 for SA 2008-09 to 2010; 39 for Neth 2015 to 2022-23); HS 75* v Z (Rotterdam) 2019; BB 4-35 v Z (Rotterdam) 2019 – separate matches. HS 205* Titans v Warriors (Benoni) 2014-15. Sm HS 102* v Hants (Taunton) 2016. BB 5-174 v Lancs (Southport) 2022. LO HS 165* v Surrey (Taunton) 2017 (RLC). LO BB 5-26 Titans v Knights (Centurion) 2012-13. T20 HS 89*. T20 BB 6-20.

UMEED, Andrew Robert Isaac (High School of Glasgow), b Glasgow 19 Apr 1996. 6'1". RHB, LB. Squad No 1. Scotland 2015. Warwickshire 2016-17, scoring 101 v Durham (Birmingham) on debut. Somerset debut 2022. HS 113 Wa v Lancs (Birmingham) 2017. Sm HS 4 v Kent (Canterbury) 2022. LO HS 56 v Sussex (Taunton) 2022 (RLC).

RELEASED/RETIRED

(Having made a County 1st XI appearance in 2022)

De LANGE, M. – see GLOUCESTERSHIRE.

HILDRETH, James Charles (Millfield S), b Milton Keynes, Bucks 9 Sep 1984. 5'10", RHB, RMF. Somerset 2003-22; cap 2007; testimonial 2017. MCC 2015. F-c Tour (EL): WI 2010-11. 1000 runs (7); most – 1620 (2015). HS 303* v Warwks (Taunton) 2009. BB 2-39 v Hants (Taunton) 2004. LO HS 159 v Glamorgan (Taunton) 2018 (RLC). LO BB 2-26 v Worcs (Worcester) 2008 (FPT). T20 HS 107*. T20 BB 3-24.

NO**IMAM-UL-HAQ**, b Lahore, Pakistan 12 Dec 1995. Nephew of Inzamam-ul-Haq (Multan, UB, Faisalabad, Rawalpindi, NB, WAPDA, Yorkshire and Pakistan 1985-86 to 2007-08). LHB, LB. Lahore Shalimar 2012-13. Khan Research Labs 2013-14 to 2015-16. Habib Bank 2016-17 to 2017-18. Baluchistan 2019-20 to date. Somerset 2022. **Tests** (P): 20 (2018 to 2022-23); HS 157 v A (Rawalpindi) 2021-22. **LOI** (P): 56 (2017-18 to 2022-23); HS 151 v E (Bristol) 2019. **IT20** (P): 2 (2019 to 2019-20); HS 14 v A (Perth) 2019-20. F-c Tours (P): E 2018, 2020; A 2019-20; SA 2018-19; SL 2022; Ire 2018. HS 202* Baluchistan v K Pakh (Lahore) 2021-22. Sm HS 90 v Glos (Taunton) 2022. BB 1-4 HB v WAPDA (Karachi) 2016-17. LO HS 151 (see LOI). LO BB –. T20 HS 94.

NO**RENSHAW, Matt**hew Thomas, b Middlesbrough, Yorks 28 Mar 1996. 6'0". LHB, OB. Queensland 2014-15 to date. Somerset 2018-22; cap 2022. Kent 2019. Big Bash: BH 2017-18 to date; AS 2020-21 to 2021-22. **Tests** (A): 14 (2016-17 to 2022-23); HS 184 v P (Sydney) 2016-17; BB –. F-c Tours (A): SA 2017-18; I 2016-17, 2018-19 (Aus A), 2022-23; B 2017; UAE 2018-19 (v P). HS 200* Q v NSW (Sydney, DO) 2022-23. Sm HS 146 v Essex (Chelmsford) 2022. BB 3-29 v Lancs (Southport) 2022. LO HS 156* Q v SA (Adelaide) 2021-22. LO BB 2-17 v Surrey (Oval) 2019 (RLC). T20 HS 90*. T20 BB 1-2.

RELEASED/RETIRED continued on p 168

SOMERSET 2022

RESULTS SUMMARY

	Place	Won	Lost	Drew	NR
LV= Insurance County Champ (Div 1)	7th	3	6	5	
Royal London One-Day Cup (Group A)	8th	1	7		
Vitality Blast (South Group)	SF	11	5		

LV= INSURANCE COUNTY CHAMPIONSHIP AVERAGES

BATTING AND FIELDING

Cap		M	I	NO	HS	Runs	Avge	100	50	Ct/St
2018	T.B.Abell	13	22	2	150*	1039	51.95	5	4	14
2022	M.T.Renshaw	8	13	–	146	620	47.69	2	1	11
	G.A.Bartlett	7	12	1	111	456	41.45	1	2	2
	T.Banton	6	9	–	126	346	38.44	1	2	2
	J.E.K.Rew	7	12	3	101*	337	37.44	1	1	18
	L.P.Goldsworthy	10	17	2	130	558	37.20	1	3	1
2015	L.Gregory	11	18	3	110*	532	35.46	1	3	13
	Imam-ul-Haq	3	6	1	90	177	35.40	–	2	–
2021	J.H.Davey	8	11	5	31*	187	31.16	–	–	5
	T.A.Lammonby	14	25	1	110	685	28.54	1	2	7
	Sajid Khan	4	5	1	53*	110	27.50	–	1	2
2007	J.C.Hildreth	6	10	–	87	256	25.60	–	3	3
	J.A.Brooks	7	9	3	32	109	18.16	–	–	3
2018	R.E.van der Merwe	3	6	–	55	105	17.50	–	1	–
2017	S.M.Davies	8	14	–	51	234	16.71	–	1	26
2016	C.Overton	9	13	1	44	200	16.66	–	–	13
2017	M.J.Leach	7	8	2	34*	93	15.50	–	–	1
2022	P.M.Siddle	8	12	4	42	105	13.12	–	–	1
	K.L.Aldridge	8	12	2	41	128	12.80	–	–	4
	B.G.F.Green	4	8	–	20	92	11.50	–	–	4
	M.de Lange	3	4	1	13*	22	7.33	–	–	1

Also batted (1 match each): E.O.Leonard 0*, 8; A.R.I.Umeed 4, 3; G.S.Virdi 15* (2 ct).

BOWLING

	O	M	R	W	Avge	Best	5wI	10wM
C.Overton	240.5	60	647	36	17.97	7- 57	3	1
J.H.Davey	159.2	35	449	21	21.38	3- 25	–	–
P.M.Siddle	241.1	65	646	27	23.92	6- 51	1	–
J.A.Brooks	183.5	28	662	23	28.78	4- 40	–	–
K.L.Aldridge	192.1	24	704	23	30.60	6-110	1	–
M.J.Leach	173	51	412	13	31.69	5- 49	1	–
L.Gregory	233.5	38	796	15	53.06	4- 62	–	–

Also bowled:

M.T.Renshaw	31	2	125	6	20.83	3- 29	–	–
M.de Lange	56	15	167	5	33.40	2- 38	–	–
R.E.van der Merwe	83.2	6	301	8	37.62	5-174	1	–
T.A.Lammonby	56.2	10	190	5	38.00	3- 35	–	–
T.B.Abell	58.2	3	231	5	46.20	2- 24	–	–
Sajid Khan	132	23	356	5	71.20	2- 60	–	–

T.Banton 1-1-0-0; L.P.Goldsworthy 5-0-24-0; B.G.F.Green 33.4-8-123-4; E.O.Leonard 18-2-69-1; G.S.Virdi 25-1-121-0.

Somerset played no first-class fixtures outside the County Championship in 2022. The First-Class Averages (pp 221–234) give the records of Somerset players in all first-class county matches, with the exception of J.A.Brooks and M.J.Leach, whose first-class figures for Somerset are as above.

SOMERSET RECORDS

FIRST-CLASS CRICKET

Highest Total	For 850-7d		v	Middlesex	Taunton	2007
	V 811		by	Surrey	The Oval	1899
Lowest Total	For 25		v	Glos	Bristol	1947
	V 22		by	Glos	Bristol	1920
Highest Innings	For 342	J.L.Langer	v	Surrey	Guildford	2006
	V 424	A.C.MacLaren	for	Lancashire	Taunton	1895

Highest Partnership for each Wicket

1st	346	L.C.H.Palairet/ H.T.Hewett	v	Yorkshire	Taunton	1892
2nd	450	N.R.D.Compton/J.C.Hildreth	v	Cardiff MCCU	Taunton Vale	2012
3rd	319	P.M.Roebuck/M.D.Crowe	v	Leics	Taunton	1984
4th	310	P.W.Denning/I.T.Botham	v	Glos	Taunton	1980
5th	320	J.D.Francis/I.D.Blackwell	v	Durham UCCE	Taunton	2005
6th	265	W.E.Alley/K.E.Palmer	v	Northants	Northampton	1961
7th	279	R.J.Harden/G.D.Rose	v	Sussex	Taunton	1997
8th	236	P.D.Trego/R.C.Davies	v	Lancashire	Manchester	2016
9th	183	C.H.M.Greetham/H.W.Stephenson	v	Leics	Weston-s-Mare	1963
	183	C.J.Tavaré/N.A.Mallender	v	Sussex	Hove	1990
10th	163	I.D.Blackwell/N.A.M.McLean	v	Derbyshire	Taunton	2003

Best Bowling	For 10-49	E.J.Tyler	v	Surrey	Taunton	1895
(Innings)	V 10-35	A.Drake	for	Yorkshire	Weston-s-Mare	1914
Best Bowling	For 16-83	J.C.White	v	Worcs	Bath	1919
(Match)	V 17-86	K.J.Abbott	for	Hampshire	Southampton[2]	2019

Most Runs – Season	2761	W.E.Alley	(av 58.74)	1961
Most Runs – Career	21142	H.Gimblett	(av 36.96)	1935-54
Most 100s – Season	11	S.J.Cook		1991
Most 100s – Career	52	M.E.Trescothick		1993-2018
Most Wkts – Season	169	A.W.Wellard	(av 19.24)	1938
Most Wkts – Career	2165	J.C.White	(av 18.03)	1909-37
Most Career W-K Dismissals	1007	H.W.Stephenson	(698 ct; 309 st)	1948-64
Most Career Catches in the Field	443	M.E.Trescothick		1993-2019

LIMITED-OVERS CRICKET

Highest Total	50ov	413-4		v	Devon	Torquay	1990
	40ov	377-9		v	Sussex	Hove	2003
	T20	265-5		v	Derbyshire	Taunton	2022
Lowest Total	50ov	58		v	Middlesex	Southgate	2000
	40ov	58		v	Essex	Chelmsford	1977
	T20	82		v	Kent	Taunton	2010
Highest Innings	50ov	177	S.J.Cook	v	Sussex	Hove	1990
	40ov	184	M.E.Trescothick	v	Glos	Taunton	2008
	T20	151*	C.H.Gayle	v	Kent	Taunton	2015
Best Bowling	50ov	8-66	S.R.G.Francis	v	Derbyshire	Derby	2004
	40ov	6-16	Abdur Rehman	v	Notts	Taunton	2012
	T20	6- 5	A.V.Suppiah	v	Glamorgan	Cardiff	2011

SURREY

Formation of Present Club: 22 August 1845
Inaugural First-Class Match: 1864
Colours: Chocolate
Badge: Prince of Wales' Feathers
County Champions (since 1890): (20) 1890, 1891, 1892, 1894, 1895, 1899, 1914, 1952, 1953, 1954, 1955, 1956, 1957, 1958, 1971, 1999, 2000, 2002, 2018, 2022
Joint Champions: (1) 1950
NatWest Trophy Winners: (1) 1982
Benson and Hedges Cup Winners: (3) 1974, 1997, 2001
Pro 40/National League (Div 1) Winners: (1) 2003
Sunday League Winners: (1) 1996
Clydesdale Bank 40 Winners: (1) 2011
Twenty20 Cup Winners: (1) 2003

Chief Executive: Steve Elworthy, The Kia Oval, London, SE11 5SS ● Tel: 0203 946 0100 ● Email: enquiries@surreycricket.com ● Web: www.kiaoval.com ● Twitter: @surreycricket (118,123 followers)

Director of Cricket: Alec Stewart. **Head Coach:** Gareth Batty. **Assistant Coaches:** Azhar Mahmood, Jade Dernbach and Jim Troughton. **Captains:** R.J.Burns (f-c) and C.J.Jordan (T20). **Overseas Players:** S.A.Abbott, S.P.Narine (T20 only) and K.A.J.Roach. **2023 Testimonial:** None. **Head Groundsman:** Lee Fortiss. **Scorer:** Debbie Beesley. ‡ New registration. NQ Not qualified for England.

NQABBOTT, **Sean** Anthony, b Windsor, NSW, Australia 29 Feb 1992. 6'1". RHB, RMF. Squad No 77. New South Wales 2011-12 to date. Surrey debut 2021. IPL: RCB 2015; SH 2022. Big Bash: ST 2011-12 to 2012-13; SS 2013-14 to date. Manchester Originals 2022. **LOI** (A): 8 (2014-15 to 2022-23); HS 49 v P (Lahore) 2021-22; BB 2-1 v NZ (Cairns) 2022. **IT20** (A): 9 (2014-15 to 2022-23); HS 12* v I (Canberra) 2020-21; BB 2-14 v P (Perth) 2019-20. F-c Tour (Aus A): I 2015. HS 102* NSW v Tas (Adelaide) 2020-21. Sy HS 40 and Sy BB 2-5 v Glos (Oval) 2021. BB 7-45 NSW v Tas (Hobart) 2018-19. LO HS 50 NSW v SA (Sydney, DO) 2013-14. LO BB 5-43 NSW v Tas (N Sydney) 2018-19. T20 HS 41. T20 BB 5-16.

ATKINSON, Angus ('**Gus**') Alexander Patrick (Bradfield C), b Chelsea, Middx 19 Jan 1998. 6'2". RHB, RM. Squad No 37. Debut (Surrey) 2020. HS 91 v SL Dev (Guildford) 2022. CC HS 66 and BB 3-26 v Northants (Oval) 2022. LO HS 15 v Notts (Guildford) 2021 (RLC). LO BB 4-43 v Yorks (Scarborough) 2021 (RLC). T20 HS 14. T20 BB 4-36.

BARNWELL, **Nathan** André (Caterham S), b Ashford, Kent 3 Feb 2003. 6'0". RHB, RFM. Squad No 29. Surrey 2nd XI debut 2018. Awaiting 1st XI debut.

BLAKE, **Josh**ua William (Trinity S, Croydon), b Carshalton 18 Sep 1998. 6'0". RHB, WK, occ LBG. Squad No 18. Awaiting f-c debut. Surrey 2nd XI debut 2021. LO HS 44 v Leics (Guildford) 2022 (RLC).

BURNS, **Rory** Joseph (City of London Freemen's S), b Epsom 26 Aug 1990. 5'10". LHB, WK, occ RM. Squad No 17. Debut (Surrey) 2011; cap 2014; captain 2018 to date. MCC 2016. MCC Univs 2010. *Wisden* 2018. **Tests**: 32 (2018-19 to 2021-22); HS 133 v A (Birmingham) 2019. F-c Tours: A 2021-22; SA 2019-20; WI 2018-19; NZ 2019-20; I 2020-21; SL 2018-19. 1000 runs (7); most – 1402 (2018). HS 219* v Hants (Oval) 2017. BB 1-18 v Middx (Lord's) 2013. LO HS 95 v Glos (Bristol) 2015 (RLC). T20 HS 56*.

163

CLARK, Jordan (Sedbergh S), b Whitehaven, Cumbria 14 Oct 1990. Elder brother of G.Clark (*see DURHAM*). 6'4". RHB, RMF, occ WK. Squad No 16. Lancashire 2015-18. Surrey debut 2019; cap 2022. Big Bash: HH 2018-19. Oval Invincibles 2021. HS 140 La v Surrey (Oval) 2017. Sy HS 137 v Glos (Bristol) 2022, sharing Sy record 8th wkt partnership of 244 with J.L.Smith. BB 6-21 v Hants (Oval) 2021. Hat-trick La v Yorks (Manchester) 2018, dismissing J.E.Root, K.S.Williamson and J.M.Bairstow. LO HS 79* and LO BB 4-34 La v Worcs (Manchester) 2017 (RLC). T20 HS 60. T20 BB 4-22.

CURRAN, Samuel Matthew (Wellington C), b Northampton 3 Jun 1998. Son of K.M.Curran (Glos, Natal, Northants, Boland and Zimbabwe 1980-81 to 1999), grandson of K.P.Curran (Rhodesia 1947-48 to 1954-55), younger brother of T.K.Curran (*see below*) and B.J.Curran (*see NORTHAMPTONSHIRE*). 5'9". LHB, LMF. Squad No 58. Debut (Surrey) 2015, taking 5-101 v Kent (Oval); cap 2018. IPL: KXIP 2019; CSK 2020-21 to 2021. Oval Invincibles 2021 to date. YC 2018. *Wisden* 2018. **ECB Central Contract 2022-23. Tests**: 24 (2018 to 2021); HS 78 v I (Southampton) 2018; BB 4-58 v SA (Centurion) 2019-20. **LOI**: 23 (2018 to 2022-23); HS 95* v I (Pune) 2020-21; BB 5-48 v SL (Oval) 2021. **IT20**: 36 (2019-20 to 2022-23); HS 24 v NZ (Auckland) 2019-20; BB 5-10 Afg (Perth) 2022-23 – E record. F-c Tours: SA 2019-20; WI 2018-19; NZ 2019-20; SL 2016-17 (EL), 2018-19, 2019-20, 2020-21; UAE 2016-17 (v Afg)(EL). HS 126 v Kent (Oval) 2022. BB 7-58 v Durham (Chester-le-St) 2016. LO HS 95* (*see LOI*). LO BB 5-48 (*see LOI*). T20 HS 72*. T20 BB 5-10.

CURRAN, Thomas Kevin (Hilton C, Durban), b Cape Town, South Africa 12 Mar 1995. Son of K.M.Curran (Glos, Natal, Northants, Boland and Zimbabwe 1980-81 to 1999), grandson of K.P.Curran (Rhodesia 1947-48 to 1954-55), elder brother of S.M.Curran (*see above*) and B.J.Curran (*see NORTHAMPTONSHIRE*). 6'0". RHB, RFM. Squad No 59. Debut (Surrey) 2014; cap 2016. IPL: KKR 2018; RR 2020-21; DC 2021. Big Bash: SS 2018-19 to 2021-22. Oval Invincibles 2021 to date. **Tests**: 2 (2017-18); HS 39 v A (Sydney) 2017-18; BB 1-65 v A (Melbourne) 2017-18. **LOI**: 28 (2017 to 2021); HS 47* v Ire (Dublin) 2019; BB 5-35 v A (Perth) 2017-18. **IT20**: 30 (2017 to 2021); HS 14* v NZ (Nelson) 2019-20; BB 4-36 v WI (Gros Islet) 2018-19. F-c Tours: A 2017-18; SL 2016-17 (EL); UAE 2016-17 (v Afg)(EL). HS 115 v Northants (Northampton) 2022. 50 wkts (1): 76 (2015). BB 7-20 v Glos (Oval) 2015. LO HS 47* (*see LOI*). LO BB 5-16 EL v UAE (Dubai, DSC) 2016-17. T20 HS 62. T20 BB 5-35.

DUNN, Matthew Peter (Bearwood C, Wokingham), b Egham 5 May 1992. 6'1". LHB, RFM. Squad No 4. Debut (Surrey) 2010. MCC 2015. HS 31* v Kent (Guildford) 2014. BB 5-43 v Somerset (Guildford) 2019. LO HS 34 v Warwks (Oval) 2022 (RLC). LO BB 2-32 Eng Dev XI v Sri Lanka A (Manchester) 2011. T20 HS 2. BB 3-8.

EVANS, Laurie John (Whitgift S; The John Fisher S; St Mary's C, Durham U), b Lambeth, London 12 Oct 1987. 6'0". RHB, RM. Squad No 10. Durham UCCE 2007. Surrey debut 2009; signed white-ball contract in 2022. Warwickshire 2010-16. Northamptonshire 2016 (on loan). Sussex 2017-19. MCC 2007. Big Bash: SS 2021-22. Oval Invincibles 2021. Manchester Originals 2022. HS 213* and BB 1-29 Wa v Sussex (Birmingham) 2015, sharing Wa 6th wkt record partnership of 327 with T.R.Ambrose. Sy HS 98 and Sy HS 3 v Bangladeshis (Oval) 2010. LO HS 134* Sx v Kent (Canterbury) 2017 (RLC). LO BB 1-29 Sx v Middx (Lord's) 2019 (RLC). T20 HS 108*. T20 BB 1-5.

FOAKES, Benjamin Thomas (Tendring TC), b Colchester, Essex 15 Feb 1993. 6'1". RHB, WK. Squad No 7. Essex 2011-14. Surrey debut 2015; cap 2016. MCC 2016. **ECB Central Contract 2022-23. Tests**: 20 (2018-19 to 2022-23); HS 113* v SA (Manchester) 2022; made 107 v SL (Galle) 2018-19 on debut. **LOI**: 1 (2019); HS 61* v Ire (Dublin) 2019. **IT20**: 1 (2019) did not bat. F-c Tours: WI 2017-18 (EL); 2018-19, 2021-22; NZ 2022-23; I 2020-21; P 2022-23; SL 2013-14 (EL), 2016-17 (EL), 2018-19; UAE 2016-17 (v Afg)(EL). HS 141* v Hants (Southampton) 2016. LO HS 92 v Somerset (Taunton) 2016 (RLC). T20 HS 75*.

GEDDES, Benedict Brodie Albert (St John's S, Leatherhead), b Epsom 31 Jul 2001. 6'1". RHB. Squad No 14. Debut (Surrey) 2021. Surrey 2nd XI debut 2019. HS 124 v Kent (Oval) 2022. LO HS 73 v Leics (Guildford) 2022 (RLC). T20 HS 28.

JACKS, William George (St George's C, Weybridge), b Chertsey 21 Nov 1998. 6'1". RHB, OB. Squad No 9. Debut (Surrey) 2018; cap 2022. Big Bash: HH 2020-21. Oval Invincibles 2021 to date. **Tests**: 2 (2022-23); HS 31 v P (Multan) 2022-23; BB 6-161 v P (Rawalpindi) 2022-23. **LOI**: 2 (2022-23); HS 26 and BB 1-18 v B (Mirpur) 2022-23. **IT20**: 2 (2022-23); HS 40 v P (Karachi) 2022-23. F-c Tours: I 2018-19 (EL); P 2022-23. HS 150* v Essex (Oval) 2022. BB 6-161 (*see Tests*). Sy BB 4-65 v Kent (Beckenham) 2022. LO HS 121 v Glos (Oval) 2018 (RLC). LO BB 2-32 v Middx (Oval) 2019 (RLC). T20 HS 108*. T20 BB 4-15.

JORDAN, Christopher James (Comber Mere S, Barbados; Dulwich C), b Christ Church, Barbados 4 Oct 1988. 6'1". RHB, RFM. Squad No 34. Debut (Surrey) 2007; returned in 2022 as T20 captain. Barbados 2011-12 to 2012-13. Sussex 2013-19; cap 2014. IPL: RCB 2016; SH 2017-18; KXIP 2020-21; PK 2021; CSK 2022. Big Bash: AS 2016-17; ST 2018-19; PS 2019-20; SS 2021-22 to date. Southern Brave 2021 to date. **Tests**: 8 (2014 to 2014-15); HS 35 v SL (Lord's) 2014; BB 4-18 v I (Oval) 2014. **LOI**: 35 (2013 to 2022-23); HS 38* v SL (Oval) 2014; BB 5-29 v SL (Manchester) 2014. **IT20**: 85 (2013-14 to 2022-23); HS 36 v NZ (Wellington) 2019-20; BB 4-6 v WI (Basseterre) 2018-19. F-c Tour: WI 2014-15. HS 166 Sx v Northants (Northampton) 2019. Sy HS 79* and Sy BB 4-57 v Essex (Chelmsford) 2011. 50 wkts (1): 61 (2013). BB 7-43 Barbados v CC&C (Bridgetown) 2012-13. CC BB 6-48 Sx v Yorks (Leeds) 2013. LO HS 55 Sx v Surrey (Guildford) 2016 (RLC). LO BB 5-28 Sx v Middx (Hove) 2016 (RLC). T20 HS 73. T20 BB 4-6.

KIMBER, Nicholas John Henry (William Farr C of E S), b Lincoln 16 Jan 2001. Younger brother of L.P.J.Kimber (*see LEICESTERSHIRE*) and J.F.Kimber (Lincolnshire 2016-18). 5'11". RHB, RMF. Squad No 12. Awaiting f-c debut. Nottinghamshire 2nd XI 2019. LO HS 84 v Warwks (Oval) 2022 (RLC). LO BB 2-15 v Durham (Gosforth) 2022 (RLC).

LAWES, Thomas Edward (Cranleigh S), b Singapore 25 Dec 2002. 6'0". RHB, RMF. Squad No 30. Debut (Surrey) 2022. Surrey 2nd XI debut 2021. HS 32* v Essex (Oval) 2022. BB 4-31 v Yorks (Oval) 2022. LO HS 75 v Notts (Mansfield) 2022 (RLC). LO BB 2-20 v Somerset (Oval) 2022 (RLC). T20 HS 6. T20 BB –.

McKERR, Conor (St John's C, Johannesburg), b Johannesburg, South Africa 19 Jan 1998. 6'6". RHB, RFM. Squad No 3. UK passport, qualified for England in March 2020. Derbyshire 2017 (on loan), taking wkt of J.D.Libby with 4th ball in f-c cricket. Surrey debut 2017. Kent 2022 (on loan). HS 37 v Warwks (Oval) 2022. BB 5-54 (10-141 match) De v Northants (Northampton) 2017. Sy BB 4-62 v Notts (Oval) 2018. LO HS 26* v Glamorgan (Cardiff) 2019 (RLC). LO BB 4-64 v Warwks (Oval) 2021 (RLC). T20 HS 7*. T20 BB 2-19.

MAJID, Yousef (Cranleigh S), b Sough, Bucks 8 Sep 2003. 6'2". LHB, SLA. Squad No 68. Awaiting f-c debut. Surrey 2nd XI debut 2021. England U19 2022. LO HS 5* v Warwks (Oval) 2022 (RLC). LO BB 3-74 v Glos (Oval) 2022 (RLC).

MORIARTY, Daniel Thornhill (Rondesbosch Boys' HS), b Reigate 2 Dec 1999. 6'0". LHB, SLA. Squad No 21. Debut (Surrey) 2020, taking 5-64 v Middx (Oval). Southern Brave 2022. Surrey 2nd XI debut 2019. Essex 2nd XI 2019. MCC YC 2019. South Africa U19 2016. HS 29 v SL Dev (Guildford) 2022. CC HS 8 v Essex (Oval) 2021. BB 6-60 v Glos (Oval) 2021. LO HS 5 v Glamorgan (Cardiff) 2021 (RLC). LO BB 4-30 v Somerset (Oval) 2021 (RLC). T20 HS 9*. T20 BB 3-25.

NQ**NARINE, Sunil** Philip, b Arima, Trinidad 26 May 1988. 5'10". LHB, OB. Trinidad & Tobago 2008-09 to 2012-13. Surrey debut 2022 (T20 only). IPL: KKR 2012 to date. Big Bash: SS 2012-13; MR 2016-17. Oval Invincibles 2022 to date. **Tests** (WI): 6 (2012 to 2013-14); HS 22* v B (Dhaka) 2012-13; BB 6-91 v NZ (Hamilton) 2013-14. **LOI** (WI): 65 (2011-12 to 2016-17); HS 36 v B (Khulna) 2012-13; BB 6-27 v SA (Providence) 2016. **IT20** (WI): 51 (2011-12 to 2019); HS 30 v P (Dubai, DSC) 2016-17; BB 4-12 v NZ (Lauderhill) 2012. F-c Tours (WI): E 2012; NZ 2013-14; B 2012-13. HS 40* WI A v Bangladesh A (Gros Islet) 2011-12. BB 8-17 (13-39 match) T&T v CC&C (Cave Hill) 2011-12. LO HS 51 T&T v Barbados (Bridgetown) 2017-18. LO BB 6-9 T&T v Guyana (Port of Spain) 2014-15. T20 HS 79. T20 BB 5-19.

OVERTON, Jamie (West Buckland S), b Barnstaple, Devon 10 Apr 1994. Twin brother of Craig Overton (*see SOMERSET*). 6'5". RHB, RFM. Squad No 88. Somerset 2012-20; cap 2019. Northamptonshire 2019 (on loan). Surrey debut 2020. Devon 2011. **ECB Pace Bowling Development Contract 2022-23. Tests**: 1 (2022); HS 97 and BB 1-61 v NZ (Leeds) 2022. F-c Tour (EL): UAE 2018-19 (v PA). HS 120 Sm v Warwks (Birmingham) 2020. Sy HS 93 v Kent (Beckenham) 2022. BB 6-61 v Yorks (Scarborough) 2022. Hat-trick Sm v Notts (Nottingham) 2018. LO HS 40* Sm v Glos (Taunton) 2016 (RLC). LO BB 4-42 Sm v Durham (Chester-le-St) 2012 (CB40). T20 HS 48. T20 BB 5-47.

PATEL, Ryan Samir (Whitgift S), b Sutton 26 Oct 1997. 5'10". LHB, RMF. Squad No 26. Debut (Surrey) 2017. HS 126 v SL Dev (Guildford) 2022. CC HS 102 v Somerset (Oval) 2022. BB 6-5 v Somerset (Guildford) 2018. LO HS 131 v Notts (Guildford) 2021 (RLC). LO BB 2-65 v Hants (Oval) 2019 (RLC). T20 HS 5*. T20 BB –.

POPE, Oliver John Douglas (Cranleigh S), b Chelsea, Middx 2 Jan 1998. 5'9". RHB, WK. Squad No 32. Debut (Surrey) 2017; cap 2018. Welsh Fire 2022. **ECB Central Contract 2022-23. Tests**: 35 (2018 to 2022-23); HS 145 v NZ (Nottingham) 2022. F-c Tours: A 2021-22; SA 2019-20; NZ 2019-20, 2022-23; I 2018-19 (EL), 2020-21; P 2022-23; SL 2019-20. 1000 runs (3): most – 1156 (2022). Sy HS 274 v Glamorgan (Oval) 2021. LO HS 93* EL v Pakistan A (Abu Dhabi) 2018-19. T20 HS 62.

REIFER, Nico Malik Julian (Queen's C, Bridgetown; Whitgift S), b Bridgetown, Barbados 11 Nov 2000. 5'11". RHB, RM. Squad No 27. Debut (Surrey) 2021. Surrey 2nd XI debut 2018. HS 68 v SL Dev (Guildford) 2022. LO HS 70 v Somerset (Oval) 2022 (RLC). T20 HS 4.

ᴺᵠ**ROACH, Kemar** Andre Jamal, b St Lucy, Barbados 30 Jun 1988. 6'1". RHB, RFM. Squad No 66. Barbados 2007-08 to 2019-20. Worcestershire 2011. Surrey debut 2021. IPL: DC 2009-10. Big Bash: BH 2012-13 to 2013-14. **Tests** (WI): 76 (2009 to 2022-23); HS 41 v NZ (Kingston) 2012; BB 6-48 v B (St George's) 2009. **LOI** (WI): 95 (2008 to 2021-22); HS 34 v I (Port of Spain) 2013; BB 6-27 v Netherlands (Delhi) 2010-11. **IT20** (WI): 11 (2008 to 2012-13); HS 3* and BB 2-25 v SA (North Sound) 2010. F-c Tours (WI): E 2012, 2017, 2020; A 2009-10, 2015-16, 2022-23; SA 2014-15, 2022-23; NZ 2008-09, 2017-18, 2020-21; I 2011-12, 2019-20 (v Afg); SL 2010-11, 2015-16, 2021-22; Z 2017-18, 2022-23; B 2011-12, 2018-19, 2020-21. HS 53 Barbados v Leeward Is (Basseterre) 2015-16. Sy HS 29 v Essex (Oval) 2022. BB 8-40 (10-80 match) v Hants (Oval) 2021. LO HS 34 (*see LOI*). LO BB 6-27 (*see LOI*). T20 HS 12. T20 BB 3-18.

ROY, Jason Jonathan (Whitgift S), b Durban, South Africa 21 Jul 1990. 6'0". RHB, RM. Squad No 20. Debut (Surrey) 2010; cap 2014. IPL: GL 2017; DD 2018; SH 2021. Big Bash: ST 2014-15; SS 2016-17 to 2017-18; PS 2020-21. Oval Invincibles 2021 to date. **ECB Increment Contract 2022-23. Tests**: 5 (2019); HS 72 v Ire (Lord's) 2019. **LOI**: 116 (2015 to 2022-23); HS 180 v A (Melbourne) 2017-18 – E record. **IT20**: 64 (2014 to 2022); HS 78 v NZ (Delhi) 2015-16. 1000 runs (1): 1078 (2014). HS 143 v Lancs (Oval) 2015. BB 3-9 v Glos (Bristol) 2014. LO HS 180 (*see LOI*). LO BB –. T20 HS 145*. T20 BB 1-23.

SIBLEY, Dominic Peter (Whitgift S, Croydon), b Epsom 5 Sep 1995. 6'3". RHB, OB. Squad No 45. Debut (Surrey) 2013. Warwickshire 2017-22; cap 2019. MCC 2019. *Wisden* 2020. **Tests**: 22 (2019-20 to 2021); HS 133* v SA (Cape Town) 2019-20. F-c Tours: SA 2019-20; NZ 2019-20; I 2020-21; SL 2019-20, 2020-21. 1000 runs (1): 1428 (2019). HS 244 v Kent (Canterbury) 2019. Sy HS 242 v Yorks (Oval) 2013. LO HS 115 Wa v West Indies A (Birmingham) 2018. LO BB 1-20 v Essex (Chelmsford) 2016 (RLC). T20 HS 74*. T20 BB 2-33.

SMITH, Jamie Luke (Whitgift S), b Epsom 12 Jul 2000. 5'10". RHB, WK. Squad No 11. Debut (Surrey) 2018-19, scoring 127 v MCC (Dubai, ICCA). Surrey 2nd XI debut. England U19 2018-19. F-c Tour (EL): SL 2022-23. HS 234* v Glos (Bristol) 2022, sharing Sy record 8th wkt partnership of 244 with J.Clark. LO HS 85 v Durham (Chester-le-St) 2021 (RLC). T20 HS 60.

STEEL, Cameron Tate (Scotch C, Perth, Australia; Millfield S; Durham U), b San Francisco, USA 13 Sep 1995. 5'10". RHB, LB. Squad No 44. Durham MCCU 2014-16. Durham 2017-20. Hampshire 2021 (on loan). Surrey debut 2021. HS 224 Du v Leics (Leicester) 2017. Sy HS 48 v Northants (Northampton) 2022. BB 3-65 v Lancs (Manchester) 2022. LO HS 77 Du v Notts (Nottingham) 2017 (RLC). LO BB 4-33 v Leics (Leicester) 2021 (RLC). T20 HS 37. T20 BB 2-60.

TAYLOR, James Philip Arthur (Trentham HS), b Stoke-on-Trent, Staffs 19 Jan 2001. Younger brother of T.A.I.Taylor (*see NORTHAMPTONSHIRE*). RHB, RM. Squad No 25. Derbyshire 2017-19. Surrey debut 2020. Derbyshire 2nd XI 2016-19. HS 31* v Warwks (Birmingham) 2022. BB 3-26 De v Leeds/Brad MCCU (Derby) 2019. Sy BB 3-56 v Hants (Oval) 2022. LO HS 6* and LO BB 2-66 De v Australia A (Derby) 2019. T20 HS 3. T20 BB 1-6.

TOPLEY, Reece James William (Royal Hospital S, Ipswich), b Ipswich, Suffolk 21 February 1994. Son of T.D.Topley (Surrey, Essex, GW 1985-94); nephew of P.A.Topley (Kent 1972-75). 6'7". RHB, LFM. Squad No 24. Essex 2011-15; cap 2013. Hampshire 2016-17. Sussex 2019. Surrey debut 2021. Big Bash: MR 2021-22. Oval Invincibles 2021 to date. **ECB Increment Contract 2022-23. LOI**: 22 (2015 to 2022-23); HS 6* v I (Oval) 2022; BB 6-24 v I (Lord's) 2022 – E record. **IT20**: 22 (2015 to 2022-23); HS 9 v I (Southampton) 2022; BB 3-22 v I (Nottingham) 2022. F-c Tour (EL): SL 2013-14. HS 16 H v Yorks (Southampton) 2017. Sy HS 10 v Middx (Lord's) 2021. BB 6-29 (11-85 match) Ex v Worcs (Chelmsford) 2013. Sy BB 5-66 v Glos (Bristol) 2021. LO HS 19 Ex v Somerset (Taunton) 2011 (CB40). LO BB 6-24 (*see LOI*). T20 HS 14*. T20 BB 4-20.

VIRDI, Guramar Singh ('Amar') (Guru Nanak Sikh Ac, Hayes), b Chiswick, Middx 19 Jul 1998. 5'10". RHB, OB. Squad No 19. Debut (Surrey) 2017. Somerset 2022 (on loan). Surrey 2nd XI debut 2016. England U19 2016 to 2017. HS 47 v Northants (Northampton) 2021. BB 8-61 (14-139 match) v Notts (Nottingham) 2019. LO HS 8 and LO BB 1-36 v Warwks (Oval) 2022 (RLC) and 8 v Middx (Radlett) 2022 (RLC).

NQWORRALL, Daniel James (Kardina International C; U of Melbourne), b Melbourne, Australia 10 Jul 1991. 6'0". RHB, RFM. Squad No 8. UK passport. S Australia 2012-13 to 2021-22. Gloucestershire 2018-21; cap 2018. Surrey debut 2022. Big Bash: MS 2013-14 to 2019-20; AS 2020-21 to 2021-22. **LOI** (A): 3 (2016-17); HS 6* v SA (Centurion) 2016-17; BB 1-43 v SA (Benoni) 2016-17. HS 50 Gs v Glamorgan (Bristol) 2018. Sy HS 44* v Kent (Beckenham) 2022. BB 7-64 (10-148 match) SA v WA (Adelaide) 2018-19. CC BB 6-56 (11-122 match) v Essex (Oval) 2022. LO HS 31* SA v WA (Perth) 2021-22. LO BB 5-62 SA v Vic (Hobart) 2017-18. T20 HS 62*. T20 BB 4-23.

RELEASED/RETIRED

(Having made a County 1st XI appearance in 2022)

NQAMLA, Hashim Mahomed, b Durban, South Africa 31 Mar 1983. Younger brother of A.M.Amla (Natal B, KZN, Dolphins 1997-98 to 2012-13). 6'0". RHB, RM/OB. KZN 1999-00 to 2003-04. Dolphins 2004-05 to 2011-12. Essex 2009. Nottinghamshire 2010; cap 2010. Surrey debut 2013-22; cap 2021. Derbyshire 2015. Cape Cobras 2015-16 to 2018-19. Hampshire 2018. IPL: KXIP 2016-17. *Wisden* 2012. **Tests** (SA): 124 (2004-05 to 2018-19, 14 as captain); 1000 runs (3); most – 1249 (2010); HS 311* v E (Oval) 2012; BB –. **LOI** (SA): 181 (2007-08 to 2019, 9 as captain); 1000 runs (2); most – 1062 (2015); HS 159 v Ire (Canberra) 2014-15. **IT20** (SA): 44 (2008-09 to 2018, 2 as captain); HS 97* v A (Cape Town) 2015-16. F-c Tours (SA) (C=Captain): E 2008, 2012, 2017; A 2008-09, 2012-13, 2016-17; WI 2010; NZ 2011-12, 2016-17; I 2004-05, 2007-08 (SA A), 2007-08, 2009-10, 2015-16C; P 2007-08; SL 2005-06 (SA A), 2006, 2014C, 2018; Z 2004 (SA A), 2007 (SA A), 2014C; B 2007-08, 2015C; UAE 2010-11, 2013-14 (v P). 1000 runs (0+2); most – 1126 (2005-06). HS 311* (*see Tests*). CC HS 215* v Hants (Oval) 2021. BB 1-10 SA A v India A (Kimberley) 2001-02. LO HS 159 (*see LOI*). T20 HS 104*.

De GRANDHOMME, C. – *see LANCASHIRE*.

GUMBS, Sheridon Sohan Emmanuel (Bradfield C), b Slough, Berks 25 May 2004. LHB, WK, occ LBG. Awaiting f-c debut. Surrey 2nd XI debut 2021. LO HS 66 v Somerset (Oval) 2022 (RLC).

HARDIE, Aaron Mark, b Bournemouth, Dorset 7 Jan 1999. RHB, RM. W Australia 2018-19 to date. Surrey debut 2022. Big Bash: PS: 2018-19 to date. F-c Tour (Aus A): SL 2022. HS 174* WA v Vic (Perth) 2021-22. Sy HS 46 and Sy BB 1-19 v Yorks (Scarborough) 2022. BB 4-24 WA v Vic (Perth) 2021-22 – separate matches. LO HS 58 Aus A v Sri Lanka A (Colombo, SSC) 2022. LO BB 3-28 WA v Vic (Melbourne SK) 2021-22. T20 HS 90*. T20 BB 3-31.

NQ**POLLARD, Kieron** Adrian, b Tacarigua, Trinidad 12 May 1987. RHB, RMF. Trinidad & Tobago 2006-07 to 2014-15, scoring 126 (inc 7 sixes) v Barbados on debut. Somerset 2010-11 (T20 only). Surrey 2022 (T20 only). IPL: MI 2009-10 to date. Big Bash: AS 2012-13 to 2016-17; MR 2017-18. London Spirit 2022. **LOI** (WI): 123 (2006-07 to 2021-22, 24 as captain); HS 119 v I (Chennai) 2011-12; BB 3-27 v SA (Roseau) 2010. **IT20** (WI): 101 (2008 to 2021-22, 38 as captain); HS 75* v NZ (Auckland) 2020-21; BB 4-25 v Ire (Basseterre) 2019-20. HS 174 T&T v Barbados (Pointe-a-Pierre) 2008-09. BB 5-36 T&T v Windward Is (Couva) 2014-15. LO HS 119 (*see LOI*). LO BB 5-17 T&T v Barbados (North Sound) 2020-21. T20 HS 104. T20 BB 4-15.

SOMERSET RELEASED/RETIRED (continued from p 160)

NQ**ROSSOUW, Rilee** Roscoe, b Bloemfontein, South Africa, 9 Oct 1989. 6'1". LHB, OB. Free State 2007-08 to 2012-13. Eagles 2008-09 to 2009-10. Knights 2010-11 to 2016-17. Hampshire 2017-19. Somerset 2022 (T20 only). IPL: RCB 2014-15. Big Bash: MR 2020-21; ST 2022-23. Oval Invincibles 2022. **LOI** (SA): 36 (2014 to 2016-17); HS 132 v WI (Centurion) 2014-15; BB 1-17 v Z (Harare) 2014. **IT20** (SA): 26 (2014-15 to 2022-23); HS 109 v B (Sydney) 2022-23. F-c Tours (SA A): A 2014; SL 2010; B 2010. 1000 runs (0+1): 1261 (2009-10). HS 319 Eagles v Titans (Centurion) 2009-10, sharing in 3rd highest 2nd wkt partnership in all f-c cricket of 480 with D.Elgar. CC HS 120* H v Lancs (Manchester) 2018. BB 1-1 Knights v Cobras (Cape Town) 2013-14. LO HS 156 H v Somerset (Taunton) 2017 (RLC). LO BB 1-17 (*see LOI*). T20 HS 121. T20 BB 1-3.

NQ**SAJID KHAN**, b Peshawar, Pakistan 3 Sep 1993. RHB, OB. Peshawar 2016-17 to 2018-19. Khan Research Laboratories 2017-18. Khyber Pakhtunkhwa 2019-20 to date. **Tests** (P): 7 (2021 to 2021-22); HS 21 v A (Lahore (2021-22); BB 8-42 (12-128 match) v B (Mirpur) 2021-22. HS 105 Peshawar v Islamabad (Lahore) 2016-17. Sm HS 53* v Warwks (Birmingham) 2022. BB 8-42 (*see Tests*). Sm BB 2-60 v Kent (Canterbury) 2022. LO HS 52 K Pakh v Sindh (Karachi) 2020-21. LO BB 3-14 K Pakh v Sindh (Karachi) 2020-21. T20 HS 33*. T20 BB 2-25.

SALE, O.R.T. – *see NORTHAMPTONSHIRE.*

WALLER, Maximilian Thomas Charles (Millfield S; Bournemouth U), b Salisbury, Wiltshire 3 March 1988. 6'0". RHB, LB. Somerset 2009-18; cap 2021; testimonial 2023. Dorset 2007-08. HS 28 v Hants (Southampton) 2009. BB 3-33 v Cardiff MCCU (Taunton Vale) 2012. CC BB 2-27 v Sussex (Hove) 2009. LO HS 25* v Glamorgan (Taunton) 2013 (Y40). LO BB 3-37 v Glos (Bristol) 2017 (RLC). T20 HS 17. T20 BB 4-16.

SURREY 2022

RESULTS SUMMARY

	Place	Won	Lost	Tied	Drew	NR
LV= Insurance County Champ (Div 1)	1st	8	1		5	
All First-Class Matches		8	1		6	
Royal London One-Day Cup (Group A)	7th	2	5	1		
Vitality Blast (South Group)	QF	10	4			1

LV= INSURANCE COUNTY CHAMPIONSHIP AVERAGES
BATTING AND FIELDING

Cap		M	I	NO	HS	Runs	Avge	100	50	Ct/St
2018	S.M.Curran	5	6	–	126	454	75.66	1	4	6
2016	B.T.Foakes	9	12	4	132*	586	73.25	1	3	44/1
2018	O.J.D.Pope	8	11	1	136	700	70.00	2	5	17
2022	W.G.Jacks	11	15	3	150*	648	54.00	2	3	11
	B.B.A.Geddes	3	4	–	124	176	44.00	1	–	3
2022	J.Clark	11	14	3	137	481	43.72	1	4	2
2014	R.J.Burns	14	23	2	132	842	40.09	3	2	4
2021	H.M.Amla	14	21	3	133	718	39.88	2	3	4
	J.L.Smith	8	11	1	234*	379	37.90	1	1	10
	A.A.P.Atkinson	4	4	1	66*	110	36.66	–	1	1
	R.S.Patel	14	23	4	102	719	35.95	1	3	11
	J.Overton	10	15	3	93	355	29.58	–	2	8
	T.E.Lawes	6	8	3	32*	112	22.40	–	–	1
	C.T.Steel	5	7	–	48	128	18.28	–	–	5
	D.J.Worrall	9	8	1	44*	116	16.57	–	–	2
	K.A.J.Roach	7	8	2	29	84	14.00	–	–	1

Also batted: T.K.Curran (2 matches – cap 2016) 115, 11, 0 (3 ct); C.de Grandhomme (3) 11, 11, 66 (2 ct); A.M.Hardie (1) 46, 40*; C.McKerr (3) 0, 37 (1 ct); D.T.Moriarty (1) 2*, 1*; J.P.A.Taylor (3) 31*, 0*, 9; R.J.W.Topley (3) 1, 0.

BOWLING

	O	M	R	W	Avge	Best	5wI	10wM
T.E.Lawes	153	32	427	18	23.72	4- 31	–	–
D.J.Worrall	327	78	942	39	24.15	6- 56	2	1
J.Overton	263.4	37	872	34	25.64	6- 61	2	–
K.A.J.Roach	213.2	53	656	25	26.24	5- 72	2	–
A.A.P.Atkinson	111.2	16	375	13	28.84	3- 26	–	–
J.Clark	341	66	1058	30	35.26	4- 52	–	–
W.G.Jacks	264.3	39	799	17	47.00	4- 65	–	–

Also bowled:

	O	M	R	W	Avge	Best	5wI	10wM
C.de Grandhomme	52.5	10	170	7	24.28	4- 39	–	–
C.T.Steel	66.2	2	264	9	29.33	3- 65	–	–
R.J.W.Topley	105.4	31	284	9	31.55	3- 55	–	–
D.T.Moriarty	37.1	6	163	5	32.60	5-163	1	–
C.McKerr	74	13	274	6	45.66	3- 39	–	–

R.J.Burns 9-1-21-0; S.M.Curran 41-10-120-3; T.K.Curran 28-6-96-0; A.M.Hardie 31-7-85-2; R.S.Patel 78.1-7-274-3; J.P.A.Taylor 71-13-228-4.

The First-Class Averages (pp 221–234) give the records of Surrey players in all first-class county matches (Surrey's other opponents being the Sri Lanka Cricket Development XI), with the exception of C.de Grandhomme, B.T.Foakes, C.McKerr, J.Overton and O.J.D.Pope, whose first-class figures for Surrey are as above.

SURREY RECORDS
FIRST-CLASS CRICKET

Highest Total	For 811		v	Somerset	The Oval	1899
	V 863		by	Lancashire	The Oval	1990
Lowest Total	For 14		v	Essex	Chelmsford	1983
	V 16		by	MCC	Lord's	1872
Highest Innings	For 357*	R.Abel	v	Somerset	The Oval	1899
	V 366	N.H.Fairbrother	for	Lancashire	The Oval	1990

Highest Partnership for each Wicket

1st	428	J.B.Hobbs/A.Sandham	v	Oxford U	The Oval	1926
2nd	371	J.B.Hobbs/E.G.Hayes	v	Hampshire	The Oval	1909
3rd	413	D.J.Bicknell/D.M.Ward	v	Kent	Canterbury	1990
4th	448	R.Abel/T.W.Hayward	v	Yorkshire	The Oval	1899
5th	318	M.R.Ramprakash/Azhar Mahmood	v	Middlesex	The Oval	2005
6th	298	A.Sandham/H.S.Harrison	v	Sussex	The Oval	1913
7th	262	C.J.Richards/K.T.Medlycott	v	Kent	The Oval	1987
8th	244	J.L.Smith/J.Clark	v	Glos	Bristol	2022
9th	168	E.R.T.Holmes/E.W.J.Brooks	v	Hampshire	The Oval	1936
10th	173	A.Ducat/A.Sandham	v	Essex	Leyton	1921

Best Bowling	For 10-43	T.Rushby	v	Somerset	Taunton	1921
(Innings)	V 10-28	W.P.Howell	for	Australians	The Oval	1899
Best Bowling	For 16-83	G.A.R.Lock	v	Kent	Blackheath	1956
(Match)	V 15-57	W.P.Howell	for	Australians	The Oval	1899

Most Runs – Season	3246	T.W.Hayward	(av 72.13)	1906
Most Runs – Career	43554	J.B.Hobbs	(av 49.72)	1905-34
Most 100s – Season	13	T.W.Hayward		1906
	13	J.B.Hobbs		1925
Most 100s – Career	144	J.B.Hobbs		1905-34
Most Wkts – Season	252	T.Richardson	(av 13.94)	1895
Most Wkts – Career	1775	T.Richardson	(av 17.87)	1892-1904
Most Career W-K Dismissals	1221	H.Strudwick	(1035 ct; 186 st)	1902-27
Most Career Catches in the Field	605	M.J.Stewart		1954-72

LIMITED-OVERS CRICKET

Highest Total	50ov	496-4		v	Glos	The Oval	2007
	40ov	386-3		v	Glamorgan	The Oval	2010
	T20	250-6		v	Kent	Canterbury	2018
Lowest Total	50ov	74		v	Kent	The Oval	1967
	40ov	64		v	Worcs	Worcester	1978
	T20	88		v	Kent	The Oval	2012
Highest Innings	50ov	268	A.D.Brown	v	Glamorgan	The Oval	2002
	40ov	203	A.D.Brown	v	Hampshire	Guildford	1997
	T20	131*	A.J.Finch	v	Sussex	Hove	2018
Best Bowling	50ov	7-33	R.D.Jackman	v	Yorkshire	Harrogate	1970
	40ov	7-30	M.P.Bicknell	v	Glamorgan	The Oval	1999
	T20	6-24	T.J.Murtagh	v	Middlesex	Lord's	2005

SUSSEX

Formation of Present Club: 1 March 1839
Substantial Reorganisation: August 1857
Inaugural First-Class Match: 1864
Colours: Dark Blue, Light Blue and Gold
Badge: County Arms of Six Martlets
County Champions: (3) 2003, 2006, 2007
Gillette/NatWest/C&G Trophy Winners: (5) 1963, 1964, 1978, 1986, 2006
Pro 40/National League (Div 1) Winners: (2) 2008, 2009
Sunday League Winners: (1) 1982
Twenty20 Cup Winners: (1) 2009

Chief Executive: Rob Andrew, The 1st Central County Ground, Eaton Road, Hove BN3 3AN ● Tel: 01273 827100 ● Email: info@sussexcricket.co.uk ● Web: www.sussexcricket.co.uk ● Twitter: @SussexCCC (132,927 followers)

Director of Pathways and Partnerships: Keith Greenfield. **Head Coach**: Paul Farbrace. **Batting Coach**: Grant Flower. **Lead Fast Bowling Coach**: James Kirtley. **Captains**: tba and R.S.Bopara (T20). **Overseas Players**: C.A.Pujara, Shadab Khan (T20 only) and S.P.D.Smith. **2023 Testimonial**: None. **Head Groundsman**: Ben Gibson. **Scorer**: Graham Irwin. **Vitality Blast Name**: Sussex Sharks. ‡ New registration. NQ Not qualified for England.

ALSOP, Thomas Philip (Lavington S), b High Wycombe, Bucks 26 Nov 1995. Younger brother of O.J.Alsop (Wiltshire 2010-12). 5'11". LHB, WK, occ SLA. Squad No 45. Hampshire 2014-21; cap 2021. Sussex debut 2022 MCC 2017. F-c Tours (EL): SL 2016-17. UAE 2016-17 (v Afg). HS 150 H v Warwks (Birmingham) 2019 and 150 v Leics (Hove) 2022. BB 2-59 H v Yorks (Leeds) 2016. Sx BB –. LO HS 189* v Middx (Hove) 2022 (RLC). T20 HS 85.

ARCHER, Jofra Chioke (Christchurch Foundation), b Bridgetown, Barbados 1 Apr 1995. 6'3". RHB, RF. Squad No 22. Debut (Sussex) 2016; cap 2017. IPL: RR 2018 to 2020-21. Big Bash: HH 2017-18 to 2018-19. *Wisden* 2019. Missed entire 2022 season due to injury. **ECB Central Contract 2022-23. Tests**: 13 (2019 to 2020-21); HS 30 v NZ (Mt Maunganui) 2019-20; BB 6-45 v A (Leeds) 2019. **LOI**: 21 (2019 to 2022-23); HS 8* v A (Manchester) 2020; BB 6-40 v SA (Kimberley) 2022-23. **IT20**: 13 (2019 to 2022-23); HS 18* and BB 4-33 v I (Ahmedabad) 2020-21. F-c Tours: SA 2019-20; NZ 2019-20; I 2020-21. HS 81* v Northants (Northampton) 2017. 50 wkts (1): 61 (2017). BB 7-67 v Kent (Hove) 2017. LO HS 45 v Essex (Chelmsford) 2017 (RLC). LO BB 6-40 (*see LOI*). T20 HS 36. T20 BB 4-18.

ATKINS, Jamie Ardley (Eastbourne C), b Redhill, Surrey 20 May 2002. 6'6". RHB, RMF. Squad No 32. Debut (Sussex) 2021. HS 17 v Worcs (Worcester) 2022. BB 5-51 v Kent (Canterbury) 2021.

BOPARA, Ravinder Singh (Brampton Manor S; Barking Abbey Sports C), b Newham, London 4 May 1985. 5'8". RHB, RM. Squad No 23. Essex 2002-19; cap 2005; benefit 2015; captain (Lo only) 2016. Auckland 2009-10. Dolphins 2010-11. Sussex debut 2020 (T20 only). MCC 2006, 2008. IPL: KXIP 2009 to 2009-10; SH 2015. Big Bash: SS 2013-14. London Spirit 2021 to date. YC 2008. **Tests**: 13 (2007-08 to 2012); HS 143 v WI (Lord's) 2009; BB 1-39 v SL (Galle) 2007-08. **LOI**: 120 (2006-07 to 2014-15); HS 101* v Ire (Dublin) 2013; BB 4-38 v B (Birmingham) 2010. **IT20**: 38 (2008 to 2014); HS 65* v A (Hobart) 2013-14; BB 4-10 v WI (Oval) 2011. F-c Tours: WI 2008-09, 2010-11 (EL); SL 2007-08, 2011-12. 1000 runs (1): 1256 (2008). HS 229 Ex v Northants (Chelmsford) 2007. BB 5-49 Ex v Derbys (Chelmsford) 2016. LO HS 201* Ex v Leics (Leicester) 2008 (FPT) – Ex record. LO BB 5-63 Dolphins v Warriors (Pietermaritzburg) 2010-11. T20 HS 105*. T20 BB 6-16.

171

CARSON, Jack Joshua (Bainbridge Ac; Hurstpierpoint C), b Craigavon, Co Armagh 3 Dec 2000. 6'2". RHB, OB. Squad No 16. Debut (Sussex) 2020. Sussex 2nd XI debut 2018. F-c Tour (EL): SL 2022-23. HS 87 v Worcs (Worcester) 2021. BB 5-85 v Yorks (Hove) 2021.

CARTER, Oliver James (Eastbourne C), b Eastbourne 2 Nov 2001. 5'8½". RHB, WK. Squad No 11. Debut (Sussex) 2021. Sussex 2nd XI debut 2018. HS 185 v Glamorgan (Cardiff) 2022. LO HS 59 v Glos (Hove) 2021 (RLC). T20 HS 2.

CLARK, Thomas Geoffrey Reeves (Ardingly C), b Haywards Heath 27 Feb 2001. 6'2". LHB, RM. Squad No 27. Debut (Sussex) 2019. Sussex 2nd XI debut 2017. HS 138 v Leics (Leicester) 2022. BB 3-21 v Durham (Hove) 2022. LO HS 104 v Surrey (Hove) 2022 (RLC).

COLES, James Matthew (Magdalen Coll S), b Aylesbury, Bucks 2 Apr 2004. 6'0½". RHB, SLA. Squad No 30. Debut (Sussex) 2020, aged 16y 157d – youngest ever player for the county. HS 59 v Leics (Hove) 2022. BB 3-91 v Durham (Chester-le-St) 2022. LO HS 32 v Essex (Chelmsford) 2021 (RLC). LO BB 3-27 v Worcs (Worcester) 2021 (RLC).

CROCOMBE, Henry Thomas (Bede's S, Upper Dicker), b Eastbourne 20 Sep 2001. 6'2". RHB, RMF. Squad No 5. Debut (Sussex) 2020. Sussex 2nd XI debut 2018. HS 46* v Northants (Hove) 2021. BB 4-84 v Glamorgan (Cardiff) 2022. LO HS 9* v Glos (Hove) 2021 (RLC). LO BB 3-33 v Middx (Hove) 2022 (RLC). T20 HS 2*. T20 BB 3-31.

CURRIE, Bradley James (Poole GS; Millfield S; Bournemouth U), b Poole, Dorset 8 Nov 1998. Elder brother of S.W.Currie (*see HAMPSHIRE*). RHB, LMF. Squad No 12. Debut (Sussex) 2022, taking 6-93 v Middx (Lord's). Somerset 2nd XI 2016. Surrey 2nd XI 2017-19. Hampshire 2nd XI 2019. Durham 2nd XI 2021. Gloucestershire 2nd XI 2021. Dorset 2016-21. HS 7 v Worcs (Hove) 2022. BB 6-93 (*see above*). LO HS 3* v Lancs (Hove) 2022 (RLC). LO BB 3-38 v Somerset (Taunton) 2022 (RLC).

FINN, Steven Thomas (Parmiter's S, Garston), b Watford, Herts 4 Apr 1989. 6'7½". RHB, RFM. Squad No 44. Middlesex 2005-21; cap 2009. Otago 2011-12. Sussex debut/cap 2022. Manchester Originals 2021. YC 2010. **Tests**: 36 (2009-10 to 2016-17); HS 56 v NZ (Dunedin) 2012-13; BB 6-79 v A (Birmingham) 2015. **LOI**: 69 (2010-11 to 2017); HS 35 v A (Brisbane) 2010-11; BB 5-33 v I (Brisbane) 2014-15. **IT20**: 21 (2011 to 2015); HS 8* v I (Colombo, RPS) 2012-13; BB 3-16 v NZ (Pallekele) 2012-13. F-c Tours: A 2010-11, 2013-14; SA 2015-16; NZ 2012-13; I 2012-13; SL 2011-12; B 2009-10, 2016-17; UAE 2011-12 (v P). HS 56 (*see Tests*) and 56 M v Sussex (Hove) 2019. Sx HS 10* v Middx (Lord's) 2022. 50 wkts (2): most – 64 (2010). BB 9-37 (14-106 match) M v Worcs (Worcester) 2010. Sx BB 3-84 v Notts (Hove) 2022. LO HS 42* M v Glamorgan (Cardiff) 2014 (RLC). LO BB (*see LOI*) and 5-33 M v Derbys (Lord's) 2011 (CB40). T20 HS 11*. T20 BB 5-16.

FOREMAN, Albert ('**Bertie**') Michael (Hurstpierpoint C), b Worthing 13 May 2004. Grandson of D.J.Foreman (W Province and Sussex 1951-52 to 1967 and football for Brighton & HA). 5'9". LHB, OB. Squad No 13. Sussex 2nd XI debut 2021. England U19 2022 to 2022-23. Awaiting 1st XI debut.

GARTON, George Henry Simmons (Hurstpierpoint C), b Brighton 15 Apr 1997. 5'10½". LHB, LF. Squad No 15. Debut (Sussex) 2016. IPL: RCB 2021. Big Bash: AS 2021-22. Southern Brave 2021 to date. **IT20**: 1 (2021-22); HS 2 and BB 1-57 v WI (Bridgetown) 2021-22. HS 97 v Glamorgan (Cardiff) 2021. BB 5-26 v Essex (Hove) 2020. LO HS 38 v Essex (Chelmsford) 2019 (RLC). LO BB 4-43 EL v Sri Lanka A (Canterbury) 2016. T20 HS 46. T20 BB 4-16.

HAINES, Thomas Jacob (Tanbridge House S, Horsham; Hurstpierpoint C), b Crawley 28 Oct 1998. 5'10". LHB, RM. Squad No 20. Debut (Sussex) 2016; cap 2021; captain 2022. Sussex 2nd XI debut 2014. F-c Tour (EL): SL 2022-23. 1000 runs (1): 1176 (2021). HS 243 v Derbys (Derby) 2022. BB 3-50 v Worcs (Worcester) 2022. LO HS 123 v Middx (Hove) 2021 (RLC). T20 HS 27.

HUDSON-PRENTICE, Fynn Jake (Warden Park S, Cuckfield; Bede's S, Upper Dicker), b Haywards Heath, 12 Jan 1996. 6'0½". RHB, RMF. Squad No 33. Debut (Sussex) 2015. Derbyshire 2019-21. HS 99 De v Middx (Derby) 2019. Sx HS 67 v Middx (Hove) 2021. BB 5-68 De v Notts (Nottingham) 2021. Sx BB 2-49 v Worcs (Worcester) 2021. LO HS 93 De v Somerset (Taunton) 2021 (RLC). LO BB 3-37 De v Notts (Derby) 2021 (RLC). T20 HS 49*. T20 BB 3-36.

HUNT, Sean Frank (Howard of Effingham S), b Guildford, Surrey 7 Dec 2001. 6'5½". RHB, LMF. Squad No 21. Debut (Sussex) 2021. Surrey 2nd XI 2019. HS 13* v Glamorgan (Hove) 2022. BB 3-47 v Lancs (Manchester) 2021. LO HS 2 and LO BB 2-59 v Notts (Nottingham) 2022 (RLC).

IBRAHIM, Danial Kashif (Eastbourne C; Bede's S, Upper Dicker), b Burnley, Lancs 8 Aug 2004. 5'10". RHB, RM. Squad No 40. Debut (Sussex) 2021, aged 16y 298d, scoring 55 v Yorks (Leeds) on 2nd day to become the youngest-ever to score a fifty in the County Championship. Sussex 2nd XI debut 2021. HS 100* v Glamorgan (Hove) 2022. BB 2-9 v Worcs (Worcester) 2021. LO HS 50 v Glos (Hove) 2022 (RLC). BB 2-54 v Essex (Chelmsford) 2021 (RLC).

KARVELAS, Aristides (St Benedict's C, Johannesburg; U of South Africa), b Alberton, South Africa 20 Mar 1994. 6'5". RHB, RMF. Squad No 36. Gauteng 2018-19. Central Gauteng 2019-20 to 2020-21. Sussex debut 2022. IT20 (Greece): 1 (2022); HS 10 v Italy (Vantaa) 2022. HS 57 v Middx (Lord's) 2022. BB 6-71 Gauteng v NW (Potchefstroom) 2018-19 – on debut. Sx BB 2-42 v Notts (Nottingham) 2022. LO HS 33 C Gauteng v WP (Cape Town) 2019-20. LO BB 5-16 C Gauteng v Boland (Johannesburg) 2019-20. T20 HS 10. T20 BB –.

LENHAM, Archie David (Bede's S, Upper Dicker), b Eastbourne 23 Jul 2004. Grandson of L.J.Lenham (Sussex 1956-70); son of N.J.Lenham (Sussex 1984-97); younger brother of S.H.Lenham (Sussex 2nd XI). 5'8½". RHB, LBG. Squad No 41. Debut (Sussex) 2021. Sussex 2nd XI debut 2021. HS 48 and BB 4-84 v Leics (Leicester) 2022. LO HS 18* v Notts (Nottingham) 2022 (RLC). LO BB 4-59 v Lancs (Sedbergh) 2021 (RLC) – on debut. T20 HS 7*. T20 BB 4-26. Became second youngest debutant in Blast aged 16y, 323d.

‡NQMcANDREW, Nathan John, b Woollongong, NSW, Australia 14 Jul 1993. RHB, RFM. Squad No 43. Auckland 2015-16. S Australia 2021-22 to date. Warwickshire 2022. Big Bash: ST 2015-16 to date. F-c Tour (Aus A): SL 2022. HS 92 Aus A v Sri Lanka A (Hambantota) 2022. CC HS 63 Wa v Hants (Southampton) 2022. BB 5-84 SA v WA (Perth) 2021-22. CC BB 4-85 Wa v Lancs (Manchester) 2022. LO HS 55 SA v Q (Brisbane, AB) 2022-23. LO BB 3-22 SA v Vic (Adelaide) 2022-23. T20 HS 30. T20 BB 4-32.

MILLS, Tymal Solomon (Mildenhall TC), b Dewsbury, Yorks 12 Aug 1992. 6'1". RHB, LF. Squad No 7. Essex 2011-14. Sussex debut 2015; has played T20 only since start of 2016. IPL: RCB 2017; MI 2022. Big Bash: BH 2016-17; HH 2017-18; PS 2021-22. Southern Brave 2021 to date. IT20: 12 (+1 ICC World XI 2018) (2016 to 2022); HS 7 v I (Southampton) 2022; BB 3-27 v B (Abu Dhabi) 2021-22. F-c Tour (EL): SL 2013-14. HS 31* EL v Sri Lanka A (Colombo, RPS) 2013-14. CC HS 30 Ex v Kent (Canterbury) 2014. Sx HS 8 v Worcs (Hove) 2015. BB 4-25 Ex v Glamorgan (Cardiff) 2012. Sx BB 2-28 v Hants (Southampton) 2015. LO HS 3* v Notts (Hove) 2015 (RLC). LO BB 3-23 Ex v Durham (Chelmsford) 2013 (Y40). T20 HS 27. T20 BB 4-22.

ORR, Alistair Graham Hamilton (Bede's S, Upper Dicker), b Eastbourne 6 Apr 2001. 6'1". LHB, RM. Squad No 6. Debut (Sussex) 2021. Sussex 2nd XI debut 2018. 1000 runs (1): 1047 (2022). HS 198 v Glamorgan (Hove) 2022. LO HS 206 v Somerset (Taunton) 2022 (RLC) – Sx record. T20 HS 41.

^{NQ}**PUJARA, Cheteshwar** Arvindbhai, b Rajkot, India 25 Jan 1988. 5'11". RHB, LB. Squad No 8. Son of A.S.Pujara (Saurashtra 1976-77 to 1979-80), nephew of B.S.Pujara (Saurashtra 1983-84 to 1996-97). Saurashtra 2005-06 to date. Derbyshire 2014. Yorkshire 2015-18. Nottinghamshire 2017; cap 2017. Sussex debut/cap 2022. IPL: KKR 2009-10; RCB 2011-13; KXIP 2014. **Tests** (I): 101 (2010-11 to 2022-23); 1000 runs (1): 1140 (2017); HS 206* v E (Ahmedabad) 2012-13. **LOI** (I): 5 (2013 to 2014); HS 27 v B (Dhaka) 2014. F-c Tours (I): E 2010 (I A), 2014, 2018, 2021, 2022; A 2006 (I A), 2014-15, 2018-19, 2020-21; SA 2010-11, 2013 (I A), 2013-14, 2017-18, 2021-22; WI 2012 (I A), 2016, 2019; NZ 2013-14, 2019-20; SL 2015, 2017; Z/Ken 2007-08 (I A). B 2022-23. 1000 runs (1+3); most – 2064 (2016-17). HS 352 Saur v Karnataka (Rajkot) 2012-13. CC HS 231 v Middx (Lord's) 2022. BB 2-4 Saur v Rajasthan (Jaipur) 2007-08. LO HS 174 v Surrey (Hove) 2022 (RLC). T20 HS 100*.

RAWLINS, Delray Millard Wendell (Bede's S, Upper Dicker), b Bermuda 14 Sep 1997. 6'1". LHB, SLA. Squad No 9. Debut (Sussex) 2017. MCC 2018. Bermuda (l-o and T20) 2019 to date. Southern Brave 2021. Oxfordshire 2017. **IT20** (Ber): 23 (2019 to 2022-23); HS 91 v Argentina (Buenos Aires) 2022-23; BB 4-10 v Argentina (Buenos Aires) 2022-23 – separate matches. HS 100 v Lancs (Manchester) 2019. BB 3-19 v Durham (Hove) 2019. LO HS 91 v Glos (Hove) 2022 (RLC). LO BB 3-22 v Leics (Hove) 2022 (RLC). T20 HS 91. T20 BB 4-10.

ROBINSON, Oliver Edward ('Ollie') (King's S, Canterbury), b Margate, Kent 1 Dec 1993. 6'5". RHB, RMF. Squad No 25. Debut (Sussex) 2015; cap 2019. Yorkshire 2013 (l-o only). Hampshire 2014 (l-o only). **ECB Central Contract 2022-23. Tests**: 16 (2021 to 2022-23); HS 42 v NZ (Lord's) 2021; BB 5-49 v SA (Oval) 2022. F-c Tours: A 2019-20 (EL), 2021-22; NZ 2022-23; P 2022-23. HS 110 v Durham (Chester-le-St) 2015, on debut, sharing Sx record 10th wkt partnership of 164 with M.E.Hobden. 50 wkts (3); most – 81 (2018). BB 9-78 (13-128 match) v Glamorgan (Cardiff) 2021. LO HS 30 v Kent (Canterbury) 2015 (RLC). LO BB 3-31 v Kent (Hove) 2018 (RLC). T20 HS 31. T20 BB 4-15.

‡^{NQ}**SHADAB KHAN**, b Mianwali, Punjab, Pakistan 4 Oct 1998. 5'10". RHB, LBG. Squad No 29. Rawalpindi 2016-17. SNGPL 2017-18. Northern 2019-20. Yorkshire 2022 (T20 only). Joins Sussex in 2023 (T20 only). Big Bash: BH 2017-18; SS 2021-22; HH 2022-23. **Tests** (P): 6 (2017 to 2020); HS 56 v E (Leeds) 2018; BB 3-31 v Ire (Dublin) 2016. **LOI** (P): 53 (2017 to 2022); HS 86 v WI (Multan) 2022; BB 4-28 v Z (Bulawayo) 2018. **IT20** (P): 84 (2016-17 to 2022-23); HS 52 v SA (Sydney) 2022-23; BB 4-8 v Hong Kong (Sharjah) 2022. F-c Tours (P): E 2016 (PA), 2018, 2020; SA 2018-19; WI 2017; Z 2016-17 (PA); Ire 2018. HS 132 PA v Zimbabwe A (Bulawayo) 2016-17. BB 6-77 (10-157 match) P v Northants (Northampton) 2018. LO HS 86 (*see LOI*). LO BB 4-28 (*see LOI*). T20 HS 91. T20 BB 5-28.

^{NQ}**SMITH, Steven** Peter Devereux, b Kogarah, Sydney, NSW, Australia 2 Jun 1989. RHB, LBG. Squad No 49. NSW 2007-08 to date. Worcestershire 2010 (T20 only). IPL: PW 2012-13; RR 2014 to 2020-21; RPS 2016-17; DC 2021. Big Bash: SS 2011-12 to date. **Tests** (A): 95 (2010 to 2022-23, 38 as captain); 1000 runs (4); most – 1474 (2015); HS 239 v E (Perth) 2017-18; BB 3-18 v E (Lord's) 2013. **LOI** (A): 139 (2009-10 to 2022-23, 51 as captain); 1000 runs (1): 1154 (2016); HS 164 v NZ (Sydney) 2016-17; BB 3-16 v Z (Harare) 2014. **IT20** (A): 63 (2009-10 to 2022-23, 8 as captain); HS 90 v E (Cardiff) 2015; BB 3-20 v WI (Gros Islet) 2010. F-c Tours (A)(C=Captain): E 2010 (v P), 2013, 2015, 2019; SA 2013-14; 2017-18C; WI 2015; NZ 2015-16C; I 2014-11, 2012-13, 2016-17C I 2022-23; P 2021-22 SL 2016C, 2022; B 2017C; UAE (v P) 2014-15. HS 239 (*see Tests*). BB 7-64 NSW v SA (Sydney) 2009-10. LO HS 164 (*see LOI*). LO BB 3-16 (*see LOI*). T20 HS 125*. T20 BB 4-13.

TEAR, Charles Joseph (Seaford S), b Chichester 12 Jun 2004. 5'8½". RHB, WK. Squad No 28. Debut (Sussex) 2022. Sussex 2nd XI debut 2021. England U19 2022-23. HS 56 v Glamorgan (Hove) 2022.

WARD, Harrison David (Tiffin's S, Oxford), b Oxford 25 Oct 1999. 6'1½". LHB, OB. Squad No 35. Debut (Sussex) 2021. Sussex 2nd XI debut 2016. Hampshire 2nd XI 2019. Oxfordshire 2015-18. England U19 2018. HS 19 v Derbys (Hove) 2021. LO HS 37 v Glos (Hove) 2022 (RLC). LO BB –. T20 HS 33. T20 BB 1-5.

(Having made a County 1st XI appearance in 2022)

BEER, William Andrew Thomas (Reigate GS; Collyer's C, Horsham), b Crawley 8 Oct 1988. 5'10". RHB, LB. Sussex 2008-21; cap 2022. HS 97 v Glos (Arundel) 2019. BB 6-29 (11-91 match) v South Africa A (Arundel) 2017. CC BB 3-31 v Worcs (Worcester) 2010. LO HS 75 v Essex (Chelmsford) 2019 (RLC). LO BB 3-27 v Warwks (Hove) 2012 (CB40). T20 HS 37. T20 BB 3-14.

BURROWS, George Davidson (Liverpool John Moores U), b Wigan, Lancs 22 Jun 1998. 6'5". RHB, RFM. Lancashire 2020. Sussex 2022. HS 2 and Sx BB 1-89 v Worcs (Worcester) 2022. BB 2-20 La v Derbys (Liverpool) 2020.

ᴺᵠ**FAHEEM ASHRAF**, b Kasur, Pakistan 16 Jan 1994. LHB, RFM. Faisalabad 2013-14. Faisalabad Wolves 2014-15. National Bank 2015-16. Habib Bank 2016-17 to 2018-19. Central Punjab 2019-20 to date. Sussex 2022. Northamptonshire 2019 (T20 only). Big Bash: HH 2022-23. **Tests** (P): 16 (2018 to 2022-23); HS 91 v NZ (Mt Maunganui) 2020-21; BB 3-42 v SA (Johannesburg) 2018-19. **LOI** (P): 31 (2017 to 2021); HS 28 v A (Sharjah) 2018-19; BB 5-22 v Z (Bulawayo) 2018-19. **IT20** (P): 42 (2017 to 2021); HS 31 v NZ (Auckland) 2020-21; BB 3-5 v Scot (Edinburgh) 2018. F-c Tours (P): E 2018; SA 2018-19; WI 2021; NZ 2020-21; B 2021-22. HS 116 Faisalabad v Multan (Faisalabad) 2013-14 – on debut. Sx HS 33 and Sx BB 1-91 v Durham (Chester-le-St) 2022. BB 6-65 HB v KRL (Karachi) 2016-17. LO HS 71 Faisalabad W v Hyderabad Hawks (Lahore) 2014-15. LO BB 5-22 (*see LOI*). T20 HS 55. T20 BB 6-19.

ᴺᵠ**McCOY, Obed** Christopher, b St Vincent, Grenadines 4 Jan 1997. 6'3". LHB, LFM. Windward Is 2017-18 to 2019-20. Sussex 2022 (T20 only). IPL: RR 2022. **LOI** (WI): 2 (2018-19); HS 0*; BB 2-38 v I (Pune) 2018-19. **IT20** (WI): 27 (2018-19 to 2022-23); HS 23* v NZ (Kingston) 2022; BB 6-17 v I (Basseterre) 2022 – WI record. HS 11* Wind Is v T&T (Tarouba) 2019-20. BB 3-56 Wind Is v Guyana (Gros Islet) 2017-18. LO HS 14* Wind Is v CC&C (Cave Hill) 2017-18. LO BB 2-28 Wind Is v T&T (Bridgetown) 2017-18. T20 HS 23*. T20 BB 6-17.

ᴺᵠ**MOHAMMAD RIZWAN**, b Peshawar, Pakistan 1 Jun 1992. 5'7". RHB, WK, occ RM. Peshawar 2008-09 to 2012-13. SNGPL 2012-13 to 2018-19. Khyber Pakhtunkhwa 2019-20. Sussex 2022. *Wisden* 2020. **Tests** (P): 27 (2016-17 to 2022-23, 2 as captain); HS 115* v SA (Rawalpindi) 2020-21. **LOI** (P): 52 (2015 to 2022-23); HS 115 v A (Sharjah) 2018-19. **IT20** (P): 55 (2015 to 2022-23); HS 104* v SA (Lahore) 2020-21. F-c Tours (P)(C=Captain): E 2020; A 2019-20; WI 2021; NZ 2016-17, 2020-21C; SL 2022; Z 2020-21; B 2021-22. HS 224 SNGPL v NBP (Karachi) 2014-15. Sx HS 130 v Derbys (Hove) 2022. BB 2-10 SNGPL v FATA (Abbottabad) 2018-19. LO HS 141* Pakistan A v EL (Abu Dhabi) 2018-19. T20 HS 110*. T20 BB 1-22.

ᴺᵠ**PHILIPPE, Josh**ua Ryan (Carine HS), b Subiaco, W Australia 1 Jun 1997. RHB, WK. W Australia 2017-18 to date. Sussex 2022 (T20 only). IPL: RCB 2020-21. Big Bash: PS 2017-18; SS 2018-19 to date. **LOI** (A): 3 (2021); HS 39 v WI (Bridgetown) 2021. **IT20** (A): 10 (2020-21 to 2021); HS 45 v NZ (Dunedin) 2020-21. HS 129 WA v Q (Brisbane) 2021-22. LO HS 137 WA v SA (Adelaide, KR) 2021-22. T20 HS 99*.

ᴺᵠ**RASHID KHAN** Arman, b Nangarhar, Afghanistan 20 Sep 1998. RHB, LBG. Afghanistan 2016-17 to date. Sussex 2018-22 (T20 only). IPL: SH 2017-21; GT 2022. Big Bash: AS 2017-18 to date. Trent Rockets 2021 to date. **Tests** (Afg): 5 (2018 to 2020-21); HS 51 v B (Chittagong) 2019; BB 7-137 v Z (Abu Dhabi) 2020-21. **LOI** (Afg): 86 (2015-16 to 2022-23); HS 60* v Ire (Belfast) 2016; BB 7-18 v WI (Gros Islet) 2017 – 4th best analysis in all LOI. **IT20** (Afg): 77 (2015-16 to 2022-23); HS 48* v A (Adelaide) 2022-23; BB 5-3 v Ire (Greater Noida) 2016-17. HS 52 and BB 8-74 (12-122 match) Afg v EL (Abu Dhabi) 2016-17. LO HS 60* (*see LOI*). LO BB 7-18 (*see LOI*). T20 HS 56*. T20 BB 6-17.

RELEASED/RETIRED continued on p 182

SUSSEX 2022

RESULTS SUMMARY

		Place	Won	Lost	Drew	NR
LV= Insurance County Champ (Div 2)		7th	1	6	7	
Royal London One-Day Cup (Group A)		SF	6	3		
Vitality Blast (South Group)		7th	4	10		

LV= INSURANCE COUNTY CHAMPIONSHIP AVERAGES BATTING AND FIELDING

Cap		M	I	NO	HS	Runs	Avge	100	50	Ct/St
2022	C.A.Pujara	8	13	3	231	1094	109.40	5	–	3
2022	Mohammad Rizwan	5	7	1	130	342	57.00	1	2	12
2021	T.J.Haines	12	21	2	243	941	49.52	3	3	4
	A.G.H.Orr	12	23	1	198	1047	47.59	3	3	4
	T.P.Alsop	13	24	2	150	930	42.27	4	4	14
	O.J.Carter	9	15	–	185	629	41.93	1	5	20
	T.G.R.Clark	13	24	1	138	765	33.26	2	4	9
	C.J.Tear	2	4	–	56	124	31.00	–	1	2
	J.J.Carson	3	5	1	58	108	27.00	–	1	1
	D.M.W.Rawlins	8	13	–	75	341	26.23	–	2	1
	J.M.Coles	5	8	1	59	179	25.57	–	2	2
	A.D.Lenham	6	10	2	48	177	22.12	–	–	2
	D.K.Ibrahim	6	11	2	100*	197	21.88	1	–	–
	A.Karvelas	2	4	–	57	73	18.25	–	1	–
	F.J.Hudson-Prentice	3	6	–	51	81	13.50	–	1	1
	Faheem Ashraf	3	5	–	33	65	13.00	–	–	1
2019	O.E.Robinson	3	4	–	26	49	12.25	–	–	–
	J.A.Atkins	3	5	2	17	36	12.00	–	–	–
	H.T.Crocombe	9	12	1	36	128	11.63	–	–	2
	S.F.Hunt	8	12	6	13*	43	7.16	–	–	1
2022	S.T.Finn	5	7	2	10*	34	6.80	–	–	2
	B.J.Currie	4	7	4	7	15	5.00	–	–	1

Also batted: A.P.Beard (3 matches) 11*, 4, 25 (3 ct); J.A.Brooks (2) 36, 8, 21; G.D.Burrows (2) 0, 2, 0; M.S.Crane (2) 13, 8 (1 ct); G.H.S.Garton (1) 53; T.L.Seifert (1) 5, 5 (4 ct; 2 st); G.Stewart (1) 18, 67*.

BOWLING

	O	M	R	W	Avge	Best	5wI	10wM
O.E.Robinson	95.1	28	266	17	15.64	5-60	2	–
B.J.Currie	98.4	17	396	15	26.40	6-93	1	–
S.F.Hunt	211.4	36	727	18	40.38	3-72	–	–
H.T.Crocombe	214.5	29	766	15	51.06	4-84	–	–
D.M.W.Rawlins	251	36	884	13	68.00	3-72	–	–
Also bowled:								
J.A.Brooks	62	8	230	8	28.75	5-46	1	–
T.G.R.Clark	82	16	232	6	38.66	3-21	–	–
A.P.Beard	96.3	12	325	7	46.42	3-51	–	–
T.J.Haines	146	30	376	8	47.00	3-50	–	–
J.J.Carson	58	5	236	5	47.20	2-40	–	–
M.S.Crane	74	5	294	5	58.80	2-28	–	–
J.M.Coles	109	5	490	8	61.25	3-91	–	–
S.T.Finn	141	17	464	7	66.28	3-84	–	–
A.D.Lenham	126.1	10	457	6	76.16	4-84	–	–

T.P.Alsop 2.5-0-21-0; J.A.Atkins 55.1-6-254-4; G.D.Burrows 44.2-188-1; Faheem Ashraf 54-3-310-2; G.H.S.Garton 21-3-95-1; F.J.Hudson-Prentice 22-3-86-0; D.K.Ibrahim 68.3-4-263-3; A.Karvelas 53.5-18-168-4; Mohammad Rizwan 2-0-5-0; C.A.Pujara 2-1-8-0; G.Stewart 27-6-77-2.

Sussex played no first-class fixtures outside the County Championship in 2022. The First-Class Averages (pp 221–234) give the records of Sussex players in all first-class county matches, with the exception of A.P.Beard, J.A.Brooks, M.S.Crane, C.A.Pujara, O.E.Robinson and G.Stewart, whose first-class figures for Sussex are as above.

SUSSEX RECORDS

FIRST-CLASS CRICKET

Highest Total	For	742-5d		v	Somerset	Taunton	2009
	V	756-4d		by	Leics	Hove	2022
Lowest Total	For	19		v	Surrey	Godalming	1830
		19		v	Notts	Hove	1873
	V	18		by	Kent	Gravesend	1867
Highest Innings	For	344*	M.W.Goodwin	v	Somerset	Taunton	2009
	V	322	E.Paynter	for	Lancashire	Hove	1937

Highest Partnership for each Wicket

1st	490	E.H.Bowley/J.G.Langridge	v	Middlesex	Hove	1933
2nd	385	E.H.Bowley/M.W.Tate	v	Northants	Hove	1921
3rd	385*	M.H.Yardy/M.W.Goodwin	v	Warwicks	Hove	2006
4th	363	M.W.Goodwin/C.D.Hopkinson	v	Somerset	Taunton	2009
5th	297	J.H.Parks/H.W.Parks	v	Hampshire	Portsmouth	1937
6th	335	L.J.Wright/B.C.Brown	v	Durham	Hove	2014
7th	344	K.S.Ranjitsinhji/W.Newham	v	Essex	Leyton	1902
8th	291	R.S.C.Martin-Jenkins/M.J.G.Davis	v	Somerset	Taunton	2002
9th	178	H.W.Parks/A.F.Wensley	v	Derbyshire	Horsham	1930
10th	164	O.E.Robinson/M.E.Hobden	v	Durham	Chester-le-St[2]	2015

Best Bowling	For	10- 48	C.H.G.Bland	v	Kent	Tonbridge	1899
(Innings)	V	9- 11	A.P.Freeman	for	Kent	Hove	1922
Best Bowling	For	17-106	G.R.Cox	v	Warwicks	Horsham	1926
(Match)	V	17- 67	A.P.Freeman	for	Kent	Hove	1922

Most Runs – Season	2850	J.G.Langridge	(av 64.77)		1949
Most Runs – Career	34150	J.G.Langridge	(av 37.69)		1928-55
Most 100s – Season	12	J.G.Langridge			1949
Most 100s – Career	76	J.G.Langridge			1928-55
Most Wkts – Season	198	M.W.Tate	(av 13.47)		1925
Most Wkts – Career	2211	M.W.Tate	(av 17.41)		1912-37
Most Career W-K Dismissals	1176	H.R.Butt	(911 ct; 265 st)		1890-1912
Most Career Catches in the Field	779	J.G.Langridge			1928-55

LIMITED-OVERS CRICKET

Highest Total	50ov	400-4		v	Middlesex	Hove	2022
	40ov	399-4		v	Worcs	Horsham	2011
	T20	242-5		v	Glos	Bristol	2016
Lowest Total	50ov	49		v	Derbyshire	Chesterfield	1969
	40ov	59		v	Glamorgan	Hove	1996
	T20	67		v	Hampshire	Hove	2004
Highest Innings	50ov	206	A.G.H.Orr	v	Somerset	Taunton	2022
	40ov	163	C.J.Adams	v	Middlesex	Arundel	1999
	T20	153*	L.J.Wright	v	Essex	Chelmsford	2014
Best Bowling	50ov	6- 9	A.I.C.Dodemaide	v	Ireland	Downpatrick	1990
	40ov	7-41	A.N.Jones	v	Notts	Nottingham	1986
	T20	5-11	Mushtaq Ahmed	v	Essex	Hove	2005

WARWICKSHIRE

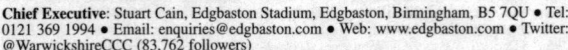

Formation of Present Club: 8 April 1882
Substantial Reorganisation: 19 January 1884
Inaugural First-Class Match: 1894
Colours: Dark Blue, Gold and Silver
Badge: Bear and Ragged Staff
County Champions: (8) 1911, 1951, 1972, 1994, 1995, 2004, 2012, 2021
Gillette/NatWest Trophy Winners: (5) 1966, 1968, 1989, 1993, 1995
Benson and Hedges Cup Winners: (2) 1994, 2002
Sunday League Winners: (3) 1980, 1994, 1997
Clydesdale Bank 40 Winners: (1) 2010
Royal London Cup Winners: (1) 2015
Twenty20 Cup Winners: (1) 2014

Chief Executive: Stuart Cain, Edgbaston Stadium, Edgbaston, Birmingham, B5 7QU ● Tel: 0121 369 1994 ● Email: enquiries@edgbaston.com ● Web: www.edgbaston.com ● Twitter: @WarwickshireCCC (83,762 followers)

1st Team Coach: Mark Robinson. **Batting Coach**: Tony Frost. **Bowling Coach**: Stuart Barnes. **Assistant Coaches**: Mohammed Sheikh and Ian Westwood. **Captain**: W.H.M.Rhodes. **Overseas Players**: Hasan Ali and G.J.Maxwell (T20 only). **2023 Testimonial**: None. **Head Groundsman**: Gary Barwell. **Scorer**: Mel Smith. **T20 Blast Name**: Birmingham Bears. ‡ New registration. NQ Not qualified for England.

ALI, Moeen Munir (Moseley S), b Birmingham 18 Jun 1987. Brother of A.K.Ali (Worcs, Glos and Leics 2000-12), cousin of Kabir Ali (Worcs, Rajasthan, Hants and Lancs 1999-2014). 6'0". LHB, OB. Squad No 1. Debut (Warwickshire) 2005. Worcestershire 2007-19; captain 2020-22 (T20 only). Moors SC 2011-12. MT 2012-13. MCC 2012. IPL: RCB 2018 to 2020-21; CSK 2021 to date. Birmingham Phoenix 2021 to date. PCA 2013. *Wisden* 2014. **ECB Central Contract 2022-23. Tests**: 64 (2014 to 2021); 1000 runs (1): 1078 (2016); HS 155* v SL (Chester-le-St) 2016; BB 6-53 v SA (Lord's) 2017. Hat-trick v SA (Oval) 2017. **LOI**: 129 (2013-14 to 2022-23, 1 as captain); HS 128 v Scotland (Christchurch) 2014-15; BB 4-46 v A (Manchester) 2018. **IT20**: 72 (2013-14 to 2022-23, 11 as captain); HS 72* v A (Cardiff) 2015; BB 3-24 v WI (Bridgetown) 2021-22. F-c Tours: A 2017-18; SA 2015-16; WI 2014-15, 2018-19; NZ 2017-18; I 2016-17, 2020-21; SL 2013-14 (EL), 2018-19; B 2016-17; UAE 2015-16 (v P). 1000 runs (2); most – 1420 (2013). HS 250 Wo v Glamorgan (Worcester) 2013; Wa HS 68 v Durham (Chester-le-St) 2006. BB 6-29 (12-96 match) Wo v Lancs (Manchester) 2012; Wa BB 2-50 v Lancs (Birmingham) 2006. LO HS 158 Wo v Sussex (Horsham) 2011 (CB40). LO BB 4-33 Wo v Notts (Nottingham) 2018 (RLC). T20 HS 121*. T20 BB 5-34.

‡BARNARD, Edward George (Shrewsbury S), b Shrewsbury, Shrops 20 Nov 1995. Younger brother of M.R.Barnard (Oxford MCCU 2010). 6'1". RHB, RMF. Squad No 30. Worcestershire 2015-22. Shropshire 2012. HS 163* Wo v Notts (Nottingham) 2022. BB 6-37 (11-89 match) Wo v Somerset (Taunton) 2018. LO HS 85* Wo v Hants (Southampton) 2022 (RLC). LO BB 3-26 Wo v Yorks (Worcester) 2019 (RLC). T20 HS 43*. T20 BB 3-29.

BENJAMIN, Christopher Gavin (St Andrew's C, Johannesburg; Durham U), b Johannesburg, South Africa 29 Apr 1999. 5'11". RHB, RMF, WK. Squad No 12. Durham MCCU 2019. Warwickshire debut 2021, scoring 127 v Lancs (Manchester); also scored fifties on RLC and T20 debuts. Durham 2022 (on loan); cap 2022. Essex 2nd XI 2018-19. Derbyshire 2nd XI 2021. HS 127 (*see above*). LO HS 50 v Glamorgan (Cardiff) 2021 (RLC). T20 HS 68*.

BETHELL, Jacob Graham (Rugby S), b Bridgetown, Barbados 23 Oct 2003. 5'10". LHB, SLA. Squad No 2. Debut (Warwickshire) 2021. Gloucestershire 2022 (on loan); cap 2022. Welsh Fire 2022. Warwickshire 2nd XI debut 2019. HS 61 Gs v Somerset (Bristol) 2022. Wa HS 15 v Yorks (Leeds) 2021. LO HS 66 v Yorks (York) 2021 (RLC). LO BB 4-36 v Glamorgan (Cardiff) 2021 (RLC). T20 HS 21. T20 BB 1-21.

BRIGGS, Danny Richard (Isle of Wight C), b Newport, IoW, 30 Apr 1991. 6'2". RHB, SLA. Squad No 14. Hampshire 2009-15; cap 2012. Sussex 2016-19. Warwickshire debut 2021; cap 2021. Big Bash: AS 2020-21. Southern Brave 2021. Oval Invincibles 2022. **LOI:** 1 (2011-12); BB 2-39 v P (Dubai) 2011-12. **IT20:** 7 (2012 to 2013-14); HS 0*; BB 2-25 v A (Chester-le-St) 2013. F-c Tours (EL): WI 2010-11; I 2018-19. HS 120* Sx v South Africa A (Arundel) 2017. CC HS 66* v Essex (Birmingham) 2021. BB 6-65 H v Windward Is (Roseau) 2010-11. CC BB 6-65 H v Notts (Southampton) 2011. Wa BB 4-31 v Essex (Birmingham) 2022. LO HS 37* Sx v Essex (Chelmsford) 2019 (RLC). LO BB 4-32 H v Glamorgan (Cardiff) 2012 (CB40). T20 HS 35*. T20 BB 5-19.

BROOKES, Ethan Alexander (Solihull S & SFC), b Solihull 23 May 2001. Younger brother of H.J.H.Brookes (*see below*). 6'1". RHB, RMF. Squad No 77. Debut (Warwickshire) 2019. Warwickshire 2nd XI debut 2018. Staffordshire 2019. HS 15* v Glamorgan (Cardiff) 2020. BB –. LO HS 63 v Leics (Birmingham) 2021 (RLC). LO BB 3-15 v Northants (Birmingham) 2021 (RLC).

BROOKES, Henry James Hamilton (Tudor Grange Acad, Solihull), b Solihull 21 Aug 1999. Elder brother of E.A.Brookes (*see above*). 6'3". RHB, RMF. Squad No 10. Debut (Warwickshire) 2017. Birmingham Phoenix 2022. Warwickshire 2nd XI debut 2016. England U19 2016-17 to 2017. HS 84 v Kent (Birmingham) 2019. BB 4-54 v Northants (Birmingham) 2018. LO HS 12* v Derbys (Derby) 2019 (RLC). LO BB 3-50 v Yorks (Birmingham) 2019 (RLC). T20 HS 31*. T20 BB 5-25.

BURGESS, Michael Gregory Kerran (Cranleigh S; Loughborough U), b Epsom, Surrey 8 Jul 1994. 6'1". RHB, WK, occ RM. Squad No 61. Loughborough MCCU 2014-15. Leicestershire 2016. Sussex 2017-19. Warwickshire debut 2019; cap 2021. HS 178 v Surrey (Birmingham) 2022. BB 1-17 v Northants (Northampton) 2022. LO HS 93 v Surrey (Oval) 2022 (RLC). T20 HS 56.

DAVIES, Alexander Luke (Queen Elizabeth GS, Blackburn), b Darwen, Lancs 23 Aug 1994. 5'7". RHB, WK. Squad No 71. Lancashire 2012-21; cap 2017. Warwickshire debut 2022. Southern Brave 2021 to date. F-c Tour (EL): WI 2017-18. 1000 runs (1): 1046 (2017). HS 147 La v Northants (Northampton) 2019. Wa HS 121 v Lancs (Birmingham) 2022. LO HS 147 La v Durham (Manchester) 2018 (RLC). T20 HS 94*.

GARRETT, George Anthony (Shrewsbury S), Harpenden, Herts 4 Mar 2000. 6'3". RHB, RM. Squad No 44. Debut (Warwickshire) 2019. Warwickshire 2nd XI debut 2019. HS 24 v Essex (Birmingham) 2019. BB 2-53 v Notts (Nottingham) 2019. LO HS 18 v Leics (Leicester) 2022 (RLC). LO BB 3-50 v Leics (Birmingham) 2021 (RLC). T20 BB 1-19.

HAIN, Samuel Robert (Southport S, Gold Coast), b Hong Kong 16 July 1995. 5'10". RHB, OB. Squad No 16. Debut (Warwickshire) 2014; cap 2018. MCC 2018. Big Bash: BH 2022-23. Manchester Originals 2021. Welsh Fire 2022. UK passport (British parents). 1000 runs (1): 1137 (2022). HS 208 v Northants (Birmingham) 2014. BB –. LO HS 161* v Worcs (Worcester) 2019 (RLC). T20 HS 112*.

HANNON-DALBY, Oliver James (Brooksbank S, Leeds Met U), b Halifax, Yorkshire 20 Jun 1989. 6'7". LHB, RMF. Squad No 20. Yorkshire 2008-12. Warwickshire debut 2013; cap 2019. F-c Tour (MCC): Nepal 2019-20. HS 40 v Somerset (Taunton) 2014. 50 wkts (1): 53 (2022). BB 6-33 (12-110 match) v Glos (Bristol) 2020. LO HS 21* Y v Warwks (Scarborough) 2012 (CB40). LO BB 5-27 v Glamorgan (Birmingham) 2015 (RLC). T20 HS 14*. T20 BB 4-20.

179

‡NOHASAN ALI, b Mandi Bahauddin, Pakistan 7 Feb 1994. 5'8". RHB, RMF. Squad No 32. Sialkot 2013-14. Sialkot Stallions 2014-15. Islamabad 2015-16 to 2016-17. Central Punjab 2019-20 to date. Lancashire 2022; cap 2022. Southern Punjab 2022-23. **Tests** (P): 22 (2017 to 2022-23); HS 30 v Z (Harare) 2021; BB 5-27 v Z (Harare) 2021 – separate matches. **LOI** (P): 60 (2016 to 2022); HS 59 v SA (Durban) 2018-19; BB 5-34 v SL (Abu Dhabi) 2017-18. **IT20** (P): 50 (2016 to 2022); HS 23 v NZ (Wellington) 2017-18; BB 4-18 v Z (Harare) 2021. F-c Tours (P): E 2016 (PA), 2018; SA 2018-19; WI 2017, 2021; SL 2022; Z 2020-21; B 2021. HS 106* C Punjab v Khyber Paktunkhwa (Karachi) 2020-21. CC HS 19 La v Hants (Southampton) 2022. 50 wkts (0+1): 55 (2020-21). BB 8-107 Sialkot S v State Bank (Sialkot) 2014-15. CC BB 6-47 La v Glos (Manchester) 2022. LO HS 59 (see LOI). LO BB 5-34 (see LOI). T20 HS 45. T20 BB 5-20.

JOHAL, Manraj Singh (Sandwell C; Oldbury Ac), b Birmingham 12 Oct 2001. 6'0". RHB, RFM. Squad No 5. Debut (Warwickshire) 2021. Staffordshire 2019. HS 19 and BB 3-29 v Lancs (Lord's) 2021. LO HS 10 v Yorks (York) 2021 (RLC). LO BB 2-35 v Northants (Birmingham) 2021 (RLC). No 1st XI appearances in 2022.

KHAN, Amir (Cockshut Hill S), b 15 Sep 2005. 5'10". LHB, OB. Squad No 3. Warwickshire 2nd XI debut 2021. Awaiting 1st XI debut.

LINTOTT, Jacob ('Jake') Benedict (Queen's C, Taunton), b Taunton, Somerset 22 Apr 1993. 5'11". RHB, SLA. Squad No 23. Debut (Warwickshire) 2021. Hampshire 2017 (T20 only). Gloucestershire 2018 (T20 only). Southern Brave 2021 to date. Dorset 2011-15. Wiltshire 2016-19. HS 15 v Worcs (Worcester) 2021. BB – . LO HS 21 EL v South Africans (Worcester) 2022. T20 HS 41. T20 BB 4-20.

MADDY, George William, b 13 Oct 2005. Son of D.L.Maddy (Leicestershire, Warwickshire and England 1994-2013). 5'10". LHB, WK. Squad No 8. Awaiting f-c debut. Warwickshire 2nd XI debut 2021. LO HS 7 v Somerset (Birmingham) 2022 (RLC).

‡NOMAXWELL, Glenn James, b Kew, Melbourne, Australia 14 Oct 1988. 5'9". RHB, OB. Victoria 2010-11 to date. Hampshire 2014. Yorkshire 2015. Lancashire 2019. Joins Warwickshire in 2023 (T20 only). IPL: DD 2012-18; MI 2013 to 2013-13; KXIP 2014 to 2020-21; RCB 2021 to date. Big Bash: MR 2011-12; MS 2012-13 to 2021-22. London Spirit 2022. **Tests** (A): 7 (2012-13 to 2017); HS 104 v I (Ranchi) 2016-17; BB 4-127 v I (Hyderabad) 2012-13. **LOI** (A): 127 (2012 to 2022); HS 108 v E (Manchester) 2020; BB 4-46 v E (Perth) 2014-15. **IT20** (A): 98 (2012 to 2022-23); HS 145* v SL (Pallekele) 2016; BB 3-10 v E (Hobart) 2017-18. F-c Tours (A): I 2012-13, 2016-17; SA/Z 2013 (Aus A); B 2017; UAE 2014-15 (v P). HS 278 Vic v NSW (Sydney, NO) 2017-18. CC HS 140 Y v Durham (Scarborough) 2015. BB 5-40 La v Middx (Lord's) 2019. LO HS 146 H v Lancs (Manchester) 2014 (RLC). LO BB 4-46 (see LOI). T20 HS 154*. T20 BB 3-10.

MILES, Craig Neil (Bradon Forest S, Swindon; Filton C, Bristol), b Swindon, Wilts 20 July 1994. Brother of A.J.Miles (Cardiff MCCU 2012). 6'4". RHB, RMF. Squad No 18. Gloucestershire 2011-18; cap 2011. Warwickshire debut 2019. Northern Superchargers 2022. HS 62* Gs v Worcs (Cheltenham) 2014. Wa HS 32 v Surrey (Birmingham) 2022. 50 wkts (3); most – 58 (2018). BB 6-63 Gs v Northants (Northampton) 2015. Wa BB 5-28 v Lancs (Lord's) 2021. Hat-trick Gs v Essex (Cheltenham) 2016. LO HS 31* v Surrey (Oval) 2021 (RLC). LO BB 4-29 Gs v Yorks (Scarborough) 2015 (RLC). T20 HS 11*. T20 BB 3-19.

MOUSLEY, Daniel Richard (Bablake S, Coventry), b Birmingham 8 Jul 2001. 5'11". LHB, OB. Squad No 80. Debut (Warwickshire) 2019. Birmingham Phoenix 2022. Staffordshire 2019. England U19 2018-19. HS 71 v Glamorgan (Cardiff) 2020. BB – . LO HS 105 Burgher Rec v Nugegoda (Colombo) 2021-22. LO BB 3-32 Burgher Rec v SL Air Force (Colombo) 2021-22. T20 HS 63*. T20 BB 1-3.

NORWELL, Liam Connor (Redruth SS), b Bournemouth, Dorset 27 Dec 1991. 6'3". RHB, RMF. Squad No 24. Gloucestershire 2011-18, taking 6-46 v Derbys (Bristol) on debut; cap 2011. Warwickshire debut 2019. HS 102 Gs v Derbys (Bristol) 2016. Wa HS 64 v Surrey (Birmingham) 2019. 50 wkts (3); most – 68 (2015). BB 9-62 (13-100 match) v Hants (Birmingham) 2022. LO HS 16 Gs v Somerset (Bristol) 2017 (RLC). LO BB 6-52 Gs v Leics (Leicester) 2012 (CB40). T20 HS 2*. T20 BB 3-27.

RHODES, William Michael Henry (Cottingham HS, Cottingham SFC, Hull), b Nottingham 2 Mar 1995. 6'2". LHB, RMF. Squad No 35. Yorkshire 2014-15 to 2016. Essex 2016 (on loan). Warwickshire debut 2018; cap 2020; captain 2020 to date. MCC 2019. F-c tour (MCC): Nepal 2019-20. HS 207 v Worcs (Worcester) 2020. BB 5-17 v Essex (Chelmsford) 2019. LO HS 69 v Notts (Birmingham) 2022 (RLC). LO BB 3-40 v Notts (Birmingham) 2021 (RLC). T20 HS 79. T20 BB 4-34.

‡**RUSHWORTH, Chris**topher (Castle View CS, Sunderland), b Sunderland, Co Durham 11 Jul 1986. Cousin of P.Mustard (Durham, Mountaineers, Auckland, Lancashire and Gloucestershire 2002-17). 6'2". RHB, RMF. Squad No 22. Durham 2010-22; cap 2010; testimonial 2019. MCC 2013, 2015. Northumberland 2004-05. PCA 2015. HS 57 Du v Kent (Canterbury) 2017. 50 wkts (6); most – 88 (2015) – Du record. BB 9-52 (15-95 match – Du record) Du v Northants (Chester-le-St) 2014. Hat-trick Du v Hants (Southampton) 2015. LO HS 38* Du v Derbys (Chester-le-St) 2015 (RLC). LO BB 5-31 Du v Notts (Chester-le-St) 2010 (CB40). T20 HS 5. T20 BB 3-14.

SHAIKH, Hamza (Eden Boys S), b 29 May 2006. 5'11". RHB, LB. Squad No 15. Awaiting f-c debut. Warwickshire 2nd XI debut 2021. LO HS 25 v Sussex (Birmingham) 2022 (RLC).

ᴺᵠ**SIMMONS, Che** Brandon (Sandwell C), b Barbados 18 Dec 2003. 6'1". RHB, RFM. Squad No 99. Warwickshire 2nd XI debut 2021. Awaiting 1st XI debut. Will qualify for England in 2024 thanks to UK passport.

SMITH, Kai (King's S, Canterbury), b Dubai 28 Nov 2004. RHB, WK. Awaiting f-c debut. Warwickshire 2nd XI debut 2021. LO HS 29* v Notts (Birmingham) 2022 (RLC).

WOAKES, Christopher Roger (Barr Beacon Language S, Walsall), b Birmingham 2 March 1989. 6'2". RHB, RFM. Squad No 19. Debut (Warwickshire) 2006; cap 2009. Wellington 2012-13. MCC 2009. IPL: KKR 2017; RCB 2018; DC 2021. Big Bash: ST 2013-14. Herefordshire 2006-07. Wisden 2016. PCA 2020. **ECB Central Contract 2022-23.** Tests: 45 (2013 to 2021-22); HS 137* v I (Lord's) 2018; BB 6-17 v Ire (Lord's) 2019. LOI: 112 (2010-11 to 2022-23); HS 95* v SL (Nottingham) 2016; BB 6-45 v A (Brisbane) 2010-11. IT20: 27 (2010-11 to 2022-23); HS 37 v P (Sharjah) 2015-16; BB 3-4 v A (Canberra) 2022-23. F-c Tours: A 2017-18, 2021-22; SA 2015-16, 2019-20; WI 2010-11 (EL), 2021-22; NZ 2017-18, 2019-20; I 2016-17; SL 2013-14 (EL), 2019-20; B 2016-17; UAE 2015-16 (v P). HS 152* v Derbys (Derby) 2013. 50 wkts (3); most – 59 (2016). BB 9-36 v Durham (Birmingham) 2016. LO HS 95* (see LOI). LO BB 6-45 (see LOI). T20 HS 57*. T20 BB 4-21.

YATES, Robert Michael (Warwick S), b Solihull 19 Sep 1999. 6'0". LHB, OB. Squad No 17. Debut (Warwickshire) 2019. Warwickshire 2nd XI debut 2017. Staffordshire 2018. HS 141 v Somerset (Birmingham) 2019. BB 2-54 v Worcs (Worcester) 2021. LO HS 114 v Sussex (Birmingham) 2022 (RLC). LO BB 1-27 v Surrey (Oval) 2021 (RLC). T20 HS 37. T20 BB 1-13.

RELEASED/RETIRED

(Having made a County 1st XI appearance in 2022, even if not
formally contracted. Some may return in 2023.)

ᴺᵠ**BRATHWAITE, Carlos** Ricardo, b Christ Church, Barbados 18 Jul 1988. RHB, RFM. CC&C 2010-11. Barbados 2011-12 to 2015-16. Sagicor HPC 2014. Kent 2018 (T20 only). Warwickshire 2021-22 (T20 only); T20 captain 2022. IPL: DD 2016-17; SH 2018; KKR 2019. Big Bash: ST 2016-17; SS 2017-18 to 2020-21. Manchester Originals 2021. Tests (WI): 3 (2015-16 to 2016); HS 69 v A (Sydney) 2015-16; BB 1-30 v A (Melbourne) 2015-16. LOI (WI): 44 (2011-12 to 2019); HS 101 v NZ (Manchester) 2019; BB 5-27 v PNG (Harare) 2017-18. IT20 (WI): 41 (2011-12 to 2019); HS 37* v P (Port of Spain) 2016-17; BB 3-20 v E (Chester-le-St) 2017. F-c Tours (WI): A 2015-16; SL 2014-15 (WI A). HS 109 Bar v T&T (Bridgetown) 2013-14. BB 7-90 CC&C v T&T (St Augustine) 2010-11 – on debut. LO HS 113 WI v SL Board Pres (Colombo, CC) 2015-16. LO BB 5-27 (see LOI). T20 HS 64*. T20 BB 4-14.

HOSE, A.J. – see WORCESTERSHIRE.

LAMB, M.J. – *see DERBYSHIRE*.

McANDREW, N.J. – *see SUSSEX*.

NQ**PANDYA, Krunal** Himanshu, b Ahmedabad, India 24 Mar 1991. Older brother of H.H.Pandya (Baroda and India 2013-14 to date). LHB, SLA. Baroda 2016-17 to date. Warwickshire 2022 (l-o only). IPL: MI 2016-21; LSG 2022. **LOI** (I): 5 (2020-21 to 2021); HS 58* v E (Pune) 2020-21; BB 1-26 v SL (Colombo, RPS) 2021. **IT20** (I): 19 (2018-19 to 2021); HS 26* v NZ (Hamilton) 2018-19; BB 4-36 v A (Sydney) 2018-19. HS 160 and BB 4-40 Baroda v Railways (Delhi) 2018-19. LO HS 133* Baroda v Chhattisgarh (Surat) 2020-21. LO BB 6-41 Baroda v Goa (Alur) 2018-19. T20 HS 86. T20 BB 4-15.

SIBLEY, D.P. – *see SURREY*.

NQ**SIRAJ, Mohammed**, b Hyderabad, India 13 Mar 1994. RHB, RMF. Hyderabad 2015-16 to 2019-20. Warwickshire 2022. IPL: SH 2017; RCB 2018 to date. **Tests** (I): 18 (2020-21 to 2022-23); HS 16* v E (Chennai) 2021-22; BB 5-73 v A (Brisbane) 2020-21. **LOI** (I): 21 (2018-19 to 2022-23); HS 9 v B (Mirpur) 2022-23; BB 4-32 v SL (Thiruvananthapuram) 2022-23. **IT20** (I): 8 (2017-18 to 2022-23); HS 5 v SA (Indore) 2022-23; BB 4-17 v NZ (Napier) 2022-23. F-c Tours (I): E 2018 (IA), 2021, 2022; A 2020-21; SA 2017 (IA), 2021-22; WI 2019 (IA); NZ 2018-19 (IA), 2019-20 (IA); B 2022-23. HS 46 Hyderabad v Vidarbha (Hyderabad) 2019-20. Wa HS 21* and Wa BB 5-82 v Somerset (Birmingham) 2022. BB 8-59 (11-136 match) India A v Australia A (Bangalore) 2018. LO HS 36* Hyderabad v Delhi (Delhi) 2018-19. LO BB 5-37 Hyderabad v Chhattisgarh (Secunderabad) 2017-18. T20 HS 14*. T20 BB 4-17.

STIRLING, P.R. – *see IRELAND*.

STONE, O.P. – *see NOTTINGHAMSHIRE*.

NQ**YADAV, Jayant**, b Delhi, India 22 Jan 1990. RHB, OB. Haryana 2011-12 to date. Warwickshire 2022. IPL: DD 2015-17; MI 2019-21. **Tests** (I): 6 (2016-17 to 2021-22); HS 104 v E (Mumbai) 2016-17; BB 4-49 v NZ (Mumbai) 2021-22. **LOI** (I): 2 (2016-17 to 2021-22); HS 2 v SA (Cape Town) 2021-22; BB 1-8 v NZ (Visakhapatnam) 2016-17. F-c Tours (IA): E 2018; A 2016. HS 211 Haryana v Karnataka (Hubli) 2012-13. Wa HS 29 v Somerset (Birmingham) 2022. BB 7-58 Haryana v Jammu & Kashmir (Jammu) 2019-20. Wa BB 5-90 v Glos (Bristol) 2022. LO HS 71 India EP v Sri Lanka EP (Colombo) 2018-19. LO BB 3-21 Haryana v Kerala (Alur) 2015-16. T20 HS 39. T20 BB 4-22.

SUSSEX RELEASED/RETIRED (continued from p 175)

NQ**SEIFERT, Tim** Louis, b Wanganui, New Zealand 14 Dec 1994. RHB, WK. Northern Districts 2014-15 to date. Sussex 2022. IPL: KKR 2021; DC 2022. **LOI** (NZ): 3 (2018-19); HS 22 v SL (Mt Maunganui) 2018-19. **IT20** (NZ): 40 (2017-18 to 2021-22); HS 84* v P (Hamilton) 2020-21. F-c Tours (NZA): I 2017-18; UAE (v P) 2018-19. HS 167* ND v Otago (Alexandra) 2017-18. Sx HS 5 v Glamorgan (Cardiff) 2022. LO HS 104 ND v Canterbury (Christchurch) 2016-17. T20 HS 107.

WRIGHT, Luke James (Belvoir HS; Ratcliffe C; Loughborough U), b Grantham, Lincs 7 Mar 1985. Younger brother of A.S.Wright (Leicestershire 2001-02). 5'11". RHB, RMF. Leicestershire 2003 (one f-c match). Sussex 2004-18; cap 2007; T20 captain & benefit 2015; captain 2016-17; captain 2020-22. IPL: PW 2012-13. Big Bash: MS 2011-12 to 2017-18. **LOI**: 50 (2007 to 2013-14); HS 52 v NZ (Birmingham) 2008; BB 2-34 v NZ (Bristol) 2008 and 2-34 v A (Southampton) 2010. **IT20**: 51 (2007-08 to 2013-14); HS 99* v P (Colombo, RPS) 2012-13; BB 2-24 v NZ (Hamilton) 2012-13. F-c Tour (EL): NZ 2008-09. 1000 runs (1): 1220 (2015). HS 226* v Worcs (Worcester) 2015, sharing Sx record 6th wkt partnership of 335 with B.C.Brown. BB 5-65 v Derbys (Derby) 2010. LO HS 166 v Middx (Lord's) 2019 (RLC). LO BB 4-12 v Middx (Hove) 2004 (NL). T20 HS 153* v Essex (Chelmsford) 2014 – Sx record. T20 BB 3-17.

T.I.Hinley left the staff without making a County 1st XI appearance in 2022.

WARWICKSHIRE 2022

RESULTS SUMMARY

	Place	Won	Lost	Tied	Drew	NR
LV= Insurance County Champ (Div 1)	8th	2	6		6	
Royal London One-Day Cup (Group A)	6th	4	3	1		
Vitality Blast (North Group)	QF	9	6			

LV= INSURANCE COUNTY CHAMPIONSHIP AVERAGES
BATTING AND FIELDING

Cap		M	I	NO	HS	Runs	Avge	100	50	Ct/St
2018	S.R.Hain	12	21	3	202*	1137	63.16	3	6	12
	M.J.Lamb	8	11	1	155*	487	48.70	2	1	3
2019	D.P.Sibley	14	25	3	142*	935	42.50	3	5	9
2021	M.G.K.Burgess	12	18	–	178	745	41.38	2	3	37/1
	N.J.McAndrew	7	9	1	63	278	34.75	–	2	2
2020	W.M.H.Rhodes	14	24	2	111*	689	31.31	1	2	11
	A.L.Davies	13	24	1	121	649	28.21	1	3	14
	C.G.Benjamin	5	9	1	47	175	21.87	–	–	4
	L.C.Norwell	4	6	3	36*	63	21.00	–	–	–
	D.R.Mousley	4	7	1	43	110	18.33	–	–	6
	R.M.Yates	10	17	–	104	298	17.52	1	1	9
	C.N.Miles	7	8	2	32	103	17.16	–	–	4
	H.J.H.Brookes	9	12	1	55	183	16.63	–	1	2
2021	D.R.Briggs	13	20	2	65	297	16.50	–	1	3
	J.Yadav	2	4	–	29	54	13.50	–	–	1
2019	O.J.Hannon-Dalby	14	19	10	19*	81	9.00	–	–	4
	J.G.Bethell	3	4	–	6	13	3.25	–	–	4

Also batted (1 match each): G.A.Garrett 0, 10* (1 ct); R.N.Sidebottom 1, 2; M.Siraj 21*; B.T.J.Wheal 4, 1.

BOWLING

	O	M	R	W	Avge	Best	5wI	10wM
L.C.Norwell	116.5	30	358	22	16.27	9-62	2	1
J.Yadav	100.5	18	274	12	22.83	5-90	1	–
O.J.Hannon-Dalby	472.2	141	1256	53	23.69	6-40	3	–
N.J.McAndrew	203.3	30	757	20	37.85	4-85	–	–
D.R.Briggs	409.3	83	1319	31	42.54	4-31	–	–
H.J.H.Brookes	241.1	33	899	18	49.94	3-26	–	–
C.N.Miles	186.5	27	724	11	65.81	4-85	–	–

Also bowled:

M.Siraj	40	147	114	6	19.00	5-82	1	–
W.M.H.Rhodes	180	39	559	8	69.87	2-44	–	–

J.G.Bethell 32-2-136-0; M.G.K.Burgess 6.2-3-17-1; A.L.Davies 1-0-1-0; G.A.Garrett 21-5-78-1; S.R.Hain 0.1-0-4-0; M.J.Lamb 15-1-60-1; D.R.Mousley 5-0-35-0; R.N.Sidebottom 7-0-57-1; B.T.J.Wheal 28.4-1-137-2; R.M.Yates 29.1-5-100-2.

Warwickshire played no first-class fixtures outside the County Championship in 2022. The First-Class Averages (pp 221–234) give the records of Warwickshire players in all first-class county matches, with the exception of C.G.Benjamin, J.G.Bethell, R.N.Sidebottom, M.Siraj and B.T.J.Wheal, whose first-class figures for Warwickshire are as above.

WARWICKSHIRE RECORDS

FIRST-CLASS CRICKET

Highest Total	For 810-4d		v	Durham	Birmingham	1994
	V 887		by	Yorkshire	Birmingham	1896
Lowest Total	For 16		v	Kent	Tonbridge	1913
	V 15		by	Hampshire	Birmingham	1922
Highest Innings	For 501*	B.C.Lara	v	Durham	Birmingham	1994
	V 322	I.V.A.Richards	for	Somerset	Taunton	1985

Highest Partnership for each Wicket

1st	377*	N.F.Horner/K.Ibadulla	v	Surrey	The Oval	1960
2nd	465*	J.A.Jameson/R.B.Kanhai	v	Glos	Birmingham	1974
3rd	327	S.P.Kinneir/W.G.Quaife	v	Lancashire	Birmingham	1901
4th	470	A.I.Kallicharran/G.W.Humpage	v	Lancashire	Southport	1982
5th	335	J.O.Troughton/T.R.Ambrose	v	Hampshire	Birmingham	2009
6th	327	L.J.Evans/T.R.Ambrose	v	Sussex	Birmingham	2015
7th	289*	I.R.Bell/T.Frost	v	Sussex	Horsham	2004
8th	228	A.J.W.Croom/R.E.S.Wyatt	v	Worcs	Dudley	1925
9th	233	I.J.L.Trott/J.S.Patel	v	Yorkshire	Birmingham	2009
10th	214	N.V.Knight/A.Richardson	v	Hampshire	Birmingham	2002

Best Bowling	For	10-41	J.D.Bannister	v	Comb Servs	Birmingham	1959
(Innings)	V	10-36	H.Verity	for	Yorkshire	Leeds	1931
Best Bowling	For	15-76	S.Hargreave	v	Surrey	The Oval	1903
(Match)	V	17-92	A.P.Freeman	for	Kent	Folkestone	1932

Most Runs – Season	2417	M.J.K.Smith	(av 60.42)		1959
Most Runs – Career	35146	D.L.Amiss	(av 41.64)		1960-87
Most 100s – Season	9	A.I.Kallicharran			1984
	9	B.C.Lara			1994
Most 100s – Career	78	D.L.Amiss			1960-87
Most Wkts – Season	180	W.E.Hollies	(av 15.13)		1946
Most Wkts – Career	2201	W.E.Hollies	(av 20.45)		1932-57
Most Career W-K Dismissals	800	E.J.Smith	(662 ct; 138 st)		1904-30
Most Career Catches in the Field	422	M.J.K.Smith			1956-75

LIMITED-OVERS CRICKET

Highest Total	50ov	392-5		v	Oxfordshire	Birmingham	1984
	40ov	321-7		v	Leics	Birmingham	2010
	T20	261-2		v	Notts	Nottingham	2022
Lowest Total	50ov	94		v	Glos	Bristol	2000
	40ov	59		v	Yorkshire	Leeds	2001
	T20	63		v	Notts	Birmingham	2021
Highest Innings	50ov	206	A.I.Kallicharran	v	Oxfordshire	Birmingham	1984
	40ov	137	I.R.Bell	v	Yorkshire	Birmingham	2005
	T20	158*	B.B.McCullum	v	Derbyshire	Birmingham	2015
Best Bowling	50ov	7-32	R.G.D.Willis	v	Yorkshire	Birmingham	1981
	40ov	6-15	A.A.Donald	v	Yorkshire	Birmingham	1995
	T20	5-19	N.M.Carter	v	Worcs	Birmingham	2005

WORCESTERSHIRE

Formation of Present Club: 11 March 1865
Inaugural First-Class Match: 1899
Colours: Dark Green and Black
Badge: Shield Argent a Fess between three Pears Sable
County Championships: (5) 1964, 1965, 1974, 1988, 1989
NatWest Trophy Winners: (1) 1994
Benson and Hedges Cup Winners: (1) 1991
Pro 40/National League (Div 1) Winners: (1) 2007
Sunday League Winners: (3) 1971, 1987, 1988
Twenty20 Cup Winners: (1) 2018

Chief Executive: tba, County Ground, New Road, Worcester, WR2 4QQ ● Tel: 01905 748474 Email: info@wccc.co.uk ● Web: www.wccc.co.uk ● Twitter: @WorcsCCC (87,624 followers)

Head Coach: Alan Richardson. **Assistant Head Coach**: Kadeer Ali. **Captains**: B.L.D'Oliveira (f-c and T20) and J.D.Libby (50 ov). **Vice Captains**: J.D.Libby (f-c) and J.A.Haynes (white ball). **Overseas Players**: Azhar Ali, M.G.Bracewell and M.J.Santner (both T20 only). **2023 Testimonial**: O.B.Cox. **Head Groundsman**: tba. **Scorer**: Sue Drinkwater. **Vitality Blast Name**: Worcestershire Rapids. ‡ New registration. ᴺQ Not qualified for England.

Worcestershire revised their capping policy in 2002 and now award players with their County Colours when they make their Championship debut.

ᴺQ**AZHAR ALI**, b Lahore, Pakistan 19 Feb 1985. RHB, LB. Squad No 79. Lahore Blues 2001-02. KRL 2002-03 to 2011-12. Lahore 2003-04. Punjab 2008-09 to 2010-11. SNGPL 2012-13 to 2018-19. Somerset 2018-21; cap 2019. Central Punjab 2019-20 to date. Worcestershire debut/cap 2022. Tests (P): 97 (2010 to 2021-22, 9 as captain); 1000 runs (1): 1198 (2016); HS 302* v WI (Dubai, DSC) 2016-17; BB 2-35 v SL (Pallekele) 2015. **LOI** (P): 53 (2011 to 2017-18, 31 as captain); HS 102 v Z (Lahore) 2015; BB 2-26 v E (Dubai, DSC) 2015-16. F-c Tours (P)(C=Captain): E 2010, 2016, 2018, 2020C; A 2009 (PA), 2016-17, 2019-20C; SA 2012-13, 2018-19; WI 2011, 2016-17, 2021; NZ 2010-11, 2016-17, 2020-21; SL 2009 (PA), 2012, 2014, 2015, 2022; Z 2011, 2013, 2021; B 2011-12, 2014-15, 2021-22; Ire 2018. HS 302* (*see Tests*). CC HS 225 v Leics (Worcester) 2022. BB 4-34 KRL v Peshawar (Peshawar) 2002-03. CC BB 1-5 Sm v Essex (Taunton) 2018. Wo BB 1-12 v Leics (Leicester) 2022. LO HS 132* SNGPL v Lahore Blues (Islamabad) 2015-16. LO BB 5-23 Lahore Whites v Peshawar (Karachi) 2001 – on debut. T20 HS 72. T20 BB 3-10.

BAKER, Josh Oliver (Warkwood Middle S; Malvern C), b Redditch 16 May 2003. 6'3". RHB, SLA. Squad No 33. Debut (Worcestershire) 2021. HS 61* v Middx (Lord's) 2021. BB 4-51 v Leics (Leicester) 2022. LO HS 25 v Durham (Worcester) 2021 (RLC). LO BB 2-53 v Sussex (Worcester) 2021 (RLC). T20 HS 5. T20 BB 2-26.

‡ᴺQ**BRACEWELL, Michael** Gordon, b Masterton, New Zealand 14 Feb 1991. Son of M.A.Bracewell (Otago 1977-78); nephew of B.P.Bracewell (C Districts, Otago, N Distsricts & New Zealand 1977-78 to 1989-90), D.W.Bracewell (Canterbury & C Districts 1974-75 to 1979-80) and J.G.Bracewell (Otago, Auckland & New Zealand 1978-79 to 1989-90); cousin of D.A.J.Bracewell (C Districts, Northamptonshire & New Zealand 2008-09 to date). LHB, OB. Squad No 4. Otago 2010-11 to 2016-17. Wellington 2017-18 to date. Joins Worcestershire in 2023 for T20 only. Tests (NZ): 6 (2022 to 2022-23); HS 74* and BB 4-75 v P (Karachi) 2022-23. **LOI** (NZ): 19 (2021-22 to 2022); HS 140 v I (Hyderabad) 2022-23; BB 3-21 v Neth (Hamilton) 2021-22. **IT20** (NZ): 16 (2022 to 2022-23); HS 61* v Scot (Edinburgh) 2022; BB 3-5 v Ire (Belfast) 2022. F-c Tours (NZ): E 2014 (NZA), 2022; P 2022-23. HS 190 Otago v Wellington (Dunedin) 2012-13. BB 5-43 Wellington v Auckland (Auckland) 2019-20. LO HS 140 (*see LOI*). LO BB 3-21 (*see LOI*). T20 HS 141*. T20 BB 4-28.

BROWN, Patrick Rhys (Bourne GS, Lincs), b Peterborough, Cambs 23 Aug 1998. 6'2". RHB, RMF. Squad No 36. Debut (Worcestershire) 2017. Birmingham Phoenix 2021. Oval Invincibles 2022. Worcestershire 2nd XI debut 2016. Lincolnshire 2016. **IT20:** 4 (2019-20); HS 4* v NZ (Wellington) 2019-20; BB 1-29 v NZ (Napier) 2019-20. HS 5* v Sussex (Worcester) 2017. LO BB 2-15 v Leics (Worcester) 2017. LO HS 3 v Somerset (Worcester) 2019 (RLC). LO BB 3-53 v Kent (Worcester) 2018 (RLC). T20 HS 9*. T20 BB 4-21.

CORNALL, Taylor Ryan, b Lytham St Anne's, Lancs 9 Oct 1998. 6'0". LHB. Squad No 57. Leeds/Bradford MCCU 2019. Worcestershire debut 2022. Lancashire 2021 (l-o only). Lancashire 2nd XI 2018-21. Kent 2nd XI 2021. Worcestershire 2nd XI debut 2021. HS 31* v Middx (Northwood) 2022. LO HS 97 v Essex (Worcester) 2022 (RLC). LO BB 2-23 v Derbys (Worcester) 2022 (RLC).

COX, Oliver Ben (Bromsgrove S), b Wordsley, Stourbridge 2 Feb 1992. 5'10". RHB, WK. Squad No 10. Debut (Worcestershire) 2009; testimonial 2023. MCC 2017, 2019. HS 124 v Glos (Cheltenham) 2017. LO HS 122* v Kent (Worcester) 2018 (RLC). T20 HS 61*.

COX, Oliver Hugo ('**Olly**') (Malvern C), b Peterborough, Canada 21 Nov 2003. 5'8". RHB, OB. Squad No 14. Worcestershire 2nd XI debut 2022. Herefordshire 2022. Awaiting 1st XI debut.

CULLEN, Henry James (St Benedict's HS, Alcester; St Augustine's SFC, Redditch), b Redditch 29 Apr 2003. RHB, WK. Squad No 13. Awaiting f-c debut. Worcestershire 2nd XI debut 2021. Herefordshire 2021-22. LO HS 8 v Derbys (Worcester) 2022 (RLC).

DAVIDSON, Oliver Forbes (Bromsgrove S), b Edinburgh, Scotland 28 Jul 2004. Younger brother of J.J.Davidson (Herefordshire 2022). LHB, SLA. Awaiting f-c debut. Worcestershire 2nd XI debut 2022. Herefordshire 2022. **LOI** (Scot): 1 (2022); HS 14 v UAE (Pearland) 2022; BB – . LO HS 14 (*see LOI*). LO BB – .

D'OLIVEIRA, Brett Louis (Worcester SFC), b Worcester 28 Feb 1992. Son of D.B.D'Oliveira (Worcs 1982-95), grandson of B.L.D'Oliveira (Worcs, EP and England 1964-80). 5'9". RHB, LB. Squad No 15. Debut (Worcestershire) 2012; captain 2022 to date. MCC 2018. Birmingham Phoenix 2022. HS 202* v Glamorgan (Cardiff) 2016. BB 7-92 v Glamorgan (Cardiff) 2019. LO HS 123 and LO BB 3-8 v Essex (Chelmsford) 2021 (RLC). T20 HS 71. T20 BB 4-20.

EDAVALATH, Rehaan Mahamood (Newcastle-under-Lyme S; Malvern C), b Wolverhampton, Staffs 4 Mar 2004. 5'9". RHB, OB. Squad No 11. Worcestershire 2nd XI debut 2021. Awaiting 1st XI debut.

EVITTS, Reeve Lee (John Taylor HS), b Lichfield, Staffs 22 Jan 2005. RHB, RMF. Awaiting f-c debut. Worcestershire 2nd XI debut 2021. LO HS 10 v Lancs (Manchester) 2022 (RLC) - only 1st XI appearance. LO BB – .

FINCH, Adam William (Kingswinford S; Oldswinford Hospital SFC), b Wordsley, Stourbridge 28 May 2000. 6'4". RHB, RMF. Squad No 61. Debut (Worcestershire) 2019. Surrey 2020 (on loan). Worcestershire 2nd XI debut 2017. England U19 2018 to 2018-19. HS 33 and Wo BB 3-59 v Notts (Nottingham) 2022. BB 4-38 Sy v Essex (Chelmsford) 2020. LO HS 24 and LO BB 3-54 v Derbys (Worcester) 2022 (RLC). T20 HS 6. T20 BB 3-38.

GIBBON, Benjamin James, b Chester 9 Jun 2000. 6'3". RHB, LMF. Squad No 21. Lancashire 2nd XI 2019-21. Debut (Worcestershire) 2022. Worcestershire 2nd XI debut 2021. Cheshire 2019-21. HS 20 v Notts (Worcester) 2022. BB 4-87 v Glamorgan (Cardiff) 2022. LO HS 11 v Derbys (Worcester) 2022 (RLC). LO BB 2-33 v Hants (Southampton) 2022 (RLC).

HAYNES, Jack Alexander (Malvern C), b Worcester 30 Jan 2001. Son of G.R.Haynes (Worcestershire 1991-99); younger brother of J.L.Haynes (Worcestershire 2nd XI 2015-16). 6'1". RHB, OB. Squad No 17. Debut (Worcestershire) 2019. Oval Invincibles 2022. Worcestershire 2nd XI debut 2016. England U19 2018. HS 133 v Derbys (Derby) 2021. LO HS 153 v Essex (Chelmsford) 2021 (RLC). T20 HS 61.

‡**HOSE, Adam** John (Carisbrooke S), b Newport, IoW 25 Oct 1992. 6'2". RHB, RMF. Squad No 54. Somerset 2016-17. Warwickshire 2018-19. Big Bash: AS 2022-23. Northern Superchargers 2022. HS 111 Wa v Notts (Birmingham) 2019. LO HS 101* Sm v Glos (Bristol) 2017 (RLC). T20 HS 119.

KASHIF ALI (Dunstable C), b Kashmir, Pakistan 7 Feb 1998. 5'8". RHB, LB. Squad No 27. Debut (Worcestershire) 2022. Bedfordshire 2021. HS 52 v Derbys (Worcester) 2022. BB –. LO HS 114 v Kent (Worcester) 2022 (RLC) – on debut. T20 HS 46*. T20 BB –.

LEACH, Joseph (Shrewsbury S; Leeds U), b Stafford 30 Oct 1990. Elder brother of S.G.Leach (Oxford MCCU 2014-16). 6'1". RHB, RMF. Squad No 23. Leeds/Bradford MCCU 2012. Worcestershire debut 2012; captain 2017-21. Staffordshire 2008-09. HS 114 v Glos (Cheltenham) 2013. 50 wkts (3); most – 69 (2017). BB 6-44 v Glamorgan (Worcester) 2022. LO HS 88 v Kent (Worcester) 2021 (RLC). LO BB 4-30 v Northants (Worcester) 2015 (RLC). T20 HS 24. T20 BB 5-33.

LIBBY, Jacob ('**Jake**') Daniel (Plymouth C; UWIC), b Plymouth, Devon 3 Jan 1993. 5'9". RHB, OB. Squad No 2. Cardiff MCCU 2014. Nottinghamshire 2014-19, scoring 108 v Sussex (Nottingham) on debut. Northamptonshire 2016 (on loan). Worcestershire debut 2020. Cornwall 2011-14. 1000 runs (1): 1104 (2021). HS 215 v Sussex (Hove) 2022. BB 2-10 v Middx (Worcester) 2022. LO HS 126* v Derbys (Worcester) 2022 (RLC). LO BB 2-47 v Lancs (Manchester) 2022 (RLC). T20 HS 78*. T20 BB 1-11.

MORRIS, Charles Andrew John (King's C, Taunton; Oxford Brookes U), b Hereford 6 Jul 1992. 6'0". RHB, RMF. Squad No 31. Oxford MCCU 2012-14. Worcestershire debut 2013. MCC Univs 2012. Devon 2011-12. HS 53* v Australians (Worcester) 2019. CC HS 50 v Leics (Worcester) 2021. 50 wkts (2); most – 56 (2014). BB 7-45 v Leics (Leicester) 2019. LO HS 25* v Durham (Worcester) 2021 (RLC). LO BB 4-33 v Durham (Gosforth) 2018 (RLC). T20 HS 7*. T20 BB 3-21.

PENNINGTON, Dillon Young (Wrekin C), b Shrewsbury, Shrops 26 Feb 1999. 6'2". RHB, RMF. Squad No 22. Debut (Worcestershire) 2018. Birmingham Phoenix 2021. Worcestershire 2nd XI debut 2017. Shropshire 2017. HS 56 v Essex (Chelmsford) 2021. BB 5-32 v Derbys (Worcester) 2021. LO HS 35 v Derbys (Worcester) 2022 (RLC). LO BB 5-67 v West Indies A (Worcester) 2018. T20 HS 10*. T20 BB 4-9.

POLLOCK, Edward John (RGS Worcester; Shrewsbury S; Collingwood C, Durham U), b High Wycombe, Bucks 10 Jul 1995. Son of A.J.Pollock (Cambridge U 1982-84); younger brother of A.W.Pollock (Cambridge MCCU & U 2013-15). 5'10". LHB, OB. Squad No 7. Durham MCCU 2015-17. Worcestershire debut 2018. Warwickshire 2017-21 (white-ball only). Herefordshire 2014-16. HS 113 v Middx (Northwood) 2022. LO HS 103* Wa v Derbys (Derby) 2021 (RLC). T20 HS 77.

RODERICK, Gareth Hugh (Maritzburg C), b Durban, South Africa 29 Aug 1991. 6'0". RHB, WK. Squad No 9. UK passport, qualifying for England in October 2018. KZN 2010-11 to 2011-12. Gloucestershire 2013-20; cap 2013; captain 2016-17. Worcestershire debut 2021. HS 172* v Glamorgan (Cardiff) 2022. LO HS 104 Gs v Leics (Leicester) 2015 (RLC). T20 HS 32.

NQ**SANTNER, Mitchell** Josef, b Hamilton, New Zealand 5 Feb 1992. LHB, SLA. Squad No 74. N Districts 2011-12 to date. Worcestershire debut 2016. IPL: CSK 2019 to date. **Tests** (NZ): 24 (2015-16 to 2021); HS 126 and BB 3-53 v E (Mt Maunganui) 2019-20. **LOI** (NZ): 93 (2015 to 2019-20); HS 67 v E (Christchurch) 2017-18; BB 5-50 v Ire (Dublin) 2017. **IT20** (NZ): 83 (2015 to 2019-20); HS 77* v Neth (Hague) 2022; BB 4-11 v I (Nagpur) 2015-16. F-c Tours (NZ): E 2015, 2021; A 2015-16, 2019-20; SA 2016; I 2016-17; SL 2019; Z 2016. HS 136 and BB 5-51 ND v CD (Mt Maunganui) 2022-23. CC HS 23* v Glamorgan (Cardiff) 2016. LO HS 86 ND v CD (New Plymouth) 2014-15. LO BB 5-50 (*see LOI*). T20 HS 92*. T20 BB 4-11.

STANLEY, Mitchell Terry (Idsall S, Shifnal; Shrewsbury SFC), b Telford, Shrops 17 Mar 2001. 6'2". RHB, RFM. Squad No 38. Awaiting f-c debut. Manchester Originals 2022. Worcestershire 2nd XI debut 2021. Shropshire 2021. T20 HS 7. T20 BB 2-24.

TONGUE, Joshua Charles (King's S, Worcester; Worcester SFC), b Redditch 15 Nov 1997. 6'5". RHB, RM. Squad No 24. Debut (Worcestershire) 2016. HS 45* v Notts (Worcester) 2022. BB 6-97 v Glamorgan (Worcester) 2017. LO HS 34 v Warwks (Worcester) 2019 (RLC). LO BB 2-35 v Lancs (Manchester) 2019 (RLC). T20 HS 2*. T20 BB 2-32.

WAITE, Matthew James (Brigshaw HS), b Leeds 24 Dec 1995. 6'0". RHB, RFM. Squad No 6. Yorkshire 2017-22. Worcestershire debut 2022. HS 59* Y v Surrey (Scarborough) 2022. Wo HS 16 v Middx (Worcester) 2022. BB 5-16 Y v Leeds/Brad MCCU (Leeds) 2019. CC BB 4-35 v Leics (Worcester) 2022. LO HS 71 Y v Warwks (Birmingham) 2017 (RLC). LO BB 5-59 Y v Leics (Leicester) 2021 (RLC). T20 HS 35*. T20 BB 3-18.

RELEASED/RETIRED

(Having made a County 1st XI appearance in 2022)

ALI, M.M. – *see WARWICKSHIRE.*

BANTON, Jacques (Bromsgrove S; King's C, Taunton), b Perpignan, France 6 Jul 2001. Son of C.Banton (Nottinghamshire 1995); younger brother of T. Banton (*see SOMERSET*). 5'10". RHB, SLA. Worcestershire 2nd XI debut 2019. Awaiting f-c debut. LO HS 33 and LO BB 3-15 v Sussex (Worcester) 2021 (RLC). T20 HS 0. T20 BB 1-6.

BARNARD, E.G. – *see WARWICKSHIRE.*

NO**BRAVO, Dwayne** John, b Santa Cruz, Trinidad 7 Oct 1983. Older half-brother of D.M.Bravo (Trinidad & Tobago, Nottinghamshire and WI 2006-07 to date). RHB, RMF. Trinidad & Tobago 2001-02 to 2012-13. Kent 2006. Surrey 2016 (T20 only). Middlesex 2018 (T20 only). Worcestershire 2022 (T20 only). IPL: MI 2007-08 to 2009-10; CSK 2011 to date; GL 2016. Big Bash: SS 2011-12; MR 2013-14 to 2017-18; MS 2018-19. Northern Superchargers 2022. **Tests** (WI): 40 (2004 to 2010-11, 1 as captain): HS 113 v A (Hobart) 2005-06; BB 6-55 v E (Manchester) 2004. **LOI** (WI): 164 (2004 to 2014-15, 37 as captain): HS 112* v E (Ahmedabad) 2006-07; BB 6-43 v Z (St George's) 2012-13. **IT20** (WI): 91 (2005-06 to 2021-22, 6 as captain): HS 66* v I (Lord's) 2009; BB 4-19 v SA (St George's) 2021. F-c Tours (WI): E 2002 (WI A), 2004, 2007; A 2005-06, 2009-10; SA 2007-08; NZ 2005-06; P 2006-07; SL 2010-11. HS 197 T&T v West Indies B (Couva) 2003-04. CC HS 76 K v Lancs (Canterbury) 2006. BB 6-11 T&T v Windward Is (St George's) 2002-03. CC BB 6-112 K v Notts (Nottingham) 2006. LO HS 112* (*see LOI*). LO BB 6-43 (*see LOI*). T20 HS 70*. T20 BB 5-23.

FELL, Thomas Charles (Oakham S; Oxford Brookes U), b Hillingdon, Middx 17 Oct 1993. 6'1". RHB, WK, occ OB. Oxford MCCU 2013. Worcestershire 2013-22. 1000 runs (1): 1127 (2015). HS 171 v Middx (Worcester) 2015. LO HS 116* v Lancs (Worcester) 2016 (RLC). T20 HS 28.

NO**MOHAMMAD HASNAIN**, b Hyderabad, Pakistan 5 Apr 2000. RHB, RF. Pakistan Television 2018-19. Sindh 2021-22. Worcestershire 2022. Big Bash: ST 2021-22. Oval Invincibles 2022. **LOI** (P): 9 (2018-19 to 2022-23); HS 28 v E (Leeds) 2019; BB 5-26 v Z (Rawalpindi) 2020-21. **IT20** (P): 27 (2019 to 2022-23); HS 8* v SL (Dubai, DSC) 2022; BB 3-37 v SL (Lahore) 2019-20. HS 5 Sindh v Khyber Pakh (Faisalabad) 2021-22. Wo HS 2 and Wo BB 2-35 v Derbys (Worcester) 2022. BB 2-32 Pak TV v Multan (Multan) 2018-19. LO HS 28 (*see LOI*). LO BB 6-19 P U23s v Sri Lanka U23s (Cox's Bazar) 2019-20. T20 HS 22. T20 BB 4-25.

MUNRO, C. – *see NOTTINGHAMSHIRE.*

J.J.Dell left the staff without making a County 1st XI appearance in 2022.

WORCESTERSHIRE 2022

RESULTS SUMMARY

	Place	Won	Lost	Drew	NR
LV= Insurance County Champ (Div 2)	4th	4	3	7	
Royal London One-Day Cup (Group B)	9th	2	6		
Vitality Blast (North Group)	9th	2	11		1

LV= INSURANCE COUNTY CHAMPIONSHIP AVERAGES
BATTING AND FIELDING

Cap†		M	I	NO	HS	Runs	Avge	100	50	Ct/St
2021	G.H.Roderick	8	9	3	172*	447	74.50	2	1	31/1
2015	E.G.Barnard	14	18	3	163*	895	59.66	3	5	7
2012	B.L.D'Oliveira	13	18	5	169*	768	59.07	3	2	6
2019	J.A.Haynes	13	19	2	133	811	47.70	3	1	13
2022	Azhar Ali	11	16	–	225	656	41.00	1	3	4
2019	A.W.Finch	3	4	2	33	82	41.00	–	–	1
2020	J.D.Libby	14	21	1	215	688	34.40	2	1	2
2022	E.J.Pollock	13	20	–	113	645	32.25	2	3	12
2012	J.Leach	8	9	–	87	266	29.55	–	3	3
2009	O.B.Cox	7	9	2	55	167	23.85	–	2	22/1
2021	J.O.Baker	10	12	1	43	178	16.18	–	–	8
2022	T.R.Cornall	5	7	1	31*	89	14.83	–	–	2
2018	D.Y.Pennington	12	13	2	44	132	12.00	–	–	3
2022	B.J.Gibbon	7	6	2	20	37	9.25	–	–	1
2014	C.A.J.Morris	8	9	–	29	72	8.00	–	–	3

Also batted: T.C.Fell (1 match – cap 2013) 17 (2 ct); Kashif Ali (1 – cap 2022) 52, 6; Mohammad Hasnain (1 – cap 2022) 1, 2; J.C.Tongue (3 – cap 2017) 45*, 39*; M.J.Waite (3 – cap 2022) 13*, 5, 16 (2 ct).

BOWLING

	O	M	R	W	Avge	Best	5wI	10wM
M.J.Waite	64.2	19	222	12	18.50	4-35	–	–
J.Leach	238.3	58	767	34	22.55	6-44	1	–
D.Y.Pennington	322.2	59	996	44	22.63	4-31	–	–
C.A.J.Morris	212.5	53	642	21	30.57	2-10	–	–
B.J.Gibbon	184	30	713	20	35.65	4-87	–	–
E.G.Barnard	357.2	65	1235	31	39.83	4-26	–	–
J.O.Baker	298	46	1026	23	44.60	4-51	–	–

Also bowled:
J.C.Tongue	65	12	216	5	43.20	2-29		
A.W.Finch	70.2	6	343	5	68.60	3-59		

Azhar Ali 10-0-42-1; T.R.Cornall 1-0-4-0; B.L.D'Oliveira 75-8-262-3; Kashif Ali 2-0-16-0 J.D.Libby 22.3-5-56-2; Mohammad Hasnain 26.1-3-98-2.

Worcestershire played no first-class fixtures outside the County Championship in 2022. The First-Class Averages (pp 221–234) give the records of Worcestershire players in all first-class county matches, with the exception of M.J.Waite whose first-class figures for Worcestershire are as above.

† Worcestershire revised their capping policy in 2002 and now award players with their County Colours when they make their Championship debut.

WORCESTERSHIRE RECORDS

FIRST-CLASS CRICKET

Highest Total	For	701-6d		v	Surrey	Worcester	2007
	V	701-4d		by	Leics	Worcester	1906
Lowest Total	For	24		v	Yorkshire	Huddersfield	1903
	V	30		by	Hampshire	Worcester	1903
Highest Innings	For	405*	G.A.Hick	v	Somerset	Taunton	1988
	V	331*	J.D.B.Robertson	for	Middlesex	Worcester	1949

Highest Partnership for each Wicket

1st	309	H.K.Foster/F.L.Bowley	v	Derbyshire	Derby	1901
2nd	316	S.C.Moore/V.S.Solanki	v	Glos	Cheltenham	2005
3rd	438*	G.A.Hick/T.M.Moody	v	Hampshire	Southampton[1]	1997
4th	330	B.F.Smith/G.A.Hick	v	Somerset	Taunton	2006
5th	393	E.G.Arnold/W.B.Burns	v	Warwicks	Birmingham	1909
6th	265	G.A.Hick/S.J.Rhodes	v	Somerset	Taunton	1988
7th	256	D.A.Leatherdale/S.J.Rhodes	v	Notts	Nottingham	2002
8th	184	S.J.Rhodes/S.R.Lampitt	v	Derbyshire	Kidderminster	1991
9th	181	J.A.Cuffe/R.D.Burrows	v	Glos	Worcester	1907
10th	136	A.G.Milton/S.J.Magoffin	v	Somerset	Worcester	2018

Best Bowling	For	9- 23	C.F.Root	v	Lancashire	Worcester	1931
(Innings)	V	10- 51	J.Mercer	for	Glamorgan	Worcester	1936
Best Bowling	For	15- 87	A.J.Conway	v	Glos	Moreton-in-M	1914
(Match)	V	17-212	J.C.Clay	for	Glamorgan	Swansea	1937

Most Runs – Season	2654	H.H.I.H.Gibbons	(av 52.03)	1934
Most Runs – Career	34490	D.Kenyon	(av 34.18)	1946-67
Most 100s – Season	10	G.M.Turner		1970
	10	G.A.Hick		1988
Most 100s – Career	106	G.A.Hick		1984-2008
Most Wkts – Season	207	C.F.Root	(av 17.52)	1925
Most Wkts – Career	2143	R.T.D.Perks	(av 23.73)	1930-55
Most Career W-K Dismissals	1095	S.J.Rhodes	(991 ct; 104 st)	1985-2004
Most Career Catches in the Field	528	G.A.Hick		1984-2008

LIMITED-OVERS CRICKET

Highest Total	50ov	404-3		v	Devon	Worcester	1987
	40ov	376-6		v	Surrey	The Oval	2010
	T20	227-6		v	Northants	Kidderminster	2007
Lowest Total	50ov	58		v	Ireland	Worcester	2009
	40ov	86		v	Yorkshire	Leeds	1969
	T20	53		v	Lancashire	Manchester	2016
Highest Innings	50ov	192	C.J.Ferguson	v	Leics	Worcester	2018
	40ov	160	T.M.Moody	v	Kent	Worcester	1991
	T20	127	T.Kohler-Cadmore	v	Durham	Worcester	2016
Best Bowling	50ov	7-19	N.V.Radford	v	Beds	Bedford	1991
	40ov	6-16	Shoaib Akhtar	v	Glos	Worcester	2005
	T20	5-24	A.Hepburn	v	Notts	Worcester	2017

YORKSHIRE

Formation of Present Club: 8 January 1863
Substantial Reorganisation: 10 December 1891
Inaugural First-Class Match: 1864
Colours: Dark Blue, Light Blue and Gold
Badge: White Rose
County Championships (since 1890): (32) 1893, 1896, 1898, 1900, 1901, 1902, 1905, 1908, 1912, 1919, 1922, 1923, 1924, 1925, 1931, 1932, 1933, 1935, 1937, 1938, 1939, 1946, 1959, 1960, 1962, 1963, 1966, 1967, 1968, 2001, 2014, 2015
Joint Champions: (1) 1949
Gillette/C&G Trophy Winners: (3) 1965, 1969, 2002
Benson and Hedges Cup Winners: (1) 1987
Sunday League Winners: (1) 1983
Twenty20 Cup Winners: (0); best – Finalist 2012

Acting Chief Executive: Stephen Vaughan, Headingley Pavilion, Kirkstall Lane, Headingley, Leeds, LS6 3DP ● Tel: 0344 504 3099 ● Email: cricket@yorkshireccc.com ● Web: www.yorkshireccc.com ● Twitter: @Yorkshireccc (160,767 followers)

MD Cricket: Darren Gough. **Head Coach**: Ottis Gibson. **Assistant Coaches**: Kabir Ali and Alastair Maiden. **Captain**: Shan Masood. **Overseas Players**: Shan Masood, N.Wagner and D.Wiese (T20 only). **2023 Testimonial**: J.M.Bairstow. **Head Groundsman**: Richard Robinson. **Scorers**: John Potter and John Virr. **Vitality Blast Name**: Yorkshire Vikings. ‡ New registration. NQ Not qualified for England.

BAIRSTOW, Jonathan Marc (St Peter's S, York; Leeds Met U), b Bradford 26 Sep 1989. Son of D.L.Bairstow (Yorkshire, GW and England 1970-90); brother of A.D.Bairstow (Derbyshire 1995). 6'0". RHB, WK, occ RM. Squad No 21. Debut (Yorkshire) 2009; cap 2011; testimonial 2023. IPL: SH 2019-21; PK 2022. Welsh Fire 2021. Inaugural winner of Young Wisden Schools Cricketer of the Year 2008. YC 2011. PCA 2022. **ECB Central Contract 2022-23. Tests**: 89 (2012 to 2022); 1000 runs (2); most – 1470 (2016); HS 167* v SL (Lord's) 2016. Took a world record 70 dismissals in 2016, as well as scoring a record number of runs in a calendar year for a keeper. **LOI**: 95 (2011 to 2022); 1000 runs (1): 1025 (2018); HS 141* v WI (Southampton) 2017. **IT20**: 66 (2011 to 2022); HS 90 v SA (Bristol) 2022. F-c Tours: A 2013-14, 2017-18, 2021-22; SA 2014-15 (EL), 2015-16, 2019-20; WI 2010-11 (EL), 2018-19, WI 2021-22; NZ 2017-18; I 2012-13, 2016-17, 2020-21; SL 2013-14 (EL), 2018-19, 2020-21; B 2016-17; UAE 2015-16 (v P). 1000 runs (3); most – 1286 (2016). HS 246 v Hants (Leeds) 2016. LO HS 174 v Durham (Leeds) 2017 (RLC). T20 HS 114.

BEAN, Finlay Joseph (Q Ethelburga's C), b Harrogate 16 Apr 2002. LHB, WK. Squad No 33. Debut (Yorkshire) 2022. Yorkshire 2nd XI Debut 2019. Warwickshire 2nd XI 2022. HS 53 v Essex (Leeds) 2022. LO HS 61 v Kent (Canterbury) 2022 (RLC).

BESS, Dominic Mark (Blundell's S), b Exeter, Devon 22 Jul 1997. Cousin of Z.G.G.Bess (Devon 2015 to date), J.J.Bess (Devon 2007-18) and L.F.O.Bess (Devon 2017 to date). 5'11". RHB, OB. Squad No 47. Somerset 2016-19. Yorkshire debut 2019 (on loan); cap 2021. MCC 2018, 2019. Devon 2015-16. **Tests**: 14 (2018 to 2020-21); HS 57 v P (Lord's) 2018; BB 5-30 v SL (Galle) 2020-21. F-c Tours: A 2019-20 (EL), 2021-22 (EL); SA 2019-20; WI 2017-18 (EL); I 2018-19 (EL), 2020-21; SL 2019-20, 2020-21. HS 107 MCC v Essex (Bridgetown) 2018. CC HS 92 Sm v Hants (Taunton) 2018. Y HS 91* v Essex (Leeds) 2019. BB 7-43 v Northants (Northampton) 2021. LO HS 27* v Hants (Scarborough) 2022 (RLC). LO BB 3-35 EL v Pakistan A (Abu Dhabi) 2018-19. T20 HS 24. T20 BB 3-15.

BROOK, Harry Cherrington (Sedbergh S), b Keighley 22 Feb 1999. 5'11''. RHB, RM. Squad No 88. Debut (Yorkshire) 2016. Big Bash: HH 2021-22. Northern Superchargers 2021. Yorkshire 2nd XI debut 2015. England U19 2016-17 to 2017. YC 2021. **ECB Increment Contract 2022-23. Tests**: 6 (2022 to 2022-23); HS 186 and BB 1-25 v NZ (Wellington) 2022-23. **LOI**: 3 (2022-23); HS 80 v SA (Bloemfontein) 2022-23. **IT20**: 20 (2021-22 to 2022-23); HS 81* v P (Karachi) 2022-23. F-c Tours: A 2021-22 (EL); NZ 2022-23; P 2022-23. HS 194 v Kent (Leeds) 2022. BB 3-15 v Glamorgan (Cardiff) 2021. LO HS 103 v Leics (Leeds) 2019 (RLC). T20 HS 102*. T20 BB 1-13.

CHOHAN, Jafer Ali (Harrow S; Loughborough U), b Camden, Middx 11 Jul 2002. RHB, LB. Squad No 5. Berkshire 2022. Awaiting 1st XI debut.

CLIFF, Benjamin Michael (Brighouse HS; Huddersfield New C), b Halifax 23 Oct 2002. RHB, RFM. Squad No 26. Awaiting f-c debut. Yorkshire 2nd XI debut 2021. England U19 2022. LO HS –. LO BB 1-44 v Northants (York) 2022 (RLC) – only 1st XI appearance.

COAD, Benjamin Oliver (Thirsk S & SFC), b Harrogate 10 Jan 1994. 6'2''. RHB, RM. Squad No 10. Debut (Yorkshire) 2016; cap 2018. HS 69 v Essex (Leeds) 2022. 50 wkts (1): 53 (2017). BB 6-25 v Lancs (Leeds) 2017. LO HS 24 v Hants (Scarborough) 2022 (RLC). LO BB 4-63 v Derbys (Leeds) 2017 (RLC). T20 HS 7. T20 BB 3-40.

DUKE, Harry George (QEGS, Wakefield; Leeds U), b Wakefield 6 Sep 2001. 5'8''. RHB, WK, occ RM. Squad No 22. Debut (Yorkshire) 2021. Yorkshire 2nd XI debut 2019. HS 54 v Sussex (Leeds) 2021. LO HS 125 v Leics (Leicester) 2021 (RLC). T20 HS –.

‡NQ**EDWARDS, Michael** William (St Augustus C), b Manly, NSW, Australia 23 Dec 1994. 6'7''. RHB, RFM. UK passport through British-born parents. New South Wales 2017-18 to date. Sydney Sixers 2017-18 to 2021-22. Middlesex 2nd XI 2013. Kent 2nd XI 2022. HS 12 NSW v Vic (Melbourne, SK) 2022-23. BB 2-48 NSW v SA (Sydney) 2017-18. LO HS 11 NSW v SA (Sydney, HO) 2017-18. LO BB 4-31 NSW v Tas (Perth) 2017-18. T20 HS 0*. T20 BB 1-19.

FISHER, Matthew David (Easingwold SS), b York 9 Nov 1997. 6'1''. RHB, RFM. Squad No 7. Debut (Yorkshire) 2015; cap 2018. MCC 2018. **ECB Pace Bowling Development Contract 2022-23. Tests**: 1 (2021-22); HS 0* and BB 1-67 v WI (Bridgetown) 2021-22. F-c Tours: A 2021-22 (EL); WI 2021-22; SL 2022-23. HS 53 and BB 5-34 EL v Sri Lanka A (Galle) 2022-23. Y HS 47* v Kent (Leeds) 2019. Y BB 5-41 v Somerset (Scarborough) 2021. LO HS 36* v Worcs (Worcester) 2017 (RLC). LO BB 3-32 v Leics (Leeds) 2015 (RLC). T20 HS 19. T20 BB 5-22.

FRAINE, William Alan Richard (Silcoates S; Bromsgrove SFC; Durham U), b Huddersfield, Yorks 13 Jun 1996. 6'2''. RHB, RM. Squad No 31. Durham MCCU 2017-18. Nottinghamshire 2018. Yorkshire debut 2019. Northern Supercharges 2021. HS 106 v Surrey (Scarborough) 2019. LO HS 143 v Northants (York) 2022 (RLC). T20 HS 44*.

HILL, George Christopher Hindley (Sedbergh S), b Keighley 24 Jan 2001. 6'2½''. RHB, RMF. Squad No 18. Debut (Yorkshire) 2020. Yorkshire 2nd XI debut 2018. England U19 2018-19. HS 151* v Northants (Northampton) 2022. BB 6-26 v Lancs (Manchester) 2022. LO HS 130 v Worcs (Scarborough) 2022 (RLC). LO BB 3-47 v Warwks (York) 2021 (RLC). T20 HS 19*. T20 BB 1-9.

LEECH, Dominic James (Nunthorpe Ac; Q Ethelburga's S, York), b Middlesbrough 10 Jan 2001. 6'2½''. RHB, RMF. Squad No 8. Debut (Yorkshire) 2020. Yorkshire 2nd XI debut 2018. HS 1 v Notts (Nottingham) 2020. BB 2-72 v Derbys (Leeds) 2020. T20 HS 1*. T20 BB 3-13.

LUXTON, William Andrew (Bradford GS), b Keighley 6 May 2003. RHB, OB. Squad No 68. Yorkshire 2nd XI debut 2021. Debut (Yorkshire) 2022. HS 31 v Surrey (Scarborough) 2022. LO HS 84 v Northants (York) 2022 (RLC).

LYTH, Adam (Caedmon S, Whitby; Whitby Community C), b Whitby 25 Sep 1987. 5'8". LHB, RM. Squad No 9. Debut (Yorkshire) 2007; cap 2010; testimonial 2020-21. MCC 2017. Big Bash: PS 2022-23. Northern Superchargers 2021 to date. PCA 2014. *Wisden* 2014. **Tests**: 7 (2015); HS 107 v NZ (Leeds) 2015. F-c Tours (EL): SA 2014-15; WI 2010-11. 1000 runs (3); most – 1619 (2014). HS 251 v Lancs (Manchester) 2014. BB 2-9 v Middx (Scarborough) 2016. LO HS 144 v Lancs (Manchester) 2018 (RLC). LO BB 2-27 v Derbys (Leeds) 2019 (RLC). T20 HS 161 v Northants (Leeds) 2017 – Y & UK record; 6th highest score in all T20 cricket. T20 BB 5-31.

MALAN, Dawid Johannes (Paarl HS), b Roehampton, Surrey 3 Sep 1987. Son of D.J.Malan (WP B and Transvaal B 1978-79 to 1981-82), elder brother of C.C.Malan (Loughborough MCCU 2009-10). 6'0". LHB, LB. Squad No 29. Boland 2005-06. Middlesex 2008-19, scoring 132* v Northants (Uxbridge) on debut; cap 2010; T20 captain 2016-19; captain 2018-19. Yorkshire debut/cap 2020. MCC 2010-11, 2013. IPL: PK 2021. Big Bash: HH 2020-21. Trent Rockets 2021 to date. **ECB Increment Contract 2022-23**. **Tests**: 22 (2017 to 2021-22); HS 140 v A (Perth) 2017-18; BB 2-33 v A (Adelaide) 2021-22. **LOI**: 18 (2019 to 2022-23); HS 134 v A (Adelaide) 2022-23; BB 1-5 v Neth (Amstelveen) 2022. **IT20**: 56 (2017 to 2022-23); HS 103* v NZ (Napier) 2019-20; BB 1-27 v NZ (Hamilton) 2017-18. F-c Tours: A 2017-18, 2021-22; WI (EL). 1000 runs (3); most – 1137 runs (2014). HS 219 v Derbys (Leeds) 2020. BB 5-61 M v Lancs (Liverpool) 2012. Y BB 2-24 v Notts (Nottingham) 2020. LO HS 185* EL v Sri Lanka A (Northampton) 2016. LO BB 4-25 PDSC v Partex (Savar) 2014-15. T20 HS 117. T20 BB 2-10.

MIKE, Benjamin Wentworth Munro (Loughborough GS), b Nottingham 24 Aug 1998. Son of G.W.Mike (Nottinghamshire 1989-96). 6'1". RHB, RM. Squad No 16. Leicestershire 2018-22. Warwickshire 2019 (on loan). Yorkshire debut 2022. Leicestershire 2nd XI debut 2017. HS 99* Le v Middx (Lord's) 2022. Y HS 14 and Y BB 1-91 v Surrey (Oval) 2022. BB 5-37 Le v Sussex (Hove) 2018 – on debut. LO HS 41 Le v Northants (Leicester) 2019 (RLC). LO BB 3-34 Le v Surrey (Leicester) 2021 (RLC). T20 HS 37. T20 BB 4-22.

MILNES, Matthew Edward (West Bridgford CS; Durham U), b Nottingham 29 Jul 1994. 6'1". RHB, RMF. Squad No 4. Durham MCCU 2014. Nottinghamshire 2018. Kent 2019-22; cap 2021. Welsh Fire 2021. Oval Invincibles 2022. T20 HS 78 K v Yorks (Canterbury) 2021. 50 wkts (1): 58 (2019). BB 6-53 K v Leics (Leicester) 2021. LO HS 26 and LO BB 5-79 K v Hants (Canterbury) 2019 (RLC). T20 HS 14*. T20 BB 5-22.

RASHID, Adil Usman (Belle Vue S, Bradford), b Bradford 17 Feb 1988. 5'8". RHB, LBG. Squad No 3. Debut (Yorkshire) 2006; cap 2008; testimonial 2018. Signed white ball only contract in 2020. MCC 2007-09. IPL: PK 2021. Big Bash: AS 2015-16. Northern Superchargers 2021 to date. YC 2007. Match double (114, 48, 8-157 and 2-45) for England U19 v India U19 (Taunton) 2006. **ECB Central Contract 2022-23. Tests**: 19 (2015-16 to 2018-19), taking 5-64 v P (Abu Dhabi) on debut; HS 61 v P (Dubai, DSC) 2015-16; BB 5-49 v SL (Colombo, SSC) 2018-19. **LOI**: 125 (2009 to 2022-23); HS 69 v NZ (Birmingham) 2015; BB 5-27 v Ire (Bristol) 2017. **IT20**: 93 (2009 to 2022-23); HS 22 v WI (Bridgetown) 2021-22; BB 4-2 v WI (Dubai) 2021-22. F-c Tours: WI 2010-11 (EL), 2018-19; I 2007-08 (EL), 2016-17; SL 2018-19; B 2006-07 (Eng A), 2016-17; UAE 2015-16 (v P). HS 180 v Somerset (Leeds) 2013. 50 wkts (2); most – 65 (2008). BB 7-107 v Hants (Southampton) 2008. LO HS 71 v Glos (Leeds) 2014 (RLC). LO BB 5-27 (see *LOI*). T20 HS 36*. T20 BB 4-2.

REVIS, Matthew Liam (Ilkley GS), b Steeton 15 Nov 2001. 6'4½". RHB, RM. Squad No 77. Debut (Yorkshire) 2019. Yorkshire 2nd XI debut 2019. HS 53* v Warwks (Leeds) 2022. BB 3-43 v Northants (Northampton) 2022. LO HS 58* v Somerset (Taunton) 2021 (RLC). LO BB 4-77 v Hants (Scarborough) 2022 (RLC). T20 HS 12*. T20 BB 2-18.

ROOT, Joseph Edward (King Ecgbert S, Sheffield; Worksop C), b Sheffield 30 Dec 1990. Elder brother of W.T.Root (*see GLAMORGAN*). 6'0". RHB, OB. Squad No 66. Debut (Yorkshire) 2010; cap 2012. Trent Rockets 2021 to date. YC 2012. *Wisden* 2013. PCA 2021. **ECB Central Contract 2022-23. Tests**: 129 (2012-13 to 2022-23, 64 as captain); 1000 runs (4); most – 1708 (2021); HS 254 v P (Manchester) 2016; BB 5-8 v I (Ahmedabad) 2020-21. **LOI**: 158 (2012-13 to 2022); HS 133* v B (Oval) 2017; BB 3-52 v Ire (Lord's) 2017. **IT20**: 32 (2012-13 to 2019); HS 90* v A (Southampton) 2013; BB 2-9 v WI (Kolkata) 2015-16. F-c Tours(C=Captain): A 2013-14, 2017-18C, 2021-22C; SA 2015-16, 2019-20C; WI 2014-15, 2018-19C, 2021-22C; NZ 2012-13, 2017-18C, 2019-20C, 2022-23; I 2012-13, 2016-17, 2020-21C; P 2022-23; SL 2018-19C, 2019-20C, 2020-21C; B 2016-17; UAE 2015-16 (v P). 1000 runs (3); most – 1228 (2013). HS 254 (*see Tests*). CC HS 236 v Derbys (Leeds) 2013. BB 5-8 (*see Tests*). LO HS 133* (*see LOI*). LO BB 3-52 (*see LOI*). T20 HS 92*. T20 BB 2-7.

‡NOSHAN MASOOD, b Kuwait 14 Oct 1989. LHB, RMF. Squad No 94. Karachi Whites 2007-08. Habib Bank 2009-10 to 2013-14. Durham MCCU 2011. Federal Areas 2011-12. Islamabad 2012-13. United Bank 2015-16 to 2017-18. National Bank 2018-19. Southern Punjab 2019-20 to 2020-21. Baluchistan 2021-22. Derbyshire 2022; cap 2022. Joins Yorkshire in 2023 as captain. **Tests** (P): 28 (2013-14 to 2022-23); HS 156 v E (Manchester) 2020; BB 1-6 v SA (Centurion) 2018-19. **LOI** (P): 6 (2018-19 to 2022-23); HS 50 v A (Dubai) 2018-19. **IT20** (P): 19 (2022-23); HS 65* v E (Karachi) 2022-23. F-c Tours (P): E 2016, 2020; A 2019-20; SA 2018-19; WI 2010-11 (P A), 2016-17; NZ 2020-21; SL 2015 (P A). 1000 runs (1+1); most – 1123 (2012-13). HS 239 De v Sussex (Derby) 2022. BB 2-52 DU v Warwks (Durham) 2011. LO HS 182* Islamabad v Rawalpindi (Rawalpindi) 2017-18. LO BB 2-0 HB v Islamabad Leopards (Islamabad) 2010-11. T20 HS 103*.

SHUTT, Jack William (Kirk Balk S; Thomas Rotherham C), b Barnsley 24 Jun 1997. 6'0". RHB, OB. Squad No 24. Debut (Yorkshire) 2020. HS 7* v Durham (Chester-le-St) 2020. BB 2-14 v Notts (Nottingham) 2020. LO HS 1* (twice). LO BB 4-46 v Glamorgan (Cardiff) 2022 (RLC). T20 HS 0*. T20 BB 5-11.

TATTERSALL, Jonathan Andrew (King James S, Knaresborough), b Harrogate 15 Dec 1994. 5'8". RHB, WK, occ LB. Squad No 12. Debut (Yorkshire) 2018; cap 2022. Gloucestershire 2021 (on loan). Surrey 2021 (on loan). HS 180* v Surrey (Scarborough) 2022. LO HS 89 v Hants (Southampton) 2018 (RLC). T20 HS 53*.

THOMPSON, Jordan Aaron (Benton Park S), b Leeds 9 Oct 1996. 5'11". LHB, RM. Squad No 44. Debut (Yorkshire) 2019; cap 2022. Big Bash: HH 2021-22. Northern Superchargers 2021. London Spirit 2022. HS 98 v Notts (Nottingham) 2020. BB 5-31 Leics (Leeds) 2020. LO BB – . T20 HS 74. T20 BB 4-44.

VAGADIA, Yash (Teesside HS; Durham U), b Newcastle upon Tyne 7 May 2004. RHB, OB. Squad No 45. Yorkshire 2nd XI debut 2021. Awaiting 1st XI debut.

NOWAGNER, Neil, b Pretoria, South Africa 13 Mar 1986. LHB, LMF. Squad No 13. Northerns 2005-06 to 2007-08. Titans 2006-07 to 2007-08. Otago 2008-09 to 2017-18. Northamptonshire 2014. Lancashire 2016. Essex 2017-18. Northern Districts 2018-19 to date. **Tests** (NZ): 62 (2012 to 2022-23); HS 66* v WI (Wellington) 2020-21; BB 7-39 v WI (Wellington) 2017-18. F-c Tours (NZ): E 2013, 2015, 2021, 2022; A 2019-20; SA 2012-13, 2016; WI 2012, 2014; I 2016-17; Z 2007 (SA Acad), 2016; B 2013-14; UAE 2018-19 (v P). HS 70 Otago v Wellington (Queenstown) 2009-10. Ex HS 50 v Surrey (Chelmsford) 2017. 50 wkts (0+2); most – 51 (2010-11, 2012-13). BB 7-39 (*see Tests*). CC BB 6-48 Ex v Somerset (Taunton) 2017. LO HS 45* ND v Northland (Whangarei) 2022-23. LO BB 5-31 ND v Auckland (Hamilton) 2022-23. T20 HS 16*. T20 BB 4-33.

WHARTON, James Henry (Holmfirth HS; Greenhead C), b Huddersfield 1 Feb 2001. 6'4". RHB, OB. Squad No 23. Debut (Yorkshire) 2022. Yorkshire 2nd XI debut 2018. HS 23 v Surrey (Scarborough) 2022. T20 HS 8.

NQWIESE, David (Witbank HS), b Roodepoort, South Africa 18 May 1985. 6'3". RHB, RMF. Squad No 96. Easterns 2005-06 to 2011-12. Titans 2009-10 to 2016-17. Sussex 2016-20; cap 2016. Joins Yorkshire in 2023 for T20 only. IPL: RCB 2015-16. London Spirit 2021. Northern Superchargers 2022. **LOI** (SA/Nam): 15 (6 for SA 2015 to 2015-16; 9 for Nam 2021-22 to 2022); HS 67 Nam v UAE (Dubai) 2021-22; BB 3-50 SA v E (Cape Town) 2015-16. **IT20** (SA/NAM): 39 (20 for SA 2013 to 2015-16; 19 for Nam 2021-22 to 2022-23); HS 66* Nam v Neth (Abu Dhabi) 2021-22; BB 5-23 SA v WI (Durban) 2014-15. F-c Tour (SA A): A 2014. HS 208 Easterns v GW (Benoni) 2008-09. UK HS 139 Sx v Cardiff MCCU (Hove) 2019. CC HS 106 Sx v Warwks (Birmingham) 2018. BB 6-58 Titans v Knights (Centurion) 2014-15. CC BB 5-26 Sx v Middx (Lord's) 2019. LO HS 171 Sx v Hants (Southampton) 2019 (RLC). LO BB 5-25 Easterns v Boland (Benoni) 2010-11. T20 HS 79*. T20 BB 5-19.

RELEASED/RETIRED

(Having made a County 1st XI appearance in 2022)

NQALLEN, Finnley Hugh (St Kentigern C), b Auckland, New Zealand 22 Apr 1999. RHB, WK. Auckland 2017-18 to 2019-20. Wellington 2020-21 to date. Lancashire 2021 (T20 only). Birmingham Phoenix 2021. **LOI** (NZ): 19 (2022 to 2022-23); HS 96 v WI (Bridgetown) 2022. **IT20** (NZ): 28 (2020-21 to 2022); HS 101 v Scot (Edinburgh) 2022. HS 66 Auckland v Wellington (Auckland) 2019-20. BB 1-15 Wellington v Otago (Wellington) 2020-21. LO HS 128 (in 59 balls) Wellington v Otago (Wellington) 2020-21. LO BB 1-32 Auckland v ND (Whangarei) 2019-20. T20 HS 101.

NQDRAKES, Dominic Conneil, b Barbados 2 Jun 1998. Son of V.C.Drakes (Barbados, Sussex, Border, Nottinghamshire, Warwickshire, Leicestershire and West Indies 1991-92 to 2003-04). LHB, LFM. Barbados 2017-18 to date. Yorkshire 2022. **IT20** (WI): 10 (2021-22 to 2022); HS 5 v P (Karachi) 2021-22 and 5 v I (Lauderhill) 2022; BB 1-19 v NZ (Kingston) 2022. HS 33 and BB 2-11 Bar v Jamaica (Bridgetown) 2017-18. Y HS 21 and Y BB 1-37 v Hants (Southampton) 2022. LO HS 38* WI Emerging v Leeward Is (Port of Spain) 2019-20. LO BB 4-44 Bar v USA (Cave Hill) 2018-19. T20 HS 48*. T20 BB 3-26.

NQGABRIEL, Shannon Terry, b Trinidad 28 Apr 1988. RHB, RF. Trinidad & Tobago 2009-10 to date. Worcestershire 2015. Gloucestershire 2019; cap 2019. Yorkshire 2022. **Tests** (WI): 58 (2012 to 2022-23); HS 20* v E (St George's) 2015; BB 8-62 v SL (Gros Islet) 2018. **LOI** (WI): 25 (2016 to 2019); HS 12* v NZ (Christchurch) 2017-18; BB 3-17 v SA (Bridgetown) 2016. **IT20** (WI): 2 (2012-13 to 2013); HS – ; BB 3-44 v P (Kingstown) 2013. F-c Tours (WI): E 2012, 2017, 2020; A 2015-16; SA 2014-15, 2022-23; NZ 2013-14, 2017-18, 2020-21; I 2013-14, 2018-19; SL 2014-15 (WI A), 2015-16, 2021-22; Z 2017-18, 2022-23; B 2018-19, 2020-21; UAE (v P) 2016-17. HS 20* (see Tests). BB 8-62 (see Tests). CC BB 5-31 Wo v Middx (Worcester) 2015. Y HS 5 and Y BB 2-18 v Surrey (Scarborough) 2022. LO HS 12* (see LOI). LO BB 5-33 T&T v Windward Is (Coolidge) 2016-17. T20 HS 2*. T20 BB 3-19.

NQHARIS RAUF, b Rawalpindi, Pakistan 7 Nov 1993. 5'11". RHB, RFM. Northern 2019-20 to date. Yorkshire 2022. Big Bash: MS 2019-20 to 2021-22. **Tests** (P): 1 (2022-23); HS 12 and BB 1-78 v E (Rawalpindi) 2022-23. **LOI** (P): 18 (2020-21 to 2022-23); HS 7 v A (Lahore) 2021-22; BB 4-65 v E (Birmingham) 2021. **IT20** (P): 57 (2019-20 to 2022-23); HS 13* v I (Dubai, DSC) 2022; BB 4-22 v NZ (Sharjah) 2021-22. HS 12 (see Tests). Y HS 6 v Northants (Northampton) 2022. BB 6-47 Northern v Central Punjab (Karachi) 2021-22. Y BB 5-65 v Kent (Leeds) 2022. LO HS 8 Baluchistan v Khyber Pakhtunkhwa (Rawalpindi) 2018-19. LO BB 4-65 (see LOI). T20 HS 19. T20 BB 5-27.

NO **KARUNARATNE**, Frank **Dimuth** Madushanka (St Joseph's C), b Colombo, Sri Lanka 28 Apr 1988. 6'0". LHB, RM. Sinhalese Sports Club 2008-09 to date. Basnahira North 2009-10. Dambulla District 2017-18. Colombo District 2021-22. Yorkshire 2022. **Tests** (SL): 83 (2012-13 to 2022-23, 25 as captain); HS 244 v B (Pallekele) 2021; BB 1-12 v SA (Port Elizabeth) 2018-19. **LOI** (SL): 34 (2011 to 2020-21, 17 as captain); HS 97 v A (Oval) 2019; BB –. F-c Tours (SL)(C=Capt): E 2011 (SL A), 2014, 2016; A 2012-13, 2018-19; SA 2012 (SL A), 2016-17, 2018-19C, 2020-21C; WI 2013 (SL A), 2020-21C; NZ 2014-15 2015-16, 2018-19, 2022-23C; I 2017-18, 2021-22C; P 2019-20C; Z 2016-17, 2019-20C; B 2013-14, 2017-18, 2022C; UAE 2013-14 (v P), 2017-18 (v P). 1000 runs (0+1): 1186 (2009-10). HS 244 (see Tests). Y HS 36 v Northants (Northampton) 2022 and 36 v Essex (Chelmsford) 2022. BB 1-6 SL A v WI A (Pallekele) 2016-17. LO HS 132 Sinhalese v KY (Kurunegala) 2017-18. LO BB 2-13 Sinhalese v Saracens (Colombo, SSC) 2009-10. T20 HS 80.

KOHLER-CADMORE, T. – see SOMERSET.

LOTEN, T.W. – see NOTTINGHAMSHIRE.

PATTERSON, Steven Andrew (Malet Lambert CS; St Mary's SFC, Hull; Leeds U), b Beverley 3 Oct 1983. 6'4". RHB, RMF. Yorkshire 2005-22; cap 2012; testimonial 2017; captain 2018 (part) to 2022 (part). Bradford/Leeds UCCE 2003 (not f-c). HS 63* v Warwks (Birmingham) 2016. 50 wkts (2); most – 53 (2012). BB 6-40 v Essex (Chelmsford) 2018. LO HS 25* v Worcs (Leeds) 2006 (P40). LO BB 6-32 v Derbys (Leeds) 2010. T20 HS 3*. T20 BB 4-30.

SHADAB KHAN – see SUSSEX.

SULLIVAN, Harris Alexander, b Leeds 17 Dec 2002. Younger brother of J.R.Sullivan (Yorkshire 2021 – l-o only). LHB. SLA. Awaiting f-c debut. Yorkshire 2nd XI debut 2021. LO HS 12 v Lancs (York) 2022 (RLC). LO BB 2-23 v Derbys (Chesterfield) 2022 (RLC).

WAITE, M.J. – see WORCESTERSHIRE.

WILLEY, D.J. – see NORTHAMPTONSHIRE.

G.S.Ballance, B.D.Birkhead, J.R.Sullivan and S.Wisniewski left the staff without making a County 1st XI appearance in 2022.

YORKSHIRE 2022

RESULTS SUMMARY

	Place	Won	Lost	Tied	Drew	NR
LV= Insurance County Champ (Div 1)	9th	1	6		7	
Royal London One-Day Cup (Group B)	5th	4	4			
Vitality Blast (North Group)	SF	8	7	1		

LV= INSURANCE COUNTY CHAMPIONSHIP AVERAGES
BATTING AND FIELDING

Cap		M	I	NO	HS	Runs	Avge	100	50	Ct/St
2021	H.C.Brook	8	12	3	194	967	107.44	3	6	8
2020	D.J.Malan	5	8	–	152	528	66.00	1	4	1
2012	J.E.Root	3	4	–	147	234	58.50	1	1	2
2022	J.A.Tattersall	7	12	2	180*	480	48.00	1	1	14/5
2019	T.Kohler-Cadmore	6	11	1	100	346	34.60	1	2	18/1
	M.L.Revis	8	11	3	53*	267	33.37	–	2	8
2010	A.Lyth	14	24	–	183	790	32.91	2	3	17
	G.C.H.Hill	14	24	1	151*	729	31.69	2	–	6
2021	D.M.Bess	13	19	2	89	499	29.35	–	4	6
	M.J.Waite	5	8	1	59*	198	28.28	–	1	1
2018	B.O.Coad	5	9	3	69	146	24.33	–	1	1
	F.J.Bean	3	6	–	53	138	23.00	–	1	1
	F.D.M.Karunaratne	3	4	–	36	89	22.25	–	–	1
	H.G.Duke	8	12	1	48	239	21.72	–	–	19/1
	W.A.R.Fraine	7	13	1	53	203	16.91	–	1	7
2022	J.A.Thompson	14	21	3	51	277	15.38	–	1	2
2012	S.A.Patterson	13	19	3	20	131	8.18	–	–	3
	J.H.Wharton	3	6	–	23	45	7.50	–	–	2
	Haris Rauf	4	4	1	6	15	5.00	–	–	2

Also played: D.C.Drakes (1 match) 6, 21; M.D.Fisher (2 – cap 2022) 2, 16*, 7 (1 ct); S.T.Gabriel (2) 0, 5, 2 (1 ct); T.W.Loten (2) 6, 5 (2 ct); W.A.Luxton (1) 31, 14; B.W.M.Mike (1) 8, 14 (1 ct); J.W.Shutt 1*, 4, 0* (1 ct).

BOWLING

	O	M	R	W	Avge	Best	5wI	10wM
M.D.Fisher	60.1	16	178	11	16.18	4- 19	–	–
B.O.Coad	132.2	35	359	18	19.94	3- 20	–	–
G.C.H.Hill	148.4	33	422	20	21.10	6- 26	1	–
S.A.Patterson	427	132	1020	37	27.56	5- 46	2	–
Haris Rauf	126	24	473	15	31.53	5- 65	1	–
J.A.Thompson	421	90	1459	42	34.73	5- 60	1	–
D.M.Bess	490	106	1545	36	42.91	5-126	1	–
M.L.Revis	163.1	35	660	13	50.76	3- 43	–	–

Also bowled:
S.T.Gabriel   45.4   4   222   5   44.40 2- 18   –   –
H.C.Brook 26-3-63-0; D.C.Drakes 27.2-7-86-2; H.G.Duke 0.4-0-1-0; T.W.Loten 48.1-11-152-4; A.Lyth 12.5-5-18-0; D.J.Malan 12.4-3-42-0; B.W.M.Mike 14-0-91-1; J.E.Root 22-2-57-0; J.W.Shutt 19-1-96-3; J.A.Tattersall 6-0-47-2; M.J.Waite 94-23-310-4.

Yorkshire played no first-class fixtures outside the County Championship in 2022. The First-Class Averages (pp 221–234) give the records of Yorkshire players in all first-class county matches, with the exception of H.C.Brook, B.W.M.Mike, J.E.Root and M.J.Waite, whose first-class figures for Yorkshire are as above.

YORKSHIRE RECORDS

FIRST-CLASS CRICKET

Highest Total	For	887		v	Warwicks	Birmingham	1896
	V	681-7d		by	Leics	Bradford	1996
Lowest Total	For	23		v	Hampshire	Middlesbrough	1965
	V	13		by	Notts	Nottingham	1901
Highest Innings	For	341	G.H.Hirst	v	Leics	Leicester	1905
	V	318*	W.G.Grace	for	Glos	Cheltenham	1876

Highest Partnership for each Wicket

1st	555	P.Holmes/H.Sutcliffe	v	Essex	Leyton	1932
2nd	346	W.Barber/M.Leyland	v	Middlesex	Sheffield	1932
3rd	346	J.J.Sayers/A.McGrath	v	Warwicks	Birmingham	2009
4th	372	J.E.Root/J.M.Bairstow	v	Surrey	Leeds	2016
5th	340	E.Wainwright/G.H.Hirst	v	Surrey	The Oval	1899
6th	305	A.Lyth/J.A.Tattersall	v	Surrey	Scarborough[2]	2022
7th	366*	J.M.Bairstow/T.T.Bresnan	v	Durham	Chester-le-St[2]	2015
8th	292	R.Peel/Lord Hawke	v	Warwicks	Birmingham	1896
9th	246	T.T.Bresnan/J.N.Gillespie	v	Surrey	The Oval	2007
10th	149	G.Boycott/G.B.Stevenson	v	Warwicks	Birmingham	1982

Best Bowling	For	10-10	H.Verity	v	Notts	Leeds	1932
(Innings)	V	10-37	C.V.Grimmett	for	Australians	Sheffield	1930
Best Bowling	For	17-91	H.Verity	v	Essex	Leyton	1933
(Match)	V	17-91	H.Dean	for	Lancashire	Liverpool	1913

Most Runs – Season	2883	H.Sutcliffe	(av 80.08)	1932
Most Runs – Career	38558	H.Sutcliffe	(av 50.20)	1919-45
Most 100s – Season	12	H.Sutcliffe		1932
Most 100s – Career	112	H.Sutcliffe		1919-45
Most Wkts – Season	240	W.Rhodes	(av 12.72)	1900
Most Wkts – Career	3597	W.Rhodes	(av 16.02)	1898-1930
Most Career W-K Dismissals	1186	D.Hunter	(863 ct; 323 st)	1888-1909
Most Career Catches in the Field	665	J.Tunnicliffe		1891-1907

LIMITED-OVERS CRICKET

Highest Total	50ov	411-6		v	Devon	Exmouth	2004
	40ov	352-6		v	Notts	Scarborough	2001
	T20	260-4		v	Northants	Leeds	2017
Lowest Total	50ov	76		v	Surrey	Harrogate	1970
	40ov	54		v	Essex	Leeds	2003
	T20	81		v	Warwicks	Birmingham	2021
Highest Innings	50ov	175	T.M.Head	v	Leics	Leicester	2016
	40ov	191	D.S.Lehmann	v	Notts	Scarborough	2001
	T20	161	A.Lyth	v	Northants	Leeds	2017
Best Bowling	50ov	7-27	D.Gough	v	Ireland	Leeds	1997
	40ov	7-15	R.A.Hutton	v	Worcs	Leeds	1969
	T20	6-19	T.T.Bresnan	v	Lancashire	Leeds	2017

PROFESSIONAL UMPIRES' TEAM 2023

† New appointment. See page 82 for key to abbreviations.

BAILEY, Robert John (Biddulph HS), b Biddulph, Staffs 28 Oct 1963. 6'3". RHB, OB. Northamptonshire 1982-99; cap 1985; benefit 1993; captain 1996-97. Derbyshire 2000-01; cap 2000. Staffordshire 1980. YC 1984. **Tests**: 4 (1988 to 1989-90); HS 43 v WI (Oval) 1988. **LOI**: 4 (1984-85 to 1989-90); HS 43* v SL (Oval) 1988. F-c Tours: SA 1991-92 (Nh); WI 1989-90; Z 1994-95 (Nh). 1000 runs (13); most – 1987 (1990). HS 224* Nh v Glamorgan (Swansea) 1986. BB 5-54 Nh v Notts (Northampton) 1993. F-c career: 374 matches; 21844 runs @ 40.52, 47 hundreds; 121 wickets @ 42.51; 272 ct. Appointed 2006. Umpired 24 LOI (2011 to 2021). **ICC International Panel 2011-19.**

BAINTON, Neil Laurence, b Romford, Essex 2 October 1970. No f-c appearances. Appointed 2006.

BALDWIN, Paul Kerr, b Epsom, Surrey 18 Jul 1973. No f-c appearances. Umpired 18 LOI (2006 to 2009). Reserve List 2010-14. Appointed 2015.

BLACKWELL, Ian David (Brookfield Community S), b Chesterfield, Derbys 10 Jun 1978. 6'2". LHB, SLA. Derbyshire 1997-99. Somerset 2000-08; cap 2001; captain 2006 (*part*). Durham 2009-12. Warwickshire 2012 (on loan). MCC 2012. **Tests**: 1 (2005-06); HS 4 and BB-v I (Nagpur) 2005-06. **LOI**: 34 (2002-03 to 2005-06); HS 82 v I (Colombo) 2002-03; BB 3-26 v A (Adelaide) 2002-03. F-c Tour: I 2005-06. 1000 runs (3); most – 1256 (2005). HS 247* Sm v Derbys (Taunton) 2003 – off 156 balls and including 204 off 98 balls in reduced post-lunch session. BB 7-52 Du v Australia A (Chester-le-St) 2012. CC BB 7-85 Du v Lancs (Manchester) 2009. F-c career: 210 matches; 11595 runs @ 39.57, 27 hundreds; 398 wickets @ 35.91; 66 ct. Reserve List 2015-17. Appointed 2018.

BURNS, Michael (Walney CS), b Barrow-in-Furness, Lancs 6 Feb 1969. 6'0". RHB, RM, WK. Warwickshire 1992-96. Somerset 1997-2005; cap 1999; captain 2003-04. 1000 runs (2); most – 1133 (2003). HS 221 Sm v Yorks (Bath) 2001. BB 6-54 Sm v Leics (Taunton) 2001. F-c career: 154 matches; 7648 runs @ 32.68, 8 hundreds; 68 wickets @ 42.42; 142 ct, 7 st. Appointed 2016. Umpired 6 LOI (2020 to 2022). **ICC International Panel 2020 to date.**

COOK, Nicholas Grant Billson (Lutterworth GS), b Leicester 17 Jun 1956. 6'0". RHB, SLA. Leicestershire 1978-85; cap 1982. Northamptonshire 1986-94; cap 1987; benefit 1995. **Tests**: 15 (1983 to 1989); HS 31 v A (Oval) 1989; BB 6-65 (11-83 match) v P (Karachi) 1983-84. **LOI**: 3 (1983-84 to 1989-90); HS – ; BB 2-18 v P (Peshawar) 1987-88. F-c Tours: NZ 1979-80 (DHR), 1983-84; P 1983-84, 1987-88; SL 1985-86 (Eng B); Z 1980-81 (Le), 1984-85 (EC). HS 75 Le v Somerset (Taunton) 1980. 50 wkts (8); most – 90 (1982). BB 7-34 (10-97 match) Nh v Essex (Chelmsford) 1992. F-c career: 356 matches; 3137 runs @ 11.66; 879 wickets @ 29.01; 197 ct. Appointed 2009.

DEBENHAM, Benjamin John, b Chelmsford, Essex 11 Oct 1967. LHB. No f-c appearances. Reserve List 2012-17. Appointed 2018.

GOUGH, Michael Andrew (English Martyrs RCS; Hartlepool SFC), b Hartlepool, Co Durham 18 Dec 1979. Son of M.P.Gough (Durham 1974-77). 6'5". RHB, OB. Durham 1998-2003. F-c Tours (Eng A): NZ 1999-00; B 1999-00. HS 123 Du v CU (Cambridge) 1998. CC HS 103 Du v Essex (Colchester) 2002. BB 5-56 Du v Middx (Chester-le-St) 2001. F-c career: 67 matches; 2952 runs @ 25.44, 2 hundreds; 30 wickets @ 45.00; 57 ct. Reserve List 2006-08. Appointed 2009. Umpired 29 Tests (2016 to 2022-23) and 74 LOI (2013 to 2022-23). **ICC Elite Panel 2020 to date.**

HARRIS, Anthony Charles, b Durban, South Africa 23 Nov 1973. No f-c appearances. Appointed 2022.

HARTLEY, Peter John (Greenhead GS; Bradford C), b Keighley, Yorks 18 Apr 1960. 6'0". RHB, RMF. Warwickshire 1982. Yorkshire 1985-97; cap 1987; benefit 1996. Hampshire 1998-2000; cap 1998. F-c Tours (Y): SA 1991-92; WI 1986-87; Z 1995-96. HS 127* Y v Lancs (Manchester) 1988. 50 wkts (7); most – 81 (1995). BB 9-41 (inc hat-trick, 4 wkts in 5 balls and 5 in 9; 11-68 match) Y v Derbys (Chesterfield) 1995. Hat-trick 1995. F-c career: 232 matches; 4321 runs @ 19.91, 2 hundreds; 683 wickets @ 30.21; 68 ct. Appointed 2003. Umpired 6 LOI (2007 to 2009). **ICC International Panel 2006-09.**

HASSAN ADNAN (MAO C, Lahore), b Lahore, Pakistan 15 May 1975. 5'9". RHB, OB. Islamabad 1994-95 to 2000-01. WAPDA 1997-98 to 2010-11. Gujranwala 1997-98 to 1998-99. Derbyshire 2003-07; cap 2004. Lahore 2003-04. Pakistan Customs 2009-10. Suffolk 2008-12. 1000 runs (1): 1380 (2004). HS 191 De v Somerset (Taunton) 2005. BB 1-4 De v Glos (Derby) 2006. F-c career: 137 matches; 7609 runs @ 37.11, 10 hundreds; 4 wickets @ 88.00; 76 ct. Reserve list 2020-21. Appointed 2022.

ILLINGWORTH, Richard Keith (Salts GS), b Bradford, Yorks 23 Aug 1963. 5'11". RHB, SLA. Worcestershire 1982-2000; cap 1986; benefit 1997. Natal 1988-89. Derbyshire 2001. Wiltshire 2005. **Tests**: 9 (1991 to 1995-96); HS 28 v SA (Pt Elizabeth) 1995-96; BB 4-96 v WI (Nottingham) 1995. Took wicket of P.V.Simmons with his first ball in Tests – v WI (Nottingham) 1991. **LOI**: 25 (1991 to 1995-96); HS 14 v P (Melbourne) 1991-92; BB 3-33 v Z (Albury) 1991-92. F-c Tours: SA 1995-96; NZ 1991-92; P 1990-91 (Eng A); SL 1990-91 (Eng A); Z 1989-90 (Eng A), 1990-91 (Wo), 1993-94 (Wo), 1996-97 (Wo). HS 120* Wo v Warwks (Worcester) 1987 – as night-watchman. Scored 106 for England A v Z (Harare) 1989-90 – also as night-watchman. 50 wkts (5); most – 75 (1990). BB 7-50 Wo v OU (Oxford) 1985. F-c career: 376 matches; 7027 runs @ 22.45, 4 hundreds; 831 wickets @ 31.54; 161 ct. Appointed 2006. Umpired 62 Tests (2012-13 to 2022-23) and 77 LOI (2010 to 2022). **ICC Elite Panel 2013 to date.**

KETTLEBOROUGH, Richard Allan (Worksop C), b Sheffield, Yorks 15 Mar 1973. 6'0". LHB, RM. Yorkshire 1994-97. Middlesex 1998-99. F-c Tour (Y): Z 1995-96. HS 108 Y v Essex (Leeds) 1996. BB 2-26 Y v Notts (Scarborough) 1996. F-c career: 33 matches; 1258 runs @ 25.16, 1 hundred; 3 wickets @ 81.00; 20 ct. Appointed 2006. Umpired 77 Tests (2010-11 to 2022-23) and 95 LOI (2009 to 2022). **ICC Elite Panel 2011 to date.**

LLONG, Nigel James (Ashford North S), b Ashford, Kent 11 Feb 1969. 6'0". LHB, OB. Kent 1990-98; cap 1993. F-c Tour (K): Z 1992-93. HS 130 K v Hants (Canterbury) 1996. BB 5-21 K v Middx (Canterbury) 1996. F-c career: 68 matches; 3024 runs @ 31.17, 6 hundreds; 35 wickets @ 35.97; 59 ct. Appointed 2002. Umpired 62 Tests (2007-08 to 2019-20) and 130 LOI (2006 to 2019-20). **ICC Elite Panel 2012-20.**

LLOYD, Graham David (Hollins County HS), b Accrington, Lancs 1 Jul 1969. Son of D.Lloyd (Lancs and England 1965-83). 5'9". RHB, RM. Lancashire 1988-2002; cap 1992; benefit 2001. **LOI**: 6 (1996 to 1998-99); HS 22 v A (Oval) 1997. F-c Tours: A 1992-93 (Eng A); WI 1995-96 (La). 1000 runs (5); most – 1389 (1992). HS 241 La v Essex (Chelmsford) 1996. BB 1-4. F-c career: 203 matches; 11279 runs @ 38.23, 24 hundreds; 2 wickets @ 220.00; 140 ct. Reserve List 2009-13. Appointed 2014.

LUNGLEY, Tom (St John Houghton SS; SE Derbyshire C), b Derby 25 Jul 1979. 6'1". LHB, RM. Derbyshire 2000-10; cap 2007. HS 50 De v Warwks (Derby) 2008. 50 wkts (1): 59 (2007). BB 5-20 De v Leics (Derby) 2007. F-c career: 55 matches; 885 runs @ 14.50; 149 wickets @ 32.10; 25 ct. Reserve list 2015-21. Appointed 2022.

MALLENDER, Neil Alan (Beverley GS), b Kirk Sandall, Yorks 13 Aug 1961. 6'0". RHB, RFM. Northamptonshire 1980-86 and 1995-96; cap 1984. Somerset 1987-94; cap 1987; benefit 1994. Otago 1983-84 to 1992-93; captain 1990-91 to 1992-93. **Tests**: 2 (1992); HS 4 v P (Oval) 1992; BB 5-50 v P (Leeds) 1992 – on debut. F-c Tour (Nh): Z 1994-95. HS 100* Otago v CD (Palmerston N) 1991-92. UK HS 87* Sm v Sussex (Hove) 1990. 50 wkts (6); most – 56 (1983). BB 7-27 Otago v Auckland (Auckland) 1984-85. UK BB 7-41 Nh v Derbys (Northampton) 1982. F-c career: 345 matches; 4709 runs @ 17.18, 1 hundred; 937 wickets @ 26.31; 111 ct. Appointed 1999. Umpired 3 Tests (2003-04) and 22 LOI (2001 to 2003-04). **ICC Elite Panel 2004.**

MIDDLEBROOK, James Daniel (Pudsey Crawshaw S), b Leeds, Yorks 13 May 1977. 6'1". RHB, OB. Yorkshire 1998-2015. Essex 2002-09; cap 2003. Northamptonshire 2010-14, cap 2011. MCC 2010, 2013. HS 127 Ex v Middx (Lord's) 2007. 50 wkts (1): 56 (2003). BB 6-78 Nh v Kent (Northampton) 2013. Hat-trick Ex v Kent (Canterbury) 2003. F-c career: 226 matches; 7873 runs @ 27.72, 10 hundreds; 475 wickets @ 38.15; 112 ct. Reserve list 2017-21. Appointed 2022.

MILLNS, David James (Garibaldi CS; N Notts C; Nottingham Trent U), b Clipstone, Notts 27 Feb 1965. 6'3". LHB, RF. Nottinghamshire 1988-89, 2000-01; cap 2000. Leicestershire 1990-99; cap 1991; benefit 1999. Tasmania 1994-95. Boland 1996-97. F-c Tours: A 1992-93 (Eng A); SA 1996-97 (Le). HS 121 Le v Northants (Northampton) 1997. 50 wkts (4); most – 76 (1994). BB 9-37 (12-91 match) Le v Derbys (Derby) 1991. F-c career: 171 matches; 3082 runs @ 22.01, 3 hundreds; 553 wickets @ 27.35; 47 ct. Reserve list 2007-08. Appointed 2009. Umpired 6 LOI (2020 to 2022). **ICC International Panel 2020 to date.**

NAEEM ASHRAF b Lahore, Pakistan 10 Nov 1972. LHB, LFM. Lahore City 1987-88 to 1998-99. National Bank of Pakistan 1992-93 to 1999-00. Lahore Whites 2000-01. **LOI** (P): 2 (1995); HS 16 v SL (Sharjah) 1995; BB – v SA. HS 139 Lahore City v Gujranwala (Gujranwala) 1997-98. BB 7-41 (10-70 match) NBP v Allied Bank (Lahore) 1997-98. F-c career: 86 matches; 3009 runs @ 26.16, 5 hundreds; 289 wickets @ 24.12; 47 ct. Appointed 2022.

NEWELL, Mark (Hazelwick SS; City of Westminster C), b Crawley, Sussex 19 Dec 1973. Brother of K.Newell (Sussex, Matabeleland and Glamorgan 1995-2001). 6'1½". RHB, OB. Sussex 1996-98. Derbyshire 1999. Buckinghamshire 2007. HS 135* Sx v Derbys (Horsham) 1998. BB –. 24 matches; 889 runs @ 23.39; 3 hundreds; 17 ct. Reserve list 2017-21. Appointed 2022.

O'SHAUGHNESSY, Steven Joseph (Harper Green SS, Franworth), b Bury, Lancs 9 Sep 1961. 5'10½". RHB, RM. Lancashire 1980-87; cap 1985. Worcestershire 1988-89. Scored 100 in 35 min to equal world record for La v Leics (Manchester) 1983. 1000 runs (1): 1167 (1984). HS 159* La v Somerset (Bath) 1984. BB 4-66 La v Notts (Nottingham) 1982. F-c career: 112 matches; 3720 runs @ 24.31, 5 hundreds; 114 wickets @ 36.03; 57 ct. Reserve List 2009-10. Appointed 2011.

POLLARD, Paul Raymond (Gedling CS), b Carlton, Nottingham 24 Sep 1968. 5'11". LHB, RM. Nottinghamshire 1987-98; cap 1992. Worcestershire 1999-2001. F-c Tour (Nt): SA 1996-97. 1000 runs (3); most – 1463 (1993). HS 180 Nt v Derbys (Nottingham) 1993. BB 2-79 Nt v Glos (Bristol) 1993. F-c career: 192 matches; 9685 runs @ 31.44, 15 hundreds; 4 wkts @ 68.00; 158 ct. Reserve List 2012-17. Appointed 2018.

PRATT, Neil, b Bishop Auckland, Co Durham 8 Jun 1972. Brother of A.Pratt (Durham 1997-2004) and G.Pratt (Durham 2000-06). RHB, RM. No f-c appearances. Reserve list 2020-21. Appointed 2022.

REDFERN, Suzanne, b Mansfield, Notts 26 Oct 1977. LHB, LM. MBE 2018. **Tests**: 6 (1995-96 to 1999); HS 30 v NZ (Worcester) 1996; BB 2-27 v I (Shenley) 1999. **LOI**: 15 (1995 to 1999); HS 27 v I (Nottingham) 1999; BB 4-21 v SA (Bristol) 1997. Test career: 6 matches; 146 runs @ 29.20; 6 wickets @ 64.50; 5 ct. Appointed 2022.

ROBINSON, Robert Timothy (Dunstable GS; High Pavement SFC; Sheffield U), b Sutton in Ashfield, Notts 21 Nov 1958. 6'0". RHB, RM. Nottinghamshire 1978-99; cap 1983; captain 1988-95; benefit 1992. *Wisden* 1985. **Tests**: 29 (1984-85 to 1989); HS 175 v A (Leeds) 1985. **LOI**: 26 (1984-85 to 1988); HS 83 v P (Sharjah) 1986-87. F-c Tours: A 1987-88; SA 1989-90 (Eng XI), 1996-97 (Nt); NZ 1987-88; WI 1985-86; I/SL 1984-85; P 1987-88. 1000 runs (14) inc 2000 (1): 2032 (1984). HS 220* Nt v Yorks (Nottingham) 1990. BB 1-22. F-c career: 425 matches; 27571 runs @ 42.15, 63 hundreds; 4 wickets @ 72.25; 257 ct. Appointed 2007. Umpired 17 LOI (2013 to 2021). **ICC International Panel 2012-19.**

SAGGERS, Martin John (Springwood HS, King's Lynn; Huddersfield U), b King's Lynn, Norfolk 23 May 1972. 6'2". RHB, RMF. Durham 1996-98. Kent 1999-2009; cap 2001; benefit 2009. MCC 2004. Essex 2007 (on loan). Norfolk 1995-96. **Tests**: 3 (2003-04 to 2004); HS 1 and BB 2-29 v B (Chittagong) 2003-04 – on debut. F-c Tour: B 2003-04. HS 64 K v Worcs (Canterbury) 2004. 50 wkts (4); most – 83 (2002). BB 7-79 K v Durham (Chester-le-St) 2000. F-c career: 119 matches; 1165 runs @ 11.20; 415 wickets @ 25.33; 27 ct. Reserve List 2010-11. Appointed 2012. Umpired 3 LOI (2020 to 2022). **ICC International Panel 2020 to date.**

SHANMUGAM, Surendiran ('Suri')(Sri Krishna C of Engineering & Technology; Manchester U), b Coimbatore, Tamil Nadu, India 2 Jun 1984. Appointed 2022.

SHANTRY, Jack David (Priory SS; Shrewsbury SFC; Liverpool U), b Shrewsbury, Shrops 29 Jan 1988. Son of B.K.Shantry (Gloucestershire 1978-79), brother of A.J.Shantry (Northants, Warwicks, Glamorgan 2003-11). 6'4". LHB, LM. Worcestershire 2009-17. Shropshire 2007-09. HS 106 v Glos (Worcester) 2016. 50 wkts (2); most – 67 (2015). BB 7-60 v Oxford MCCU (Oxford) 2013. CC BB 7-69 v Essex (Worcester) 2013. F-c career: 92 matches; 1640 runs @ 19.06, 2 hundreds; 266 wickets @ 29.25; 30 ct. Appointed 2022.

TAYLOR, Billy Victor (Bitterne Park S, Southampton), b Southampton 11 Jan 1977. Younger brother of J.L.Taylor (Wiltshire 1998-2002). 6'3". LHB, RMF. Sussex 1999-2003. Hampshire 2004-09; cap 2006; testimonial 2010. Wiltshire 1996-98. HS 40 v Essex (Southampton) 2004. BB 6-32 v Middlesex (Southampton) 2006 (inc hat-trick). F-c career: 54 matches; 431 runs @10.26; 136 wickets @ 33.34; 6 ct. Reserve list 2011-16. Appointed 2017.

WARREN, Russell John (Kingsthorpe Upper S), b Northampton 10 Sep 1971. 6'1". RHB, OB, WK. Northamptonshire 1992-2002; cap 1995. Nottinghamshire 2003-06; cap 2004. 1000 runs (1): 1030 (2001). HS 201* Nh v Glamorgan (Northampton) 2001. F-c career: 146 matches; 7776 runs @ 36.67, 15 hundreds; 128 ct, 5 st. Reserve List: 2015-17. Appointed 2018.

WATTS, Christopher Mark (Stalham HS; Paston C), b Acle, Norfolk 3 Jul 1967. No f-c appearances. Reserve list 2015-21. Appointed 2022.

WHARF, Alexander George (Buttershaw Upper S; Thomas Danby C), b Bradford, Yorks 4 Jun 1975. 6'5". RHB, RMF. Yorkshire 1994-97. Nottinghamshire 1998-99. Glamorgan 2000-08, scoring 100* v OU (Oxford) on debut; cap 2000; benefit 2009. **LOI**: 13 (2004 to 2004-05); HS 9 v India (Lord's) 2004; BB 4-24 v Z (Harare) 2004-05. F-c Tour (Eng A): WI 2005-06. HS 128* Gm v Glos (Bristol) 2007. 50 wkts (1): 52 (2003). BB 6-59 Gm v Glos (Bristol) 2005. F-c career: 121 matches; 3570 runs @ 23.03, 6 hundreds; 293 wickets @ 37.34; 63 ct. Reserve List 2011-13. Appointed 2014. Umpired 4 Tests (2021 to 2022-23) and 11 LOI (2018 to 2022). **ICC International Panel 2018 to date.**

WHITE, Robert Allan (Stowe S; Durham U; Loughborough U), b Chelmsford, Essex 15 Oct 1979. 5'11". RHB, LB. Northamptonshire 2000-12; cap 2008. Loughborough UCCE 2003. British U 2003. 1000 runs (1): 1037 (2008). HS 277 and BB 2-30 v Glos (Northampton) 2002 – highest maiden f-c hundred in UK; included 107 before lunch on first day. F-c career: 112 matches; 5706 runs @ 32.98, 8 hundreds; 18 wickets @ 59.50; 67 ct. Reserve list 2018-21. Appointed 2022.

Test Match and LOI statistics to 8 March 2023.

TOURING TEAMS REGISTER 2022

INDIA

Full Names	Birthdate	Birthplace	Team	Type	F-C Debut
BUMRAH, Jasprit Jasbirsingh	06.12.93	Ahmedabad	Gujarat	RHB/RFM	2013-14
GILL, Shubman	08.09.99	Firozpur	Punjab	RHB/OB	2017-18
IYER, Shreyas Santosh	06.12.94	Bombay	Mumbai	RHB/OB	2014-15
JADEJA, Ravindrasinh Anirudsinh	06.12.88	Navagam-Khed	Saurashtra	LHB/SLA	2006-07
KOHLI, Virat	05.11.88	Delhi	Delhi	RHB/RM	2006-07
MOHAMMED SHAMI	03.09.90	Jonagar	Bengal	RHB/RFM	2010-11
PANT, Rishabh Rajendra	04.10.97	Haridwar	Delhi	LHB/WK	2015-16
PUJARA, Cheteshwar Arvindbhai	25.01.88	Rajkot	Saurashtra	RHB/LB	2005-06
SIRAJ, Mohammed	13.03.94	Hyderabad	Hyderabad	RHB/RFM	2015-16
THAKUR, Shardul Narendra	16.10.91	Palghar	Mumbai	RHB/RFM	2012-13
VIHARI, Gade Hanuma	13.10.93	Kakinada	Andhra	RHB/OB	2010-11

NEW ZEALAND

Full Names	Birthdate	Birthplace	Team	Type	F-C Debut
BLUNDELL, Thomas Ackland	01.09.90	Wellington	Wellington	RHB/WK	2012-13
BOULT, Trent Alexander	22.07.89	Rotorua	Northern D	RHB/LFM	2008-09
BRACEWELL, Michael Gordon	14.02.91	Masterton	Wellington	LHB/OB	2010-11
CONWAY, Devon Philip	08.07.91	Johannesburg, SA	Wellington	LHB/RM	2008-09
DE GRANDHOMME, Colin	22.07.86	Harare, Zim	Northern D	RHB/RMF	2005-06
HENRY, Matthew James	14.12.91	Christchurch	Canterbury	RHB/RFM	2010-11
JAMIESON, Kyle Alex	30.12.94	Auckland	Auckland	RHB/RFM	2014-15
LATHAM, Thomas William Maxwell	02.04.92	Christchurch	Canterbury	LHB/WK	2010-11
MITCHELL, Daryl Joseph	20.05.91	Hamilton	Canterbury	RHB/RM	2011-12
NICHOLLS, Henry Michael	15.11.91	Christchurch	Canterbury	LHB/OB	2011-12
PATEL, Ajaz Yunus	21.10.88	Bombay, India	Central D	LHB/SLA	2012-13
SOUTHEE, Timothy Grant	11.12.88	Whangarei	Northern D	RHB/RMF	2006-07
WAGNER, Neil	13.03.86	Pretoria, SA	Northern D	LHB/LMF	2005-06
WILLIAMSON, Kane Stuart	08.08.90	Tauranga	Northern D	RHB/OB	2007-08
YOUNG, William Alexander	22.11.92	New Plymouth	Central D	RHB/OB	2011-12

SOUTH AFRICA

Full Names	Birthdate	Birthplace	Team	Type	F-C Debut
ELGAR, Dean	11.06.87	Welkom	Northerns	LHB/SLA	2005-06
ERWEE, Sarel Johannes	10.11.89	Pietermaritzburg	KZN Coastal	LHB/OB	2008-09
HARMER, Simon Ross	10.02.89	Pretoria	Northerns	RHB/OB	2009-10
JANSEN, Marco	01.05.00	Potchefstroom	Eastern P	RHB/LF	2018-19
MAHARAJ, Keshav Athmanand	07.02.90	Durban	KZN Coastal	LHB/SLA	2006-07
MARKRAM, Aiden Kyle	04.10.94	Pretoria	Northerns	RHB/OB	2014-15
MULDER, Peter Wiaan Adriaan	19.02.98	Johannesburg	Gauteng	RHB/RMF	2016-17
NGIDI, Lungisani True-man	29.03.96	Durban	Northerns	RHB/RFM	2015-16
NORTJE, Anrich Arno	16.11.93	Uitenhage	Warriors	RHB/RF	2012-13
PETERSEN, Keegan Darryl	08.08.93	Paarl	KZN Coastal	RHB/LB	2011-12
RABADA, Kagiso	25.05.95	Johannesburg	Gauteng	LHB/RF	2013-14
RICKELTON, Ryan David	11.07.96	Johannesburg	Gauteng	LHB/WK	2015-16
VAN DER DUSSEN, Hendrik Erasmus	07.02.89	Pretoria	Gauteng	RHB/LB	2007-08
VERREYNNE, Kyle	12.05.97	Pretoria	Western P	RHB/WK	2014-15
ZONDO, Khayelihle	07.03.90	Durban	KZN Coastal	RHB/OB	2007-08

SRI LANKA DEVELOPMENT XI

Full Names	Birthdate	Birthplace	Team	Type	F-C Debut
BANDARA, K.Nadeeja Ashen	23.11.98	Galle	Police	RHB/LB	2017-18
CHANDIMA, Korale K.Avishka T.	13.09.01	Ragama	Ragama	RHB/RM	2021-22
CROOSPULLE, Dian Lasith Shenan	10.10.98	Negombo	Ace Capital	RHB/OB	2017-18
DANIEL, Ashian Angelo	20.02.01	Moratuwa	Nondescripts	RHB/OB	2020
De SILVA, Demuni Amshi Oren	11.11.01	Galle	Nondescripts	RHB/RFM	2021-22
De SILVA, H.K.Manelker	08.08.98	Colombo	Sebastianites	LHB/RMF	2017-18
FERNANDO, K.Nishan Madushka	10.09.99	Moratuwa	Ragama	RHB/WK	2018-19
FERNANDO, M.Nuwanidu Keshawa	13.10.99	Colombo	Sinhalese	RHB/OB	2016-17
GUNATHILAKE, Santhush N.S.	14.09.99	Colombo	Tamil Union	RHB/RM	2018-19
LAKSHAN, P.A.Dhananjaya	05.10.98	Galle	Colts	LHB/RMF	2018-19
MADUSHAN, W.P.Udith	15.06.97	Hambantota	Saracens	RHB/RFM	2016-17
MALINGA, Lamahewage Nipun	27.02.00	Galle	Ragama	RHB/RFM	2019-20
PERERA, D.K.Avishka Lakmal	26.04.01	Colombo	Colts	RHB/RM	2018-19
PERERA, Nipun Dananjaya	28.09.00	Chilaw	Sinhalese	LHB/OB	2018-19
RANSIKA, W.A.Nipun	02.06.99	Galle	Nondescripts	LHB/RM	2018-19
RODRIGO, Yasiru Hasanjala	24.02.03	Nugegoda	Lankan	LHB/LM	2022
THILAKARATNE, Dilum Sudeera	04.10.00	Galle	Tamil Union	RHB/SLA	2018-19
WELLALAGE, Dulith Nethmika	09.01.03	Colombo	Colts	LHB/SLA	2018-19

THE 2022 FIRST-CLASS SEASON
STATISTICAL HIGHLIGHTS

FIRST TO INDIVIDUAL TARGETS

1000 RUNS	Shan Masood	Derbyshire	26 June
2000 RUNS	–	Most – 1273 W.L.Madsen (Derbyshire)	
50 WICKETS	M.J.Potts	Durham and England	1 July
100 WICKETS	–	Most – 78 M.J.Potts (Durham and England)	

TEAM HIGHLIGHTS († Team record)
HIGHEST INNINGS TOTALS

795-5d†	Glamorgan v Leicestershire	Leicester
756-4d†	Leicestershire v Sussex	Hove
673-7d	Surrey v Kent	The Oval
671-9d	Surrey v Kent	Beckenham

Setting the world record for the highest total not to include a century.

662-5d	Nottinghamshire v Durham	Nottingham
658-9d	Sri Lanka Development v Kent	Canterbury
652-6d	Hampshire v Kent	Canterbury
642-7d	Durham v Worcestershire	Chester-le-St
624-9d	Lancashire v Somerset	Southport
618-8d	Nottinghamshire v Derbyshire	Derby
605-6d	Somerset v Essex	Chelmsford
603	Surrey v Gloucestershire	Bristol

HIGHEST FOURTH INNINGS TOTAL

378-3	England (set 378) v India	Birmingham
370-3	Middlesex (set 370) v Sussex	Hove

LOWEST INNINGS TOTALS

57	Hampshire v Kent	Southampton
59	Essex v Lancashire	Chelmsford
69	Somerset v Hampshire	Taunton
73	Lancashire v Essex	Chelmsford
93	Leicestershire v Nottinghamshire	Nottingham
99	Leicestershire v Nottinghamshire	Leicester

HIGHEST MATCH AGGREGATES

1675-35	New Zealand (553 & 284) v England (539 & 299-5)	Nottingham
1564-14	Sussex (588 & 220-1d) v Leicestershire (756-4d)	Hove
1562-25	Leicestershire (584 & 183) v Glamorgan (795-5d)	Leicester

LOWEST MATCH AGGREGATE

370-40	Lancashire (131 & 73) v Essex (107 & 59)	Chelmsford

BATSMEN'S MATCH (Qualification: 1200 runs, average 60 per wicket)

(111.71)	1564-14	Sussex (588 & 220-1d) v Leicestershire (756-4d)	Hove
(80.72)	1453-18	Kent (595-8d & 200-1d) v Sri Lanka Dev (658-9d)	Canterbury
(76.11)	1294-17	Durham (642-7d & 102-0) v Worcestershire (550)	Chester-le-St
(66.05)	1321-20	Durham (580-6d & 170-1d) v Worcestershire (309 & 262-3)	Worcester
(65.00)	1365-21	Surrey (673-7d) v Kent (331 & 361-4)	The Oval
(62.48)	1562-25	Leicestershire (584 & 183) v Glamorgan (795-5d)	Leicester

LARGE MARGINS OF VICTORY

462 runs	Nottinghamshire (662-5d & 121-2d) beat Durham (207 & 114)	Nottingham
352 runs	Somerset (389 & 337-4d) beat Northamptonshire (265 & 109)	Taunton
Inns & 260 runs	Essex (573) beat Kent (164 & 149)	Canterbury
Inns & 259 runs	Worcestershire (577-6d) beat Leicestershire (148 & 170)	Worcester
Inns & 246 runs	Somerset (591-7d) beat Gloucestershire (186 & 159)	Bristol

NARROW MARGINS OF VICTORY

5 runs	Warwicks (272-4d & 177) beat Hampshire (311 & 133)	Birmingham
12 runs	Essex (238 & 223) beat Hampshire (163 & 286)	Chelmsford
1 wkt	Essex (180 & 84-9) beat Somerset (109 & 154)	Taunton
1 wkt	Essex (225 & 162-9) beat Yorkshire (134 & 252)	Leeds

ALL ELEVEN SCORING DOUBLE FIGURES

Surrey (671-9d, lowest score 12) v Kent   Beckenham

FOUR HUNDREDS IN AN INNINGS

4	Surrey (673-7d) v Kent	The Oval
4	Nottinghamshire (662-5d) v Durham	Nottinghamshire

SIX OR MORE FIFTIES IN AN INNINGS

7	Surrey (671-9d) v Kent	Beckenham

Equalling the County Championship record for the most fifties in an innings.

6	Leicestershire (584) v Glamorgan	Leicester

ALL ELEVEN PLAYERS BOWLING IN AN INNINGS

Nottinghamshire v Middlesex (261-1d)   Nottingham

MOST EXTRAS IN AN INNINGS

	B	LB	W	NB		
81	28	26	1	26	Worcestershire (550) v Durham	Chester-le-St
64	11	15	–	38	Glamorgan (437) v Leicestershire	Cardiff
61	8	11	–	42	Sussex (588) v Leicestershire	Hove

Under ECB regulations, Test matches excluded, two penalty extras were scored for each no-ball.

BATTING HIGHLIGHTS
TREBLE HUNDREDS

K.K.Jennings	318	Lancashire v Somerset	Southport
D.L.Lloyd	313*	Glamorgan v Derbyshire	Cardiff
S.A.Northeast	410*†	Glamorgan v Leicestershire	Leicester

The third highest score in English f-c cricket.

DOUBLE HUNDREDS

C.N.Ackermann	277*	Leicestershire v Sussex	Hove
Azhar Ali	225	Worcestershire v Leicestershire	Worcester
J.J.Bohannon	231	Lancashire v Gloucestershire	Manchester
N.L.J.Browne	234*	Essex v Somerset	Chelmsford
C.D.J.Dent	207*	Gloucestershire v Surrey	Bristol
B.M.Duckett	241	Nottinghamshire v Derbyshire	Derby
K.N.M.Fernando	269	Sri Lanka Development v Kent	Canterbury
S.R.Hain	202*	Warwickshire v Northamptonshire	Birmingham
T.J.Haines	243‡	Sussex v Derbyshire	Derby

K.K.Jennings	238		Lancashire v Yorkshire	Leeds
M.A.Jones	206		Durham v Middlesex	Chester-le-St
J.D.Libby	215		Worcestershire v Sussex	Hove
P.W.A.Mulder	235*		Leicestershire v Sussex	Hove
C.A.Pujara (3)	201*‡		Sussex v Derbyshire	Derby
	203		Sussex v Durham	Hove
	231		Sussex v Middlesex	Lord's
R.Ravindra	217		Durham v Worcestershire	Chester-le-St
Shan Masood	239‡		Derbyshire v Sussex	Derby
	219		Derbyshire v Leicestershire	Leicester

In successive matches; only the third to achieve this feat in the County Championship this century.
‡ *The third instance in all CC history when three double centuries have been scored in the same match.*

| B.T.Slater | 225* | | Nottinghamshire v Durham | Chester-le-St |
| J.L.Smith | 234* | | Surrey v Gloucestershire | Bristol |

HUNDREDS IN THREE CONSECUTIVE INNINGS

B.G.Compton	129		Kent v Essex	Chelmsford
	104*	115	Kent v Lancashire	Canterbury
S.R.Dickson		186	Durham v Sussex	Hove
	104	105	Durham v Worcestershire	Worcester

HUNDRED IN EACH INNINGS OF A MATCH

T.B.Abell	111	115	Somerset v Northamptonshire	Taunton
J.M.Bairstow	106	114*	England v India	Birmingham
D.J.Bell-Dummond	102	107*	Kent v Surrey	The Oval
B.G.Compton	104*	115	Kent v Lancashire	Canterbury
A.N.Cook	107	102*	Essex v Yorkshire	Chelmsford
S.R.Dickson	104	105	Durham v Worcestershire	Worcester
J.L.du Plooy	122*	134	Derbyshire v Durham	Chester-le-St
N.R.T.Gubbins	101*	130	Hampshire v Lancashire	Southampton
B.D.Guest	109	138	Derbyshire v Glamorgan	Derby
T.J.Haines	108*	177	Sussex v Glamorgan	Hove

FASTEST HUNDRED AGAINST GENUINE BOWLING

| S.J.Mullaney (100*) 55 balls | | Nottinghamshire v Middlesex | Lord's |

MOST SIXES IN AN INNINGS

| 17 | B.A.Stokes (161) | Durham v Worcestershire | Worcester |

200 RUNS IN A DAY

B.M.Duckett (0-237*)	Nottinghamshire v Derbyshire	Derby
K.K.Jennings (61*-318)	Lancashire v Somerset	Southport
D.L.Lloyd (0-203*)	Glamorgan v Derbyshire	Cardiff
S.A.Northeast (50*-308*)	Glamorgan v Leicestershire	Leicester
Shan Masood (0-201*)	Derbyshire v Sussex	Derby

150 RUNS OR MORE FROM BOUNDARIES IN AN INNINGS

Runs	6s	4s		
198	3	45	S.A.Northeast	Glamorgan v Leicestershire	Leicester
184	4	40	D.L.Lloyd	Glamorgan v Derbyshire	Cardiff
170	1	41	C.N.Ackermann	Leicestershire v Sussex	Hove
160	2	37	K.N.M.Fernando	Sri Lanka Development v Kent	Canterbury

HUNDRED ON FIRST-CLASS DEBUT

| S.W.Mead | 106* | Kent v Sri Lanka Development | Canterbury |

HUNDRED ON FIRST-CLASS DEBUT IN BRITAIN

K.K.A.T.Chandima	103*	Sri Lanka Development v Surrey	Guildford
D.L.S.Croospulle	136	Sri Lanka Development v Kent	Canterbury
K.N.M.Fernando	269	Sri Lanka Development v Kent	Canterbury
R.Ravindra	217	Durham v Worcestershire	Chester-le-St
R.D.Rickelton	103	Northamptonshire v Warwickshire	Northampton

CARRYING BAT THROUGH COMPLETED INNINGS

B.G.Compton	104*	Kent (260) v Lancashire	Canterbury

Compton scored 115 in the second innings and was the last man out, becoming only the 12th batter in f-c history to bat throughout both completed innings.

S.T.Evans	50*	Leicestershire (93) v Nottinghamshire	Nottingham
T.J.Haines	108*	Sussex (258) v Glamorgan	Hove
A.Z.Lees	182*	Durham (383) v Glamorgan	Cardiff
D.P.Sibley (2)	142*	Warwickshire (315) v Lancashire	Manchester
	120*	Warwickshire (274) v Gloucestershire	Bristol

LONG INNINGS (Qualification 600 mins and/or 400 balls)

Mins	Balls			
553	467	J.J.Bohannon (231)	Lancashire v Gloucestershire	Manchester
630	454	N.L.J.Browne (234*)	Essex v Somerset	Chelmsford
638	494	S.R.Hain (202*)	Warwickshire v Northamptonshire	Birmingham
654	491	T.J.Haines (243)	Sussex v Derbyshire	Derby
540	408	K.K.Jennings (238)	Lancashire v Yorkshire	Leeds
582	426	K.K.Jennings (318)	Lancashire v Somerset	Southport
603	450	S.A.Northeast (410*)	Glamorgan v Leicestershire	Leicester
533	403	C.A.Pujara (231)	Sussex v Middlesex	Lord's
605	445	B.T.Slater (225*)	Nottinghamshire v Durham	Chester-le-St
568	430	J.L.Smith (234*)	Surrey v Gloucestershire	Bristol

FIRST-WICKET PARTNERSHIP OF 100 IN EACH INNINGS

180/186	L.W.P.Wells/K.K.Jennings Lancashire v Yorkshire	Manchester

OTHER NOTABLE PARTNERSHIPS

Qualifications: 1st-4th wkts: 250 runs; 5th-6th: 225; 7th: 200; 8th: 175; 9th: 150; 10th: 100; highest partnership for that wicket otherwise. († Team record)

First Wicket

328	A.G.H.Orr/T.J.Haines	Sussex v Glamorgan	Hove
313	A.Z.Lees/S.R.Dickson	Durham v Sussex	Hove
296	M.S.Harris/C.D.J.Dent	Gloucestershire v Surrey	Bristol
287	R.S.Vasconcelos/W.A.Young	Northamptonshire v Warwicks	Birmingham
251	L.M.Reece/B.A.Godleman	Derbyshire v Leicestershire	Derby

Second Wicket

402†	H.Hameed/B.M.Duckett	Nottinghamshire v Derbyshire	Derby
328†	E.J.Byrom/C.A.Ingram	Glamorgan v Sussex	Cardiff
294	D.L.S.Croospulle/K.N.M.Fernando	Sri Lanka Dev v Kent	Canterbury

Third Wicket

351	T.J.Haines/C.A.Pujara	Sussex v Derbyshire	Derby
306	C.A.Ingram/S.A.Northeast	Glamorgan v Leicestershire	Leicester
292	Shan Masood/W.L.Madsen	Derbyshire v Sussex	Derby
281	Azhar Ali/J.A.Haynes	Worcestershire v Leics	Worcester
276	B.D.Guest/W.L.Madsen	Derbyshire v Glamorgan	Derby

Fourth Wicket

269*	J.E.Root/J.M.Bairstow	England v India	Birmingham
269	D.J.Malan/H.C.Brook	Yorkshire v Kent	Canterbury
254	J.A.Leaning/J.M.Cox	Kent v Gloucestershire	Canterbury

Fifth Wicket

477*†	C.N.Ackermann/P.W.A.Mulder	Leiestershire v Sussex	Hove

The highest fifth-wicket partnership in all English f-c cricket

273†	L.A.Dawson/B.C.Brown	Hampshire v Kent	Canterbury
264	D.I.Stevens/G.F.Linde	Kent v Sri Lanka Dev	Canterbury
254*	S.R.Hain/M.J.Lamb	Warwickshire v Northants	Birmingham
248	B.D.Guest/J.L.du Plooy	Derbyshire v Durham	Chester-le-St
236	D.J.Mitchell/T.A.Blundell	New Zealand v England	Nottingham

Sixth Wicket

461*†	S.A.Northeast/C.B.Cooke	Glamorgan v Leicestershire	Leicester

The second highest sixth-wicket partnership in all f-c cricket and the highest in England.

305†	A.Lyth/J.A.Tattersall	Yorkshire v Surrey	Scarborough

Seventh Wicket

241	J.M.Bairstow/J.Overton	England v New Zealand	Leeds

Eighth Wicket

244†	J.L.Smith/J.Clark	Surrey v Gloucestershire	Bristol
213*†	B.A.Raine/P.Coughlin	Durham v Worcestershire	Chester-le-St

Ninth Wicket

124	A.A.P.Atkinson/J.Overton	Surrey v Northamptonshire	The Oval

Tenth Wicket

122	M.G.K.Burgess/O.J.Hannon-Dalby	Warwickshire v Surrey	Birmingham
101	A.H.T.Donald/J.K.Fuller	Hampshire v Gloucestershire	Southampton

BOWLING HIGHLIGHTS
EIGHT OR MORE WICKETS IN AN INNINGS

S.R.Harmer (2)	8- 46	Essex v Hampshire	Chelmsford
	8-112	Essex v Gloucestershire	Chelmsford
L.C.Norwell	9- 62	Warwickshire v Hampshire	Birmingham
D.Paterson	8- 52	Nottinghamshire v Worcestershire	Nottingham
T.J.Price	8- 27	Gloucestershire v Warwickshire	Bristol

TEN OR MORE WICKETS IN A MATCH

K.J.Abbott	10-113	Hampshire v Yorkshire	Scarborough
T.E.Bailey	11-110	Lancashire v Kent	Manchester
S.J.Cook	10- 60	Essex v Kent	Canterbury
L.A.Dawson	10-139	Hampshire v Essex	Chelmsford
S.R.Harmer (2)	15-207	Essex v Hampshire	Chelmsford
	13-156	Essex v Gloucestershire	Chelmsford
M.J.Leach	10-166	England v New Zealand	Leeds
L.C.Norwell	13-100	Warwickshire v Hampshire	Birmingham
C.Overton	13- 87	Somerset v Essex	Taunton
D.Paterson	10-117	Nottinghamshire v Worcestershire	Nottingham
M.J.Potts (2)	11-101	Durham v Glamorgan	Chester-le-St
	13-101	Durham v Leicestershire	Leicester
T.J.Price	10- 73	Gloucestershire v Warwickshire	Bristol
T.S.Roland-Jones	10-107	Middlesex v Durham	Lord's
C.Rushworth	11-106	Durham v Derbyshire	Chester-le-St
D.J.Worrall	11-122	Surrey v Essex	The Oval
Zafar Gohar	10-196	Gloucestershire v Northamptonshire	Cheltenham

FIVE WICKETS ON FIRST-CLASS DEBUT IN BRITAIN

B.J.Currie	6-93	Sussex v Middlesex	Lord's
J.A.Turner	5-31	Hampshire v Sri Lanka Dev	Southampton

HAT-TRICK

K.J.Abbott	Hampshire v Gloucestershire	Cheltenham
G.P.Balderson	Lancashire v Essex	Chelmsford
T.J.Price	Gloucestershire v Kent	Canterbury

MOST RUNS CONCEDED IN AN INNINGS

D.M.W.Rawlins	49-3-223-0	Sussex v Leicestershire	Hove

The most runs conceded by any bowler in English f-c cricket without taking a wicket

MOST OVERS BOWLED IN AN INNINGS

Zafar Gohar	65-20-135-4	Gloucestershire v Lancashire	Manchester

WICKET-KEEPING HIGHLIGHTS
SIX WICKET-KEEPING DISMISSALS IN AN INNINGS

S.W.Billings	7ct	Kent v Warwickshire	Birmingham
C.B.Cooke	6ct	Glamorgan v Middlesex	Cardiff
B.D.Guest	6ct	Derbyshire v Worcestershire	Worcester
G.H.Roderick	6ct	Worcestershire v Middlesex	Worcester
J.A.Simpson	6ct	Middlesex v Nottinghamshire	Lord's

NINE WICKET-KEEPING DISMISSALS IN A MATCH

S.W.Billings	12ct	Kent v Warwickshire	Birmingham

Joint third most dismissals in all f-c cricket, and equal most catches in all f-c cricket.

B.D.Guest	9ct	Derbyshire v Worcestershire	Worcester
J.A.Simpson	9ct	Middlesex v Durham	Lord's

NO BYES CONCEDED IN AN INNINGS OF 550

642-7d	G.H.Roderick	Worcestershire v Durham	Chester-le-St
584	C.B.Cooke	Glamorgan v Leicestershire	Leicester
580-6d	O.B.Cox	Worcestershire v Durham	Worcester
551-8d	O.J.Carter	Sussex v Derbyshire	Hove
551-8d	J.A.Simpson	Middlesex v Nottinghamshire	Nottingham
550-5d	B.D.Guest	Derbyshire v Glamorgan	Cardiff

FIELDING HIGHLIGHTS
FOUR OR MORE CATCHES IN THE FIELD IN AN INNINGS

A.N.Cook	4ct	Essex v Somerset	Taunton
T.Kohler-Cadmore	4ct	Yorkshire v Hampshire	Scarborough
W.L.Madsen	4ct	Derbyshire v Middlesex	Chesterfield

SIX OR MORE CATCHES IN THE FIELD IN A MATCH

Z.Crawley	6ct	England v India	Birmingham

ALL-ROUND HIGHLIGHTS
HUNDRED AND FIVE WICKETS IN AN INNINGS

R.Ahmed	122	5-114	Leicestershire v Derbyshire	Derby
A.K.Dal	112*	5- 40	Derbyshire v Worcestershire	Worcester

LV= INSURANCE COUNTY CHAMPIONSHIP 2022 FINAL TABLES

DIVISION 1

		P	W	L	T	D	Bonus Bat	Points Bowl	Deduct Points	Total Points
1	**SURREY**	14	8	1	–	5	48	34	–	250
2	Lancashire	14	7	1	–	6	32	39	6	225
3	Hampshire	14	9	4	–	1	37	37	2	224
4	Essex	14	7	3	–	4	24	34	–	202
5	Kent	14	4	5	–	5	30	27	3	158
6	Northamptonshire	14	2	5	–	7	31	35	–	154
7	Somerset	14	3	6	–	5	28	33	–	149
8	Warwickshire	14	2	6	–	6	26	36	1	141
9	Yorkshire	14	1	6	–	7	33	35	2	138
10	Gloucestershire	14	2	8	–	4	26	29	5	114

DIVISION 2

		P	W	L	T	D	Bonus Bat	Points Bowl	Deduct Points	Total Points
1	Nottinghamshire	14	8	2	–	4	45	40	4	241
2	Middlesex	14	6	2	–	6	45	36	–	225
3	Glamorgan	14	6	3	–	5	43	37	–	216
4	Worcestershire	14	4	3	–	7	38	36	–	194
5	Derbyshire	14	3	3	–	8	37	36	–	185
6	Durham	14	3	3	–	8	41	32	11	174
7	Sussex	14	1	6	–	7	35	29	6	128
8	Leicestershire	14	–	9	–	5	26	28	1	93

SCORING OF CHAMPIONSHIP POINTS 2022

(a) For a win, 16 points, plus any points scored in the first innings.

(b) In a tie, each side to score eight points, plus any points scored in the first innings.

(c) In a drawn match, each side to score eight points, plus any points scored in the first innings (see also paragraph (e) below).

(d) **First Innings Points** (awarded only for performances **in the first 110 overs** of each first innings and retained whatever the result of the match).

  (i) A maximum of five batting points to be available as under:
      200 to 249 runs – 1 point; 250 to 299 runs – 2 points; 300 to 349 runs – 3 points; 350 to 399 runs – 4 points; 400 runs or over – 5 points.

  (ii) A maximum of three bowling points to be available as under:
      3 to 5 wickets taken – 1 point; 6 to 8 wickets taken – 2 points; 9 to 10 wickets taken – 3 points.

(e) If a match is abandoned without a ball being bowled, each side to score five points.

(f) The bottom two sides from Division 1 were relegated, with the top two sides in Division 2 being promoted. Should any sides in the Championship table be equal on points, the following tie-breakers will be applied in the order stated: most wins, fewest losses, team achieving most points in contests between teams level on points, most wickets taken, most runs scored.

COUNTY CHAMPIONSHIP RESULTS 2022

DIVISION 1

	ESSEX	GLOS	HANTS	KENT	LANCS	N'HANTS	SOM'T	SURREY	WARKS	YORKS
ESSEX		C'ford	C'ford	C'ford	C'ford	C'ford	C'ford			C'ford
		Ex 9w	Ex 12	Drawn	Drawn	Drawn	Drawn			Drawn
GLOS			Chelt		Bristol	Chelt	Bristol	Bristol	Bristol	Bristol
			H 6w		Drawn	Nh 2w	Sm I/246	Drawn	Gs 3w	Y 6w
HANTS	So'ton			So'ton	So'ton	So'ton	So'ton		So'ton	So'ton
	H 87			K 77	Drawn	H I/4	H I/113		H 8w	H 2w
KENT	Cant	Cant	Cant		Cant	Cant		Cant	Beck	
	Ex I/260	K 8w	H I/51		La 10w	Nh 203		K I/151		
LANCS	Man	Man		Man			S'port	Man	Man	Man
	Ex I/56	La I/57		La 184			Drawn	La I/130	Drawn	Drawn
N'HANTS	No'ton	No'ton	No'ton		No'ton			No'ton	No'ton	
	E 47	Drawn	Drawn		La 4w			Drawn	Drawn	
SOM'T	Taunton	Taunton	Taunton			Taunton		Taunton	Taunton	
	Ex 1w	Drawn	H 10w			Sm 352		Sy 3w	Sm I/82	
SURREY	Oval		Oval	Oval		Oval	Oval		Oval	Oval
	Sy 6w		Sy I/17	Drawn		Sy I/5	Sy 3w		Sy 6w	Sy 10w
WARKS	Birm		Birm	Birm	Birm	Birm	Birm	Birm		Birm
	Wa 10w		Wa 5	K 177	La 4w	Drawn	Drawn	Drawn		Drawn
YORKS	Leeds	Leeds	Scarb	Leeds	Leeds			Scarb	Leeds	
	Ex 1w	Gs 18	H 7w	Drawn	Drawn			Sy 4w	Drawn	

DIVISION 2

	DERBYS	DURHAM	GLAM	LEICS	MIDDX	NOTTS	SUSSEX	WORCS
DERBYS		Derby	Derby	Derby	Cfield	Derby	Derby	Derby
		Drawn	Drawn	Drawn	De 6w	Drawn	Drawn	Drawn
DURHAM	C-le-St		C-le-St	C-le-St	C-le-St	C-le-St	C-le-St	C-le-St
	Drawn		Du 58	Drawn	Drawn	Nt I/141	Du I/140	Drawn
GLAM	Cardiff	Cardiff		Cardiff	Cardiff	Cardiff	Cardiff	Cardiff
	Gm I/24	Drawn		Gm 6w	M I/82	Drawn	Gm 5w	Drawn
LEICS	Leics	Leics	Leics		Leics	Leics	Leics	
	De I/68	Du 7w	Gm I/28		M 80	Nt I/9	Drawn	
MIDDX	Lord's	Lord's	Lord's	Lord's		Lord's	Lord's	N'wood
	Drawn	M 6w	M 10w	M 10w		Drawn	Drawn	Wo 7w
NOTTS	N'ham	N'ham	N'ham	N'ham	N'ham		N'ham	N'ham
	Nt 10w	Nt 462	Gm 7w	Nt 241	Drawn		Nt 256	Nt 5w
SUSSEX	Hove	Hove	Hove	Hove	Hove	Hove		Hove
	Sx 5w	Drawn	Drawn	Drawn	M 7w	Nt 10w		Drawn
WORCS	Worcs	Worcs	Worcs	Worcs	Worcs	Worcs	Worcs	
	De 98	Drawn	Gm 3w	Wo I/259	Drawn	Wo I/79	Wo I/34	

COUNTY CHAMPIONS

The English County Championship was not officially constituted until December 1889. Prior to that date there was no generally accepted method of awarding the title; although the 'least matches lost' method existed, it was not consistently applied. Rules governing playing qualifications were agreed in 1873 and the first unofficial points system 15 years later.

Research has produced a list of champions dating back to 1826, but at least seven different versions exist for the period from 1864 to 1889 (see *The Wisden Book of Cricket Records*). Only from 1890 can any authorised list of county champions commence.

That first official Championship was contested between eight counties: Gloucestershire, Kent, Lancashire, Middlesex, Nottinghamshire, Surrey, Sussex and Yorkshire. The remaining counties were admitted in the following seasons: 1891 – Somerset, 1895 – Derbyshire, Essex, Hampshire, Leicestershire and Warwickshire, 1899 – Worcestershire, 1905 – Northamptonshire, 1921 – Glamorgan, and 1992 – Durham.

The Championship pennant was introduced by the 1951 champions, Warwickshire, and the Lord's Taverners' Trophy was first presented in 1973. The first sponsors, Schweppes (1977-83), were succeeded by Britannic Assurance (1984-98), PPP Healthcare (1999-2000), CricInfo (2001), Frizzell (2002-05), Liverpool Victoria (2006-15) and Specsavers (from 2016). Based on their previous season's positions, the 18 counties were separated into two divisions in 2000. From 2000 to 2005 the bottom three Division 1 teams were relegated and the top three Division 2 sides promoted. This was reduced to two teams from the end of the 2006 season.

1890	Surrey	1936	Derbyshire	1981	Nottinghamshire
1891	Surrey	1937	Yorkshire	1982	Middlesex
1892	Surrey	1938	Yorkshire	1983	Essex
1893	Yorkshire	1939	Yorkshire	1984	Essex
1894	Surrey	1946	Yorkshire	1985	Middlesex
1895	Surrey	1947	Middlesex	1986	Essex
1896	Yorkshire	1948	Glamorgan	1987	Nottinghamshire
1897	Lancashire	1949	Middlesex	1988	Worcestershire
1898	Yorkshire		Yorkshire	1989	Worcestershire
1899	Surrey	1950	Lancashire	1990	Middlesex
1900	Yorkshire		Surrey	1991	Essex
1901	Yorkshire	1951	Warwickshire	1992	Essex
1902	Yorkshire	1952	Surrey	1993	Middlesex
1903	Middlesex	1953	Surrey	1994	Warwickshire
1904	Lancashire	1954	Surrey	1995	Warwickshire
1905	Yorkshire	1955	Surrey	1996	Leicestershire
1906	Kent	1956	Surrey	1997	Glamorgan
1907	Nottinghamshire	1957	Surrey	1998	Leicestershire
1908	Yorkshire	1958	Surrey	1999	Surrey
1909	Kent	1959	Yorkshire	2000	Surrey
1910	Kent	1960	Yorkshire	2001	Yorkshire
1911	Warwickshire	1961	Hampshire	2002	Surrey
1912	Yorkshire	1962	Yorkshire	2003	Sussex
1913	Kent	1963	Yorkshire	2004	Warwickshire
1914	Surrey	1964	Worcestershire	2005	Nottinghamshire
1919	Yorkshire	1965	Worcestershire	2006	Sussex
1920	Middlesex	1966	Yorkshire	2007	Sussex
1921	Middlesex	1967	Yorkshire	2008	Durham
1922	Yorkshire	1968	Yorkshire	2009	Durham
1923	Yorkshire	1969	Glamorgan	2010	Nottinghamshire
1924	Yorkshire	1970	Kent	2011	Lancashire
1925	Yorkshire	1971	Surrey	2012	Warwickshire
1926	Lancashire	1972	Warwickshire	2013	Durham
1927	Lancashire	1973	Hampshire	2014	Yorkshire
1928	Lancashire	1974	Worcestershire	2015	Yorkshire
1929	Nottinghamshire	1975	Leicestershire	2016	Middlesex
1930	Lancashire	1976	Middlesex	2017	Essex
1931	Yorkshire	1977	Kent	2018	Surrey
1932	Yorkshire		Middlesex	2019	Essex
1933	Yorkshire	1978	Kent	2021	Warwickshire
1934	Lancashire	1979	Essex	2022	Surrey
1935	Yorkshire	1980	Middlesex		

COUNTY CHAMPIONSHIP FIXTURES 2023

DIVISION 1

	ESSEX	HANTS	KENT	LANCS	MIDDX	N'HANTS	NOTTS	SOM'T	SURREY	WARKS
ESSEX		C'ford	C'ford	C'ford	C'ford			C'ford	C'ford	C'ford
HANTS	So'ton				So'ton	So'ton	So'ton	So'ton	So'ton	So'ton
KENT	Cant	Cant		Cant		Cant	Cant		Cant	Cant
LANCS	B'pool	S'port			Man	Man	Man	Man	Man	
MIDDX	Lord's		Lord's			N'wood	Lord's	Lord's	Lord's	Lord's
N'HANTS	No'ton	No'ton	No'ton	No'ton	No'ton		No'ton	No'ton		
NOTTS	N'ham	N'ham	N'ham	N'ham	N'ham			N'ham		N'ham
SOM'T		Taunton	Taunton	Taunton		Taunton	Taunton		Taunton	Taunton
SURREY		Oval	Oval	Oval	Oval	Oval	Oval			Oval
WARKS	Birm		Birm	Birm	Birm	Birm		Birm	Birm	

DIVISION 2

	DERBYS	DURHAM	GLAM	GLOS	LEICS	SUSSEX	WORCS	YORKS
DERBYS		Derby	Derby	Derby	Derby	Derby	Derby	Cfield
DURHAM	C-le-St		C-le-St	C-le-St	C-le-St	C-le-St	C-le-St	C-le-St
GLAM	Cardiff	Cardiff		Cardiff	Cardiff	Cardiff	Cardiff	Cardiff
GLOS	Bristol	Bristol	Chelt		Bristol	Bristol	Chelt	Bristol
LEICS	Leics	Leics	Leics	Leics		Leics	Oakham	Leics
SUSSEX	Hove	Hove	Hove	Hove	Hove		Hove	Hove
WORCS	Worcs	Worcs	Worcs	Worcs	Worcs	Worcs		Worcs
YORKS	Scar	Scar	Leeds	Leeds	Leeds	Leeds	Leeds	

ROYAL LONDON ONE-DAY CUP 2022

This latest format of limited-overs competition was launched in 2014, and is now the only List-A tournament played in the UK. The top team from each group went through to the semi-finals, with a home draw; the second team from each group (drawn at home) played off against the third team from the other division to qualify for the semi-finals. The winner was decided in the final at Trent Bridge.

GROUP A		P	W	L	T	NR	Pts	Net RR
1	Sussex	8	6	2	–	–	12	+1.92
2	Leicestershire	8	6	2	–	–	12	+0.03
3	Nottinghamshire	8	5	3	–	–	10	+1.14
4	Middlesex	8	5	3	–	–	10	+0.32
5	Gloucestershire	8	5	3	–	–	10	+0.02
6	Warwickshire	8	4	3	1	–	9	–0.36
7	Surrey	8	2	5	1	–	5	–0.97
8	Somerset	8	1	7	–	–	2	–1.63
9	Durham	8	1	7	–	–	0	–0.65

GROUP B		P	W	L	T	NR	Pts	Net RR
1	Hampshire	8	7	1	–	–	14	+0.59
2	Lancashire	8	5	2	–	1	11	+0.55
3	Kent	8	4	3	–	1	9	–0.81
4	Glamorgan	8	4	4	–	–	8	–0.04
5	Yorkshire	8	4	4	–	–	8	–0.12
6	Essex	8	3	4	–	1	7	+0.81
7	Derbyshire	8	3	4	–	1	5	–0.35
8	Northamptonshire	8	2	6	–	–	4	–0.06
9	Worcestershire	8	2	6	–	–	4	–0.45

Win = 2 points. Tie (T)/No Result (NR) = 1 point.

Positions of counties finishing equal on points are decided by most wins or, if equal, the team that achieved the most points in the matches played between them; if still equal, the team with the higher net run rate (ie deducting from the average runs per over scored by that team in matches where a result was achieved, the average runs per over scored against that team). In the event the teams still cannot be separated, the winner will be decided by drawing lots.

Durham deducted two points for disciplinary breaches; Derbyshire deducted two points after a player's bat failed a bat-gauge test.

Statistical Highlights in 2022

Highest total	400-4	Sussex v Middlesex	Hove
Biggest win (runs)	216	Sussex (378-6) beat Surrey (162)	Hove
Biggest win (wkts)	10 (229 balls)	Notts (124-0) beat Somerset (119)	Taunton
Most runs	658 (ave 94.00)	S.S.Eskinazi (Middlesex)	
Highest innings	206*	O.G.Robinson	Kent v Worcestershire	Worcester
	206	A.G.H.Orr	Sussex v Somerset	Taunton
Most sixes (inns)	12	B.G.F.Green	Somerset v Durham	Taunton
Highest partnership	245*	S.A.Northeast/W.T.Root Glamorgan v Worcs	Worcester
Most wickets	22 (ave 14.59)	B.A.Hutton (Nottinghamshire)	
Best bowling	7-26	B.A.Hutton	Nottinghamshire v Leics	Leicester
Most economical	10-4-15-2	B.O.Coad	Yorkshire v Derbyshire	Chesterfield
Most expensive	9-0-110-0	M.K.Andersson	Middlesex v Sussex	Hove
Most w/k dismissals	14	B.C.Brown (Hampshire)	
Most catches	12	M.Montgomery (Nottinghamshire)	

2022 ROYAL LONDON ONE-DAY CUP FINAL
KENT v LANCASHIRE

At Trent Bridge, Nottingham, on 17 September.

Result: **KENT** won by 21 runs.

Toss: Kent. Award: J.D.M.Evison.

KENT		Runs	Balls	4/6	Fall
B.G.Compton	c Croft b Bailey	0	4	–	1- 0
J.D.M.Evison	b Lamb	97	111	14/1	3-212
† O.G.Robinson	c Lavelle b Hurt	43	48	6	2- 79
* J.L.Denly	b Hurt	78	69	8/1	4-245
A.J.Blake	c Jennings b Bailey	38	32	4/1	5-284
D.I.Stevens	not out	33	31	2	
G.Stewart	run out	1	2	–	6-287
H.Z.Finch	not out	4	4	–	
H.W.Podmore					
Hamidullah Qadri					
N.N.Gilchrist					
Extras	(B 2, LB 1, NB 2, W 7)	12			
Total	(6 wkts; 50 overs)	306			

LANCASHIRE		Runs	Balls	4/6	Fall
L.W.P.Wells	c and b Stewart	16	14	3	1- 40
* K.K.Jennings	c Blake b Qadri	72	62	11	3-126
J.J.Bohannon	c Stewart b Podmore	5	21	–	2- 71
S.J.Croft	c Blake b Gilchrist	72	83	7	5-212
D.J.Vilas	b Evison	11	16	–	4-153
R.P.Jones	lbw b Stewart	29	46	–	8-249
† G.I.D.Lavelle	c Evison b Gilchrist	6	8	–	6-220
D.J.Lamb	c Gilchrist b Stewart	20	14	2/1	7-248
T.E.Bailey	b Gilchrist	16	11	1	9-267
L.J.Hurt	b Evison	12	11	1	10-285
W.S.A.Williams	not out	8	7	–	
Extras	(LB 9, NB 2, W 2, Pen 5)	18			
Total	(48.4 overs)	285			

LANCASHIRE	O	M	R	W	KENT	O	M	R	W
Bailey	10	0	46	2	Stewart	7	0	42	3
Williams	10	0	62	0	Gilchrist	10	0	65	3
Lamb	10	0	57	1	Stevens	8	0	45	0
Hurt	10	1	64	2	Podmore	5	0	21	1
Wells	8	0	53	0	Hamidullah Qadri	9	0	43	1
Croft	2	0	21	0	Evison	6.4	0	34	2
					Denly	3	0	21	0

Umpires: P.R.Pollard and R.J.Warren

SEMI-FINALS

At The Rose Bowl, Southampton, on 30 August. Toss: Kent. **KENT** won by three wickets. Hampshire 310-9 (50; N.R.T.Gubbins 75, A.H.T.Donald 54, F.S.Organ 54). Kent 313-7 (49; O.G.Robinson 95, D.I.Stevens 84*, H.Z.Finch 52, J.O.I.Campbell 3-72).

At County Ground, Hove, 30 August. Toss: Lancashire. **LANCASHIRE** won by 65 runs. Lancashire 319-8 (50; D.J.Vilas 121, D.J.Lamb 57, G.I.D.Lavelle 50, F.J.Hudson-Prentice 3-43). Sussex 254 (46.3; A.G.H.Orr 71, L.J.Hurt 3-43).

PRINCIPAL LIST A RECORDS 1963-2022

These records cover all the major limited-overs tournaments played by the counties since the inauguration of the Gillette Cup in 1963.

Highest Totals		496-4		Surrey v Glos	The Oval	2007
		445-8		Notts v Northants	Nottingham	2016
Highest Total Batting Second		429		Glamorgan v Surrey	The Oval	2002
Lowest Totals		23		Middlesex v Yorks	Leeds	1974
		36		Leics v Sussex	Leicester	1973
Largest Victory (Runs)		346		Somerset beat Devon	Torquay	1990
		304		Sussex beat Ireland	Belfast	1996
Highest Scores	268		A.D.Brown	Surrey v Glamorgan	The Oval	2002
	206*		O.G.Robinson	Kent v Worcestershire	Worcester	2022
	206		A.I.Kallicharran	Warwicks v Oxfords	Birmingham	1984
	206		A.G.H.Orr	Surrey v Somerset	Taunton	2022
	203		A.D.Brown	Surrey v Hampshire	Guildford	1997
Fastest Hundred	36 balls		G.D.Rose	Somerset v Devon	Torquay	1990
	43 balls		R.R.Watson	Scotland v Somerset	Edinburgh	2003
	44 balls		M.A.Ealham	Kent v Derbyshire	Maidstone	1995
	44 balls		T.C.Smith	Lancashire v Worcs	Worcester	2012
	44 balls		D.I.Stevens	Kent v Sussex	Canterbury	2013
Most Sixes (Inns)	15		R.N.ten Doeschate	Essex v Scotland	Chelmsford	2013

Highest Partnership for each Wicket

1st	342	M.J.Lumb/M.H.Wessels	Notts v Northants	Nottingham	2016
2nd	302	M.E.Trescothick/C.Kieswetter	Somerset v Glos	Taunton	2008
3rd	309*	T.S.Curtis/T.M.Moody	Worcs v Surrey	The Oval	1994
4th	245*	S.A.Northeast/W.T.Root	Glamorgan v Worcs	Worcester	2022
5th	221*	R.R.Sarwan/M.A.Hardinges	Glos v Lancashire	Manchester	2005
6th	232	D.Wiese/B.C.Brown	Sussex v Hampshire	Southampton	2019
7th	170	D.R.Brown/A.F.Giles	Warwicks v Essex	Birmingham	2005
8th	174	R.W.T.Key/J.C.Tredwell	Kent v Surrey	The Oval	2007
9th	155	C.M.W.Read/A.J.Harris	Notts v Durham	Nottingham	1984
10th	82	G.Chapple/P.J.Martin	Lancashire v Worcs	Manchester	1996

Best Bowling	8-21	M.A.Holding	Derbyshire v Sussex	Hove	1988
	8-26	K.D.Boyce	Essex v Lancashire	Manchester	1971
	8-31	D.L.Underwood	Kent v Scotland	Edinburgh	1987
	8-66	S.R.G.Francis	Somerset v Derbys	Derby	2004
Four Wkts in Four Balls		A.Ward	Derbyshire v Sussex	Derby	1970
		S.M.Pollock	Warwickshire v Leics	Birmingham	1996
		V.C.Drakes	Notts v Derbyshire	Nottingham	1999
		D.A.Payne	Gloucestershire v Essex	Chelmsford	2010
		G.R.Napier	Essex v Surrey	Chelmsford	2013

Most Economical Analyses

8-8-0-0	B.A.Langford	Somerset v Essex	Yeovil	1969
8-7-1-1	D.R.Doshi	Notts v Northants	Northampton	1977
12-9-3-1	J.Simmons	Lancashire v Suffolk	Bury St Eds	1985
8-6-2-3	F.J.Titmus	Middlesex v Northants	Northampton	1972

Most Expensive Analyses

9-0-110-0	M.K.Andersson	Middlesex v Sussex	Hove	2022
9-0-108-3	S.D.Thomas	Glamorgan v Surrey	The Oval	2002
10-0-107-0	J.W.Dernbach	Surrey v Essex	The Oval	2008
11-0-103-0	G.Welch	Warwicks v Lancs	Birmingham	1995
10-0-101-1	M.J.J.Critchley	Derbyshire v Worcs	Worcester	2016

Century and Five Wickets in an Innings

154*, 5-26	M.J.Procter	Glos v Somerset	Taunton	1972
206, 6-32	A.I.Kallicharran	Warwicks v Oxfords	Birmingham	1984
103, 5-41	C.L.Hooper	Kent v Sussex	Maidstone	1993
113, 5-40	A.R.Roberts	Bedfords v Derbyshire CB	Tottenhow	2002
125, 5-41	I.R.Bell	Warwicks v Essex	Chelmsford	2003

Most Wicket-Keeping Dismissals in an Innings

8 (8 ct)	D.J.S.Taylor	Somerset v British Us	Taunton	1982
8 (8 ct)	D.J.Pipe	Worcs v Herts	Hertford	2001

Most Catches in an Innings by a Fielder

5	V.J.Marks	Combined Us v Kent	Oxford	1976
5	J.M.Rice	Hampshire v Warwicks	Southampton	1978
5	D.J.G.Sales	Northants v Essex	Northampton	2007

VITALITY BLAST 2022

In 2022, the Twenty20 competition was again sponsored by Vitality. Between 2003 and 2009, three regional leagues competed to qualify for the knockout stages, but this was reduced to two leagues in 2010, before returning to the three-division format in 2012. Since 2014, the competition has reverted to two regional leagues, except for 2020 when, due to Covid constraints, the three-division format applied.

NORTH GROUP

		P	W	L	T	NR	Pts	Net RR
1.	Warwickshire (4)	14	9	5	–	–	18	+1.21
2.	Lancashire (3)	14	8	4	1	1	18	+0.43
3.	Derbyshire (8)	14	9	5	–	–	18	+0.05
4.	Yorkshire (2)	14	7	6	1	–	15	+0.72
5.	Nottinghamshire (1)	14	7	6	–	1	15	+0.05
6.	Leicestershire (6)	14	8	6	–	–	14	+0.05
7.	Northamptonshire (9)	14	6	6	–	2	14	–0.04
8.	Durham (7)	14	3	10	–	1	7	–0.64
9.	Worcestershire (5)	14	2	11	–	1	5	–1.80

Leicestershire were deducted two points for breaches relating to onfield discipline.

SOUTH GROUP

		P	W	L	T	NR	Pts	Net RR
1.	Surrey (5)	14	10	3	–	1	21	+0.63
2.	Somerset (2)	14	10	4	–	–	20	+0.63
3.	Essex (7)	14	9	4	–	1	19	+0.88
4.	Hampshire (4)	14	9	5	–	–	18	+0.19
5.	Gloucestershire (6)	14	6	6	–	2	14	+0.02
6.	Glamorgan (9)	14	5	7	–	2	12	–0.15
7.	Sussex (3)	14	4	10	–	–	8	–0.39
8.	Middlesex (8)	14	4	10	–	–	8	–0.98
9.	Kent (1)	14	3	11	–	–	6	–0.67

QUARTER-FINALS:	YORKSHIRE beat Surrey by 1 run at The Oval.
	HAMPSHIRE beat Warwickshire by 104 runs at Birmingham.
	LANCASHIRE beat Essex by seven wickets at Manchester.
	SOMERSET beat Derbyshire by 191 runs at Taunton.
SEMI-FINALS:	LANCASHIRE beat Yorkshire by six wickets at Birmingham.
	HAMPSHIRE beat Somerset by 37 runs at Birmingham.

LEADING AGGREGATES AND RECORDS 2022

BATTING (600 runs)	M	I	NO	HS	Runs	Avge	100	50	R/100b	Sixes
J.M.Vince (Hants)	16	16	2	129*	678	48.42	2	4	146.1	21
R.R.Rossouw (Som't)	16	16	3	93	623	47.92	–	7	192.2	42

BOWLING (24 wkts)	O	M	R	W	Avge	BB		4wR/Over
R.J.Gleeson (Lancs)	56.0	1	457	25	18.28	5-33	2	8.16
Naveen-ul-Haq (Leics)	50.2	–	388	24	16.16	5-11	3	7.70

Highest total	265-5	Somerset v Derbyshire	Taunton
Biggest win (runs)	191	Somerset (265-5) beat Derbyshire (74)	Taunton
Biggest win (wkts)	10	Yorkshire (106-0) beat Warwicks (101)	Birmingham
Highest innings	129*	J.M.Vince Hampshire v Somerset	Taunton
Most sixes	42	R.R.Rossouw (Somerset)	
Highest partnership	174*	S.R.Hain/A.J.Hose Warwickshire v Notts	Nottingham
Best bowling	5-11	Naveen-ul-Haq Leicestershire v Worcs	Worcester
Most economical	4-0-11-5	Naveen-ul-Haq Leicestershire v Worcs	Worcester
Most expensive	4-0-82-0	M.H.McKiernan Derbyshire v Somerset	Taunton
Most w/k dismissals	21	A.L.Davies (Warwickshire)	
Most catches	15	T.H.David (Lancashire)	

2022 VITALITY BLAST FINAL
HAMPSHIRE v LANCASHIRE

At Edgbaston, Birmingham, on 16 July (floodlit).
Result: **HAMPSHIRE** won by 1 run.
Toss: Hampshire. Award: B.R.McDermott.

HAMPSHIRE		Runs	Balls	4/6	Fall
* J.M.Vince	b Gleeson	5	5	–	1- 11
† B.R.McDermott	b Parkinson	62	36	4/4	5- 90
T.J.Prest	c Hartley b Wood	2	7	–	2- 15
J.J.Weatherley	c Croft b Parkinson	9	13	1	3- 58
L.A.Dawson	c Vilas b Parkinson	2	6	–	4- 67
R.A.Whiteley	c Jennings b Wood	22	20	1	6-105
J.K.Fuller	c Jennings b Lamb	10	7	–/1	6-105
N.T.Ellis	c David b Parkinson	2	5	–	7-111
C.P.Wood	not out	20	17	1/1	
M.S.Crane	not out	7	5	–	
B.T.J.Wheal					
Extras	(B 6, LB 1, NB 2, W 2)	11			
Total	**(8 wkts; 20 overs)**	**152**			

LANCASHIRE		Runs	Balls	4/6	Fall
† P.D.Salt	c Prest b Wood	10	4	1/1	1- 12
K.K.Jennings	c sub (S.W.Currie) b Dawson	24	20	1/1	3- 77
S.J.Croft	c McDermott b Crane	36	25	5	2- 72
* D.J.Vilas	c Vince b Dawson	23	21	2/1	4-104
L.W.P.Wells	run out	27	24	2/1	7-142
T.H.David	lbw b Fuller	8	11	–	5-118
D.J.Lamb	c Vince b Fuller	2	7	–	6-124
L.Wood	run out	9	5	1	8-146
T.W.Hartley	not out	1	2	–	
R.J.Gleeson	not out	2	3	–	
M.W.Parkinson					
Extras	(B 1, NB 4, W 4)	9			
Total	**(8 wkts; 20 overs)**	**151**			

LANCASHIRE	O	M	R	W	HAMPSHIRE	O	M	R	W
Hartley	4	0	24	0	Wood	4	0	38	1
Gleeson	4	0	27	1	Wheal	2	0	28	0
Wood	4	0	26	2	Ellis	4	0	23	0
Lamb	3	0	21	1	Dawson	4	0	23	2
Parkinson	4	0	26	4	Crane	3	0	19	1
Wells	1	0	21	0	Fuller	3	0	19	2

Umpires: G.D.Lloyd and DJ.Millns

TWENTY20 CUP WINNERS

2003	Surrey	2010	Hampshire	2017	Nottinghamshire
2004	Leicestershire	2011	Leicestershire	2018	Worcestershire
2005	Somerset	2012	Hampshire	2019	Essex
2006	Leicestershire	2013	Northamptonshire	2020	Nottinghamshire
2007	Kent	2014	Warwickshire	2021	Kent
2008	Middlesex	2015	Lancashire	2022	Hampshire
2009	Sussex	2016	Northamptonshire		

PRINCIPAL TWENTY20 CUP RECORDS 2003-22

Highest Total	265-5		Somerset v Derbyshire	Taunton	2022
Highest Total Batting 2nd	233-6		Sussex v Essex	Chelmsford	2022
Lowest Total	44		Glamorgan v Surrey	The Oval	2019
Largest Victory (Runs)	191		Somerset v Derbyshire	Taunton	2022
Largest Victory (Balls)	82		Nottinghamshire v Worcs	Nottingham	2021
Highest Scores	161	A.Lyth	Yorkshire v Northants	Leeds	2017
	158*	B.B.McCullum	Warwickshire v Derbys	Birmingham	2015
	153*	L.J.Wright	Sussex v Essex	Chelmsford	2014
	152*	G.R.Napier	Essex v Sussex	Chelmsford	2008
	151*	C.H.Gayle	Somerset v Kent	Taunton	2015
Fastest Hundred	34 balls	A.Symonds	Kent v Middlesex	Maidstone	2004
Most Sixes (Innings)	16	G.R.Napier	Essex v Sussex	Chelmsford	2008
Most Runs in Career	5026	L.J.Wright	Sussex		2004-22

Highest Partnership for each Wicket

1st	207	J.L.Denly/D.J.Bell-Drummond	Kent v Essex	Chelmsford	2017
2nd	186	J.L.Langer/C.L.White	Somerset v Glos	Taunton	2006
3rd	174*	S.R.Hain/A.J.Hose	Warwickshire v Notts	Nottingham	2022
4th	159*	L.J.Wright/M.W.Machan	Sussex v Essex	Chelmsford	2014
5th	171	A.J.Hose/D.R.Mousley	Warwickshire v Northants	Birmingham	2020
6th	141*	H.C.Brook/J.A.Thompson	Yorkshire v Worcestershire	Leeds	2021
7th	88	D.A.Douthwaite/W.J.Weighell	Glamorgan v Middlesex	Radlett	2021
8th	86*	J.A.Simpson/T.G.Southee	Middlesex v Hampshire	Southampton	2017
9th	69	C.J.Anderson/J.H.Davey	Somerset v Surrey	The Oval	2017
10th	59	H.H.Streak/J.E.Anyon	Warwickshire v Worcs	Birmingham	2005

Best Bowling

	7-18	C.N.Ackermann	Leics v Warwicks	Leicester	2019
	6- 5	A.V.Suppiah	Somerset v Glamorgan	Cardiff	2011
	6-16	T.G.Southee	Essex v Glamorgan	Chelmsford	2011
	6-19	T.T.Bresnan	Yorkshire v Lancashire	Leeds	2017
	6-19	Shaheen Shah Afridi	Hampshire v Middlesex	Southampton	2020
	6-21	A.J.Hall	Northants v Worcs	Northampton	2008
	6-24	T.J.Murtagh	Surrey v Middlesex	Lord's	2005
	6-28	J.K.Fuller	Middlesex v Hampshire	Southampton	2018
Most Wkts in Career	205	D.R.Briggs	Hampshire, Sussex, Warwickshire		2010-22

Most Economical Innings Analyses (Qualification: 4 overs)

4-1-4-3	S.R.Patel	Nottinghamshire v Worcs	Nottingham	2021

Most Maiden Overs in an Innings

4-2-9-1	M.Morkel	Kent v Surrey	Beckenham	2007
4-2-5-2	A.C.Thomas	Somerset v Hampshire	Southampton	2010
4-2-14-1	S.M.Curran	Surrey v Sussex	Hove	2018

Most Expensive Innings Analyses

4-0-82-0	M.H.McKiernan	Derbyshire v Somerset	Taunton	2022
4-0-77-0	B.W.Sanderson	Northants v Yorkshire	Leeds	2017

Most Wicket-Keeping Dismissals in Career

114	J.S.Foster	Essex		2003-17

Most Wicket-Keeping Dismissals in an Innings

5 (5 ct)	M.J.Prior	Sussex v Middlesex	Richmond	2006
5 (4 ct, 1 st)	G.L.Brophy	Yorkshire v Durham	Chester-le-St	2008
5 (3 ct, 2 st)	B.J.M.Scott	Worcs v Yorkshire	Worcester	2011
5 (4 ct, 1 st)	G.C.Wilson	Surrey v Hampshire	The Oval	2014
5 (5 ct)	N.J.O'Brien	Leics v Northants	Leicester	2014
5 (3 ct, 2 st)	J.A.Simpson	Middlesex v Surrey	Lord's	2014
5 (4 ct, 1 st)	C.B.Cooke	Glamorgan v Surrey	Cardiff	2016
5 (3 ct, 2 st)	A.L.Davies	Warwickshire v Leics	Birmingham	2022
5 (3 ct, 2 st)	J.R.Bracey	Gloucestershire v Sussex	Hove	2022

Most Catches in Career

122	S.J.Croft	Lancashire		2006-22

Most Catches in an Innings by a Fielder

5	M.W.Machan	Sussex v Glamorgan	Hove	2016

YOUNG CRICKETER OF THE YEAR

This annual award, made by The Cricket Writers' Club, is currently restricted to players qualified for England, Andrew Symonds meeting that requirement at the time of his award, and under the age of 23 on 1st May. In 1986 their ballot resulted in a dead heat. Up to 7 March 2022 their selections have gained a tally of 2,897 international Test match caps (shown in brackets).

1950	R.Tattersall (16)	1975	A.Kennedy	1999	A.J.Tudor (10)
1951	P.B.H.May (66)	1976	G.Miller (34)	2000	P.J.Franks
1952	F.S.Trueman (67)	1977	I.T.Botham (102)	2001	O.A.Shah (6)
1953	M.C.Cowdrey (114)	1978	D.I.Gower (117)	2002	R.Clarke (2)
1954	P.J.Loader (13)	1979	P.W.G.Parker (1)	2003	J.M.Anderson (179)
1955	K.F.Barrington (82)	1980	G.R.Dilley (41)	2004	I.R.Bell (118)
1956	B.Taylor	1981	M.W.Gatting (79)	2005	A.N.Cook (161)
1957	M.J.Stewart (8)	1982	N.G.Cowans (19)	2006	S.C.J.Broad (161)
1958	A.C.D.Ingleby-Mackenzie	1983	N.A.Foster (29)	2007	A.U.Rashid (19)
1959	G.Pullar (28)	1984	R.J.Bailey (4)	2008	R.S.Bopara (13)
1960	D.A.Allen (39)	1985	D.V.Lawrence (5)	2009	J.W.A.Taylor (7)
1961	P.H.Parfitt (37)	1986 {	A.A.Metcalfe	2010	S.T.Finn (36)
1962	P.J.Sharpe (12)		J.J.Whitaker (1)	2011	J.M.Bairstow (89)
1963	G.Boycott (108)	1987	R.J.Blakey (2)	2012	J.E.Root (129)
1964	J.M.Brearley (39)	1988	M.P.Maynard (4)	2013	B.A.Stokes (91)
1965	A.P.E.Knott (95)	1989	N.Hussain (96)	2014	A.Z.Lees (10)
1966	D.L.Underwood (86)	1990	M.A.Atherton (115)	2015	J.A.Leaning
1967	A.W.Greig (58)	1991	M.R.Ramprakash (52)	2016	B.M.Duckett (9)
1968	R.M.H.Cottam (4)	1992	I.D.K.Salisbury (15)	2017	D.W.Lawrence (11)
1969	A.Ward (5)	1993	M.N.Lathwell (2)	2018	S.M.Curran (24)
1970	C.M.Old (46)	1994	J.P.Crawley (37)	2019	T.Banton
1971	J.Whitehouse	1995	A.Symonds (26 – Australia)	2020	Z.Crawley (33)
1972	D.R.Owen-Thomas	1996	C.E.W.Silverwood (6)	2021	H.C.Brook (6)
1973	M.Hendrick (30)	1997	B.C.Hollioake (2)	2022	J.M.Cox
1974	P.H.Edmonds (51)	1998	A.Flintoff (79)		

THE PROFESSIONAL CRICKETERS' ASSOCIATION

PLAYER OF THE YEAR

Founded in 1967, the Professional Cricketers' Association introduced this award, decided by their membership, in 1970. The award, now known as the Reg Hayter Cup, is presented at the PCA's Annual Awards Dinner in London.

1970 {	M.J.Procter	1987	R.J.Hadlee	2005	A.Flintoff
	J.D.Bond	1988	G.A.Hick	2006	M.R.Ramprakash
1971	L.R.Gibbs	1989	S.J.Cook	2007	O.D.Gibson
1972	A.M.E.Roberts	1990	G.A.Gooch	2008	M.van Jaarsveld
1973	P.G.Lee	1991	Waqar Younis	2009	M.E.Trescothick
1974	B.Stead	1992	C.A.Walsh	2010	N.M.Carter
1975	Zaheer Abbas	1993	S.L.Watkin	2011	M.E.Trescothick
1976	P.G.Lee	1994	B.C.Lara	2012	N.R.D.Compton
1977	M.J.Procter	1995	D.G.Cork	2013	M.M.Ali
1978	J.K.Lever	1996	P.V.Simmons	2014	A.Lyth
1979	J.K.Lever	1997	S.P.James	2015	C.Rushworth
1980	R.D.Jackman	1998	M.B.Loye	2016	B.M.Duckett
1981	R.J.Hadlee	1999	S.G.Law	2017	S.R.Patel
1982	M.D.Marshall	2000	M.E.Trescothick	2018	J.L.Denly
1983	K.S.McEwan	2001	D.P.Fulton	2019	B.A.Stokes
1984	R.J.Hadlee	2002	M.P.Vaughan	2020	C.R.Woakes
1985	N.V.Radford	2003	Mushtaq Ahmed	2021	J.E.Root
1986	C.A.Walsh	2004	A.Flintoff	2022	J.M.Bairstow

2022 FIRST-CLASS AVERAGES

These averages involve the 459 players who appeared in the 136 first-class matches played by 23 teams in England and Wales during the 2022 season.

'Cap' denotes the season in which the player was awarded a 1st XI cap by the county he represented in 2022. If he played for more than one county in 2022, the county(ies) who awarded him his cap is (are) underlined. Durham and Gloucestershire now cap players on first-class debut. Worcestershire now award county colours when players make their Championship debut.

Team abbreviations: De – Derbyshire; Du – Durham; E – England; Ex – Essex; Gm – Glamorgan; Gs – Gloucestershire; H – Hampshire; I – India; K – Kent; La – Lancashire; Le – Leicestershire; M – Middlesex; Nh – Northamptonshire; Nt – Nottinghamshire; NZ – New Zealand; SA – South Africa; Sm – Somerset; SLD – Sri Lanka Cricket Development XI; Sy – Surrey; Sx – Sussex; Wa – Warwickshire; Wo – Worcestershire; Y – Yorkshire.

† Left-handed batsman. Cap: a dash (–) denotes a non-county player. A blank denotes uncapped by his current county.

BATTING AND FIELDING

	Cap	M	I	NO	HS	Runs	Avge	100	50	Ct/St
K.J.Abbott (H)	2017	13	18	3	57*	233	15.53	–	1	–
T.B.Abell (Sm)	2018	13	22	2	150*	1039	51.95	5	4	14
C.N.Ackermann (Le)	2019	12	23	2	277*	744	35.42	2	2	16
R.Ahmed (Le)		3	6	–	122	195	32.50	1	–	2
B.W.Aitchison (De)		6	10	2	25*	119	14.87	–	–	4
T.E.Albert (H)		1	1	1	69*	69	–	–	1	2
K.L.Aldridge (Sm)		8	12	2	41	128	12.80	–	–	4
B.M.J.Allison (Ex)		3	5	2	69*	164	54.66	–	2	1
† T.P.Alsop (Sx)		13	24	2	150	930	42.27	4	4	14
H.M.Amla (Sx)	2021	14	21	3	133	718	39.88	2	3	4
† J.M.Anderson (E/La)	2003	10	9	6	9	33	11.00	–	–	4
M.K.Andersson (M)		5	6	1	62	234	46.80	–	2	–
J.A.Atkins (Sx)		3	5	2	17	36	12.00	–	–	–
A.A.P.Atkinson (Sy)		5	5	1	91	201	50.25	–	2	1
† M.H.Azad (Le)		11	21	1	104	579	28.95	1	4	3
Azhar Ali (Wo)	2022	11	16	–	225	656	41.00	1	3	4
T.E.Bailey (La)	2018	13	16	2	59	208	14.85	–	1	1
J.M.Bairstow (E)	–	6	11	2	162	681	75.66	4	1	12
J.O.Baker (Wo)	2021	10	12	1	43	178	16.18	–	–	8
G.P.Balderson (La)		11	16	3	97	253	19.46	–	1	3
J.T.Ball (Nt)	2016	1	2	–	20	20	10.00	–	–	–
E.R.Bamber (M)	2022	10	12	3	37*	109	12.11	–	–	3
K.N.A.Bandara (SLD)	–	1	1	–	9	9	9.00	–	–	–
T.Banton (Sm)		6	9	–	126	346	38.44	1	2	2
† K.H.D.Barker (H)	2021	14	22	2	76	595	29.75	–	4	1
E.G.Barnard (Wo)	2015	14	18	3	163*	895	59.66	3	5	7
E.Barnes (Le)		10	17	2	46	260	17.33	–	–	4
N.A.Barnwell (Sy)		1	1	–	22	22	22.00	–	–	–
G.A.Bartlett (Sm)		7	12	1	111	456	41.45	1	2	2
† F.J.Bean (Y)		3	6	–	53	138	23.00	–	1	1
A.P.Beard (Ex/Sx)		6	7	3	33	99	24.75	–	–	1
D.G.Bedingham (Du)	2020	12	17	3	191	664	47.42	2	2	9
G.J.Bell (La)		2	3	–	24	42	14.00	–	–	1
D.J.Bell-Drummond (K)	2015	14	25	4	149	923	43.95	4	3	6
C.G.Benjamin (Du/Wa)	2022	7	12	2	82*	290	29.00	–	1	8
G.K.Berg (Nh)		6	8	1	75	207	29.57	–	2	1
D.M.Bess (Y)	2021	13	19	2	89	499	29.35	–	4	6
† J.G.Bethell (Gs/Wa)	2022	4	6	–	61	111	18.50	–	1	4
T.R.Bevan (Gm)		1	1	–	48	48	48.00	–	–	–

	Cap	M	I	NO	HS	Runs	Avge	100	50	Ct/St
S.W.Billings (E/K)	2015	7	8	1	44	179	25.57	–	–	28/1
J.M.Bird (K)		3	5	2	53*	85	28.33	–	1	–
T.A.Blundell (NZ)		3	6	1	106	383	76.60	1	3	10
J.J.Bohannon (La)	2021	14	20	–	231	805	40.25	3	1	6
S.G.Borthwick (Du)	2009	14	24	2	96	764	34.72	–	7	19
T.A.Boult (NZ)	–	3	6	3	17	55	18.33	–	–	3
M.G.Bracewell (NZ)	–	2	4	–	49	96	24.00	–	–	–
† J.R.Bracey (Gs)	2016	14	27	1	177	702	27.00	2	3	47/4
D.R.Briggs (Wa)	2021	13	20	2	65	297	16.50	–	1	3
† S.C.J.Broad (E/Nt)	2008	11	11	2	45*	197	21.88	–	–	5
H.C.Brook (E/Y)	2021	9	13	3	194	979	97.90	3	6	9
H.J.H.Brookes (Wa)		9	12	1	55	183	16.63	–	1	2
J.A.Brooks (Sm/Sx)		9	12	3	36	174	19.33	–	–	3
B.C.Brown (H)		13	20	2	157	696	38.66	1	4	42/1
† N.L.J.Browne (Ex)	2015	14	26	3	234*	797	34.65	2	2	10
N.L.Buck (Nh)		1	2	1	13	14	14.00	–	–	–
S.G.Budinger (Le)		3	6	–	64	126	21.00	–	1	3
J.J.Bumrah (I)	–	1	2	1	31*	38	38.00	–	–	1
M.G.K.Burgess (Wa)	2021	12	18	–	178	745	41.38	2	3	37/1
† R.J.Burns (Sy)	2014	14	23	2	132	842	40.09	3	2	4
G.D.Burrows (Sx)		2	3	–	2	2	0.66	–	–	–
J.J.Bushnell (Du)	2022	4	7	2	66	216	43.20	–	1	–
† E.J.Byrom (Gm)		8	13	1	176	588	49.00	2	2	3
H.R.C.Came (De)		5	9	–	78	300	33.33	–	3	3
J.O.I.Campbell (H)		1								1
K.S.Carlson (Gm)	2021	12	22	1	91	491	23.38	–	3	6
B.A.Carse (Du)	2016	2	4	1	28	63	21.00	–	–	–
J.J.Carson (Sx)		3	5	1	58	108	27.00	–	1	–
O.J.Carter (Sx)		9	15	–	185	629	41.93	1	5	20
H.W.R.Cartwright (De)		3	6	2	71*	96	24.00	–	1	3
K.K.A.T.Chandima (SLD)	–	1	2	1	103*	151	151.00	1	–	1
Z.J.Chappell (Gs)	2022	4	8	1	20	51	7.28	–	–	1
† B.G.Charlesworth (Gs)	2018	5	10	–	64	208	20.80	–	2	5
J.Clark (Sy)	2022	11	14	3	137	481	43.72	1	4	2
† T.G.R.Clark (Sx)		13	24	1	138	765	33.26	2	4	9
J.M.Clarke (Nt)	2021	14	22	3	95	682	35.89	–	5	13
B.O.Coad (Y)	2018	5	9	3	69	146	24.33	–	1	1
J.J.Cobb (Nh)	2018	8	14	1	88	327	25.15	–	2	3
J.M.Coles (Sx)		5	8	1	59	179	25.57	–	2	2
B.G.Compton (K)		13	25	3	140	1193	54.22	4	6	7
S.Conners (De)	2022	14	15	3	23	65	5.41	–	–	6
† D.P.Conway (NZ)	–	3	6	–	52	151	25.16	–	1	–
† A.N.Cook (Ex)	2005	14	25	2	145	966	42.00	4	2	20
S.J.Cook (Ex)	2020	12	20	7	38	179	13.76	–	–	5
C.B.Cooke (Gm)	2016	13	21	6	191*	840	56.00	2	5	51/5
† T.R.Cornall (Wo)	2022	5	7	1	31*	89	14.83	–	–	2
P.Coughlin (Du)	2012	5	6	2	100*	157	39.25	1	–	4
J.M.Cox (K)		12	20	–	158	917	45.85	2	6	14
O.B.Cox (Wo)	2009	7	9	2	55	167	23.85	–	2	22/1
M.S.Crane (H/Sx)	2021	3	2	–	13	21	10.50	–	–	1
Z.Crawley (E/K)	2019	16	30	1	84	743	25.62	–	5	21
M.J.J.Critchley (Ex)		13	20	–	132	446	22.30	1	1	9
H.T.Crocombe (Sx)		9	12	1	36	126	11.63	–	–	2
S.J.Croft (La)	2010	14	20	1	155	837	44.05	2	3	9
† D.L.S.Croospulle (SLD)	–	3	5	–	136	260	52.00	1	–	3
B.C.Cullen (M)		1	1	1	1	1	1.00	–	–	1
T.N.Cullen (Gm)		2	4	–	21	47	11.75	–	–	8
† B.J.Curran (Nh)		2	3	–	18	28	9.33	–	–	3

	Cap	M	I	NO	HS	Runs	Avge	100	50	Ct/St
† S.M.Curran (Sy)	2018	5	6	–	126	454	75.66	1	4	6
T.K.Curran (Sy)	2016	2	3	–	115	126	42.00	1	–	3
B.J.Currie (Sx)		4	7	4	7	15	5.00	–	–	1
A.K.Dal (De)	2022	13	19	6	146*	957	73.61	3	5	7
A.S.Dale (Gs)	2022	8	14	8	36*	71	11.83	–	–	–
A.A.Daniel (SLD)	–	1	1	–	21	21	21.00	–	–	1
J.H.Davey (Sm)	2021	8	11	5	31*	187	31.16	–	–	5
A.L.Davies (Wa)		13	24	1	121	649	28.21	1	3	14
† J.L.B.Davies (M)		3	4	–	25	39	9.75	–	–	3
† S.M.Davies (Sm)	2017	8	14	–	51	234	16.71	–	1	26
W.S.Davis (Le)		3	5	2	32*	52	17.33	–	–	1
L.A.Dawson (H)	2013	12	18	1	171	587	34.52	1	3	18
J.M.de Caires (M)		3	6	–	80	101	16.83	–	1	1
C.de Grandhomme (NZ/Sy)		4	5	1	66	130	32.50	–	1	2
M.de Lange (Sm)		3	4	1	13*	22	7.33	–	–	1
D.A.O.de Silva (SLD)	–	1	1	1	1*	1	–	–	–	–
† H.K.M.de Silva (SLD)	–	1	1	–	16	16	16.00	–	–	–
J.L.Denly (K)	2008	8	13	1	141	524	43.66	1	3	2
† C.D.J.Dent (Gs)	2010	10	19	1	207*	714	39.66	2	4	6
S.R.Dickson (Du)	2020	10	18	–	186	858	47.66	4	2	5
B.L.D'Oliveira (Wo)	2012	13	18	5	169*	768	59.07	3	2	6
A.H.T.Donald (H)		10	15	–	94	414	27.60	–	3	20
† D.C.Drakes (Y)		1	2	–	21	27	13.50	–	–	–
G.S.Drissell (Du)	2022	3	5	1	16	48	12.00	–	–	1
† J.L.du Plooy (De)	2022	14	23	3	134	845	42.25	2	5	6
† B.M.Duckett (Nt)	2020	10	14	–	241	1012	72.28	3	5	8
J.A.Duffy (K)		2	2	1	1	1	0.50	–	–	2
H.G.Duke (Y)		8	12	1	48	239	21.72	–	–	19/1
E.J.H.Eckersley (Du)	2019	8	11	1	58	143	14.30	–	1	22/1
† D.Elgar (SA)	–	3	5	–	47	107	21.40	–	–	4
† S.J.Erwee (SA)	–	3	5	–	73	127	25.40	–	1	3
S.S.Eskinazi (M)	2018	8	12	1	118	437	39.72	2	1	9
S.T.Evans (Le)		9	18	2	77*	457	28.56	–	4	1
J.D.M.Evison (K/Le/Nt)		6	9	1	109*	216	27.00	1	–	2
† Faheem Ashraf (Sx)		3	5	–	33	65	13.00	–	–	1
T.C.Fell (Wo)	2013	1	1	–	17	17	17.00	–	–	2
K.N.M.Fernando (SLD)	–	3	5	–	269	326	65.20	1	–	3
M.N.K.Fernando (SLD)	–	3	5	1	99	187	46.75	–	2	1
M.G.A.Finan (Le)		3	6	2	58	102	25.50	–	1	1
A.W.Finch (Wo)	2019	3	4	2	33	82	41.00	–	–	–
H.Z.Finch (K)		1	2	–	24	24	12.00	–	–	1
S.T.Finn (Y)	2022	5	7	2	10*	34	6.80	–	–	2
M.D.Fisher (Y)	2022	2	3	1	16*	25	12.50	–	–	1
L.J.Fletcher (Nt)	2014	10	9	3	51	132	22.00	–	2	2
B.T.Foakes (E/Sy)	2016	15	21	7	132*	826	59.00	2	4	70/1
W.A.R.Fraine (Y)		7	13	1	53	203	16.91	–	1	7
J.K.Fuller (H)	2022	13	21	4	78*	527	31.00	–	2	6
S.T.Gabriel (Y)		2	3	–	5	7	2.33	–	–	1
G.A.Garrett (Wa)		1	2	1	10*	10	10.00	–	–	1
† G.H.S.Garton (Sx)		1	1	–	53	53	53.00	–	1	–
E.N.Gay (Nh)		14	25	–	145	825	33.00	2	4	20
B.B.A.Geddes (Sy)		4	5	–	124	280	56.00	2	–	3
B.J.Gibbon (Wo)	2022	7	6	2	20	37	9.25	–	–	1
O.J.Gibson (Du)	2022	7	7	2	6	7	1.40	–	–	1
N.N.Gilchrist (K)		8	13	–	14	57	4.38	–	–	2
S.Gill (Gm/I)		4	6	–	119	265	44.16	1	1	4
† B.A.Godleman (De)	2015	12	20	–	158	468	23.40	1	–	3
L.P.Goldsworthy (Sm)		10	17	2	130	558	37.20	1	3	1

	Cap	M	I	NO	HS	Runs	Avge	100	50	Ct/St
D.C.Goodman (Gs)	2021	1	2	–	18	19	9.50	–	–	3
A.W.Gorvin (Gm)		3	4	–	23	27	6.75	–	–	2
B.G.F.Green (Sm)		4	8	–	20	92	11.50	–	–	4
L.Gregory (Sm)	2015	11	18	3	110*	532	35.46	1	3	13
† N.R.T.Gubbins (H)	2022	14	24	3	130	754	35.90	2	2	4
B.D.Guest (De)	2022	14	24	–	138	923	38.45	4	2	52
S.N.S.Gunathilake (SLD)		3	4	1	58*	122	40.66	–	2	4
S.R.Hain (Wa)	2018	12	21	3	202*	1137	63.16	3	6	12
† T.J.Haines (Sx)	2021	12	21	2	243	941	49.52	3	3	4
H.Hameed (Nt)	2020	14	24	3	196	1235	58.80	4	7	6
Hamidullah Qadri (K)		4	6	1	87	242	48.40	–	2	–
M.A.H.Hammond (Gs)	2013	14	27	2	169	836	33.44	1	6	10
P.S.P.Handscomb (M)		5	8	1	79	220	31.42	–	1	9
† O.J.Hannon-Dalby (Wa)	2019	14	19	10	19*	81	9.00	–	–	2
A.M.Hardie (Sy)		1	2	1	46	86	86.00	–	1	–
Haris Rauf (Y)		4	4	1	6	15	5.00	–	–	2
S.R.Harmer (Ex/SA)	2018	12	20	3	75*	414	24.35	–	4	9
J.A.R.Harris (Gm)	2010	11	13	3	34	162	16.20	–	–	1
† M.S.Harris (Gs)	2022	9	17	–	159	726	42.70	3	2	8
† T.W.Hartley (La)		5	6	–	19	55	13.75	–	–	3
Hasan Ali (La)	2022	3	6	–	19	39	6.50	–	–	–
J.A.Haynes (Wo)	2019	13	19	2	153	811	47.70	3	1	13
T.G.Helm (M)	2019	7	8	4	51	207	51.75	–	2	1
† B.E.Hendricks (Le)		6	11	5	22	118	19.66	–	–	1
M.J.Henry (K/NZ)		3	6	–	34	97	16.16	–	–	2
R.F.Higgins (Gs/M)	2018	14	23	1	199	692	31.45	1	4	5
J.C.Hildreth (Sm)	2007	6	10	–	87	256	25.60	–	3	3
G.C.H.Hill (Y)		14	24	1	151*	729	31.69	2	–	6
L.J.Hill (Le)	2021	7	13	–	104	503	38.69	1	4	1
M.G.Hogan (Gm)	2013	14	13	4	19*	91	10.11	–	–	3
† M.D.E.Holden (M)		14	21	2	91	749	39.42	–	6	4
I.G.Holland (H)		14	24	1	99	519	22.56	–	3	13
† L.B.K.Hollman (M)	2021	12	15	–	82	518	34.53	–	4	11
F.J.Hudson-Prentice (Sx)		3	6	–	51	81	13.50	–	1	–
A.L.Hughes (De)	2017	1	2	–	49	82	41.00	–	–	1
S.F.Hunt (Sx)		8	12	6	13*	43	7.16	–	–	1
L.J.Hurt (De)		1	2	–	49	62	31.00	–	–	–
B.A.Hutton (Nt/Sy)	2021	7	9	2	20*	104	14.85	–	–	3
D.K.Ibrahim (Sx)		6	11	2	100*	197	21.88	1	–	1
Imam-ul-Haq (Sm)		3	6	1	90	177	35.40	–	2	–
† C.A.Ingram (Gm)	2017	5	9	1	178	596	66.22	3	1	4
S.S.Iyer (I)		–	1	2	19	34	17.00	–	–	2
W.G.Jacks (Sy)	2022	11	15	3	150*	648	54.00	2	3	11
† R.A.Jadeja (I)		1	2	–	104	127	63.50	1	–	–
L.W.James (Nt)		13	19	2	164*	890	52.35	3	5	9
K.A.Jamieson (NZ)		–	2	4	14	21	5.25	–	–	–
M.Jansen (SA)		–	2	3	–	48	82	27.33	–	–	5
† K.K.Jennings (La)	2018	11	17	–	318	1233	72.52	5	2	12
M.A.Jones (Du)	2018	10	18	1	206	878	51.64	2	5	1
R.P.Jones (La)		5	7	1	66	206	34.33	–	2	14
† F.D.M.Karunaratne (Y)		3	4	–	36	89	22.25	–	–	1
A.Karvelas (Sx)		2	4	–	57	73	18.25	–	1	–
Kashif Ali (Wo)	2022	1	2	–	52	58	29.00	–	1	–
† D.C.Kelly (H)		1	–	–	–	–	–	–	–	1
M.L.Kelly (Nh)		5	7	1	42	151	25.16	–	–	2
R.I.Keogh (Nh)	2019	14	25	–	130	804	32.16	3	2	3
H.L.Kerr (De)		1	2	–	16	24	12.00	–	–	1
S.C.Kerrigan (Nh)		7	10	2	43	140	17.50	–	–	5

	Cap	M	I	NO	HS	Runs	Avge	100	50	Ct/St
F.I.N.Khushi (Ex)		6	10	–	164	250	25.00	1	–	2
L.P.J.Kimber (Le)		11	19	–	104	503	26.47	1	3	6
T.Kohler-Cadmore (Y)	2019	6	11	1	100	346	34.60	1	2	18/1
V.Kohli (I)	–	1	2	–	20	31	15.50	–	–	1
M.Labuschagne (Gm)	2019	5	10	1	130	377	41.88	1	2	4
T.C.Lace (Gs)	2020	5	8	–	73	184	23.00	–	2	–
R.A.S.Lakmal (De)		5	3	1	5	6	3.00	–	–	1
† P.A.D.Lakshan (SLD)		2	3	1	24	55	27.50	–	–	
D.J.Lamb (La)		4	5	2	41*	78	26.00	–	–	2
M.J.Lamb (Wa)		8	11	1	155*	487	48.70	2	1	3
† T.A.Lammonby (Sm)		14	25	1	110	685	28.54	1	2	7
† T.W.M.Latham (NZ)	–	3	6	–	76	121	20.16	–	1	–
G.I.D.Lavelle (La)		2	4	–	30	49	12.25	–	–	10/1
T.E.Lawes (Sy)		7	9	3	32*	120	20.00	–	–	1
D.W.Lawrence (Ex)	2017	12	19	–	120	420	22.10	1	1	10
J.Leach (Wo)	2012	8	9	–	87	266	29.55	–	3	3
† M.J.Leach (E/Sm)	2017	14	15	4	34*	127	11.54	–	–	2
J.A.Leaning (Y)	2021	12	20	1	128	777	40.89	2	4	16
† A.Z.Lees (Du/E)	2018	14	26	2	182*	978	40.75	2	4	6
A.D.Lenham (Sx)		6	10	2	48	177	22.12	–	–	2
E.O.Leonard (Sm)		1	2	1	8	8	8.00	–	–	
J.D.Libby (Wo)	2020	14	21	1	215	688	34.40	2	1	2
† G.F.Linde (K)		7	9	1	107	216	27.00	1	–	3
D.L.Lloyd (Gm)	2019	14	25	2	313*	899	39.08	1	5	9
T.W.Loten (Y)		2	2	–	6	11	5.50	–	–	1
M.J.Luckett (K)		1								1
W.A.Luxton (Y)		1	2	–	31	45	22.50	–	–	
† A.Lyth (Y)	2010	14	24	–	183	790	32.91	2	3	17
S.J.C.McAlindon (Du)	2022	2	2	2	26*	44	–	–	–	
N.J.McAndrew (Wa)		7	9	1	63	278	34.75	–	2	2
C.McKerr (K/Sy)		5	5	–	37	44	8.80	–	–	2
M.H.McKiernan (De)		4	5	–	101	174	34.80	1	1	1
T.S.S.Mackintosh (Du)	2022	4	4	–	51	90	22.50	–	1	21
L.D.McManus (Nh)		10	16	2	62*	410	29.28	–	4	27
† N.J.Maddinson (Du)	2022	6	11	1	90	339	33.90	–	2	7
W.L.Madsen (De)	2011	14	24	3	176	1273	60.61	3	10	22
W.P.U.Madushan (SLD)	–	2	1	1	13*	13	–	–	–	
K.A.Maharaj (SA)	–	3	5	–	41	79	15.80	–	–	1
S.Mahmood (La)	2021	1	1	1	17*	17	–	–	–	
† D.J.Malan (Y)	2020	5	8	–	152	528	66.00	1	4	1
P.J.Malan (M)		5	6	–	93	200	33.33	–	2	1
L.N.Malinga (SLD)	–	1	1	–	0	0	0.00	–	–	
A.K.Markram (SA)	–	2	3	–	16	36	12.00	–	–	3
S.W.Mead (K)		1	1	1	106*	106	–	1	–	
F.S.Middleton (H)		1	1	–	64	64	64.00	–	1	
B.W.M.Mike (Le/Y)		9	16	1	99*	437	29.13	–	4	4
C.N.Miles (Wa)		7	8	2	32	103	17.16	–	–	4
M.E.Milnes (K)	2021	10	17	3	67	268	19.14	–	1	2
D.J.Mitchell (NZ)	–	3	6	1	190	538	107.60	3	2	6
Mohammad Abbas (H)	2022	12	16	9	8	21	3.00	–	–	3
† Mohammad Amir (Gs)	2022	2	2	–	18	18	9.00	–	–	
Mohammad Hasnain (Wo)	2022	1	2	–	2	3	1.50	–	–	
Mohammad Rizwan (Sx)	2022	5	7	1	130	342	57.00	1	2	12
Mohammed Shami (I)	–	1	2	–	16	29	14.50	–	–	
M.Montgomery (Nt)		4	8	–	178	369	46.12	1	1	8
T.J.Moores (Nt)	2021	13	17	2	81*	385	25.66	–	1	38/1
† D.T.Moriarty (Sy)		2	3	2	29	32	32.00	–	–	1
† J.P.Morley (La)		3	3	3	2*	3	–	–	–	3

	Cap	M	I	NO	HS	Runs	Avge	100	50	Ct/St
C.A.J.Morris (Wo)	2014	8	9	–	29	72	8.00	–	–	3
† D.R.Mousley (Wa)		4	7	1	43	110	18.33	–	–	6
P.W.A.Mulder (Le/SA)		9	17	1	235*	706	44.12	2	2	2
S.J.Mullaney (Nt)	2013	14	21	2	192	993	52.26	3	4	15
C.S.Mumford (H)		1	–	–	–	–	–	–	–	–
† T.J.Murtagh (M)	2008	10	13	3	15	48	4.80	–	–	1
T.S.Muyeye (K)		6	10	–	85	272	27.20	–	3	7
Naseem Shah (Gm)	2022	1	2	–	19	26	13.00	–	–	–
† J.D.S.Neesham (Nh)		1	2	–	91	124	62.00	–	1	3
M.G.Neser (Gm)	2021	9	12	1	62	277	25.18	–	1	4
L.T.Ngidi (SA)		2	3	1	4*	4	2.00	–	–	–
† H.M.Nicholls (NZ)		2	4	–	30	59	14.75	–	–	–
S.A.Northeast (Gm)	2022	14	24	4	410*	1189	59.45	2	5	13
A.A.Nortje (SA)		3	5	2	28*	45	15.00	–	–	–
L.C.Norwell (Wa)		4	6	3	36*	63	21.00	–	–	–
F.S.Organ (H)		15	26	3	118	726	30.25	2	3	4
M.K.O'Riordan (K)		1	2	1	102*	133	133.00	1	–	–
A.G.H.Orr (Sx)		12	23	1	198	1047	47.59	3	3	4
C.Overton (Sm)	2016	9	13	1	44	200	16.66	–	–	13
J.Overton (E/Sy)		11	16	3	97	452	34.76	–	3	8
† R.R.Pant (I)		1	2	–	146	203	101.50	1	–	4
C.F.Parkinson (Le)	2022	13	23	6	49	397	23.35	–	–	2
M.W.Parkinson (E/La)	2019	11	13	3	17*	97	9.70	–	–	1
† A.Y.Patel (Gm/NZ)		5	6	1	51*	117	23.40	–	1	4
R.K.Patel (Le)		8	15	–	99	418	27.86	–	3	5
† R.S.Patel (Sy)		15	24	3	126	845	40.23	2	3	15
D.Paterson (Nt)	2021	12	12	7	16	50	10.00	–	–	1
S.A.Patterson (Y)	2012	13	19	3	20	131	8.18	–	–	3
† L.A.Patterson-White (Nt)		14	17	1	54	379	23.68	–	2	8
† J.L.Pattinson (Nt)	2017	8	10	2	45*	239	29.87	–	–	1
D.A.Payne (Gs)	2011	6	8	5	17*	25	8.33	–	–	3
D.Y.Pennington (Wo)	2018	12	13	2	44	132	12.00	–	–	3
M.S.Pepper (Ex)		2	4	–	7	13	3.25	–	–	6
D.K.A.L.Perera (SLD)		1	2	–	18	31	15.50	–	–	–/1
† N.D.Perera (SLD)		3	5	1	150*	244	61.00	1	1	2
K.D.Petersen (Du/SA)	2022	9	16	2	78	409	29.21	–	2	4
H.W.Petrie (H)		1	–	–	–	–	–	–	–	1
T.H.S.Pettman (De/K)		3	3	2	3*	3	3.00	–	–	1
G.D.Phillips (Gs)	2021	2	4	–	125	212	53.00	1	1	1
H.W.Podmore (K)	2019	3	5	–	56	91	18.20	–	1	–
† E.J.Pollock (Wo)	2022	13	20	–	113	645	32.25	2	3	12
O.J.D.Pope (E/Sy)	2018	15	24	2	145	1156	52.54	3	8	22
J.A.Porter (Ex)	2015	8	10	4	4*	9	1.50	–	–	1
M.J.Potts (Du/E)	2017	15	17	2	40	149	9.93	–	–	6
N.J.Potts (De)		5	7	–	13	46	6.57	–	–	2
T.J.Prest (H)		1	1	–	35	35	35.00	–	–	1
O.J.Price (Gs)	2021	8	15	–	68	386	25.73	–	5	11
T.J.Price (Gs)	2020	8	15	2	39	190	14.61	–	–	2
† L.A.Procter (Nh)	2020	13	23	5	144*	961	53.38	3	4	4
C.A.Pujara (I/Sx)	2022	9	15	3	231	1173	97.75	5	1	3
M.R.Quinn (K)		10	15	9	19*	58	9.66	–	–	2
† K.Rabada (SA)		3	5	1	36	48	12.00	–	–	1
B.A.Raine (Du)	2011	13	18	4	103*	366	26.14	1	1	2
† W.A.N.Ransika (SLD)		1	1	–	0	0	0.00	–	–	–
† R.Ravindra (Du)	2022	1	2	1	217	263	263.00	1	–	–
† D.M.W.Rawlins (Sx)		8	13	–	75	341	26.23	–	2	1
† L.M.Reece (De)	2019	12	21	2	116	620	32.63	1	3	8
N.M.J.Reifer (Sy)		1	1	–	68	68	68.00	–	1	1

	Cap	M	I	NO	HS	Runs	Avge	100	50	Ct/St
† M.T.Renshaw (Sm)	2022	8	13	–	146	620	47.69	2	1	11
M.L.Revis (Y)		8	11	3	53*	267	33.37	–	2	8
† J.E.K.Rew (Sm)		7	12	3	101*	337	37.44	1	1	18
G.H.Rhodes (Le)		3	6	–	23	48	8.00	–	–	2
W.M.H.Rhodes (Wa)	2020	14	24	2	111*	689	31.31	1	2	11
† R.D.Rickelton (Nh/SA)		5	10	1	133	558	62.00	2	4	2
K.A.J.Roach (Sy)		7	8	2	29	84	14.00	–	–	1
O.E.Robinson (E/Sx)	2019	5	6	–	26	69	11.50	–	–	–
O.G.Robinson (K)	2022	12	20	2	86*	497	27.61	–	4	28/1
S.D.Robson (M)	2013	13	22	3	149	708	37.26	3	2	18
G.H.Roderick (Wo)	2021	8	9	3	172*	447	74.50	2	1	31/1
† Y.H.Rodrigo (SLD)	–	2	2	–	25	42	21.00	–	–	–
T.S.Roland-Jones (M)	2012	13	17	5	85	354	29.50	–	3	4
J.E.Root (E/Y)	2012	10	16	3	176	849	65.30	4	2	13
† W.T.Root (Gm)	2021	9	14	1	99*	418	32.15	–	4	3
A.M.Rossington (Ex)		12	18	1	100	424	24.94	1	2	28/4
C.Rushworth (Du)	2010	11	11	5	33	65	10.83	–	–	3
N.Saini (K)		2	4	1	5*	8	2.66	–	–	–
Sajid Khan (Sm)		4	5	1	53*	110	27.50	–	1	2
J.J.G.Sales (Nh)		4	8	–	71	159	19.87	–	1	1
M.E.T.Salisbury (Du)	2018	5	4	–	45	59	14.75	–	–	–
P.D.Salt (La)		7	8	–	97	349	43.62	–	2	19/1
A.G.Salter (Gm)	2022	12	17	2	45*	284	18.93	–	–	4
B.W.Sanderson (Nh)	2018	13	20	6	38	209	14.92	–	–	–
G.F.B.Scott (Gs)	2020	4	8	–	77	160	20.00	–	1	2
G.L.S.Scrimshaw (De)		2	3	2	8*	12	12.00	–	–	–
T.A.R.Scriven (Le)		3	6	–	65	178	29.66	–	2	–
T.L.Seifert (Sx)		1	2	–	5	10	5.00	–	–	4/2
† Shaheen Shah Afridi (M)		3	3	–	29	76	25.33	–	–	2
† Shan Masood (De)		8	13	–	239	1074	82.61	3	4	5
J.Shaw (Gs)	2016	5	9	2	29	97	13.85	–	–	1
J.W.Shutt (Y)		2	3	2	4	5	5.00	–	–	1
D.P.Sibley (Wa)	2019	14	25	3	142*	935	42.50	3	5	9
P.M.Siddle (Sm)	2022	8	12	4	42	105	13.12	–	–	1
R.N.Sidebottom (De/Wa)		4	5	1	31*	34	8.50	–	–	–
J.A.Simpson (M)	2011	14	19	3	132	1039	64.93	3	6	46/2
J.Singh (K)		3	2	1	14*	18	18.00	–	–	–
M.Siraj (I/Wa)		2	3	2	21*	25	25.00	–	–	–
B.T.Slater (Nt)	2021	14	24	3	225*	703	33.47	1	2	6
J.L.Smith (Sy)		9	12	1	234*	424	38.54	1	1	12
S.Snater (Ex)	2022	14	22	2	79*	463	23.15	–	4	2
T.G.Southee (NZ)	–	3	6	–	33	86	14.33	–	–	4
C.T.Steel (Sy)		6	8	–	48	141	17.62	–	–	7
S.Steel (Le)		1	2	–	18	18	9.00	–	–	1
M.T.Steketee (Ex)		5	8	2	18	56	9.33	–	–	–
D.I.Stevens (K)	2005	6	8	1	168	316	45.14	1	1	1
G.Stewart (K/Sx)		7	12	2	90	316	31.60	–	4	1
† B.A.Stokes (Du/E)	2010	10	15	1	161	652	46.57	2	3	6
M.D.Stoneman (M)	2022	14	24	3	128	1025	48.80	3	4	6
H.J.Swindells (Le)		14	25	–	67	454	18.16	–	3	25/1
A.R.Sylvester (De)		1	2	1	11*	11	–	–	–	–
J.A.Tattersall (Y)	2022	7	12	2	180*	480	48.00	1	1	14/5
C.Z.Taylor (Gm)		3	5	1	23*	57	14.25	–	–	–
J.M.R.Taylor (Gs)	2010	4	6	–	71	172	28.66	–	2	4
J.P.A.Taylor (Sy)		3	3	2	31*	40	40.00	–	–	–
M.D.Taylor (Gs)	2013	6	9	2	24*	69	9.85	–	–	2
T.A.I.Taylor (Nh)		10	17	3	60*	221	15.78	–	1	6
C.J.Tear (Sx)		2	4	–	56	124	31.00	–	1	2

	Cap	M	I	NO	HS	Runs	Avge	100	50	Ct/St
S.N.Thakur (I)	–	1	2	–	4	5	2.50	–	–	–
D.S.Thilakaratne (SLD)	–	2	2	–	33	38	19.00	–	–	–
J.A.Thompson (Y)	2022	14	21	3	51	277	15.38	–	1	2
A.T.Thomson (De)		11	15	2	54	234	18.00	–	2	5
J.C.Tongue (Wo)	2017	3	2	2	45*	84	–	–	–	–
R.J.W.Topley (Sy)		3	2	–	1	1	0.50	–	–	–
† L.Trevaskis (Du)	2017	11	15	5	88	337	33.70	–	2	3
J.A.Turner (H)		1	1	–	0	0	0.00	–	–	–
A.R.I.Umeed (Sm)		1	2	–	4	7	3.50	–	–	–
G.L.van Buuren (Gs)	2016	12	20	2	127*	502	27.88	1	1	8
H.E.van der Dussen (SA)	–	2	3	–	41	76	25.33	–	–	–
T.van der Gugten (Gm)	2018	9	12	7	62	203	40.60	–	1	1
R.E.van der Merwe (Sm)		3	6	–	55	105	17.50	–	1	–
† R.S.Vasconcelos (Nh)	2021	13	23	–	156	576	25.04	1	2	18/1
K.Verreynne (SA)	–	3	5	1	21	61	15.25	–	–	8/1
G.H.Vihari (I)		1	2	–	20	31	15.50	–	–	–
D.J.Vilas (La)	2018	13	18	–	124	567	31.50	2	2	11
J.M.Vince (H)	2013	14	24	2	111	839	38.13	1	6	19
G.S.Virdi (Sm/Sy)		2	2	2	15*	19	–	–	–	3
† N.Wagner (NZ)	–	1	2	–	4	4	2.00	–	–	–
M.J.Waite (Wo/Y)	2022	8	11	2	59*	232	25.77	–	1	3
† T.N.Walallawita (M)		2	3	–	3	5	1.66	–	–	1
R.I.Walker (Le)		3	6	1	64	103	20.60	–	1	1
† P.I.Walter (Ex)		7	11	1	141	415	41.50	1	2	5
J.D.Warner (Gs)	2021	2	4	1	32*	59	19.66	–	–	–
† M.S.Washington Sundar (La)		2	4	1	34*	52	17.33	–	–	1
† M.R.J.Watt (De)		3	4	1	55*	57	19.00	–	1	–
J.J.Weatherley (H)	2021	8	13	–	168	396	30.46	1	2	12
† W.J.Weighell (Gm)		4	4	–	45	95	23.75	–	–	1
N.R.Welch (Le)		2	2	–	3	5	2.50	–	–	–
† D.N.Wellalage (SLD)	–	2	2	–	46	90	45.00	–	–	1
† L.W.P.Wells (La)	2022	14	22	3	175*	991	52.15	3	4	10
T.Westley (Es)	2013	14	25	3	90	641	29.13	–	4	3
J.H.Wharton (Y)		3	6	–	23	45	7.50	–	–	2
B.T.J.Wheal (Gs/H/Wa)	2022/2021	5	9	5	13*	40	10.00	–	–	2
A.J.A.Wheater (Ex)	2020	4	7	1	37	118	19.66	–	–	7
† C.J.White (Nh)		9	14	6	14*	55	6.87	–	–	3
R.G.White (M)		6	9	–	81	263	29.22	–	2	7
† R.A.Whiteley (H)		1	1	1	55*	55	–	–	1	–
L.B.Williams (Nh)		3	6	1	30	69	13.80	–	–	1
W.S.A.Williams (La)		8	11	6	29*	86	17.20	–	–	4
K.S.Williamson (NZ)	–	2	4	–	48	96	24.00	–	–	2
† L.Wood (La)		8	10	–	50	188	18.80	–	1	2
D.J.Worrall (Sy)		9	8	1	44*	116	16.57	–	–	2
C.J.C.Wright (Le)	2021	13	22	7	36*	279	18.60	–	–	5
J.Yadav (Wa)		2	4	–	29	54	13.50	–	–	1
U.T.Yadav (M)		3	4	2	44*	85	42.50	–	–	1
† R.M.Yates (Wa)		10	17	–	104	298	17.52	1	1	9
W.A.Young (Nh/NZ)		13	24	–	134	805	33.54	1	5	13
† Zafar Gohar (Gs)	2021	11	21	3	81	493	27.38	–	4	5
† S.A.Zaib (Nh)		7	13	1	124	301	25.08	1	1	3
K.Zondo (SA)	–	1	2	–	23	39	19.50	–	–	–

BOWLING

See BATTING AND FIELDING section for details of matches and caps

	Cat	O	M	R	W	Avge	Best	5wI	10wM
K.J.Abbott (H)	RFM	405.1	100	1159	58	19.98	6- 36	4	1
T.B.Abell (Sm)	RM	58.2	3	231	5	46.20	2- 24	–	–
C.N.Ackermann (Le)	OB	135.3	10	460	5	92.00	2- 69	–	–
R.Ahmed (Le)	LB	74.2	5	271	9	30.11	5-114	1	–
B.W.Aitchison (De)	RFM	194.3	41	599	20	29.95	4- 40	–	–
K.L.Aldridge (Sm)	RM	192.1	24	704	23	30.60	6-110	1	–
B.M.J.Allison (Ex)	RFM	65.1	18	161	12	13.41	5- 32	1	–
T.P.Alsop (Sx)	SLA	2.5	0	21	0				
J.M.Anderson (E/La)	RFM	322.5	101	751	39	19.25	5- 60	1	–
M.K.Andersson (M)	RM	132.2	8	560	11	50.90	3- 87	–	–
J.A.Atkins (Sx)	RMF	55.1	6	254	4	63.50	2- 79	–	–
A.A.P.Atkinson (Sy)	RM	141.2	18	495	16	30.93	3- 26	–	–
M.H.Azad (Le)	OB	1	0	6	0				
Azhar Ali (Wo)	LB	10	0	42	1	42.00	1- 12	–	–
T.E.Bailey (La)	RMF	461.3	113	1176	52	22.61	6- 64	3	1
J.O.Baker (Wo)	SLA	298	46	1026	23	44.60	4- 51	–	–
G.P.Balderson (La)	RM	226.2	42	737	22	33.50	5- 14	1	–
J.T.Ball (Nt)	RFM	21	7	60	3	20.00	3- 60	–	–
E.R.Bamber (M)	RMF	324.4	79	958	25	38.32	3- 18	–	–
K.N.A.Bandara (SLD)	LB	22	0	94	1	94.00	1- 50	–	–
T.Banton (Sm)		1	1	0	0				
K.H.D.Barker (H)	LMF	449.3	127	1164	52	22.38	6- 27	3	–
E.G.Barnard (Wo)	RMF	357.2	65	1235	31	39.83	4- 26	–	–
E.Barnes (Le)	RMF	201.1	18	868	19	45.68	5-101	1	–
N.A.Barnwell (Sy)	RFM	23	1	100	1	100.00	1- 68	–	–
A.P.Beard (Ex/Sx)	RFM	139.3	14	518	12	43.16	3- 51	–	–
D.J.Bell-Drummond (K)	RMF	84.1	10	273	9	30.33	3- 37	–	–
G.K.Berg (Nh)	RMF	181.3	48	505	13	38.84	5- 58	1	–
D.M.Bess (Y)	OB	490	66	1545	36	42.91	5-126	1	–
J.G.Bethell (Gs/Wa)	SLA	34	2	151	0				
T.R.Bevan (Gm)	RM	2	0	6	0				
J.M.Bird (K)	RFM	64	12	226	3	75.33	3- 85	–	–
S.G.Borthwick (Du)	LBG	116.3	6	441	2	220.50	1- 43	–	–
T.A.Boult (NZ)	LFM	121.2	22	463	16	28.93	5-106	1	–
M.G.Bracewell (NZ)	OB	47.4	2	285	5	57.00	3- 62	–	–
D.R.Briggs (Wa)	SLA	409.3	83	1319	31	42.54	4- 31	–	–
S.C.J.Broad (E/Nt)	RFM	357.4	76	1121	45	24.91	4- 41	–	–
H.C.Brook (E/Y)	RM	26	3	63	0				
H.J.H.Brookes (Wa)	RMF	241.1	33	899	18	49.94	3- 26	–	–
J.A.Brooks (Sm/Sx)	RFM	245.5	36	892	31	28.77	5- 46	1	–
N.L.Buck (Nh)	RMF	37.4	5	153	3	51.00	2- 63	–	–
J.J.Bumrah (I)	RMF	36	4	142	5	28.40	3- 68	–	–
M.G.K.Burgess (Wa)	RM	6.2	3	17	1	17.00	1- 17	–	–
R.J.Burns (Sy)	RM	9	1	21	0				
G.D.Burrows (Sx)	RFM	44	2	188	1	188.00	1- 89	–	–
J.J.Bushnell (Du)	RM	27.5	0	107	1	107.00	1- 15	–	–
E.J.Byrom (Gm)	OB	3	1	12	0				
H.R.C.Came (De)	OB	8	1	37	0				
J.O.I.Campbell (H)	LMF	5.3	2	17	0				
K.S.Carlson (Gm)	OB	21.4	2	65	1	65.00	1- 17	–	–
B.A.Carse (Du)	RF	40	3	212	2	106.00	2- 31	–	–
J.J.Carson (Sx)	OB	58	5	236	5	47.20	2- 40	–	–
Z.J.Chappell (Gs)	RFM	106.1	17	340	9	37.77	3- 70	–	–
B.G.Charlesworth (Gs)	RM/OB	19	3	71	2	35.50	1- 20	–	–
J.Clark (Sy)	RMF	341	66	1058	30	35.26	4- 52	–	–

229

	Cat	O	M	R	W	Avge	Best	5wI	10wM
T.G.R.Clark (Sx)	RM	82	16	232	6	38.66	3- 21	–	–
J.M.Clarke (Nt)	RM	6	0	26	0				
B.O.Coad (Y)	RMF	132.2	35	359	18	19.94	3- 20	–	–
J.J.Cobb (Nh)	OB	19.4	5	78	2	39.00	1- 5	–	–
J.M.Coles (Sx)	SLA	109	5	490	8	61.25	3- 91	–	–
B.G.Compton (K)	OB	3	0	13	0				
S.Conners (De)	RM	453.5	60	1790	50	35.80	5- 51	2	–
A.N.Cook (Ex)	OB	1	0	8	0				
S.J.Cook (Ex)	RFM	375.5	115	828	51	16.23	7- 33	1	1
C.B.Cooke (Gm)	RM	4	0	15	0				
T.R.Cornall (Wo)		1	0	4	0				
P.Coughlin (Du)	RM	135	34	403	12	33.58	3- 33	–	–
M.S.Crane (H/Sx)	LB	97	5	402	5	80.40	2- 28	–	–
M.J.J.Critchley (Ex)	LB	198.1	25	749	19	39.42	4-114	–	–
H.T.Crocombe (Sx)	RMF	214.5	29	766	15	51.06	4- 84	–	–
S.J.Croft (La)	RMF	10	1	33	0				
B.C.Cullen (M)	RMF	28	3	145	1	145.00	1- 68	–	–
B.J.Curran (Nh)	OB	8	1	31	1	31.00	1- 31	–	–
S.M.Curran (Sy)	LMF	41	10	120	3	40.00	2- 43	–	–
T.K.Curran (Sy)	RFM	28	6	96	0				
B.J.Currie (Sx)	LMF	98.4	17	396	15	26.40	6- 93	1	–
A.K.Dal (De)	RM	332.4	62	1016	34	29.88	5- 40	1	–
A.S.Dale (Gs)	RFM	164.5	25	645	18	35.83	4- 72	–	–
A.A.Daniel (SLD)	OB	13	1	30	0				
J.H.Davey (Sm)	RMF	159.2	35	449	21	21.38	3- 25	–	–
A.L.Davies (Wa)		1	0	1	0				
W.S.Davis (Le)	RFM	81	12	361	4	90.25	3-107	–	–
L.A.Dawson (H)	SLA	261.4	52	680	24	28.33	7- 68	1	1
J.M.de Caires (M)	RM	43	4	153	1	153.00	1- 49	–	–
C.de Grandhomme (NZ/Sy)	RMF	64.4	13	197	8	24.62	4- 39	–	–
M.de Lange (Sm)	RF	56	15	167	5	33.40	2- 38	–	–
D.A.O.de Silva (SLD)	RFM	32	3	124	2	62.00	2-124	–	–
H.K.M.de Silva (SLD)	RMF	12	1	32	0				
J.L.Denly (K)	LB	59	6	224	5	44.80	2- 31	–	–
B.L.D'Oliveira (Wo)	LB	75	8	262	3	87.33	2- 2	–	–
D.C.Drakes (Y)	LFM	27.2	7	86	2	43.00	1- 37	–	–
G.S.Drissell (Du)	OB	55	3	217	0				
J.L.du Plooy (De)	SLA	43	4	170	2	85.00	1- 0	–	–
B.M.Duckett (Nt)	OB	7	0	15	1	15.00	1- 15	–	–
J.A.Duffy (K)	RFM	62	4	320	8	40.00	5- 66	1	–
H.G.Duke (Y)	RM	0.4	0	1	0				
S.S.Eskinazi (M)		1	1	0	0				
J.D.M.Evison (K/Le/Nt)	RM	83	9	336	4	84.00	3- 67	–	–
Faheem Ashraf (Sx)	RFM	54	3	310	2	155.00	1- 91	–	–
M.N.K.Fernando (SLD)	OB	41	2	121	2	60.50	2- 78	–	–
M.G.A.Finan (Le)	LFM	75.2	8	362	13	27.84	5- 58	1	–
A.W.Finch (Wo)	RMF	70.2	6	343	5	68.60	3- 59	–	–
S.T.Finn (Sx)	RFM	141	17	464	7	66.28	3- 84	–	–
M.D.Fisher (Y)	RFM	60.1	16	178	11	16.18	4- 19	–	–
L.J.Fletcher (Nt)	RMF	284.5	74	801	29	27.62	4- 23	–	–
J.K.Fuller (H)	RFM	205.2	16	806	28	28.78	4- 34	–	–
S.T.Gabriel (Y)	RF	45.4	4	222	5	44.40	2- 18	–	–
G.A.Garrett (Wa)	RM	21	5	78	1	78.00	1- 16	–	–
G.H.S.Garton (Sx)	LF	21	3	95	1	95.00	1- 50	–	–
E.N.Gay (Nh)	RM	21	0	73	1	73.00	1- 12	–	–
B.B.A.Geddes (Sy)		2	0	12	0				
B.J.Gibbon (Wo)	LMF	184	30	713	20	35.65	4- 87	–	–
O.J.Gibson (Du)	RFM	146	22	533	8	66.62	2- 25	–	–

230

	Cat	O	M	R	W	Avge	Best	5wI	10wM
N.N.Gilchrist (K)	RFM	224.1	26	892	33	27.03	6- 61	1	–
L.P.Goldsworthy (Sm)	SLA	5	0	24	0			–	–
D.C.Goodman (Gs)	RM	21	3	65	1	65.00	1- 32	–	–
A.W.Gorvin (Gm)	RM	66	14	187	5	37.40	2- 35	–	–
B.G.F.Green (Sm)	RFM	33.4	8	123	4	30.75	3- 31	–	–
L.Gregory (Sm)	RMF	233.5	38	796	15	53.06	4- 62	–	–
N.R.T.Gubbins (H)	LB	1	0	4	0			–	–
S.N.S.Gunathilake (SLD)	RM	25	6	78	0			–	–
S.R.Hain (Wa)	OB	0.1	0	4	0			–	–
T.J.Haines (Sx)	RM	146	30	376	8	47.00	3- 50	–	–
H.Hameed (Nt)	LB	12	2	39	0			–	–
Hamidullah Qadri (K)	OB	100.5	10	422	8	52.75	6-129	1	–
M.A.H.Hammond (Gs)	OB	54	7	249	1	249.00	1- 6	–	–
O.J.Hannon-Dalby (Wa)	RMF	472.2	141	1256	53	23.69	6- 40	3	–
A.M.Hardie (Sy)	RM	31	7	85	2	42.50	1- 19	–	–
Haris Rauf (Y)	RFM	126	24	473	15	31.53	5- 65	1	–
S.R.Harmer (Ex/SA)	OB	446	119	1293	60	21.55	8- 46	7	2
J.A.R.Harris (Gm)	RFM	317	46	1181	31	38.09	5- 90	1	–
T.W.Hartley (La)	SLA	81.2	31	144	11	13.09	5- 52	1	–
Hasan Ali (La)	RMF	184	42	515	25	20.60	6- 47	2	–
T.G.Helm (M)	RMF	200.5	43	637	29	21.96	5-109	1	–
B.E.Hendricks (Le)	LFM	148	15	563	4	140.75	2- 97	–	–
M.J.Henry (K/NZ)	RFM	125	23	421	14	30.07	5- 45	1	–
R.F.Higgins (Gs/M)	RMF	413.4	102	1268	36	35.22	4- 59	–	–
G.C.H.Hill (Y)	RMF	148.4	33	422	20	21.10	6- 26	1	–
L.J.Hill (Le)	RM	2	0	15	0			–	–
M.G.Hogan (Gm)	RFM	418.4	78	1235	45	27.44	4- 43	–	–
I.G.Holland (H)	RMF	162.2	40	503	19	26.47	3- 85	–	–
L.B.K.Hollman (M)	LB	229	18	993	19	52.26	4-122	–	–
F.J.Hudson-Prentice (Sx)	RMF	22	3	86	0			–	–
A.L.Hughes (De)	RM	11	0	44	0			–	–
S.F.Hunt (Sx)	LMF	211.4	36	727	18	40.38	3- 72	–	–
L.J.Hurt (De)	RMF	20	0	110	0			–	–
B.A.Hutton (Nt/Sy)	RM	231.3	45	712	26	27.38	4- 76	–	–
D.K.Ibrahim (Sx)	RM	68.3	4	263	3	87.66	1- 47	–	–
C.A.Ingram (Gm)	LB	38	3	142	4	35.50	2- 46	–	–
W.G.Jacks (Sy)	RM	264.3	39	799	17	47.00	4- 65	–	–
R.A.Jadeja (I)	SLA	20.4	3	65	0			–	–
L.W.James (Nt)	RMF	125	17	381	6	63.50	3- 49	–	–
K.A.Jamieson (NZ)	RFM	48.3	10	165	6	27.50	4- 79	–	–
M.Jansen (SA)	LF	31.3	3	118	9	13.11	5- 35	1	–
M.A.Jones (Du)	OB	1	0	1	0			–	–
A.Karvelas (Sx)	RMF	53.5	18	168	4	42.00	2- 42	–	–
Kashif Ali (Wo)	LB	2	0	16	0			–	–
D.C.Kelly (H)	RM	29.1	9	83	3	27.66	2- 55	–	–
M.L.Kelly (Nh)	RMF	142	24	500	8	62.50	2- 50	–	–
R.I.Keogh (Nh)	OB	334	56	1028	34	30.23	5- 31	1	–
H.L.Kerr (De)	LFM	24.4	2	82	3	27.33	3- 63	–	–
S.C.Kerrigan (Nh)	SLA	244	37	822	10	82.20	5- 43	1	–
L.P.J.Kimber (Le)	OB	22	4	69	2	34.50	1- 8	–	–
M.Labuschagne (Gm)	LB	79.5	8	287	10	28.70	3- 35	–	–
R.A.S.Lakmal (De)	RMF	213.5	50	605	15	40.33	5- 82	1	–
P.A.D.Lakshan (SLD)	RMF	37	7	149	4	37.25	2- 43	–	–
D.J.Lamb (La)	RMF	66	8	240	7	34.28	3- 43	–	–
M.J.Lamb (Wa)	RM	15	1	60	1	60.00	1- 54	–	–
T.A.Lammonby (Sm)	LM	56.2	10	190	5	38.00	3- 35	–	–
T.E.Lawes (Sy)	RMF	163	34	461	21	21.95	4- 31	–	–
D.W.Lawrence (Ex)	LB	45.3	4	216	3	72.00	3- 98	–	–

	Cat	O	M	R	W	Avge	Best	5wI	10wM
J.Leach (Wo)	RMF	238.3	58	767	34	22.55	6- 44	1	–
M.J.Leach (E/Sm)	SLA	369.1	101	992	29	34.20	5- 49	3	1
J.A.Leaning (K)	RMF	134.3	12	509	7	72.71	2- 36	–	–
A.D.Lenham (Sx)	LBG	126.1	10	457	6	76.16	4- 84	–	–
E.O.Leonard (Sm)	RMF	18	2	69	1	69.00	1- 69	–	–
J.D.Libby (Wo)	OB	22.3	5	56	2	28.00	2- 10	–	–
G.F.Linde (K)	SLA	245	30	859	14	61.35	3- 43	–	–
D.L.Lloyd (Gm)	RM	184	28	708	9	78.66	2- 36	–	–
T.W.Loten (Y)	RMF	48.1	11	152	4	38.00	2- 31	–	–
M.J.Luckett (K)	RFM	15.3	2	73	2	36.50	2- 73	–	–
A.Lyth (Y)	RM	12	5	18	0				
S.J.C.McAlindon (Du)	RFM	36.1	3	191	4	47.75	2- 63	–	–
N.J.McAndrew (Wa)	RM	203.3	30	757	20	37.85	4- 85	–	–
C.McKerr (K/Sy)	RFM	99	16	372	8	46.50	3- 39	–	–
M.H.McKiernan (De)	LB	42	1	146	4	36.50	1- 10	–	–
N.J.Maddinson (Du)	SLA	12	2	40	0				
W.L.Madsen (De)	OB	45	18	102	1	102.00	1- 12	–	–
W.P.U.Madushan (SLD)	RFM	53	3	205	4	51.25	2- 73	–	–
K.A.Maharaj (SA)	SLA	34.4	4	113	4	28.25	2- 35	–	–
S.Mahmood (La)	RFM	45	15	90	4	22.50	2- 44	–	–
D.J.Malan (Y)	LB	12	4	32	0				
P.J.Malan (M)	RMF	8	0	26	0				
L.N.Malinga (SLD)	RFM	26	3	106	1	106.00	1- 87	–	–
B.W.M.Mike (Le/Y)	RM	148	10	800	17	47.05	4- 15	–	–
C.N.Miles (Wa)	RMF	186.5	27	724	11	65.81	4- 85	–	–
M.E.Milnes (K)	RMF	253	43	901	21	42.90	4- 11	–	–
D.J.Mitchell (NZ)	RM	5.1	0	24	0				
Mohammad Abbas (H)	RMF	374.1	121	881	50	17.62	6- 45	1	–
Mohammad Amir (Gs)	LFM	67	20	170	6	28.33	3- 33	–	–
Mohammad Hasnain (Wo)	RF	26.1	3	98	2	49.00	2- 35	–	–
Mohammad Rizwan (Sx)	RM	2	0	5	0				
Mohammed Shami (I)	RFM	37	6	142	2	71.00	2- 78	–	–
M.Montgomery (Nt)	OB	1	0	4	0				
T.J.Moores (Nt)	RM	1	0	5	0				
D.T.Moriarty (Sy)	SLA	57.1	7	249	6	41.50	5-163	1	–
J.P.Morley (La)	SLA	117.2	18	355	12	29.58	5- 69	1	–
C.A.J.Morris (Wo)	RMF	212.5	53	642	21	30.57	2- 10	–	–
D.R.Mousley (Wa)	OB	6.5	0	35	0				
P.W.A.Mulder (Le/SA)	RMF	183	27	727	14	51.92	4-125	–	–
S.J.Mullaney (Nt)	RMF	151.3	26	393	15	26.20	3- 29	–	–
T.J.Murtagh (M)	RMF	334.1	83	920	30	30.66	3- 40	–	–
T.S.Muyeye (K)	OB	49.5	3	192	3	64.00	2- 70	–	–
Naseem Shah (Gs)	RF	11	1	41	1	41.00	1- 41	–	–
J.D.S.Neesham (Nh)	RM	19	1	83	1	83.00	1- 43	–	–
M.G.Neser (Gm)	RMF	328	65	931	37	25.16	4- 50	–	–
L.T.Ngidi (SA)	RFM	30	6	88	2	44.00	1- 15	–	–
S.A.Northeast (Gm)	LB	3	0	10	0				
A.A.Nortje (SA)	RF	53	4	248	10	24.80	3- 47	–	–
L.C.Norwell (Wa)	RMF	116.5	30	358	22	16.27	9- 62	2	1
F.S.Organ (H)	OB	119	14	398	11	36.18	3- 57	–	–
M.K.O'Riordan (K)	OB	9	0	26	1	26.00	1- 26	–	–
C.Overton (Sm)	RMF	240.5	60	647	36	17.97	7- 57	3	1
J.Overton (E/Sy)	RFM	300.4	41	1018	36	28.27	6- 61	2	–
C.F.Parkinson (Le)	SLA	442.4	62	1487	30	49.56	5-128	1	–
M.W.Parkinson (E/La)	LB	412	74	1059	34	31.14	4- 66	–	–
A.Y.Patel (Gm/NZ)	SLA	171	37	541	14	38.64	5- 68	1	–
R.S.Patel (Sy)	RMF	88.1	7	306	4	76.50	1- 26	–	–
D.Paterson (Nt)	RFM	404	89	1252	56	22.35	8- 52	2	1

232

	Cat	O	M	R	W	Avge	Best	5wI	10wM
S.A.Patterson (Y)	RMF	427	132	1020	37	27.56	5-46	2	–
L.A.Patterson-White (Nt)	SLA	452.1	106	1146	41	27.95	5-54	2	–
J.L.Pattinson (Nt)	RFM	261.1	43	964	33	29.21	5-56	1	–
D.A.Payne (Gs)	LMF	179.4	29	573	17	33.70	4-51	–	–
D.Y.Pennington (Wo)	RMF	322.2	59	996	44	22.63	4-31	–	–
N.D.Perera (SLD)	OB	1	0	4	0				
H.W.Petrie (H)	RFM	27	6	71	4	17.75	3-48	–	–
T.H.S.Pettman (De/K)	RFM	72.5	17	247	9	27.44	3-40	–	–
G.D.Phillips (Gs)	OB	29.4	3	123	1	123.00	1- 8	–	–
H.W.Podmore (K)	RMF	88.2	9	295	6	49.16	2-11	–	–
J.A.Porter (Ex)	RFM	190.1	37	587	19	30.89	4-64	–	–
M.J.Potts (Du/E)	RFM	564	141	1597	78	20.47	7-40	6	2
N.J.Potts (De)	RFM	113.5	13	428	12	35.66	4-50	–	–
T.J.Prest (H)	OB	10.3	0	47	0				
O.J.Price (Gs)	OB	24	5	85	1	85.00	1-14	–	–
T.J.Price (Gs)	RM	195.4	48	643	32	20.09	8-27	3	1
L.A.Procter (Nh)	RM	169.1	49	528	12	44.00	3-68	–	–
C.A.Pujara (I/Sx)	LB	1	0	8	0				
M.R.Quinn (K)	RMF	291.5	62	886	30	29.53	6-23	1	–
K.Rabada (SA)	RF	74	9	327	14	23.35	5-52	1	–
B.A.Raine (Du)	RMF	464.2	110	1187	47	25.25	5-43	2	–
W.A.N.Ransika (SLD)	RFM	13	2	40	0				
R.Ravindra (Du)	SLA	9	0	28	0				
D.M.W.Rawlins (Sx)	SLA	251	36	884	13	68.00	3-72	–	–
L.M.Reece (De)	LM	145.3	25	503	10	50.30	3-26	–	–
M.T.Renshaw (Sm)	OB	31	2	125	6	20.83	3-29	–	–
M.L.Revis (Y)	RM	163.1	35	660	13	50.76	3-43	–	–
G.H.Rhodes (Le)	OB	19	1	78	1	78.00	1-64	–	–
W.M.H.Rhodes (Wa)	RMF	180	39	559	8	69.87	2-44	–	–
K.A.J.Roach (WI)	RF	213.2	53	656	25	26.24	5-72	2	–
O.E.Robinson (E/Sx)	RMF	153.2	39	446	29	15.37	5-49	3	–
S.D.Robson (M)	LB	23.3	4	96	3	32.00	2-28	–	–
Y.H.Rodrigo (SLD)	LM	50	6	212	3	70.66	2-90	–	–
T.S.Roland-Jones (M)	RFM	475.5	111	1260	67	18.80	6-35	4	1
J.E.Root (E/Y)	OB	54	5	190	2	95.00	1-23	–	–
W.T.Root (Gm)	RM	4	0	26	0				
C.Rushworth (Du)	RMF	332.4	85	930	34	27.35	7-44	1	1
N.Saini (K)	RFM	57	8	262	11	23.81	5-72	1	–
Sajid Khan (Sm)	OB	132	23	356	5	71.20	2-60	–	–
J.J.G.Sales (Nh)	RM	22	1	138	2	69.00	2-52	–	–
M.E.T.Salisbury (Du)	RMF	147	31	484	6	80.66	2-71	–	–
A.G.Salter (Gm)	OB	390.3	62	1083	33	32.81	7-45	2	–
B.W.Sanderson (Nh)	RMF	449	127	1164	41	28.39	5-66	1	–
G.F.B.Scott (Gs)	RM	17	4	77	0				
G.L.S.Scrimshaw (De)	RMF	31.1	2	116	4	29.00	2-22	–	–
T.A.R.Scriven (Le)	RMF	50	6	168	4	42.00	2-44	–	–
Shaheen Shah Afridi (M)	LFM	101.5	16	356	14	25.42	3-35	–	–
J.Shaw (Gs)	RMF	84	15	343	6	57.16	2-56	–	–
J.W.Shutt (Y)	OB	19	1	96	3	32.00	2-41	–	–
P.M.Siddle (Sm)	RMF	241.1	65	646	27	23.92	6-51	1	–
R.N.Sidebottom (De/Wa)	RMF	62	6	273	8	34.12	4-50	–	–
J.Singh (K)	RFM	51.2	5	264	2	132.00	1-64	–	–
M.Siraj (I/Wa)	RFM	66.3	16	278	10	27.80	5-82	1	–
B.T.Slater (Nt)	OB	60	12	82	3	27.33	1- 1	–	–
S.Snater (Ex)	RM	316	84	886	36	24.61	6-10	2	–
T.G.Southee (NZ)	RMF	122.5	16	531	9	59.00	4-55	–	–
C.T.Steel (Sy)	LB	70.2	2	285	9	31.66	3-65	–	–
S.Steel (Le)	OB	6.4	0	33	1	33.00	1-20	–	–

233

	Cat	O	M	R	W	Avge	Best	5wI	10wM
M.T.Steketee (Ex)	RFM	134.2	26	481	10	48.10	4-130	–	–
D.I.Stevens (K)	RM	152	34	451	6	75.16	2- 54	–	–
G.Stewart (K/Sx)	RMF	186.2	28	633	13	48.69	3- 81	–	–
B.A.Stokes (Du/E)	RFM	193.5	26	688	22	31.27	4- 33	–	–
M.D.Stoneman (M)	OB	31	1	123	1	123.00	1- 34	–	–
H.J.Swindells (Le)		1	0	3	0				
A.R.Sylvester (De)	RM	19	0	95	0				
J.A.Tattersall (Y)	LB	6	0	47	2	23.50	2- 27	–	–
C.Z.Taylor (Gm)	OB	20	1	71	0				
J.M.R.Taylor (Gs)	OB	18	0	91	1	91.00	1- 75	–	–
J.P.A.Taylor (Sy)	RM	71	13	228	4	57.00	3- 56	–	–
M.D.Taylor (Gs)	LMF	143	37	410	8	51.25	3- 85	–	–
T.A.I.Taylor (Nh)	RMF	258.5	61	800	25	32.00	5- 49	1	–
S.N.Thakur (I)	RFM	18	0	113	1	113.00	1- 48	–	–
D.S.Thilakaratne (SLD)	SLA	61.3	13	217	2	108.50	1- 40	–	–
J.A.Thompson (Y)	RM	421	90	1459	42	34.73	5- 60	1	–
A.T.Thomson (De)	OB	375.5	92	1109	22	50.40	4-103	–	–
J.C.Tongue (Wo)	RM	65	12	216	5	43.20	2- 29	–	–
R.J.W.Topley (Sy)	LFM	105.4	31	284	9	31.55	3- 55	–	–
L.Trevaskis (Du)	SLA	262.4	49	842	16	52.62	5-128	1	–
J.A.Turner (H)	RFM	16	6	31	5	6.20	5- 31	1	–
G.L.van Buuren (Gs)	SLA	101.1	10	354	8	44.25	3- 53	–	–
T.van der Gugten (Gm)	RFM	241	46	708	24	29.50	4- 60	–	–
R.E.van der Merwe (Sm)	SLA	83.2	6	301	8	37.62	5-174	1	–
R.S.Vasconcelos (Nh)	OB	6	0	34	0				
G.S.Virdi (Sm/Sy)	OB	60.2	5	261	4	65.25	3- 67	–	–
N.Wagner (NZ)	LMF	20	3	108	2	54.00	2- 75	–	–
M.J.Waite (Wo/Y)	RFM	158.2	42	532	16	33.25	4- 35	–	–
T.N.Walallawitta (M)	SLA	18	1	76	1	76.00	1- 45	–	–
R.I.Walker (Le)	RFM	73	13	285	7	40.71	3- 84	–	–
P.I.Walter (Ex)	LMF	28	2	97	1	97.00	1- 19	–	–
J.D.Warner (Gs)	RFM	30.2	3	144	1	144.00	1- 20	–	–
M.S.Washington Sundar (La)	OB	68	6	198	8	24.75	5- 76	1	–
M.R.J.Watt (De)	SLA	109.1	35	317	9	35.22	2- 37	–	–
W.J.Weighell (Gm)	RMF	100.5	18	346	6	57.66	2- 25	–	–
D.N.Wellalage (SLD)	SLA	54.3	10	152	5	30.40	5-143	1	–
L.W.P.Wells (La)	LB	98.5	14	271	4	67.75	2- 41	–	–
T.Westley (Ex)	OB	2	0	19	0				
B.T.J.Wheal (Gs/H/Wa)	RMF	127.5	17	503	14	35.92	4- 59	–	–
C.J.White (Nh)	RFM	296	83	786	37	21.24	6- 38	2	–
R.A.Whiteley (Wo)	LM	4	0	22	0				
L.B.Williams (Nh)	RMF	69	7	343	2	171.50	2-114	–	–
W.S.A.Williams (La)	RMF	292.4	93	614	36	17.05	5- 41	1	–
L.Wood (La)	LFM	206.4	37	658	15	43.86	3- 34	–	–
D.J.Worrall (Sy)	RFM	327	78	942	39	24.15	6- 56	2	1
C.J.C.Wright (Le)	RFM	374.4	60	1324	27	45.70	3- 26	–	–
J.Yadav (Wa)	OB	100.5	18	274	12	22.83	5- 90	1	–
U.T.Yadav (M)	RFM	105	24	286	4	71.50	1- 25	–	–
R.M.Yates (Wa)	OB	29.1	5	100	2	50.00	1- 4	–	–
Zafar Gohar (Gs)	SLA	449.1	94	1335	47	28.40	5- 40	5	1
S.A.Zaib (Nh)	SLA	22	3	94	1	94.00	1- 14	–	–

FIRST-CLASS CAREER RECORDS

Compiled by Philip Bailey

The following career records are for all players who appeared in first-class, county cricket and The Hundred during the 2022 season, and are complete to the end of that season. Some players who did not appear in 2022 but may do so in 2023 are included.

BATTING AND FIELDING

'1000' denotes instances of scoring 1000 runs in a season. Where these have been achieved outside the British Isles they are shown after a plus sign.

	M	I	NO	HS	Runs	Avge	100	50	1000	Ct/St
Abbott, K.J.	142	192	38	97*	2882	18.71	–	11	–	20
Abell, T.B.	107	190	18	150*	5996	34.86	13	32	1	81
Ackermann, C.N.	152	266	30	277*	9472	40.13	20	57	0+1	154
Ahmed, R.	3	6	0	122	195	32.50	1	–	–	2
Aitchison, B.W.	22	31	6	50	327	13.08	–	1	–	18
Albert, T.E.	1	1	1	69*	69	–	–	1	–	2
Aldridge, K.L.	9	12	2	41	128	12.80	–	–	–	4
Ali, M.M.	198	339	27	250	11334	36.32	20	69	2	119
Allen, F.H.	16	28	2	66	526	20.23	–	3	–	17
Allison, B.M.J.	6	9	2	69*	233	33.28	–	3	–	2
Alsop, T.P.	76	129	8	150	3493	28.86	8	18	–	93
Amla, H.M.	265	439	37	311*	19521	48.55	57	93	0+2	192
Anderson, J.M.	280	357	151	81	1949	9.46	–	1	–	157
Andersson, M.K.	31	54	4	92	1094	21.88	–	7	–	15
Archer, J.C.	43	63	10	81*	1201	22.66	–	6	–	21
Atkins, J.A.	8	14	7	17	57	8.14	–	–	–	0
Atkinson, A.A.P.	9	13	2	91	274	24.90	–	2	–	1
Azad, M.H.	52	87	8	152	2900	36.70	7	16	1	21
Azhar Ali	240	415	33	302*	15005	39.28	43	67	–	156
Bailey, T.E.	86	112	15	68	1713	17.65	–	8	–	16
Bairstow, J.M.	202	338	37	246	13130	43.62	30	65	3	502/24
Baker, J.O.	15	19	3	61*	262	16.37	–	1	–	12
Balderson, G.P.	22	32	6	97	620	23.84	–	4	–	3
Ball, J.T.	68	104	24	49*	1044	13.05	–	–	–	13
Bamber, E.R.	36	56	14	37*	420	10.00	–	–	–	7
Bandara, K.N.A.	26	37	5	106	1256	39.25	1	8	–	24
Banton, T.	28	47	1	126	1194	25.95	1	8	–	14
Barker, K.H.D.	153	210	34	125	4992	28.36	6	24	–	38
Barnard, E.G.	92	132	22	163*	3753	34.11	5	20	–	59
Barnes, E.	22	30	6	83*	523	21.79	–	2	–	8
Barnwell, N.A.	1	1	0	22	22	22.00	–	–	–	0
Bartlett, G.A.	47	79	5	137	2167	29.28	6	7	–	12
Bean, F.J.	3	6	0	53	138	23.00	–	1	–	1
Beard, A.P.	28	31	14	58*	333	19.58	–	1	–	10
Bedingham, D.G.	67	108	12	257	4697	48.92	13	18	1	59
Beer, W.A.T.	28	36	8	97	797	28.46	–	4	–	6
Behrendorff, J.P.	31	45	13	39*	389	12.15	–	–	–	11
Bell, G.J.	2	3	0	24	42	14.00	–	–	–	1
Bell-Drummond, D.J.	141	243	22	206*	7339	33.20	15	35	1	55
Benjamin, C.G.	12	21	2	127	534	28.10	1	1	–	11
Berg, G.K.	148	219	27	130*	5434	28.30	2	30	–	73
Bess, D.M.	79	118	17	107	2413	23.89	1	12	–	32
Bethell, J.G.	5	8	0	61	134	16.75	–	1	–	5
Bevan, T.R.	1	1	0	48	48	48.00	–	–	–	0
Billings, S.W.	82	118	12	171	3536	33.35	6	15	–	206/12
Bird, J.M.	105	146	37	64	1388	12.73	–	4	–	54

	M	I	NO	HS	Runs	Avge	100	50	1000	Ct/St
Blake, A.J.	46	72	6	105*	1511	22.89	1	6	–	25
Blatherwick, J.M.	6	7	2	11	23	4.60	–	–	–	1
Blundell, T.A.	86	145	19	153	4636	36.79	11	22	–	199/8
Bohannon, J.J.	51	70	6	231	2740	42.81	6	13	–	25
Bopara, R.S.	221	357	40	229	12821	40.44	31	55	1	118
Borthwick, S.G.	196	329	27	216	10526	34.85	20	58	4	254
Boult, T.A.	113	136	56	61	1212	15.15	–	2	–	59
Bracewell, M.G.	98	175	13	190	5358	33.07	11	22	–	94
Bracey, J.R	67	119	9	177	3639	33.08	9	17	–	135/4
Brathwaite, C.R.	39	64	9	109	1522	27.67	1	9	–	20
Bravo, D.J.	100	180	7	197	5302	30.64	8	30	–	89
Briggs, D.R.	134	178	43	120*	2479	18.36	1	5	–	45
Broad, S.C.J.	253	354	61	169	5666	19.33	1	25	–	92
Brook, H.C.	57	91	5	194	3079	35.80	7	17	–	45
Brookes, E.A.	3	3	1	15*	21	10.50	–	–	–	0
Brookes, H.J.H.	28	41	4	84	671	18.13	–	4	–	10
Brooks, J.A.	148	187	65	109*	2048	16.78	1	5	–	35
Brown, B.C.	170	270	38	163	9345	40.28	23	48	2	476/22
Brown, P.R.	5	6	4	5*	14	7.00	–	–	–	2
Browne, N.L.J.	123	202	15	255	6994	37.40	18	30	3	89
Buck, N.L.	101	142	39	53	1489	14.45	–	3	–	18
Budinger, S.G.	3	6	0	64	126	21.00	–	1	–	3
Bumrah, J.J.	58	76	37	55*	392	10.05	–	1	–	17
Burgess, M.G.K.	65	95	4	178	3219	35.37	5	16	–	128/7
Burns, R.J.	173	300	17	219*	11633	41.10	24	65	7	137
Burrows, G.D.	4	4	0	2	3	0.75	–	–	–	0
Bushnell, J.J.	4	7	2	66	216	43.20	–	1	–	0
Buttleman, W.E.L.	1	1	0	0	0	0.00	–	–	–	3
Buttler, J.C.	122	199	16	152	5888	32.17	7	33	–	274/3
Byrom, E.J.	42	74	4	176	2173	31.04	5	7	–	20
Came, H.R.C.	13	20	1	78	440	23.15	–	3	–	5
Campbell, J.O.I.	4	4	2	2	2	1.00	–	–	–	1
Carlson, K.S.	60	105	7	191	2921	29.80	7	12	–	25
Carse, B.A.	35	45	11	77*	867	25.50	–	2	–	5
Carson, J.J.	22	37	5	87	553	17.28	–	4	–	5
Carter, M.	17	27	2	33	241	9.64	–	–	–	16
Carter, O.J.	15	27	1	185	864	33.23	1	6	–	34
Cartwright, H.W.R.	68	117	12	170*	3709	35.32	7	18	–	33
Chandima, K.K.A.T.	4	6	1	103*	223	44.60	1	–	–	7
Chappell, Z.J.	30	47	8	96	710	18.20	–	2	–	6
Charlesworth, B.G.	23	37	2	77*	737	21.05	–	6	–	10
Christian, D.T.	83	141	17	131*	3783	30.50	5	16	–	90
Clark, G.	37	67	2	109	1626	25.01	1	10	–	25
Clark, J.	75	104	12	140	2581	28.05	2	16	–	11
Clark, T.G.R.	25	46	3	138	1128	26.23	2	6	–	17
Clarke, J.M.	107	182	14	194	6291	37.44	18	28	1	57
Coad, B.O.	53	72	24	69	749	15.60	–	1	–	3
Cobb, J.J.	135	232	23	148*	5483	26.23	4	32	–	57
Cockbain, I.A.	57	97	7	151*	2684	29.82	5	15	–	36
Coles, J.M.	8	14	2	59	272	22.66	–	2	–	2
Compton, B.G.	23	43	8	140	1770	50.57	6	8	1	16
Conners, S.	31	37	9	39	244	8.71	–	–	–	7
Conway, D.P.	120	195	23	327*	8169	47.49	21	37	–	100
Cook, A.N.	338	593	44	294	25807	47.00	73	119	9+1	369
Cook, S.J.	59	68	24	38	445	10.11	–	–	–	9
Cooke, C.B.	116	195	32	205*	6428	39.43	10	38	–	248/12
Cooke, J.M.	14	19	2	68	279	16.41	–	1	–	14
Cornall, T.R.	7	11	1	31*	132	13.20	–	–	–	4

236

	M	I	NO	HS	Runs	Avge	100	50	1000	Ct/St
Coughlin, P.	51	77	10	100*	1728	25.79	1	8	–	29
Cox, J.M.	32	53	3	238*	1891	37.82	3	10	–	31
Cox, O.B.	142	226	31	124	5344	27.40	4	30	–	394/16
Cracknell, J.B.	1	2	0	13	20	10.00	–	–	–	–
Crane, M.S.	51	67	20	29	532	11.31	–	–	–	12
Crawley, Z.	87	154	4	267	4508	30.05	6	27	–	85
Critchley, M.J.J.	80	134	13	137*	3700	30.57	5	19	1	51
Crocombe, H.T.	22	37	7	46*	256	8.53	–	–	–	3
Croft, S.J.	205	309	30	156	9629	34.51	16	55	–	199
Croospulle, D.L.S.	29	51	1	157	1752	35.04	2	12	–	26
Cullen, B.C.	7	9	0	34	105	11.66	–	–	–	2
Cullen, T.N.	22	35	3	63	629	19.65	–	4	–	58/1
Curran, B.J.	29	48	4	83*	1229	27.93	–	7	–	22
Curran, S.M.	79	120	14	126	3186	30.05	1	22	–	25
Curran, T.K.	61	84	11	115	1367	18.72	1	5	–	23
Currie, B.J.	4	7	4	7	15	5.00	–	–	–	1
Currie, S.W.	2	4	0	38	43	10.75	–	–	–	3
Dal, A.K.	40	62	13	146*	1800	36.73	4	9	–	24
Dale, A.S.	10	18	9	36*	78	8.66	–	–	–	0
Daniel, A.A.	8	11	0	38	110	10.00	–	–	–	2
Davey, J.H.	58	88	24	75*	1263	19.73	–	4	–	20
Davies, A.L.	107	167	9	147	5422	34.31	6	36	1	195/19
Davies, J.L.B.	6	9	0	25	87	9.66	–	–	–	4
Davies, S.M.	252	420	39	200*	14285	37.49	25	68	6	614/34
Davis, W.S.	35	48	17	42	388	12.51	–	–	–	7
Dawson, L.A.	176	285	30	171	8399	32.93	11	45	1	183
de Caires, J.M.	5	10	0	80	129	12.90	–	1	–	2
de Grandhomme, C.	126	202	29	174*	6592	38.10	15	36	–	113
de Lange, M.	98	132	18	113	1900	16.66	1	5	–	41
de Leede, B.F.W.	1	2	1	56*	61	61.00	–	1	–	–
Denly, J.L.	229	393	26	227	13244	36.08	30	67	4	91
Dent, C.D.J.	169	305	26	268	10425	37.36	20	62	4	171
de Silva, D.A.O.	2	2	1	1*	1	1.00	–	–	–	9
de Silva, H.K.M.	18	25	3	39	504	22.90	–	–	–	9
Dickson, S.R.	87	147	10	318	4770	34.81	14	17	–	68
D'Oliveira, B.L.	91	148	11	202*	4408	32.17	11	13	–	40
Donald, A.H.T.	58	101	5	234	3024	31.50	3	18	1	55
Douthwaite, D.A.	27	41	3	100*	1085	28.55	1	6	–	7
Drakes, D.C.	2	3	0	33	60	20.00	–	–	–	1
Drissell, G.S.	10	16	1	19	125	8.33	–	–	–	1
Duckett, B.M.	118	199	10	282*	7857	41.57	22	35	3	93/3
Duffy, J.A.	78	104	30	71	914	12.35	–	1	–	34
Duke, H.G.	17	25	2	54	436	18.95	–	2	–	50/1
Dunn, M.P.	43	50	22	31*	197	7.03	–	–	–	10
du Plooy, J.L.	88	143	18	186	5388	43.10	15	29	–	65
Eckersley, E.J.H.	147	252	20	158	7314	31.52	16	28	1	270/5
Edwards, M.W.	3	6	0	11	24	4.00	–	–	–	1
Elgar, D.	231	405	29	268	15661	41.65	44	66	0+2	189
Ellis, N.T.	7	10	0	41	164	16.40	–	–	–	2
Erwee, S.J.	103	176	11	200*	6298	38.16	11	38	–	83
Eskinazi, S.S.	73	128	8	179	3915	32.62	9	15	–	69
Evans, L.J.	73	125	6	213*	3495	29.36	6	18	–	58
Evans, S.T.	32	54	3	138	1445	28.33	4	6	–	9
Evison, J.D.M.	12	19	1	109*	463	25.72	1	1	–	4
Faheem Ashraf	60	89	11	116	2214	28.38	2	10	–	30
Fell, T.C.	97	163	7	171	4485	28.75	6	19	1	75
Fernando, K.N.M.	26	41	3	269	1796	47.26	4	8	–	41/1
Fernando, M.N.K.	19	31	1	109	872	29.06	1	4	–	12

237

	M	I	NO	HS	Runs	Avge	100	50	1000	Ct/St
Finan, M.G.A.	3	6	2	58	102	25.50	–	1	–	1
Finch, A.W.	17	23	9	33	209	14.92	–	–	–	1
Finch, H.Z.	55	93	6	135*	2329	26.77	4	13	–	69
Finn, S.T.	164	202	65	56	1317	9.61	–	2	–	51
Fisher, M.D.	24	32	7	47*	337	13.48	–	–	–	9
Fletcher, L.J.	140	200	36	92	2301	14.03	–	7	–	31
Foakes, B.T.	141	221	40	141*	7136	39.42	13	38	–	332/30
Fraine, W.A.R.	30	50	2	106	1032	21.50	1	3	–	18
Fuller, J.K.	72	99	14	93	1861	21.89	–	8	–	29
Gabriel, S.T.	120	168	67	20*	514	5.08	–	–	–	27
Garrett, G.A.	4	6	3	24	42	14.00	–	–	–	1
Garton, G.H.S.	25	35	6	97	622	21.44	–	5	–	14
Gay, E.N.	28	48	1	145	1337	28.44	3	6	–	30
Geddes, B.B.A.	5	7	0	124	299	42.71	2	–	–	3
Gibbon, B.J.	7	6	2	20	37	9.25	–	–	–	1
Gibson, O.J.	7	7	2	6	7	1.40	–	–	–	1
Gilchrist, N.N.	18	23	1	25	147	6.68	–	–	–	4
Gill, S.	38	65	7	268	3121	53.81	8	16	–	24
Gleeson, R.J.	34	39	16	31	259	11.26	–	–	–	8
Glover, B.D.	10	15	6	12*	38	4.22	–	–	–	1
Godleman, B.A.	185	331	15	227	10027	31.73	23	44	2	108
Goldsworthy, L.P.	20	32	3	130	855	29.48	1	3	–	2
Goodman, D.C.	5	7	3	18	39	9.75	–	–	–	3
Gorvin, A.W.	3	4	0	23	27	6.75	–	–	–	2
Green, B.G.F.	13	25	1	54	416	17.33	–	1	–	9
Gregory, L.	109	160	18	137	3490	24.57	4	14	–	69
Gubbins, N.R.T.	107	190	7	201*	6271	34.26	13	34	1	42
Guest, B.D.	29	48	1	138	1448	30.80	5	3	–	83/3
Gunathilake, S.N.S.	15	24	2	130	950	43.18	2	7	–	11
Haider Ali	11	18	0	206	978	54.33	3	4	–	6
Hain, S.R.	107	172	17	208	6061	39.10	14	34	1	102
Haines, T.J.	46	81	3	243	2949	37.80	8	11	1	12
Hales, A.D.	107	182	6	236	6655	37.81	13	38	3	84
Hameed, H.	101	171	16	196	5438	35.08	12	31	2	63
Hamidullah Qadri	19	33	12	87	368	17.52	–	2	–	6
Hammond, M.A.H.	50	90	7	169	2397	28.87	3	15	–	44
Handscomb, P.S.P.	139	234	16	215	8155	37.40	17	46	–	230/4
Hannon-Dalby, O.J.	97	121	47	40	578	7.81	–	–	–	12
Hardie, A.M.	13	22	8	174*	740	52.85	2	2	–	7
Haris Rauf	8	7	3	9*	30	7.50	–	–	–	5
Harmer, S.R.	186	273	53	102*	5271	23.95	2	28	–	184
Harris, J.A.R.	164	237	55	87*	4114	22.60	–	18	–	45
Harris, M.S.	133	240	15	250*	8876	39.44	22	36	0+1	72
Harrison, C.G.	2	3	1	37*	65	32.50	–	–	–	1
Hartley, T.W.	10	12	4	25	151	18.87	–	–	–	7
Hasan Ali	65	95	22	106*	1117	15.30	1	3	–	20
Haynes, J.A.	32	49	4	133	1706	37.91	3	7	–	23
Helm, T.G.	41	57	14	52	815	18.95	–	3	–	11
Hendricks, B.E.	105	126	41	68	883	10.38	–	1	–	30
Henry, M.J.	83	110	17	81	1837	19.75	–	6	–	35
Higgins, R.F.	65	103	11	199	2854	31.02	6	11	–	20
Hildreth, J.C.	286	471	32	303*	18000	41.00	47	81	7	250
Hill, G.C.H.	23	37	2	151*	1025	29.28	2	2	–	7
Hill, L.J.	62	106	10	145	2906	30.27	5	14	–	100/3
Hogan, M.G.	186	252	99	57	2452	16.02	–	4	–	84
Holden, M.D.E.	67	118	7	153	3105	27.97	3	15	–	25
Holland, I.G.	59	96	8	146*	2271	25.80	3	12	–	34
Hollman, L.B.K.	18	24	1	82	694	30.17	–	4	–	14

	M	I	NO	HS	Runs	Avge	100	50	1000	Ct/St
Hose, A.J.	19	35	1	111	746	21.94	1	4	–	5
Howell, B.A.C.	86	136	13	163	3378	27.46	2	18	–	52
Hudson-Prentice, F.J.	30	51	7	99	1006	22.86	–	5	–	7
Hughes, A.L.	79	138	12	142	3483	27.64	6	13	–	55
Hunt, S.F.	14	22	10	13*	55	4.58	–	–	–	1
Hurt, L.J.	4	5	0	49	103	20.60	–	–	–	0
Hutton, B.A.	73	109	14	74	1658	17.45	–	5	–	46
Ibrahim, D.K.	12	22	2	100*	525	26.25	1	3	–	3
Imam-ul-Haq	62	110	17	202*	3797	40.82	9	19	–	36
Ingram, C.A.	117	206	17	190	7271	38.47	17	31	–	79
Iyer, S.S.	59	101	4	202*	5014	51.69	13	26	0+1	45
Jacks, W.G.	41	59	8	150*	1790	35.09	3	12	–	43
Jadeja, R.A.	114	169	28	331	6579	46.65	12	34	–	90
James, L.W.	28	41	4	164*	1525	41.21	3	10	–	11
Jamieson, K.A.	47	64	11	67	980	18.49	–	5	–	12
Jansen, M.	25	43	7	88	833	23.13	–	5	–	10
Jennings, K.K.	159	271	17	318	9311	36.65	25	33	2	133
Jones, M.A.	23	39	2	206	1321	35.70	2	8	–	5
Jones, R.P.	44	63	6	122	1580	27.71	2	8	–	52
Jordan, C.J.	114	159	23	166	3443	25.31	3	15	–	137
Karunaratne, F.D.M.	187	328	24	244	13992	46.02	44	62	0+1	171/1
Karvelas, A.	17	21	3	57	288	16.00	–	1	–	7
Kashif Ali	1	2	0	52	58	29.00	–	1	–	0
Kelly, D.C.	1	–	–	–	–	–	–	–	–	1
Kelly, M.L.	43	57	13	89	795	18.06	–	1	–	17
Keogh, R.I.	111	184	10	221	5257	30.21	14	16	–	27/1
Kerr, H.L.	5	9	2	88	216	30.85	–	2	–	3
Kerrigan, S.C.	124	152	50	62*	1423	13.95	–	3	–	45
Khushi, F.I.N.	10	15	0	164	375	25.00	1	1	–	7
Kimber, L.P.J.	17	28	1	104	753	27.88	1	6	–	13
Klaassen, F.J.	5	8	3	14*	45	9.00	–	–	–	3
Kohler-Cadmore, T.	83	137	9	176	4158	32.48	10	18	1	126/1
Kohli, V.	134	221	17	254*	10323	50.60	34	36	0+1	133
Labuschagne, M.	115	202	15	215	8537	45.65	23	44	1+2	103
Lace, T.C.	38	69	5	143	1914	29.90	4	9	–	22
Lakmal, R.A.S.	135	173	37	58*	1522	11.19	–	1	–	47
Lakshan, P.A.D.	20	35	3	141	914	28.56	2	3	–	10
Lamb, D.J.	23	30	6	125	653	27.20	1	3	–	9
Lamb, M.J.	41	67	8	173	1843	31.23	3	8	–	14
Lammonby, T.A.	33	58	5	116	1536	28.98	5	4	–	18
Latham, T.W.M.	137	236	15	264*	9497	42.97	23	51	–	175/1
Lavelle, G.I.D.	5	9	0	32	105	11.66	–	–	–	17/1
Lawes, T.E.	1	3	2	32*	120	20.00	–	–	–	1
Lawrence, D.W.	107	170	16	161	5559	36.09	12	27	1	76
Leach, J.	114	166	22	114	3562	24.73	2	22	–	28
Leach, M.J.	126	174	45	92	1698	13.16	–	3	–	47
Leaning, J.A.	98	157	18	220*	4756	34.21	8	26	–	88
Leech, D.J.	3	2	1	1	1	1.00	–	–	–	0
Lees, A.Z.	144	249	16	275*	8182	35.11	19	39	2	96
Lenham, A.D.	7	12	2	48	206	20.60	–	–	–	1
Leonard, E.O.	2	4	2	8	18	9.00	–	–	–	1
Libby, J.D.	89	151	12	215	4864	34.99	12	19	1	31
Lilley, A.M.	16	20	5	63	444	29.60	–	2	–	5
Linde, G.F.	68	98	10	148*	2669	30.32	5	12	–	36
Lintott, J.B.	1	1	0	15	15	15.00	–	–	–	1
Livingstone, L.S.	62	94	14	224	3069	38.36	7	15	–	74
Lloyd, D.L.	97	166	15	313*	4666	30.90	6	21	–	50
Loten, T.W.	7	9	0	58	137	15.22	–	1	–	2

	M	I	NO	HS	Runs	Avge	100	50	1000	Ct/St
Luckett, M.J.	1	–	–	–	–	–	–	–	–	1
Luxton, W.A.	1	2	0	31	45	22.50	–	–	–	0
Lynn, C.A.	41	71	8	250	2743	43.53	6	12	–	26
Lyth, A.	209	350	16	251	12503	37.43	29	64	3	278
McAlindon, S.J.C.	2	2	2	26*	44	–	–	–	–	0
McAndrew, N.J.	19	26	3	92	745	32.39	–	5	–	7
McCoy, O.C.	4	6	4	11*	15	7.50	–	–	–	3
McDermott, B.R.	45	80	9	107*	2403	33.84	2	17	–	33
McIlroy, J.P.	2	1	0	0	0	0.00	–	–	–	0
McKerr, C.	19	20	4	37	177	11.06	–	–	–	4
McKiernan, M.H.	8	12	0	101	307	25.58	1	2	–	8
Mackintosh, T.S.S.	4	4	0	51	90	22.50	–	1	–	21
McManus, L.D.	65	93	10	132*	2286	27.54	1	13	–	149/13
Maddinson, N.J.	111	193	14	224	7041	39.33	15	35	–	80
Madsen, W.L.	214	381	27	231*	14125	39.90	35	76	6	240
Madushan, W.P.U.	16	19	7	29	163	13.58	–	–	–	6
Maharaj, K.A.	148	214	27	114*	3834	20.50	2	16	–	55
Mahmood, S.	28	34	15	49	296	15.57	–	–	–	5
Malan, D.J.	205	350	21	219	12659	38.47	28	67	3	205
Malan, P.J.	177	291	23	264	12316	45.95	38	50	0+2	114
Malinga, L.N.	10	12	2	80	128	12.80	–	1	–	4
Markram, A.K.	86	148	8	204*	6009	42.92	17	27	0+2	86
Maxwell, G.J.	67	112	10	278	4061	39.81	7	23	–	55
Mead, S.W.	1	1	1	106*	106	–	1	–	–	1
Middleton, F.S.	1	1	0	64	64	64.00	–	1	–	1
Mike, B.W.M.	37	59	5	99*	1324	24.51	–	10	–	10
Miles, C.N.	96	133	23	62*	1727	15.70	–	5	–	28
Mills, T.S.	32	38	15	31*	260	11.30	–	–	–	9
Milnes, M.E.	45	69	18	78	900	17.64	–	2	–	17
Mitchell, D.J.	88	141	18	190	4987	40.54	13	27	–	101
Mohammad Abbas	144	202	79	40	769	6.25	–	–	–	39
Mohammad Amir	69	104	16	66	1384	15.72	–	2	–	15
Mohammad Hasnain	7	8	0	5	16	2.00	–	–	–	2
Mohammad Rizwan	109	165	28	224	5997	43.77	13	30	–	305/19
Mohammed Shami	84	117	34	56*	984	11.85	–	2	–	22
Montgomery, M.	8	14	1	178	544	41.84	1	2	–	12
Moores, T.J.	64	102	6	106	2243	23.36	2	6	–	182/5
Morgan, E.J.G.	102	169	18	209*	5042	33.39	11	24	1	76/1
Moriarty, D.T.	8	9	2	29	45	6.42	–	–	–	2
Morley, J.P.	4	4	3	6	6	6.00	–	–	–	3
Morris, C.A.J.	77	100	49	53*	642	12.58	–	2	–	15
Mousley, D.R.	7	12	1	71	262	23.81	–	1	–	7
Mulder, P.W.A.	57	97	15	235*	2857	34.84	7	9	–	42
Mullaney, S.J.	171	284	11	192	9377	34.34	19	49	1	163
Mumford, C.S.	1	–	–	–	–	–	–	–	–	0
Munro, C.	48	74	4	281	3611	51.58	13	15	–	21
Murtagh, T.J.	258	346	100	74*	4333	17.61	–	11	–	69
Muyeye, T.S.	10	16	2	89	414	29.57	–	4	–	7
Narine, S.P.	13	18	6	40*	213	17.75	–	–	–	10
Naseem Shah	27	33	10	31	160	6.95	–	–	–	4
Naveen-ul-Haq	10	13	1	34	93	7.75	–	–	–	5
Neesham, J.D.S.	68	114	10	147	3373	32.43	5	18	–	70
Neser, M.G.	81	111	14	121	2384	24.57	1	12	–	33
Ngidi, L.T.	28	37	16	15	109	5.19	–	–	–	11
Nicholls, H.M.	103	168	12	174	6072	38.92	13	33	–	81
Nijjar, A.S.S.	14	16	5	53	239	21.72	–	1	–	3
Northeast, S.A.	196	330	27	410*	12028	39.69	27	61	5	102
Nortje, A.A.	63	86	22	79*	879	13.73	–	4	–	13

240

	M	I	NO	HS	Runs	Avge	100	50	1000	Ct/St
Norwell, L.C.	91	120	45	102	1058	14.10	1	2	–	18
Organ, F.S.	33	55	2	118	1315	24.81	3	6	–	15
O'Riordan, M.K.	14	19	4	102*	510	34.00	1	1	–	5
Orr, A.G.H.	19	37	1	198	1595	44.30	4	7	1	5
Overton, C.	116	170	20	138	3135	20.90	1	13	–	95
Overton, J.	88	124	25	120	2112	21.33	1	12	–	52
Pandya, K.H.	9	17	0	160	486	28.58	2	2	–	4
Pant, R.R.	55	89	7	308	3975	48.47	10	18	–	180/18
Parkinson, C.F.	54	83	16	75	1285	19.17	–	1	–	8
Parkinson, M.W.	43	51	21	21*	250	8.33	–	–	–	8
Patel, A.Y.	78	110	30	52	1149	14.36	–	2	–	54
Patel, R.K.	20	32	0	99	731	22.84	–	3	–	15
Patel, R.S.	47	76	7	126	2021	29.28	3	7	–	32
Patel, S.R.	231	376	20	257*	12692	35.65	26	64	4	140
Paterson, D.	129	158	50	59	1352	12.51	–	1	–	44
Patterson, S.A.	185	226	48	63	2699	15.16	–	4	–	37
Patterson-White, L.A.	34	46	6	101	1041	26.02	1	6	–	15
Pattinson, J.L.	89	114	23	89*	1998	21.95	–	5	–	24
Payne, D.A.	115	142	47	67*	1779	18.72	–	6	–	40
Pennington, D.Y.	37	53	11	56	441	10.50	–	1	–	9
Pepper, M.S.	11	17	0	92	278	16.35	–	2	–	15
Perera, D.K.A.L.	3	6	0	47	138	23.00	–	–	–	1/1
Perera, N.D.	12	20	1	150*	855	45.00	2	5	–	10
Petersen, K.D.	118	198	18	225*	7255	40.30	17	35	0+1	91/4
Petrie, H.W.	1									1
Pettman, T.H.S.	10	11	3	54*	125	15.62	–	1	–	4
Philippe, J.R.	29	55	3	129	1650	31.73	2	12	–	60
Phillips, G.D.	46	80	6	138*	2948	39.83	7	19	–	43
Podmore, H.W.	53	76	19	66*	1050	18.42	–	4	–	12
Pollard, K.A.	27	44	2	174	1584	37.71	4	7	–	42
Pollock, E.J.	18	27	1	113	829	31.88	2	4	–	13
Pope, O.J.D.	77	121	15	274	5376	50.71	15	21	3	88
Porter, J.A.	110	128	49	34	469	5.93	–	–	–	28
Potts, M.J.	33	42	8	81	531	15.61	–	2	–	11
Potts, N.J.	5	7	0	13	46	6.57	–	–	–	2
Prest, T.J.	3	2	0	35	53	26.50	–	–	–	2
Price, O.J.	12	22	0	68	496	22.54	–	5	–	15
Price, T.J.	15	26	6	71	367	18.35	–	1	–	3
Procter, L.A.	124	199	24	144*	5866	33.52	7	31	–	30
Pujara, C.A.	235	389	42	352	18121	52.22	55	71	1+3	150/1
Qais Ahmad	12	17	2	46*	226	15.06	–	1	–	7
Quinn, M.R.	52	66	23	50	450	10.46	–	1	–	9
Rabada, K.	74	105	17	48*	1046	11.88	–	–	–	35
Rahane, A.M.	167	285	27	265*	11981	46.43	36	53	0+3	172
Raine, B.A.	109	169	22	103*	3263	22.19	1	13	–	21
Ransika, W.A.N.	9	10	3	15	64	9.14	–	–	–	4
Rashid, A.U.	175	251	41	180	6822	32.48	10	37	–	79
Rashid Khan	9	11	1	52	231	23.10	–	2	–	0
Ravindra, R.	36	61	8	217	2149	40.54	4	12	–	21
Rawlins, D.M.W.	37	64	1	100	1468	23.30	1	9	–	9
Reece, L.M.	88	158	10	184	4656	31.45	8	26	–	39
Reifer, N.M.J.	1	1	0	68	68	68.00	–	1	–	1
Renshaw, M.T.	89	159	10	184	5428	36.42	15	14	–	90
Revis, M.L.	10	15	3	53*	310	25.83	–	2	–	9
Rew, J.E.K.	8	13	3	101*	339	33.90	1	1	–	19/1
Rhodes, G.H.	34	62	8	90	1212	22.44	–	7	–	18
Rhodes, W.M.H.	85	140	8	207	4586	34.74	8	21	–	57
Richardson, K.W.	34	52	4	49	664	13.83	–	–	–	10

241

	M	I	NO	HS	Runs	Avge	100	50	1000	Ct/St
Rickelton, R.D.	43	74	6	202*	3531	51.92	12	14	–	94/1
Roach, K.A.J.	145	198	41	53	2094	13.33	–	3	–	42
Robinson, O.E.	78	115	19	110	1882	19.60	1	7	–	25
Robinson, O.G.	48	77	5	143	2205	30.62	4	11	–	143/2
Robson, S.D.	189	335	23	253	11720	37.56	29	44	3	186
Roderick, G.H.	115	183	26	172*	5516	35.13	8	33	–	309/6
Rodrigo, Y.H.	2	2	0	25	42	21.00	–	–	–	0
Roelofsen, G.	47	70	6	224*	2594	40.53	8	10	–	106/11
Roland-Jones, T.S.	133	187	37	103*	3316	22.10	1	14	–	37
Root, J.E.	192	336	29	254	15117	49.24	40	73	3	208
Root, W.T.	53	88	6	229	2611	31.84	6	9	–	15
Rossington, A.M.	103	163	15	138*	5060	34.18	8	34	–	227/17
Rossouw, R.R.	108	190	10	319	7363	40.90	19	33	0+1	118
Roy, J.J.	87	144	11	143	4850	36.46	9	23	1	75
Rushworth, C.	155	210	70	57	1670	11.92	–	1	–	34
Rutherford, H.D.	122	212	3	239	7683	36.76	17	39	0+1	75
Rymell, J.S.	3	3	0	14	23	7.66	–	–	–	2
Saini, N.	56	59	23	42*	340	9.44	–	–	–	15
Sajid Khan	53	76	6	105	1253	17.90	1	4	–	34
Sales, J.J.G.	7	14	2	71	271	22.58	–	2	–	2
Salisbury, M.E.T.	43	65	11	45	513	9.50	–	–	–	4
Salt, P.D.	45	74	2	148	2316	32.16	4	12	–	52/1
Salter, A.G.	78	115	23	90	2134	23.19	–	9	–	35
Sams, D.R.	5	10	0	88	255	25.50	–	2	–	2
Sanderson, B.W.	88	117	39	42	725	9.29	–	–	–	11
Santner, M.J.	56	85	5	126	2344	29.30	3	14	–	46
Schadendorf, D.J.	1	1	0	24	24	24.00	–	–	–	4
Scott, G.F.B.	25	39	5	77	604	17.76	–	2	–	10
Scrimshaw, G.L.S.	5	8	5	8*	17	5.66	–	–	–	1
Scriven, T.A.R.	5	9	0	68	262	29.11	–	3	–	1
Seifert, T.L.	55	94	6	167*	2986	33.93	6	14	–	137/12
Shadab Khan	17	24	2	132	595	27.04	1	3	–	11
Shaheen Shah Afridi	34	41	8	29	266	8.06	–	–	–	5
Shan Masood	144	246	11	239	9016	38.36	21	41	1+1	88
Shaw, J.	48	67	13	42	663	12.27	–	–	–	9
Shutt, J.W.	5	7	5	7*	12	6.00	–	–	–	3
Sibley, D.P.	114	195	19	244	6834	38.82	18	35	1	78
Siddle, P.M.	205	278	56	103*	3722	16.76	1	6	–	60
Sidebottom, R.N.	27	37	17	31*	135	6.75	–	–	–	5
Simpson, J.A.	187	295	44	167*	8504	33.88	10	48	1	582/30
Singh, J.	5	4	1	14*	20	6.66	–	–	–	1
Siraj, M.	53	69	16	46	412	7.77	–	–	–	13
Sisodiya, P.	4	7	1	38	83	13.83	–	–	–	2
Slater, B.T.	116	209	13	225*	6569	33.51	10	33	1	46
Smith, J.L.	35	54	5	234*	1819	37.12	5	5	–	40/3
Smith, R.A.J.	31	46	6	57*	693	17.32	–	2	–	4
Smith, S.P.D.	146	253	28	239	12661	56.27	44	56	–	227
Smith, T.M.J.	55	77	14	84	1422	22.57	–	4	–	17
Snater, S.	27	35	6	79*	648	22.34	–	5	–	4
Southee, T.G.	129	176	16	156	2682	16.76	1	7	–	82
Sowter, N.A.	13	23	4	57*	292	15.36	–	2	–	12
Steel, C.T.	49	84	2	224	2222	27.09	3	11	–	26
Steel, S.	3	6	0	39	66	11.00	–	–	–	2
Steketee, M.T.	59	80	16	53	944	14.75	–	2	–	21
Stevens, D.I.	326	508	34	237	16676	35.18	38	82	3	205
Stewart, G.	34	53	12	103	1121	24.91	1	8	–	4
Stirling, P.R.	70	110	5	146	2932	27.92	6	14	–	40
Stokes, B.A.	166	282	14	258	9506	35.47	21	48	–	132

	M	I	NO	HS	Runs	Avge	100	50	1000	Ct/St
Stone, O.P.	44	58	12	60	708	15.39	–	1	–	17
Stoneman, M.D.	222	385	11	197	13138	35.12	29	66	6	97
Stubbs, T.	8	10	0	132	465	46.50	2	1	–	11
Swindells, H.J.	39	61	5	171*	1503	26.83	2	7	–	75/3
Sylvester, A.R.	1	2	1	11*	11	–	–	–	–	0
Tattersall, J.A.	42	66	8	180*	2020	34.82	2	11	–	101/9
Taylor, C.Z.	11	17	3	106	425	30.35	1	2	–	2
Taylor, J.M.R.	86	133	9	156	3605	29.07	7	11	–	45
Taylor, J.P.A.	9	11	5	31*	104	17.33	–	–	–	1
Taylor, M.D.	72	95	35	56	792	13.20	–	1	–	9
Taylor, T.A.I.	54	83	13	80	1358	19.40	–	6	–	20
Tear, C.J.	2	4	0	56	124	31.00	–	1	–	2
Thakur, S.N.	70	98	7	87	1508	16.57	–	9	–	19
Thilakaratne, D.S.	8	9	2	54	246	35.14	–	1	–	3
Thompson, J.A.	34	50	4	98	958	20.82	–	4	–	8
Thomson, A.T.	29	39	2	54	615	16.62	–	2	–	11
Tongue, J.C.	42	54	12	45*	543	12.92	–	–	–	4
Toole, R.L.	17	23	13	17*	59	5.90	–	–	–	5
Topley, R.J.W.	46	54	22	16	132	4.12	–	–	–	8
Trevaskis, L.	25	38	8	88	878	29.26	–	6	–	7
Turner, A.J.	43	70	6	110	2129	33.26	3	10	–	45
Turner, J.A.	1	1	0	0	0	0.00	–	–	–	–
Tye, A.J.	9	10	0	10	52	5.20	–	–	–	1
Umeed, A.R.I.	16	27	1	113	504	19.38	2	–	–	13
van Buuren, G.L.	108	169	25	235	5811	40.35	12	35	–	60
van der Dussen, H.E.	135	228	26	175	8447	41.81	17	47	0+1	91
van der Gugten, T.	67	94	30	85*	1147	17.92	–	5	–	17
van der Merwe, R.E.	80	128	16	205*	3587	32.02	6	22	–	61
van Meekeren, P.A.	8	14	3	34	106	9.63	–	–	–	2
Vasconcelos, R.S.	65	116	7	185*	3700	33.94	8	17	–	107/7
Verreynne, K.	60	92	13	216*	3880	49.11	6	23	–	167/12
Vihari, G.H.	102	166	23	302*	7868	55.02	22	42	0+1	95/1
Vilas, D.J.	189	282	30	266	10270	40.75	24	46	1	466/20
Vince, J.M.	189	313	22	240	11347	38.99	27	46	2	169
Virdi, G.S.	41	50	26	47	229	9.54	–	–	–	10
Wagner, N.	191	250	55	70	3260	16.71	–	9	–	58
Waite, M.J.	16	22	3	59*	392	20.63	–	1	–	4
Walallawita, T.N.	11	15	5	20*	81	8.10	–	–	–	3
Walker, R.I.	3	6	1	64	103	20.60	–	1	–	1
Waller, M.T.C.	9	10	1	28	91	10.11	–	–	–	5
Walter, P.I.	35	46	7	141	1465	37.56	1	7	–	12
Ward, H.D.	3	6	0	19	30	5.00	–	–	–	2
Warner, J.D.	7	9	4	32*	97	19.40	–	–	–	1
Washington Sundar, M.S.	19	28	3	159	850	34.00	1	5	–	9
Watt, M.R.J.	7	7	2	81*	185	37.00	–	2	–	2
Weatherley, J.J.	58	94	4	168	2223	24.70	2	10	–	49
Weighell, W.J.	24	35	4	84	676	21.80	–	3	–	7
Welch, N.R.	7	9	0	83	184	20.44	–	1	–	1
Wellalage, D.N.	12	17	0	74	391	23.00	–	1	–	6
Wells, B.J.J.	1	1	0	40	40	40.00	–	–	–	–
Wells, L.W.P.	168	277	21	258	9383	36.65	22	40	2	91
Westley, T.	213	353	26	254	11490	35.13	24	53	1	126
Wharton, J.H.	3	6	0	23	45	7.50	–	–	–	2
Wheal, B.T.J.	46	57	21	46*	402	11.16	–	–	–	15
Wheater, A.J.A.	162	234	29	204*	7216	35.20	12	39	–	282/21
White, C.	17	25	13	15*	93	7.75	–	–	–	3
White, G.G.	39	55	5	65	659	13.18	–	2	–	12
White, R.G.	39	63	5	120	1478	25.48	2	8	–	51/2

	M	I	NO	HS	Runs	Avge	100	50	1000	Ct/St
Whiteley, R.A.	90	146	14	130*	3632	27.51	3	20	–	60
Whiteman, S.M.	74	121	8	176*	4235	37.47	9	23	–	175/6
Willey, D.J.	77	108	16	104*	2515	27.33	2	14	–	18
Williams, L.B.	70	97	34	83*	927	14.71	–	3	–	33
Williams, W.S.A.	49	68	20	38	646	13.45	–	–	–	20
Williamson, K.S.	156	267	21	284*	12179	49.50	34	60	–	138
Wood, C.P.	43	62	6	105*	1326	23.67	1	6	–	14
Wood, L.	60	88	16	119	1882	26.13	2	7	–	19
Wood, T.A.	11	19	0	31	202	10.63	–	–	–	9
Worrall, D.J.	72	105	37	50	883	12.98	–	1	–	19
Wright, C.J.C.	189	249	55	87	3567	18.38	–	13	–	36
Wright, L.J.	144	223	23	226*	7622	38.11	17	38	1	58
Yadav, J.	66	103	13	211	2248	24.97	3	9	–	33
Yadav, U.T.	106	126	51	128*	1146	15.28	1	1	–	37/1
Yates, R.M.	43	72	3	141	1954	28.31	7	6	–	44
Young, W.A.	106	178	13	162	6674	40.44	13	39	–	64
Zafar Gohar	62	93	12	100*	1908	23.55	1	9	–	26
Zaib, S.A.	40	64	5	135	1407	23.84	2	7	–	12
Zondo, K.	134	215	17	203*	6269	31.66	13	30	–	74

BOWLING

'50wS' denotes instances of taking 50 or more wickets in a season. Where these have been achieved outside the British Isles they are shown after a plus sign.

	Runs	Wkts	Avge	Best	5wI	10wM	50wS
Abbott, K.J.	11641	553	21.05	9- 40	37	6	4+1
Abell, T.B.	1797	58	30.98	4- 39	–	–	–
Ackermann, C.N.	3484	78	44.66	5- 69	1	–	–
Ahmed, R.	271	9	30.11	5-114	1	–	–
Aitchison, B.W.	1602	60	26.70	6- 28	1	–	–
Aldridge, K.L.	805	23	35.00	6-110	1	–	–
Ali, M.M.	14490	382	37.93	6- 29	12	2	–
Allen, F.H.	15	1	15.00	1- 15	–	–	–
Allison, B.M.J.	394	17	23.17	5- 32	1	–	–
Alsop, T.P.	102	3	34.00	2- 59	–	–	–
Amla, H.M.	277	1	277.00	1- 10	–	–	–
Anderson, J.M.	26085	1065	24.49	7- 19	53	6	4
Andersson, M.K.	1965	66	29.77	4- 25	–	–	–
Archer, J.C.	4510	181	24.91	7- 67	8	1	1
Atkins, J.A.	723	24	30.12	5- 51	2	–	–
Atkinson, A.A.P.	795	25	31.80	3- 26	–	–	–
Azad, M.H.	23	1	23.00	1- 15	–	–	–
Azhar Ali	2200	48	45.83	4- 34	–	–	–
Bailey, T.E.	7286	309	23.57	7- 37	13	3	3
Bairstow, J.M.	1	0					
Baker, J.O.	1434	35	40.97	4- 51	–	–	–
Balderson, G.P.	1460	43	33.95	5- 14	1	–	–
Ball, J.T.	5873	206	28.50	6- 49	6	–	1
Bamber, E.R.	3275	125	26.20	5- 41	2	–	1
Bandara, K.N.A.	269	6	44.83	2- 4	–	–	–
Banton, T.	0	0					
Barker, K.H.D.	12243	497	24.63	7- 46	21	1	4
Barnard, E.G.	7763	261	29.74	6- 37	5	1	–
Barnes, E.	1699	40	42.47	5-101	1	–	–
Barnwell, N.A.	100	1	100.00	1- 68	–	–	–
Bartlett, G.A.	27	0					
Beard, A.P.	2016	61	33.04	4- 21	–	–	–
Bedingham, D.G.	18	0					
Beer, W.A.T.	1550	43	36.04	6- 29	2	1	–

244

	Runs	Wkts	Avge	Best	5wI	10wM	50wS
Behrendorff, J.P.	3002	126	23.82	9-37	6	2	–
Bell-Drummond, D.J.	606	22	27.54	3-37	–	–	–
Berg, G.K.	9883	316	31.27	6-56	7	–	–
Bess, D.M.	7046	216	32.62	7-43	13	1	–
Bethell, J.G.	151	0					
Bevan, T.R.	6	0					
Billings, S.W.	4	0					
Bird, J.M.	10522	424	24.81	7-18	18	5	0+2
Blake, A.J.	138	3	46.00	2- 9	–	–	–
Blatherwick, J.M.	428	11	38.90	4-28	–	–	–
Blundell, T.A.	65	1	65.00	1-15	–	–	–
Bohannon, J.J.	562	13	43.23	3-46	–	–	–
Bopara, R.S.	9381	257	36.50	5-49	3	–	–
Borthwick, S.G.	8997	222	40.52	6-70	3	–	–
Boult, T.A.	11634	433	26.86	6-30	18	1	–
Bracewell, M.G.	1568	32	49.00	5-43	1	–	–
Bracey, J.R.	35	0					
Brathwaite, C.R.	2098	88	23.84	7-90	2	–	–
Bravo, D.J.	5918	177	33.43	6-11	7	–	–
Briggs, D.R.	11431	334	34.22	6-45	8	–	–
Broad, S.C.J.	24013	899	26.71	8-15	31	4	–
Brook, H.C.	442	8	55.25	3-15	–	–	–
Brookes, E.A.	76	0					
Brookes, H.J.H.	2965	73	40.61	4-54	–	–	–
Brooks, J.A.	14276	518	27.55	6-65	21	–	4
Brown, B.C.	109	1	109.00	1-48	–	–	–
Brown, P.R.	266	7	38.00	2-15	–	–	–
Browne, N.L.J.	175	0					
Buck, N.L.	9288	272	34.14	6-34	8	–	–
Bumrah, J.J.	5179	220	23.54	6-27	14	–	–
Burgess, M.G.K.	31	1	31.00	1-17	–	–	–
Burns, R.J.	170	2	85.00	1-18	–	–	–
Burrows, G.D.	315	5	63.00	2-20	–	–	–
Bushnell, J.J.	107	1	107.00	1-15	–	–	–
Buttler, J.C.	11	0					
Byrom, E.J.	119	2	59.50	2-64	–	–	–
Came, H.R.C.	37	0					
Campbell, J.O.I.	278	1	278.00	1-43	–	–	–
Carlson, K.S.	403	8	50.37	5-28	1	–	–
Carse, B.A.	3026	97	31.19	6-26	5	–	–
Carson, J.J.	2047	60	34.11	5-85	2	–	–
Carter, M.	1989	50	39.78	7-56	2	1	–
Cartwright, H.W.R.	1723	52	33.13	4-23	–	–	–
Chandima, K.K.A.T.	4	0					
Chappell, Z.J.	2446	68	35.97	6-44	1	–	–
Charlesworth, B.G.	342	10	34.20	3-25	–	–	–
Christian, D.T.	5679	163	34.84	5-24	3	–	–
Clark, G.	58	2	29.00	1-10	–	–	–
Clark, J.	5356	161	33.26	6-21	4	–	–
Clark, T.G.R.	352	7	50.28	3-21	–	–	–
Clarke, J.M.	48	0					
Coad, B.O.	4255	210	20.26	6-25	9	2	1
Cobb, J.J.	1685	20	84.25	2-11	–	–	–
Cockbain, I.A.	44	1	44.00	1-23	–	–	–
Coles, J.M.	617	11	56.09	3-91	–	–	–
Compton, B.G.	13	0					
Conners, S.	2981	90	33.12	5-51	3	–	1
Conway, D.P.	467	9	51.88	3-36	–	–	–

	Runs	Wkts	Avge	Best	5wI	10wM	50wS
Cook, A.N.	224	7	32.00	3- 13	–	–	–
Cook, S.J.	4126	213	19.37	7- 23	11	3	2
Cooke, C.B.	34	0					
Cooke, J.M.	359	3	119.66	1- 26	–	–	–
Cornall, T.R.	4	0					
Coughlin, P.	3812	113	33.73	5- 49	3	1	–
Cox, J.M.	3	0					
Crane, M.S.	5323	124	42.92	5- 35	3	–	–
Crawley, Z.	33	0					
Critchley, M.J.J.	5657	133	42.53	6- 73	3	1	–
Crocombe, H.T.	1767	38	46.50	4- 84	–	–	–
Croft, S.J.	3090	72	42.91	6- 41	1	–	–
Croospulle, D.L.S.	395	6	65.83	3- 35	–	–	–
Cullen, B.C.	648	14	46.28	3- 30	–	–	–
Curran, B.J.	50	1	50.00	1- 31	–	–	–
Curran, S.M.	6121	203	30.15	7- 58	7	1	–
Curran, T.K.	5709	195	29.27	7- 20	7	1	1
Currie, B.J.	396	15	26.40	6- 93	1	–	–
Currie, S.W.	167	7	23.85	4-109	–	–	–
Dal, A.K.	1590	54	29.44	5- 40	1	–	–
Dale, A.S.	718	22	32.63	4- 72	–	–	–
Daniel, A.A.	737	25	29.48	5- 75	1	–	–
Davey, J.H.	3539	161	21.98	5- 21	4	–	–
Davies, A.L.	7	0					
Davis, W.S.	3100	91	34.06	7-146	2	–	–
Dawson, L.A.	8524	247	34.51	7- 51	5	1	–
de Caires, J.M.	160	1	160.00	1- 49	–	–	–
de Grandhomme, C.	6070	205	29.60	6- 24	2	–	–
de Lange, M.	10238	339	30.20	7- 23	11	2	–
Denly, J.L.	3208	77	41.66	4- 36	–	–	–
Dent, C.D.J.	831	9	92.33	2- 21	–	–	–
de Silva, D.A.O.	217	4	54.25	2-124	–	–	–
de Silva, H.K.M.	133	3	44.33	3- 13	–	–	–
Dickson, S.R.	53	2	26.50	1- 15	–	–	–
D'Oliveira, B.L.	3919	75	52.25	7- 92	2	–	–
Douthwaite, D.A.	2156	52	41.46	4- 48	–	–	–
Drakes, D.C.	137	4	34.25	2- 11	–	–	–
Drissell, G.S.	721	8	90.12	4- 83	–	–	–
Duckett, B.M.	99	2	49.50	1- 15	–	–	–
Duffy, J.A.	7328	218	33.61	7- 89	9	–	–
Duke, H.G.	1	0					
Dunn, M.P.	4237	117	36.21	5- 43	4	–	–
du Plooy, J.L.	1413	27	52.33	3- 76	–	–	–
Eckersley, E.J.H.	74	2	37.00	2- 29	–	–	–
Edwards, M.W.	190	5	38.00	2- 48	–	–	–
Elgar, D.	2798	56	49.96	4- 22	–	–	–
Ellis, N.T.	879	35	25.11	6- 43	2	–	–
Erwee, S.J.	424	7	60.57	2- 15	–	–	–
Eskinazi, S.S.	4	0					
Evans, L.J.	270	2	135.00	1- 29	–	–	–
Evans, S.T.	46	0					
Evison, J.D.M.	692	22	31.45	5- 21	1	–	–
Faheem Ashraf	4598	150	30.65	6- 65	6	–	–
Fell, T.C.	17	0					
Fernando, M.N.K.	322	3	107.33	2- 78	–	–	–
Finan, M.G.A.	362	13	27.84	5- 58	1	–	–
Finch, A.W.	1490	33	45.15	4- 38	–	–	–
Finch, H.Z.	118	2	59.00	1- 9	–	–	–

	Runs	Wkts	Avge	Best	5wI	10wM	50wS
Finn, S.T.	16711	570	29.31	9- 37	15	1	2
Fisher, M.D.	1983	75	26.44	5- 41	2	–	–
Fletcher, L.J.	11439	438	26.11	7- 37	10	1	1
Foakes, B.T.	6	0					
Fraine, W.A.R.	25	0					
Fuller, J.K.	6100	190	32.10	6- 24	5	1	–
Gabriel, S.T.	10052	323	31.12	8- 62	9	1	–
Garrett, G.A.	380	9	42.22	2- 53	–	–	–
Garton, G.H.S.	1985	54	36.75	5- 26	1	–	–
Gay, E.N.	95	2	47.50	1- 8	–	–	–
Geddes, B.B.A.	12	0					
Gibbon, B.J.	713	20	35.65	4- 87	–	–	–
Gibson, O.J.	533	8	66.62	2- 25	–	–	–
Gilchrist, N.N.	1564	63	24.82	6- 61	2	–	–
Gill, S.	43	0					
Gleeson, R.J.	3053	143	21.34	6- 43	10	1	–
Glover, B.D.	827	24	34.45	4- 83	–	–	–
Godleman, B.A.	35	0					
Goldsworthy, L.P.	69	0					
Goodman, D.C.	317	6	52.83	2- 19	–	–	–
Gorvin, A.W.	187	5	37.40	2- 35	–	–	–
Green, B.G.F.	233	6	38.83	3- 31	–	–	–
Gregory, L.	8541	318	26.85	6- 32	15	2	1
Gubbins, N.R.T.	119	5	23.80	4- 41	–	–	–
Gunathilake, S.N.S.	471	9	52.33	2- 36	–	–	–
Haider Ali	31	0					
Hain, S.R.	35	0					
Haines, T.J.	856	18	47.55	3- 50	–	–	–
Hales, A.D.	173	3	57.66	2- 63	–	–	–
Hameed, H.	60	0					
Hamidullah Qadri	1396	33	42.30	6-129	2	–	–
Hammond, M.A.H.	702	6	117.00	2- 37	–	–	–
Handscomb, P.S.P.	79	0					
Hannon-Dalby, O.J.	8061	277	29.10	6- 33	11	1	1
Hardie, A.M.	896	34	26.35	4- 24	–	–	–
Haris Rauf	857	31	27.64	6- 47	2	–	–
Harmer, S.R.	21078	816	25.83	9- 80	50	12	5+2
Harris, J.A.R.	15764	539	29.24	9- 34	16	2	3
Harris, M.S.	64	0					
Harrison, C.G.	113	3	37.66	1- 30	–	–	–
Hartley, T.W.	611	21	29.09	5- 52	1	–	–
Hasan Ali	6511	274	23.76	8-107	18	4	0+1
Helm, T.G.	3409	116	29.38	5- 36	4	–	–
Hendricks, B.E.	8639	336	25.71	7- 29	19	2	0+1
Henry, M.J.	8926	363	24.58	7- 23	17	3	1
Higgins, R.F.	5157	214	24.09	7- 42	7	1	2
Hildreth, J.C.	492	6	82.00	2- 39	–	–	–
Hill, G.C.H.	604	28	21.57	6- 26	1	–	–
Hill, L.J.	43	0					
Hogan, M.G.	16858	681	24.75	7- 92	24	2	3
Holden, M.D.E.	460	5	92.00	2- 59	–	–	–
Holland, I.G.	2429	82	29.62	6- 60	1	–	–
Hollman, L.B.K.	1356	32	42.37	5- 65	2	1	–
Howell, B.A.C.	3222	96	33.56	5- 57	1	–	–
Hudson-Prentice, F.J.	1459	47	31.04	5- 68	1	–	–
Hughes, A.L.	1941	37	52.45	4- 46	–	–	–
Hunt, S.F.	1214	31	39.16	3- 47	–	–	–
Hurt, L.J.	358	7	51.14	4- 27	–	–	–

247

	Runs	Wkts	Avge	Best	5wI	10wM	50wS
Hutton, B.A.	6572	248	26.50	8-57	11	2	–
Ibrahim, D.K.	499	6	83.16	2- 9	–	–	–
Imam-ul-Haq	74	1	74.00	1- 4	–	–	–
Ingram, C.A.	2275	54	42.12	4-16	–	–	–
Iyer, S.S.	401	4	100.25	2-29	–	–	–
Jacks, W.G.	1119	21	53.28	4-65	–	–	–
Jadeja, R.A.	11025	453	24.33	7-31	28	7	0+3
James, L.W.	982	26	37.76	4-51	–	–	–
Jamieson, K.A.	3758	168	22.36	8-74	11	2	–
Jansen, M.	2109	99	21.30	6-40	3	–	–
Jennings, K.K.	988	30	32.93	3-37	–	–	–
Jones, M.A.	1	0					
Jones, R.P.	49	2	24.50	1- 4	–	–	–
Jordan, C.J.	10730	335	32.02	7-43	10	–	1
Karunaratne, F.D.M.	500	4	125.00	1- 6	–	–	–
Karvelas, A.	1217	48	25.35	6-71	2	–	–
Kashif Ali	16	0					
Kelly, D.C.	83	3	27.66	2-55	–	–	–
Kelly, M.L.	3764	119	31.63	6-67	5	–	–
Keogh, R.I.	5361	128	41.88	9-52	2	1	–
Kerr, H.L.	315	11	28.63	3-63	–	–	–
Kerrigan, S.C.	11521	364	31.65	9-51	16	3	2
Kimber, L.P.J.	170	4	42.50	1- 8	–	–	–
Klaassen, F.J.	422	9	46.88	4-44	–	–	–
Kohli, V.	338	3	112.66	1-19	–	–	–
Labuschagne, M.	3557	75	47.42	3-35	–	–	–
Lakmal, R.A.S.	11700	362	32.32	6-68	10	–	–
Lakshan, P.A.D.	719	22	32.68	3-24	–	–	–
Lamb, D.J.	1458	48	30.37	4-55	–	–	–
Lamb, M.J.	364	9	40.44	2-38	–	–	–
Lammonby, T.A.	515	11	46.81	3-35	–	–	–
Latham, T.W.M.	18	1	18.00	1- 7	–	–	–
Lawes, T.E.	461	21	21.95	4-31	–	–	–
Lawrence, D.W.	847	20	42.35	3-98	–	–	–
Leach, J.	10523	402	26.17	6-44	15	1	3
Leach, M.J.	10630	385	27.61	8-85	25	4	3
Leaning, J.A.	1322	21	62.95	2-20	–	–	–
Leech, D.J.	213	4	53.25	2-72	–	–	–
Lees, A.Z.	96	3	32.00	2-51	–	–	–
Lenham, A.D.	528	7	75.42	4-84	–	–	–
Leonard, E.O.	154	2	77.00	1-68	–	–	–
Libby, J.D.	527	9	58.55	2-10	–	–	–
Lilley, A.M.	1428	43	33.20	5-23	2	–	–
Linde, G.F.	6169	236	26.13	7-29	15	3	–
Lintott, J.B.	103	0					
Livingstone, L.S.	1552	43	36.09	6-52	1	–	–
Lloyd, D.L.	4078	91	44.81	4-11	–	–	–
Loten, T.W.	152	4	38.00	2-31	–	–	–
Luckett, M.J.	73	2	36.50	2-73	–	–	–
Lynn, C.A.	64	0					
Lyth, A.	1723	36	47.86	2- 9	–	–	–
McAlindon, S.J.C.	191	4	47.75	2-63	–	–	–
McAndrew, N.J.	1898	58	32.72	5-84	1	–	–
McCoy, O.C.	278	6	46.33	3-56	–	–	–
McDermott, B.R.	75	0					
McIlroy, J.P.	131	1	131.00	1-12	–	–	–
McKerr, C.	1426	46	31.00	5-54	2	1	–
McKiernan, M.H.	210	6	35.00	2- 3	–	–	–

	Runs	Wkts	Avge	Best	5wI	10wM	50wS
Maddinson, N.J.	437	8	54.62	2- 10	–	–	–
Madsen, W.L.	1944	38	51.15	3- 45	–	–	–
Madushan, W.P.U.	1314	20	65.70	3-103	–	–	–
Maharaj, K.A.	15175	559	27.14	9-129	34	7	–
Mahmood, S.	2182	80	27.27	5- 47	1	–	–
Malan, D.J.	2548	63	40.44	5- 61	1	–	–
Malan, P.J.	513	20	25.65	5- 35	1	–	–
Malinga, L.N.	645	11	58.63	3- 68	–	–	–
Markram, A.K.	398	6	66.33	2- 27	–	–	–
Maxwell, G.J.	3174	77	41.22	5- 40	1	–	–
Mike, B.W.M.	3115	80	38.93	5- 37	1	–	–
Miles, C.N.	9324	334	27.91	6- 63	17	1	3
Mills, T.S.	2008	55	36.50	4- 25	–	–	–
Milnes, M.E.	4056	140	28.97	6- 53	4	–	1
Mitchell, D.J.	2715	90	30.16	5- 44	1	–	–
Mohammad Abbas	12088	589	20.52	8- 46	39	11	2+2
Mohammad Amir	6020	266	22.63	7- 61	13	2	0+1
Mohammad Hasnain	590	12	49.16	2- 32	–	–	–
Mohammad Rizwan	136	4	34.00	2- 10	–	–	–
Mohammed Shami	8580	319	26.89	7- 79	12	2	–
Montgomery, M.	4	0					
Moores, T.J.	5	0					
Morgan, E.J.G.	94	2	47.00	2- 24	–	–	–
Moriarty, D.T.	1112	41	27.12	6- 60	5	1	–
Morley, J.P.	426	17	25.05	5- 69	1	–	–
Morris, C.A.J.	7042	237	29.71	7- 45	7	–	2
Mousley, D.R.	72	0					
Mulder, P.W.A.	3898	136	28.66	7- 25	1	–	–
Mullaney, S.J.	4900	135	36.29	5- 32	1	–	–
Munro, C.	1640	58	28.27	4- 36	–	–	–
Murtagh, T.J.	22835	929	24.58	7- 82	38	4	9
Muyeye, T.S.	192	3	64.00	2- 70	–	–	–
Narine, S.P.	1398	65	21.50	8- 17	8	3	–
Naseem Shah	2239	84	26.65	6- 59	4	–	–
Naveen-ul-Haq	782	31	25.22	8- 35	1	–	–
Neesham, J.D.S.	4095	124	33.02	5- 65	2	–	–
Neser, M.G.	6875	281	24.46	6- 57	7	–	–
Ngidi, L.T.	1946	87	22.36	6- 37	6	–	–
Nicholls, H.M.	26	0					
Nijjar, A.S.S.	806	19	42.42	2- 28	–	–	–
Northeast, S.A.	157	1	157.00	1- 60	–	–	–
Nortje, A.A.	5819	221	26.33	6- 44	8	–	–
Norwell, L.C.	8560	347	24.66	9- 62	16	4	3
Organ, F.S.	818	34	24.05	5- 25	1	–	–
O'Riordan, M.K.	459	11	41.72	3- 50	–	–	–
Overton, C.	9516	412	23.09	7- 57	16	1	1
Overton, J.	6791	221	30.72	6- 61	6	–	–
Pandya, K.H.	369	14	26.35	4- 40	–	–	–
Pant, R.R.	9	1	9.00	1- 9	–	–	–
Parkinson, C.F.	5279	134	39.39	8-148	5	2	1
Parkinson, M.W.	3441	136	25.30	7-126	4	1	–
Patel, A.Y.	9278	287	32.32	10-119	20	4	–
Patel, R.S.	1159	19	61.00	6- 5	1	–	–
Patel, S.R.	13650	357	38.23	7- 68	5	1	–
Paterson, D.	10966	474	23.13	8- 52	17	2	2+2
Patterson, S.A.	13486	489	27.57	6- 40	10	–	2
Patterson-White, L.A.	2442	87	28.06	5- 41	4	–	–
Pattinson, J.L.	8232	350	23.52	6- 32	13	–	–

	Runs	Wkts	Avge	Best	5wI	10wM	50wS
Payne, D.A.	9705	328	29.58	6- 26	6	1	–
Pennington, D.Y.	3221	114	28.25	5- 32	1	–	–
Perera, N.D.	56	1	56.00	1- 25	–	–	–
Petersen, K.D.	327	3	109.00	3- 49	–	–	–
Petrie, H.W.	71	4	17.75	3- 48	–	–	–
Pettman, T.H.S.	945	42	22.50	5- 19	2	–	–
Phillips, G.D.	1352	35	38.62	4- 70	–	–	–
Podmore, H.W.	4470	167	26.76	6- 36	4	–	1
Pollard, K.A.	436	14	31.14	5- 36	1	–	–
Porter, J.A.	9983	409	24.40	7- 41	13	2	5
Potts, M.J.	3019	120	25.15	7- 40	6	2	1
Potts, N.J.	428	12	35.66	4- 50	–	–	–
Prest, T.J.	52	0					
Price, O.J.	185	1	185.00	1- 14	–	–	–
Price, T.J.	1091	48	22.72	8- 27	3	1	–
Procter, L.A.	4829	133	36.30	7- 71	4	–	–
Pujara, C.A.	165	6	27.50	2- 4	–	–	–
Qais Ahmad	1395	68	20.51	7- 41	5	3	–
Quinn, M.R.	5014	171	29.32	7- 76	2	1	–
Rabada, K.	7584	329	23.05	9- 33	15	5	0+1
Rahane, A.M.	75	0					
Raine, B.A.	9434	366	25.77	6- 27	12	–	3
Ransika, W.A.N.	469	11	42.63	3- 34	–	–	–
Rashid, A.U.	17949	512	35.05	7-107	20	1	2
Rashid Khan	1287	69	18.65	8- 74	8	3	–
Ravindra, R.	1910	34	56.17	6- 89	1	–	–
Rawlins, D.M.W.	2275	31	73.38	3- 19	–	–	–
Reece, L.M.	3670	123	29.83	7- 20	4	–	1
Renshaw, M.T.	458	11	41.63	3- 29	–	–	–
Revis, M.L.	679	15	45.26	3- 43	–	–	–
Rhodes, G.H.	806	7	115.14	2- 83	–	–	–
Rhodes, W.M.H.	2835	87	32.58	5- 17	2	–	–
Richardson, K.W.	3505	102	34.36	5- 69	1	–	–
Rickelton, R.D.	7	0					
Roach, K.A.J.	12261	478	25.65	8- 40	20	2	–
Robinson, O.E.	7268	351	20.70	9- 78	21	5	3
Robson, S.D.	373	11	33.90	2- 0	–	–	–
Rodrigo, Y.H.	212	3	70.66	2- 90	–	–	–
Roland-Jones, T.S.	12107	495	24.45	7- 52	24	5	3
Root, J.E.	3327	68	48.92	5- 8	1	–	–
Root, W.T.	266	8	33.25	3- 29	–	–	–
Rossington, A.M.	86	0					
Rossouw, R.R.	70	3	23.33	1- 1	–	–	–
Roy, J.J.	495	14	35.35	3- 9	–	–	–
Rushworth, C.	13637	603	22.61	9- 52	30	5	6
Rutherford, H.D.	107	1	107.00	1- 26	–	–	–
Saini, N.	4526	159	28.46	6- 32	5	–	–
Sajid Khan	5477	195	28.08	8- 42	11	2	0+1
Sales, J.J.G.	292	5	58.40	2- 52	–	–	–
Salisbury, M.E.T.	3876	117	33.12	6- 37	1	–	–
Salt, P.D.	32	1	32.00	1- 32	–	–	–
Salter, A.G.	5900	134	44.02	7- 45	2	–	–
Sams, D.R.	494	13	38.00	4- 55	–	–	–
Sanderson, B.W.	7161	328	21.83	8- 73	17	3	3
Santner, M.J.	4061	86	47.22	4-111	–	–	–
Scott, G.F.B.	622	10	62.20	2- 34	–	–	–
Scrimshaw, G.L.S.	270	7	38.57	2- 22	–	–	–
Scriven, T.A.R.	247	7	35.28	2- 24	–	–	–

250

	Runs	Wkts	Avge	Best	5wI	10wM	50wS
Shadab Khan	1753	68	25.77	6- 77	2	1	–
Shaheen Shah Afridi	3368	139	24.23	8- 39	5	1	–
Shan Masood	607	8	75.87	2- 52	–	–	–
Shaw, J.	4161	112	37.15	5- 79	2	–	–
Shutt, J.W.	200	5	40.00	2- 14	–	–	–
Sibley, D.P.	271	4	67.75	2-103	–	–	–
Siddle, P.M.	18653	701	26.60	8- 54	27	–	0+1
Sidebottom, R.N.	2083	67	31.08	6- 35	1	1	–
Simpson, J.A.	23	0					
Singh, J.	404	9	44.88	4- 51	–	–	–
Siraj, M.	4945	200	24.72	8- 59	6	2	–
Sisodiya, P.	369	15	24.60	4- 79	–	–	–
Slater, B.T.	203	3	67.66	1- 1	–	–	–
Smith, R.A.J.	2413	69	34.97	5- 87	1	–	–
Smith, S.P.D.	3633	69	52.65	7- 64	1	–	–
Smith, T.M.J.	4171	82	50.86	4- 35	–	–	–
Snater, S.	1815	87	20.86	7- 98	7	–	–
Southee, T.G.	13680	511	26.77	8- 27	25	1	–
Sowter, N.A.	1032	20	51.60	3- 42	–	–	–
Steel, C.T.	1043	31	33.64	3- 65	–	–	–
Steel, S.	49	1	49.00	1- 20	–	–	–
Steketee, M.T.	5479	204	26.85	7- 44	4	1	–
Stevens, D.I.	14648	591	24.78	8- 75	31	2	4
Stewart, G.	2424	74	32.75	6- 22	2	–	–
Stirling, P.R.	1118	27	41.40	2- 21	–	–	–
Stokes, B.A.	11081	371	29.86	7- 67	7	1	–
Stone, O.P.	3717	150	24.78	8- 80	6	1	–
Stoneman, M.D.	301	1	301.00	1- 34	–	–	–
Stubbs, T.	68	1	68.00	1- 13	–	–	–
Swindells, H.J.	3	0					
Sylvester, A.R.	95	0					
Tattersall, J.A.	47	2	23.50	2- 27	–	–	–
Taylor, C.Z.	636	7	90.85	2- 16	–	–	–
Taylor, J.M.R.	3436	76	45.21	4- 16	–	–	–
Taylor, J.P.A.	594	17	34.94	3- 26	–	–	–
Taylor, M.D.	6292	188	33.46	5- 15	6	–	1
Taylor, T.A.I.	4667	150	31.11	6- 47	5	1	–
Thakur, S.N.	6575	234	28.09	7- 61	13	–	0+1
Thilakaratne, D.S.	889	20	44.45	4- 86	–	–	–
Thompson, J.A.	2759	108	25.54	5- 31	3	–	–
Thomson, A.T.	2066	49	42.16	6-138	1	–	–
Tongue, J.C.	3611	143	25.25	6- 97	6	–	–
Toole, R.L.	1454	53	27.43	6- 54	1	–	–
Topley, R.J.W.	4382	163	26.88	6- 29	8	2	–
Trevaskis, L.	1554	32	48.56	5- 78	2	–	–
Turner, A.J.	521	12	43.41	6-111	1	–	–
Turner, J.A.	31	5	6.20	5- 31	1	–	–
Tye, A.J.	991	27	36.70	3- 47	–	–	–
Umeed, A.R.I.	73	2	36.50	1- 19	–	–	–
van Buuren, G.L.	3345	103	32.47	4- 12	–	–	–
van der Dussen, H.E.	257	5	51.40	2- 39	–	–	–
van der Gugten, T.	5997	216	27.76	7- 42	10	1	1
van der Merwe, R.E.	5069	150	33.79	5-174	1	–	–
van Meekeren, P.A.	785	21	37.38	4- 60	–	–	–
Vasconcelos, R.S.	43	0					
Vihari, G.H.	1170	27	43.33	3- 17	–	–	–
Vilas, D.J.	9	0					
Vince, J.M.	1116	23	48.52	5- 41	1	–	–

	Runs	Wkts	Avge	Best	5wI	10wM	50wS
Virdi, G.S.	3778	123	30.71	8- 61	5	1	–
Wagner, N.	20996	783	26.81	7- 39	36	2	0+2
Waite, M.J.	1115	39	28.58	5- 16	1	–	–
Walallawita, T.N.	647	10	64.70	3- 28	–	–	–
Walker, R.I.	285	7	40.71	3- 84	–	–	–
Waller, M.T.C.	493	10	49.30	3- 33	–	–	–
Walter, P.I.	810	16	50.62	3- 44	–	–	–
Ward, H.D.	2	0					
Warner, J.D.	426	10	42.60	3- 35	–	–	–
Washington Sundar, M.S.	1305	44	29.65	6- 87	3	1	–
Watt, M.R.J.	639	17	37.58	3- 60	–	–	–
Weatherley, J.J.	250	5	50.00	1- 2	–	–	–
Weighell, W.J.	2206	65	33.93	7- 32	2	–	–
Wellalage, D.N.	1081	34	31.79	5-143	1	–	–
Wells, L.W.P.	3629	82	44.25	5- 63	1	–	–
Westley, T.	2724	59	46.16	4- 55	–	–	–
Wheal, B.T.J.	3668	109	33.65	6- 51	1	–	–
Wheater, A.J.A.	86	1	86.00	1- 86	–	–	–
White, C.	1365	55	24.81	6- 38	2	–	–
White, G.G.	2730	65	42.00	6- 44	1	–	–
Whiteley, R.A.	2119	41	51.68	2- 6	–	–	–
Willey, D.J.	5895	198	29.77	5- 29	6	1	–
Williams, L.B.	6004	211	28.45	7- 75	7	1	–
Williams, W.S.A.	3271	152	21.51	5- 26	3	–	–
Williamson, K.S.	3721	86	43.26	5- 75	1	–	–
Wood, C.P.	3174	105	30.22	5- 39	3	–	–
Wood, L.	4644	132	35.18	5- 40	3	–	–
Worrall, D.J.	7461	273	27.32	7- 64	11	2	–
Wright, C.J.C.	17644	540	32.67	7- 53	17	–	2
Wright, L.J.	4862	120	40.51	5- 65	3	–	–
Yadav, J.	5782	185	31.25	7- 58	9	1	–
Yadav, U.T.	9749	331	29.45	7- 48	15	2	–
Yates, R.M.	317	6	52.83	2- 54	–	–	–
Young, W.A.	8	0					
Zafar Gohar	6986	236	29.60	7- 79	15	4	–
Zaib, S.A.	730	21	34.76	6-115	2	–	–
Zondo, K.	1638	43	38.09	6- 52	2	–	–

LIMITED-OVERS CAREER RECORDS

Compiled by Philip Bailey

The following career records, to the end of the 2022 season, include all players currently registered with first-class counties or teams in The Hundred. These records are restricted to performances in limited-overs matches of 'List A' status as defined by the Association of Cricket Statisticians and Historians now incorporated by ICC into their Classification of Cricket. The following matches qualify for List A status and are included in the figures that follow: Limited-Overs Internationals; Other International matches (e.g. Commonwealth Games, 'A' team internationals); Premier domestic limited-overs tournaments in Test status countries; Official tourist matches against the main first-class teams.

The following matches do NOT qualify for inclusion: World Cup warm-up games; Tourist matches against first-class teams outside the major domestic competitions (e.g. Universities, Minor Counties etc.); Festival, pre-season friendly games and Twenty20 Cup matches.

	M	Runs	Avge	HS	100	50	Wkts	Avge	Best	Econ
Abbott, K.J.	112	536	16.24	56	–	1	149	29.62	5-43	5.22
Abell, T.B.	26	649	30.90	106	1	1	2	13.00	2-19	4.33
Ackermann, C.N.	87	2356	36.24	152*	2	16	44	39.63	4-48	4.80
Ahmed, R.	7	89	44.50	40*	–	–	5	63.60	2-25	5.74
Aitchison, B.W.	13	60	8.57	19	–	–	15	29.00	4-39	4.80
Albert, T.E.	9	339	48.42	84*	–	2	0	–	–	–
Aldridge, K.L.	14	38	5.42	12	–	–	19	31.05	5-50	6.34
Ali, M.M.	238	5318	28.13	158	11	20	169	44.83	4-33	5.37
Allison, B.M.J.	9	25	25.00	21*	–	–	7	55.71	2-33	6.17
Alsop, T.P.	62	2099	36.82	189*	5	10	0	–	–	44/6
Anderson, J.M.	261	378	9.00	28	–	–	358	28.57	5-23	4.82
Andersson, M.K.	12	270	67.50	44*	–	–	10	65.20	2-48	7.39
Archer, J.C.	31	219	18.25	45	–	–	51	26.76	5-42	4.98
Atkinson, A.A.P.	2	15	15.00	15	–	–	5	22.60	4-43	7.06
Azhar Ali	176	6463	46.49	132*	18	36	69	33.79	5-23	5.51
Bailey, T.E.	29	184	16.72	45	–	–	42	28.14	3-22	5.00
Bairstow, J.M.	163	5556	41.46	174	14	25	–	–	–	99/9
Baker, J.O.	8	86	21.50	25	–	–	7	49.14	2-53	6.21
Baker, S.	11	12	6.00	7*	–	–	19	25.42	6-46	6.36
Balderson, G.P.	13	242	34.57	106*	1	–	13	32.15	3-25	5.42
Ball, J.T.	95	198	8.60	28	–	–	118	33.51	5-51	5.87
Bamber, E.R.	9	46	15.33	21	–	–	15	28.80	3-41	5.44
Banton, T.	24	658	29.90	112	2	4	0	–	–	16/1
Barker, K.H.D.	65	617	19.90	56	–	1	73	32.56	4-33	5.72
Barnard, E.G.	59	921	29.70	85*	–	5	65	37.29	3-26	5.84
Barnes, E.	12	77	19.25	33*	–	–	15	37.33	2-32	5.93
Barnwell, N.A.	2	32	16.00	31	–	–	0	–	0-17	8.50
Bartlett, G.A.	23	523	30.76	108	1	1	0	–	–	–
Bean, F.J.	3	74	24.66	61	–	1	0	–	–	–
Beard, A.P.	6	79	15.80	22*	–	–	7	43.28	3-51	6.78
Bedingham, D.G.	28	796	33.16	104*	2	6	0	–	0-25	3.84
Bell, G.J.	1	35	35.00	35	–	–	0	–	–	–
Bell-Drummond, D.J.	89	3381	42.26	171*	6	22	5	24.20	2-22	4.68
Benjamin, C.G.	1	50	50.00	50	–	1	0	–	–	–
Benkenstein, L.M.	6	72	14.40	55	–	1	11	17.90	6-42	5.32
Berg, G.K.	113	1590	22.08	75	–	7	120	29.25	5-26	5.09
Bess, D.M.	26	176	10.35	27*	–	–	21	55.66	3-35	5.87
Bethell, J.G.	8	141	23.50	66	–	1	11	27.36	4-36	5.28
Bevan, T.R.	4	158	39.50	134	1	–	0	–	–	–
Billings, S.W.	100	3030	42.08	175	7	20	–	–	–	87/8

253

	M	Runs	Avge	HS	100	50	Wkts	Avge	Best	Econ
Blake, A.J.	116	2447	30.97	116	1	15	5	55.40	2-13	6.29
Blake, J.W.	8	163	23.28	44	–	–	0	–	–	–
Blatherwick, J.M.	6	11	11.00	5*	–	–	6	36.33	3-57	7.78
Bohannon, J.J.	31	648	29.45	75	–	4	1	208.00	1-33	8.32
Bopara, R.S.	323	9845	40.18	201*	15	60	248	29.02	5-63	5.33
Borthwick, S.G.	115	1822	24.62	88	–	11	81	43.39	5-38	6.02
Bracey, J.R.	22	942	47.10	113*	2	6	1	23.00	1-23	22/2
Briggs, D.R.	107	402	12.56	37*	–	–	112	37.39	4-32	5.11
Broad, S.C.J.	151	620	11.92	45*	–	–	216	30.51	5-23	5.27
Brook, H.C.	15	343	31.18	103	1	1	0	–	0-19	6.33
Brookes, E.A.	16	226	20.54	63	–	2	9	35.55	3-15	7.32
Brookes, H.J.H.	12	13	4.33	12*	–	–	17	35.35	3-50	6.54
Brooks, J.A.	45	130	9.28	28	–	–	50	33.74	4-38	4.95
Brown, B.C.	88	1545	26.18	105	1	10	0	–	–	82/12
Brown, P.R.	10	3	3.00	3	–	–	12	36.50	3-53	6.28
Browne, N.L.J.	25	606	27.54	99	–	3	0	–	–	–
Budinger, S.G.	17	523	32.68	89	–	4	0	–	0-17	17.00
Burgess, M.G.K.	33	853	29.41	93	–	6	0	–	–	27/3
Burns, R.J.	57	1722	35.14	95	–	12	0	–	–	–
Bushnell, J.J.	3	54	18.00	25	–	–	0	–	–	–
Buttleman, W.E.L.	7	68	9.71	23	–	–	0	–	–	–
Buttler, J.C.	227	6410	44.51	162*	12	38	0	–	–	239/39
Byrom, E.J.	7	49	9.80	18	–	–	0	–	–	–
Came, H.R.C.	14	286	23.83	57	–	1	0	–	–	–
Campbell, J.O.I.	14	1	0.50	1*	–	–	23	25.91	4-44	5.45
Carlson, K.S.	35	821	27.36	82	–	6	10	20.00	4-41	5.42
Carse, B.A.	16	79	15.80	31	–	–	22	27.50	5-61	5.57
Carter, M.	16	65	7.22	21*	–	–	23	27.17	4-40	5.34
Carter, O.J.	9	163	27.16	59	–	2	0	–	–	11/2
Chappell, Z.J.	23	209	20.90	59*	–	1	30	36.10	3-35	6.35
Charlesworth, B.G.	10	451	50.11	99*	–	3	0	–	0-13	6.50
Clark, G.	49	1588	33.78	141*	4	6	4	12.50	3-18	5.55
Clark, J.	51	954	30.77	79*	–	5	34	45.17	4-34	6.34
Clark, T.G.R.	12	355	32.27	104	1	1	0	–	0-17	5.66
Clarke, J.M.	62	1846	34.18	139	4	9	0	–	–	22/2
Cliff, B.M.	1	0	–	0	–	–	1	44.00	1-44	8.80
Coad, B.O.	33	79	13.16	24	–	–	36	36.61	4-63	5.11
Cobb, J.J.	99	3330	38.27	146*	7	21	35	48.91	3-34	5.84
Coles, J.M.	12	117	19.50	32	–	–	17	23.05	3-27	5.11
Compton, B.G.	19	812	45.11	110	2	7	0	–	–	–
Conners, S.	9	12	6.00	5	–	–	14	28.57	5-28	5.40
Cook, A.N.	178	6510	39.93	137	13	38	0	–	–	3.33
Cook, S.J.	13	15	5.00	6	–	–	14	36.64	3-37	4.79
Cooke, C.B.	92	2616	34.88	161	3	14	0	–	–	58/5
Cornall, T.R.	9	310	44.28	97	–	3	3	43.33	2-23	6.09
Coughlin, P.	33	341	17.05	77	–	1	20	49.35	3-36	5.71
Cox, J.M.	1	21	21.00	21	–	–	0	–	–	1/-
Cox, O.B.	81	1624	31.23	122*	1	8	0	–	–	91/9
Cracknell, J.B.	9	158	22.57	71	–	1	0	–	–	10/2
Crane, M.S.	39	112	28.00	28*	–	–	67	29.98	4-30	6.08
Crawley, Z.	26	840	36.52	120	1	5	0	–	0-17	8.50
Critchley, M.J.J.	43	685	27.40	64*	–	2	31	54.00	4-48	6.56
Crocombe, H.T.	11	20	6.66	9*	–	–	12	40.75	3-33	6.03
Croft, S.J.	174	4820	38.25	127	4	34	66	41.74	4-24	5.57
Cullen, H.J.	4	11	5.50	8	–	–	0	–	–	–
Curran, S.M.	65	774	22.76	95*	–	2	82	32.18	5-48	5.55

254

	M	Runs	Avge	HS	100	50	Wkts	Avge	Best	Econ
Curran, T.K.	86	739	21.11	47*	–	–	126	28.83	5-16	5.57
Currie, B.J.	8	4	4.00	3*	–	–	12	26.00	3-38	4.87
Currie, S.W.	14	139	17.37	43*	–	–	24	24.33	3-25	6.05
Dal, A.K.	19	254	19.53	52	–	1	2	94.50	1-16	5.10
Dale, A.S.	2	0	–	0	–	–	2	33.00	2-42	4.71
Das, R.J.	7	202	28.85	63	–	1	0	–	–	–
Davey, J.H.	92	1280	23.27	91	–	6	114	26.78	6-28	5.33
Davidson, O.F.	2	16	16.00	14	–	–	0	–	0-30	5.93
Davies, A.L.	49	1380	32.09	147	1	7	0	–	–	48/11
Davies, J.L.B.	5	164	32.80	70	–	2	0	–	–	–
Davies, S.M.	197	5959	34.84	127*	9	37	0	–	–	160/42
Davis, W.S.	9	48	16.00	15*	–	–	8	51.50	2-40	6.92
Dawson, L.A.	159	3499	33.00	113*	3	18	161	30.04	6-47	4.72
de Caires, J.M.	3	68	22.66	43	–	–	1	95.00	1-13	5.27
de Grandhomme, C.	156	3116	25.96	151	3	11	84	42.88	4-37	5.10
de Lange, M.	98	776	15.52	58*	–	2	170	26.03	5-49	5.54
de Leede, B.F.W.	29	567	20.25	89	–	2	12	45.25	3-50	6.18
Denly, J.L.	166	5195	36.84	150*	8	29	55	26.18	4-35	5.11
Dent, C.D.J.	82	2294	32.30	151*	5	6	12	34.33	4-43	5.64
Dickson, S.R.	57	1403	29.85	103*	1	9	0	–	0-20	10.00
D'Oliveira, B.L.	73	1320	25.38	123	1	7	58	41.15	3- 8	5.27
Donald, A.H.T.	39	651	18.60	76	–	4	0	–	–	–
Doneathy, L.	11	188	31.33	69*	–	2	8	39.00	4-36	6.59
Douthwaite, D.A.	11	145	29.00	52*	–	1	13	32.84	3-43	5.93
Drissell, G.S.	10	146	29.20	37*	–	–	5	58.00	1-21	5.14
Duckett, B.M.	74	2385	38.46	220*	3	16	0	–	–	39/3
Duke, H.G.	17	536	35.73	125	2	2	0	–	–	9/3
Dunn, M.P.	18	66	13.20	34	–	–	19	38.10	2-32	6.13
du Plooy, J.L.	45	1865	58.28	155	5	10	11	35.36	3-19	5.84
Edwards, M.W.	9	29	9.66	11	–	–	10	40.70	4-31	5.78
Ellis, N.T.	15	109	18.16	31	–	–	21	25.66	5-38	4.99
Eskinazi, S.S.	30	1434	55.15	182	6	3	0	–	–	–
Evans, S.T.	3	37	18.50	20	–	–	0	–	–	–
Evison, J.D.M.	15	402	33.50	109	1	3	11	32.90	3-62	6.62
Evitts, R.L.	1	10	10.00	10	–	–	0	–	0-21	3.50
Finan, M.G.A.	1	0	–	0*	–	–	0	–	0-46	9.20
Finch, A.W.	14	71	14.20	24	–	–	14	43.42	3-54	6.17
Finch, H.Z.	50	1470	35.85	108	1	11	0	–	0- 2	9.00
Finn, S.T.	143	411	12.08	42*	–	–	199	29.27	5-33	5.14
Fisher, M.D.	34	228	28.50	36*	–	–	32	42.68	3-32	5.92
Fletcher, L.J.	79	505	20.20	53*	–	1	87	35.25	5-56	5.67
Foakes, B.T.	73	1941	37.32	92	–	18	0	–	–	86/11
Fraine, W.A.R.	21	582	34.23	143	1	2	0	–	–	–
Fuller, J.K.	69	884	23.26	55*	–	2	79	33.03	6-35	5.92
Garrett, G.A.	10	39	9.75	8*	–	–	12	39.00	3-50	6.00
Garton, G.H.S.	24	103	11.44	38	–	–	29	34.24	4-43	6.32
Gay, E.N.	16	521	40.07	131	1	2	0	–	0-19	6.33
Geddes, B.B.A.	12	299	27.18	73	–	2	0	–	–	–
Gibbon, B.J.	5	11	5.50	11	–	–	7	35.42	2-33	5.90
Gibson, O.J.	7	21	5.25	6	–	–	11	29.18	3-54	6.37
Gilchrist, N.N.	16	53	8.83	33	–	–	22	29.04	5-45	6.89
Gleeson, R.J.	21	53	6.62	13	–	–	28	29.14	5-47	5.82
Glover, B.D.	16	101	16.83	27	–	–	14	49.42	3-43	6.11
Godleman, B.A.	76	2827	42.83	137	7	13	0	–	–	–
Goldsworthy, L.P.	16	632	48.61	111	1	5	6	78.83	2-58	5.56
Goodman, D.C.	2	0	–	0	–	–	0	–	0-15	5.83

	M	Runs	Avge	HS	100	50	Wkts	Avge	Best	Econ
Gorvin, A.W.	7	20	–	12*	–	–	3	63.33	2-41	4.87
Greatwood, T.L.	7	14	14.00	7*	–	–	9	33.55	2-30	6.04
Green, B.G.F.	13	356	50.85	157	1	1	12	37.58	3-64	5.74
Gregory, L.	79	1323	24.96	105*	1	8	110	27.66	4-23	5.95
Gubbins, N.R.T.	72	2771	40.75	141	7	16	6	47.33	4-38	5.68
Guest, B.D.	16	413	29.50	88	–	3	0	–	–	15/2
Gumbs, S.S.E.	4	104	26.00	66	–	1	0	–	–	–
Haider Ali	21	708	33.71	118	1	4	0	–	–	–
Hain, S.R.	59	2810	58.54	161*	10	15	0	–	–	–
Haines, T.J.	8	301	37.62	123	1	1	0	–	–	–
Hales, A.D.	175	6260	38.40	187*	17	32	1	–	0- 4	15.00
Hameed, H.	30	972	40.50	114	2	6	0	–	–	–
Hamidullah Qadri	18	137	27.40	42*	–	–	20	35.55	4-36	5.91
Hammond, M.A.H.	8	185	30.83	95	–	1	5	19.40	2-18	5.10
Hannon-Dalby, O.J.	51	118	14.75	21*	–	–	81	31.09	5-27	6.22
Hardie, A.M.	9	135	27.00	58	–	1	11	28.90	3-28	5.67
Harding, J.C.	3	12	12.00	12	–	–	2	47.50	2-33	6.78
Harmer, S.R.	94	1144	21.18	44*	–	3	96	38.45	4-42	4.92
Harris, J.A.R.	72	469	13.40	117	1	–	96	31.79	4-38	5.89
Harris, M.B.	4	27	13.50	12	–	–	7	41.28	3-98	7.41
Harris, M.S.	61	1953	34.26	127	2	12	0	–	–	–
Harrison, A.	1	5	5.00	5	–	–	0	–	0-23	7.66
Hasan Ali	85	579	16.08	59	–	2	138	27.65	5-34	5.58
Hayes, J.P.H.	2	1	–	1*	–	–	2	45.00	2-58	6.42
Haynes, J.A.	8	395	49.37	153	1	2	0	–	–	–
Heldreich, F.J.	5	5	5.00	5	–	–	3	73.66	2-69	7.62
Helm, T.G.	40	206	12.87	30	–	–	56	31.10	5-33	5.75
Henry, M.J.	139	657	12.39	48*	–	–	230	26.55	6-45	5.24
Higgins, R.F.	33	680	28.33	81*	–	3	24	35.20	4-50	5.54
Hill, G.C.H.	17	407	33.91	130	1	2	10	24.90	3-47	5.29
Hill, L.J.	57	1308	26.16	118	3	5	0	–	–	30/2
Hogan, M.G.	79	187	18.70	27	–	–	118	27.27	5-44	4.87
Holden, M.D.E.	24	845	42.25	166	1	5	1	104.00	1-29	4.95
Holland, I.G.	37	640	24.61	75	–	4	37	33.02	4-12	5.01
Hollman, L.B.K.	12	108	12.00	20	–	–	21	27.80	4-34	5.61
Hose, A.J.	30	765	31.87	101*	1	4	0	–	–	–
Howell, B.A.C.	87	2090	35.42	122	1	13	79	34.15	3-37	5.21
Hudson-Prentice, F.J.	13	374	46.75	93	–	3	10	39.90	3-37	6.41
Hunt, S.F.	2	3	3.00	2	–	–	2	49.50	2-59	6.60
Hutton, B.A.	32	351	21.93	46	–	–	44	29.13	7-26	5.56
Ibrahim, D.K.	14	174	17.40	50	–	1	5	65.80	2-54	5.57
Ingram, C.A.	193	7926	48.03	155	19	50	43	34.37	4-39	5.55
Jacks, W.G.	22	506	24.09	121	1	2	11	38.45	2-32	5.26
James, L.W.	16	278	23.16	54	–	1	5	9.60	5-48	5.33
Jennings, K.K.	82	2794	42.33	139	5	19	11	60.90	2-19	5.82
Jones, M.A.	14	479	34.21	119	1	3	0	–	–	–
Jones, R.P.	28	710	41.76	85*	–	6	2	61.00	1- 3	6.00
Jordan, C.J.	84	634	15.46	55	–	1	121	30.02	5-28	5.73
Karvelas, A.	22	150	18.75	33	–	–	37	21.56	5-16	4.53
Kashif Ali	4	206	51.50	114	1	1	0	–	–	–
Kelly, D.C.	1	17	17.00	17	–	–	0	–	0-36	6.00
Keogh, R.I.	59	1592	33.16	134	2	14	16	70.06	3-32	5.36
Kerrigan, S.C.	39	35	2.91	10	–	–	34	43.91	4-48	5.30
Khushi, F.I.N.	12	558	46.50	118	3	1	0	–	–	–
Killeen, M.J.	3	49	16.33	32	–	–	2	50.50	1-17	4.59
Kimber, L.P.J.	17	569	37.93	102	1	5	7	23.14	4-61	6.48

	M	Runs	Avge	HS	100	50	Wkts	Avge	Best	Econ
Kimber, N.J.H.	10	196	28.00	84	–	1	6	44.83	2-15	7.47
King, S.I.M.	1	11	11.00	11	–	–	0	–	–	–
Klaassen, F.J.	29	85	7.72	13	–	–	43	25.74	3-23	4.61
Kohler-Cadmore, T.	56	1808	34.11	164	3	10	0	–	–	–
Labuschagne, M.	63	2072	34.53	135	2	16	11	73.45	3-46	6.37
Lace, T.C.	15	205	15.76	48	–	–	2	10.00	2-20	10.00
Lakmal, R.A.S.	174	482	9.83	38*	–	–	242	28.44	5-31	5.30
Lamb, D.J.	18	292	41.71	86*	–	2	28	29.92	5-30	5.63
Lamb, M.J.	19	549	42.23	119*	1	2	4	54.00	4-35	5.83
Lavelle, G.I.D.	17	290	32.22	61*	–	3	0	–	–	18/1
Lawes, T.E.	8	318	53.00	75	–	4	8	44.50	2-20	6.13
Lawrence, D.W.	28	670	26.80	115	1	4	11	54.27	3-35	6.25
Leach, J.	52	841	29.00	88	–	3	56	40.35	4-30	5.86
Leach, M.J.	17	22	7.33	18	–	–	21	33.19	3- 7	4.79
Leaning, J.A.	54	1123	28.79	131*	2	5	10	32.70	5-22	5.68
Lees, A.Z.	65	2165	40.09	126*	4	17	0	–	–	–
Lenham, A.D.	11	71	17.75	18*	–	–	10	49.10	4-59	6.21
Leonard, E.O.	4	1	–	1*	–	–	3	55.33	2-84	7.54
Libby, J.D.	22	688	40.47	126*	1	5	4	47.50	2-47	5.13
Lilley, A.M.	36	471	19.62	60	–	1	21	38.14	4-30	5.64
Linde, G.F.	72	1372	26.38	93*	–	10	94	30.41	6-47	5.30
Lintott, J.B.	1	21	21.00	21	–	–	0	–	0-89	8.90
Livingstone, L.S.	67	1802	35.33	129	1	11	29	44.10	3-51	5.27
Lloyd, D.L.	51	1053	24.48	92	–	6	21	38.19	5-53	5.93
Loten, T.W.	8	85	42.50	43*	–	–	6	40.00	2-37	6.10
Luxton, W.A.	12	295	29.50	84	–	2	0	–	–	–
Lynn, C.A.	50	1597	36.29	135	2	12	1	45.00	1- 3	3.91
Lyth, A.	122	3765	35.18	144	5	18	6	62.16	2-27	6.21
McAlindon, S.J.C.	7	123	30.75	50	–	1	7	42.14	4-29	6.14
McAndrew, N.J.	7	67	13.40	25	–	–	6	53.83	2-54	6.77
McDermott, B.R.	31	1434	49.44	133	5	8	0	–	–	–
McIlroy, J.P.	3	10	–	10*	–	–	5	21.40	2-13	3.96
McKerr, C.	24	107	8.91	26*	–	–	36	29.58	4-64	6.07
McKiernan, M.H.	14	305	30.50	72*	–	1	6	60.16	1-14	6.44
Mackintosh, T.S.S.	8	130	16.25	36	–	–	0	–	–	–
McManus, L.D.	44	893	30.79	107	1	3	0	–	–	33/10
Maddy, G.W.	2	7	7.00	7	–	–	0	–	–	–
Madsen, W.L.	105	3323	41.53	138	6	19	16	35.81	3-27	5.14
Maharaj, K.A.	121	863	16.92	50*	–	1	154	29.91	5-34	4.76
Mahmood, S.	34	137	17.12	45	–	–	64	24.14	6-37	5.56
Majid, Y.	8	10	10.00	5*	–	–	9	34.66	3-74	5.57
Malan, D.J.	157	5430	42.09	185*	11	27	41	32.07	4-25	5.84
Malan, P.J.	127	5053	45.93	169*	14	26	1	274.00	1-28	6.71
Martindale, B.J.R.	1	1	1.00	1	–	–	0	–	0-13	6.50
Maxwell, G.J.	196	5323	33.90	146	5	33	101	45.28	4-46	5.48
Middleton, F.S.	10	235	26.11	64	–	1	0	–	–	–
Mike, B.W.M.	10	159	19.87	41	–	–	10	37.60	3-34	7.54
Miles, C.N.	41	146	12.16	31*	–	–	51	35.98	4-29	6.26
Miller, A.H.	4	56	56.00	31	–	–	0	–	–	–
Mills, T.S.	23	7	1.75	3*	–	–	22	35.77	3-23	5.97
Milnes, M.E.	12	101	16.83	26	–	–	19	34.05	5-79	6.75
Mohammad Abbas	55	137	7.61	15*	–	–	75	29.21	4-31	4.88
Montgomery, M.	21	732	48.80	104	1	5	5	66.40	2-48	6.03
Moores, T.J.	21	566	35.37	76	–	5	0	–	–	18/5
Moriarty, D.T.	10	8	4.00	5	–	–	15	23.80	4-30	4.36
Morley, J.P.	13	7	7.00	6	–	–	11	39.09	2-22	4.62

257

	M	Runs	Avge	HS	100	50	Wkts	Avge	Best	Econ
Morris, C.A.J.	41	110	15.71	25*	–	–	44	37.38	4-33	5.94
Mousley, D.R.	9	338	37.55	105	1	2	7	25.42	3-32	4.23
Mulder, P.W.A.	50	1171	36.59	116*	2	6	53	31.11	4-47	5.22
Mullaney, S.J.	123	2611	35.28	124	2	19	100	34.58	4-29	5.21
Munro, C.	139	4197	36.49	174*	9	22	24	63.33	3-45	5.46
Murtagh, T.J.	214	828	10.09	35*	–	–	277	29.84	5-21	5.00
Muyeye, T.S.	11	221	24.55	40	–	1	1	33.00	1-17	3.30
Narine, S.P.	100	625	12.01	51	–	1	163	20.85	6- 9	3.72
Naveen-ul-Haq	23	92	10.22	30	–	–	34	34.47	5-40	5.94
Neser, M.G.	59	747	23.34	122	1	2	69	34.76	4-41	5.31
Nijjar, A.S.S.	20	204	18.54	32*	–	–	20	41.85	2-26	5.09
Northeast, S.A.	113	3277	34.86	177*	5	18	0	–	–	–
Norwell, L.C.	26	63	6.30	16	–	–	33	35.63	6-52	5.46
Ogborne, A.R.J.	5	39	39.00	27*	–	–	4	61.25	3-49	6.44
Organ, F.S.	19	260	18.57	79	–	2	10	47.80	3-39	4.60
O'Riordan, M.K.	5	119	39.66	60	–	1	1	157.00	1-77	7.47
Orr, A.G.H.	14	670	47.85	206	2	3	0	–	–	–
Overton, C.	75	824	22.27	66*	–	2	95	32.16	5-18	5.32
Overton, J.	42	399	17.34	40*	–	–	57	30.54	4-42	6.28
Parkinson, C.F.	13	222	27.75	52*	–	1	4	147.25	1-34	6.40
Parkinson, M.W.	30	50	16.66	15*	–	–	47	28.04	5-51	5.23
Patel, R.K.	20	491	25.84	118	1	2	0	–	–	–
Patel, R.S.	21	730	45.62	131	3	3	4	47.00	2-65	6.55
Patel, S.R.	245	6270	35.22	136*	8	33	225	33.29	6-13	5.40
Paterson, D.	101	348	11.60	29	–	–	137	30.75	5-19	5.30
Patterson-White, L.A.	15	192	19.20	62*	–	1	24	19.87	5-19	5.00
Payne, D.A.	68	211	19.18	40	–	–	111	25.87	7-29	5.78
Pennington, D.Y.	10	75	25.00	35	–	–	18	31.11	5-67	6.15
Pepper, M.S.	5	40	13.33	34	–	–	0	–	–	–
Pettman, T.H.S.	3	5	–	5*	–	–	4	35.25	4-44	6.13
Phillips, G.D.	52	1737	35.44	156	5	3	14	31.64	3-40	32/2
Podmore, H.W.	26	183	15.25	40	–	–	27	45.48	4-57	6.30
Pollock, E.J.	31	677	24.17	103*	1	2	0	–	–	–
Pope, O.J.D.	31	767	33.34	93*	–	5	0	–	–	–
Porter, J.A.	37	51	10.20	10*	–	–	37	38.02	4-29	4.93
Potts, M.J.	11	56	14.00	30	–	–	16	25.43	4-62	5.98
Potts, N.J.	5	8	8.00	6*	–	–	4	58.00	2-63	6.69
Prest, T.J.	16	510	31.87	181	1	3	3	27.00	2-28	7.36
Price, O.J.	10	256	28.44	45	–	–	4	28.75	2-34	5.75
Price, T.J.	8	121	20.16	45	–	–	6	67.33	4-70	6.73
Procter, L.A.	48	820	32.80	97	–	5	26	41.92	3-29	5.74
Pujara, C.A.	112	5069	56.95	174	14	31	0	–	0- 8	8.00
Quinn, M.R.	44	143	11.91	36	–	–	59	37.28	4-71	6.20
Rahane, A.M.	167	6054	39.56	187	10	42	4	12.75	2-36	5.77
Raine, B.A.	29	423	21.15	83	–	1	30	40.63	3-31	5.68
Rashid, A.U.	235	1792	18.66	71	–	2	311	32.04	5-27	5.46
Rashid Khan	85	1135	21.01	60*	–	5	162	18.73	7-18	4.18
Rawlins, D.M.W.	20	510	28.33	91	–	4	17	39.00	3-22	5.14
Reece, L.M.	47	1238	32.57	136	3	6	25	47.56	4-35	6.02
Reifer, N.M.J.	18	276	25.09	70	–	2	0	–	–	–
Revis, M.L.	17	279	21.46	58*	–	1	17	33.00	4-77	5.72
Rew, J.E.K.	10	333	33.30	114	1	1	0	–	–	–
Rhodes, W.M.H.	47	1177	28.70	113	1	5	30	38.63	3-40	6.03
Richards, J.A.	7	137	34.25	46	–	–	5	37.00	2-37	5.72
Richardson, K.W.	91	467	13.34	36	–	–	147	29.27	6-48	5.28
Roach, K.A.J.	119	400	13.33	34	–	–	156	29.69	6-27	5.01

258

	M	Runs	Avge	HS	100	50	Wkts	Avge	Best	Econ
Robinson, O.E.	15	122	15.25	30	–	–	16	38.93	3-31	5.97
Robinson, O.G.	26	821	39.09	206*	1	4	0	–	–	14/1
Robson, S.D.	32	1241	42.79	111	3	8	5	51.40	2-23	6.94
Roderick, G.H.	64	1425	29.68	104	2	9	0	–	–	56/6
Roland-Jones, T.S.	79	684	21.37	65	–	1	126	25.24	4-10	5.19
Root, J.E.	196	7420	47.87	133*	17	44	39	50.56	3-52	5.59
Root, W.T.	40	1100	40.74	113*	3	5	6	51.66	2-36	6.36
Rossington, A.M.	49	1381	37.32	97	–	11	0	–	–	34/5
Roy, J.J.	202	6935	38.10	180	17	36	0	–	0-12	12.00
Rushworth, C.	87	215	11.31	38*	–	–	140	24.40	5-31	5.17
Russell, A.K.	8	5	–	3*	–	–	5	83.00	2-69	6.28
Rymell, J.S.	13	421	35.08	121	1	1	0	–	–	–
Sale, O.R.T.	3	13	13.00	13	–	–	3	60.66	3-80	7.58
Sales, J.J.G.	11	134	26.80	34*	–	–	3	98.33	2-65	6.32
Salisbury, M.E.T.	17	10	10.00	5*	–	–	17	38.35	4-55	5.66
Salt, P.D.	24	863	39.22	137*	2	4	0	–	–	6/–
Salter, A.G.	48	472	22.47	51	–	1	30	50.13	3-37	5.17
Sams, D.R.	14	302	27.45	62	–	2	21	24.71	5-46	5.17
Sanderson, B.W.	45	157	10.46	31	–	–	56	29.50	3-17	5.43
Santner, M.J.	110	1704	28.40	86	–	7	121	32.68	5-50	4.66
Schadendorf, D.J.	17	147	14.70	44*	–	–	0	–	–	13/4
Scrimshaw, G.L.S.	4	13	–	13*	–	–	4	37.50	2-41	7.50
Scriven, T.A.R.	11	105	17.50	42	–	–	7	36.85	2-46	5.50
Shadab Khan	68	829	26.74	86	–	–	93	31.03	4-28	5.20
Shaikh, H.	4	62	20.66	25	–	–	0	–	–	–
Shan Masood	102	4743	57.14	182*	14	29	2	8.50	2- 0	4.25
Shaw, J.	10	14	3.50	8*	–	–	8	60.75	4-36	6.23
Shutt, J.W.	11	3	3.00	1*	–	–	10	32.30	4-46	5.90
Sibley, D.P.	29	763	31.79	115	3	1	1	62.00	1-20	6.88
Siddle, P.M.	71	294	11.30	62	–	1	91	30.83	4-22	4.73
Simpson, J.A.	96	1607	25.50	82*	–	8	0	–	–	90/19
Singh, F.	12	134	19.14	45	–	–	9	43.00	2- 7	6.17
Sisodiya, P.	4	13	6.50	7	–	–	6	29.66	3-76	5.23
Slater, B.T.	53	2438	56.69	148*	6	16	0	–	0-17	5.66
Smeed, W.C.F.	1	0	0.00	0	–	–	0	–	–	–
Smith, J.L.	15	425	42.50	85	–	3	0	–	–	13/2
Smith, K.	8	86	21.50	29*	–	–	0	–	–	–
Smith, S.P.D.	179	6478	46.94	164	14	40	47	39.14	3-16	5.43
Smith, T.M.J.	99	605	20.86	65	–	2	87	39.55	4-26	5.26
Snater, S.	31	276	18.40	64	–	1	42	31.00	5-29	5.79
Sowter, N.A.	19	134	14.88	31	–	–	36	25.77	6-62	5.52
Steel, C.T.	22	334	22.26	77	–	3	14	37.42	4-33	5.56
Steel, S.	10	296	32.88	68	–	3	3	48.66	1-31	5.84
Stewart, G.	20	216	15.42	49	–	–	23	30.04	4-42	5.44
Stokes, B.A.	175	4764	36.93	164	7	27	137	33.55	5-61	5.77
Stone, O.P.	30	122	24.40	24*	–	–	24	42.62	4-71	5.45
Stoneman, M.D.	99	3286	37.77	144*	7	19	1	41.00	1- 8	11.18
Stubbs, T.	11	275	27.50	82	–	1	0	–	0-11	5.50
Swindells, H.J.	19	389	25.93	75	–	4	0	–	–	16/3
Tattersall, J.A.	32	697	31.68	89	–	7	0	–	–	27/3
Taylor, C.Z.	3	53	17.66	36	–	–	3	30.33	1- 6	5.05
Taylor, J.M.R.	67	1758	39.95	95	–	16	40	32.65	4-31	5.35
Taylor, J.P.A.	2	6	–	6*	–	–	3	31.00	2-66	7.15
Taylor, M.D.	35	105	21.00	51*	–	1	27	52.03	3-39	5.43
Taylor, T.A.I.	22	489	48.90	98*	–	5	24	42.41	3-24	6.21
Thomas, J.F.	4	12	4.00	10	–	–	1	69.00	1-39	7.66

	M	Runs	Avge	HS	100	50	Wkts	Avge	Best	Econ
Thompson, J.A.	1	0	–	0	–	–	0	–	0-43	8.60
Thomson, A.T.	18	320	32.00	68*	–	2	22	28.22	3-25	5.35
Tongue, J.C.	15	99	19.80	34	–	–	16	45.50	2-35	6.92
Topley, R.J.W.	65	65	8.12	19	–	–	110	24.78	6-24	5.43
Trevaskis, L.	25	315	19.68	59*	–	2	23	40.82	3-38	4.89
Turner, J.A.	15	34	11.33	12	–	–	27	19.59	5-25	5.18
Tye, A.J.	52	324	16.20	44	–	–	113	21.46	6-46	5.52
Umeed, A.R.I.	6	132	22.00	56	–	1	0	–	–	–
van Buuren, G.L.	78	1656	29.57	119*	1	8	63	32.76	5-35	4.74
van der Gugten, T.	63	400	17.39	49	–	–	76	33.31	5-24	5.37
van der Merwe, R.E.	188	2901	26.86	165*	1	11	251	26.62	5-26	4.87
van Meekeren, P.A.	63	143	9.53	15*	–	–	75	28.68	5-48	5.24
Vasconcelos, R.S.	42	1265	32.43	112	3	7	0	–	–	31/3
Vilas, D.J.	177	5102	37.24	166	10	24	0	–	–	175/29
Vince, J.M.	142	5063	40.50	190	10	24	3	54.00	1-18	5.58
Virdi, G.S.	6	28	5.60	8	–	–	2	76.00	1-36	5.62
Waite, M.J.	29	606	33.66	71	–	1	42	26.23	5-59	5.79
Walallawita, T.N.	9	83	11.85	29	–	–	5	87.20	2-54	5.45
Walker, R.I.	5	53	26.50	23	–	–	4	46.75	2-51	5.96
Walter, P.I.	16	253	25.30	50	–	1	14	31.00	4-37	7.07
Ward, H.D.	8	141	17.62	37	–	–	0	–	0-18	8.80
Warner, J.D.	10	0	0.00	0*	–	–	8	49.62	3-42	5.51
Watt, M.R.J.	67	396	14.14	44	–	–	75	31.48	5-33	4.29
Weatherley, J.J.	27	664	28.86	105*	1	4	8	27.62	4-25	4.05
Welch, N.R.	15	327	23.35	127*	1	1	0	–	–	–
Wells, B.J.J.	12	201	20.10	76	–	1	0	–	–	–
Wells, L.W.P.	43	745	21.28	88	–	5	23	38.04	3-19	5.20
Westley, T.	105	3603	38.74	134	7	28	31	40.06	4-60	4.99
Wheal, B.T.J.	28	63	7.00	18*	–	–	44	26.22	4-38	5.24
White, C.	12	38	9.50	10*	–	–	17	29.11	4-20	6.08
White, G.G.	89	558	15.08	41*	–	–	94	29.82	6-37	5.00
White, R.G.	15	239	23.90	55	–	1	0	–	–	19/3
Whiteley, R.A.	81	1660	27.66	131	1	10	14	40.21	4-58	6.66
Whiteman, S.M.	45	841	24.02	79	–	6	0	–	–	36/4
Willey, D.J.	143	1960	25.45	167	3	7	168	30.16	5-30	5.61
Wood, C.P.	79	400	12.90	41	–	–	106	27.96	5-22	5.38
Wood, L.	4	73	73.00	52	–	1	5	25.00	2-36	5.95
Wood, T.A.	12	254	25.40	109	1	–	3	31.00	1-13	5.47
Worrall, D.J.	43	128	10.66	31*	–	–	50	38.88	5-62	5.39
Wright, C.J.C.	116	308	11.84	42	–	–	121	35.57	6-35	5.50
Yates, R.M.	16	760	47.50	114	2	6	4	78.50	1-27	5.54
Zafar Gohar	75	874	17.83	62	–	5	107	29.19	5-56	4.86
Zaib, S.A.	25	477	25.10	136	1	1	15	42.93	4-23	5.75

TWENTY20 CAREER RECORDS

Compiled by Philip Bailey

The following career records, to the end of the 2022 season, include all players currently registered with first-class counties or teams in The Hundred. Performances in The Hundred are included.

	M	Runs	Avge	HS	100	50	Wkts	Avge	Best	Econ
Abbott, K.J.	153	324	13.33	30	–	–	157	28.36	5-14	8.24
Abbott, K.J.	156	324	13.50	30	–	–	157	28.56	5-14	8.27
Abbott, S.A.	116	582	11.19	41	–	–	142	21.88	5-16	8.60
Abell, T.B.	71	1686	33.72	101*	1	10	2	50.00	1-11	10.00
Ackermann, C.N.	153	3478	27.82	85	–	19	73	27.58	7-18	7.22
Ahmed, R.	19	100	11.11	33	–	–	21	22.57	4-22	7.38
Aitchison, B.W.	3	2	2.00	2	–	–	4	31.50	2-30	12.60
Albert, T.E.	11	101	20.20	24*	–	–	0	–	–	–
Aldridge, K.L.	1	0	–	0	–	–	0	–	–	–
Ali, M.M.	247	5348	24.87	121*	2	28	174	24.68	5-34	7.61
Allison, B.M.J.	14	12	6.00	6*	–	–	12	30.00	3-33	9.64
Alsop, T.P.	52	1111	25.25	85	–	5	0	–	–	19/3
Anderson, J.M.	44	23	5.75	16	–	–	41	32.14	3-23	8.47
Andersson, M.K.	23	185	10.27	25*	–	–	17	25.35	3-32	10.30
Archer, J.C.	121	551	17.21	36	–	–	153	22.52	4-18	7.65
Atkinson, A.A.P.	23	44	7.33	14	–	–	33	17.66	4-36	8.61
Azhar Ali	49	985	21.88	72	–	3	15	18.86	3-10	6.35
Bailey, T.E.	28	21	4.20	10	–	–	26	25.11	5-17	9.32
Bairstow, J.M.	180	4304	30.52	114	3	25	–	–	–	101/15
Baker, J.O.	8	14	3.50	5	–	–	3	68.66	2-26	9.36
Baker, S.	3	0	0.00	0	–	–	2	37.50	2-28	10.00
Ball, J.T.	109	55	7.85	18*	–	–	142	22.35	4-11	8.93
Bamber, E.R.	5	3	–	3*	–	–	0	–	0-10	11.54
Banton, T.	98	2166	23.04	107*	2	12	0	–	–	58/6
Barker, K.H.D.	65	383	13.67	46	–	–	69	23.01	4-19	7.90
Barnard, E.G.	102	751	15.97	43*	–	–	60	38.96	3-29	9.00
Barnes, E.	5	7	7.00	7	–	–	2	57.50	2-27	11.50
Bartlett, G.A.	8	148	21.14	82*	–	1	0	–	–	–
Beard, A.P.	15	31	15.50	13	–	–	18	21.72	4-29	9.30
Bedingham, D.G.	55	1014	20.28	73	–	6	0	–	–	15/1
Bell, G.J.	1	31	31.00	31	–	–	0	–	–	–
Bell-Drummond, D.J.	136	3716	29.49	112*	1	29	5	38.20	2-19	10.32
Benjamin, C.G.	34	603	30.15	68*	–	3	0	–	–	–
Berg, G.K.	104	1198	21.78	90	–	3	80	28.33	4-20	7.75
Bess, D.M.	32	48	6.85	24	–	–	25	27.88	3-15	7.57
Bethell, J.G.	13	103	8.58	21	–	–	1	96.00	1-21	8.72
Bevan, T.R.	2	25	12.50	21	–	–	0	–	–	–
Billings, S.W.	242	4654	23.98	95*	–	25	0	–	–	132/23
Blake, A.J.	152	2150	20.87	71*	–	10	1	96.00	1-17	7.38
Bohannon, J.J.	25	127	10.58	35	–	–	0	–	–	–
Bopara, R.S.	429	8388	27.14	105*	1	43	258	25.62	6-16	7.52
Borthwick, S.G.	116	729	17.78	62	–	1	82	25.69	4-18	8.21
Bracey, J.R.	43	723	21.26	70	–	3	0	–	–	20/12
Briggs, D.R.	220	235	11.75	35*	–	–	239	22.59	5-19	7.35
Broad, S.C.J.	85	152	7.60	18*	–	–	100	21.44	4-24	7.19
Brook, H.C.	83	2125	34.27	102*	1	8	1	26.00	1-13	13.00
Brookes, H.J.H.	37	125	9.61	31*	–	–	46	25.00	5-25	9.11
Brooks, J.A.	71	77	12.83	33*	–	–	61	27.95	5-21	7.60
Brown, B.C.	82	840	15.00	68	–	1	0	–	–	41/7
Brown, P.R.	70	54	10.80	9*	–	–	80	25.55	4-21	9.19

	M	Runs	Avge	HS	100	50	Wkts	Avge	Best	Econ
Browne, N.L.J.	14	165	16.50	38	–	–	0	–	–	
Budinger, S.G.	10	96	12.00	24	–	–	2	10.50	2-21	5.25
Burgess, M.G.K.	52	491	14.87	56	–	1	0	–	–	21/12
Burns, R.J.	68	826	17.20	56*	–	2	0	–	–	28/2
Bushnell, J.J.	2	33	–	25*	–	–	0	–	–	
Buttleman, W.E.L.	14	222	17.07	56*	–	1	0	–	–	3/1
Buttler, J.C.	327	8530	33.71	124	6	56	0	–	–	182/34
Byrom, E.J.	28	336	15.27	54*	–	1	0	–	–	
Came, H.R.C.	17	278	17.37	56	–	1	0	–	–	
Campbell, J.O.I.	2	6	6.00	6	–	–	1	21.00	1-21	10.50
Carlson, K.S.	46	626	16.47	58	–	1	0	–	0- 1	6.00
Carse, B.A.	51	514	17.72	51	–	1	29	44.41	3-30	8.89
Carter, M.	59	145	11.15	23*	–	–	57	24.75	3-14	7.68
Carter, O.J.	4	2	1.00	2	–	–	0	–	–	1/1
Chappell, Z.J.	24	80	10.00	16	–	–	26	24.15	3-19	9.21
Charlesworth, L.A.	1	1	1.00	1	–	–	1	32.00	1-32	10.66
Clark, G.	84	1874	24.02	91*	–	11	0	–	0- 8	15.23
Clark, J.	107	1048	21.83	60	–	1	60	30.33	4-22	8.97
Clarke, J.M.	136	3353	26.61	136	3	21	0	–	–	46/4
Coad, B.O.	12	14	4.66	7	–	–	13	24.84	3-40	8.93
Cobb, J.J.	190	3915	24.46	103	1	24	76	30.23	5-25	7.75
Conners, S.	18	7	2.33	2*	–	–	13	31.30	3-25	11.20
Cook, A.N.	32	892	31.85	100*	1	5	0	–	–	
Cook, S.J.	49	39	6.50	18	–	–	55	23.63	4-15	8.31
Cooke, C.B.	138	2174	22.64	72	–	6	0	–	–	83/12
Coughlin, P.	61	737	21.67	53	–	1	62	24.24	5-42	9.62
Cox, J.M.	52	1066	31.35	94	–	6	0	–	–	32/5
Cox, O.B.	141	2164	26.39	61*	–	5	0	–	–	64/31
Cracknell, J.B.	32	773	24.93	77	–	4	0	–	–	
Crane, M.S.	79	83	20.75	12*	–	–	88	23.06	4-24	7.83
Crawley, Z.J.	47	1284	29.86	108*	1	5	0	–	–	
Critchley, M.J.J.	92	1329	22.15	80*	–	4	77	25.32	4-36	7.70
Crocombe, H.T.	9	6	–	2*	–	–	7	35.42	3-31	11.27
Croft, S.J.	226	4936	30.85	94*	–	28	78	28.34	3- 6	7.42
Cullen, B.C.	23	61	12.20	20*	–	–	34	19.32	4-32	9.63
Curran, S.M.	131	1682	21.29	72*	–	9	124	27.65	5-30	8.61
Curran, T.K.	166	1295	20.55	62	–	3	185	25.82	4-22	8.85
Currie, S.W.	16	7	2.33	3	–	–	22	18.00	4-24	8.60
Dal, A.K.	21	159	15.90	35	–	–	0	–	0- 8	8.00
Dale, A.S.	1	0	0.00	0	–	–	0	–	0-44	14.66
Das, R.J.	3	45	15.00	23	–	–	0	–	–	
Davey, J.H.	75	309	19.31	24	–	–	90	20.96	4-18	8.70
Davies, A.L.	111	2290	25.44	94*	–	15	0	–	–	70/15
Davies, J.L.B.	14	250	19.23	47	–	–	0	–	–	
Davies, S.M.	153	2850	20.95	99*	–	16	0	–	–	69/24
Davis, W.S.	26	13	3.25	5*	–	–	18	30.22	3-24	8.79
Dawson, L.A.	216	2222	18.21	82	–	5	167	25.85	5-17	7.21
de Caires, J.M.	2	38	19.00	24	–	–	0	–	–	
de Grandhomme, C.	231	3817	23.56	86	–	15	69	40.46	3- 4	9.46
de Kock, Q.	283	8235	32.67	140*	5	50	0	–	–	203/45
de Lange, M.	136	372	10.94	28*	–	–	152	25.32	5-20	8.70
de Leede, B.F.W.	32	612	30.60	91*	–	4	27	16.62	3-19	8.81
Denly, J.L.	260	6194	26.47	127	5	32	46	24.63	4-19	7.83
Dent, C.D.J.	74	1434	23.90	87	–	7	5	33.60	1- 4	8.40
Dickson, S.R.	32	568	28.40	53	–	3	1	9.00	1- 9	9.00
D'Oliveira, B.L.	121	1781	24.06	71	–	10	62	31.79	4-20	7.61
Donald, A.H.T.	58	947	18.94	76	–	5	0	–	–	
Doneathy, L.	2	10	10.00	5*	–	–	1	19.00	1-19	9.50

262

	M	Runs	Avge	HS	100	50	Wkts	Avge	Best	Econ
Douthwaite, D.A.	43	526	20.23	53	–	2	31	29.87	3-28	8.99
Drissell, G.S.	2	0	–	0	–	–	0	–	0-14	14.00
Duckett, B.M.	167	4035	29.88	96	–	26	0	–	–	80/2
Duke, H.G.	4	0	–	0	–	–	0	–	–	–
Dunn, M.P.	23	4	2.00	2	–	–	27	22.88	3- 8	9.15
du Plessis, F.	311	8074	31.05	120*	4	50	50	18.34	5-19	6.96
du Plooy, J.L.	88	1954	32.03	92	–	11	13	17.00	4-15	7.80
Dwarshuis, B.J.	98	420	16.80	66	–	1	117	24.13	5-26	8.32
Edwards, M.W.	3	0	–	0*	–	–	2	42.00	1-19	9.33
Ellis, N.T.	69	209	9.95	20	–	–	79	24.43	4-28	7.90
Eskinazi, S.S.	64	1955	35.54	102*	1	14	0	–	–	–
Evison, J.D.M.	1	0	–	0	–	–	0	–	0-15	15.00
Finch, A.W.	6	9	9.00	6	–	–	7	26.42	3-38	9.73
Finch, H.Z.	26	307	18.05	47	–	–	0	–	–	–
Finn, S.T.	144	79	8.77	11*	–	–	176	22.43	5-16	8.19
Fisher, M.D.	39	61	8.71	19	–	–	43	26.23	5-22	9.10
Fletcher, L.J.	105	181	6.96	27	–	–	116	25.30	5-32	8.45
Foakes, B.T.	77	856	21.40	75*	–	4	0	–	–	38/10
Fraine, W.A.R.	34	411	18.68	44*	–	–	0	–	–	–
Fuller, J.K.	137	1382	21.93	53*	–	2	129	23.89	6-28	8.67
Garrett, G.A.	2	0	–	0	–	–	1	39.00	1-19	9.75
Garton, G.H.S.	63	452	18.08	46	–	–	61	26.14	4-16	9.11
Gay, E.N.	4	67	22.33	30	–	–	0	–	0- 8	8.00
Geddes, B.B.A.	6	44	7.33	28	–	–	0	–	–	–
Gleeson, R.J.	75	51	5.66	8	–	–	85	23.95	5-33	8.18
Glover, B.D.	36	27	6.75	15	–	–	44	19.13	4-12	7.77
Godleman, B.A.	96	1867	22.49	92	–	12	0	–	–	–
Goldsworthy, L.P.	25	257	19.76	48	–	–	23	21.47	3-14	7.96
Greatwood, T.L.	2	0	–	0	–	–	1	69.00	1-35	9.85
Green, B.G.F.	35	322	18.94	43*	–	–	32	23.34	5-29	8.96
Gregory, L.C.	182	2183	20.59	76*	–	6	151	26.66	5-24	9.01
Gubbins, N.R.T.	40	515	14.30	53	–	1	1	30.00	1-22	6.00
Guest, B.D.	32	393	23.11	54	–	1	0	–	–	22/5
Haider Ali	81	1726	25.38	91*	–	10	0	–	–	–
Hain, S.R.	97	2811	36.98	112*	1	19	0	–	–	–
Haines, T.J.	1	27	27.00	27	–	–	0	–	–	–
Hales, A.D.	359	10104	30.71	116*	5	63	0	–	0- 2	14.00
Hamidullah Qadir	1	0	–	0	–	–	0	–	0-12	12.00
Hammond, M.A.H.	80	1461	21.17	63	–	3	0	–	0-17	8.50
Hannon-Dalby, O.J.	60	53	10.60	14*	–	–	75	24.38	4-20	8.76
Hardie, A.M.	31	275	16.17	45	–	–	16	33.56	3-31	9.10
Harmer, S.R.	138	960	17.14	43	–	–	122	27.10	4-19	7.46
Harris, J.A.R.	60	168	10.50	18	–	–	48	34.41	4-23	9.35
Harris, M.B.	2	7	–	7*	–	–	4	15.75	2-26	9.00
Harris, M.S.	48	970	21.08	85	–	4	0	–	–	–
Harrison, C.G.	34	130	10.83	23	–	–	28	23.03	4-17	7.80
Hartley, T.W.	59	131	16.37	19*	–	–	53	25.81	4-16	7.57
Hasan Ali	149	477	12.23	45	–	–	190	22.23	5-20	7.89
Hatzoglou, P.	30	19	4.75	12*	–	–	34	24.32	3-43	7.86
Haynes, J.A.	19	408	22.66	61	–	2	0	–	–	–
Heldreich, F.J.	18	8	4.00	4	–	–	21	23.85	3-22	8.49
Helm, T.G.	72	193	13.78	28*	–	–	86	24.06	5-11	8.91
Henry, M.J.	100	468	13.37	44	–	–	102	28.54	4-43	8.65
Higgins, R.F.	101	1554	25.06	77*	–	4	73	23.61	5-13	9.08
Hill, G.C.H.	14	72	12.00	19*	–	–	2	42.50	1- 9	8.09
Hill, L.J.	79	971	18.32	59	–	3	0	–	–	31/3
Hogan, M.G.	115	81	8.10	17*	–	–	132	23.35	5-17	7.96
Holden, M.D.E.	38	853	25.08	102*	1	3	0	–	0-12	12.00

	M	Runs	Avge	HS	100	50	Wkts	Avge	Best	Econ
Holland, I.G.	23	238	26.44	65	–	1	15	22.80	2- 3	6.19
Hollman, L.B.K.	33	476	21.63	51	–	1	27	23.07	3-18	8.09
Horton, A.J.	4	1	1.00	1*	–	–	0	–	–	0/1
Hose, A.J.	93	2435	31.21	119	2	15	0	–	–	–
Howell, B.A.C.	178	2341	22.95	57	–	6	183	22.06	5-18	7.18
Hudson-Prentice, F.J.	30	319	17.72	49*	–	–	28	24.89	3-36	9.29
Hutton, B.A.	9	50	16.66	18*	–	–	5	51.00	2-28	8.89
Imran Tahir	373	339	8.69	23	–	–	466	19.89	5-23	6.96
Inglis, J.P.	79	1964	30.21	118*	2	12	0	–	–	48/14
Ingram, C.A.	319	7740	29.09	127*	4	47	38	32.81	4-32	7.88
Jacks, W.G.	100	2492	29.31	108*	1	20	23	25.47	4-15	7.19
James, L.W.	7	48	9.60	20	–	–	2	33.00	1-23	11.00
Jennings, K.K.	84	1577	32.85	108	1	7	22	28.54	4-37	7.38
Jones, M.A.	15	319	24.53	44	–	–	0	–	–	–
Jones, R.P.	25	273	34.12	61*	–	1	0	–	0-10	10.00
Jordan, C.J.	292	1571	15.10	73	–	1	305	27.28	4- 6	8.56
Karvelas, A.	1	10	10.00	10	–	–	0	–	0-10	3.33
Kashif Ali	9	140	28.00	46*	–	–	0	–	0-14	14.00
Keogh, R.I.	85	1074	26.85	59*	–	4	16	27.43	3-30	8.28
Kerrigan, S.C.	24	9	–	4*	–	–	20	29.75	3-17	6.91
Khushi, F.I.N.	9	171	19.00	67	–	1	0	–	–	–
Kimber, L.P.J.	12	148	18.50	53	–	1	0	–	–	–
Klaassen, F.J.	90	73	6.08	13	–	–	97	26.37	5-19	8.60
Kohler-Cadmore, T.	130	3435	29.61	127	1	26	0	–	–	72/2
Labuschagne, M.	32	786	28.07	93*	–	4	24	22.75	3-13	8.95
Lace, T.C.	1	5	5.00	5	–	–	0	–	–	–
Lakmal, R.A.S.	66	143	9.53	33	–	–	69	24.86	5-34	8.07
Lamb, D.J.	51	230	12.77	29*	–	–	40	27.27	3-23	8.61
Lamb, M.J.	10	168	24.00	39	–	–	0	–	0- 9	9.00
Lammonby, T.A.	62	773	20.34	90	–	1	15	30.53	2-32	9.19
Lavelle, G.I.D.	2	18	9.00	12	–	–	0	–	–	–
Lawes, T.E.	1	6	6.00	6	–	–	0	–	0-35	11.66
Lawrence, D.W.	86	1861	26.58	86	–	11	32	21.81	4-20	7.76
Leach, J.	54	261	10.44	24	–	–	52	26.05	5-33	9.57
Leach, M.J.	2	0	–	0	–	–	5	12.00	3-28	7.50
Leaning, J.A.	91	1700	27.41	81*	–	7	15	21.80	3-15	7.60
Leech, D.J.	3	1	–	1*	–	–	5	9.20	3-13	6.57
Lees, A.Z.	56	1350	28.72	77*	–	8	0	–	–	–
Lenham, A.D.	20	15	15.00	7*	–	–	12	34.00	4-26	8.00
Leonard, E.O.	1	0	–	0	–	–	1	8.00	1- 8	4.00
Libby, J.D.	52	1150	30.26	78*	–	5	1	77.00	1-11	8.55
Lilley, A.M.	122	1731	21.10	99*	–	5	50	32.02	3-26	7.57
Linde, G.F.	119	1192	18.33	52*	–	2	122	23.65	4-19	7.34
Lintott, J.B.	64	193	12.06	41	–	–	76	21.80	4-20	7.53
Little, J.B.	76	144	12.00	27*	–	–	94	20.85	5-13	7.38
Livingstone, L.S.	200	4967	28.87	103	2	29	83	24.20	4-17	8.11
Lloyd, D.L.	79	1620	23.47	97*	–	10	6	31.16	2-13	8.90
Lynn, C.A.	241	6659	31.86	113*	4	44	3	31.00	2-15	7.15
Lyth, A.	166	4089	26.72	161	1	28	25	27.08	5-31	7.75
McAndrew, N.J.	41	147	18.37	30	–	–	34	33.55	3-40	9.30
McDermott, B.R.	119	3059	31.53	127	3	17	0	–	–	67/6
McIlroy, J.P.	2	0	–	0	–	–	5	12.60	3-31	9.00
McKerr, C.	12	16	4.00	7*	–	–	9	30.88	2-19	9.26
McKiernan, M.H.	29	171	11.40	26	–	–	24	27.83	3- 9	8.24
McManus, L.D.	75	725	15.76	60*	–	2	0	–	–	37/16
Madsen, W.L.	151	3702	30.34	100*	1	24	22	34.31	2-20	8.03
Maharaj, K.A.	122	539	18.58	45*	–	–	98	28.87	4-15	6.70
Mahmood, S.	59	56	9.33	11*	–	–	74	22.51	4-14	8.84

	M	Runs	Avge	HS	100	50	Wkts	Avge	Best	Econ
Malan, D.J.	277	7558	32.71	117	5	47	23	31.39	2-10	7.64
Malan, P.J.	52	1635	39.87	140*	1	11	2	15.00	2-30	7.50
Maxwell, G.J.	366	8309	28.26	154*	5	46	130	31.90	3-10	7.64
Mike, B.W.M.	42	483	20.12	37	–	–	30	26.40	4-22	9.94
Miles, C.N.	47	57	7.12	11*	–	–	50	25.24	3-19	8.69
Miller, A.H.	1	5	5.00	5	–	–	0	–	–	–
Miller, D.A.	401	8750	36.00	120*	3	42	0	–	–	10.33
Mills, T.S.	172	131	6.55	27	–	–	198	24.02	4-22	8.04
Milnes, M.E.	47	64	8.00	14*	–	–	45	30.68	5-22	9.29
Mohammad Abbas	32	32	10.66	15*	–	–	26	37.34	3-22	8.59
Montgomery, M.	2	30	–	30*	–	–	0	–	–	–
Moores, T.J.	112	1700	22.97	80*	–	6	0	–	–	61/21
Moriarty, D.T.	36	29	7.25	9*	–	–	31	25.77	3-25	7.30
Morris, C.A.J.	32	21	10.50	7*	–	–	32	29.59	3-21	9.56
Mousley, D.R.	16	359	29.91	63*	–	4	6	24.16	1- 3	7.25
Mulder, P.W.A.	49	640	25.60	63	–	5	34	27.05	2-10	8.27
Mullaney, S.J.	172	1657	17.26	79	–	3	121	28.37	4-19	7.90
Munro, C.	357	8917	30.53	114*	5	52	31	32.80	4-15	9.21
Murtagh, T.J.	109	227	9.08	40*	–	–	113	25.61	6-24	8.16
Muyeye, T.S.	6	81	13.50	41	–	–	0	–	–	–
Naish, W.L.	1	0	0.00	0	–	–	0	–	–	–
Narine, S.P.	435	3355	15.38	79	–	13	474	20.89	5-19	5.99
Naveen-ul-Haq	115	205	8.20	20*	–	–	143	22.13	5-11	7.94
Neser, M.G.	88	441	13.36	40*	–	–	92	25.80	3-13	8.37
Nijjar, A.S.S.	35	92	9.20	27*	–	–	29	32.96	3-22	8.13
Noor Ahmad	43	54	9.00	13*	–	–	43	27.09	4-10	7.38
Northeast, S.A.	141	3476	30.49	114	1	24	0	–	–	–
Norwell, L.C.	26	5	5.00	2*	–	–	13	56.69	3-27	9.63
Organ, F.S.	3	21	7.00	9	–	–	3	18.00	2-21	6.75
O'Riordan, M.K.	3	15	15.00	13*	–	–	3	18.33	2-24	5.50
Orr, A.G.H.	8	166	20.75	41	–	–	0	–	–	–
Overton, C.	70	347	15.77	35*	–	–	70	27.34	4-25	8.80
Overton, J.	83	567	17.18	48	–	–	67	29.70	5-47	9.37
Parkinson, C.F.	83	249	11.31	27*	–	–	94	23.00	4-20	7.55
Parkinson, M.W.	91	45	3.75	12*	–	–	128	18.60	4- 9	7.66
Parnell, W.D.	237	1788	19.43	99	–	5	240	25.74	5-30	7.82
Patel, R.K.	28	403	16.79	57	–	1	0	–	–	–
Patel, S.	7	7	3.50	5*	–	–	0	–	0- 8	10.28
Patel, S.R.	377	6214	25.15	90*	–	33	321	25.55	4- 5	7.27
Paterson, D.	102	163	8.57	24*	–	–	108	24.87	4-24	8.00
Payne, D.A.	126	65	4.33	10	–	–	155	22.94	5-24	8.48
Pennington, D.Y.	43	55	9.16	10*	–	–	42	26.92	4- 9	9.29
Pepper, M.S.	42	878	28.32	86*	–	4	0	–	–	–
Phillips, G.D.	185	4980	32.98	116*	4	34	16	27.43	2-11	103/10
Podmore, H.W.	23	37	5.28	9	–	–	23	26.91	3-13	9.08
Pollock, E.J.	56	1072	19.85	77	–	6	0	–	–	–
Pope, O.J.D.	47	1055	31.02	62	–	3	0	–	–	–
Porter, J.A.	25	5	5.00	1*	–	–	19	33.47	4-20	9.06
Potts, M.J.	42	127	21.16	40*	–	–	49	23.55	3- 8	8.50
Prest, T.J.	21	451	23.73	64	–	4	2	21.50	1- 8	7.16
Pretorius, D.	182	2328	20.60	77*	–	5	137	27.04	5-17	8.36
Price, O.J.	1	33	33.00	33	–	–	0	–	0-23	11.50
Price, T.J.	2	25	25.00	25	–	–	0	–	0-16	9.20
Procter, L.A.	37	240	14.11	25*	–	–	14	31.28	3-22	8.87
Pujara, C.A.	64	1356	29.47	100*	1	7	0	–	–	–
Quinn, M.R.	72	29	14.50	8*	–	–	72	28.61	4-20	8.76
Rahane, A.M.	219	5528	29.24	105*	2	40	1	5.00	1- 5	5.00
Raine, B.A.	102	1170	19.18	113	1	4	90	26.62	3- 7	8.81

265

	M	Runs	Avge	HS	100	50	Wkts	Avge	Best	Econ
Rashid, A.U.	232	741	11.76	36*	–	–	265	22.43	4- 2	7.46
Rashid Khan	353	1679	12.34	56*	–	1	482	17.93	6-17	6.37
Rawlins, D.M.W.	75	1384	23.06	69	–	5	34	28.08	3-21	7.29
Reece, L.M.	81	1676	22.95	97*	–	13	29	30.79	3-33	8.51
Reifer, N.M.J.	2	4	2.00	4	–	–	0	–	–	–
Revis, M.L.	18	36	9.00	12*	–	–	14	29.07	2-18	9.92
Rew, J.E.K.	1	47	47.00	47	–	–	0	–	–	–
Rhodes, W.M.H.	56	659	14.64	79	–	1	36	20.58	4-34	9.01
Richardson, K.W.	152	370	12.33	45	–	–	198	21.73	4-22	8.00
Roach, K.A.J.	46	59	7.37	12	–	–	28	43.89	3-18	8.08
Robinson, O.E.	49	92	7.07	31	–	–	45	29.02	4-15	8.86
Robinson, O.G.	32	469	18.76	56	–	2	0	–	–	12/6
Robson, S.D.	7	128	25.60	60	–	1	0	–	–	–
Roderick, G.H.	48	262	13.10	32	–	–	0	–	–	27/1
Roland-Jones, T.S.	60	326	14.81	40	–	–	74	23.33	5-21	8.70
Root, J.E.	88	2083	32.54	92*	–	13	22	30.68	2- 7	8.56
Root, W.T.	40	499	21.69	41*	–	–	0	–	0- 6	12.33
Rossington, A.M.	121	2305	20.95	95	–	12	0	–	–	54/22
Roy, J.J.	295	7694	27.97	122*	5	52	1	39.00	1-23	13.00
Rushworth, C.	85	20	3.33	5	–	–	78	27.19	3-14	7.84
Russell, A.D.	428	7176	26.47	121*	2	27	381	25.54	5-15	8.54
Russell, A.K.	2	1	–	1*	–	–	1	55.00	1-27	7.85
Rymell, J.S.	1	21	21.00	21	–	–	0	–	–	–
Sale, O.R.T.	10	20	10.00	14*	–	–	13	26.23	3-32	10.43
Sales, J.J.G.	2	23	23.00	12	–	–	0	–	0-16	14.50
Salisbury, M.E.T.	8	2	–	1*	–	–	10	25.60	2-19	8.93
Salt, P.D.	158	3640	25.45	78*	–	25	0	–	–	72/11
Salter, A.G.	94	385	13.27	39*	–	–	67	29.19	4-12	8.25
Sams, D.R.	106	1008	15.75	98*	–	5	121	25.45	4-14	8.70
Sanderson, B.W.	67	59	8.42	12*	–	–	73	26.21	4-21	8.97
Sangha, T.S.	28	32	16.00	17*	–	–	37	18.43	4-14	7.46
Santner, M.J.	137	1433	23.11	92*	–	3	135	24.41	4-11	7.04
Scrimshaw, G.L.S.	34	19	19.00	5*	–	–	44	22.90	3-20	8.89
Scriven, T.A.R.	2	2	2.00	2	–	–	0	–	0- 8	8.00
Shadab Khan	205	1883	18.64	91	–	6	234	22.53	5-28	7.23
Shamsi, T.	201	78	5.57	15*	–	–	233	21.83	5-24	7.23
Shan Masood	108	2781	27.26	103*	1	18	0	–	–	–
Shaw, J.	29	6	3.00	4	–	–	22	28.36	3-32	8.91
Shutt, J.W.	13	0	0.00	0*	–	–	16	20.43	5-11	7.78
Sibley, D.P.	35	859	29.62	74*	–	7	5	67.60	2-33	8.89
Siddle, P.M.	101	69	4.92	11*	–	–	125	21.19	5-16	7.62
Simpson, J.A.	155	2582	22.25	84*	–	9	0	–	–	83/29
Singh, J.	2	0	–	0	–	–	0	–	0-17	21.50
Sisodiya, P.	33	29	14.50	9*	–	–	32	29.50	3-26	7.80
Slater, B.T.	15	305	21.78	57	–	1	0	–	–	–
Smeed, W.C.F.	55	1471	29.42	101*	1	8	0	–	–	–
Smith, J.L.	38	502	25.10	60	–	3	0	–	–	18/1
Smith, S.P.D.	229	4724	30.08	101	1	21	54	19.55	4-13	7.68
Smith, T.M.J.	162	343	16.33	36*	–	–	162	23.00	5-16	7.33
Snater, S.	30	78	11.14	16*	–	–	24	34.41	3-42	10.21
Sodhi, I.S.	214	336	9.88	51	–	1	243	23.90	6-11	7.81
Sowter, N.A.	86	193	10.15	37*	–	–	81	26.53	4-23	7.93
Stanley, M.T.	9	9	9.00	7	–	–	8	29.75	2-24	10.50
Steel, C.T.	7	112	16.00	37	–	–	2	64.50	2-60	11.72
Steel, S.	41	909	25.25	72	–	6	17	33.41	3-20	7.15
Stewart, G.	42	301	13.08	51	–	1	37	30.02	3-33	8.65
Stoinis, M.P.	203	4128	30.57	147*	1	20	89	27.66	4-15	8.90
Stokes, B.A.	148	2865	24.91	107*	2	9	86	31.03	4-16	8.52

266

	M	Runs	Avge	HS	100	50	Wkts	Avge	Best	Econ
Stone, O.P.	61	86	9.55	22*	–	–	61	27.63	4-21	8.69
Stoneman, M.D.	77	1343	20.04	89*	–	8	0	–	–	–
Stubbs, T.	34	784	30.15	80*	–	4	5	44.40	2- 6	9.06
Swindells, H.J.	26	382	18.19	63	–	3	0	–	–	8/3
Tattersall, J.A.	42	442	23.26	53*	–	1	0	–	–	28/6
Taylor, C.Z.	16	138	12.54	23	–	–	5	17.20	2- 9	7.81
Taylor, J.M.R.	116	1527	21.81	80	–	2	27	35.40	4-16	8.12
Taylor, J.P.A.	2	3	3.00	3	–	–	1	34.00	1- 6	17.00
Taylor, M.D.	45	59	11.80	18*	–	–	36	33.16	3-16	8.92
Taylor, T.A.I.	33	214	13.37	50*	–	1	30	29.00	4-27	9.42
Thompson, J.A.	78	691	15.70	74	–	4	74	25.13	4-21	9.45
Thomson, A.T.	20	89	14.83	28	–	–	15	28.93	4-35	8.18
Tongue, J.C.	7	3	–	2*	–	–	4	40.75	2-32	8.57
Topley, R.J.W.	124	70	10.00	14*	–	–	160	21.84	4-20	8.22
Trevaskis, L.	54	346	15.72	31*	–	–	47	27.61	4-16	7.59
Tye, A.J.	195	551	11.72	44	–	–	274	20.70	5-17	8.11
van Buuren, G.L.	72	781	22.97	64	–	4	47	25.46	5- 8	7.08
van der Gugten, T.	110	294	12.25	40*	–	–	123	21.78	5-21	8.08
van der Merwe, R.E.	280	2848	22.07	89*	–	10	252	25.52	5-32	7.24
van Meekeren, P.A.	80	107	6.29	18	–	–	75	26.36	4-11	7.79
Vasconcelos, R.S.	26	562	26.76	78*	–	2	0	–	–	14/2
Vilas, D.J.	209	3956	28.87	75*	–	16	0	–	–	112/30
Vince, J.M.	311	8339	30.65	129*	4	49	3	29.00	1- 5	6.69
Wade, M.S.	194	3772	26.56	130*	1	22	0	–	–	101/14
Wahab Riaz	319	1600	14.15	53	–	1	379	22.24	5- 8	7.44
Waite, M.J.	25	103	10.30	35*	–	–	18	31.77	3-18	9.66
Walallawita, T.N.	14	23	4.60	10	–	–	11	27.18	3-18	8.08
Walker, R.I.	13	28	5.60	19*	–	–	17	22.82	3-15	9.27
Walter, P.I.	85	1067	22.70	76	–	4	43	25.34	3-20	8.75
Ward, H.D.	19	277	18.46	33	–	–	1	5.00	1- 5	5.00
Warner, J.D.	1	1	1.00	1	–	–	0	–	0-15	7.50
Watt, M.R.J.	76	198	9.90	22	–	–	79	26.00	5-27	7.61
Weatherley, J.J.	49	1068	25.42	71	–	3	0	–	0- 9	9.00
Welch, N.R.	10	274	30.44	46	–	–	0	–	–	–
Wells, B.J.J.	1	42	42.00	42	–	–	0	–	–	–
Wells, L.W.P.	24	232	13.64	42	–	–	12	31.66	2-26	8.05
Westley, T.	107	2529	29.75	109*	2	10	8	38.75	2-27	7.56
Wharton, J.H.	2	12	6.00	8	–	–	0	–	–	–
Wheal, B.T.J.	53	31	6.20	16	–	–	68	21.42	5-38	8.41
White, G.G.	144	467	14.59	37*	–	–	120	26.80	5-22	8.10
White, R.G.	3	11	11.00	11*	–	–	0	–	–	–
Whiteley, R.A.	178	2966	24.51	91*	–	6	4	45.25	1-10	10.64
Whiteman, S.M.	45	653	17.64	68	–	3	0	–	–	22/6
Wiese, D.	311	3594	23.64	79*	–	8	248	26.10	5-19	8.37
Willey, D.J.	233	3358	24.15	118	2	14	233	22.73	4- 7	7.91
Wood, C.P.	168	446	11.15	27	–	–	179	26.27	5-32	8.22
Wood, L.	80	144	9.60	33*	–	–	71	27.19	4-20	8.34
Wood, T.A.	8	242	40.33	67	–	2	0	–	–	–
Worrall, D.J.	67	159	14.45	62*	–	1	53	33.90	4-23	8.08
Wright, C.J.C.	62	30	4.28	6*	–	–	53	34.60	4-24	9.00
Yates, R.M.	15	252	16.80	53	–	1	1	66.00	1-13	8.25
Zafar Gohar	61	255	15.00	32*	–	–	67	23.04	4-14	7.72
Zaib, S.A.	40	601	24.04	92	–	3	2	81.00	1-20	8.52
Zampa, A.	208	254	6.68	23	–	–	242	21.94	6-19	7.28

FIRST-CLASS CRICKET RECORDS

To the end of the 2022 season

TEAM RECORDS
HIGHEST INNINGS TOTALS

1107	Victoria v New South Wales	Melbourne	1926-27
1059	Victoria v Tasmania	Melbourne	1922-23
952-6d	Sri Lanka v India	Colombo	1997-98
951-7d	Sind v Baluchistan	Karachi	1973-74
944-6d	Hyderabad v Andhra	Secunderabad	1993-94
918	New South Wales v South Australia	Sydney	1900-01
912-8d	Holkar v Mysore	Indore	1945-46
910-6d	Railways v Dera Ismail Khan	Lahore	1964-65
903-7d	England v Australia	The Oval	1938
900-6d	Queensland v Victoria	Brisbane	2005-06
887	Yorkshire v Warwickshire	Birmingham	1896
880	Jharkhand v Nagaland	Kolkata	2021-22
864-9d	Boost Region v Speen Ghar Region	Kandahar	2021-22
863	Lancashire v Surrey	The Oval	1990
860-6d	Tamil Nadu v Goa	Panjim	1988-89
850-7d	Somerset v Middlesex	Taunton	2007

Excluding penalty runs in India, there have been 38 innings totals of 800 runs or more in first-class cricket. Tamil Nadu's total of 860-6d was boosted to 912 by 52 penalty runs.

HIGHEST SECOND INNINGS TOTAL

770	New South Wales v South Australia	Adelaide	1920-21

HIGHEST FOURTH INNINGS TOTAL

654-5	England (set 696 to win) v South Africa	Durban	1938-39

HIGHEST MATCH AGGREGATE

2376-37	Maharashtra v Bombay	Poona	1948-49

RECORD MARGIN OF VICTORY

Innings and 851 runs: Railways v Dera Ismail Khan   Lahore   1964-65

MOST RUNS IN A DAY

721	Australians v Essex	Southend	1948

MOST HUNDREDS IN AN INNINGS

6	Holkar v Mysore	Indore	1945-46

LOWEST INNINGS TOTALS

12	†Oxford University v MCC and Ground	Oxford	1877
12	Northamptonshire v Gloucestershire	Gloucester	1907
13	Auckland v Canterbury	Auckland	1877-78
13	Nottinghamshire v Yorkshire	Nottingham	1901
14	Surrey v Essex	Chelmsford	1983
15	MCC v Surrey	Lord's	1839
15	†Victoria v MCC	Melbourne	1903-04
15	†Northamptonshire v Yorkshire	Northampton	1908
15	Hampshire v Warwickshire	Birmingham	1922

† *Batted one man short*

There have been 29 instances of a team being dismissed for under 20.

LOWEST MATCH AGGREGATE BY ONE TEAM'

34 (16 and 18)	Border v Natal	East London	1959-60

LOWEST COMPLETED MATCH AGGREGATE BY BOTH TEAMS

105	MCC v Australians	Lord's	1878

FEWEST RUNS IN AN UNINTERRUPTED DAY'S PLAY

95	Australia (80) v Pakistan (15-2)	Karachi	1956-57

Before 1949 a match was considered to be tied if the scores were level after the fourth innings, even if the side batting last had wickets in hand when play ended. Law 22 was amended in 1948 and since then a match has been tied only when the scores are level after the fourth innings has been completed. There have been 41 tied first-class matches since then. The most recent is:

Central Punjab (257-9d & 355) v Khyber Pakhtunkhwa (300 & 312)　　Karachi　　　2021-22

BATTING RECORDS
35,000 RUNS IN A CAREER

	Career	I	NO	HS	Runs	Avge	100
J.B.Hobbs	1905-34	1315	106	316*	**61237**	50.65	197
F.E.Woolley	1906-38	1532	85	305*	**58969**	40.75	145
E.H.Hendren	1907-38	1300	166	301*	**57611**	50.80	170
C.P.Mead	1905-36	1340	185	280*	**55061**	47.67	153
W.G.Grace	1865-1908	1493	105	344	**54896**	39.55	126
W.R.Hammond	1920-51	1005	104	336*	**50551**	56.10	167
H.Sutcliffe	1919-45	1088	123	313	**50138**	51.95	149
G.Boycott	1962-86	1014	162	261*	**48426**	56.83	151
T.W.Graveney	1948-71/72	1223	159	258	**47793**	44.91	122
G.A.Gooch	1973-2000	990	75	333	**44846**	49.01	128
T.W.Hayward	1893-1914	1138	96	315*	**43551**	41.79	104
D.L.Amiss	1960-87	1139	126	262*	**43423**	42.86	102
M.C.Cowdrey	1950-76	1130	134	307	**42719**	42.89	107
A.Sandham	1911-37/38	1000	79	325	**41284**	44.82	107
G.A.Hick	1983/84-2008	871	84	405*	**41112**	52.23	136
L.Hutton	1934-60	814	91	364	**40140**	55.51	129
M.J.K.Smith	1951-75	1091	139	204	**39832**	41.84	69
W.Rhodes	1898-1930	1528	237	267*	**39802**	30.83	58
J.H.Edrich	1956-78	979	104	310*	**39790**	45.47	103
R.E.S.Wyatt	1923-57	1141	157	232	**39405**	40.04	85
D.C.S.Compton	1936-64	839	88	300	**38942**	51.85	123
G.E.Tyldesley	1909-36	961	106	256*	**38874**	45.46	102
J.T.Tyldesley	1895-1923	994	62	295*	**37897**	40.60	86
K.W.R.Fletcher	1962-88	1167	170	228*	**37665**	37.77	63
C.G.Greenidge	1970-92	889	75	273*	**37354**	45.88	92
J.W.Hearne	1909-36	1025	116	285*	**37252**	40.98	96
L.E.G.Ames	1926-51	951	95	295	**37248**	43.51	102
D.Kenyon	1946-67	1159	59	259	**37002**	33.63	74
W.J.Edrich	1934-58	964	92	267*	**36965**	42.39	86
J.M.Parks	1949-76	1227	172	205*	**36673**	34.76	51
M.W.Gatting	1975-98	861	123	258	**36549**	49.52	94
D.Denton	1894-1920	1163	70	221	**36479**	33.37	69
G.H.Hirst	1891-1929	1215	151	341	**36323**	34.13	60
I.V.A.Richards	1971/72-93	796	63	322	**36212**	49.40	114
A.Jones	1957-83	1168	72	204*	**36049**	32.89	56
W.G.Quaife	1894-1928	1203	185	255*	**36012**	35.37	72
R.E.Marshall	1945/46-72	1053	59	228*	**35725**	35.94	68
M.R.Ramprakash	1987-2012	764	93	301*	**35659**	53.14	114
G.Gunn	1902-32	1061	82	220	**35208**	35.96	62

HIGHEST INDIVIDUAL INNINGS

501*	B.C.Lara	Warwickshire v Durham	Birmingham	1994
499	Hanif Mohammed	Karachi v Bahawalpur	Karachi	1958-59
452*	D.G.Bradman	New South Wales v Queensland	Sydney	1929-30
443*	B.B.Nimbalkar	Maharashtra v Kathiawar	Poona	1948-49
437	W.H.Ponsford	Victoria v Queensland	Melbourne	1927-28

429	W.H.Ponsford	Victoria v Tasmania	Melbourne	1922-23
428	Aftab Baloch	Sind v Baluchistan	Karachi	1973-74
424	A.C.MacLaren	Lancashire v Somerset	Taunton	1895
410*	S.A.Northeast	Glamorgan v Leicestershire	Leicester	2022
405*	G.A.Hick	Worcestershire v Somerset	Taunton	1988
400*	B.C.Lara	West Indies v England	St John's	2003-04
394	Naved Latif	Sargodha v Gujranwala	Gujranwala	2000-01
390	S.C.Cook	Lions v Warriors	East London	2009-10
385	B.Sutcliffe	Otago v Canterbury	Christchurch	1952-53
383	C.W.Gregory	New South Wales v Queensland	Brisbane	1906-07
380	M.L.Hayden	Australia v Zimbabwe	Perth	2003-04
377	S.V.Manjrekar	Bombay v Hyderabad	Bombay	1990-91
375	B.C.Lara	West Indies v England	St John's	1993-94
374	D.P.M.D.Jayawardena	Sri Lanka v South Africa	Colombo	2006
369	D.G.Bradman	South Australia v Tasmania	Adelaide	1935-36
366	N.H.Fairbrother	Lancashire v Surrey	The Oval	1990
366	M.V.Sridhar	Hyderabad v Andhra	Secunderabad	1993-94
365*	C.Hill	South Australia v NSW	Adelaide	1900-01
365*	G.St A.Sobers	West Indies v Pakistan	Kingston	1957-58
364	L.Hutton	England v Australia	The Oval	1938
359*	V.M.Merchant	Bombay v Maharashtra	Bombay	1943-44
359*	S.B.Gohel	Gujarat v Orissa	Jaipur	2016-17
359	R.B.Simpson	New South Wales v Queensland	Brisbane	1963-64
357*	R.Abel	Surrey v Somerset	The Oval	1899
357	D.G.Bradman	South Australia v Victoria	Melbourne	1935-36
356	B.A.Richards	South Australia v W Australia	Perth	1970-71
355*	G.R.Marsh	W Australia v S Australia	Perth	1989-90
355*	K.P.Pietersen	Surrey v Leicestershire	The Oval	2015
355	B.Sutcliffe	Otago v Auckland	Dunedin	1949-50
354*	L.D.Chandimal	Sri Lanka Army v Saracens	Katunayake	2020
353	V.V.S.Laxman	Hyderabad v Karnataka	Bangalore	1999-00
352	W.H.Ponsford	Victoria v New South Wales	Melbourne	1926-27
352	C.A.Pujara	Saurashtra v Karnataka	Rajkot	2012-13
351*	S.M.Gugale	Maharashtra v Delhi	Mumbai	2016-17
351	K.D.K.Vithanage	Tamil Union v SL Air	Katunayake	2014-15
350	Rashid Israr	Habib Bank v National Bank	Lahore	1976-77

There have been 236 triple hundreds in first-class cricket, W.V.Raman (313) and Arjan Kripal Singh (302*) for Tamil Nadu v Goa at Panjim in 1988-89 providing the only instance of two batsmen scoring 300 in the same innings.

MOST HUNDREDS IN SUCCESSIVE INNINGS

6	C.B.Fry	Sussex and Rest of England	1901
6	D.G.Bradman	South Australia and D.G.Bradman's XI	1938-39
6	M.J.Procter	Rhodesia	1970-71

TWO DOUBLE HUNDREDS IN A MATCH

244	202*	A.E.Fagg	Kent v Essex	Colchester	1938
201	231	A.K.Perera	Nondescripts v Sinhalese	Colombo (PSO)	2018-19

TRIPLE HUNDRED AND HUNDRED IN A MATCH

333	123	G.A.Gooch	England v India	Lord's	1990
319	105	K.C.Sangakkara	Sri Lanka v Bangladesh	Chittagong	2013-14

DOUBLE HUNDRED AND HUNDRED IN A MATCH MOST TIMES

4	Zaheer Abbas	Gloucestershire	1976-81

TWO HUNDREDS IN A MATCH MOST TIMES

8	Zaheer Abbas	Gloucestershire and PIA	1976-82
8	R.T.Ponting	Tasmania, Australia and Australians	1992-2006

MOST HUNDREDS IN A SEASON

18   D.C.S.Compton   1947   16   J.B.Hobbs   1925

100 HUNDREDS IN A CAREER

	Total		100th Hundred	
	Hundreds	Inns	Season	Inns
J.B.Hobbs	197	1315	1923	821
E.H.Hendren	170	1300	1928-29	740
W.R.Hammond	167	1005	1935	679
C.P.Mead	153	1340	1927	892
G.Boycott	151	1014	1977	645
H.Sutcliffe	149	1088	1932	700
F.E.Woolley	145	1532	1929	1031
G.A.Hick	136	871	1998	574
L.Hutton	129	814	1951	619
G.A.Gooch	128	990	1992-93	820
W.G.Grace	126	1493	1895	1113
D.C.S.Compton	123	839	1952	552
T.W.Graveney	122	1223	1964	940
D.G.Bradman	117	338	1947-48	295
I.V.A.Richards	114	796	1988-89	658
M.R.Ramprakash	114	764	2008	676
Zaheer Abbas	108	768	1982-83	658
A.Sandham	107	1000	1935	871
M.C.Cowdrey	107	1130	1973	1035
T.W.Hayward	104	1138	1913	1076
G.M.Turner	103	792	1982	779
J.H.Edrich	103	979	1977	945
L.E.G.Ames	102	951	1950	915
G.E.Tyldesley	102	961	1934	919
D.L.Amiss	102	1139	1986	1081

MOST 400s: 2 – B.C.Lara, W.H.Ponsford

MOST 300s or more: 6 – D.G.Bradman; 4 – W.R.Hammond, W.H.Ponsford

MOST 200s or more: 37 – D.G.Bradman; 36 – W.R.Hammond; 22 – E.H.Hendren

MOST RUNS IN A MONTH

1294 (avge 92.42)   L.Hutton   Yorkshire   June 1949

MOST RUNS IN A SEASON

Runs			I	NO	HS	Avge	100	Season
3816	D.C.S.Compton	Middlesex	50	8	246	90.85	18	1947
3539	W.J.Edrich	Middlesex	52	8	267*	80.43	12	1947
3518	T.W.Hayward	Surrey	61	8	219	66.37	13	1906

The feat of scoring 3000 runs in a season has been achieved 28 times, the most recent instance being by W.E.Alley (3019) in 1961. The highest aggregate in a season since 1969 is 2755 by S.J.Cook in 1991.

1000 RUNS IN A SEASON MOST TIMES

28   W.G.Grace (Gloucestershire), F.E.Woolley (Kent)

HIGHEST BATTING AVERAGE IN A SEASON

(Qualification: 12 innings)

Avge			I	NO	HS	Runs	100	Season
115.66	D.G.Bradman	Australians	26	5	278	2429	13	1938
106.50	K.C.Sangakkara	Surrey	16	2	200	1491	8	2017
104.66	D.R.Martyn	Australians	14	5	176*	942	5	2001
103.54	M.R.Ramprakash	Surrey	24	2	301*	2278	8	2006
102.53	G.Boycott	Yorkshire	20	5	175*	1538	6	1979
102.00	W.A.Johnston	Australians	17	16	28*	102	–	1953
101.70	G.A.Gooch	Essex	30	3	333	2746	12	1990

Avge			I	NO	HS	Runs	100	Season
101.30	M.R.Ramprakash	Surrey	25	5	266*	2026	10	2007
100.12	G.Boycott	Yorkshire	30	5	233	2503	13	1971

FASTEST HUNDRED AGAINST AUTHENTIC BOWLING
35 min	P.G.H.Fender	Surrey v Northamptonshire	Northampton	1920

FASTEST DOUBLE HUNDRED
103 min	Shafiqullah Shinwari	Kabul Region v Boost Region	Asadabad	2017-18

FASTEST TRIPLE HUNDRED
181 min	D.C.S.Compton	MCC v NE Transvaal	Benoni	1948-49

MOST SIXES IN AN INNINGS
23	C.Munro	Central Districts v Auckland	Napier	2014-15

MOST SIXES IN A MATCH
24	Shafiqullah Shinwari	Kabul v Boost	Asadabad	2017-18

MOST SIXES IN A SEASON
80	I.T.Botham	Somerset and England		1985

MOST BOUNDARIES IN AN INNINGS
72	B.C.Lara	Warwickshire v Durham	Birmingham	1994

MOST RUNS OFF ONE OVER
36	G.St A.Sobers	Nottinghamshire v Glamorgan	Swansea	1968
36	R.J.Shastri	Bombay v Baroda	Bombay	1984-85

Both batsmen hit for six all six balls of overs bowled by M.A.Nash and Tilak Raj respectively.

MOST RUNS IN A DAY
390*	B.C.Lara	Warwickshire v Durham	Birmingham	1994

There have been 19 instances of a batsman scoring 300 or more runs in a day.

LONGEST INNINGS
1015 min	R.Nayyar (271)	Himachal Pradesh v Jammu & Kashmir	Chamba	1999-00

HIGHEST PARTNERSHIPS FOR EACH WICKET
First Wicket
561	Waheed Mirza/Mansoor Akhtar	Karachi W v Quetta	Karachi	1976-77
555	P.Holmes/H.Sutcliffe	Yorkshire v Essex	Leyton	1932
554	J.T.Brown/J.Tunnicliffe	Yorkshire v Derbys	Chesterfield	1898

Second Wicket
580	Rafatullah Mohmand/Aamer Sajjad	WAPDA v SSGC	Sheikhupura	2009-10
576	S.T.Jayasuriya/R.S.Mahanama	Sri Lanka v India	Colombo	1997-98
480	D.Elgar/R.R.Rossouw	Eagles v Titans	Centurion	2009-10
475	Zahir Alam/L.S.Rajput	Assam v Tripura	Gauhati	1991-92
465*	J.A.Jameson/R.B.Kanhai	Warwickshire v Glos	Birmingham	1974

Third Wicket
624	K.C.Sangakkara/D.P.M.D.Jayawardena	Sri Lanka v South Africa	Colombo	2006
594*	S.M.Gugale/A.R.Bawne	Maharashtra v Delhi	Mumbai	2016-17
539	S.D.Jogiyani/R.A.Jadeja	Saurashtra v Gujarat	Surat	2012-13
523	M.A.Carberry/N.D.McKenzie	Hampshire v Yorkshire	Southampton	2011

Fourth Wicket
577	V.S.Hazare/Gul Mahomed	Baroda v Holkar	Baroda	1946-47
574*	C.L.Walcott/F.M.M.Worrell	Barbados v Trinidad	Port-of-Spain	1945-46
538	D.Abrar/S.Gani	Bihar v Mizoram	Kolkata	2021-22
502*	F.M.M.Worrell/J.D.C.Goddard	Barbados v Trinidad	Bridgetown	1943-44
470	A.I.Kallicharran/G.W.Humpage	Warwickshire v Lancs	Southport	1982

Fifth Wicket
520*	C.A.Pujara/R.A.Jadeja	Saurashtra v Orissa	Rajkot	2008-09
494	Marchall Ayub/Mehrab Hossain Jr	Central Zone v East Zone	Bogra	2012-13

479	Misbah-ul-Haq/Usman Arshad	Sui NGP v Lahore Shalimar	Lahore	2009-10
477*	C.N.Ackermann/P.W.A.Mulder	Leicestershire v Sussex	Hove	2022

Sixth Wicket

487*	G.A.Headley/C.C.Passailaigue	Jamaica v Tennyson's	Kingston	1931-32
461*	S.A.Northeast/C.B.Cooke	Glamorgan v Leicestershire	Leicester	2022
428	W.W.Armstrong/M.A.Noble	Australians v Sussex	Hove	1902
417	W.P.Saha/L.R.Shukla	Bengal v Assam	Kolkata	2010-11

Seventh Wicket

460	Bhupinder Singh jr/P.Dharmani	Punjab v Delhi	Delhi	1994-95
399	A.N.Khare/A.J.Mandal	Chhattisgarh v Uttarakhand	Naya Raipur	2019-20
371	M.R.Marsh/S.M.Whiteman	Australia A v India A	Brisbane	2014
366*	J.M.Bairstow/T.T.Bresnan	Yorkshire v Durham	Chester-le-Street	2015

Eighth Wicket

433	V.T.Trumper/A.Sims	Australians v C'bury	Christchurch	1913-14
392	A.Mishra/J.Yadav	Haryana v Karnataka	Hubli	2012-13
332	I.J.L.Trott/S.C.J.Broad	England v Pakistan	Lord's	2010

Ninth Wicket

283	J.Chapman/A.Warren	Derbys v Warwicks	Blackwell	1910
268	J.B.Commins/N.Boje	SA 'A' v Mashonaland	Harare	1994-95
261	W.L.Madsen/T.Poynton	Derbys v Northants	Northampton	2012

Tenth Wicket

307	A.F.Kippax/J.E.H.Hooker	NSW v Victoria	Melbourne	1928-29
249	C.T.Sarwate/S.N.Banerjee	Indians v Surrey	The Oval	1946
239	Aqil Arshad/Ali Raza	Lahore Whites v Hyderabad	Lahore	2004-05

BOWLING RECORDS
2000 WICKETS IN A CAREER

	Career	Runs	Wkts	Avge	100w
W.Rhodes	1898-1930	69993	**4187**	16.71	23
A.P.Freeman	1914-36	69577	**3776**	18.42	17
C.W.L.Parker	1903-35	63817	**3278**	19.46	16
J.T.Hearne	1888-1923	54352	**3061**	17.75	15
T.W.J.Goddard	1922-52	59116	**2979**	19.84	16
W.G.Grace	1865-1908	51545	**2876**	17.92	10
A.S.Kennedy	1907-36	61034	**2874**	21.23	15
D.Shackleton	1948-69	53303	**2857**	18.65	20
G.A.R.Lock	1946-70/71	54709	**2844**	19.23	14
F.J.Titmus	1949-82	63313	**2830**	22.37	16
M.W.Tate	1912-37	50571	**2784**	18.16	13+1
G.H.Hirst	1891-1929	51282	**2739**	18.72	15
C.Blythe	1899-1914	42136	**2506**	16.81	14
D.L.Underwood	1963-87	49993	**2465**	20.28	10
W.E.Astill	1906-39	57783	**2431**	23.76	9
J.C.White	1909-37	43759	**2356**	18.57	14
W.E.Hollies	1932-57	48656	**2323**	20.94	14
F.S.Trueman	1949-69	42154	**2304**	18.29	12
J.B.Statham	1950-68	36999	**2260**	16.37	13
R.T.D.Perks	1930-55	53771	**2233**	24.07	16
J.Briggs	1879-1900	35431	**2221**	15.95	12
D.J.Shepherd	1950-72	47302	**2218**	21.32	12
E.G.Dennett	1903-26	42571	**2147**	19.82	12
T.Richardson	1892-1905	38794	**2104**	18.43	10
T.E.Bailey	1945-67	48170	**2082**	23.13	9
R.Illingworth	1951-83	42023	**2072**	20.28	10
F.E.Woolley	1906-38	41066	**2068**	19.85	8
N.Gifford	1960-88	48731	**2068**	23.56	4
G.Geary	1912-38	41339	**2063**	20.03	11

	Career	Runs	Wkts	Avge	100w
D.V.P.Wright	1932-57	49307	**2056**	23.98	10
J.A.Newman	1906-30	51111	**2032**	25.15	9
A.Shaw	1864-97	24580	**2026**+1	12.12	9
S.Haigh	1895-1913	32091	**2012**	15.94	11

ALL TEN WICKETS IN AN INNINGS

This feat has been achieved 82 times in first-class matches (excluding 12-a-side fixtures).
Three Times: A.P.Freeman (1929, 1930, 1931)
Twice: V.E.Walker (1859, 1865); H.Verity (1931, 1932); J.C.Laker (1956)
Instances since 1945:

W.E.Hollies	Warwickshire v Notts	Birmingham	1946
J.M.Sims	East v West	Kingston on Thames	1948
J.K.R.Graveney	Gloucestershire v Derbyshire	Chesterfield	1949
T.E.Bailey	Essex v Lancashire	Clacton	1949
R.Berry	Lancashire v Worcestershire	Blackpool	1953
S.P.Gupte	President's XI v Combined XI	Bombay	1954-55
J.C.Laker	Surrey v Australians	The Oval	1956
K.Smales	Nottinghamshire v Glos	Stroud	1956
G.A.R.Lock	Surrey v Kent	Blackheath	1956
J.C.Laker	England v Australia	Manchester	1956
P.M.Chatterjee	Bengal v Assam	Jorhat	1956-57
J.D.Bannister	Warwicks v Combined Services	Birmingham (M & B)	1959
A.J.G.Pearson	Cambridge U v Leicestershire	Loughborough	1961
N.I.Thomson	Sussex v Warwickshire	Worthing	1964
P.J.Allan	Queensland v Victoria	Melbourne	1965-66
I.J.Brayshaw	Western Australia v Victoria	Perth	1967-68
Shahid Mahmood	Karachi Whites v Khairpur	Karachi	1969-70
E.E.Hemmings	International XI v W Indians	Kingston	1982-83
P.Sunderam	Rajasthan v Vidarbha	Jodhpur	1985-86
S.T.Jefferies	Western Province v OFS	Cape Town	1987-88
Imran Adil	Bahawalpur v Faisalabad	Faisalabad	1989-90
G.P.Wickremasinghe	Sinhalese v Kalutara	Colombo	1991-92
R.L.Johnson	Middlesex v Derbyshire	Derby	1994
Naeem Akhtar	Rawalpindi B v Peshawar	Peshawar	1995-96
A.Kumble	India v Pakistan	Delhi	1998-99
D.S.Mohanty	East Zone v South Zone	Agartala	2000-01
O.D.Gibson	Durham v Hampshire	Chester-le-Street	2007
M.W.Olivier	Warriors v Eagles	Bloemfontein	2007-08
Zulfiqar Babar	Multan v Islamabad	Multan	2009-10
P.M.Pushpakumara	Colombo v Saracens	Moratuwa	2018-19
S.A.Whitehead	SW Districts v Easterns	Oudtshoorn	2021-22
A.Y.Patel	New Zealand v India	Mumbai	2021-22

MOST WICKETS IN A MATCH

19	J.C.Laker	England v Australia	Manchester	1956

MOST WICKETS IN A SEASON

Wkts		Season	Matches	Overs	Mdns	Runs	Avge
304	A.P.Freeman	1928	37	1976.1	423	5489	18.05
298	A.P.Freeman	1933	33	2039	651	4549	15.26

The feat of taking 250 wickets in a season has been achieved on 12 occasions, the last instance being by A.P.Freeman in 1933. 200 or more wickets in a season have been taken on 59 occasions, the last being by G.A.R.Lock (212 wickets, average 12.02) in 1957.

The highest aggregates of wickets taken in a season since the reduction of County Championship matches in 1969 are as follows:

Wkts		Season	Matches	Overs	Mdns	Runs	Avge
134	M.D.Marshall	1982	22	822	225	2108	15.73
131	L.R.Gibbs	1971	23	1024.1	295	2475	18.89
125	F.D.Stephenson	1988	22	819.1	196	2289	18.31
121	R.D.Jackman	1980	23	746.2	220	1864	15.40

Since 1969 there have been 50 instances of bowlers taking 100 wickets in a season.

MOST HAT-TRICKS IN A CAREER

7	D.V.P.Wright
6	T.W.J.Goddard, C.W.L.Parker
5	S.Haigh, V.W.C.Jupp, A.E.G.Rhodes, F.A.Tarrant

ALL-ROUND RECORDS
THE 'DOUBLE'

3000 runs and 100 wickets: J.H.Parks (1937)
2000 runs and 200 wickets: G.H.Hirst (1906)
2000 runs and 100 wickets: F.E.Woolley (4), J.W.Hearne (3), W.G.Grace (2), G.H.Hirst (2), W.Rhodes (2), T.E.Bailey, D.E.Davies, G.L.Jessop, V.W.C.Jupp, J.Langridge, F.A.Tarrant, C.L.Townsend, L.F.Townsend
1000 runs and 200 wickets: M.W.Tate (3), A.E.Trott (2), A.S.Kennedy
Most Doubles: 16 – W.Rhodes; 14 – G.H.Hirst; 10 – V.W.C.Jupp
Double in Debut Season: D.B.Close (1949) – aged 18, the youngest to achieve this feat.

The feat of scoring 1000 runs and taking 100 wickets in a season has been achieved on 305 occasions, R.J.Hadlee (1984) and F.D.Stephenson (1988) being the only players to complete the 'double' since the reduction of County Championship matches in 1969.

WICKET-KEEPING RECORDS
1000 DISMISSALS IN A CAREER

	Career	Dismissals	Ct	St
R.W.Taylor	1960-88	**1649**	1473	176
J.T.Murray	1952-75	**1527**	1270	257
H.Strudwick	1902-27	**1497**	1242	255
A.P.E.Knott	1964-85	**1344**	1211	133
R.C.Russell	1981-2004	**1320**	1192	128
F.H.Huish	1895-1914	**1310**	933	377
B.Taylor	1949-73	**1294**	1083	211
S.J.Rhodes	1981-2004	**1263**	1139	124
D.Hunter	1889-1909	**1253**	906	347
H.R.Butt	1890-1912	**1228**	953	275
J.H.Board	1891-1914/15	**1207**	852	355
H.Elliott	1920-47	**1206**	904	302
J.M.Parks	1949-76	**1181**	1088	93
R.Booth	1951-70	**1126**	948	178
L.E.G.Ames	1926-51	**1121**	703	418
C.M.W.Read	1997-2017	**1104**	1051	53
D.L.Bairstow	1970-90	**1099**	961	138
G.Duckworth	1923-47	**1096**	753	343
H.W.Stephenson	1948-64	**1082**	748	334
J.G.Binks	1955-75	**1071**	895	176
T.G.Evans	1939-69	**1066**	816	250
A.Long	1960-80	**1046**	922	124
G.O.Dawkes	1937-61	**1043**	895	148
R.W.Tolchard	1965-83	**1037**	912	125
W.L.Cornford	1921-47	**1017**	675	342

MOST DISMISSALS IN AN INNINGS

9	(8ct, 1st)	Tahir Rashid	Habib Bank v PACO	Gujranwala	1992-93
9	(7ct, 2st)	W.R.James	Matabeleland v Mashonaland CD	Bulawayo	1995-96
8	(8ct)	A.T.W.Grout	Queensland v W Australia	Brisbane	1959-60
8	(8ct)	D.E.East	Essex v Somerset	Taunton	1985
8	(8ct)	S.A.Marsh	Kent v Middlesex	Lord's	1991
8	(6ct, 2st)	T.J.Zoehrer	Australians v Surrey	The Oval	1993
8	(7ct, 1st)	D.S.Berry	Victoria v South Australia	Melbourne	1996-97
8	(7ct, 1st)	Y.S.S.Mendis	Bloomfield v Kurunegala Youth	Colombo	2000-01
8	(7ct, 1st)	S.Nath	Assam v Tripura (on debut)	Gauhati	2001-02
8	(8ct)	J.N.Batty	Surrey v Kent	The Oval	2004
8	(8ct)	Golam Mabud	Sylhet v Dhaka	Dhaka	2005-06
8	(8ct)	A.Z.M.Dyili	Eastern Province v Free State	Port Elizabeth	2009-10
8	(8ct)	D.C.de Boorder	Otago v Wellington	Wellington	2009-10
8	(8ct)	R.S.Second	Free State v North West	Bloemfontein	2011-12
8	(8ct)	T.L.Tsolekile	South Africa A v Sri Lanka A	Durban	2012
8	(7ct, 1st)	M.A.R.S.Fernando	Chilaw Marians v Colts	Columbo (SSC)	2017-18

MOST DISMISSALS IN A MATCH

14	(11ct, 3st)	I.Khaleel	Hyderabad v Assam	Guwahati	2011-12
13	(11ct, 2st)	W.R.James	Matabeleland v Mashonaland CD	Bulawayo	1995-96
12	(8ct, 4st)	E.W.Pooley	Surrey v Sussex	The Oval	1868
12	(9ct, 3st)	D.Tallon	Queensland v NSW	Sydney	1938-39
12	(9ct, 3st)	H.B.Taber	NSW v South Australia	Adelaide	1968-69
12	(12ct)	P.D.McGlashan	Northern Districts v Central Districts	Whangarei	2009-10
12	(11ct, 1st)	T.L.Tsolekile	Lions v Dolphins	Johannesburg	2010-11
12	(12ct)	Kashif Mahmood	Lahore Shalimar v Abbottabad	Abbottabad	2010-11
12	(12ct)	R.S.Second	Free State v North West	Bloemfontein	2011-12
12	(12ct)	S.W.Billings	Kent v Warwickshire	Birmingham	2022

MOST DISMISSALS IN A SEASON

128	(79ct, 49st)	L.E.G.Ames			1929

FIELDING RECORDS
700 CATCHES IN A CAREER

1018	F.E.Woolley	1906-38	784	J.G.Langridge	1928-55
887	W.G.Grace	1865-1908	764	W.Rhodes	1898-1930
830	G.A.R.Lock	1946-70/71	758	C.A.Milton	1948-74
819	W.R.Hammond	1920-51	754	E.H.Hendren	1907-38
813	D.B.Close	1949-86	709	G.A.Hick	1983/84-2008

MOST CATCHES IN AN INNINGS

7	M.J.Stewart	Surrey v Northamptonshire	Northampton	1957
7	A.S.Brown	Gloucestershire v Nottinghamshire	Nottingham	1966
7	R.Clarke	Warwickshire v Lancashire	Liverpool	2011

MOST CATCHES IN A MATCH

10	W.R.Hammond	Gloucestershire v Surrey	Cheltenham	1928
9	R.Clarke	Warwickshire v Lancashire	Liverpool	2011
9	P.S.P.Handscomb	Victoria v Tasmania	Melbourne	2021-22

MOST CATCHES IN A SEASON

78	W.R.Hammond	1928	77	M.J.Stewart	1957

LIMITED-OVERS INTERNATIONALS CAREER RECORDS

These records, complete to 7 March 2023, include all players registered for county cricket for the 2023 season at the time of going to press, plus those who have appeared in LOI matches for ICC full member countries since 25 November 2021. Some players who may return to LOI action have also been listed, even if their most recent game was earlier than this date.

ENGLAND – BATTING AND FIELDING

	M	I	NO	HS	Runs	Avge	100	50	Ct/St
R.Ahmed	1	1	–	2	2	2.00	–	–	1
M.M.Ali	129	103	15	128	2212	25.13	3	6	42
J.M.Anderson	194	79	43	28	273	7.58	–	–	53
J.C.Archer	21	11	6	8*	32	6.40	–	–	6
J.M.Bairstow	95	86	8	141*	3634	46.58	11	15	48/3
J.T.Ball	18	6	2	28	38	9.50	–	–	5
G.S.Ballance ‡	16	15	1	79	279	21.21	–	2	8
T.Banton	6	5	–	58	134	26.80	–	1	2
S.W.Billings	28	23	2	118	702	33.42	1	5	19/1
R.S.Bopara	120	109	21	101*	2695	30.62	1	14	35
S.G.Borthwick	2	2	–	15	18	9.00	–	–	–
D.R.Briggs	1								–
S.C.J.Broad	121	68	25	45*	529	12.30	–	–	27
H.C.Brook	3	3	–	80	86	28.66	–	1	–
J.C.Buttler	165	138	26	162*	4647	41.49	11	24	204/34
B.A.Carse	9	6	2	31	77	19.25	–	–	1
A.N.Cook	92	92	4	137	3204	36.40	5	19	36
Z.Crawley	3	3	1	58*	97	48.50	–	1	4
S.M.Curran	23	16	3	95*	318	24.46	–	1	5
T.K.Curran	28	17	9	47*	303	37.87	–	–	5
S.M.Davies	8	8	–	87	244	30.50	–	1	8
L.A.Dawson	6	5	–	20	63	12.60	–	–	2
J.L.Denly	16	13	–	87	446	34.30	–	4	7
B.M.Duckett	6	6	–	63	146	24.33	–	2	3
S.T.Finn	69	30	13	35	136	8.00	–	–	15
B.T.Foakes	1	1	1	61*	61	–	–	–	2/1
L.Gregory	3	2	–	77	117	58.50	–	1	–
A.D.Hales	70	67	3	171	2419	37.79	6	14	27
W.G.Jacks	2	2	–	26	27	13.50	–	–	–
C.J.Jordan	35	24	9	38*	184	12.26	–	–	19
L.S.Livingstone	12	10	2	66*	250	31.25	–	1	6
S.Mahmood	8	2	–	12	20	10.00	–	–	1
D.J.Malan	18	18	4	134	769	54.92	4	3	7
E.J.G.Morgan †	225	207	32	148	6957	39.75	13	42	78
C.Overton	7	5	2	32	68	22.66	–	–	4
M.W.Parkinson	5	1	1	7*	7	–	–	–	1
S.R.Patel	36	22	7	70*	482	32.13	–	1	7
D.A.Payne	1								–
M.J.Potts	1	1	1	3*	3	–	–	–	–
A.U.Rashid	125	59	20	69	734	18.82	–	1	40
T.S.Roland-Jones	1	1	1	37*	37	–	–	–	–
J.E.Root	158	147	23	133*	6207	50.05	16	36	78
J.J.Roy	116	110	3	180	4271	39.91	12	21	46
P.D.Salt	14	12	–	122	460	38.33	1	2	4
J.A.Simpson	3	2	–	17	20	10.00	–	–	9
B.A.Stokes	105	90	15	102*	2924	38.98	3	21	49
O.P.Stone	8	4	2	9*	14	7.00	–	–	–

	M	I	NO	HS	Runs	Avge	100	50	Ct/St
R.J.W.Topley	22	10	7	6*	18	6.00	–	–	5
J.M.Vince	25	22	–	102	616	28.00	1	3	10
D.J.Willey	64	37	15	51	538	24.45	–	2	26
C.R.Woakes	112	78	22	95*	1386	24.75	–	5	47
L.Wood	1	1	–	10	10	10.00	–	–	–
M.A.Wood	59	19	11	14	72	9.00	–	–	13

ENGLAND – BOWLING

	O	M	R	W	Avge	Best	4wI	R/Over
R.Ahmed	10	0	62	1	62.00	1-62	–	6.20
M.M.Ali	934.2	13	4940	99	49.89	4-46	1	5.28
J.M.Anderson	1597.2	125	7861	269	29.22	5-23	13	4.92
J.C.Archer	189.5	14	913	42	21.73	6-40	1	4.80
J.T.Ball	157.5	5	980	21	46.66	5-51	1	6.20
R.S.Bopara	310	11	1523	40	38.07	4-38	1	4.91
S.G.Borthwick	9	0	72	0	–	–	–	8.00
D.R.Briggs	10	0	39	2	19.50	2-39	–	3.90
S.C.J.Broad	1018.1	56	5364	178	30.13	5-23	10	5.26
B.A.Carse	67.4	0	382	12	31.83	5-61	1	5.64
S.M.Curran	161.2	8	946	26	36.38	5-48	2	5.86
T.K.Curran	218	8	1290	34	37.94	5-35	3	5.91
L.A.Dawson	44	0	284	5	56.80	2-70	–	6.45
J.L.Denly	17	0	101	1	101.00	1-24	–	5.94
S.T.Finn	591.4	38	2996	102	29.37	5-33	6	5.06
L.Gregory	19	1	97	4	24.25	3-44	–	5.10
W.G.Jacks	11	0	45	1	45.00	1-18	–	4.09
C.J.Jordan	276.4	5	1660	46	36.08	5-29	1	6.00
L.S.Livingstone	25	0	145	6	24.16	2-30	–	5.80
S.Mahmood	69.5	0	320	14	22.85	4-42	1	4.58
D.J.Malan	2.3	0	17	1	17.00	1- 5	–	6.80
C.Overton	51.2	2	291	5	58.20	2-23	–	5.66
M.W.Parkinson	34.4	0	203	5	40.60	2-28	–	5.85
S.R.Patel	197.5	4	1091	24	45.45	5-41	1	5.51
D.A.Payne	9	1	38	1	38.00	1-38	–	4.22
M.J.Potts	4	0	33	0	–	–	–	8.25
A.U.Rashid	1043.5	11	5894	183	32.20	5-27	10	5.64
T.S.Roland-Jones	7	2	34	1	34.00	1-34	–	4.85
J.E.Root	258.5	2	1495	26	57.50	3-52	–	5.77
B.A.Stokes	518.2	8	3137	74	42.39	5-61	2	6.05
O.P.Stone	53	2	317	8	39.62	4-85	1	5.98
R.J.W.Topley	168.2	14	892	33	27.03	6-24	2	5.29
J.M.Vince	7	0	38	1	38.00	1-18	–	5.42
D.J.Willey	469.3	27	2622	84	31.21	5-30	5	5.58
C.R.Woakes	886.1	50	4837	160	30.23	6-45	13	5.45
L.Wood	10	0	59	0	–	–	–	5.90
M.A.Wood	495.5	17	2690	71	37.88	4-33	2	5.42

† E.J.G.Morgan has also made 23 appearances for Ireland (see below).
‡ G.S.Ballance has also made 2 appearances for Zimbabwe (see below).

AUSTRALIA – BATTING AND FIELDING

	M	I	NO	HS	Runs	Avge	100	50	Ct/St
S.A.Abbott	8	6	–	49	105	17.50	–	–	3
A.C.Agar	20	16	4	46	257	21.41	–	–	10
J.P.Behrendorff	12	6	3	11*	21	7.00	–	–	3
A.T.Carey	62	57	11	106	1629	35.41	1	7	71/8
P.J.Cummins	75	47	15	36	324	10.12	–	–	19
N.T.Ellis	3	3	2	3*	6	6.00	–	–	–
A.J.Finch	146	142	3	153*	5406	38.89	17	30	71
C.D.Green	13	11	6	89*	290	58.00	–	1	5
J.R.Hazlewood	69	23	19	23*	81	20.25	–	–	22
T.M.Head	51	48	3	152	1823	40.51	3	13	13
J.P.Inglis	2	2	–	10	15	7.50	–	–	2
M.P.Kuhnemann	4	2	–	15	16	8.00	–	–	–
M.Labuschagne	27	26	1	108	804	32.16	1	6	10
B.R.McDermott	5	5	–	104	223	44.60	1	1	–
M.R.Marsh	69	65	9	102*	1814	32.39	1	13	31
G.J.Maxwell	127	116	14	108	3482	34.13	2	23	79
M.G.Neser	2	2	–	6	8	4.00	–	–	–
J.A.Richardson	15	9	4	29	93	18.60	–	–	5
K.W.Richardson	25	12	7	24*	75	15.00	–	–	7
P.M.Siddle	20	6	3	10*	31	10.33	–	–	1
S.P.D.Smith	139	124	15	164	4917	45.11	12	29	78
M.A.Starc	107	60	22	52*	469	12.34	–	1	37
M.P.Stoinis	57	52	7	146*	1296	28.80	1	6	14
M.J.Swepson	3	1	–	2	2	2.00	–	–	–
A.J.Tye	7	7	3	19	57	14.25	–	–	1
D.A.Warner	141	139	6	179	6007	45.16	19	27	61
D.J.Worrall	3	1	1	6*	6	–	–	–	1
A.Zampa	76	35	13	36	206	9.36	–	–	16

AUSTRALIA – BOWLING

	O	M	R	W	Avge	Best	4wI	R/Over
S.A.Abbott	57	7	311	9	34.55	2- 1	–	5.45
A.C.Agar	164	4	877	18	48.72	2-31	–	5.34
J.P.Behrendorff	107.3	7	568	16	35.50	5-44	1	5.28
P.J.Cummins	656.2	43	3424	124	27.61	5-70	7	5.21
N.T.Ellis	23	0	140	3	46.66	1-36	–	6.08
A.J.Finch	47.2	0	259	4	64.75	1- 2	–	5.47
C.D.Green	4	0	27	0	–	–	–	6.75
J.R.Hazlewood	604.2	48	2766	108	25.61	6-52	4	4.57
T.M.Head	140.3	0	818	14	58.42	2-22	–	5.82
M.P.Kuhnemann	38	3	191	6	31.83	2-26	–	5.02
M.Labuschagne	30.5	1	197	2	98.50	2-19	–	6.38
M.R.Marsh	351.5	9	1913	54	35.42	5-33	2	5.43
G.J.Maxwell	539.2	11	3007	60	50.11	4-46	3	5.57
M.G.Neser	16.4	1	120	2	60.00	2-46	–	7.19
J.A.Richardson	135	11	793	27	29.37	4-26	1	5.87
K.W.Richardson	218.4	11	1240	39	31.79	5-68	1	5.67
P.M.Siddle	150.1	10	743	17	43.70	3-55	–	4.94
S.P.D.Smith	179.2	1	971	28	34.67	3-16	–	5.41
M.A.Starc	918.1	47	4670	211	22.13	6-28	20	5.08
M.P.Stoinis	276	2	1647	37	44.51	3-16	–	5.96
M.J.Swepson	26.2	0	161	3	53.66	2-53	–	6.11
A.J.Tye	64.3	1	392	12	32.66	5-46	1	6.07
D.A.Warner	1	0	8	0	–	–	–	8.00

AUSTRALIA – BOWLING (continued)

	O	M	R	W	Avge	Best	4wI	R/Over
D.J.Worrall	26.2	0	171	1	171.00	1-43	–	6.49
A.Zampa	669	10	3641	127	28.66	5-35	7	5.44

SOUTH AFRICA – BATTING AND FIELDING

	M	I	NO	HS	Runs	Avge	100	50	Ct/St
K.J.Abbott	28	13	4	23	76	8.44	–	–	7
T.Bavuma	23	22	2	113	910	45.50	3	2	21
Q.de Kock	137	137	7	178	5901	45.39	17	29	180/12
M.de Lange	4	–	–	–	–	–	–	–	–
B.C.Fortuin	3	2	1	1	1	1.00	–	–	–
M.Z.Hamza	1	1	–	56	56	56.00	–	1	–
R.R.Hendricks	27	27	2	102	694	27.76	1	5	16
C.A.Ingram	31	29	3	124	843	32.42	3	3	12
M.Jansen	5	4	1	32*	60	20.00	–	–	–
H.Klaasen	33	31	5	123*	933	35.88	1	5	33/5
G.F.Linde	2	2	1	18	27	27.00	–	–	3
S.S.B.Magala	5	3	1	5*	7	3.50	–	–	2
K.A.Maharaj	27	13	2	28	159	14.45	–	–	4
J.N.Malan	23	22	2	177*	958	47.90	3	4	11
A.K.Markram	47	44	3	96	1189	29.00	–	5	20
D.A.Miller	152	130	40	139	3780	42.00	5	20	68
P.W.A.Mulder	12	10	4	19*	81	13.50	–	–	5
L.T.Ngidi	42	15	10	19*	67	13.40	–	–	8
A.A.Nortje	19	5	1	10	25	6.25	–	–	3
W.D.Parnell	72	42	14	56	570	20.35	–	1	13
D.Paterson	4	–	–	–	–	–	–	–	2
A.L.Phehlukwayo	74	47	16	69*	742	23.93	–	2	16
D.Pretorius	27	13	1	50	192	16.00	–	1	11
K.Rabada	88	36	16	31*	317	15.85	–	–	29
T.Shamsi	41	8	6	9*	18	9.00	–	–	8
H.E.van der Dussen	41	35	10	134	1679	67.16	4	11	17
R.E.van der Merwe †	13	7	3	12	39	9.75	–	–	3
K.Verreynne	12	10	1	95	371	41.22	–	4	9
D.Wiese ‡	6	6	1	41*	102	20.40	–	–	–
K.Zondo	6	6	1	54	146	29.20	–	1	1

SOUTH AFRICA – BOWLING

	O	M	R	W	Avge	Best	4wI	R/Over
K.J.Abbott	217.1	13	1051	34	30.91	4-21	2	4.83
T.Bavuma	6.1	0	22	0	–	–	–	3.56
M.de Lange	34.5	1	198	10	19.80	4-46	1	5.68
B.C.Fortuin	13	2	72	2	36.00	1-20	–	5.53
R.R.Hendricks	7	0	47	1	47.00	1-13	–	6.71
C.A.Ingram	1	0	17	0	–	–	–	17.00
M.Jansen	44.1	1	268	5	53.60	2-53	–	6.06
H.Klaasen	5	0	33	0	–	–	–	6.60
G.F.Linde	15	1	72	3	24.00	2-32	–	4.80
S.S.B.Magala	36	0	255	6	42.50	3-46	–	7.08
K.A.Maharaj	224.1	5	1074	29	37.03	3-25	–	4.79
A.K.Markram	84	0	481	12	40.08	2-18	–	5.72
P.W.A.Mulder	59	0	341	10	34.10	2-59	–	5.77
L.T.Ngidi	331	19	1883	71	26.52	6-58	4	5.68
A.A.Nortje	149.4	0	874	34	25.70	4-51	3	5.83

SOUTH AFRICA – BOWLING (continued)

	O	M	R	W	Avge	Best	4wI	R/Over
W.D.Parnell	532	22	2980	98	30.40	5-48	5	5.60
D.Paterson	34.5	1	217	4	54.25	3-44	–	6.22
A.L.Phehlukwayo	478.1	17	2744	87	31.54	4-22	3	5.73
D.Pretorius	190.4	9	947	35	27.05	4-36	1	4.96
K.Rabada	755.1	50	3796	137	27.70	6-16	8	5.02
T.Shamsi	331.3	7	1835	51	35.98	5-49	2	5.53
H.E.van der Dussen	1	0	3	1	3.00	1- 3	–	3.00
R.E.van der Merwe	117.3	2	561	17	33.00	3-27	–	4.77
D.Wiese	49	0	316	9	35.11	3-50	–	6.44

† R.E.van der Merwe has also made 3 appearances for Netherlands (see below).
‡ D.Wiese has also made 9 appearances for Namibia (see below).

WEST INDIES – BATTING AND FIELDING

	M	I	NO	HS	Runs	Avge	100	50	Ct/St
F.A.Allen	20	16	3	51	200	15.38	–	1	10
J.Blackwood	3	3	1	12*	23	11.50	–	–	2
N.E.Bonner	6	6	1	31	85	17.00	–	–	1
D.M.Bravo	122	117	14	124	3109	30.18	4	18	35
S.S.J.Brooks	21	21	1	101*	694	34.70	1	3	11
Y.Cariah	3	2	1	52	53	53.00	–	1	–
K.U.Carty	9	7	1	43*	145	24.16	–	–	–
R.L.Chase	33	26	3	94	553	24.04	–	2	13
J.P.Greaves	3	3	–	12	29	9.66	–	–	–
J.O.Holder	131	107	23	99*	2042	24.30	–	11	61
S.D.Hope	104	99	11	170	4308	48.95	13	21	107/11
A.J.Hosein	29	22	5	60	234	13.76	–	1	14
A.S.Joseph	54	31	13	49	332	18.44	–	–	15
B.A.King	20	20	2	91*	431	23.94	–	3	3
S.H.Lewis	1	–	–	–	–	–	–	–	1
K.R.Mayers	17	16	–	120	486	30.37	2	1	6
G.Motie	4	3	–	7	15	5.00	–	–	1
S.P.Narine	65	45	12	36	363	11.00	–	–	14
K.M.A.Paul	23	17	5	46	266	22.16	–	–	11
A.Phillip	5	2	1	21*	22	22.00	–	–	2
K.A.Pollard	123	113	9	119	2706	26.01	3	13	64
N.Pooran	52	49	6	118	1555	36.16	1	11	21/2
R.Powell	45	42	3	101	897	23.00	1	2	14
K.A.J.Roach	95	60	36	34	308	12.83	–	–	22
J.N.T.Seales	7	3	2	16*	16	16.00	–	–	1
R.Shepherd	18	14	2	50	213	17.75	–	1	5
K.Sinclair	3	1	1	3*	3	–	–	–	2
O.F.Smith	5	5	1	46	144	36.00	–	–	1
H.R.Walsh †	21	11	3	46*	128	16.00	–	–	4

WEST INDIES – BOWLING

	O	M	R	W	Avge	Best	4wI	R/Over
F.A.Allen	111	0	627	7	89.57	2-40	–	5.64
J.Blackwood	3	0	16	0	–	–	–	5.33
N.E.Bonner	10.5	0	55	1	55.00	1-29	–	5.07
Y.Cariah	25	0	152	3	50.66	2-77	–	6.08
K.U.Carty	1.1	0	10	0	–	–	–	8.57
R.L.Chase	168.5	3	812	19	42.73	3-30	–	4.80
J.O.Holder	1007.1	57	5555	153	36.30	5-27	7	5.51

	O	M	R	W	Avge	Best	4wI	R/Over
A.J.Hosein	263.2	8	1246	44	28.31	4-39	1	4.73
A.S.Joseph	461.4	20	2408	87	27.67	5-56	5	5.21
S.H.Lewis	9.5	0	67	3	22.33	3-67	–	6.81
K.R.Mayers	58.4	2	339	6	56.50	2-48	–	5.77
G.Motie	36.4	4	134	8	16.75	4-23	1	3.65
S.P.Narine	590	35	2435	92	26.46	6-27	6	4.12
K.M.A.Paul	162.4	3	977	25	39.08	3-44	–	6.00
A.Phillip	32.3	0	207	4	51.75	2-50	–	6.36
K.A.Pollard	379.1	4	2161	55	39.29	3-27	–	5.69
N.Pooran	28.1	0	174	6	29.00	4-48	1	6.17
R.Powell	46.4	0	275	3	91.66	1- 7	–	5.89
K.A.J.Roach	763.1	53	3885	125	31.08	6-27	6	5.09
J.N.T.Seales	55.1	3	321	4	80.25	1-39	–	5.81
R.Shepherd	112.1	4	601	11	54.63	3-50	–	5.35
K.Sinclair	28.2	1	123	5	24.60	4-41	1	4.34
O.F.Smith	24.1	0	122	6	20.33	2-26	–	5.04
H.R.Walsh	163.4	1	882	28	31.50	5-39	2	5.38

† H.R.Walsh has also made 1 appearance for the USA v PNG, scoring 27 and taking 0-9.

NEW ZEALAND – BATTING AND FIELDING

	M	I	NO	HS	Runs	Avge	100	50	Ct/St
F.H.Allen	17	16	–	96	482	30.12	–	4	6
T.A.Boult	99	45	24	21*	191	9.09	–	–	37
D.A.J.Bracewell	21	14	2	57	221	18.41	–	1	5
M.G.Bracewell	19	16	5	140	510	42.50	2	–	9
M.S.Chapman	7	7	2	124*	262	52.40	2	–	2
D.Cleaver	1	1	–	32	32	32.00	–	–	2
D.P.Conway	18	17	1	138	733	45.81	3	3	9
C.de Grandhomme	45	35	7	74*	742	26.50	–	4	17
J.A.Duffy	3	1	–	0	0	0.00	–	–	–
L.H.Ferguson	53	25	11	19	97	6.92	–	–	12
M.J.Guptill	198	195	19	237*	7346	41.73	18	39	104
M.J.Henry	65	25	8	48*	223	13.11	–	–	19
K.A.Jamieson	8	3	2	25*	34	34.00	–	–	2
T.W.M.Latham	123	113	14	145*	3467	35.02	7	18	103/15
A.F.Milne	42	17	7	36	168	16.80	–	–	21
D.J.Mitchell	19	16	3	100*	479	36.84	1	2	6
C.Munro	57	53	2	87	1271	24.92	–	8	22
J.D.S.Neesham	71	61	11	97*	1409	28.18	–	6	26
H.M.Nicholls	61	59	11	124*	1652	34.41	1	13	22
G.D.Phillips	15	11	1	63*	312	31.20	–	1	7
M.J.Santner	93	70	26	67	1248	28.36	–	3	37
H.B.Shipley	3	3	1	2*	2	1.00	–	–	–
I.S.Sodhi	39	19	4	25	144	9.60	–	–	10
T.G.Southee	154	93	35	55	720	12.41	–	1	43
L.R.P.L.Taylor	236	220	39	181*	8607	47.55	21	51	142
B.M.Tickner	9	5	4	4	4	4.00	–	–	4
K.S.Williamson	161	153	16	148	6554	47.83	13	42	64
W.A.Young	8	8	2	120	240	40.00	2	–	3

NEW ZEALAND – BOWLING

	O	M	R	W	Avge	Best	4wI	R/Over
T.A.Boult	908.5	69	4484	187	23.97	7-34	15	4.93
D.A.J.Bracewell	169.2	18	845	26	32.50	4-55	1	4.99
M.G.Bracewell	123	4	634	15	42.26	3-21	–	5.15

	O	M	R	W	Avge	Best	4wI	R/Over
C.de Grandhomme	258	10	1230	30	41.00	3-26	–	4.76
J.A.Duffy	26.4	1	204	7	29.14	3-52	–	7.65
L.H.Ferguson	465.5	9	2639	85	31.04	5-45	3	5.66
M.J.Guptill	18.1	0	98	4	24.50	2- 6	–	5.39
M.J.Henry	568	42	2955	116	25.47	5-30	12	5.20
K.A.Jamieson	68.4	6	296	11	26.90	3-45	–	4.31
A.F.Milne	320.1	7	1705	45	37.88	3-49	–	5.32
D.J.Mitchell	25	0	142	6	23.66	3-25	–	5.68
C.Munro	92	1	481	7	68.71	2-10	–	5.22
J.D.S.Neesham	382.3	6	2320	69	33.62	5-27	4	6.06
G.D.Phillips	20	0	131	5	26.20	1- 9	–	6.55
M.J.Santner	712.5	14	3473	90	38.58	5-50	1	4.87
H.B.Shipley	20	1	131	3	43.66	2-74	–	6.55
I.S.Sodhi	323.1	10	1754	51	34.39	4-58	1	5.42
T.G.Southee	1291.5	80	7027	210	33.46	7-33	8	5.43
L.R.P.L.Taylor	7	0	35	0	–	–	–	5.00
B.M.Tickner	75	2	498	13	38.30	4-50	1	6.64
K.S.Williamson	244.3	2	1310	37	35.40	4-22	1	5.35

INDIA – BATTING AND FIELDING

	M	I	NO	HS	Runs	Avge	100	50	Ct/St
Aavesh Khan	5	2	–	10	13	6.50	–	–	3
Arshdeep Singh	3	1	–	9	9	9.00	–	–	–
R.Ashwin	113	63	20	65	707	16.44	–	1	30
R.Bishnoi	1	1	1	4*	4	–	–	–	–
J.J.Bumrah	72	20	13	14*	47	6.71	–	–	17
Y.S.Chahal	72	14	5	18*	77	8.55	–	–	16
D.L.Chahar	13	9	3	69*	203	33.83	–	2	1
S.Dhawan	167	164	10	143	6793	44.11	17	39	83
R.D.Gaikwad	1	1	–	19	19	19.00	–	–	–
S.Gill	21	21	4	208	1254	73.76	4	5	11
D.J.Hooda	10	7	1	33	153	25.50	–	–	3
S.S.Iyer	42	38	3	113*	1631	46.60	2	14	16
V.R.Iyer	2	2	–	22	24	12.00	–	–	–
R.A.Jadeja	171	115	40	87	2447	32.62	–	13	63
I.P.Kishan	13	12	1	210	507	46.09	1	3	5/2
V.Kohli	271	262	40	183	12809	57.69	46	64	141
P.M.Krishna	14	5	3	2*	2	1.00	–	–	4
Kuldeep Yadav	78	28	16	19	146	12.16	–	–	11
B.Kumar	121	55	16	53*	552	14.15	–	1	29
Mohammed Shami	87	41	19	25	190	8.63	–	–	29
H.H.Pandya	71	52	7	92*	1518	33.73	–	9	28
R.R.Pant	30	26	1	125*	865	34.60	1	5	26/1
A.R.Patel	49	29	9	64*	381	19.05	–	2	22
C.A.Pujara	5	5	–	27	51	10.20	–	–	–
A.M.Rahane	90	87	3	111	2962	35.26	3	24	48
K.L.Rahul	51	49	7	112	1870	44.52	5	12	29/2
S.V.Samson	11	10	5	86*	330	66.00	–	2	7/2
K.R.Sen	1	1	–	2*	2	–	–	–	–
Shahbaz Ahmed	3	1	–	0	0	0.00	–	–	1
R.G.Sharma	241	234	34	264	9782	48.91	30	48	87
M.Siraj	21	8	4	9	27	6.75	–	–	4
S.N.Thakur	34	21	6	50*	298	19.86	–	1	7
Umran Malik	8	3	3	2*	2	–	–	–	1
M.S.Washington Sundar	16	9	1	51	233	29.12	–	1	4

	M	I	NO	HS	Runs	Avge	100	50	Ct/St
J.Yadav	2	2	1	2	3	3.00	–	–	1
S.A.Yadav	20	18	3	64	433	28.86	–	2	14

INDIA – BOWLING

	O	M	R	W	Avge	Best	4wI	R/Over
Aavesh Khan	35.3	2	214	3	71.33	3-66	–	6.02
Arshdeep Singh	13.1	1	89	0	–	–	–	6.75
R.Ashwin	1023.3	36	5058	151	33.49	4-25	1	4.94
R.Bishnoi	8	0	69	1	69.00	1-69	–	8.62
J.J.Bumrah	634.3	43	2941	121	24.30	6-19	7	4.63
Y.S.Chahal	623.1	14	3283	121	27.13	6-42	7	5.26
D.L.Chahar	85	5	489	16	30.56	3-27	–	5.75
D.J.Hooda	25	1	119	3	39.66	1- 6	–	4.76
S.S.Iyer	6.1	0	39	0	–	–	–	6.32
V.R.Iyer	5	0	28	0	–	–	–	5.60
R.A.Jadeja	1435.1	50	7062	189	37.36	5-36	8	4.92
V.Kohli	106.5	1	665	4	166.25	1-15	–	6.22
P.M.Krishna	112.2	7	598	25	23.92	4-12	2	5.32
Kuldeep Yadav	686.4	18	3567	130	27.43	6-25	6	5.19
B.Kumar	974.3	68	4951	141	35.11	5-42	5	5.08
Mohammed Shami	736	43	4127	159	25.95	5-69	10	5.60
H.H.Pandya	468.4	11	2620	68	38.52	4-24	1	5.59
A.R.Patel	391.3	18	1740	56	31.07	3-24	–	4.44
K.R.Sen	5	0	37	2	18.50	2-37	–	7.40
Shahbaz Ahmed	26	0	125	3	41.66	2-32	–	4.80
R.G.Sharma	98.5	2	515	8	64.37	2-27	–	5.21
M.Siraj	170.4	17	788	38	20.73	4-32	2	4.61
S.N.Thakur	254.5	9	1587	50	31.74	4-52	2	6.22
Umran Malik	55	2	355	13	27.30	3-57	–	6.45
M.S.Washington Sundar	86	2	435	16	27.18	3-30	–	5.05
J.Yadav	14	0	61	1	61.00	1- 8	–	4.35

PAKISTAN – BATTING AND FIELDING

	M	I	NO	HS	Runs	Avge	100	50	Ct/St
Abdullah Shafiq	1	1	–	2	2	2.00	–	–	–
Agha Salman	6	6	3	50*	184	61.33	–	1	3
Asif Ali	21	16	1	52	382	25.46	–	3	6
Azhar Ali	53	53	3	102	1845	36.90	3	12	8
Babar Azam	95	93	12	158	4813	59.41	17	24	44
Fakhar Zaman	65	65	4	210*	2785	45.65	8	15	31
Haider Ali	2	2	–	29	42	21.00	–	–	1
Haris Rauf	18	7	4	7	10	3.33	–	–	5
Haris Sohail	45	44	5	130	1749	44.84	2	14	17
Hasan Ali	60	35	11	59	363	15.12	–	2	13
Iftikhar Ahmed	10	9	4	32*	124	24.80	–	–	4
Imam-ul-Haq	56	56	6	151	2545	50.90	9	14	10
Kamran Ghulam	1	–	–	–	–	–	–	–	–
Khushdil Shah	10	8	2	41*	199	33.16	–	–	6
Mohammad Abbas	3	–	–	–	–	–	–	–	–
Mohammad Haris	4	3	–	6	10	3.33	–	–	4/2
Mohammad Hasnain	9	5	3	28	47	23.50	–	–	2
Mohammad Nawaz	25	20	4	53	264	16.50	–	–	10
Mohammad Rizwan	52	47	9	115	1247	32.81	2	8	44/1

	M	I	NO	HS	Runs	Avge	100	50	Ct/St
Mohammad Wasim	11	6	1	17*	51	10.20	–	–	1
Naseem Shah	5	2	1	3	3	3.00	–	–	1
Saud Shakeel	5	4	1	56	67	22.33	–	1	2
Shadab Khan	53	31	10	86	596	28.38	–	4	13
Shaheen Shah Afridi	32	16	10	19*	102	17.00	–	–	6
Shahnawaz Dahani	2	2	2	4*	4	–	–	–	–
Shan Masood	6	6	–	50	111	18.50	–	1	2
Usama Mir	3	2	–	12	18	9.00	–	–	2
Zafar Gohar	1	1	–	15	15	15.00	–	–	–
Zahid Mahmood	4	2	1	9	9	9.00	–	–	–

PAKISTAN – BOWLING

	O	M	R	W	Avge	Best	4wI	R/Over
Agha Salman	24	0	118	2	59.00	2-42	–	4.91
Asif Ali	0.5	0	9	0	–	–	–	10.80
Azhar Ali	43	0	260	4	65.00	2-26	–	6.04
Fakhar Zaman	22.3	0	111	1	111.00	1-19	–	4.93
Haris Rauf	152	7	878	30	29.26	4-65	2	5.77
Haris Sohail	107	0	613	11	55.72	3-45	–	5.72
Hasan Ali	480.2	14	2763	91	30.36	5-34	5	5.75
Iftikhar Ahmed	60	4	313	8	39.12	5-40	1	5.21
Khushdil Shah	18	0	122	2	61.00	1-50	–	6.77
Mohammad Abbas	27	0	153	1	153.00	1-44	–	5.66
Mohammad Hasnain	77.1	5	497	12	41.41	5-26	1	6.44
Mohammad Nawaz	211.3	9	1024	37	27.67	4-19	3	4.84
Mohammad Wasim	86.4	2	467	18	25.94	4-36	1	5.38
Naseem Shah	44.5	0	226	18	12.55	5-33	2	5.04
Saud Shakeel	7.5	0	37	1	37.00	1-14	–	4.72
Shadab Khan	435	10	2215	70	31.64	4-28	4	5.09
Shaheen Shah Afridi	268.3	15	1480	62	23.87	6-35	7	5.51
Shahnawaz Dahani	16	0	73	1	73.00	1-36	–	4.56
Usama Mir	30	0	145	4	36.25	2-42	–	4.83
Zafar Gohar	10	0	54	2	27.00	2-54	–	5.40
Zahid Mahmood	36	0	220	4	55.00	2-59	–	6.11

SRI LANKA – BATTING AND FIELDING

	M	I	NO	HS	Runs	Avge	100	50	Ct/St
K.I.C.Asalanka	22	21	2	110	791	41.63	1	6	5
K.N.A.Bandara	6	5	1	55*	141	35.25	–	2	3
P.V.D.Chameera	42	29	11	29	224	12.44	–	–	7
L.D.Chandimal	157	142	21	111	3854	31.5	4	24	62/8
D.M.de Silva	65	61	8	91	1393	26.28	–	8	31
P.W.H.de Silva	37	34	5	80*	710	24.48	–	4	11
D.P.D.N.Dickwella	55	52	1	116	1604	31.45	2	9	41/11
A.M.Fernando	5	2	1	1*	1	1.00	–	–	–
A.N.P.R.Fernando	49	25	17	7	35	4.37	–	–	7
M.N.K.Fernando	2	2	–	50	69	34.50	–	1	–
W.I.A.Fernando	29	29	–	127	990	34.13	3	5	14
C.D.Gunasekara	1	–	–	–	–	–	–	–	–
M.D.Gunathilleke	47	46	1	133	1601	35.57	2	11	14
C.Karunaratne	21	20	6	75	408	29.14	–	1	4
C.B.R.L.S.Kumara	17	9	4	9	26	5.20	–	–	3
R.A.S.Lakmal	86	48	22	26	244	9.38	–	–	20

	M	I	NO	HS	Runs	Avge	100	50	Ct/St
P.A.D.Lakshan	3	2	–	2	4	2.00	–	–	1
P.M.Liyanagamage	1	1	–	15	15	15.00	–	–	–
L.D.Madushanka	1	–	–	–	–	–	–	–	–
B.K.G.Mendis	93	91	6	119	2654	31.22	2	20	51/3
P.H.K.D.Mendis	7	7	1	57	127	21.16	–	1	2
C.A.K.Rajitha	16	8	6	17*	48	24.00	–	–	1
M.D.Shanaka	48	44	4	108*	1067	26.67	2	3	9
P.N.Silva	21	21	1	137	649	32.45	1	5	7
M.M.Theekshana	12	7	5	11*	31	15.50	–	–	4
J.D.F.Vandersay	20	12	2	25	89	8.90	–	–	4
R.T.M.Wanigamuni	4	4	2	26	50	25.00	–	–	1
D.N.Wellalage	9	7	1	32	109	18.16	–	–	3

SRI LANKA – BOWLING

	O	M	R	W	Avge	Best	4wI	R/Over
K.I.C.Asalanka	14	0	82	1	82.00	1- 3	–	5.85
K.N.A.Bandara	1	0	8	0	–	–	–	8.00
P.V.D.Chameera	291.1	12	1577	44	35.84	5-16	1	5.41
D.M.de Silva	278.2	1	1411	37	38.13	3-32	–	5.06
P.W.H.de Silva	297.1	10	1506	39	38.61	4-58	1	5.06
A.M.Fernando	30	1	202	1	202.00	1-64	–	6.73
A.N.P.R.Fernando	390.5	20	2339	63	37.12	4-31	2	5.98
M.N.K.Fernando	2	0	22	0	–	–	–	11.00
C.D.Gunasekara	1	0	8	0	–	–	–	8.00
M.D.Gunathilleke	67	1	371	8	46.37	3-48	–	5.53
C.Karunaratne	107	3	623	20	31.15	3-47	–	5.82
C.B.R.L.S.Kumara	124.2	1	878	20	43.90	2-26	–	7.06
R.A.S.Lakmal	646.5	36	3534	109	32.42	4-13	3	5.46
P.A.D.Lakshan	11	0	76	1	76.00	1-43	–	6.90
P.M.Liyanagamage	3	0	13	1	13.00	1-13	–	4.33
L.D.Madushanka	6	0	43	1	43.00	1-43	–	7.16
B.K.G.Mendis	3.2	0	28	0	–	–	–	8.40
P.H.K.D.Mendis	25	0	151	2	75.50	1-32	–	6.04
C.A.K.Rajitha	124	3	794	23	34.52	3-31	–	6.40
M.D.Shanaka	95	0	573	15	38.20	5-43	1	6.03
M.M.Theekshana	109	4	491	13	37.76	4-37	1	4.50
J.D.F.Vandersay	143	5	802	25	32.08	4-10	1	5.60
R.T.M.Wanigamuni	12	0	74	4	18.50	2-26	–	6.16
D.N.Wellalage	51	0	303	9	33.66	3-42	–	5.94

A.N.P.R.Fernando is also known as N.Pradeep; P.M.Liyanagamage is also known as P.Madushan; P.N.Silva is also known as P.Nissanka; R.T.M.Wanigamuni is also known as W.R.T.Mendis.

ZIMBABWE – BATTING AND FIELDING

	M	I	NO	HS	Runs	Avge	100	50	Ct/St
G.S.Ballance †	2	2	–	52	75	37.50	–	1	4
R.P.Burl	37	32	5	59	617	22.85	–	4	16
R.W.Chakabva	61	57	3	102	1188	22.00	1	4	53/5
T.L.Chatara	80	54	25	23	192	6.62	–	–	8
C.J.Chibhabha	109	109	2	99	2474	23.12	–	16	34
T.L.Chivanga	5	4	2	6*	11	5.50	–	–	1
C.R.Ervine	107	103	12	130*	2948	32.39	3	18	51

	M	I	NO	HS	Runs	Avge	100	50	Ct/St
B.N.Evans	11	9	2	33*	101	14.42	–	–	4
L.M.Jongwe	37	31	4	46	352	13.03	–	–	10
I.Kaia	14	14	1	110	384	29.53	1	2	3
T.Kaitano	8	8	–	42	126	15.75	–	–	2
C.Madande	3	3	1	24	42	21.00	–	–	2
W.N.Madhevere	26	25	–	72	487	19.48	–	4	5
T.Marumani	11	10	–	45	139	13.90	–	–	1
W.P.Masakadza	26	15	3	15	68	5.66	–	–	7
B.A.Mavuta	8	5	1	20	52	13.00	–	–	2
T.T.Munyonga	6	6	1	30*	92	18.40	–	–	1
T.K.Musakanda	16	16	1	60	308	20.53	–	1	12
B.Muzarabani	33	27	8	17	64	3.36	–	–	11
D.N.Myers	5	5	–	34	96	19.20	–	–	3
R.Ngarava	30	19	9	34*	108	10.80	–	–	4
V.M.Nyauchi	10	6	–	26	43	7.16	–	–	2
M.Shumba	6	5	1	11	27	6.75	–	–	2
Sikandar Raza	126	120	18	141	3724	36.50	6	20	51
D.T.Tiripano	38	29	8	55*	364	17.33	–	1	5
S.C.Williams	147	142	19	129*	4266	34.68	5	32	54

ZIMBABWE – BOWLING

	O	M	R	W	Avge	Best	4wI	R/Over
R.P.Burl	94.1	2	570	18	31.66	5-10	2	6.05
T.L.Chatara	659.2	53	3385	105	32.23	4-33	1	5.13
C.J.Chibhabha	279.5	12	1631	35	46.60	4-25	1	5.82
T.L.Chivanga	36.2	0	197	3	65.66	1-38	–	5.42
B.N.Evans	67.3	5	431	11	39.18	5-54	1	6.38
L.M.Jongwe	225.5	11	1282	38	33.73	5- 6	1	5.67
I.Kaia	4.4	0	22	0	–	–	–	4.71
W.N.Madhevere	101.2	1	515	9	57.22	2-40	–	5.08
W.P.Masakadza	195.1	8	983	25	39.32	4-21	1	5.03
B.A.Mavuta	46	0	266	7	38.00	2-30	–	5.78
T.T.Munyonga	1	0	10	0	–	–	–	10.00
T.K.Musakanda	2	0	11	0	–	–	–	5.50
B.Muzarabani	267.2	16	1376	46	29.91	5-49	4	5.14
D.N.Myers	2	0	13	1	13.00	1-13	–	6.50
R.Ngarava	226.2	10	1271	30	42.36	3-52	–	5.61
V.M.Nyauchi	67	5	353	7	50.42	2-65	–	5.26
M.Shumba	6.5	0	42	0	–	–	–	6.14
Sikandar Raza	655.2	23	3218	71	45.32	5-21	–	4.91
D.T.Tiripano	251.2	12	1456	36	40.44	5-63	1	5.79
S.C.Williams	756.4	32	3738	77	48.54	4-43	1	4.94

† *G.S.Ballance has also made 16 appearances for England (see above).*

BANGLADESH – BATTING AND FIELDING

	M	I	NO	HS	Runs	Avge	100	50	Ct/St
Afif Hossain	25	22	5	93*	542	31.88	–	3	10
Anamul Haque	44	41	–	120	1254	30.58	3	5	12
Ebadat Hossain	5	4	2	1*	1	0.50	–	–	1
Hasan Mahmud	6	3	–	1	1	0.33	–	–	–
Liton Das	63	63	5	176	1919	33.08	5	7	42/3
Mahmudullah	218	190	50	128*	4950	35.35	3	27	76
Mehedi Hasan	70	45	9	100*	775	21.52	1	2	30

287

	M	I	NO	HS	Runs	Avge	100	50	Ct/St
Mosaddek Hossain	43	35	10	52*	634	25.36	–	3	18
Mushfiqur Rahim	242	227	37	144	6901	36.32	8	43	206/539
Mustafizur Rahman	85	39	23	18*	105	6.56	–	–	14
Nasum Ahmed	4	1	1	18*	18	–	–	–	–
Nazmul Hossain	18	18	–	58	321	17.83	–	2	5
Nurul Hasan	6	5	3	45*	165	82.50	–	–	4/3
Shakib Al Hasan	227	215	30	134*	6976	37.70	9	52	55
Shoriful Islam	14	6	1	8	18	3.60	–	–	2
Taijul Islam	15	10	2	39*	87	10.87	–	–	1
Tamim Iqbal	234	232	11	158	8143	36.84	14	55	67
Taskin Ahmed	54	27	9	21	130	7.22	–	–	9
Yasir Ali	7	5	–	50	78	15.60	–	1	2

BANGLADESH – BOWLING

	O	M	R	W	Avge	Best	4wI	R/Over
Afif Hossain	13.4	1	68	3	22.66	1- 0	–	4.97
Ebadat Hossain	44.2	2	248	13	19.07	4-47	1	5.59
Hasan Mahmud	43.2	3	256	8	32.00	3-28	–	5.90
Mahmudullah	712.1	14	3712	82	45.26	3- 4	–	5.21
Mehedi Hasan	585.3	26	2753	84	32.77	4-25	5	4.70
Mosaddek Hossain	188.2	2	969	17	57.00	3-13	–	5.14
Mustafizur Rahman	687.3	28	3500	142	24.64	6-43	9	5.09
Nasum Ahmed	37.4	8	128	5	25.60	3-19	–	3.39
Nazmul Hossain	2.4	0	13	0	–	–	–	4.87
Shakib Al Hasan	1951.5	94	8688	300	28.96	5-29	14	4.45
Shoriful Islam	100.4	3	564	19	29.68	4-34	2	5.60
Taijul Islam	144	9	611	26	23.50	5-28	2	4.24
Tamim Iqbal	1	0	13	0	–	–	–	13.00
Taskin Ahmed	422.5	15	2370	73	32.46	5-28	5	5.60
Yasir Ali	1	0	2	0	–	–	–	2.00

IRELAND – BATTING AND FIELDING

	M	I	NO	HS	Runs	Avge	100	50	Ct/St
M.R.Adair	29	22	9	32	261	20.07	–	–	10
A.Balbirnie	89	86	6	145*	2665	33.31	8	13	27
C.Campher	19	16	1	68	471	31.40	–	4	6
M.Commins	2	1	–	6	6	6.00	–	–	1
G.J.Delany	14	13	4	22	159	17.66	–	–	4
G.H.Dockrell	105	73	24	74	928	18.93	–	3	40
S.T.Doheny	3	2	–	84	87	43.50	–	1	2
G.I.Hume	4	1	1	7*	7	–	–	–	2
J.B.Little	25	10	3	9*	26	3.71	–	–	3
A.R.McBrine	70	46	12	79	672	19.76	–	2	27
B.J.McCarthy	38	26	6	18	162	8.10	–	–	11
E.J.G.Morgan †	23	23	2	115	744	35.42	1	5	9
T.J.Murtagh	58	36	12	23*	188	7.83	–	–	16
N.A.Rock	3	2	–	5	7	3.50	–	–	2
Simi Singh	35	30	4	100*	593	22.80	1	1	13
P.R.Stirling	142	138	3	177	5230	38.74	13	26	53
H.T.Tector	26	25	5	113	1071	53.55	3	8	13
L.J.Tucker	32	26	2	83	483	20.12	–	2	39/1
C.A.Young	36	22	10	12*	82	6.83	–	–	8

IRELAND – BOWLING

	O	M	R	W	Avge	Best	4wI	R/Over
M.R.Adair	204.2	10	1217	32	38.03	4-19	2	5.95
A.Balbirnie	10	0	68	2	34.00	1-26	–	6.80
C.Campher	93.3	3	523	15	34.86	3-49	–	5.59
G.J.Delany	29	0	198	4	49.50	1-10	–	6.82
G.H.Dockrell	733.2	31	3509	93	37.73	4-24	4	4.78
G.I.Hume	29	0	175	4	43.75	2-41	–	6.03
J.B.Little	197.5	9	1116	38	29.36	4-38	3	5.64
A.R.McBrine	563.5	34	2494	76	32.81	5-29	3	4.42
B.J.McCarthy	315	11	1819	61	29.81	5-46	3	5.77
T.J.Murtagh	503.2	45	2290	74	30.94	5-21	5	4.54
Simi Singh	253.1	19	1011	39	25.92	5-10	1	3.99
P.R.Stirling	406.5	8	1942	43	45.16	6-55	2	4.77
H.T.Tector	16	0	107	2	53.50	1-20	–	6.68
C.A.Young	286.2	13	1571	59	26.62	5-46	2	5.48

† E.J.G.Morgan has also made 225 appearances for England (see above).

AFGHANISTAN – BATTING AND FIELDING

	M	I	NO	HS	Runs	Avge	100	50	Ct/St
Azmatullah Omarzai	7	4	1	15*	35	11.66	–	–	2
Fareed Ahmad	11	3	3	6*	7	–	–	–	3
Fazalhaq Farooqi	10	3	2	2*	2	2.00	–	–	1
Gulbadin Naib	75	64	8	82*	1150	20.53	–	5	22
Hashmatullah Shahidi	53	53	7	97*	1505	32.71	–	13	11
Ibrahim Zadran	8	8	1	162	433	61.85	3	–	3
Mohammad Nabi	136	121	13	116	2968	27.48	1	15	58
Mujeeb Zadran	55	27	13	18*	97	6.92	–	–	9
Najibullah Zadran	82	75	12	104*	1974	31.33	1	15	39
Naveen-ul-Haq	7	5	4	10*	21	21.00	–	–	2
Noor Ahmad	1	1	1	2*	2	–	–	–	–
Qais Ahmad	1	–	–	–	–	–	–	–	–
Rahmanullah Gurbaz	15	15	1	127	582	41.57	3	2	9/2
Rahmat Shah	88	84	3	114	3083	38.06	5	22	20
Rashid Khan	86	68	12	60*	1134	20.25	–	5	27
Riaz Hassan	3	3	–	50	86	28.66	–	1	–
Shahidullah	1	1	–	1	1	1.00	–	–	–
Sharafuddin Ashraf	19	11	4	21	66	9.42	–	–	5
Usman Ghani	17	17	–	118	435	25.58	1	2	3
Yamin Ahmadzai	9	5	2	5	9	3.00	–	–	4

AFGHANISTAN – BOWLING

	O	M	R	W	Avge	Best	4wI	R/Over
Azmatullah Omarzai	41	0	179	4	44.75	1-17	–	4.36
Fareed Ahmad	74	4	343	15	22.86	3-56	–	4.63
Fazalhaq Farooqi	79.1	5	403	17	23.70	4-49	2	5.09
Gulbadin Naib	420.3	11	2279	64	35.60	6-43	3	5.41
Hashmatullah Shahidi	3	0	25	0	–	–	–	8.33
Mohammad Nabi	1079.3	43	4628	144	32.13	4-30	4	4.28
Mujeeb Zadran	481.3	31	1956	79	24.75	5-50	4	4.06
Najibullah Zadran	5	0	30	0	–	–	–	6.00
Naveen-ul-Haq	61.3	1	356	14	25.42	4-42	1	5.78
Noor Ahmad	4	0	32	0	–	–	–	8.00
Qais Ahmad	7.4	0	32	3	10.66	3-32	–	4.17
Rahmat Shah	88.2	2	514	14	36.71	5-32	1	5.81

	O	M	R	W	Avge	Best	4wI	R/Over
Rashid Khan	724.5	28	3024	163	18.55	7-18	10	4.17
Shahidullah	3	0	16	0	–	–	–	5.33
Sharafuddin Ashraf	141.2	4	605	13	46.53	3-29	–	4.28
Usman Ghani	6.2	0	34	1	34.00	1-21	–	5.36
Yamin Ahmadzai	56.4	4	304	7	43.42	2-34	–	5.36

ASSOCIATES – BATTING AND FIELDING

	M	I	NO	HS	Runs	Avge	100	50	Ct/St
C.N.Ackermann (Neth)	4	3	–	81	96	32.00	–	1	1
J.H.Davey (Scot)	31	28	6	64	497	22.59	–	2	10
B.F.W.de Leede (Neth)	23	22	–	89	480	21.81	–	2	11
B.D.Glover (Neth)	8	6	4	18	29	14.50	–	–	3
I.G.Holland (USA)	8	8	–	75	244	30.50	–	2	3
M.A.Jones (Scot)	12	12	–	87	354	29.50	–	3	4
F.J.Klaassen (Neth)	14	11	4	13	56	8.00	–	–	4
S.Snater (Neth)	4	4	1	17*	33	11.00	–	–	5
T.van der Gugten (Neth)	8	4	–	49	54	13.50	–	–	–
R.E.van der Merwe (Neth) †	3	1	–	57	57	57.00	–	1	3
P.A.van Meekeren (Neth)	8	6	4	15*	38	19.00	–	–	1
M.R.J.Watt (Scot)	54	34	11	37*	371	16.13	–	–	13
B.T.J.Wheal (Scot)	13	7	3	14	16	4.00	–	–	3
D.Wiese (Nam) ‡	9	9	1	67	228	28.50	–	1	2

ASSOCIATES – BOWLING

	O	M	R	W	Avge	Best	4wI	R/Over
C.N.Ackermann	19	0	81	2	40.50	1-10	–	4.26
J.H.Davey	216.5	18	1082	49	22.08	6-28	3	4.99
B.F.W.de Leede	70.5	1	438	9	48.66	3-50	–	6.18
B.D.Glover	66	2	382	8	47.75	3-43	–	5.78
I.G.Holland	45.5	2	209	7	29.85	3-11	–	4.56
F.J.Klaassen	129	11	514	25	20.56	3-23	–	3.98
S.Snater	25	1	188	2	94.00	1-41	–	7.52
T.van der Gugten	54	7	195	12	16.25	5-24	1	3.61
R.E.van der Merwe	20	0	124	2	62.00	1-27	–	6.20
P.A.van Meekeren	56	5	277	9	30.77	2-28	–	4.94
M.R.J.Watt	468.4	42	1894	79	23.97	5-33	4	4.04
B.T.J.Wheal	114.3	9	508	23	22.08	3-34	–	4.43
D.Wiese	73.5	3	370	6	61.66	2-22	–	5.01

† *R.E.van der Merwe has also made 13 appearances for South Africa (see above).*
‡ *D.Wiese has also made 6 appearances for South Africa (see above).*

LIMITED-OVERS INTERNATIONALS RESULTS

1970-71 to 7 March 2023

This chart excludes all matches involving multinational teams.

	Opponents	Matches	E	A	SA	WI	NZ	I	P	SL	Z	B	Ire	Afg	Ass	Tied	NR
England	Australia	155	63	87	–	–	–	–	–	–	–	–	–	–	–	2	3
	South Africa	69	30	–	33	–	–	–	–	–	–	–	–	–	–	1	5
	West Indies	102	52	–	–	44	–	–	–	–	–	–	–	–	–	–	6
	New Zealand	91	41	–	–	–	43	–	–	–	–	–	–	–	–	3	4
	India	106	44	–	–	–	–	57	–	–	–	–	–	–	–	2	3
	Pakistan	91	56	–	–	–	–	–	32	–	–	–	–	–	–	–	3
	Sri Lanka	78	38	–	–	–	–	–	–	36	–	–	–	–	–	1	3
	Zimbabwe	30	21	–	–	–	–	–	–	–	8	–	–	–	–	–	1
	Bangladesh	24	19	–	–	–	–	–	–	–	–	5	–	–	–	–	1
	Ireland	13	10	–	–	–	–	–	–	–	–	–	2	–	–	–	1
	Afghanistan	2	2	–	–	–	–	–	–	–	–	–	–	0	–	–	–
	Associates	18	16	–	–	–	–	–	–	–	–	–	–	–	1	–	1
Australia	South Africa	103	–	48	51	–	–	–	–	–	–	–	–	–	–	3	1
	West Indies	143	–	76	–	61	–	–	–	–	–	–	–	–	–	3	3
	New Zealand	141	–	95	–	–	39	–	–	–	–	–	–	–	–	–	7
	India	143	–	80	–	–	–	53	–	–	–	–	–	–	–	–	10
	Pakistan	107	–	69	–	–	–	–	34	–	–	–	–	–	–	1	3
	Sri Lanka	102	–	63	–	–	–	–	–	35	–	–	–	–	–	–	4
	Zimbabwe	33	–	29	–	–	–	–	–	–	3	–	–	–	–	–	1
	Bangladesh	21	–	19	–	–	–	–	–	–	–	1	–	–	–	–	1
	Ireland	5	–	4	–	–	–	–	–	–	–	–	0	–	–	–	1
	Afghanistan	3	–	3	–	–	–	–	–	–	–	–	–	0	–	–	–
	Associates	16	–	16	–	–	–	–	–	–	–	–	–	–	0	–	–
S Africa	West Indies	62	–	–	44	15	–	–	–	–	–	–	–	–	–	1	2
	New Zealand	71	–	–	41	–	25	–	–	–	–	–	–	–	–	–	5
	India	90	–	–	50	–	–	37	–	–	–	–	–	–	–	–	3
	Pakistan	82	–	–	51	–	–	–	30	–	–	–	–	–	–	–	1
	Sri Lanka	80	–	–	45	–	–	–	–	33	–	–	–	–	–	1	1
	Zimbabwe	41	–	–	38	–	–	–	–	–	2	–	–	–	–	–	1
	Bangladesh	24	–	–	18	–	–	–	–	–	–	6	–	–	–	–	–
	Ireland	8	–	–	6	–	–	–	–	–	–	–	1	–	–	–	1
	Afghanistan	1	–	–	1	–	–	–	–	–	–	–	–	0	–	–	–
	Associates	19	–	–	18	–	–	–	–	–	–	–	–	–	0	–	1
W Indies	New Zealand	68	–	–	–	31	30	–	–	–	–	–	–	–	–	–	7
	India	139	–	–	–	63	–	70	–	–	–	–	–	–	–	2	4
	Pakistan	137	–	–	–	71	–	–	63	–	–	–	–	–	–	3	–
	Sri Lanka	63	–	–	–	31	–	–	–	29	–	–	–	–	–	–	3
	Zimbabwe	48	–	–	–	36	–	–	–	–	10	–	–	–	–	1	1
	Bangladesh	44	–	–	–	21	–	–	–	–	–	21	–	–	–	–	2
	Ireland	15	–	–	–	11	–	–	–	–	–	–	3	–	–	–	1
	Afghanistan	9	–	–	–	5	–	–	–	–	–	–	–	3	–	–	1
	Associates	22	–	–	–	21	–	–	–	–	–	–	–	–	1	–	–
N Zealand	India	116	–	–	–	–	50	58	–	–	–	–	–	–	–	1	7
	Pakistan	110	–	–	–	–	50	–	56	–	–	–	–	–	–	1	3
	Sri Lanka	99	–	–	–	–	49	–	–	41	–	–	–	–	–	1	8
	Zimbabwe	38	–	–	–	–	27	–	–	–	9	–	–	–	–	1	1
	Bangladesh	38	–	–	–	–	28	–	–	–	–	10	–	–	–	–	–
	Ireland	7	–	–	–	–	7	–	–	–	–	–	0	–	–	–	–
	Afghanistan	2	–	–	–	–	2	–	–	–	–	–	–	0	–	–	–
	Associates	16	–	–	–	–	16	–	–	–	–	–	–	–	0	–	–
India	Pakistan	132	–	–	–	–	–	55	73	–	–	–	–	–	–	–	4
	Sri Lanka	165	–	–	–	–	–	96	–	57	–	–	–	–	–	1	11
	Zimbabwe	66	–	–	–	–	–	54	–	–	10	–	–	–	–	2	–
	Bangladesh	39	–	–	–	–	–	31	–	–	–	7	–	–	–	–	1

	Opponents	Matches	Won													Tied	NR
			E	A	SA	WI	NZ	I	P	SL	Z	B	Ire	Afg	Ass		
	Ireland	3	–	–	–	–	–	3	–	–	–	–	0	–	–	–	–
	Afghanistan	3	–	–	–	–	–	2	–	–	–	–	–	–	–	1	–
	Associates	24	–	–	–	–	–	22	–	–	–	–	–	–	2	–	–
Pakistan	Sri Lanka	155	–	–	–	–	–	–	92	58	–	–	–	–	–	1	4
	Zimbabwe	62	–	–	–	–	–	–	54	–	4	–	–	–	–	2	2
	Bangladesh	37	–	–	–	–	–	–	32	–	–	5	–	–	–	–	–
	Ireland	7	–	–	–	–	–	–	5	–	–	–	1	–	–	–	1
	Afghanistan	4	–	–	–	–	–	–	4	–	–	–	–	0	–	–	–
	Associates	24	–	–	–	–	–	–	24	–	–	–	–	–	0	–	–
Sri Lanka	Zimbabwe	60	–	–	–	–	–	–	–	46	12	–	–	–	–	–	2
	Bangladesh	51	–	–	–	–	–	–	–	40	–	9	–	–	–	–	2
	Ireland	4	–	–	–	–	–	–	–	2	–	–	0	–	–	–	2
	Afghanistan	7	–	–	–	–	–	–	–	4	–	–	–	2	–	–	1
	Associates	17	–	–	–	–	–	–	–	16	–	–	–	–	1	–	–
Zimbabwe	Bangladesh	81	–	–	–	–	–	–	–	–	30	51	–	–	–	–	–
	Ireland	19	–	–	–	–	–	–	–	–	8	–	8	–	–	1	2
	Afghanistan	28	–	–	–	–	–	–	–	–	10	–	–	18	–	–	–
	Associates	50	–	–	–	–	–	–	–	–	38	–	–	–	9	1	2
Bangladesh	Ireland	10	–	–	–	–	–	–	–	–	–	7	2	–	–	–	1
	Afghanistan	11	–	–	–	–	–	–	–	–	–	7	–	4	–	–	–
	Associates	26	–	–	–	–	–	–	–	–	–	18	–	–	8	–	–
Ireland	Afghanistan	30	–	–	–	–	–	–	–	–	–	–	13	16	–	–	1
	Associates	61	–	–	–	–	–	–	–	–	–	–	45	–	12	2	2
Afghanistan	Associates	41	–	–	–	–	–	–	–	–	–	–	–	27	13	–	1
Associates	Associates	259	–	–	–	–	–	–	–	–	–	–	–	–	249	3	7
		4521	392	589	396	410	366	538	499	399	144	147	75	70	296	42	159

MERIT TABLE OF ALL L-O INTERNATIONALS

	Matches	Won	Lost	Tied	No Result	% Won (exc NR)
South Africa	650	396	227	6	21	62.95
Australia	972	589	340	9	34	62.79
India	1026	538	436	9	43	54.73
Pakistan	948	499	420	9	20	53.77
England	779	392	348	9	30	52.33
Afghanistan	141	70	66	1	4	51.09
West Indies	852	410	402	10	30	49.87
New Zealand	797	366	382	7	42	48.47
Sri Lanka	881	399	438	5	39	47.38
Ireland	182	75	93	3	11	43.85
Bangladesh	406	147	252	–	7	36.84
Zimbabwe	556	144	391	8	13	26.51
Associate Members (v Full*)	334	47	277	3	7	14.96

* Results of games between two Associate Members and those involving multi-national sides are excluded from this list; Associate Members have participated in 593 LOIs, 259 LOIs being between Associate Members.

TEAM RECORDS

HIGHEST TOTALS
† Batting Second

498-4	(50 overs)	England v Netherlands	Amstelveen	2022
481-6	(50 overs)	England v Australia	Nottingham	2018
444-3	(50 overs)	England v Pakistan	Nottingham	2016

443-9	(50 overs)	Sri Lanka v Netherlands	Amstelveen	2006
439-2	(50 overs)	South Africa v West Indies	Johannesburg	2014-15
438-9†	(49.5 overs)	South Africa v Australia	Johannesburg	2005-06
438-4	(50 overs)	South Africa v India	Mumbai	2015-16
434-4	(50 overs)	Australia v South Africa	Johannesburg	2005-06
418-5	(50 overs)	South Africa v Zimbabwe	Potchefstroom	2006-07
418-5	(50 overs)	India v West Indies	Indore	2011-12
418-6	(50 overs)	England v West Indies	St George's	2018-19
417-6	(50 overs)	Australia v Afghanistan	Perth	2014-15
414-7	(50 overs)	India v Sri Lanka	Rajkot	2009-10
413-5	(50 overs)	India v Bermuda	Port of Spain	2006-07
411-8†	(50 overs)	Sri Lanka v India	Rajkot	2009-10
411-4	(50 overs)	South Africa v Ireland	Canberra	2014-15
409-8	(50 overs)	India v Bangladesh	Chattogram	2022-23
408-5	(50 overs)	South Africa v West Indies	Sydney	2014-15
408-9	(50 overs)	England v New Zealand	Birmingham	2015
404-5	(50 overs)	India v Sri Lanka	Kolkata	2014-15
402-2	(50 overs)	New Zealand v Ireland	Aberdeen	2008
401-3	(50 overs)	India v South Africa	Gwalior	2009-10
399-6	(50 overs)	South Africa v Zimbabwe	Benoni	2010-11
399-9	(50 overs)	England v South Africa	Bloemfontein	2015-16
399-1	(50 overs)	Pakistan v Zimbabwe	Bulawayo	2018
398-5	(50 overs)	Sri Lanka v Kenya	Kandy	1995-96
398-5	(50 overs)	New Zealand v England	The Oval	2015
397-5	(44 overs)	New Zealand v Zimbabwe	Bulawayo	2005
397-6	(50 overs)	England v Afghanistan	Manchester	2019
393-6	(50 overs)	New Zealand v West Indies	Wellington	2014-15
392-6	(50 overs)	South Africa v Pakistan	Pretoria	2006-07
392-4	(50 overs)	India v New Zealand	Christchurch	2008-09
392-4	(50 overs)	India v Sri Lanka	Mohali	2017-18
391-4	(50 overs)	England v Bangladesh	Nottingham	2005
390-5	(50 overs)	India v Sri Lanka	Karyavattom	2022-23
389	(48 overs)	West Indies v England	St George's	2018-19
389-4	(50 overs)	Australia v India	Sydney	2020-21
387-5	(50 overs)	India v England	Rajkot	2008-09
387-5	(50 overs)	India v West Indies	Visakhapatnam	2019-20
386-6	(50 overs)	England v Bangladesh	Cardiff	2019
385-7	(50 overs)	Pakistan v Bangladesh	Dambulla	2010
385-9	(50 overs)	India v New Zealand	Indore	2022-23
384-6	(50 overs)	South Africa v Sri Lanka	Centurion	2016-17
383-6	(50 overs)	India v Australia	Bangalore	2013-14
381-6	(50 overs)	India v England	Cuttack	2016-17
381-3	(50 overs)	West Indies v Ireland	Dublin	2019
381-5	(50 overs)	Australia v Bangladesh	Nottingham	2019

The highest score for Ireland is 359-9 (v NZ, Dublin, 2022), for Zimbabwe is 351-7 (v Kenya, Mombasa, 2008-09), for Afghanistan is 338 (v Ire, Greater Noida, 2016-17) and for Bangladesh is 333-8 (v A, Nottingham, 2019).

HIGHEST MATCH AGGREGATES

872-13	(99.5 overs)	South Africa v Australia	Johannesburg	2005-06
825-15	(100 overs)	India v Sri Lanka	Rajkot	2009-10
807-16	(98 overs)	West Indies v England	St George's	2018-19

LARGEST RUNS MARGINS OF VICTORY

317 runs	India beat Sri Lanka	Karyavattom	2022-23
290 runs	New Zealand beat Ireland	Aberdeen	2008
275 runs	Australia beat Afghanistan	Perth	2014-15

272 runs	South Africa beat Zimbabwe	Benoni	2010-11
258 runs	South Africa beat Sri Lanka	Paarl	2011-12
257 runs	India beat Bermuda	Port of Spain	2006-07
257 runs	South Africa beat West Indies	Sydney	2014-15
256 runs	Australia beat Namibia	Potchefstroom	2002-03
256 runs	India beat Hong Kong	Karachi	2008
255 runs	Pakistan beat Ireland	Dublin	2016
245 runs	Sri Lanka beat India	Sharjah	2000-01
244 runs	Pakistan beat Zimbabwe	Bulawayo	2018
243 runs	Sri Lanka beat Bermuda	Port of Spain	2006-07
242 runs	England beat Australia	Nottingham	2018
234 runs	Sri Lanka beat Pakistan	Lahore	2008-09
233 runs	Pakistan beat Bangladesh	Dhaka	1999-00
232 runs	Australia beat Sri Lanka	Adelaide	1984-85
232 runs	England beat Netherlands	Amstelveen	2022
231 runs	South Africa beat Netherlands	Mohali	2010-11
229 runs	Australia beat Netherlands	Basseterre	2006-07
227 runs	India beat Bangladesh	Chattogram	2022-23
226 runs	Ireland beat UAE	Harare	2017-18

LOWEST TOTALS (Excluding reduced innings)

35	(18.0 overs)	Zimbabwe v Sri Lanka	Harare	2003-04
35	(12.0 overs)	USA v Nepal	Kirtipur	2019-20
36	(18.4 overs)	Canada v Sri Lanka	Paarl	2002-03
38	(15.4 overs)	Zimbabwe v Sri Lanka	Colombo (SSC)	2001-02
43	(19.5 overs)	Pakistan v West Indies	Cape Town	1992-93
43	(20.1 overs)	Sri Lanka v South Africa	Paarl	2011-12
44	(24.5 overs)	Zimbabwe v Bangladesh	Chittagong	2009-10
45	(40.3 overs)	Canada v England	Manchester	1979
45	(14.0 overs)	Namibia v Australia	Potchefstroom	2002-03
54	(26.3 overs)	India v Sri Lanka	Sharjah	2000-01
54	(23.2 overs)	West Indies v South Africa	Cape Town	2003-04
54	(13.5 overs)	Zimbabwe v Afghanistan	Harare	2016-17
55	(28.3 overs)	Sri Lanka v West Indies	Sharjah	1986-87
58	(18.5 overs)	Bangladesh v West Indies	Dhaka	2010-11
58	(17.4 overs)	Bangladesh v India	Dhaka	2014
58	(16.1 overs)	Afghanistan v Zimbabwe	Sharjah	2015-16
61	(22.0 overs)	West Indies v Bangladesh	Chittagong	2011-12
63	(25.5 overs)	India v Australia	Sydney	1980-81
63	(18.3 overs)	Afghanistan v Scotland	Abu Dhabi	2014-15
64	(35.5 overs)	New Zealand v Pakistan	Sharjah	1985-86
65	(24.0 overs)	USA v Australia	Southampton	2004
65	(24.3 overs)	Zimbabwe v India	Harare	2005
67	(31.0 overs)	Zimbabwe v Sri Lanka	Harare	2008-09
67	(24.4 overs)	Canada v Netherlands	King City	2013
67	(24.0 overs)	Sri Lanka v England	Manchester	2014
67	(25.1 overs)	Zimbabwe v Pakistan	Bulawayo	2018
68	(31.3 overs)	Scotland v West Indies	Leicester	1999
69	(28.0 overs)	South Africa v Australia	Sydney	1993-94
69	(22.5 overs)	Zimbabwe v Kenya	Harare	2005-06
69	(23.5 overs)	Kenya v New Zealand	Chennai	2010-11
70	(25.2 overs)	Australia v England	Birmingham	1977
70	(26.3 overs)	Australia v New Zealand	Adelaide	1985-86
70	(23.5 overs)	West Indies v Australia	Perth	2012-13
70	(24.4 overs)	Bangladesh v West Indies	St George's	2014
70	(24.4 overs)	Zimbabwe v Sri Lanka	Pallekele	2021-22

The lowest for England is 86 (v A, Manchester, 2001) and for Ireland is 77 (v SL, St George's, 2007).

LOWEST MATCH AGGREGATES

71-12	(17.2 overs)	USA (35) v Nepal (36-2)	Kirtipur	2019-20
73-11	(23.2 overs)	Canada (36) v Sri Lanka (37-1)	Paarl	2002-03
75-11	(27.2 overs)	Zimbabwe (35) v Sri Lanka (40-1)	Harare	2003-04
78-11	(20.0 overs)	Zimbabwe (38) v Sri Lanka (40-1)	Colombo (SSC)	2001-02

BATTING RECORDS
6000 RUNS IN A CAREER

		LOI	I	NO	HS	Runs	Avge	100	50
S.R.Tendulkar	I	463	452	41	200*	**18426**	44.83	49	96
K.C.Sangakkara	SL/Asia/ICC	404	380	41	169	**14234**	41.98	25	93
R.T.Ponting	A/ICC	375	365	39	164	**13704**	42.03	30	82
S.T.Jayasuriya	SL/Asia	445	433	18	189	**13430**	32.36	28	68
V.Kohli	I	271	262	40	183	**12809**	57.69	46	64
D.P.M.D.Jayawardena	SL/Asia	448	418	39	144	**12650**	33.37	19	77
Inzamam-ul-Haq	P/Asia	378	350	53	137*	**11739**	39.52	10	83
J.H.Kallis	SA/Afr/ICC	328	314	53	139	**11579**	44.36	17	86
S.C.Ganguly	I/Asia	311	300	23	183	**11363**	41.02	22	72
R.S.Dravid	I/Asia/ICC	344	318	40	153	**10889**	39.16	12	83
M.S.Dhoni	I/Asia	350	297	84	183*	**10773**	50.57	10	73
C.H.Gayle	WI/ICC	301	294	17	215	**10480**	37.83	25	54
B.C.Lara	WI/ICC	299	289	32	169	**10405**	40.48	19	63
T.M.Dilshan	SL	330	303	41	161*	**10290**	39.27	22	47
R.G.Sharma	I	241	234	32	264	**9782**	48.91	30	48
Mohammad Yousuf	P/Asia	288	272	40	141*	**9720**	41.71	15	64
A.C.Gilchrist	A/ICC	287	279	11	172	**9619**	35.89	16	55
A.B.de Villiers	SA/Afr	228	218	39	176	**9577**	53.50	25	53
M.Azharuddin	I	334	308	54	153*	**9378**	36.92	7	58
P.A.de Silva	SL	308	296	30	145	**9284**	34.90	11	64
Saeed Anwar	P	247	244	19	194	**8824**	39.21	20	43
S.Chanderpaul	WI	268	251	40	150	**8778**	41.60	11	59
Yuvraj Singh	I/Asia	304	278	40	150	**8701**	36.55	14	52
D.L.Haynes	WI	238	237	28	152*	**8648**	41.37	17	57
L.R.P.L.Taylor	NZ	236	220	39	181*	**8607**	47.55	21	51
M.S.Atapattu	SL	268	259	32	132*	**8529**	37.57	11	59
M.E.Waugh	A	244	236	20	173	**8500**	39.35	18	50
V.Sehwag	I/Asia/ICC	251	245	9	219	**8273**	35.05	15	38
Tamim Iqbal	B	234	232	11	158	**8143**	36.84	14	55
H.M.Amla	SA	181	178	14	159	**8113**	49.46	27	39
H.H.Gibbs	SA	248	240	16	175	**8094**	36.13	21	37
Shahid Afridi	P/Asia/ICC	398	369	27	124	**8064**	23.57	6	39
S.P.Fleming	NZ/ICC	280	269	21	134*	**8037**	32.40	8	49
M.J.Clarke	A	245	223	44	130	**7981**	44.58	8	58
E.J.G.Morgan	E/Ire	248	230	34	148	**7701**	39.29	14	47
S.R.Waugh	A	325	288	58	120*	**7569**	32.90	3	45
Shoaib Malik	P	287	258	40	143	**7534**	34.55	9	44
A.Ranatunga	SL	269	255	47	131*	**7456**	35.84	4	49
Javed Miandad	P	233	218	41	119*	**7381**	41.70	8	50
M.J.Guptill	NZ	198	195	19	237*	**7346**	41.73	18	39
Younus Khan	P	265	255	23	144	**7249**	31.24	7	48
Salim Malik	P	283	256	38	102	**7170**	32.88	5	47
N.J.Astle	NZ	223	217	14	145*	**7090**	34.92	16	41
G.C.Smith	SA/Afr	197	194	10	141	**6989**	37.98	10	47

Shakib Al Hasan	B	227	215	30	134*	**6976**	37.70	9	52
W.U.Tharanga	SL/Asia	235	223	17	174*	**6951**	33.74	15	37
M.G.Bevan	A	232	196	67	108*	**6912**	53.58	6	46
Mushfiqur Rahim	B	242	227	37	144	**6901**	36.32	8	43
G.Kirsten	SA	185	185	19	188*	**6798**	40.95	13	45
S.Dhawan	I	167	164	10	143	**6793**	44.11	17	39
A.Flower	Z	213	208	16	145	**6786**	35.34	4	55
I.V.A.Richards	WI	187	167	24	189*	**6721**	47.00	11	45
B.R.M.Taylor	Z	205	203	15	145*	**6684**	35.55	11	39
Mohammad Hafeez	P	218	216	15	140*	**6614**	32.90	11	38
G.W.Flower	Z	221	214	18	142*	**6571**	33.52	6	40
Ijaz Ahmed	P	250	232	29	139*	**6564**	32.33	10	37
K.S.Williamson	NZ	161	153	16	148	**6554**	47.83	13	42
A.R.Border	A	273	252	39	127*	**6524**	30.62	3	39
R.B.Richardson	WI	224	217	30	122	**6248**	33.41	5	44
J.E.Root	E	158	147	23	133*	**6207**	50.05	16	36
M.L.Hayden	A/ICC	161	155	15	181*	**6133**	43.80	10	36
B.B.McCullum	NZ	260	228	28	166	**6083**	30.41	5	32
D.M.Jones	A	164	161	25	145	**6068**	44.61	7	46
D.A.Warner	A	141	139	6	179	**6007**	45.16	19	27

The most runs for Ireland is 5230 by P.R.Stirling (138 innings) and for Afghanistan 3083 by Rahmat Shah (84 innings).

HIGHEST INDIVIDUAL INNINGS

264	R.G.Sharma	India v Sri Lanka	Kolkata	2014-15
237*	M.J.Guptill	New Zealand v West Indies	Wellington	2014-15
219	V.Sehwag	India v West Indies	Indore	2011-12
215	C.H.Gayle	West Indies v Zimbabwe	Canberra	2014-15
210*	Fakhar Zaman	Pakistan v Zimbabwe	Bulawayo	2018
210	Ishan Kishan	India v Bangladesh	Chattogram	2022-23
209	R.G.Sharma	India v Australia	Bangalore	2013-14
208*	R.G.Sharma	India v Sri Lanka	Mohali	2017-18
208	S.Gill	India v New Zealand	Hyderabad	2022-23
200*	S.R.Tendulkar	India v South Africa	Gwalior	2009-10
194*	C.K.Coventry	Zimbabwe v Bangladesh	Bulawayo	2009
194	Saeed Anwar	Pakistan v India	Madras	1996-97
193	Fakhar Zaman	Pakistan v South Africa	Johannesburg	2020-21
189*	I.V.A.Richards	West Indies v England	Manchester	1984
189*	M.J.Guptill	New Zealand v England	Southampton	2013
189	S.T.Jayasuriya	Sri Lanka v India	Sharjah	2000-01
188*	G.Kirsten	South Africa v UAE	Rawalpindi	1995-96
186*	S.R.Tendulkar	India v New Zealand	Hyderabad	1999-00
185*	S.R.Watson	Australia v Bangladesh	Dhaka	2010-11
185	F.du Plessis	South Africa v Sri Lanka	Cape Town	2016-17
183*	M.S.Dhoni	India v Sri Lanka	Jaipur	2005-06
183	S.C.Ganguly	India v Sri Lanka	Taunton	1999
183	V.Kohli	India v Pakistan	Dhaka	2011-12
181*	M.L.Hayden	Australia v New Zealand	Hamilton	2006-07
181*	L.R.P.L.Taylor	New Zealand v England	Dunedin	2017-18
181	I.V.A.Richards	West Indies v Sri Lanka	Karachi	1987-88
180*	M.J.Guptill	New Zealand v South Africa	Hamilton	2016-17
180	J.J.Roy	England v Australia	Melbourne	2017-18
179	D.A.Warner	Australia v Pakistan	Adelaide	2016-17
179	J.D.Campbell	West Indies v Ireland	Dublin	2019
178*	H.Masakadza	Zimbabwe v Kenya	Harare	2009-10
178	D.A.Warner	Australia v Afghanistan	Perth	2014-15

178	Q.de Kock	South Africa v Australia	Centurion	2016-17
177*	J.N.Malan	South Africa v Ireland	Dublin	2021
177	P.R.Stirling	Ireland v Canada	Toronto	2010
176*	E.Lewis	West Indies v England	The Oval	2017
176	A.B.de Villiers	South Africa v Bangladesh	Paarl	2017-18
176	Liton Das	Bangladesh v Zimbabwe	Sylhet	2019-20
175*	Kapil Dev	India v Zimbabwe	Tunbridge Wells	1983
175	H.H.Gibbs	South Africa v Australia	Johannesburg	2005-06
175	S.R.Tendulkar	India v Australia	Hyderabad	2009-10
175	V.Sehwag	India v Bangladesh	Dhaka	2010-11
175	C.S.MacLeod	Scotland v Canada	Christchurch	2013-14
174*	W.U.Tharanga	Sri Lanka v India	Kingston	2013
173*	J.S.Malhotra	USA v PNG	Al Amerat	2021
173	M.E.Waugh	Australia v West Indies	Melbourne	2000-01
173	D.A.Warner	Australia v South Africa	Cape Town	2016-17
172*	C.B.Wishart	Zimbabwe v Namibia	Harare	2002-03
172	A.C.Gilchrist	Australia v Zimbabwe	Hobart	2003-04
172	L.Vincent	New Zealand v Zimbabwe	Bulawayo	2005
171*	G.M.Turner	New Zealand v East Africa	Birmingham	1975
171*	R.G.Sharma	India v Australia	Perth	2015-16
171	A.D.Hales	England v Pakistan	Nottingham	2016
170*	L.Ronchi	New Zealand v Sri Lanka	Dunedin	2014-15
170	S.D.Hope	West Indies v Ireland	Dublin	2019

The highest for Afghanistan is 162 by Ibrahim Zadran (v SL, Pallekele, 2022-23).

HUNDRED ON DEBUT

D.L.Amiss	103	England v Australia	Manchester	1972
D.L.Haynes	148	West Indies v Australia	St John's	1977-78
A.Flower	115*	Zimbabwe v Sri Lanka	New Plymouth	1991-92
Salim Elahi	102*	Pakistan v Sri Lanka	Gujranwala	1995-96
M.J.Guptill	122*	New Zealand v West Indies	Auckland	2008-09
C.A.Ingram	124	South Africa v Zimbabwe	Bloemfontein	2010-11
R.J.Nicol	108*	New Zealand v Zimbabwe	Harare	2011-12
P.J.Hughes	112	Australia v Sri Lanka	Melbourne	2012-13
M.J.Lumb	106	England v West Indies	North Sound	2013-14
M.S.Chapman	124*	Hong Kong v UAE	Dubai	2015-16
K.L.Rahul	100*	India v Zimbabwe	Harare	2016
T.Bavuma	113	South Africa v Ireland	Benoni	2016-17
Imam-ul-Haq	100	Pakistan v Sri Lanka	Abu Dhabi	2017-18
R.R.Hendricks	102	South Africa v Sri Lanka	Pallekele	2018
Abid Ali	112	Pakistan v Australia	Dubai, DSC	2018-19
Rahmanullah Gurbaz	127	Afghanistan v Ireland	Abu Dhabi	2020-21

Shahid Afridi scored 102 for P v SL, Nairobi, 1996-97, in his second match having not batted in his first.

Fastest 100	31 balls	A.B.de Villiers (149)	SA v WI	Johannesburg	2014-15
Fastest 50	16 balls	A.B.de Villiers (149)	SA v WI	Johannesburg	2014-15

16 HUNDREDS

		Inns	100	E	A	SA	WI	NZ	I	P	SL	Z	B	Ire	Afg	Ass
S.R.Tendulkar	I	452	**49**	2	9	5	4	5	–	5	8	5	1	–	–	5
V.Kohli	I	262	**46**	3	8	4	9	5	–	2	10	1	4	–	–	–
R.G.Sharma	I	234	**30**	2	8	3	3	2	–	2	6	1	3	–	–	–
R.T.Ponting	A	365	**30***	5	–	2	2	6	6	1	4	1	–	–	–	1
S.T.Jayasuriya	SL	433	**28**	4	2	–	1	5	7	3	–	1	4	–	–	1
H.M.Amla	SA	178	**27**	2	1	–	5	2	2	3	5	3	2	1	–	1

297

A.B.de Villiers	SA	218	**25**	2	1	—	5	1	6	3	2	3	1	—	—	1
C.H.Gayle	WI	294	**25**	4	—	3	—	2	4	3	1	3	1	—	—	4
K.C.Sangakkara	SL	380	**25**	4	2	2	—	2	6	2	—	5	—	—	2
S.C.Ganguly	I	300	**22**	1	1	3	—	3	—	2	4	3	1	—	4
T.M.Dilshan	SL	303	**22**	2	1	2	—	3	4	2	—	2	4	—	2
L.R.P.L.Taylor	NZ	220	**21**	5	2	1	1	—	3	3	2	2	2	—	—
H.H.Gibbs	SA	240	**21**	2	3	—	5	2	2	2	1	2	1	—	1
Saeed Anwar	P	244	**20**	—	1	—	2	4	4	—	7	2	—	—
D.A.Warner	A	139	**19**	2	—	4	—	2	3	3	3	—	1	—	1
B.C.Lara	WI	289	**19**	1	3	3	—	2	—	5	2	2	1	1	—	1
D.P.M.D.Jayawardena	SL	418	**19***	5	—	1	3	4	2	—	—	1	1	1	—	1
M.J.Guptill	NZ	195	**18**	2	1	2	2	—	1	1	2	2	3	1	—	1
M.E.Waugh	A	236	**18**	1	—	2	3	3	3	1	1	3	—	—	1
Babar Azam	P	93	**17**	2	3	1	5	1	—	3	2	—	—
Q.de Kock	SA	137	**17**	3	2	—	—	6	1	3	—	1	1	1	—	—
A.J.Finch	A	142	**17**	7	—	2	—	4	2	1	—	—	—	1
S.Dhawan	I	164	**17**	—	4	3	2	—	1	4	1	—	1	—	1
D.L.Haynes	WI	237	**17**	2	6	—	2	2	4	1	—	—	—	1
J.H.Kallis	SA	314	**17**	1	1	—	4	3	2	1	3	1	—	—	1
J.E.Root	E	147	**16**	—	—	2	4	3	3	1	2	—	1	—	1
N.J.Astle	NZ	217	**16**	2	1	1	1	—	5	2	—	3	—	—	1
A.C.Gilchrist	A	279	**16***	2	—	2	—	2	2	1	1	6	1	—	—	1

* = Includes hundred scored against multi-national side.
The most for Zimbabwe is 11 by B.R.M.Taylor (203 innings), for Bangladesh 14 by Tamim Iqbal (232), for Ireland 13 by P.R.Stirling (138), and for Afghanistan 6 by Mohammad Shahzad (84).

HIGHEST PARTNERSHIP FOR EACH WICKET

1st	365	J.D.Campbell/S.D.Hope	West Indies v Ireland	Dublin	2019
2nd	372	C.H.Gayle/M.N.Samuels	West Indies v Zimbabwe	Canberra	2014-15
3rd	258	D.M.Bravo/D.Ramdin	West Indies v Bangladesh	Basseterre	2014
4th	275*	M.Azharuddin/A.Jadeja	India v Zimbabwe	Cuttack	1997-98
5th	256*	D.A.Miller/J.P.Duminy	South Africa v Zimbabwe	Hamilton	2014-15
6th	267*	G.D.Elliott/L.Ronchi	New Zealand v Sri Lanka	Dunedin	2014-15
7th	177	J.C.Buttler/A.U.Rashid	England v New Zealand	Birmingham	2015
8th	138*	J.M.Kemp/A.J.Hall	South Africa v India	Cape Town	2006-07
9th	132	A.D.Mathews/S.L.Malinga	Sri Lanka v Australia	Melbourne	2010-11
10th	106*	I.V.A.Richards/M.A.Holding	West Indies v England	Manchester	1984

BOWLING RECORDS
200 WICKETS IN A CAREER

		LOI	Balls	R	W	Avge	Best	5w	R/Over
M.Muralitharan	SL/Asia/ICC	350	18811	12326	**534**	23.08	7-30	10	3.93
Wasim Akram	P	356	18186	11812	**502**	23.52	5-15	6	3.89
Waqar Younis	P	262	12698	9919	**416**	23.84	7-36	13	4.68
W.P.J.U.C.Vaas	SL/Asia	322	15775	11014	**400**	27.53	8-19	4	4.18
Shahid Afridi	P/Asia/ICC	398	17620	13632	**395**	34.51	7-12	9	4.62
S.M.Pollock	SA/Afr/ICC	303	15712	9631	**393**	24.50	6-35	5	3.67
G.D.McGrath	A/ICC	250	12970	8391	**381**	22.02	7-15	7	3.88
B.Lee	A	221	11185	8877	**380**	23.36	5-22	9	4.76
S.L.Malinga	SL	226	10936	9760	**338**	28.87	6-38	8	5.35
A.Kumble	I/Asia	271	14496	10412	**337**	30.89	6-12	2	4.30
S.T.Jayasuriya	SL	445	14874	11871	**323**	36.75	6-29	4	4.78
J.Srinath	I	229	11935	8847	**315**	28.08	5-23	3	4.44
D.L.Vettori	NZ/ICC	295	14060	9674	**305**	31.71	5- 7	2	4.12
Shakib Al Hasan	B	227	11711	8688	**300**	28.96	5-29	4	4.45

		LOI	Balls	R	W	Avge	Best	5w	R/Over
S.K.Warne	A/ICC	194	10642	7541	293	25.73	5-33	1	4.25
Saqlain Mushtaq	P	169	8770	6275	288	21.78	5-20	6	4.29
A.B.Agarkar	I	191	9484	8021	288	27.85	6-42	2	5.07
Z.Khan	I/Asia	200	10097	8301	282	29.43	5-42	1	4.93
J.H.Kallis	SA/Afr/ICC	328	10750	8680	273	31.79	5-30	2	4.84
A.A.Donald	SA	164	8561	5926	272	21.78	6-23	2	4.15
Mashrafe Mortaza	B/Asia	220	10922	8893	270	32.93	6-26	1	4.88
J.M.Anderson	E	194	9584	7861	269	29.22	5-23	2	4.92
Abdul Razzaq	P/Asia	265	10941	8564	269	31.83	6-35	3	4.69
Harbhajan Singh	I/Asia	236	12479	8973	269	33.35	5-31	3	4.31
M.Ntini	SA/ICC	173	8687	6519	266	24.65	6-22	4	4.53
Kapil Dev	I	225	11202	6945	253	27.45	5-43	1	3.72
Shoaib Akhtar	P/Asia/ICC	163	7764	6169	247	24.97	6-16	4	4.76
K.D.Mills	NZ	170	8230	6485	240	27.02	5-25	1	4.72
M.G.Johnson	A	153	7489	6038	239	25.26	6-31	3	4.83
H.H.Streak	Z/Afr	189	9468	7129	239	29.82	5-32	1	4.51
D.Gough	E/ICC	159	8470	6209	235	26.42	5-44	2	4.39
C.A.Walsh	WI	205	10822	6918	227	30.47	5- 1	1	3.83
C.E.L.Ambrose	WI	176	9353	5429	225	24.12	5-17	4	3.48
M.A.Starc	A	107	5509	4670	211	22.13	6-28	8	5.08
T.G.Southee	NZ	154	7751	7027	210	33.46	7-33	3	5.43
Abdur Razzak	B	153	7965	6065	207	29.29	5-29	4	4.56
C.J.McDermott	A	138	7460	5018	203	24.71	5-44	1	4.03
C.Z.Harris	NZ	250	10667	7613	203	37.50	5-42	1	4.28
C.L.Cairns	NZ/ICC	215	8168	6594	201	32.80	5-42	1	4.84

The most wickets for Ireland is 114 by K.J.O'Brien (153 matches) and for Afghanistan 163 by Rashid Khan (86).

BEST FIGURES IN AN INNINGS

8-19	W.P.J.U.C.Vaas	Sri Lanka v Zimbabwe	Colombo (SSC)	2001-02
7-12	Shahid Afridi	Pakistan v West Indies	Providence	2013
7-15	G.D.McGrath	Australia v Namibia	Potchefstroom	2002-03
7-18	Rashid Khan	Afghanistan v West Indies	Gros Islet	2017
7-20	A.J.Bichel	Australia v England	Port Elizabeth	2002-03
7-30	M.Muralitharan	Sri Lanka v India	Sharjah	2000-01
7-33	T.G.Southee	New Zealand v England	Wellington	2014-15
7-34	T.A.Boult	New Zealand v West Indies	Christchurch	2017-18
7-36	Waqar Younis	Pakistan v England	Leeds	2001
7-37	Aqib Javed	Pakistan v India	Sharjah	1991-92
7-45	Imran Tahir	South Africa v West Indies	Basseterre	2016
7-51	W.W.Davis	West Indies v Australia	Leeds	1983
6- 4	S.T.R.Binny	India v Bangladesh	Dhaka	2014
6-11	S.Lamichhane	Nepal v PNG	Al Amerat	2021
6-12	A.Kumble	India v West Indies	Calcutta	1993-94
6-13	B.A.W.Mendis	Sri Lanka v India	Karachi	2008
6-14	G.J.Gilmour	Australia v England	Leeds	1975
6-14	Imran Khan	Pakistan v India	Sharjah	1984-85
6-14	M.F.Maharoof	Sri Lanka v West Indies	Mumbai	2006-07
6-15	C.E.H.Croft	West Indies v England	Kingstown	1980-81
6-16	Shoaib Akhtar	Pakistan v New Zealand	Karachi	2001-02
6-16	K.Rabada	South Africa v Bangladesh	Dhaka	2015
6-16	S.Lamichhane	Nepal v USA	Kirtipur	2019-20
6-18	Azhar Mahmood	Pakistan v West Indies	Sharjah	1999-00
6-19	H.K.Olonga	Zimbabwe v England	Cape Town	1999-00
6-19	S.E.Bond	New Zealand v Zimbabwe	Harare	2005

6-19	J.J.Bumrah	India v England	The Oval	2022
6-20	B.C.Strang	Zimbabwe v Bangladesh	Nairobi	1997-98
6-20	A.D.Mathews	Sri Lanka v India	Colombo (RPS)	2009-10
6-22	F.H.Edwards	West Indies v Zimbabwe	Harare	2003-04
6-22	M.Ntini	South Africa v Australia	Cape Town	2005-06
6-23	A.A.Donald	South Africa v Kenya	Nairobi	1996-97
6-23	A.Nehra	India v England	Durban	2002-03
6-23	S.E.Bond	New Zealand v Australia	Port Elizabeth	2002-03
6-24	Imran Tahir	South Africa v Zimbabwe	Bloemfontein	2018-19
6-24	R.J.W.Topley	England v India	Lord's	2022
6-25	S.B.Styris	New Zealand v West Indies	Port of Spain	2002
6-25	W.P.J.U.C.Vaas	Sri Lanka v Bangladesh	Pietermaritzburg	2002-03
6-25	Kuldeep Yadav	India v England	Nottingham	2018
6-26	Waqar Younis	Pakistan v Sri Lanka	Sharjah	1989-90
6-26	Mashrafe Mortaza	Bangladesh v Kenya	Nairobi	2006
6-26	Rubel Hossain	Bangladesh v New Zealand	Dhaka	2013-14
6-26	Yasir Shah	Pakistan v Zimbabwe	Harare	2015-16
6-27	Naved-ul-Hasan	Pakistan v India	Jamshedpur	2004-05
6-27	C.R.D.Fernando	Sri Lanka v England	Colombo (RPS)	2007-08
6-27	M.Kartik	India v Australia	Mumbai	2007-08
6-27	K.A.J.Roach	West Indies v Netherlands	Delhi	2010-11
6-27	S.P.Narine	West Indies v South Africa	Providence	2016
6-28	H.K.Olonga	Zimbabwe v Kenya	Bulawayo	2002-03
6-28	J.H.Davey	Scotland v Afghanistan	Abu Dhabi	2014-15
6-28	M.A.Starc	Australia v New Zealand	Auckland	2014-15
6-29	B.P.Patterson	West Indies v India	Nagpur	1987-88
6-29	S.T.Jayasuriya	Sri Lanka v England	Moratuwa	1992-93
6-29	B.A.W.Mendis	Sri Lanka v Zimbabwe	Harare	2008-09
6-29	M.K.P.A.D.Perera	Sri Lanka v South Africa	Colombo (RPS)	2018
6-30	Waqar Younis	Pakistan v New Zealand	Auckland	1993-94

The best figures for Ireland are 6-55 by P.R.Stirling (v Afg, Greater Noida, 2016-17).

HAT-TRICKS

Jalaluddin	Pakistan v Australia	Hyderabad	1982-83
B.A.Reid	Australia v New Zealand	Sydney	1985-86
C.Sharma	India v New Zealand	Nagpur	1987-88
Wasim Akram	Pakistan v West Indies	Sharjah	1989-90
Wasim Akram	Pakistan v Australia	Sharjah	1989-90
Kapil Dev	India v Sri Lanka	Calcutta	1990-91
Aqib Javed	Pakistan v India	Sharjah	1991-92
D.K.Morrison	New Zealand v India	Napier	1993-94
Waqar Younis	Pakistan v New Zealand	East London	1994-95
Saqlain Mushtaq	Pakistan v Zimbabwe	Peshawar	1996-97
E.A.Brandes	Zimbabwe v England	Harare	1996-97
A.M.Stuart	Australia v Pakistan	Melbourne	1996-97
Saqlain Mushtaq	Pakistan v Zimbabwe	The Oval	1999
W.P.J.U.C.Vaas	Sri Lanka v Zimbabwe	Colombo (SSC)	2001-02
Mohammad Sami	Pakistan v West Indies	Sharjah	2001-02
W.P.J.U.C.Vaas[1]	Sri Lanka v Bangladesh	Pietermaritzburg	2002-03
B.Lee	Australia v Kenya	Durban	2002-03
J.M.Anderson	England v Pakistan	The Oval	2003
S.J.Harmison	England v India	Nottingham	2004
C.K.Langeveldt	South Africa v West Indies	Bridgetown	2004-05
Shahadat Hossain	Bangladesh v Zimbabwe	Harare	2006
J.E.Taylor	West Indies v Australia	Mumbai	2006-07
S.E.Bond	New Zealand v Australia	Hobart	2006-07

S.L.Malinga[2]	Sri Lanka v South Africa	Providence	2006-07
A.Flintoff	England v West Indies	St Lucia	2008-09
M.F.Maharoof	Sri Lanka v India	Dambulla	2010
Abdur Razzak	Bangladesh v Zimbabwe	Dhaka	2010-11
K.A.J.Roach	West Indies v Netherlands	Delhi	2010-11
S.L.Malinga	Sri Lanka v Kenya	Colombo (RPS)	2010-11
S.L.Malinga	Sri Lanka v Australia	Colombo (RPS)	2011
D.T.Christian	Australia v Sri Lanka	Melbourne	2011-12
N.L.T.C.Perera	Sri Lanka v Pakistan	Colombo (RPS)	2012
C.J.McKay	Australia v England	Cardiff	2013
Rubel Hossain	Bangladesh v New Zealand	Dhaka	2013-14
P.Utseya	Zimbabwe v South Africa	Harare	2014
Taijul Islam	Bangladesh v Zimbabwe	Dhaka	2014-15
S.T.Finn	England v Australia	Melbourne	2014-15
J.P.Duminy	South Africa v Sri Lanka	Sydney	2014-15
K.Rabada	South Africa v Bangladesh	Mirpur	2015
J.P.Faulkner	Australia v Sri Lanka	Colombo (RPS)	2016
Taskin Ahmed	Bangladesh v Sri Lanka	Dambulla	2016-17
P.W.H.de Silva	Sri Lanka v Zimbabwe	Galle	2017
Kuldeep Yadav	India v Australia	Kolkata	2017-18
D.S.K.Madushanka	Sri Lanka v Bangladesh	Dhaka	2017-18
Imran Tahir	South Africa v Zimbabwe	Bloemfontein	2018-19
T.A.Boult	New Zealand v Pakistan	Abu Dhabi	2018-19
Mohammed Shami	India v Afghanistan	Southampton	2019
T.A.Boult	New Zealand v Australia	Lord's	2019
Kuldeep Yadav	India v West Indies	Visakhapatnam	2019-20

[1] The first three balls of the match. Took four wickets in opening over (W W W 4 wide W 0).
[2] Four wickets in four balls.

WICKET-KEEPING RECORDS
150 DISMISSALS IN A CAREER

Total			LOI	Ct	St
482†‡	K.C.Sangakkara	Sri Lanka/Asia/ICC	360	384	98
472‡	A.C.Gilchrist	Australia/ICC	287	417	55
444	M.S.Dhoni	India/Asia	350	321	123
424	M.V.Boucher	South Africa/Africa	295	402	22
287‡	Moin Khan	Pakistan	219	214	73
257	Mushfiqur Rahim	Bangladesh	242	204	53
242†‡	B.B.McCullum	New Zealand	185	227	15
238	J.C.Buttler	England	165	204	34
233	I.A.Healy	Australia	168	194	39
220‡	Rashid Latif	Pakistan	166	182	38
206‡	R.S.Kaluwitharana	Sri Lanka	187	131	75
204‡	P.J.L.Dujon	West Indies	169	183	21
192	Q.de Kock	South Africa	137	180	12
189	R.D.Jacobs	West Indies	147	160	29
188	D.Ramdin	West Indies	139	181	7
187	Kamran Akmal	Pakistan	154	156	31
181	B.J.Haddin	Australia	126	170	11
165	D.J.Richardson	South Africa	122	148	17
165†‡	A.Flower	Zimbabwe	213	133	32
163†‡	A.J.Stewart	England	170	148	15
154‡	N.R.Mongia	India	140	110	44

† Excluding catches taken in the field. ‡ Excluding matches when not wicket-keeper.
The most for Ireland is 96 by N.J.O'Brien (103 matches) and for Afghanistan 88 by Mohammad Shahzad (84).

SIX DISMISSALS IN AN INNINGS

6	(6ct)	A.C.Gilchrist	Australia v South Africa	Cape Town	1999-00
6	(6ct)	A.J.Stewart	England v Zimbabwe	Manchester	2000
6	(5ct/1st)	R.D.Jacobs	West Indies v Sri Lanka	Colombo (RPS)	2001-02
6	(6ct)	A.C.Gilchrist	Australia v England	Sydney	2002-03
6	(6ct)	A.C.Gilchrist	Australia v Namibia	Potchefstroom	2002-03
6	(5ct/1st)	A.C.Gilchrist	Australia v Sri Lanka	Colombo (RPS)	2003-04
6	(6ct)	M.V.Boucher	South Africa v Pakistan	Cape Town	2006-07
6	(5ct/1st)	M.S.Dhoni	India v England	Leeds	2007
6	(6ct)	A.C.Gilchrist	Australia v India	Baroda	2007-08
6	(5ct/1st)	A.C.Gilchrist	Australia v India	Sydney	2007-08
6	(6ct)	M.J.Prior	England v South Africa	Nottingham	2008
6	(6ct)	J.C.Buttler	England v South Africa	The Oval	2013
6	(6ct)	M.H.Cross	Scotland v Canada	Christchurch	2013-14
6	(5ct/1st)	Q.de Kock	South Africa v New Zealand	Mt Maunganui	2014-15
6	(6ct)	Sarfraz Ahmed	Pakistan v South Africa	Auckland	2014-15

FIELDING RECORDS
100 CATCHES IN A CAREER

Total			LOI	Total			LOI
218	D.P.M.D.Jayawardena	Sri Lanka/Asia	448	118	T.M.Dilshan	Sri Lanka	330
160	R.T.Ponting	Australia/ICC	375	113	Inzamam-ul-Haq	Pakistan/Asia	378
156	M.Azharuddin	India	334	111	S.R.Waugh	Australia	325
142	L.R.P.L.Taylor	New Zealand	236	109	R.S.Mahanama	Sri Lanka	213
141	V.Kohli	India	271	108	P.D.Collingwood	England	197
140	S.R.Tendulkar	India	463	108	M.E.Waugh	Australia	244
133	S.P.Fleming	New Zealand/ICC	280	108	H.H.Gibbs	South Africa	248
131	J.H.Kallis	South Africa/Africa/ICC	328	108	S.M.Pollock	South Africa/Africa/ICC	303
130	Younus Khan	Pakistan	265	106	M.J.Clarke	Australia	245
130	M.Muralitharan	Sri Lanka/Asia/ICC	350	106	M.E.K.Hussey	Australia	185
127	A.R.Border	Australia	273	105	G.C.Smith	South Africa/Africa	197
127	Shahid Afridi	Pakistan/Asia/ICC	398	105	J.N.Rhodes	South Africa	245
124	C.H.Gayle	West Indies/ICC	301	104	M.J.Guptill	New Zealand	198
124	R.S.Dravid	India/Asia/ICC	344	102	S.K.Raina	India	226
123	S.T.Jayasuriya	Sri Lanka/Asia	445	100	I.V.A.Richards	West Indies	187
120	C.L.Hooper	West Indies	227	100	S.C.Ganguly	India/Asia	311
120	B.C.Lara	West Indies/ICC	299				

The most for Zimbabwe is 86 by G.W.Flower (221), for Bangladesh 76 by Mahmudullah (218), for Ireland 68 by W.T.S.Porterfield (148), and for Afghanistan 58 by Mohammad Nabi (136).

FIVE CATCHES IN AN INNINGS

5	J.N.Rhodes	South Africa v West Indies	Bombay (BS)	1993-94

APPEARANCE RECORDS
250 MATCHES

463	S.R.Tendulkar	India	344	R.S.Dravid	India/Asia/ICC
448	D.P.M.D.Jayawardena	Sri Lanka/Asia	334	M.Azharuddin	India
445	S.T.Jayasuriya	Sri Lanka/Asia	330	T.M.Dilshan	Sri Lanka
404	K.C.Sangakkara	Sri Lanka/Asia/ICC	328	J.H.Kallis	South Africa/Africa/ICC
398	Shahid Afridi	Pakistan/Asia/ICC	325	S.R.Waugh	Australia
378	Inzamam-ul-Haq	Pakistan/Asia	322	W.P.J.U.C.Vaas	Sri Lanka/Asia
375	R.T.Ponting	Australia/ICC	311	S.C.Ganguly	India/Asia
356	Wasim Akram	Pakistan	308	P.A.de Silva	Sri Lanka
350	M.S.Dhoni	India/Asia	304	Yuvraj Singh	India/Asia
350	M.Muralitharan	Sri Lanka/Asia/ICC	303	S.M.Pollock	South Africa/Africa/ICC

301	C.H.Gayle	West Indies/ICC
299	B.C.Lara	West Indies/ICC
295	M.V.Boucher	South Africa/Africa
295	D.L.Vettori	New Zealand/ICC
288	Mohammad Yousuf	Pakistan/Asia
287	A.C.Gilchrist	Australia/ICC
287	Shoaib Malik	Pakistan
283	Salim Malik	Pakistan
280	S.P.Fleming	New Zealand/ICC
273	A.R.Border	Australia
271	V.Kohli	India
271	A.Kumble	India/Asia

269	A.Ranatunga	Sri Lanka
268	M.S.Atapattu	Sri Lanka
268	S.Chanderpaul	West Indies
265	Abdul Razzaq	Pakistan/Asia
265	Younus Khan	Pakistan
262	Waqar Younis	Pakistan
260	B.B.McCullum	New Zealand
251	V.Sehwag	India/Asia/ICC
250	C.Z.Harris	New Zealand
250	Ijaz Ahmed	Pakistan
250	G.D.McGrath	Australia/ICC

The most for England is 225 by E.J.G.Morgan, for Zimbabwe 221 by G.W.Flower, for Bangladesh 242 by Mushfiqur Rahim, for Ireland 153 by K.J.O'Brien, and for Afghanistan 136 by Mohammad Nabi.

The most consecutive appearances is 185 by S.R.Tendulkar for India (Apr 1990-Apr 1998).

100 MATCHES AS CAPTAIN

			W	L	T	NR	% Won (exc NR)
230	R.T.Ponting	Australia/ICC	165	51	2	12	75.68
218	S.P.Fleming	New Zealand	98	106	1	13	47.80
200	M.S.Dhoni	India	110	74	5	11	58.20
193	A.Ranatunga	Sri Lanka	89	95	1	8	48.10
178	A.R.Border	Australia	107	67	1	3	61.14
174	M.Azharuddin	India	90	76	2	6	53.57
150	G.C.Smith	South Africa/Africa	92	51	1	6	63.88
147	S.C.Ganguly	India/Asia	76	66	–	5	53.52
139	Imran Khan	Pakistan	75	59	1	4	55.55
138	W.J.Cronje	South Africa	99	35	1	3	73.33
129	D.P.M.D.Jayawardena	Sri Lanka	71	49	1	8	58.67
126	E.J.G.Morgan	England	76	40	2	8	64.40
125	B.C.Lara	West Indies	59	59	–	7	50.42
118	S.T.Jayasuriya	Sri Lanka	66	47	2	3	57.39
113	W.T.S.Porterfield	Ireland	50	55	2	6	46.72
109	Wasim Akram	Pakistan	66	41	2	–	60.55
106	A.D.Mathews	Sri Lanka	49	51	1	5	48.51
106	S.R.Waugh	Australia	67	35	3	1	63.80
105	I.V.A.Richards	West Indies	67	36	–	2	65.04
103	A.B.de Villers	South Africa	59	39	1	4	59.59

The most for Zimbabwe is 86 by A.D.R.Campbell, for Bangladesh 88 by Mashrafe Mortaza, and for Afghanistan 59 by Asghar Afghan.

150 LOI UMPIRING APPEARANCES

222	Alim Dar	Pakistan	16.02.2000	to	13.01.2023
209	R.E.Koertzen	South Africa	09.12.1992	to	09.06.2010
200	B.F.Bowden	New Zealand	23.03.1995	to	06.02.2016
181	S.A.Bucknor	West Indies	18.03.1989	to	29.03.2009
174	D.J.Harper	Australia	14.01.1994	to	19.03.2011
174	S.J.A.Taufel	Australia	13.01.1999	to	02.09.2012
172	D.R.Shepherd	England	09.06.1983	to	12.07.2005
154	R.B.Tiffin	Zimbabwe	25.10.1992	to	22.07.2018

ICC MEN'S T20 WORLD CUP 2022-23

The eighth ICC Men's T20 World Cup was held in Australia between 16 October and 13 November.

GROUP ONE

	Team	P	W	L	T	NR	Pts	Net RR
1	New Zealand	5	3	1	–	1	7	+2.11
2	England	5	3	1	–	1	7	+0.47
3	Australia	5	3	1	–	1	7	–0.17
4	Sri Lanka	5	2	3	–	–	4	–0.42
5	Ireland	5	1	3	–	1	3	–1.61
6	Afghanistan	5	–	3	–	2	2	–0.57

GROUP TWO

	Team	P	W	L	T	NR	Pts	Net RR
1	India	5	4	1	–	–	8	+1.31
2	Pakistan	5	3	2	–	–	6	+1.02
3	South Africa	5	2	2	–	1	5	+0.87
4	Netherlands	5	2	3	–	–	4	–0.84
5	Bangladesh	5	2	3	–	–	4	–1.17
6	Zimbabwe	5	1	3	–	1	3	–1.13

England's Group Stage games:

Perth Stadium, 22 October. Toss: England. **ENGLAND** won by five wickets. Afghanistan 112 (19.4; S.M.Curran 5-10). England 113-5 (18.1). Award: S.M.Curran.
S.M.Curran's figures of 5-10 were an England record analysis.

Melbourne Cricket Ground, 26 October. Toss: England. **IRELAND** won by 5 runs (DLS method). Ireland 157 (19.2; A.Balbirnie 62, M.A.Wood 3-34). England 105-5 (14.3). Award: A.Balbirnie.

Melbourne Cricket Ground, 28 October. MATCH ABANDONED v Australia without a ball being bowled.

Woolloongabba, Brisbane, 1 November. Toss: England. **ENGLAND** won by 20 runs. England 179-6 (20; J.C.Buttler 73, A.D.Hales 52). New Zealand 159-6 (20; G.D.Phillips 62, K.S.Williamson 40). Award: J.C.Buttler.

Sydney Cricket Ground, 5 November. Toss: Sri Lanka. **ENGLAND** won by four wickets. Sri Lanka 141-8 (20; P.N.Silva 67, M.A.Wood 3-26). England 144-6 (19.4; A.D.Hales 47, B.A.Stokes 42). Award: A.U.Rashid (1-16).

Semi-finals

Sydney Cricket Ground, 9 November. Toss: New Zealand. **PAKISTAN** won by seven wickets. New Zealand 152-4 (20; D.J.Mitchell 53*, K.S.Williamson 46). Pakistan 153-3 (19.1; Mohammad Rizwan 57, Babar Azam 53). Award: Mohammad Rizwan.

Adelaide Oval, 10 November. Toss: England. **ENGLAND** won by ten wickets. India 168-6 (20; H.H.Pandya 63, V.Kohli 50, C.J.Jordan 3-43). England 170-0 (16; A.D.Hales 86*, J.C.Buttler 80*). Award: A.D.Hales.
A.D.Hales and J.C.Buttler shared the highest partnership in ICC T20 World Cup history.

Statistical Highlights in ICC Men's T20 World Cup 2022-23

Highest total	205-5	South Africa v Bangladesh	Sydney
Biggest victory (runs)	104	South Africa beat Bangladesh	Sydney
Biggest victory (wkts)	10	England beat India	Adelaide
Biggest victory (balls)	37	Pakistan beat Netherlands	Perth
Most runs	296 (ave 98.66)	V.Kohli (India)	
Highest innings	109	R.R.Rossouw	South Africa v Bangladesh	Sydney
Most sixes (inns)	8	R.R.Rossouw	South Africa v Bangladesh	Sydney
Highest partnership	170*	J.C.Buttler/A.D.Hales England v India	Adelaide
Most wickets	15 (ave 13.26)	P.W.H.de Silva (Sri Lanka)	
Best bowling	5-10	S.M.Curran	England v Afghanistan	Perth
Most expensive	4-0-59-0	B.J.McCarthy	Ireland v Scotland	Hobart
	4-0-59-0	M.R.Adair	Ireland v Australia	Brisbane
Most w/k dismissals	9	J.C.Buttler (England), S.A.Edwards (Netherlands)	
Most catches	9	M.D.Shanaka (Sri Lanka)	

Overall ICC Men's T20 World Cup Records 2007-08 to 2022-23

Highest total	260-6	Sri Lanka v Kenya Johannesburg	2007-08
Biggest victory (runs)	172	Sri Lanka beat Kenya Johannesburg	2007-08
Biggest victory (balls)	90	Sri Lanka beat Netherlands Chattogram	2013-14
Most runs	1141 (ave 81.50)	V.Kohli (India)	
Highest innings	123	B.B.McCullum New Zealand v Bangladesh Pallekele	2012-13
Most sixes (inns)	11	C.H.Gayle West Indies v England Mumbai	2015-16
Highest partnership	170*	J.C.Buttler/A.D.Hales England v India Adelaide	2022-23
Most wickets	47 (ave 18.63)	Shakib Al Hasan (Bangladesh)	
Best bowling	6-8	B.A.W.Mendis Sri Lanka v Zimbabwe Hambantota	2012-13
Most expensive	4-0-64-0	S.T.Jayasuriya Sri Lanka v Pakistan Johannesburg	2007-08
Most w/k dismissals	32	M.S.Dhoni (India)	
Most catches	23	A.B.de Villiers (South Africa)	
Most catches (inns)	4	D.J.Sammy West Indies v Ireland Providence	2010

ICC MEN'S T20 WORLD CUP FINAL
ENGLAND v PAKISTAN

At Melbourne Cricket Ground, on 13 November (floodlit).

Result: **ENGLAND** won by five wickets.

Toss: England. Award: S.M.Curran. Series award: S.M.Curran.

PAKISTAN		Runs	Balls	4/6	Fall
† Mohammad Rizwan	b Curran	15	14	–/1	1- 29
* Babar Azam	c and b Rashid	32	28	2	3- 84
Mohammad Haris	c Stokes b Rashid	8	12	1	2- 45
Shan Masood	c Livingstone b Curran	38	28	2/1	5-121
Iftikhar Ahmed	c Buttler b Stokes	0	6	–	4- 85
Shadab Khan	c Woakes b Jordan	20	14	2	6-123
Mohammad Nawaz	c Livingstone b Curran	5	7	–	7-129
Mohammad Wasim	c Livingstone b Jordan	4	8	–	8-131
Shaheen Shah Afridi	not out	5	3	1	
Haris Rauf	not out	1	1	–	
Naseem Shah					
Extras	(B 1, LB 1, NB 1, W 6)	9			
Total	**(8 wkts; 20 overs)**	**137**			

England		Runs	Balls	4/6	Fall
*†J.C.Buttler	c Rizwan b Rauf	26	17	3/1	3- 45
A.D.Hales	b Afridi	1	2	–	1- 7
P.D.Salt	c Ahmed b Rauf	10	9	2	2- 32
B.A.Stokes	not out	52	49	5/1	
H.C.Brook	c Afridi b Khan	20	23	–	4- 84
M.M.Ali	b Wasim	19	13	3	5-132
L.S.Livingstone	not out	1	1	–	
S.M.Curran					
C.R.Woakes					
C.J.Jordan					
A.U.Rashid					
Extras	(LB 1, W 8)	9			
Total	**(5 wkts; 19 overs)**	**138**			

ENGLAND	O	M	R	W	PAKISTAN	O	M	R	W
Stokes	4	0	32	1	Shaheen Shah Afridi	2.1	0	13	1
Woakes	3	0	26	0	Naseem Shah	4	0	30	0
Curran	4	0	12	3	Haris Rauf	4	0	23	2
Rashid	4	1	22	2	Shadab Khan	4	0	20	1
Jordan	4	0	27	2	Mohammad Wasim	4	0	38	1
Livingstone	1	0	16	0	Iftikhar Ahmed	0.5	0	13	0

Umpires: H.D.P.K.Dharmasena and M.Erasmus

PREVIOUS WINNERS

Season	Hosts	Winners
2007-08	South Africa	India
2009	England	Pakistan
2010	West Indies	England
2012-13	Sri Lanka	West Indies
2013-14	Bangladesh	Sri Lanka
2015-16	India	West Indies
2021-22	Oman/UAE	Australia

ENGLAND TWENTY20 INTERNATIONALS CAREER RECORDS

These records, complete to 8 March 2023, include all players registered for county cricket for the 2023 season at the time of going to press.

BATTING AND FIELDING

	M	I	NO	HS	Runs	Avge	100	50	Ct/St
M.M.Ali	71	61	15	72*	1044	22.69	–	7	15
J.M.Anderson	19	4	3	1*	1	1.00	–	–	3
J.C.Archer	12	2	1	18*	19	19.00	–	–	4
J.M.Bairstow	66	60	12	90	1337	27.85	–	8	45/1
J.T.Ball	2	–	–	–	–	–	–	–	1
T.Banton	14	14	–	73	327	23.35	–	2	9
S.W.Billings†	36	32	5	87	474	17.55	–	2	17/2
R.S.Bopara	38	35	10	65*	711	28.44	–	3	7
S.G.Borthwick	1	1	–	14	14	14.00	–	–	1
D.R.Briggs	7	1	1	0*	0	–	–	–	1
S.C.J.Broad	56	26	10	18*	118	7.37	–	–	21
H.C.Brook	20	17	3	81*	372	26.57	–	1	10
P.R.Brown	4	1	1	4*	4	–	–	–	2
J.C.Buttler	103	95	20	101*	2602	34.69	1	19	56/10
A.N.Cook	4	4	–	26	61	15.25	–	–	1
M.S.Crane	2	–	–	–	–	–	–	–	–
S.M.Curran	35	21	8	24	158	12.15	–	–	12
T.K.Curran	30	13	7	14*	64	10.66	–	–	8
S.M.Davies	5	5	–	33	102	20.40	–	–	2/1
L.A.Dawson	11	5	1	34	57	14.25	–	–	2
J.L.Denly	13	12	2	30	125	12.50	–	–	4
B.M.Duckett	8	8	2	70*	242	40.33	–	1	4
S.T.Finn	21	3	3	8*	14	–	–	–	6
B.T.Foakes	1	–	–	–	–	–	–	–	1
G.H.S.Garton	1	1	–	2	2	2.00	–	–	–
R.J.Gleeson	6	2	–	2	2	1.00	–	–	4
L.Gregory	9	7	1	15	45	7.50	–	–	–
A.D.Hales	75	75	8	116*	2074	30.95	1	12	39
W.G.Jacks	2	2	–	40	40	20.00	–	–	–
C.J.Jordan	84	50	22	36	422	15.07	–	–	42
L.S.Livingstone	29	24	5	103	423	22.26	1	–	15
S.Mahmood	12	7	4	7*	22	7.33	–	–	2
D.J.Malan	55	53	8	103*	1748	38.84	1	14	22
T.S.Mills†	12	4	2	7	8	4.00	–	–	2
E.J.G.Morgan	115	107	21	91	2458	28.58	–	14	46
M.W.Parkinson	6	4	–	5	5	1.25	–	–	1
S.D.Parry	5	1	–	1	1	1.00	–	–	2
S.R.Patel	18	14	2	67	189	15.75	–	1	3
A.U.Rashid	92	29	15	22	91	6.50	–	–	26
J.E.Root	32	30	5	90*	893	35.72	–	5	18
J.J.Roy	64	64	1	78	1522	24.15	–	8	19
P.D.Salt	13	12	1	88*	245	22.27	–	2	8/1
B.A.Stokes	43	36	9	52*	585	21.66	–	1	22
O.P.Stone	1	1	–	0	0	0.00	–	–	–
R.J.W.Topley	22	7	5	9	13	6.50	–	–	5
J.M.Vince	17	17	–	59	463	27.23	–	2	7
D.J.Willey	43	26	11	33*	226	15.06	–	–	17
C.R.Woakes	26	11	6	37	126	25.20	–	–	8

	M	I	NO	HS	Runs	Avge	100	50	Ct/St
L.Wood	2	–	–	–	–	–	–	–	–
M.A.Wood	27	3	3	5*	11	–	–	–	3

BOWLING

	O	M	R	W	Avge	Best	4wI	R/Over
M.M.Ali	129.1	1	1081	40	27.02	3-24	–	8.36
J.M.Anderson	70.2	1	552	18	30.66	3-23	–	7.84
J.C.Archer	47	0	371	14	26.50	4-33	1	7.89
J.T.Ball	7	0	83	2	41.50	1-39	–	11.85
R.S.Bopara	53.4	1	387	16	24.18	4-10	1	7.21
S.G.Borthwick	4	0	15	1	15.00	1-15	–	3.75
D.R.Briggs	18	0	199	5	39.80	2-25	–	11.05
S.C.J.Broad	195.3	2	1491	65	22.93	4-24	1	7.62
P.R.Brown	13	0	128	3	42.66	1-29	–	9.84
M.S.Crane	8	0	62	1	62.00	1-38	–	7.75
S.M.Curran	115.4	1	892	41	21.75	5-10	1	7.71
T.K.Curran	98	1	907	29	31.27	4-36	1	9.25
L.A.Dawson	34	0	242	6	40.33	3-27	–	7.11
J.L.Denly	12	0	93	7	13.28	4-19	1	7.75
S.T.Finn	80	0	583	27	21.59	3-16	–	7.28
G.H.S.Garton	4	0	57	1	57.00	1-57	–	14.25
R.J.Gleeson	21	1	187	9	20.77	3-15	–	8.90
L.Gregory	13	0	117	2	58.50	1-10	–	9.00
C.J.Jordan	294.5	2	2571	95	27.06	4- 6	3	8.72
L.S.Livingstone	50	0	405	15	27.00	3-17	–	8.10
S.Mahmood	38	0	398	7	56.85	3-33	–	10.47
D.J.Malan	2	0	27	1	27.00	1-27	–	13.50
T.S.Mills	41.4	1	361	12	31.16	3-27	–	8.37
M.W.Parkinson	20	0	198	7	28.28	4-47	1	9.90
S.D.Parry	16	0	138	3	46.00	2-33	–	8.62
S.R.Patel	42	0	321	7	45.85	2- 6	–	7.64
A.U.Rashid	320.2	4	2378	93	25.56	4- 2	2	7.42
J.E.Root	14	0	139	6	23.16	2- 9	–	9.92
B.A.Stokes	102	1	856	26	32.92	3-26	–	8.39
O.P.Stone	4	0	36	0	–	–	–	9.00
R.J.W.Topley	78.1	0	649	22	29.50	3-22	–	8.30
D.J.Willey	144.1	1	1180	51	23.13	4- 7	1	8.18
C.R.Woakes	86.3	1	680	27	25.18	3- 4	–	7.86
L.Wood	8	0	73	3	24.33	3-24	–	9.12
M.A.Wood	97.3	1	807	44	18.34	3- 9	–	8.27

† *S.W.Billings and T.S.Mills also played one game for an ICC World XI v West Indies at Lord's in 2018.*

INTERNATIONAL TWENTY20 RECORDS

From 1 January 2019, the ICC granted official IT20 status to all 20-over matches between its 105 members. As a result, there has been a vast increase in the number of games played, many featuring very minor nations. In the records that follow, except for the first-ranked record, only those IT20s featuring a nation that has also played a full LOI are listed.

MATCH RESULTS
2004-05 to 1 March 2023

	Opponents	Matches	Won													Tied	NR
			E	A	SA	WI	NZ	I	P	SL	Z	B	Ire	Afg	Ass		
England	Australia	23	11	10	–	–	–	–	–	–	–	–	–	–	–	–	2
	South Africa	25	12	–	12	–	–	–	–	–	–	–	–	–	–	–	1
	West Indies	24	10	–	–	14	–	–	–	–	–	–	–	–	–	–	–
	New Zealand	23	13	–	–	–	8	–	–	–	–	–	–	–	–	1	1
	India	23	11	–	–	–	–	12	–	–	–	–	–	–	–	–	–
	Pakistan	29	18	–	–	–	–	–	9	–	–	–	–	–	–	1	1
	Sri Lanka	14	10	–	–	–	–	–	–	4	–	–	–	–	–	–	–
	Zimbabwe	1	1	–	–	–	–	–	–	–	0	–	–	–	–	–	–
	Bangladesh	1	1	–	–	–	–	–	–	–	–	0	–	–	–	–	–
	Ireland	2	0	–	–	–	–	–	–	–	–	–	1	–	–	–	1
	Afghanistan	3	3	–	–	–	–	–	–	–	–	–	–	0	–	–	–
	Associates	2	0	–	–	–	–	–	–	–	–	–	–	–	2	–	–
Australia	South Africa	22	–	14	8	–	–	–	–	–	–	–	–	–	–	–	–
	West Indies	19	–	9	–	10	–	–	–	–	–	–	–	–	–	–	–
	New Zealand	16	–	10	–	–	5	–	–	–	–	–	–	–	–	1	–
	India	26	–	10	–	–	–	15	–	–	–	–	–	–	–	–	–
	Pakistan	25	–	11	–	–	–	–	12	–	–	–	–	–	–	1	1
	Sri Lanka	26	–	15	–	–	–	–	–	10	–	–	–	–	–	1	–
	Zimbabwe	3	–	2	–	–	–	–	–	–	1	–	–	–	–	–	–
	Bangladesh	10	–	6	–	–	–	–	–	–	–	4	–	–	–	–	–
	Ireland	2	–	2	–	–	–	–	–	–	–	–	0	–	–	–	–
	Afghanistan	1	–	1	–	–	–	–	–	–	–	–	–	0	–	–	–
	Associates	1	–	1	–	–	–	–	–	–	–	–	–	–	0	–	–
S Africa	West Indies	16	–	–	10	6	–	–	–	–	–	–	–	–	–	–	–
	New Zealand	15	–	–	11	–	4	–	–	–	–	–	–	–	–	–	–
	India	24	–	–	10	–	–	13	–	–	–	–	–	–	–	–	1
	Pakistan	22	–	–	10	–	–	–	12	–	–	–	–	–	–	–	–
	Sri Lanka	17	–	–	11	–	–	–	–	5	–	–	–	–	–	1	–
	Zimbabwe	6	–	–	5	–	–	–	–	–	0	–	–	–	–	–	1
	Bangladesh	8	–	–	8	–	–	–	–	–	–	0	–	–	–	–	–
	Ireland	5	–	–	5	–	–	–	–	–	–	–	0	–	–	–	–
	Afghanistan	2	–	–	2	–	–	–	–	–	–	–	–	0	–	–	–
	Associates	3	–	–	2	–	–	–	–	–	–	–	–	–	1	–	–
W Indies	New Zealand	19	–	–	–	4	10	–	–	–	–	–	–	–	–	3	2
	India	25	–	–	–	7	–	17	–	–	–	–	–	–	–	–	1
	Pakistan	21	–	–	–	3	–	–	15	–	–	–	–	–	–	–	3
	Sri Lanka	15	–	–	–	7	–	–	–	8	–	–	–	–	–	–	–
	Zimbabwe	4	–	–	–	3	–	–	–	–	1	–	–	–	–	–	–
	Bangladesh	16	–	–	–	9	–	–	–	–	–	5	–	–	–	–	2
	Ireland	8	–	–	–	3	–	–	–	–	–	–	3	–	–	–	2
	Afghanistan	7	–	–	–	4	–	–	–	–	–	–	–	3	–	–	–
	Associates	1	–	–	–	0	–	–	–	–	–	–	–	–	1	–	–
N Zealand	India	25	–	–	–	–	10	12	–	–	–	–	–	–	–	3	–
	Pakistan	29	–	–	–	–	11	–	18	–	–	–	–	–	–	–	–
	Sri Lanka	20	–	–	–	–	11	–	–	7	–	–	–	–	–	1	1
	Zimbabwe	6	–	–	–	–	6	–	–	–	0	–	–	–	–	–	–
	Bangladesh	17	–	–	–	–	14	–	–	–	–	3	–	–	–	–	–
	Ireland	5	–	–	–	–	5	–	–	–	–	–	0	–	–	–	–
	Afghanistan	1	–	–	–	–	1	–	–	–	–	–	–	0	–	–	–
	Associates	9	–	–	–	–	9	–	–	–	–	–	–	–	0	–	–

	Opponents	Matches	E	A	SA	WI	NZ	I	P	SL	Z	B	Ire	Afg	Ass	Tied	NR
India	Pakistan	12	–	–	–	–	–	8	3	–	–	–	–	–	–	1	–
	Sri Lanka	29	–	–	–	–	–	19	–	9	–	–	–	–	–	–	1
	Zimbabwe	8	–	–	–	–	–	6	–	–	2	–	–	–	–	–	–
	Bangladesh	12	–	–	–	–	–	11	–	–	–	1	–	–	–	–	–
	Ireland	5	–	–	–	–	–	5	–	–	–	–	0	–	–	–	–
	Afghanistan	4	–	–	–	–	–	4	–	–	–	–	–	0	–	–	–
	Associates	6	–	–	–	–	–	5	–	–	–	–	–	–	0	–	1
Pakistan	Sri Lanka	23	–	–	–	–	–	–	13	10	–	–	–	–	–	–	–
	Zimbabwe	18	–	–	–	–	–	–	16	–	2	–	–	–	–	–	–
	Bangladesh	18	–	–	–	–	–	–	16	–	–	2	–	–	–	–	–
	Ireland	1	–	–	–	–	–	–	1	–	–	–	0	–	–	–	–
	Afghanistan	3	–	–	–	–	–	–	3	–	–	–	–	0	–	–	–
	Associates	11	–	–	–	–	–	–	11	–	–	–	–	–	0	–	–
Sri Lanka	Zimbabwe	3	–	–	–	–	–	–	–	3	0	–	–	–	–	–	–
	Bangladesh	13	–	–	–	–	–	–	–	9	–	4	–	–	–	–	–
	Ireland	3	–	–	–	–	–	–	–	3	–	–	0	–	–	–	–
	Afghanistan	4	–	–	–	–	–	–	–	3	–	–	–	1	–	–	–
	Associates	9	–	–	–	–	–	–	–	8	–	–	–	–	1	–	–
Zimbabwe	Bangladesh	20	–	–	–	–	–	–	–	–	7	13	–	–	–	–	–
	Ireland	12	–	–	–	–	–	–	–	–	6	–	6	–	–	–	–
	Afghanistan	15	–	–	–	–	–	–	–	–	1	–	–	14	–	–	–
	Associates	27	–	–	–	–	–	–	–	–	18	–	–	7	2	–	–
Bangladesh	Ireland	5	–	–	–	–	–	–	–	–	–	3	1	–	–	–	1
	Afghanistan	9	–	–	–	–	–	–	–	–	–	3	–	6	–	–	–
	Associates	15	–	–	–	–	–	–	–	–	–	11	–	4	–	–	–
Ireland	Afghanistan	23	–	–	–	–	–	–	–	–	–	–	6	16	–	1	–
	Associates	73	–	–	–	–	–	–	–	–	–	–	42	–	27	1	3
Afghanistan	Associates	38	–	–	–	–	–	–	–	–	–	–	–	30	8	–	–
Associates	Associates	917	–	–	–	–	–	–	–	–	–	–	–	–	882	8	27
		2003	90	91	94	70	94	127	129	79	38	49	59	70	933	26	54

MATCH RESULTS SUMMARY

	Matches	Won	Lost	Tied	NR	% Won (ex NR)
India	199	127	63	4	5	65.46
Afghanistan	110	70	39	1	0	63.63
Pakistan	212	129	75	3	5	62.31
South Africa	165	94	67	1	3	58.02
England	170	90	72	2	6	54.87
Australia	174	91	76	3	4	53.52
New Zealand	185	94	78	9	4	51.93
Sri Lanka	176	79	92	3	2	45.40
Ireland	144	59	76	2	7	43.06
West Indies	175	70	92	3	10	42.42
Bangladesh	144	49	92	0	3	34.75
Zimbabwe	123	38	82	2	1	31.14
Associates (v Full)	195	51	137	3	4	26.70

Results of games between two Associate Members and Pakistan's three IT20s v a World XI in 2017 (W2, L1) and West Indies' IT20 v an ICC World XI in 2018 (W1) are excluded from these figures.

INTERNATIONAL TWENTY20 RECORDS

(To 1 March 2023)

TEAM RECORDS
HIGHEST INNINGS TOTALS
† Batting Second

278-3	Afghanistan v Ireland	Dehradun	2018-19
263-3	Australia v Sri Lanka	Pallekele	2016
260-6	Sri Lanka v Kenya	Johannesburg	2007-08
260-5	India v Sri Lanka	Indore	2017-18
254-5	New Zealand v Scotland	Edinburgh	2022
252-3	Scotland v Netherlands	Dublin	2019
248-6	Australia v England	Southampton	2013
245-6	West Indies v India	Lauderhill	2016
245-5†	Australia v New Zealand	Auckland	2017-18
245-1	Canada v Panama	Coolidge	2021-22
244-4†	India v West Indies	Lauderhill	2016
243-5	New Zealand v West Indies	Mt Maunganui	2017-18
243-6	New Zealand v Australia	Auckland	2017-18
241-6	South Africa v England	Centurion	2009-10
241-3	England v New Zealand	Napier	2019-20
240-3	Namibia v Botswana	Windhoek	2019
240-3	India v West Indies	Mumbai	2019-20
238-3	New Zealand v West Indies	Mt Maunganui	2020-21
238-3	Nepal v Netherlands	Kirtipur	2021
237-3	India v South Africa	Guwahati	2022-23
237-5	Kenya v Lesotho	Kigali	2022-23
236-6†	West Indies v South Africa	Johannesburg	2014-15
236-3	Nepal v Bhutan	Kirtipur	2019-20
236-5	Zimbabwe v Singapore	Bulawayo	2022
234-3	Canada v Belize	Coolidge	2021-22
234-6	England v South Africa	Bristol	2022
234-4	India v New Zealand	Ahmedabad	2022-23
233-8	Afghanistan v Ireland	Greater Noida	2016-17
233-2	Australia v Sri Lanka	Adelaide	2019-20
232-6	Pakistan v England	Nottingham	2021
231-7	South Africa v West Indies	Johannesburg	2014-15
230-8†	England v South Africa	Mumbai	2015-16

The highest total for Bangladesh is 215-5 (v Sri Lanka, Colombo (RPS), 2017-18).

LOWEST COMPLETED INNINGS TOTALS
† Batting Second

10	(8.4)	Isle of Man v Spain	Cartagena	2022-23
30	(10.4)	Mali v Kenya	Kigali	2022-23
36	(15.2)	Philippines v Oman	Al Amerat	2021-22
37†	(17.2)	Panama v Canada	Coolidge	2021-22
38†	(10.4)	Hong Kong v Pakistan	Sharjah	2022
39	(10.3)	Netherlands v Sri Lanka	Chittagong	2013-14
44	(10.0)	Netherlands v Sri Lanka	Sharjah	2021-22
45†	(11.5)	West Indies v England	Basseterre	2018-19
46	(12.1)	Botswana v Namibia	Kampala	2019
48	(14.2)	Cameroon v Kenya	Benoni	2022
53	(14.3)	Nepal v Ireland	Belfast	2015
55	(14.2)	West Indies v England	Dubai (DSC)	2021-22
56†	(18.4)	Kenya v Afghanistan	Sharjah	2013-14
60†	(15.3)	New Zealand v Sri Lanka	Chittagong	2013-14
60†	(13.4)	West Indies v Pakistan	Karachi	2017-18
60	(16.5)	New Zealand v Bangladesh	Mirpur	2021

60†	(10.2)	Scotland v Afghanistan	Sharjah	2021-22
61-8		Iran v UAE	Al Amerat	2019-20
62†	(13.4)	Australia v Bangladesh	Mirpur	2021
64	(11.0)	Nepal v Oman	Al Amerat	2019-20
66-9		Cayman Islands v USA	Sandys Parish	2019
66-9		Nigeria v Ireland	Abu Dhabi	2019-20
66		Thailand v Nepal	Bangkok	2019-20
66†	(12.1)	New Zealand v India	Ahmedabad	2022-23

The lowest total for England is 80 (v India, Colombo (RPS), 2012-13).

LARGEST RUNS MARGIN OF VICTORY

257 runs	Czech Republic beat Turkey	Ilfov County	2019
208 runs	Canada beat Panama	Coolidge	2021-22
172 runs	Sri Lanka beat Kenya	Johannesburg	2007
168 runs	India beat New Zealand	Ahmedabad	2022-23
167 runs	Kenya beat Lesotho	Kigali	2022-23
155 runs	Pakistan beat Hong Kong	Sharjah	2022
145 runs	Canada beat Belize	Coolidge	2021-22
143 runs	Pakistan beat West Indies	Karachi	2017-18
143 runs	India beat Ireland	Dublin	2018
142 runs	Nepal beat Netherlands	Kirtipur	2021
141 runs	Nepal beat Bhutan	Kirtipur	2019-20
137 runs	England beat West Indies	Basseterre	2018-19

There have been 44 victories by ten wickets, with Spain beating Isle of Man by a record margin of 118 balls remaining (Cartagena, 2022-23).

BATTING RECORDS
1800 RUNS IN A CAREER

Runs			M	I	NO	HS	Avge	50	R/100B
4008	V.Kohli	I	115	107	31	122*	52.73	38	137.9
3853	R.G.Sharma	I	148	140	17	118	31.32	33	139.2
3531	M.J.Guptill	NZ	122	118	7	105	31.81	22	135.7
3355	Babar Azam	P	99	94	13	122	41.41	32	127.8
3181	P.R.Stirling	Ire	121	120	9	115*	28.65	22	134.7
3120	A.J.Finch	A	103	103	12	172	34.28	21	142.5
2894	D.A.Warner	A	99	99	11	100*	32.88	25	141.3
2635	Mohammad Rizwan	P	80	69	15	104*	48.79	24	126.6
2602	J.C.Buttler	E	103	95	20	101*	34.69	20	144.2
2514	Mohammad Hafeez	P	119	108	13	99*	26.46	14	122.0
2464	K.S.Williamson	NZ	87	85	11	95	33.29	17	123.0
2458	E.J.G.Morgan	E	115	107	21	91	28.58	14	136.1
2435	Shoaib Malik	P/ICC	124	111	33	75	31.21	9	125.6
2265	K.L.Rahul	I	72	68	8	110*	37.75	24	139.1
2243	Shakib Al Hasan	B	109	108	11	84	23.12	12	121.7
2159	G.J.Maxwell	A	98	90	14	145*	28.40	13	150.9
2156	Q.de Kock	SA	77	76	9	79*	32.17	14	135.4
2147	D.A.Miller	SA/Wd	111	96	34	106*	34.62	8	144.1
2140	B.B.McCullum	NZ	71	70	10	123	35.66	15	136.2
2122	Mahmudullah	B	121	113	23	64*	23.57	6	117.3
2074	A.D.Hales	E	75	75	8	116*	30.95	13	138.3
2015	Mohammad Shahzad	Afg	70	70	3	118*	30.07	13	133.6
1973	K.J.O'Brien	Ire	110	103	10	124	21.21	6	130.9
1934	J.P.Duminy	SA	81	75	25	96*	38.68	11	126.2
1909	L.R.P.L.Taylor	NZ	102	94	21	63	26.15	7	122.3
1899	C.H.Gayle	WI	79	75	7	117	27.92	16	137.5
1889	T.M.Dilshan	SL	80	79	12	104*	28.19	14	120.5
1857	A.Balbirnie	Ire	89	85	4	83	22.92	8	124.8

HIGHEST INDIVIDUAL INNINGS

Score	Balls				
172	76	A.J.Finch	A v Z	Harare	2018
162*	62	Hazratullah Zazai	Afg v Ire	Dehradun	2018-19
156	63	A.J.Finch	A v E	Southampton	2013
145*	65	G.J.Maxwell	A v SL	Pallekele	2016
133*	73	M.P.O'Dowd	Neth v Malay	Kirtipur	2021
127*	56	H.G.Munsey	Scot v Neth	Dublin	2019
126*	63	S.Gill	I v NZ	Ahmedabad	2022-23
125*	62	E.Lewis	WI v I	Kingston	2017
124*	71	S.R.Watson	A v I	Sydney	2015-16
124	62	K.J.O'Brien	Ire v HK	Al Amerat	2019-20
123	58	B.B.McCullum	NZ v B	Pallekele	2012-13
122*	61	V.Kohli	I v Afg	Dubai (DSC)	2022
122	60	Babar Hayat	HK v Oman	Fatullah	2015-16
122	59	Babar Azam	P v SA	Centurion	2021
119	56	F.du Plessis	SA v WI	Johannesburg	2014-15
118*	67	Mohammad Shahzad	Afg v Z	Sharjah	2015-16
118	43	R.G.Sharma	I v SL	Indore	2017-18
117*	51	R.E.Levi	SA v NZ	Hamilton	2011-12
117*	68	Shaiman Anwar	UAE v PNG	Abu Dhabi	2017
117	57	C.H.Gayle	WI v SA	Johannesburg	2007-08
117	51	S.A.Yadav	I v E	Nottingham	2022
116*	56	B.B.McCullum	NZ v A	Christchurch	2009-10
116	64	A.D.Hales	E v SL	Chittagong	2013-14
115*	75	P.R.Stirling	Ire v Z	Bready	2021
114*	70	M.N.van Wyk	SA v WI	Durban	2014-15
113*	55	G.J.Maxwell	A v I	Bengaluru	2018-19
112*	51	S.A.Yadav	I v SL	Rajkot	2022-23
112	66	Muhammad Waseem	UAE v Ire	Al Amerat	2021-22
111*	62	Ahmed Shehzad	P v B	Dhaka	2013-14
111*	61	R.G.Sharma	I v WI	Lucknow	2018-19
111*	51	S.A.Yadav	I v NZ	Mt Maunganui	2022-23
110*	51	K.L.Rahul	I v WI	Lauderhill	2016
110*	57	D.S.Airee	Nep v Malay	Kirtipur	2021-22
110*	66	Babar Azam	P v E	Karachi	2022-23

The highest score for Sri Lanka is 104* by T.M.Dilshan (v A, Pallekele, 2011), for Zimbabwe 94 by S.F.Mire (v P, Harare, 2018) and for Bangladesh 103* by Tamim Iqbal (v Oman, Dharamsala, 2015-16).

MOST SIXES IN AN INNINGS

16	Hazratullah Zazai (162*)	Afg v Ire	Dehradun		2018-19
14	A.J.Finch (156)	A v E	Southampton		2013
14	H.G.Munsey (127*)	Scot v Neth	Dublin		2019
13	R.E.Levi (117*)	SA v NZ	Hamilton		2011-12
12	E.Lewis (115*)	WI v I	Kingston		2017

HIGHEST PARTNERSHIP FOR EACH WICKET

1st	236	Hazratullah Zazai/Usmann Ghani	Afg v Ire	Dehradun	2018-19
2nd	176	S.V.Samson/D.J.Hooda	I v Ire	Dublin	2022
3rd	184	D.P.Conway/G.D.Phillips	NZ v WI	Mt Maunganui	2020-21
4th	174*	Q.de Kock/D.A.Miller	SA v I	Guwahati	2022-23
5th	119*	Shoaib Malik/Misbah-ul-Haq	P v A	Johannesburg	2007-08
	119*	C.Campher/G.H.Dockrell	Ire v Scot	Hobart	2022-23
6th	115	T.P.Ura/N.Vanua	PNG v Sing	Singapore	2022
7th	92	M.P.Stoinis/D.R.Sams	A v NZ	Dunedin	2020-21
8th	80	P.L.Mommsen/S.M.Sharif	Scot v Neth	Edinburgh	2015

9th	132*	Saber Zakhil/Saqlain Ali		Belg v Austria	Waterloo			2021
10th	62*	K.B.Ahir/N.Ahir		Pan v Arg	North Sound			2021-22

BOWLING RECORDS
70 WICKETS IN A CAREER

Wkts				Matches	Overs	Mdns	Runs	Avge	Best	R/Over
134	T.G.Southee		NZ	107	389.1	3	3179	23.72	5-18	8.16
128	Shakib Al Hasan		B	109	397.3	3	2716	21.21	5-20	6.83
126	Rashid Khan		Afg/IC	77	292.2	1	1820	14.44	5- 3	6.22
114	I.S.Sodhi		NZ	91	317.1	–	2555	22.41	4-28	8.05
107	S.L.Malinga		SL	84	299.5	1	2225	20.79	5- 6	7.42
98	Shadab Khan		P	84	299.1	3	2105	21.47	4- 8	7.03
98	Shahid Afridi		P/Wd	99	361.2	4	2396	24.44	4-11	6.63
97	Mustafizur Rahman		B	78	278.4	6	2129	21.94	5-22	7.63
95	C.J.Jordan		E	84	294.5	2	2571	27.06	4- 6	8.72
93	A.U.Rashid		E	92	320.2	4	2378	25.56	4- 2	7.42
91	M.J.Santner		NZ	83	286.2	2	2021	22.20	4-11	7.05
91	Y.S.Chahal		I	75	276.0	2	2246	24.68	6-25	8.13
90	B.Kumar		I	87	298.3	10	2079	23.10	5- 4	6.96
89	P.W.H.de Silva		SL	55	197.4	1	1345	15.11	4- 9	6.80
85	S.Lamichhane		Nep/Wd	44	166.5	3	1068	12.56	5- 9	6.40
85	Umar Gul		P	60	200.3	2	1443	16.97	5- 6	7.19
85	Saeed Ajmal		P	64	238.2	2	1516	17.83	4-19	6.36
84	Mohammad Nabi		Afg	104	324.4	5	2375	28.27	4-10	7.31
82	A.Zampa		A	72	256.5	1	1781	21.71	5-19	6.93
81	G.H.Dockrell		Ire	115	256.2	1	1833	22.62	4-20	7.15
80	M.R.Adair		Ire	61	213.5	2	1644	20.55	4-23	7.68
78	D.J.Bravo		WI	91	250.5	–	2036	26.10	4-19	8.11
74	T.A.Boult		NZ	55	209.3	2	1647	22.25	4-13	7.86
73	T.Shamsi		SA	59	214.4	1	1534	21.01	5-24	7.14
73	M.A.Starc		A	58	219.0	2	1673	22.91	4-20	7.63
72	Haris Rauf		P	57	204.4	1	1652	22.94	4-22	8.07
72	R.Ashwin		I	65	242.0	3	1672	23.22	4- 8	6.90
71	Bilal Khan		Oman	53	187.1	6	1201	16.91	4-19	6.41
70	J.J.Bumrah		I	60	213.5	9	1416	20.22	3-11	6.62

The most wickets for Zimbabwe is 56 by T.L.Chatara (50 matches).

BEST FIGURES IN AN INNINGS

6- 5	P.Aho	Nig v S Leone	Lagos	2021-22
6- 7	D.L.Chahar	I v B	Nagpur	2019-20
6- 8	B.A.W.Mendis	SL v Z	Hambantota	2012-13
6-10	J.J.Smit	Nam v Uganda	Windhoek	2022
6-16	B.A.W.Mendis	SL v A	Pallekele	2011
6-17	O.C.McCoy	WI v I	Basseterre	2022
6-17	P.K.Langat	Ken v Mali	Kigali	2022-23
6-24	J.N.Frylinck	Nam v UAE	Dubai	2021-22
6-25	Y.S.Chahal	I v E	Bangalore	2016-17
6-30	A.C.Agar	A v NZ	Wellington	2020-21
5- 3	H.M.R.K.B.Herath	SL v NZ	Chittagong	2013-14
5- 3	Rashid Khan	Afg v Ire	Greater Noida	2016-17
5- 4	Khizar Hayat	Malay v HK	Kuala Lumpur	2019-20
5- 4	B.Kumar	I v Afg	Dubai (DSC)	2022
5- 6	Umar Gul	P v NZ	The Oval	2009
5- 6	Umar Gul	P v SA	Centurion	2012-13
5- 6	S.L.Malinga	SL v NZ	Pallekele	2019
5- 9	C.Viljoen	Nam v Bots	Kampala	2019
5- 9	S.Lamichhane	Nep v Ken	Nairobi	2022
5-10	S.M.Curran	E v Afg	Perth	2022-23

5-11	Karim Janat	Afg v WI	Lucknow	2019-20
5-12	Vraj Patel	Ken v Nig	Kigali	2021-22
5-12	S.N.Netravalkar	USA v Sing	Bulawayo	2022
5-13	Elias Sunny	B v Ire	Belfast	2012
5-13	Samiullah Shenwari	Afg v Ken	Sharjah	2013-14
5-14	Imad Wasim	P v WI	Dubai	2016-17
5-15	K.M.A.Paul	WI v B	Dhaka	2018-19
5-15	D.Ravu	PNG v Vanu	Apia	2019
5-15	Aamir Kaleem	Oman v Nep	Al Amerat	2019-20

The best figures for South Africa are 5-17 by D.Pretorius (v P, Lahore, 2020-21), for New Zealand 5-18 by T.G.Southee (v P, Auckland, 2010-11), for Zimbabwe 4-8 by Sikandar Raza (v Neth, Bulawayo, 2022), and for Ireland 4-11 by A.R.Cusack (v WI, Kingston, 2013-14).

HAT-TRICKS

B.Lee	Australia v Bangladesh	Melbourne	2007-08
J.D.P.Oram	New Zealand v Sri Lanka	Colombo (RPS)	2009
T.G.Southee	New Zealand v Pakistan	Auckland	2010-11
N.L.T.C.Perera	Sri Lanka v India	Ranchi	2015-16
S.L.Malinga	Sri Lanka v Bangladesh	Colombo (RPS)	2016-17
Faheem Ashraf	Pakistan v Sri Lanka	Abu Dhabi	2017-18
Rashid Khan†	Afghanistan v Ireland	Dehradun	2018-19
S.L.Malinga†	Sri Lanka v New Zealand	Pallekele	2019
Mohammad Hasnain	Pakistan v Sri Lanka	Lahore	2019-20
Khawar Ali	Oman v Netherlands	Al Amerat	2019-20
N.Vanua	PNG v Bermuda	Dubai	2019-20
D.L.Chahar	India v Bangladesh	Nagpur	2019-20
A.C.Agar	Australia v South Africa	Johannesburg	2019-20
M.K.P.A.D.Perera	Sri Lanka v West Indies	Antigua	2020-21
N.T.Ellis	Australia v Bangladesh	Dhaka	2021
E.Otieno	Kenya v Uganda	Entebbe	2021
C.Campher†	Ireland v Netherlands	Abu Dhabi	2021-22
P.W.H.de Silva	Sri Lanka v South Africa	Sharjah	2021-22
K.Rabada	South Africa v England	Sharjah	2021-22
J.O.Holder†	West Indies v England	Bridgetown	2021-22
K.C.Karan	Nepal v PNG	Kirtipur	2021-22
J.J.Smit	Namibia v Uganda	Windhoek	2022
L.V.van Beek	Netherlands v Hong Kong	Bulawayo	2022
M.G.Bracewell	New Zealand v Ireland	Belfast	2022
K.P.Meiyappan	UAE v Sri Lanka	Geelong	2022-33
J.B.Little	Ireland v New Zealand	Adelaide	2022-23
T.G.Southee	New Zealand v India	Mt Maunganui	2022-23

† Four wickets in four balls.

WICKET-KEEPING RECORDS – 50 DISMISSALS IN A CAREER

Dis			*Matches*	*Ct*	*St*
91	M.S.Dhoni	India	98	57	34
87	Q.de Kock	South Africa	77	71	16
64	J.C.Buttler	England	103	54	10
63	D.Ramdin	West Indies	71	43	20
62	Mushfiqur Rahim	Bangladesh	102	32	30
60	Kamran Akmal	Pakistan	58	28	32
60	I.A.Karim	Kenya	44	40	20
58	Mohammad Shahzad	Afghanistan	70	30	28
53	M.S.Wade	Australia	75	47	6
50	M.H.Cross	Scotland	61	35	15

MOST DISMISSALS IN AN INNINGS

| 5 (3 ct, 2 st) | Mohammad Shahzad | Afghanistan v Oman | Abu Dhabi | 2015-16 |
| 5 (5 ct) | M.S.Dhoni | India v England | Bristol | 2018 |

315

5 (2 ct, 3 st)	I.A.Karim	Kenya v Ghana	Kampala	2019
5 (5 ct)	K.Doriga	PNG v Vanuatu	Apia	2019
5 (5 ct)	I.A.Karim	Kenya v Uganda	Kigali	2021-22
5 (4 ct, 1 st)	I.A.Karim	Kenya v Mali	Kigali	2022-23

FIELDING RECORDS – 40 CATCHES IN A CAREER

Total			*Matches*	*Total*			*Matches*
75	D.A.Miller	South Africa/Wd	111	50	A.J.Finch	Australia	103
68	M.J.Guptill	New Zealand	122	50	Shoaib Malik	Pakistan/ICC	124
58	R.G.Sharma	India	148	50	V.Kohli	India	115
56	D.A.Warner	Australia	99	46	L.R.P.L.Taylor	New Zealand	102
55	G.H.Dockrell	Ireland	104	46	E.J.G.Morgan	England	115
54	Mohammad Nabi	Afghanistan	104	46	Mahmudullah	Bangladesh	121
53	T.G.Southee	New Zealand	107				

† *Excluding catches taken as a wicket-keeper.*

MOST CATCHES IN AN INNINGS

4	D.J.G.Sammy	West Indies v Ireland	Providence	2009-10
4	P.W.Borren	Netherlands v Bangladesh	The Hague	2012
4	C.J.Anderson	New Zealand v South Africa	Port Elizabeth	2012-13
4	L.D.Chandimal	Sri Lanka v Bangladesh	Chittagong	2013-14
4	A.M.Rahane	India v England	Birmingham	2014
4	Babar Hayat	Hong Kong v Afghanistan	Dhaka	2015-16
4	D.A.Miller	South Africa v Pakistan	Cape Town	2018-19
4	L.Siaka	PNG v Vanuatu	Apia	2019
4	C.S.MacLeod	Scotland v Ireland	Dublin	2019
4	T.H.David	Singapore v Scotland	Dubai	2019-20
4	C.de Grandhomme	New Zealand v England	Wellington	2019-20
4	P.Sarraf	Nepal v Malaysia	Bangkok	2019-20
4	M.G.Erasmus	Namibia v UAE	Dubai	2021-22
4	K.Bhurtel	Nepal v Malaysia	Kirtipur	2022

APPEARANCE RECORDS – 100 APPEARANCES

148	R.G.Sharma	India	110	K.J.O'Brien	Ireland
124	Shoaib Malik	Pakistan/ICC	109	Shakib Al Hasan	Bangladesh
122	M.J.Guptill	New Zealand	107	T.G.Southee	New Zealand
121	Mahmudullah	Bangladesh	104	Mohammad Nabi	Afghanistan
121	P.R.Stirling	Ireland	103	J.C.Buttler	England
119	Mohammad Hafeez	Pakistan	103	A.J.Finch	Australia
115	G.H.Dockrell	Ireland	102	Mushfiqur Rahim	Bangladesh
115	V.Kohli	India	102	L.R.P.L.Taylor	New Zealand
115	E.J.G.Morgan	England	101	K.A.Pollard	West Indies
111	D.A.Miller	South Africa/World			

The most appearances for Sri Lanka is 85 by M.D.Shanaka, and for Zimbabwe 68 by S.C.Williams.

50 MATCHES AS CAPTAIN

			W	L	T	NR	%age wins
76	A.J.Finch	Australia	40	32	1	3	54.79
72	M.S.Dhoni	India	41	28	1	2	58.57
72	E.J.G.Morgan	England	42	27	2	1	59.15
69	K.S.Williamson	New Zealand	35	32	1	1	51.47
66	Babar Azam	Pakistan	40	21	–	5	65.57
56	W.T.S.Porterfield	Ireland	26	26	–	4	50.00
52	Asghar Stanikzai	Afghanistan	42	9	1	–	80.76
52	A.Balbirnie	Ireland	19	31	1	1	37.25
51	R.G.Sharma	India	39	12	–	–	76.47
50	V.Kohli	India	30	16	2	2	62.50

THE MEN'S HUNDRED 2022

The second edition of The Hundred, featuring eight franchise sides in matches of 100 balls per side, took place between 3 August and 3 September. The second- and third-placed sides played off for a place in the final, held at Lord's. (2021's positions in brackets.)

		P	W	L	T	NR	Pts	Net RR
1.	Trent Rockets (3)	8	6	2	–	–	12	+0.57
2.	Manchester Originals (6)	8	5	3	–	–	10	+0.90
3.	London Spirit (8)	8	5	3	–	–	10	+0.33
4.	Birmingham Phoenix (1)	8	5	3	–	–	10	–0.17
5.	Oval Invincibles (4)	8	4	4	–	–	8	+0.38
6.	Northern Superchargers (5)	8	4	4	–	–	8	+0.00
7.	Southern Brave (2)	8	3	5	–	–	6	–0.59
8.	Welsh Fire (7)	8	–	8	–	–	0	–1.44

LEADING AGGREGATES AND RECORDS 2022

BATTING (275 runs)

	M	I	NO	HS	Runs	Avge	100	50	R/100b	Sixes
D.J.Malan (Rockets)	9	9	2	98*	377	53.85	–	4	166.8	20
P.D.Salt (Originals)	10	10	1	70*	353	39.22	–	3	152.8	15
A.Lyth (Superchargers)	8	8	–	79	299	37.37	–	3	175.8	20

BOWLING (14 wkts)

	Balls	R	W	Avge	BB	4w	R/100b
P.I.Walter (Originals)	135	160	14	11.42	3-20	–	118.5
T.G.Helm (Phoenix)	142	197	14	14.07	4-17	1	138.7
J.A.Thompson (Spirit)	166	253	14	18.07	4-21	1	152.4

Highest total	208-5	Originals v Superchargers	Leeds
Biggest win (runs)	79	Originals (154-6) beat Phoenix (75)	Birmingham
Biggest win (balls)	31	Brave (109-1) beat Fire (107-7)	Southampton
Highest innings	108*	W.G.Jacks	Invincibles v Brave	The Oval
Most sixes	20	A.Lyth (Superchargers), D.J.Malan (Rockets)	
Most sixes (inns)	9	D.J.Malan	Rockets v Originals	Manchester
Highest partnership	121	P.R.Stirling/Q.de Kock	Brave v Fire	Cardiff
Best bowling	5-13	J.B.Little	Originals v Invincibles	Manchester
Most economical	20b-11-3	S.P.Narine	Invincibles v Superchargers	The Oval
	20b-11-3	T.G.Helm	Phoenix v Invincibles	The Oval
Most expensive	20b-53-1	D.Wiese	Superchargers v Originals	Leeds
Most w/k dismissals	6	A.M.Rossington (Spirit)		
Most catches	9	T.Stubbs (Originals)		

OVERALL RECORDS

Highest total	208-5	Originals v Superchargers	Leeds	2022
Biggest win (runs)	93	Phoenix (184-5) beat Fire (91)	Birmingham	2021
Biggest win (balls)	32	Brave (97-3) beat Rockets (96)	The Oval	2021
Most runs	591	D.J.Malan (Rockets)		2021-22
Highest innings	108*	W.G.Jacks	Invincibles v Brave	The Oval	2022
Most sixes	41	L.S.Livingstone (Phoenix)		2021-22
Most wickets	21	S.R.Patel (Rockets)		2021-22
Best bowling	5-13	J.B.Little	Originals v Invincibles	Manchester	2022
Most economical	20b-6-2	Mujeeb Zadran	Superchargers v Spirit	Lord's	2021
Most expensive	20b-53-1	D.Wiese	Superchargers v Originals	Leeds	2022
Most w/k dismissals	15	Q.de Kock (Brave)		2021-22
Most catches	11	A.L.Davies (Brave)		2021-22

2022 THE HUNDRED FINAL
MANCHESTER ORIGINALS v TRENT ROCKETS

At Lord's, London, on 3 September (floodlit).

Result: **TRENT ROCKETS** won by two wickets.

Toss: Manchester Originals. Award: S.J.Cook.

MANCHESTER ORIGINALS		Runs	Balls	4/6	Fall
† P.D.Salt	c Gregory b Sams	11	10	2	3- 22
* L.J.Evans	lbw b Cook	4	4	1	1- 13
W.L.Madsen	b Cook	3	6	–	2- 18
T.Stubbs	c Moores b Patel	18	18	1	4- 57
A.J.Turner	c Cook b Patel	26	13	3/1	6- 75
P.I.Walter	c Malan b Patel	0	1	–	5- 57
T.A.Lammonby	b Cook	21	18	1	7-100
T.W.Hartley	c Moores b Wood	12	15	1	8-103
R.J.Gleeson	b Cook	8	8	1	9-111
M.W.Parkinson	not out	2	5	–	
J.B.Little	not out	5	2	1	
Extras	(B 2, LB 4, W 4)	10			
Total	**(9 wkts; 100 balls)**	**120**			

TRENT ROCKETS		Runs	Balls	4/6	Fall
A.D.Hales	c Walter b Little	8	8	1	1- 16
D.J.Malan	c Stubbs b Walter	19	18	2	3- 49
T.Kohler-Cadmore	lbw b Parkinson	18	18	2	2- 45
S.R.Patel	c Turner b Hartley	9	13	–	5- 85
C.Munro	c Hartley b Parkinson	16	7	2/1	4- 68
† T.J.Moores	c Stubbs b Walter	16	15	1	6- 97
D.R.Sams	c Stubbs b Hartley	13	8	1/1	7-106
* L.Gregory	not out	17	6	1/1	
M.Carter	c Hartley b Little	0	3	–	8-107
L.Wood	not out	1	2	–	
S.J.Cook					
Extras	(W 4)	4			
Total	**(8 wkts; 98 balls)**	**121**			

ROCKETS	B	O	R	W	ORIGINALS	B	O	R	W
Wood	20	10	19	1	Gleeson	18	7	28	0
Cook	20	11	18	4	Little	20	9	18	2
Sams	15	5	20	1	Walter	20	9	21	2
Gregory	10	2	15	0	Hartley	20	6	28	2
Patel	15	5	23	3	Parkinson	15	3	21	2
Carter	20	6	19	0	Stubbs	5	1	5	0

Umpires: M.Burns and M.J.Saggers.

THE HUNDRED WINNERS

2021	Southern Brave	1	2022	Trent Rockets

Eliminator: At the Rose Bowl, Southampton, 2 September. Toss: London Spirit. **MANCHESTER ORIGINALS** won by five wickets. London Spirit 150-7 (100 balls; B.R.McDermott 59, Z.Crawley 36, P.I.Walter 3-29). Manchester Originals 151-5 (89 balls; L.J.Evans 72). Award: L.J.Evans.

IRELAND INTERNATIONALS

The following players have played for Ireland in any format of international cricket since 1 November 2021. Details correct to 17 March 2023.

ADAIR, George Ross, b Belfast 21 Apr 1994. Elder brother of M.R.Adair (*see below*). RHB, LB. Northern Knights debut 2021 (not f-c). **IT20**: 3 (2022-23): HS 65 v Z (Harare) 2022-23. LO HS 47* Northern v Munster (Belfast) 2022. LO BB –. T20 HS 111. T20 BB 2-24.

ADAIR, Mark Richard (Sullivan Upper S, Holywood), b Belfast 27 Mar 1996. Younger brother of G.R.Adair (*see above*). 6'2". RHB, RFM. Warwickshire 2015-16. Northern Knights debut 2018. Ireland Wolves 2018-19 to 2020-21. **Tests**: 1 (2019); HS 8 and BB 3-32 v E (Lord's) 2019. **LOI**: 29 (2019 to 2022-23); HS 32 v E (Dublin) 2019; BB 4-19 v Afg (Belfast) 2019. **IT20**: 61 (2019 to 2022-23); HS 38 v Z (Bready) 2019; BB 4-23 v Z (Bready) 2021. HS 91 Northern v Leinster (Dublin, Sandymount) 2018. BB 3-22 IW v Bangladesh EP (Chittagong) 2021-22. LO HS 108 Northern v Munster (Cork) 2022. LO BB 4-19 (*see LOI*). T20 HS 39. T20 BB 4-14.

BALBIRNIE, Andrew (St Andrew's C, Dublin; UWIC), b Dublin 28 Dec 1990. 6'2". RHB, OB. Cardiff MCCU 2012-13. Ireland debut 2012. Middlesex 2012-15. Leinster Lightning debut 2017. Ireland Wolves 2017-18. Glamorgan 2021. **Tests**: 3 (2018 to 2019); HS 82 v Afg (Dehradun) 2018-19. LOI: 89 (2010 to 2022-23, 25 as captain); HS 145* v Afg (Dehradun) 2018-19; BB 1-26 v Afg (Dubai, DSC) 2014-15. **IT20**: 89 (2015 to 2022-23, 52 as captain); HS 83 v Neth (Al Amerat) 2018-19. HS 205* Ire v Neth (Dublin) 2017. BB 4-23 Leinster v NW (Bready) 2017. LO HS 160* IW v Bangladesh A (Dublin, CA) 2018. LO BB 1-26 (*see LOI*). T20 HS 99*.

CAMPHER, Curtis (St Stithians C), b Johannesburg, South Africa 20 Apr 1999. RHB, RM. Ireland Wolves 2020-21. Leinster Lightning 2020 (not f-c). Munster Reds debut 2021 (not f-c). **LOI**: 19 (2020 to 2022-23); HS 68 v E (Southampton); BB 3-49 v NZ (Dublin) 2022. **IT20**: 31 (2021 to 2022-23); HS 72* v Scot (Hobart) 2022-23; BB 4-25 v USA (Lauderhill) 2021-22. HS 39 IW v Bangladesh EP (Chittagong) 2020-21. LO HS 68 (*see LOI*). LO BB 4-46 Leinster v NW (Bready) 2020. T20 HS 72*. T20 BB 4-25.

COMMINS, Murray b Cape Town, South Africa 2 Jan 1997. Son of J.T.Commins (W Province, Boland & South Africa 1985-86 to 1994-95); grandson of K.T.Commins (W Province & Boland 1951-52 to 1960-61). RHB, RMF. SW Districts 2016-17. Boland 2017-18 to 2018-19. Northern Knights 2019. Munster Reds debut 2021 (not f-c). **LOI**: 2 (2022-23); HS 6 v Z (Harare) 2022-23. HS 78 SW Districts v Northern Cape (Oudtshoorn) 2016-17. LO HS 125 Munster v Northern (Belfast) 2021. T20 HS 102.

DELANY, Gareth James, b Dublin 28 Apr 1997. Cousin of D.C.A.Delany (Leinster, Northern, Munster & Ireland 2017 to date). RHB, LBG. Leinster Lightning 2017-19. Ireland Wolves 2018-19 to 2020-21. Leicestershire 2020 (T20 only). Munster Reds debut 2021 (not f-c). **LOI**: 14 (2019-20 to 2022-23); HS 22 v E (Southampton) 2020 and 22 v NZ (Dublin) 2022; BB 1-10 v UAE (Abu Dhabi) 2020-21. **IT20**: 58 (2019 to 2022-23); HS 89* v Oman (Abu Dhabi, TO) 2019-20; BB 3-16 v WI (Hobart) 2022-23. HS 22 IW v Sri Lanka A (Colombo, SSC) 2018-19. BB 3-48 Leinster v Northern (Belfast) 2017. LO HS 104 and LO BB 5-39 IW v Namibia A (Windhoek) 2021-22. T20 HS 89*. T20 BB 3-8.

DOCKRELL, George Henry (Gonzaga C, Dublin), b Dublin 22 Jul 1992. 6'3". RHB, SLA. Ireland debut 2010. Somerset 2011-14. Sussex 2015. Leinster Lightning debut 2017. Ireland Wolves 2017-18. **Tests**: 1 (2018-19); HS 39 and BB 2-63 v Afg (Dehradun) 2018-19. **LOI**: 105 (2009-10 to 2022-23); HS 74 v NZ (Dublin) 2022; BB 4-24 v Scot (Belfast) 2013. **IT20**: 115 (2009-10 to 2022-23); HS 58* v Afg (Belfast) 2022; BB 4-20 v Neth (Dubai) 2009-10. HS 92 Leinster v NW (Bready) 2018. BB 6-27 Sm v Middx (Taunton) 2012. LO HS 100* Leinster v Northern (Dublin, SP) 2021. LO BB 5-21 Leinster v Northern (Dublin, V) 2018. T20 HS 69*. T20 BB 4-20.

DOHENY, Stephen Thomas (Catholic Uni S, Dublin), b Dublin 29 Aug 1998. RHB, WK, occ OB. Leinster Lightning 2018-19. Ireland Wolves 2018-19 to 2020-21. North West Warriors debut 2021 (not f-c). **LOI**: 3 (2022-23); HS 84 v Z (Harare) 2022-23. **IT20**: 3 (2022-23); HS 15 v Z (Harare) 2022-23. HS 58 IW v Sri Lanka A (Hambantota) 2018-19. BB 1-4 Leinster v Northern (Dublin) 2019. LO HS 97 NW v Northern (Belfast) 2022. T20 HS 74*.

GETKATE, Shane Charles, b Durban, South Africa 2 Oct 1991. Grandson of R.S.Getkate (Natal 1936-37). RHB, RMF. Northern Knights 2017-19. Ireland Wolves 2017-18. North West Warriors 2021 (not f-c). **LOI**: 4 (2019 to 2021); HS 16* v Z (Bready) 2019; BB 2-30 v Z (Belfast) 2019. **IT20**: 30 (2018-19 to 2021-22); HS 30 v UAE (Al Amerat) 2021-22; BB 3-20 v Z (Dublin) 2021. HS 70 Northern v Leinster (Comber) 2018. BB 4-62 Northern v Leinster (Dublin, CA) 2017. LO HS 120 Tuskers v SR (Bulawayo) 2022-23. LO BB 5-44 Northern v Leinster (Downpatrick) 2017. T20 HS 54. T20 BB 5-8.

HAND, Fionn (Ardgillan Community C; Queen's C, Taunton), b Dublin 1 Jul 1998. RHB, RMF. Leinster Lightning 2019. Munster Reds debut 2021 (not f-c). **IT20**: 8 (2022 to 2022-23); HS 36 v Afg (Belfast) 2022; BB 1-11 v Afg (Belfast) 2022 – separate matches. BB –. LO HS 49* Munster v NW (Cork) 2021. LO BB 2-28 Munster v Northern (Belfast) 2022. T20 HS 44*. T20 BB 2-12.

HUME, Graham Ian, b Johannesburg, South Africa 23 Nov 1990. LHB, RMF. Gauteng 2009-10 to 2012-13. KZN Inland 2013-14 to 2018-19. Dolphins 2014-15. North West Warriors debut 2019. Ireland Wolves 2020-21. **LOI**: 4 (2022 to 2022-23); HS 7* v NZ (Dublin) 2022; BB 2-41 v Z (Harare) 2022-23. **IT20**: 2 (2022 to 2022-23); HS 1 v Afg (Belfast) 2022; BB 3-17 v Z (Harare) 2022-23. HS 105 Gauteng v SW Districts (Johannesburg) 2011-12. BB 7-23 KZN Inland v Northerns (Centurion) 2017-18. LO HS 44* NW v Leinster (Dublin, SP) 2021. LO BB 4-18 NW v Northern (Bready) 2022. T20 HS 52. T20 BB 4-7.

KANE, Tyrone Edward (Catholic Uni S, Dublin; University C, Dublin), b Dublin 8 Jul 1994. RHB, RMF. Leinster 2017-19. Munster Reds debut 2021 (not f-c). **Tests**: 1 (2018); HS 14 v P (Dublin) 2018; BB –. **IT20**: 9 (2015 to 2022-23); HS 26* v Scot (Bready) 2015; BB 3-19 v PNG (Belfast) 2015. HS 75 and BB 3-45 Leinster v Northern (Dublin, CA) 2017. LO HS 78 Munster v NW (Cork) 2021. LO BB 6-42 Leinster v Northern (Belfast) 2019. T20 HS 66*. T20 BB 5-22.

LITTLE, Joshua Brian (St Andrew's C), b Dublin 1 Nov 1999. RHB, LFM. Leinster Lightning debut 2018. Ireland Wolves 2018-19. Manchester Originals 2022. **LOI**: 25 (2019 to 2022-23); HS 9* v Neth (Utrecht) 2021; BB 4-38 v Z (Harare) 2022-23. **IT20**: 53 (2016 to 2022-23); HS 15* v SA (Dublin) 2021; BB 4-23 v SL (Abu Dhabi) 2021-22. HS 27 Leinster v NW (Bready) 2018. BB 3-95 Leinster v Northern (Dublin) 2018. LO HS 22 Leinster v Munster (Dublin, SP) 2021. LO BB 4-38 *(see LOI)*. T20 HS 27*. T20 BB 5-13.

McBRINE, Andrew Robert (St Michael's C, Dublin; University C, Dublin), b Londonderry 30 Apr 1993. Son of A.McBrine (Ireland 1985-92), nephew of J.McBrine (Ireland 1986). LHB, OB. Ireland debut 2013. North West Warriors debut 2017. Ireland Wolves 2017-18. **Tests**: 2 (2018-19 to 2019); HS 11 v E (Lord's) 2019; BB 2-77 v Afg (Dehradun) 2018-19. **LOI**: 70 (2014 to 2022-23); HS 79 v SL (Dublin) 2016; BB 5-29 v Afg (Abu Dhabi) 2020-21. **IT20**: 32 (2013-14 to 2022); HS 36 v Oman (Al Amerat) 2021-22; BB 2-7 v PNG (Townsville) 2015-16. HS 77 NW v Northern (Comber) 2018. BB 4-35 NW v Northern (Bready) 2018. LO HS 117 NW v Northern (Belfast) 2022. LO BB 5-29 *(see LOI)*. T20 HS 52*. T20 BB 3-19.

McCARTHY, Barry John (St Michael's C, Dublin; University C, Dublin), b Dublin 13 Sep 1992. 5'11''. RHB, RMF. Durham 2015-18. Leinster Lightning debut 2019. **LOI**: 38 (2016 to 2021); HS 18 v Afg (Belfast) 2019; BB 5-46 v Afg (Sharjah) 2017-18. **IT20**: 7 (2016-17 to 2022-23); HS 32 v SA (Bristol) 2022; BB 4-30 v USA (Lauderhill) 2021-22. HS 51* Du v Hants (Chester-le-St) 2016. BB 6-63 Du v Kent (Canterbury) 2017. LO HS Leinster v Northern (Dublin, SP) 2022. LO BB 6-39 Leinster v Munster (Dublin, SP) 2021. T20 HS 32. T20 BB 4-18.

McCLINTOCK, William T., b Londonderry 1 Jan 1997. Twin brother of G.S.McClintock (North West Warriors 2017). RHB, RM. North West Warriors debut 2017 (not f-c). **IT20:** 5 (2021 to 2021-22); HS 15* v Z (Bready) 2021. LO HS 72* NW v Northern (Belfast) 2021. T20 HS 54.

OLPHERT, Conor James, b 28 Dec 1995. RHB, RFM. North West Warriors debut 2020 (not f-c). **IT20:** 2 (2022); HS – ; BB –. LO HS 7 NW v Leinster (Dublin, SP) 2022. LO BB 3-83 NW v Northern (Belfast) 2022. T20 HS 8. T20 BB 3-27.

PORTERFIELD, William Thomas Stuart (Strabane GS; Leeds Met U), b Londonderry 6 Sep 1984. 5'11". LHB, OB. Ireland 2006-19. Gloucestershire 2008-10; cap 2008. Warwickshire 2011-17; cap 2014. North West Warriors debut 2018. MCC 2007. **Tests:** 3 (2018 to 2019, 3 as captain); HS 32 v P (Dublin) 2018. **LOI:** 148 (2006 to 2021-22, 113 as captain); HS 139 v UAE (Dubai, ICCA) 2017-18. **IT20:** 61 (2008 to 2018, 56 as captain); HS 72 v UAE (Abu Dhabi) 2015-16. HS 207 NW v Leinster (Bready) 2018. BB 1-29 Ire v Jamaica (Spanish Town) 2009-10. LO HS 139 (*see LOI*). T20 HS 127*.

ROCK, Neil Alan, b Dublin 24 Sep 2000. LHB, WK. Northern Knights debut 2018. Ireland Wolves 2018-19. Munster Reds 2020 (T20 only). **LOI:** 3 (2021-22); HS 5 v WI (Kingston) 2021-22. **IT20:** 14 (2021 to 2022-23); HS 22 v Z (Bready) 2021. HS 85 IW v Sri Lanka A (Hambantota) 2018-19. LO HS 81 Northern v Leinster (Dublin, SP) 2022. T20 HS 58*.

SINGH, Simranjit ('Simi'), b Bathlana, Punjab, India 4 Feb 1987. RHB, OB. Leinster Lightning debut 2017. Ireland debut 2017. Ireland Wolves 2017-18. **LOI:** 35 (2017 to 2022); HS 100* v SA (Dublin) 2021; BB 5-10 v UAE (Abu Dhabi) 2020-21. **IT20:** 53 (2018 to 2022-23); HS 57* v Neth (Rotterdam) 2018; BB 3-9 v Oman (Al Amerat) 2021-22. HS 121 IW v Bangladesh A (Sylhet) 2017-18. BB 5-38 Leinster v Northern (Dublin) 2019. LO HS 121* Leinster v Northern (Dublin, V) 2018. LO BB 5-10 (*see LOI*). T20 HS 109. T20 BB 4-21.

STIRLING, Paul Robert (Belfast HS), b Belfast, N Ireland 3 Sep 1990. Father Brian Stirling was an international rugby referee. 5'10". RHB, OB. Ireland 2007-08 to date. Middlesex 2013-19; cap 2016. Northamptonshire 2020 (T20 only). Northern Knights debut 2020 (white-ball only). Warwickshire 2022 (T20 only). Southern Brave debut 2021. **Tests:** 3 (2018 to 2019); HS 36 v E (Lord's) 2019; BB – . **LOI:** 142 (2008 to 2022-23); HS 177 v Canada (Toronto) 2010 – Ire record; BB 6-55 v Afg (Greater Noida) 2016-17 – Ire record. **IT20:** 121 (2009 to 2022-23); HS 115* v Z (Bready) 2021; BB 3-21 v B (Belfast) 2012. HS 146 Ire v UAE (Dublin) 2015. CC HS 138 and BB 2-21 M v Glamorgan (Radlett) 2019. LO HS 177 (*see LOI*). LO BB 6-55 (*see LOI*). T20 HS 119. T20 BB 4-10.

TECTOR, Harry Tom, b Dublin 6 Nov 1999. Younger brother of J.B.Tector (Leinster 2017 to date). RHB, OB. Northern Knights 2018-21. Leinster Lightning debut 2022. Ireland debut 2020 (not f-c). Ireland Wolves 2018-19 to 2020-21. **LOI:** 26 (2020 to 2022-23); HS 113 v NZ (Dublin) 2022; BB 1-20 v Z (Harare) 2022-23. **IT20:** 54 (2019 to 2022-23); HS 64* v I (Dublin) 2022; BB 2-17 v Z (Harare) 2022-23. HS 146 Northern v Leinster (Dublin) 2019. BB 4-70 Northern v NW (Bready) 2018. LO HS 113 (*see LOI*). LO BB 5-36 Northern v NW (La Manga) 2019. T20 HS 91. T20 BB 4-21.

TUCKER, Lorcan John, b Dublin 10 Sep 1996. RHB, WK. Leinster Lightning debut 2017. Ireland Wolves 2018-19 to 2020-21. **LOI:** 32 (2019 to 2022-23); HS 83 v Afg (Abu Dhabi) 2020-21. **IT20:** 49 (2016 to 2022-23); HS 84 v USA (Lauderhill) 2021-22. HS 80 IW v Sri Lanka A (Hambantota) 2018-19. LO HS 109 IW v Sri Lanka A (Hambantota) 2018-19. T20 HS 84.

WHITE, Benjamin Charlie, b Dublin 29 Aug 1998. RHB, LB. Northern Knights debut 2021 (not f-c). **IT20:** 10 (2021 to 2022-23); HS 2* v SA (Belfast) 2021 and 2* v USA (Lauderhill) 2021-22; BB 2-23 v Z (Bready) 2021. HS 13 Northern v Munster (Cork) 2022. LO BB 4-49 IW v Namibia A (Windhoek) 2021-22. T20 HS 12*. T20 BB 5-13.

YOUNG, Craig Alexander (Strabane HS; North West IHE, Belfast), b Londonderry 4 Apr 1990. RHB, RM. Ireland debut 2013. North West Warriors debut 2017. Ireland Wolves 2018-19. **LOI:** 36 (2014 to 2022); HS 12* v Afg (Abu Dhabi) 2020-21; BB 5-46 v Scot (Dublin) 2014. **IT20:** 53 (2015 to 2022); HS 22 v SA (Belfast) 2021; BB 4-13 v Nigeria (Abu Dhabi) 2019-20. HS 23 and BB 5-37 NW v Northern (Eglinton) 2017. LO HS 30 IW v Netherlands A (Oak Hill) 2021. LO BB 5-46 (*see LOI*). T20 HS 22. T20 BB 5-15.

ENGLAND WOMEN INTERNATIONALS

The following players have played for England since 1 October 2021 and are still available for selection. Details correct to 1 April 2023.

BEAUMONT, Tamsin (**'Tammy'**) Tilley, b Dover, Kent 11 Mar 1991. RHB, WK. MBE 2018. Kent 2007-19. Diamonds 2007-12. Sapphires 2008. Emeralds 2011-13. Surrey Stars 2016-17. Adelaide Strikers 2016-17 to 2017-18. Southern Vipers 2018-19. Melbourne Renegades 2019-20. Lightning 2020 to date. Sydney Thunder 2020-21. London Spirit 2021. Welsh Fire 2022. *Wisden* 2018. **Tests**: 7 (2013 to 2022); HS 70 v A (Sydney) 2017-18. **LOI**: 103 (2009-10 to 2022-23); HS 168* v P (Taunton) 2016. **IT20**: 99 (2009-10 to 2021-22); HS 116 v SA (Taunton) 2018.

BELL, Lauren Katie, b Swindon, Wilts 2 Jan 2001. Younger sister of C.J.Bell (Berkshire & Buckinghamshire 2016-19). RHB, RM. Berkshire 2015-19. Southern Vipers debut 2020. Southern Brave debut 2021. **Tests**: 1 (2022); HS – ; BB 2-47 v SA (Taunton) 2022. **LOI**: 5 (2022 to 2022-23); HS 11* v I (Canterbury) 2022; BB 4-33 v WI (North Sound) 2022-23. **IT20**: 9 (2022 to 2022-23); HS – ; BB 4-12 v WI (Bridgetown) 2022-23.

BOUCHIER, Maia Emily (Dragon S; Rugby S; Oxford Brookes U), b Kensington, London 5 Dec 1998. RHB, RM. Middlesex 2014-18. Auckland 2017-18. Southern Vipers 2018 to date. Hampshire 2019. Southern Brave 2021 to date. W Australia 2021-22. Melbourne Stars 2021-22. **IT20**: 19 (2021 to 2022-23); HS 34 v I (Derby) 2022.

CAPSEY, Alice Rose (Bede's S), b Redhill, Surrey 11 Aug 2004. RHB, OB. Surrey 2019 to date. South East Stars 2020 to date. Oval Invincibles 2021 to date. **LOI**: 4 (2022 to 2022-23); HS 39 v I (Canterbury) 2022. **IT20**: 15 (2022 to 2022-23); HS 51 v Ire (Paarl) 2022-23; BB 1-10 v SA (Worcester) 2022.

CROSS, Kathryn (**'Kate'**) Laura, b Manchester, Lancs 3 Oct 1991. RHB, RMF. Lancashire 2005-19. Sapphires 2007-08. Emeralds 2012. W Australia 2017-18 to 2018-19. Brisbane Heat 2015-16. Lancashire Thunder 2016-19. Perth Scorchers 2018-19. Thunder 2020 to date. Manchester Originals 2021 to date. **Tests**: 6 (2013-14 to 2022); HS 11 v A (Canberra) 2021-22; BB 4-63 v SA (Taunton) 2022. **LOI**: 54 (2013-14 to 2022-23); HS 29 v NZ (Leicester) 2021; BB 5-24 v NZ (Lincoln) 2014-15. **IT20**: 13 (2013-14 to 2019-20); HS 0*; BB 2-18 v I (Guwahati) 2018-19.

DAVIDSON-RICHARDS, Alice Natica, b Tunbridge Wells, Kent 29 May 1994. RHB, RFM. Kent 2010-19. Sapphires 2011-12. Emeralds 2013. Otago 2018-19. South East Stars debut 2020. Yorkshire Diamonds 2016. Northern Superchargers debut 2021. **Tests**: 1 (2022); HS 107 and BB 1-39 v SA (Taunton) 2022. **LOI**: 22 (2018 to 2022-23); HS 50* v I (Hove) 2022; BB 3-35 v SA (Leicester) 2022. **IT20**: 8 (2017-18 to 2022-23); HS 24 v A (Mumbai) 2017-18; BB 3-5 v WI (Bridgetown) 2022-23.

DAVIES, Freya Ruth, b Chichester, Sussex 27 Oct 1995. RHB, RMF. Sussex 2012-19. Western Storm 2016-19. South East Stars 2020 to date. London Spirit 2021 to date. **LOI**: 9 (2019-20 to 2022-23); HS 10* v I (Lord's) 2022; BB 2-36 v B (Wellington) 2021-22. **IT20**: 25 (2018-19 to 2022-23); HS 1* v NZ (Wellington) 2020-21; BB 4-23 v NZ (Wellington) 2020-21 – separate matches.

DEAN, Charlotte (**'Charlie'**) Ellen (Portsmouth GS), b Burton-upon-Trent, Staffs 22 Dec 2000. Daughter of S.J.Dean (Staffordshire and Warwickshire 1986-2002 – List-A only). RHB, OB. Hampshire 2016-19. Southern Vipers 2017 to date. London Spirit 2021 to date. **Tests**: 1 (2021-22); HS 9 and BB 2-24 v A (Canberra) 2021-22. **LOI**: 22 (2021 to 2022-23); HS 47 v I (Lord's) 2022; BB 4-23 v I (Mt Maunganui) 2021-22. **IT20**: 10 (2021-22 to 2022-23); HS 20 v WI (Bridgetown) 2022-23; BB 4-19 v WI (Bridgetown) 2022-23 – separate matches.

DUNKLEY, Sophia Ivy Rose, b Lambeth, Surrey 16 Jul 1998. RHB, LB. Middlesex 2013-19. Surrey Stars 2016-18. Lancashire Thunder 2019. South East Stars 2020 to date. Southern Brave 2021 to date. **Tests**: 3 (2021 to 2022); HS 74* v I (Bristol) 2021; BB –. **LOI**: 28 (2021 to 2022-23); HS 107 v SA (Bristol) 2022; BB 1-1 v WI (North Sound) 2022-23. **IT20**: 44 (2018-19 to 2022-23); HS 61* v I (Chester-le-St) 2022; BB 1-6 v SL (Colombo, PSS) 2018-19.

ECCLESTONE, Sophie (Helsby HS), b Chester 6 May 1999. 5'11". RHB, SLA. Cheshire 2013-14. Lancashire 2015-19. Lancashire Thunder 2016-19. Thunder 2020 to date. Manchester Originals 2021 to date. Sydney Sixers 2022-23. **Tests**: 5 (2017-18 to 2022); HS 35 v SA (Taunton) 2022; BB 4-88 v I (Bristol) 2021. **LOI**: 55 (2016-17 to 2022-23); HS 33* v WI (Dunedin) 2021-22; BB 6-36 v SA (Christchurch) 2021-22. **IT20**: 70 (2016 to 2022-23); HS 33* v SA (Derby) 2022; BB 4-18 v NZ (Taunton) 2018.

FARRANT, Natasha ('Tash') Eleni (Sevenoaks S), b Athens, Greece 29 May 1996. LHB, LMF. Kent 2012-19. Sapphires 2013. W Australia 2016-17. Southern Vipers 2016-19. South East Stars 2020 to date. Oval Invincibles 2021. **LOI**: 6 (2013-14 to 2021-22); HS 22 v NZ (Worcester) 2021; BB 2-31 v NZ (Christchurch) 2021-22. **IT20**: 18 (2013 to 2021); HS 3* v A (Mumbai, BS) 2017-18; BB 2-15 v P (Loughborough) 2013.

GLENN, Sarah, b Derby 27 Feb 1999. RHB, LB. Derbyshire 2013-18. Worcestershire 2019. Loughborough Lightning 2017-19. Central Sparks 2020 to date. Perth Scorchers 2020-21. Trent Rockets 2021 to date. **LOI**: 9 (2019-20 to 2021); HS 11 v NZ (Dunedin) 2020-21; BB 4-18 v P (Kuala Lumpur) 2019-20. **IT20**: 46 (2019-20 to 2022-23); HS 26 v WI (Derby) 2020; BB 4-23 v I (Chester-le-St) 2022.

JONES, Amy Ellen, b Solihull, Warwicks 13 Jun 1993. RHB, WK. Warwickshire 2008-19. Diamonds 2011. Emeralds 2012. Rubies 2013. Loughborough Lightning 2016-19. Sydney Sixers 2016-17 to 2017-18. W Australia 2017-18. Perth Scorchers 2018-19 to 2020-21. Central Sparks 2020 to date. Birmingham Phoenix 2021 to date. Sydney Thunder 2022-23. **Tests**: 4 (2019 to 2022); HS 64 v A (Taunton) 2019. **LOI**: 76 (2012-13 to 2022-23); HS 94 v I (Nagpur) 2017-18. **IT20**: 85 (2013 to 2022-23); HS 89 v P (Kuala Lumpur) 2019-20.

KEMP, Freya Grace (Cunmor House S; Bede's S), b Westminster, London 21 Apr 2005. LHB, LMF. Sussex 2019 to date. Southern Vipers 2022. Southern Brave 2022. **LOI**: 2 (2022); HS 12 v I (Canterbury) 2022; BB 2-24 v I (Lord's) 2022. **IT20**: 9 (2022); HS 51* v I (Derby) 2022; BB 2-14 v SL (Birmingham) 2022.

KNIGHT, Heather Clare, b Rochdale, Lancs 26 Dec 1990. RHB, OB. OBE 2018. Devon 2008-09. Emeralds 2008-13. Berkshire 2010-19. Sapphires 2011-12. Tasmania 2014-15 to 2015-16. Hobart Hurricanes 2015-16 to 2019-20. Western Storm 2016 to date. Sydney Thunder 2020-21. London Spirit 2021. *Wisden* 2017. **Tests**: 10 (2010-11 to 2022, 5 as captain); HS 168* v A (Canberra) 2021-22; BB 2-7 v I (Bristol) 2021. **LOI**: 129 (2009-10 to 2022-23, 74 as captain); HS 106 v P (Leicester) 2017; BB 5-26 v P (Leicester) 2016. **IT20**: 98 (2010-11 to 2022-23, 65 as captain); HS 108* v Thai (Canberra) 2019-20; BB 3-9 v I (North Sound) 2018-19.

LAMB, Emma Louise, b Preston, Lancs 16 Dec 1997. Sister of D.J.Lamb (*see LANCASHIRE*). RHB, RM. Lancashire 2012-19. Thunder 2020 to date. Manchester Originals 2021 to date. **Tests**: 1 (2022); HS 38 v SA (Taunton) 2022; BB –. **LOI**: 10 (2021-22 to 2022-23); HS 102 v SA (Northampton) 2022; BB 3-42 v SA (Leicester) 2022. **IT20**: 1 (2021); HS 0*.

SCIVER-BRUNT, Katherine Helen, b Barnsley, Yorks 2 Jul 1985. Wife of N.R.Sciver-Brunt (*see below*). RHB, RMF. Yorkshire 2004-19. Sapphires 2006-08. Diamonds 2011-12. Perth Scorchers 2015-16 to 2017-18. Yorkshire Diamonds 2016-18. Northern Diamonds 2020 to date. Melbourne Stars 2020-21. Trent Rockets 2021 to date. **Tests**: 14 (2004 to 2021-22); HS 52 v A (Worcester) 2005; BB 6-69 v A (Worcester) 2009. **LOI**: 141 (2004-05 to 2022); HS 72* v A (Worcester) 2018; BB 5-18 v A (Wormsley) 2011. **IT20**: 112 (2005 to 2022-23); HS 42* v SA (Taunton) 2018; BB 4-15 v SA (Chelmsford) 2022.

SCIVER-BRUNT, Natalie Ruth (Epsom C), b Tokyo, Japan 20 Aug 1992. Wife of K.H.Sciver-Brunt (*see above*). RHB, RM. Surrey 2010-19. Rubies 2011. Emeralds 2012-13. Melbourne Stars 2015-16 to 2020-21. Surrey Stars 2016-19. Perth Scorchers 2017-18 to 2019-20. Northern Diamonds 2020 to date. Trent Rockets 2021 to date. *Wisden* 2017. **Tests**: 8 (2013-14 to 2022); HS 169* v SA (Taunton) 2022; BB 3-41 v A (Canberra) 2021-22. **LOI**: 94 (2013 to 2022-23); HS 148* v A (Christchurch) 2021-22; BB 4-59 v SA (Northampton) 2022. **IT20**: 108 (2013 to 2022-23, 10 as captain); HS 82 v WI (Derby) 2020. BB 4-15 v A (Cardiff) 2015.

SMITH, Bryony Frances, b Sutton, Surrey 12 Dec 1997. RHB, OB. Surrey 2014 to date. South East Stars 2020 to date. Welsh Fire 2021. Trent Rockets 2022. **LOI**: 1 (2019); HS – ; BB 1-20 v WI (Chelmsford) 2019. **IT20**: 8 (2017-18 to 2022); HS 16 v I (Derby) 2022; BB 1-10 v I (Chester-le-St) 2022.

WINFIELD-HILL, Lauren, b York 16 Aug 1990. RHB, WK. Yorkshire 2007-19. Diamonds 2011. Sapphires 2012. Rubies 2013. Brisbane Heat 2015-16 to 2016-17. Yorkshire Diamonds 2016-19. Hobart Hurricanes 2017-18. Adelaide Strikers 2019-20. Northern Diamonds 2020 to date. Northern Superchargers 2021. Oval Invincibles 2022. Melbourne Stars 2022-23. **Tests**: 5 (2014 to 2021-22); HS 35 v I (Wormsley) 2014 and 35 v I (Bristol) 2021. **LOI**: 55 (2013 to 2021-22); HS 123 v P (Worcester) 2016. **IT20**: 44 (2013 to 2022-23); HS 74 v SA (Birmingham) 2014 and 74 v P (Bristol) 2016.

WONG, Isabelle Eleanor Chih Ming ('**Issy**') (Shrewsbury S), b Chelsea, London 15 May 2002. RHB, RMF. Worcestershire 2018. Warwickshire 2019 to date. Southern Vipers 2019. Central Sparks 2020 to date. Birmingham Phoenix 2021 to date. Sydney Thunder 2021-22. **Tests**: 1 (2022); HS – ; BB 2-46 v SA (Taunton) 2022. **LOI**: 3 (2022); HS – ; BB 3-36 v SA (Bristol) 2022. **IT20**: 9 (2022 to 2022-23); HS 0; BB 2-10 v SL (Birmingham) 2022 and 2-10 v NZ (Birmingham) 2022.

WYATT, Danielle ('Danni') Nicole, b Stoke-on-Trent, Staffs 22 Apr 1991. RHB, OB/RM. Staffordshire 2005-12. Emeralds 2006-08. Sapphires 2011-13. Victoria 2011-12 to 2015-16. Nottinghamshire 2013-15. Melbourne Renegades 2015-16 to 2019-20. Sussex 2016-19. Lancashire Thunder 2016. Southern Vipers 2017 to date. Southern Brave 2021 to date. Brisbane Heat 2022-23. **LOI**: 102 (2009-10 to 2022-23); HS 129 v SA (Christchurch) 2021-22; BB 3-7 v SA (Cuttack) 2012-13. **IT20**: 143 (2009-10 to 2022-23); HS 124 v I (Mumbai, BS) 2017-18; BB 4-11 v SA (Basseterre) 2010.

WOMEN'S TEST CRICKET RECORDS

1934-35 to 6 April 2023
RESULTS SUMMARY

	Opponents	Tests	E	A	NZ	SA	WI	I	P	SL	Ire	H	Drawn
England	Australia	51	9	12	–	–	–	–	–	–	–	–	30
	New Zealand	23	6	–	0	–	–	–	–	–	–	–	17
	South Africa	7	2	–	–	0	–	–	–	–	–	–	5
	West Indies	3	2	–	–	–	0	–	–	–	–	–	1
	India	14	1	–	–	–	–	2	–	–	–	–	11
Australia	New Zealand	13	–	4	1	–	–	–	–	–	–	–	8
	West Indies	2	–	0	–	–	0	–	–	–	–	–	2
	India	10	–	4	–	–	–	0	–	–	–	–	6
New Zealand	South Africa	3	–	–	1	0	–	–	–	–	–	–	2
	India	6	–	–	0	–	–	0	–	–	–	–	6
South Africa	India	2	–	–	–	0	–	2	–	–	–	–	–
	Netherlands	1	–	–	–	–	1	–	–	–	–	0	–
West Indies	India	6	–	–	–	–	1	1	–	–	–	–	4
	Pakistan	1	–	–	–	–	0	–	0	–	–	–	1
Pakistan	Sri Lanka	1	–	–	–	–	–	–	0	1	–	–	–
	Ireland	1	–	–	–	–	–	–	0	–	1	–	–
		144	20	20	2	1	1	5	0	1	1	0	93

	Tests	Won	Lost	Drawn	Toss Won
England	98	20	14	64	58
Australia	76	20	10	46	27
New Zealand	45	2	10	33	21
South Africa	13	1	5	7	6
West Indies	12	1	3	8	6†
India	38	5	6	27	18†
Pakistan	3	–	2	1	1
Sri Lanka	1	1	–	–	1
Ireland	1	1	–	–	–
Netherlands	1	–	1	–	1

† Results of tosses in five of the six India v West Indies Tests in 1976-77 are not known

TEAM RECORDS – HIGHEST INNINGS TOTALS

569-6d	Australia v England	Guildford	1998
525	Australia v India	Ahmedabad	1983-84
517-8	New Zealand v England	Scarborough	1996
503-5d	England v New Zealand	Christchurch	1934-35
497	England v South Africa	Shenley	2003
467	India v England	Taunton	2002
455	England v South Africa	Taunton	2003
448-9d	Australia v England	Sydney	2017-18
440	West Indies v Pakistan	Karachi	2003-04
427-4d	Australia v England	Worcester	1998
426-7d	Pakistan v West Indies	Karachi	2003-04
426-9d	India v England	Blackpool	1986
420-8d	Australia v England	Taunton	2019
417-8d	England v South Africa	Taunton	2022
414	England v New Zealand	Scarborough	1996
414	England v Australia	Guildford	1998
404-9d	India v South Africa	Paarl	2001-02

| 403-8d | New Zealand v India | Nelson | 1994-95 |
| 400-6d | India v South Africa | Mysore | 2014-15 |

The highest totals for countries not included above are:

316	South Africa v England	Shenley	2003
193-3d	Ireland v Pakistan	Dublin	2000
108	Netherlands v South Africa	Rotterdam	2007

LOWEST INNINGS TOTALS

35	England v Australia	Melbourne	1957-58
38	Australia v England	Melbourne	1957-58
44	New Zealand v England	Christchurch	1934-35
47	Australia v England	Brisbane	1934-35
50	Netherlands v South Africa	Rotterdam	2007
53	Pakistan v Ireland	Dublin	2000

The lowest innings totals for countries not included above are:

65	India v West Indies	Jammu	1976-77
67	West Indies v England	Canterbury	1979
89	South Africa v New Zealand	Durban	1971-72

BATTING RECORDS – 1000 RUNS IN TESTS

		Career	M	I	NO	HS	Avge	100	50
1935	J.A.Brittin (E)	1979-98	27	44	5	167	49.61	5	11
1676	C.M.Edwards (E)	1996-2015	23	43	5	117	44.10	4	9
1594	R.Heyhoe-Flint (E)	1960-79	22	38	3	179	45.54	3	10
1301	D.A.Hockley (NZ)	1979-96	19	29	4	126*	52.04	4	7
1164	C.A.Hodges (E)	1984-92	18	31	2	158*	40.13	2	6
1110	S.Agarwal (I)	1984-95	13	23	1	190	50.45	4	4
1078	E.Bakewell (E)	1968-79	12	22	4	124	59.88	4	7
1030	S.C.Taylor (E)	1999-2009	15	27	2	177	41.20	4	2
1007	M.E.Maclagan (E)	1934-51	14	25	1	119	41.95	2	6
1002	K.L.Rolton (A)	1995-2009	14	22	4	209*	55.66	2	5

HIGHEST INDIVIDUAL INNINGS

242	Kiran Baluch	P v WI	Karachi	2003-04
214	M.Raj	I v E	Taunton	2002
213*	E.A.Perry	A v E	Sydney	2017-18
209*	K.L.Rolton	A v E	Leeds	2001
204	K.E.Flavell	NZ v E	Scarborough	1996
204‡	M.A.J.Goszko	A v E	Shenley	2001
200	J.Broadbent	A v E	Guildford	1998
193	D.A.Annetts	A v E	Collingham	1987
192	M.D.T.Kamini	I v SA	Mysore	2014-15
190	S.Agarwal	I v E	Worcester	1986
189	E.A.Snowball	E v NZ	Christchurch	1934-35
179	R.Heyhoe-Flint	E v A	The Oval	1976
177	S.C.Taylor	E v SA	Shenley	2003
176*	K.L.Rolton	A v E	Worcester	1998
169*	N.R.Sciver	E v SA	Taunton	2022
168*	H.C.Knight	E v A	Canberra	2021-22
167	J.A.Brittin	E v A	Harrogate	1998
161*	E.C.Drumm	E v A	Christchurch	1994-95
160	B.A.Daniels	E v NZ	Scarborough	1996
158*	C.A.Hodges	E v NZ	Canterbury	1984
157	H.C.Knight	E v A	Wormsley	2013
150	M.Kapp	SA v E	Taunton	2022

‡ *On debut*

FIVE HUNDREDS

						Opponents							
		M	*I*	*E*	*A*	*NZ*	*SA*	*WI*	*Ind*	*P*	*SL*	*Ire*
5	J.A.Brittin (E)	27	44	–	3	–	1	–	1	–	–	–

HIGHEST PARTNERSHIP FOR EACH WICKET

1st	241	Kiran Baluch/Sajjida Shah	P v WI	Karachi	2003-04
2nd	275	M.D.T.Kamini/P.G.Raut	I v SA	Mysore	2014-15
3rd	309	L.A.Reeler/D.A.Annetts	A v E	Collingham	1987
4th	253	K.L.Rolton/L.C.Broadfoot	A v E	Leeds	2001
5th	138	J.Logtenberg/C.van der Westhuizen	SA v E	Shenley	2003
6th	229	J.M.Fields/R.L.Haynes	A v E	Worcester	2009
7th	157	M.Raj/J.Goswami	I v E	Taunton	2002
8th	181	S.J.Griffiths/D.L.Wilson	A v NZ	Auckland	1989-90
9th	107	B.Botha/M.Payne	SA v NZ	Cape Town	1971-72
10th	119	S.Nitschke/C.R.Smith	A v E	Hove	2005

BOWLING RECORDS
50 WICKETS IN TESTS

Wkts		*Career*	*M*	*Balls*	*Runs*	*Avge*	*Best*	*5wI*	*10wM*
77	M.B.Duggan (E)	1949-63	17	3734	1039	13.49	7- 6	5	–
68	E.R.Wilson (A)	1948-58	11	2885	803	11.80	7- 7	4	2
63	D.F.Edulji (I)	1976-91	20	5098†	1624	25.77	6- 64	1	–
60	M.E.Maclagan (E)	1934-51	14	3432	935	15.58	7- 10	3	–
60	C.L.Fitzpatrick (A)	1991-2006	13	3603	1147	19.11	5- 29	2	–
60	S.Kulkarni (I)	1976-91	19	3320†	1647	27.45	6- 99	5	–
57	R.H.Thompson (A)	1972-85	16	4304	1040	18.24	5- 33	1	–
55	J.Lord (NZ)	1966-79	15	3108	1049	19.07	6-119	4	1
51	K.H.Brunt (E)	2004-22	14	2611	1098	21.52	6- 69	3	–
50	E.Bakewell (E)	1968-79	12	2697	831	16.62	7- 61	3	1

TEN WICKETS IN A TEST

13-226	Shaiza Khan	P v WI	Karachi	2003-04
11- 16	E.R.Wilson	A v E	Melbourne	1957-58
11- 63	J.M.Greenwood	E v WI	Canterbury	1979
11-107	L.C.Pearson	E v A	Sydney	2002-03
10- 65	E.R.Wilson	A v NZ	Wellington	1947-48
10- 75	E.Bakewell	E v WI	Birmingham	1979
10- 78	J.Goswami	I v E	Taunton	2006
10-107	K.Price	A v I	Lucknow	1983-84
10-118	D.A.Gordon	A v E	Melbourne	1968-69
10-137	J.Lord	NZ v A	Melbourne	1978-79

SEVEN WICKETS IN AN INNINGS

8-53	N.David	I v E	Jamshedpur	1995-96
7- 6	M.B.Duggan	E v A	Melbourne	1957-58
7- 7	E.R.Wilson	A v E	Melbourne	1957-58
7-10	M.E.Maclagan	E v A	Brisbane	1934-35
7-18	A.Palmer	A v E	Brisbane	1934-35
7-24	L.Johnston	A v NZ	Melbourne	1971-72
7-34	G.E.McConway	E v I	Worcester	1986
7-41	J.A.Burley	NZ v E	The Oval	1966
7-51	L.C.Pearson	E v A	Sydney	2002-03
7-59	Shaiza Khan	P v WI	Karachi	2003-04
7-61	E.Bakewell	E v WI	Birmingham	1979

HAT-TRICKS

E.R.Wilson	Australia v England	Melbourne	1957-58
Shaiza Khan	Pakistan v West Indies	Karachi	2003-04
R.M.Farrell	Australia v England	Sydney	2010-11

WICKET-KEEPING AND FIELDING RECORDS
25 DISMISSALS IN TESTS

Total			Tests	Ct	St	
58	C.Matthews	Australia	20	46	12	1984-95
43	J.Smit	England	21	39	4	1992-2006
36	S.A.Hodges	England	11	19	17	1969-79
28	B.A.Brentnall	New Zealand	10	16	12	1966-72

EIGHT DISMISSALS IN A TEST

9 (8ct, 1st)	C.Matthews	A v I	Adelaide	1990-91
8 (6ct, 2st)	L.Nye	E v NZ	New Plymouth	1991-92

SIX DISMISSALS IN AN INNINGS

8 (6ct, 2st)	L.Nye	E v NZ	New Plymouth	1991-92
6 (2ct, 4st)	B.A.Brentnall	NZ v SA	Johannesburg	1971-72
6 (6ct)	A.E.Jones	E v A	Canberra	2021-22

20 CATCHES IN THE FIELD IN TESTS

Total			Tests	
25	C.A.Hodges	England	18	1984-92
21	S.Shah	India	20	1976-91
20	L.A.Fullston	Australia	12	1984-87

APPEARANCE RECORDS
25 TEST MATCH APPEARANCES

27	J.A.Brittin	England	1979-98

12 MATCHES AS CAPTAIN

			Won	Lost	Drawn	
14	P.F.McKelvey	New Zealand	2	3	9	1966-79
12	R.Heyhoe-Flint	England	2	–	10	1966-76
12	S.Rangaswamy	India	1	2	9	1976-84

England Results Since April 2022

At County Ground, Taunton, 27-30 June. Toss: England. Result: **MATCH DRAWN**.
South Africa 284 (M.Kapp 150, K.L.Cross 4-63) and 181-5 (M.Kapp 43*). England 417-8d
(N.R.Sciver 169*, A.N.Davidson-Richards 107). England debuts: L.K.Bell,
A.N.Davidson-Richards, E.L.Lamb, I.E.C.M.Wong. Award: N.R.Sciver.

WOMEN'S LIMITED-OVERS RECORDS

1973 to 1 March 2023

RESULTS SUMMARY

	Matches	Won	Lost	Tied	No Result	% Won (exc NR)
Thailand	4	4	–	–	–	100.00
Australia	353	281	64	2	6	80.97
England	380	223	144	2	11	60.43
India	301	164	132	1	4	55.21
South Africa	227	118	94	5	10	54.37
New Zealand	370	182	178	2	8	50.27
West Indies	209	91	108	3	7	45.04
Sri Lanka	173	57	111	–	5	33.92
Trinidad & Tobago	6	2	4	–	–	33.33
Pakistan	194	57	133	1	3	29.84
Bangladesh	52	14	34	–	4	29.16
Ireland	162	45	111	–	6	28.84
Jamaica	5	1	4	–	–	20.00
Denmark	33	6	27	–	–	18.18
Netherlands	108	19	88	–	1	17.75
International XI	18	3	14	–	1	17.64
Young England	6	1	5	–	–	16.66
Scotland	8	1	7	–	–	12.50
Zimbabwe	8	1	7	–	–	12.50
Japan	5	–	5	–	–	0.00

TEAM RECORDS – HIGHEST INNINGS TOTALS

491-4	(50 overs)	New Zealand v Ireland	Dublin	2018
455-5	(50 overs)	New Zealand v Pakistan	Christchurch	1996-97
440-3	(50 overs)	New Zealand v Ireland	Dublin	2018
418	(49.5 overs)	New Zealand v Ireland	Dublin	2018
412-3	(50 overs)	Australia v Denmark	Mumbai	1997-98
397-4	(50 overs)	Australia v Pakistan	Melbourne	1996-97
378-5	(50 overs)	England v Pakistan	Worcester	2016

LARGEST RUNS MARGIN OF VICTORY

408 runs	New Zealand beat Pakistan	Christchurch	1996-97
374 runs	Australia beat Pakistan	Melbourne	1996-97

LOWEST INNINGS TOTALS

22	(23.4 overs)	Netherlands v West Indies	Deventer	2008
23	(24.1 overs)	Pakistan v Australia	Melbourne	1996-97
24	(21.3 overs)	Scotland v England	Reading	2001

BATTING RECORDS – 3300 RUNS IN A CAREER

Runs		Career	M	I	NO	HS	Avge	100	50
7805	M.Raj (I)	1999-2022	232	211	57	125*	50.68	7	64
5992	C.M.Edwards (E)	1997-2016	191	180	23	173*	38.16	9	46
5367	S.R.Taylor (WI)	2008-2022	148	143	21	171	43.99	7	38
5267	S.W.Bates (NZ)	2006-2022	148	142	15	168	41.47	12	31
4844	B.J.Clark (A)	1991-2005	118	114	12	229*	47.49	5	30
4814	K.L.Rolton (A)	1995-2009	141	132	32	154*	48.14	8	33
4639	A.E.Satterthwaite (NZ)	2007-2022	145	138	17	137*	38.33	7	27
4602	M.M.Lanning (A)	2011-2023	103	102	16	152*	53.51	15	21
4101	S.C.Taylor (E)	1998-2011	126	120	18	156*	40.20	8	23
4064	D.A.Hockley (NZ)	1982-2000	118	115	18	117	41.89	4	34
4056	S.J.Taylor (E)	2006-2019	126	119	13	147	38.26	7	20
3760	M.du Preez (SA)	2007-2022	154	141	27	116*	32.98	2	18
3727	D.J.S.Dottin (WI)	2008-2022	143	135	13	150*	30.54	3	22
3589	H.C.Knight (E)	2010-2022	129	124	25	106	36.25	2	24
3505	T.T.Beaumont (E)	2009-2022	103	95	9	168*	40.75	9	17
3492	A.J.Blackwell (A)	2003-2017	144	124	27	114	36.00	3	25
3386	E.A.Perry (A)	2007-2023	131	105	37	112*	49.79	2	29

Runs		Career	M	I	NO	HS	Avge	100	50
3330	S.F.M.Devine (NZ)	2006-2022	134	121	11	145	30.27	6	14
3322	H.Kaur (I)	2009-2022	124	105	18	171*	38.18	5	17
3315	L.Lee (SA)	2013-2022	100	99	8	132*	36.42	3	23

HIGHEST INDIVIDUAL INNINGS

232*	A.C.Kerr	New Zealand v Ireland	Dublin	2018
229*	B.J.Clark	Australia v Denmark	Mumbai	1997-98
188	D.B.Sharma	India v Ireland	Potchefstroom	2017
178*	A.C.Jayangani	Sri Lanka v Australia	Bristol	2017
176*	Sidra Ameen	Pakistan v Ireland	Lahore	2022-23
173*	C.M.Edwards	England v Ireland	Pune	1997-98
171*	H.Kaur	India v Australia	Derby	2017
171	S.R.Taylor	West Indies v Sri Lanka	Mumbai	2012-13
170	A.J.Healy	Australia v England	Christchurch	2021-22
168*	T.T.Beaumont	England v Pakistan	Taunton	2016
168	S.W.Bates	New Zealand v Pakistan	Sydney	2008-09
157	R.H.Priest	New Zealand v Sri Lanka	Lincoln	2015-16
156*	L.M.Keightley	Australia v Pakistan	Melbourne	1996-97
156*	S.C.Taylor	England v India	Lord's	2006
154*	K.L.Rolton	Australia v Sri Lanka	Christchurch	2000-01
153*	J.Logtenberg	South Africa v Netherlands	Deventer	2007
152*	M.M.Lanning	Australia v Sri Lanka	Bristol	2017
151	K.L.Rolton	Australia v Ireland	Dublin	2005
151	S.W.Bates	New Zealand v Ireland	Dublin	2018
150*	D.J.S.Dottin	West Indies v South Africa	Johannesburg	2021-22

HIGHEST PARTNERSHIP FOR EACH WICKET

1st	320	D.B.Sharma/P.G.Raut	India v Ireland	Potchefstroom	2017
2nd	295	A.C.Kerr/L.M.Kasperek	New Zealand v Ireland	Dublin	2018
3rd	244	K.L.Rolton/L.C.Sthalekar	Australia v Ireland	Dublin	2005
4th	224*	J.Logtenberg/M.du Preez	South Africa v Netherlands	Deventer	2007
5th	188*	S.C.Taylor/J.Cassar	England v Sri Lanka	Lincoln	2000-01
6th	142	S.Luus/C.L.Tryon	South Africa v Ireland	Dublin	2016
7th	122	S.Rana/P.Vastrakar	India v Pakistan	Mt Maunganui	2021-22
8th	88	N.N.D.de Silva/O.U.Ranasinghe	Sri Lanka v England	Hambantota	2018-19
9th	73	L.R.F.Askew/I.T.Guha	England v New Zealand	Chennai	2006-07
10th	76	A.J.Blackwell/K.M.Beams	Australia v India	Derby	2017

BOWLING RECORDS – 110 WICKETS IN A CAREER

		LOI	Balls	Runs	W	Avge	Best	4w	R/Over
J.Goswami (I)	2002-2022	204	10005	5622	255	22.04	6-31	9	3.37
S.Ismail (SA)	2007-2022	126	6170	3812	191	19.95	6-10	8	3.70
C.L.Fitzpatrick (A)	1993-2007	109	6017	3023	180	16.79	5-14	11	3.01
A.Mohammed (WI)	2003-2022	141	6252	3735	180	20.75	7-14	13	3.58
K.H.Sciver-Brunt (E)	2005-2022	141	6847	4081	170	24.00	5-18	8	3.57
E.A.Perry (A)	2007-2023	131	5590	4051	161	25.16	7-22	4	4.34
S.R.Taylor (WI)	2008-2022	145	5680	3343	153	21.84	4-17	5	3.53
Sana Mir (P)	2005-2019	120	5942	3665	151	24.27	5-32	8	3.70
M.Kapp (SA)	2009-2022	149	5748	3652	147	24.84	5-45	5	3.81
L.C.Sthalekar (A)	2001-2013	125	5964	3646	146	24.97	5-35	2	3.66
N.David (I)	1995-2008	97	4892	2305	141	16.34	5-20	6	2.82
D.van Niekerk (SA)	2009-2021	107	4578	2642	138	19.14	5-17	8	3.46
J.L.Gunn (E)	2004-2019	144	5906	3822	136	28.10	5-22	6	3.88
J.L.Jonassen (A)	2012-2023	88	4026	2638	135	19.54	5-27	8	3.93
L.A.Marsh (E)	2006-2019	103	5328	3463	129	26.84	5-15	4	3.89
H.A.S.D.Siriwardene (SL)	2003-2019	118	5449	3577	124	28.84	4-11	6	3.93
S.Luus (SA)	2012-2022	106	3297	2457	115	21.36	6-36	8	4.47
A.Khaka (SA)	2012-2022	87	4098	2828	113	25.02	5-26	3	4.14
M.Schutt (A)	2012-2023	79	3755	2625	112	23.43	4-18	5	4.19

SIX OR MORE WICKETS IN AN INNINGS

7-4	Sajjida Shah	Pakistan v Japan	Amsterdam	2003
7-8	J.M.Chamberlain	England v Denmark	Haarlem	1991

7-14	A.Mohammed	West Indies v Pakistan	Dhaka	2011-12
7-22	E.A.Perry	Australia v England	Canterbury	2019
7-24	S.Nitschke	Australia v England	Kidderminster	2005
6-10	J.Lord	New Zealand v India	Auckland	1981-82
6-10	M.Maben	India v Sri Lanka	Kandy	2003-04
6-10	S.Ismail	South Africa v Netherlands	Savar	2011-12
6-20	G.L.Page	New Zealand v Trinidad & T		1973
6-20	D.B.Sharma	India v Sri Lanka	Ranchi	2015-16
6-20	Khadija Tul Kubra	Bangladesh v Pakistan	Cox's Bazar	2018-19
6-31	J.Goswami	India v New Zealand	Southgate	2011
6-32	B.H.McNeill	New Zealand v England	Lincoln, NZ	2007-08
6-36	S.Luus	South Africa v Ireland	Dublin	2016
6-36	S.Ecclestone	England v South Africa	Christchurch	2021-22
6-45	S.Luus	South Africa v New Zealand	Hamilton	2019-20
6-46	A.Shrubsole	England v India	Lord's	2017
6-46	L.M.Kasperek	New Zealand v Australia	Mt Maunganui	2020-21

WICKET-KEEPING AND FIELDING RECORDS – 100 DISMISSALS IN A CAREER

Total			LOI	Ct	St
182	T.Chetty	South Africa	134	131	51
136	S.J.Taylor	England	126	85	51
133	R.J.Rolls	New Zealand	104	89	44
114	J.Smit	England	109	69	45
102	M.R.Aguillera	West Indies	112	76	26

SIX DISMISSALS IN AN INNINGS

6	(4ct, 2st)	S.L.Illingworth	New Zealand v Australia	Beckenham	1993
6	(1ct, 5st)	V.Kalpana	India v Denmark	Slough	1993
6	(2ct, 4st)	Batool Fatima	Pakistan v West Indies	Karachi	2003-04
6	(4ct, 2st)	Batool Fatima	Pakistan v Sri Lanka	Colombo (PSS)	2011

50 CATCHES IN THE FIELD IN A CAREER

Total			LOI	Career
80	S.W.Bates	New Zealand	148	2006-2022
69	J.Goswami	India	204	2002-2022
67	S.R.Taylor	West Indies	148	2008-2022
64	M.Raj	India	232	1999-2022
57	A.E.Satterthwaite	New Zealand	145	2007-2022
56	D.van Niekerk	South Africa	107	2009-2021
55	A.J.Blackwell	Australia	144	2003-2017
52	L.S.Greenway	England	126	2003-2016
52	C.M.Edwards	England	191	1997-2016
51	M.M.Lanning	Australia	103	2011-2023

FOUR CATCHES IN THE FIELD IN AN INNINGS

4	Z.J.Goss	Australia v New Zealand	Adelaide	1995-96
4	J.L.Gunn	England v New Zealand	Lincoln, NZ	2014-15
4	Nahida Khan	Pakistan v Sri Lanka	Dambulla	2017-18
4	A.C.Kerr	New Zealand v India	Queenstown	2021-22

APPEARANCE RECORDS – 150 APPEARANCES

232	M.Raj	India	1999-2022
204	J.Goswami	India	2002-2022
191	C.M.Edwards	England	1997-2016
154	M.du Preez	South Africa	2007-2022

100 CONSECUTIVE APPEARANCES

109	M.Raj	India	17.04.2004 to 07.02.2013
101	M.du Preez	South Africa	08.03.2009 to 05.02.2018

100 MATCHES AS CAPTAIN

			Won	Lost	No Result	
155	M.Raj	India	89	63	3	2004-2022
117	C.M.Edwards	England	72	38	7	2005-2016
101	B.J.Clark	Australia	83	17	1	1994-2005

WOMEN'S INTERNATIONAL TWENTY20 RECORDS

As for the men's IT20 records, in the section that follows, except for the first-ranked record and the highest partnerships, only those games featuring a nation that has also played a full LOI are listed.

MATCH RESULTS SUMMARY

	Matches	Won	Lost	Tied	NR	Win %
Zimbabwe	39	34	5	–	–	87.17
England	178	128	45	3	2	72.72
Australia	171	116	46	4	5	69.87
New Zealand	154	89	60	3	2	58.55
India	167	88	74	1	4	53.98
West Indies	159	77	73	6	3	49.35
South Africa	140	63	73	–	4	46.32
Pakistan	148	59	82	3	4	40.97
Bangladesh	96	37	59	–	–	38.54
Ireland	102	36	65	–	1	35.64
Sri Lanka	125	36	85	–	4	29.75

WOMEN'S INTERNATIONAL TWENTY20 RECORDS
TEAM RECORDS – HIGHEST INNINGS TOTALS † Batting Second

318-1	Bahrain v Saudi Arabia	Al Amerat	2021-22
255-2	Bangladesh v Maldives	Pokhara	2019-20
250-3	England v South Africa	Taunton	2018
226-3	Australia v England	Chelmsford	2019
226-2	Australia v Sri Lanka	Sydney (NS)	2019-20
217-4	Australia v Sri Lanka	Sydney (NS)	2019-20
216-1	New Zealand v South Africa	Taunton	2018
213-4	Ireland v Netherlands	Deventer	2019
213-5	England v Pakistan	Cape Town	2022-23
209-4	Australia v England	Mumbai (BS)	2017-18
205-1	South Africa v Netherlands	Potchefstroom	2010-11
205-3	Zimbabwe v Mozambique	Gaborone	2021
204-2	England v Sri Lanka	Colombo (PSS)	2018-19
199-3†	England v India	Mumbai (BS)	2017-18

LOWEST COMPLETED INNINGS TOTALS † Batting Second

6†	(12.1)	Maldives v Bangladesh	Pokhara	2019-20
6	(9.0)	Mali v Rwanda	Rwanda	2019
17	(9.2)	Eswatini v Zimbabwe	Gaborone	2021
24	(17.4)	France v Scotland	Cartagena	2021
24	(16.1)	France v Ireland	Cartagena	2021
27†	(13.4)	Malaysia v India	Kuala Lumpur	2018
30†	(18.4)	Malaysia v Pakistan	Kuala Lumpur	2018
30†	(12.5)	Bangladesh v Pakistan	Cox's Bazar	2018-19

The lowest score for England is 87 (v Australia, Hove, 2015).

BATTING RECORDS – 2400 RUNS IN A CAREER

Runs			M	I	NO	HS	Avge	50	R/100B
3820	S.W.Bates	NZ	143	140	11	124*	29.61	26	109.7
3405	M.M.Lanning	A	132	121	28	133*	36.61	17	116.3
3166	S.R.Taylor	WI	113	111	22	90	35.57	21	100.6†
3058	H.Kaur	I	151	136	27	103	28.05	11	106.3†
2969	S.F.M.Devine	NZ	119	116	14	105	29.10	18	121.2
2802	S.Mandhana	I	116	112	11	87	27.74	22	123.8
2697	D.J.S.Dottin	WI	127	125	20	112*	25.68	14	122.8†
2658	Bismah Maroof	P	132	126	28	70*	27.12	12	91.3
2605	C.M.Edwards	E	95	93	14	92*	32.97	12	106.9
2489	A.J.Healy	A	141	123	14	148*	24.40	15	126.9

† *No information on balls faced for games at Roseau on 22 and 23 February 2012.*

HIGHEST INDIVIDUAL INNINGS

Score	Balls				
161*	66	H.M.D.Rasangika	Bah v Saudi	Al Amerat	2021-22
148*	61	A.J.Healy	A v SL	Sydney (NS)	2019-20
133*	63	M.M.Lanning	A v E	Chelmsford	2019
126*	76	S.L.Kalis	Neth v Ger	Cartagena	2019
126	65	M.M.Lanning	A v Ire	Sylhet	2013-14
124*	66	S.W.Bates	NZ v SA	Taunton	2018
124	64	D.N.Wyatt	E v I	Mumbai (BS)	2017-18
117*	70	B.L.Mooney	A v E	Canberra	2017-18
116*	71	S.A.Fritz	SA v Neth	Potchefstroom	2010-11
116	52	T.T.Beaumont	E v SA	Taunton	2018

HIGHEST PARTNERSHIP FOR EACH WICKET

1st	182	S.W.Bates/S.F.M.Devine	NZ v SA	Taunton	2018
2nd	162*	H.K.Matthews/C.N.Nation	WI v Ire	Dublin	2019
3rd	236*	Nigar Sultana/Fargana Hoque	B v Mald	Pokhara	2019-20
4th	147*	K.L.Rolton/K.A.Blackwell	A v E	Taunton	2005
5th	129*	A.Gardner/G.M.Harris	A v I	Mumbai (BS)	2022-23
6th	84	M.A.A.Sanjeewani/N.N.de Silva	SL v P	Colombo (SSC)	2017-18
7th	75*	Salma Khatun/Ritu Moni	B v Ken	Kuala Lumpur	2021-22
8th	47*	A.Gardner/A.M.King	A v I	Birmingham	2022
9th	34	A.N.Kelly/C.Murray	Ire v B	Abu Dhabi	2022-23
10th	37*	P.Vastrakar/R.S.Gayakwad	I v A	Carrara	2021-22

BOWLING RECORDS – 100 WICKETS IN A CAREER

Wkts			Matches	Overs	Mdns	Runs	Avge	Best	R/Over
126	Nida Dar	P	130	418.2	10	2291	18.18	5-21	5.47
125	A.Mohammed	WI	117	395.3	6	2206	17.64	5-10	5.57
124	M.Schutt	A	96	321.3	7	1998	16.11	5-15	6.21
123	S.Ismail	SA	113	396.5	21	2291	18.62	5-12	5.77
122	E.A.Perry	A	139	396.5	8	2324	19.04	4-12	5.85
114	K.H.Sciver-Brunt	E	112	392.1	17	2188	19.19	4-15	5.57
110	S.F.M.Devine	NZ	119	302.3	6	1920	17.45	4-22	6.34
102	A.Shrubsole	E	79	266.2	10	1587	15.55	5-11	5.95
102	D.B.Sharma	I	92	321.4	11	1985	19.46	4-10	6.17

BEST FIGURES IN AN INNINGS

7- 3	F.Overdijk	Neth v Fra	Cartagena	2021
7- 3	A.Stocks	Arg v Peru	Seropedica	2022-23
6-11	E.Mbofana	Z v Eswatini	Gaborone	2021
6-17	A.E.Satterthwaite	NZ v E	Taunton	2007
5- 3	M.McColl	Scot v France	Cartagena	2021
5- 5	D.J.S.Dottin	WI v B	Providence	2018-19
5- 6	L.Phiri	Z v Bot	Gaborone	2021
5- 8	S.Luus	SA v Ire	Chennai	2015-16
5-10	A.Mohammed	WI v SA	Cape Town	2009-10
5-10	M.Strano	A v NZ	Geelong	2016-17
5-11	A.Shrubsole	E v NZ	Wellington	2011-12
5-11	J.Goswami	I v A	Visakhapatnam	2011-12

HAT-TRICKS

Asmavia Iqbal	Pakistan v England	Loughborough	2012
Ekta Bisht	Sri Lanka v India	Colombo (NCC)	2012-13
M.Kapp	South Africa v Bangladesh	Potchefstroom	2013-14
N.R.Sciver	England v New Zealand	Bridgetown	2013-14
Sana Mir	Pakistan v Sri Lanka	Sharjah	2014-15
A.M.Peterson	New Zealand v Australia	Geelong	2016-17
M.Schutt	Australia v India	Mumbai (BS)	2017-18

Fahima Khatun	Bangladesh v UAE	Utrecht		2018
A.Mohammed	West Indies v South Africa	Tarouba		2018-19
A.Shrubsole	England v South Africa	Gros Islet		2018-19
O.Kamchomphu	Thailand v Ireland	Deventer		2019
S.R.Taylor	West Indies v Pakistan	North Sound		2021
Fariha Trisna	Bangladesh v Malaysia	Sylhet		2022-23
H.Graham	Australia v India	Mumbai		2022-23

WICKET-KEEPING RECORDS – 60 DISMISSALS IN A CAREER

Dis			Matches	Ct	St
109	A.J.Healy	Australia	141	51	58
74	S.J.Taylor	England	90	23	51
72	R.H.Priest	New Zealand	75	41	31
70	T.Chetty	South Africa	82	42	28
70	M.R.Aguilleira	West Indies	95	36	34
68	T.Bhatia	India	53	23	45
62	M.V.Waldron	Ireland	88	34	28

FIVE DISMISSALS IN AN INNINGS

5 (1ct, 4st)	K.A.Knight	West Indies v Sri Lanka	Colombo (RPS)	2012-13
5 (1ct, 4st)	Batool Fatima	Pakistan v Ireland	Dublin	2013
5 (1ct, 4st)	Batool Fatima	Pakistan v Ireland	Dublin	2013
5 (3ct, 2st)	B.Bezuidenhout	New Zealand v Ireland	Dublin	2018
5 (1ct, 4st)	S.J.Bryce	Scotland v Netherlands	Arbroath	2019

FIELDING RECORDS – 40 CATCHES IN A CAREER

Total			Matches	Total			Matches
80	S.W.Bates	New Zealand	143	54	L.S.Greenway	England	85
58	J.L.Gunn	England	104	45	M.M.Lanning	Australia	132
56	N.R.Sciver-Brunt	England	108	41	E.A.Perry	Australia	139
55	H.Kaur	India	151	40	S.F.M.Devine	New Zealand	119

FOUR CATCHES IN AN INNINGS

4	L.S.Greenway	England v New Zealand	Chelmsford	2010
4	V.Krishnamurthy	India v Australia	Providence	2018-19
4	R.M.A.M.Avery	Brazil v Canada	Naucalpan	2021-22
4	J.E.Ronalds	Germany v Botswana	Rwanda	2022
4	S.W.Bates	New Zealand v West Indies	North Sound	2022-23
4	T.Brits	South Africa v England	Cape Town	2022-23

APPEARANCE RECORDS – 120 APPEARANCES

151	H.Kaur	India		132	Bismah Maharoof	Pakistan
143	S.W.Bates	New Zealand		132	M.M.Lanning	Australia
143	D.N.Wyatt	England		130	Nida Dar	Pakistan
141	A.J.Healy	Australia		127	D.J.S.Dottin	West Indies
139	E.A.Perry	Australia				

65 MATCHES AS CAPTAIN

			W	L	T	NR	%age wins
100	M.M.Lanning	Australia	76	18	1	5	80.00
96	H.Kaur	India	54	37	1	4	58.69
93	C.M.Edwards	England	68	23	1	1	73.91
73	M.R.Aguilleira	West Indies	39	29	3	2	54.92
65	H.C.Knight	England	49	14	1	1	76.56
65	Salma Khatun	Bangladesh	27	38	–	–	41.53
65	Sana Mir	Pakistan	26	36	2	1	40.62

THE WOMEN'S HUNDRED 2022

The Women's Hundred was launched in 2021, featuring eight franchise sides in matches of 100 balls per side, with all games played alongside the men's version. The second- and third-placed sides played off for a place in the final, held at Lord's.

		P	W	L	T	NR	Pts	Net RR
1.	Oval Invincibles (2)	6	5	1	–	–	10	+1.09
2.	Southern Brave (1)	6	5	1	–	–	10	+0.80
3.	Trent Rockets (7)	6	3	3	–	–	6	+0.10
4.	Birmingham Phoenix (3)	6	3	3	–	–	6	–0.03
5.	Northern Superchargers (6)	6	3	3	–	–	6	–0.11
6.	Manchester Originals (5)	6	2	4	–	–	4	–0.47
7.	London Spirit (4)	6	2	4	–	–	4	–0.55
8.	Welsh Fire (8)	6	1	5	–	–	2	–0.68

Eliminator: At The Rose Bowl, Southampton, 2 September. Toss: Trent Rockets. **SOUTHERN BRAVE** won by 2 runs. Southern Brave 134-6 (100 balls; G.L.Adams 38, T.M.McGrath 31). Trent Rockets 132-7 (100 balls; N.R.Sciver 72*). Award: T.M.McGrath.

FINAL: At Lord's, 3 September. Toss: Southern Brave. **OVAL INVINCIBLES** won by five wickets. Southern Brave 101-7 (100 balls). Oval Invincibles 105-5 (94 balls; M.Kapp 37*). Award: M.Kapp. Series award: N.R.Sciver (Rockets).

LEADING AGGREGATES AND RECORDS 2022

BATTING (225 runs)	M	I	NO	HS	Runs	Avge	100	50	R/100b	Sixes
L.Wolvaardt (Superchargers)	6	6	2	90*	286	71.50	–	2	133.6	4
S.W.Bates (Invincibles)	7	7	1	79*	232	38.66	–	1	146.8	6
N.R.Sciver (Rockets)	6	6	3	72*	228	76.00	–	2	122.5	5

BOWLING (10 wkts)	Balls	R	W	Avge	BB	4w	R/100b
A.Wellington (Brave)	160	201	17	11.82	3-17	–	125.6
L.K.Bell (Brave)	155	176	11	16.00	4-10	1	113.5

Highest total	163-2	Invincibles v Originals	Manchester
Biggest win (runs)	43	Rockets (119-5) beat Originals (76)	Manchester
Biggest win (balls)	44	Brave (94-0) beat Rockets (88-8)	Southampton
Highest innings	97*	B.L.Mooney	Spirit v Brave	Southampton
Most sixes	8	D.J.S.Dottin (Originals)	
Highest partnership	110	T.T.Beaumont/H.K.Matthews	Fire v Originals	Manchester
Best bowling	4-10	L.K.Bell	Brave v Rockets	Southampton
Most economical	20b-8-0	A.M.King	Rockets v Invincibles	Nottingham
	20b-8-3	S.Ecclestone	Originals v Phoenix	Birmingham
Most expensive	20b-40-1	H.K.Matthews	Fire v Originals	Manchester
	20b-39-1	G.A.Elwiss	Phoenix v Superchargers	Birmingham
Most w/k dismissals	6	L.Winfield-Hill (Invincibles)	
Most catches	6	E.A.Perry (Phoenix)	
Most catches (inns)	3	S.Mandhana	Brave v Originals	Southampton
	3	H.Graham	Superchargers v Brave	Leeds
	3	E.A.Russell	Superchargers v Brave	Leeds

PRINCIPAL WOMEN'S FIXTURES 2023

F   Floodlit match
100   The Hundred
TM   LV= Insurance Test Match
IT20   Vitality International Twenty20

RHF   Rachael Heyhoe Flint Trophy (50 overs)
CEC   Charlotte Edwards Cup (Twenty20)
LOI   Limited-Overs International

Sat 22 April
RHF	Nottingham	Blaze v Sparks
RHF	Leeds	Diamonds v Storm
RHF	Southampton	Vipers v Sunrisers
RHF	Manchester	Thunder v SE Stars

Sat 29 April
RHF	Worcester	Sparks v Diamonds
RHF	Beckenham	SE Stars v Vipers
RHF	Cardiff	Storm v Thunder
RHF	Chelmsford	Sunrisers v Blaze

Mon 1 May
RHF	Mansfield	Blaze v Thunder
RHF	Wormsley	Sparks v Vipers
RHF	Chelmsford	Sunrisers v Diamonds
RHF	Bristol	Storm v SE Stars

Fri 5 May
| RHF | Radlett | Sunrisers v SE Stars |

Sat 6 May
RHF	Chester-le-St	Diamonds v Blaze
RHF	Hove	Vipers v Storm
RHF	Manchester	Thunder v Sparks

Wed 10 May
RHF	Leicester	Blaze v Storm
RHF	Scarborough	Diamonds v SE Stars
RHF	Hove	Vipers v Sparks
RHF	Sale	Thunder v Sunrisers

Thu 18 May
| CEC^F | Chelmsford | Sunrisers v Sparks |

Fri 19 May
| CEC | Leeds | Diamonds v Storm |

Sat 20 May
| CEC | Beckenham | SE Stars v Blaze |

Sun 21 May
| CEC | Taunton | Storm v Thunder |

Tue 23 May
| CEC | Birmingham | Sparks v Diamonds |
| CEC | Newbury | Vipers v SE Stars |

Thu 25 May
| CEC | Lord's | Sunrisers v SE Stars |
| CEC | Manchester | Thunder v Blaze |

Fri 26 May
CEC	Leicester	Blaze v Sparks
CEC	The Oval	SE Stars v Diamonds
CEC	Southampton	Vipers v Storm

Sat 27 May
| CEC | Manchester | Thunder v Sunrisers |

Sun 28 May
| CEC | Leeds | Diamonds v Sunrisers |
| CEC | Taunton | Storm v SE Stars |

Mon 29 May
| CEC | Derby | Blaze v Vipers |
| CEC | Worcester | Sparks v Thunder |

Wed 31 May
| CEC | Southampton | Vipers v Thunder |
| CEC | Northampton | Sunrisers v Storm |

Fri 2 June
| CEC | Chester-le-St | Diamonds v Blaze |

Sat 3 June
| CEC | Birmingham | Sparks v Vipers |

Sun 4 June
CEC	Nottingham	Blaze v Sunrisers
CEC	Leeds	Diamonds v Vipers
CEC	Blackpool	Thunder v SE Stars
CEC	Bristol	Storm v Sparks

Wed 7 June
CEC	Canterbury	SE Stars v Sparks
CEC	Hove	Vipers v Sunrisers
CEC	Blackpool	Thunder v Diamonds
CEC	Cardiff	Storm v Blaze

Sat 10 June
| CEC | Worcester | Semi-final and FINAL |

Thu 15 – Sat 17 June

	Derby	England v Australia A
	Leicester	England A v Australia

Thu 22 – Mon 26 June

TM	Nottingham	**ENGLAND v AUSTRALIA**

Sat 1 July

IT20[F]	Birmingham	**England v Australia**

Sun 2 July

RHF	Worcester	Sparks v Thunder
RHF	Beckenham	SE Stars v Diamonds
RHF	Chelmsford	Sunrisers v Vipers
RHF	Bristol	Storm v Blaze

Wed 5 July

IT20[F]	The Oval	**England v Australia**

Fri 7 July

RHF	Chesterfield	Blaze v Diamonds
RHF	Guildford	SE Stars v Sparks
RHF	Southport	Thunder v Vipers

Sat 8 July

IT20[F]	Lord's	**England v Australia**

Tue 11 July

RHF	Moseley	Sparks v Storm
RHF	York	Diamonds v Thunder
RHF	Beckenham	SE Stars v Sunrisers
RHF	Newclose, IoW	Vipers v Blaze

Wed 12 July

LOI[F]	Bristol	**England v Australia**

Sat 15 July

RHF	Leeds	Diamonds v Sparks
RHF	Northampton	Sunrisers v Thunder
RHF	tbc	Storm v Vipers

Sun 16 July

LOI	Southampton	**England v Australia**

Mon 17 July

RHF	Mansfield	Blaze v SE Stars

Tue 18 July

LOI[F]	Taunton	**England v Australia**

Sat 22 July

RHF	Worcester	Sparks v Sunrisers
RHF	Beckenham	SE Stars v Storm
RHF	Arundel	Vipers v Diamonds
RHF	Sedbergh	Thunder v Blaze

Mon 24 July

RHF	Cheltenham	Storm v Sunrisers

Tue 1 August

100	Nottingham	Rockets v Brave

Wed 2 August

100	Lord's	Spirit v Invincibles
100	Cardiff	Fire v Originals

Thu 3 August

100	Leeds	Superchargers v Phoenix

Fri 4 August

100	Southampton	Brave v Fire

Sat 5 August

100	Birmingham	Phoenix v Rockets
100	Manchester	Originals v Spirit

Sun 6 August

100	The Oval	Invincibles v Fire
100	Southampton	Brave v Superchargers

Mon 7 August

100	Manchester	Originals v Phoenix

Tue 8 August

100	Lord's	Spirit v Brave

Wed 9 August

100	The Oval	Invincibles v Originals
100	Nottingham	Rockets v Superchargers

Thu 10 August

100	Birmingham	Phoenix v Fire

Fri 11 August

100	Leeds	Superchargers v Invincibles

Sat 12 August

100	Lord's	Spirit v Rockets
100	Cardiff	Fire v Brave

Sun 13 August

100	Birmingham	Phoenix v Invincibles
100	Leeds	Superchargers v Originals

Mon 14 August

100	Cardiff	Fire v Rockets

Tue 15 August

100	The Oval	Invincibles v Spirit

Wed 16 August

100	Southampton	Brave v Phoenix

Thu 17 August
100   Nottingham   Rockets v Originals

Fri 18 August
100   Lord's   Spirit v Superchargers

Sat 19 August
100   Southampton   Brave v Invincibles
100   Nottingham   Rockets v Phoenix

Sun 20 August
100   Manchester   Originals v Superchargers
100   Cardiff   Fire v Spirit

Mon 21 August
100   The Oval   Invincibles v Rockets

Tue 22 August
100   Leeds   Superchargers v Fire

Wed 23 August
100   Manchester   Originals v Brave

Thu 24 August
100   Birmingham   Phoenix v Spirit

Sat 26 August
100   The Oval   Eliminator

Sun 27 August
100   Lord's   FINAL

Sat 2 September
IT20   Chelmsford   **England v Sri Lanka**

Tue 5 September
RHF   Birmingham   Sparks v Blaze
RHF   Gosforth   Diamonds v Vipers
RHF   Guildford   SE Stars v Thunder
RHF   Radlett   Sunrisers v Storm

Wed 6 September
IT20[F]   Derby   **England v Sri Lanka**

Sat 9 September
IT20   Chester-le-St   **England v Sri Lanka**
RHF   Arundel   Vipers v Thunder

Sun 10 September
RHF   Beckenham   SE Stars v Blaze
RHF   Hove   Sunrisers v Sparks
RHF   Taunton   Storm v Diamonds

Wed 13 September
RHF   Mansfield   Blaze v Sunrisers
RHF   Southampton   Vipers v SE Stars
RHF   Sale   Thunder v Diamonds
RHF   Taunton   Storm v Sparks

Thu 14 September
LOI[F]   Leicester   **England v Sri Lanka**

Sat 16 September
RHF   Loughborough   Blaze v Vipers
RHF   Birmingham   Sparks v SE Stars
RHF   Chester-le-St   Diamonds v Sunrisers
RHF   Manchester   Thunder v Storm

Sun 17 September
LOI   Hove   **England v Sri Lanka**

Tue 19 September
LOI[F]   Leicester   **England v Sri Lanka**

Thu 21 September
RHF   tbc   Play-off

Sun 24 September
RHF   Northampton   FINAL

NATIONAL COUNTIES FIXTURES 2023

Sun 16 April   **TWENTY20 COMPETITION**
Sale	Cheshire v Northumberland (1)
Moddershall & Oulton	Staffordshire v Cumbria (1)
Sherborne S	Dorset v Herefordshire (2)
South Wilts	Wiltshire v Devon (2)
Wisbech	Cambridgeshire v Hertfordshire (3)
Bourne	Lincolnshire v Norfolk (3)
Falkland	Berkshire v Wales NC (4)
Wormsley	Oxfordshire v Buckinghamshire (4)

Sun 23 April   **TWENTY20 COMPETITION**
S Northumberland	Northumberland v Staffordshire (1)
Shifnal	Shropshire v Cheshire (1)
Wadebridge	Cornwall v Wiltshire (2)
Exmouth	Devon v Dorset (2)
Hitchin	Hertfordshire v Lincolnshire (3)
Ipswich S	Suffolk v Cambridgeshire (3)
Dunstable	Bedfordshire v Oxfordshire (4)
High Wycombe	Buckinghamshire v Berkshire (4)

Sun 30 April   **TWENTY20 COMPETITION**
Barrow	Cumbria v Northumberland (1)
Leek	Staffordshire v Shropshire (1)
Sandford	Devon v Herefordshire (2)
Milton Abbey S	Dorset v Cornwall (2)
Woodhall Spa	Lincolnshire v Suffolk (3)
Horsford, Manor P	Norfolk v Hertfordshire (3)
Wargrave	Berkshire v Bedfordshire (4)
Lisvane	Wales NC v Buckinghamshire (4)

Mon 1 May   **TWENTY20 COMPETITION**
Nantwich	Cheshire v Staffordshire (1)
Wem	Shropshire v Cumbria (1)
Werrington	Cornwall v Herefordshire (2)
tbc	Wiltshire v Dorset (2)
March Town	Cambridgeshire v Lincolnshire (3)
Ipswich S	Suffolk v Norfolk (3)
Ampthill Town	Bedfordshire v Wales NC (4)
Thame	Oxfordshire v Berkshire (4)

Sun 7 May   **TWENTY20 COMPETITION**
Netherfield	Cumbria v Cheshire (1)
S Northumberland	Northumberland v Shropshire (1)
Cornwood	Devon v Cornwall (2)
Eastnor	Herefordshire v Wiltshire (2)
Welwyn Garden City	Hertfordshire v Suffolk (3)
Horsford, Manor P	Norfolk v Cambridgeshire (3)
High Wycombe	Buckinghamshire v Bedfordshire (4)
Pontarddulais	Wales NC v Oxfordshire (4)

Sun 21 May   **TWENTY20 COMPETITION**
Tring Park	Finals Day (22 May Reserve Day)

Sun 28 May   **NCCA TROPHY**
Horsford, Manor P	Norfolk v Cheshire (3)
Sudbury	Suffolk v Shropshire (3)
Port Talbot	Wales NC v Staffordshire (4)

Mon 29 May   **NCCA TROPHY**
Brockhampton	Herefordshire v Cumbria (1)
Scunthorpe	Lincolnshire v Northumberland (1)
Henley	Berkshire v Hertfordshire (2)
Truro	Cornwall v Devon (2)
Mildenhall	Suffolk v Cheshire (3)

Marlborough C	Wiltshire v Buckinghamshire (4)

Sun 4 June	**NCCA TROPHY**
Cockermouth	Cumbria v Oxfordshire (1)
Jesmond	Northumberland v Herefordshire (1)
Exeter	Devon v Berkshire (2)
West Herts	Hertfordshire v Bedfordshire (2)
Didsbury	Cheshire v Cambridgeshire (3)
Horsford, Manor P	Norfolk v Suffolk (3)
Gerrards Cross	Buckinghamshire v Dorset (4)
Smethwick	Staffordshire v Wiltshire (4)

Sun 11 June	**NCCA TROPHY**
Brockhampton	Herefordshire v Lincolnshire (1)
Banbury	Oxfordshire v Northumberland (1)
Luton Town & I	Bedfordshire v Devon (2)
Slough	Berkshire v Cornwall (2)
Burwell & Exning	Cambridgeshire v Suffolk (3)
Oswestry	Shropshire v Norfolk (3)
Bashley (Rydal)	Dorset v Staffordshire (4)
Warminster	Wiltshire v Wales NC (4)

Sun 18 June	**NCCA TROPHY**
Bracebridge Heath	Lincolnshire v Oxfordshire (1)
Allendale	Northumberland v Cumbria (1)
Redruth	Cornwall v Bedfordshire (2)
North Devon	Devon v Hertfordshire (2)
St Georges	Shropshire v Cambridgeshire (3)
Porthill Park	Staffordshire v Buckinghamshire (4)
Panteg	Wales NC v Dorset (4)

Sun 25 June	**NCCA TROPHY**
Keswick	Cumbria v Lincolnshire (1)
tbc	Oxfordshire v Herefordshire (1)
Southill Park	Bedfordshire v Berkshire (2)
North Mymms	Hertfordshire v Cornwall (2)
Burwell & Exning	Cambridgeshire v Norfolk (3)
Toft	Cheshire v Shropshire (3)
Slough	Buckinghamshire v Wales NC (4)
Dorchester	Dorset v Wiltshire (4)

Sun 2 July	**NCCA TROPHY**
Match A	Winners Gp 1 v Runners-up Gp 3
Match B	Winners Gp 3 v Runners-up Gp 1
Match C	Winners Gp 2 v Runners-up Gp 4
Match D	Winners Gp 4 v Runners-up Gp 2

Sun 9 – Tue 11 July	**CHAMPIONSHIP**
Tring Park	Buckinghamshire v Norfolk (E1)
Bury St Edmunds	Suffolk v Staffordshire (E1)
Furness	Cumbria v Bedfordshire (E2)
Tynemouth	Northumberland v Cambridgeshire (E2)
Falkland	Berkshire v Devon (W1)
Eastnor	Herefordshire v Oxfordshire (W1)
Truro	Cornwall v Dorset (W2)
Brymbo	Wales NC v Shropshire (W2)

Sun 16 July	**NCCA TROPHY**
Semi-final	Winners Match B v Winners Match A
Semi-final	Winners Match C v Winners Match D
	(17 July Reserve Day)

Sun 23 – Tue 25 July	**CHAMPIONSHIP**
Sleaford	Lincolnshire v Suffolk (E1)
West Brom, Dartmouth	Staffordshire v Buckinghamshire (E1)
Bedford S	Bedfordshire v Northumberland (E2)
Bishop's Stortford	Hertfordshire v Cumbria (E2)

Alderley Edge	Cheshire v Herefordshire (W1)
Thame	Oxfordshire v Berkshire (W1)
Bridgnorth	Shropshire v Cornwall (W2)
Corsham	Wiltshire v Wales NC (W2)

Sun 30 July — **SHOWCASE GAMES**

tbc	Bedfordshire v Essex
tbc	Berkshire v Middlesex
tbc	Cambridgeshire v Northamptonshire
tbc	Cheshire v Yorkshire
Sedbergh	Cumbria v Lancashire
tbc	Devon v Somerset
tbc	Dorset v Hampshire
Cheltenham	Gloucestershire v Wiltshire
tbc	Herefordshire v Glamorgan
West Herts	Hertfordshire v Kent
tbc	Lincolnshire v Derbyshire
tbc	Norfolk v Nottinghamshire
tbc	Northumberland v Durham
tbc	Oxfordshire v Sussex
tbc	Shropshire v Worcestershire
Knypersley	Staffordshire v Leicestershire
tbc	Suffolk v Surrey
tbc	Wales NC v Warwickshire

Tue 1 August — **SHOWCASE GAMES**

| tbc | Cornwall v Somerset |
| Hove | Sussex v Buckinghamshire |

Sun 6 – Tue 8 August — **CHAMPIONSHIP**

Chesham	Buckinghamshire v Lincolnshire (E1)
Horsford, Manor P	Norfolk v Staffordshire (E1)
Saffron Walden	Cambridgeshire v Bedfordshire (E2)
Jesmond	Northumberland Hertfordshire (E2)
Finchampstead	Berkshire v Cheshire (W1)
Exeter	Devon v Oxfordshire (W1)
St Austell	Cornwall v Wiltshire (W2)
Wimborne	Dorset v Shropshire (W2)

Sun 13 – Tue 15 August — **CHAMPIONSHIP**

Horsford, Manor P	Norfolk v Suffolk (E1)
Checkley	Staffordshire v Lincolnshire (E1)
Carlisle	Cumbria v Northumberland (E2)
Hertford	Hertfordshire v Cambridgeshire (E2)
Chester, Boughton H	Cheshire v Devon (W1)
Eastnor	Herefordshire v Berkshire (W1)
Abergavenny	Wales NC v Cornwall (W2)
South Wilts	Wiltshire v Dorset (W2)

Sun 20 – Tue 22 August — **CHAMPIONSHIP**

Cleethorpes	Lincolnshire v Norfolk (E1)
Copdock & OI	Suffolk v Buckinghamshire (E1)
Flitwick	Bedfordshire v Hertfordshire (E2)
Peterborough	Cambridgeshire v Cumbria (E2)
Sidmouth	Devon v Herefordshire (W1)
Banbury	Oxfordshire v Cheshire (W1)
Wimborne	Dorset v Wales NC (W2)
Whitchurch	Shropshire v Wiltshire (W2)

Sun 27 August — **NCCA TROPHY**

| Wormsley | Final (28 Aug Reserve Day) |

Sun 3 – Wed 6 September — **CHAMPIONSHIP**

| West Brom, Dartmouth | Final |

Sun 29 May — **NCCA TROPHY**

| Eastnor | Herefordshire v Oxfordshire (1) |

Scunthorpe	Lincolnshire v Cumbria (1)
Bedford School	Bedfordshire v Hertfordshire (2)
Henley	Berkshire v Devon (2)
Exning	Cambridgeshire v Cheshire (3)
Mildenhall	Suffolk v Norfolk (3)
Port Talbot	Wales NC v Buckinghamshire (4)
Marlborough College	Wiltshire v Dorset (4)

Sun 5 June   NCCA TROPHY

Cockermouth	Cumbria v Herefordshire (1)
Allendale	Northumberland v Lincolnshire (1)
Truro	Cornwall v Berkshire (2)
Exeter	Devon v Bedfordshire (2)
Manor Park	Norfolk v Cambridgeshire (3)
Oswestry	Shropshire v Suffolk (3)
High Wycombe	Buckinghamshire v Wiltshire (4)
Himley	Staffordshire v Wales NC (4)

Sun 12 June   NCCA TROPHY

Brockhampton	Herefordshire v Northumberland (1)
Banbury	Oxfordshire v Cumbria (1)
Southill Park	Bedfordshire v Cornwall (2)
Hertford	Hertfordshire v Devon (2)
Exning	Cambridgeshire v Shropshire (3)
Chester Boughton	Cheshire v Norfolk (3)
Dorchester	Dorset v Buckinghamshire (4)
Warminster	Wiltshire v Staffordshire (4)

Sun 19 June   NCCA TROPHY

Bracebridge Heath	Lincolnshire v Herefordshire (1)
Jesmond	Northumberland v Oxfordshire (1)
Wargrave	Berkshire v Bedfordshire (2)
Redruth	Cornwall v Hertfordshire (2)
Wem	Shropshire v Cheshire (3)
Sudbury	Suffolk v Cambridgeshire (3)
Dartmouth, West Brom	Staffordshire v Dorset (4)
Llandysul	Wales NC v Wiltshire (4)

Sun 26 June   NCCA TROPHY

Keswick	Cumbria v Northumberland (1)
Aston Rowant	Oxfordshire v Lincolnshire (1)
Sidmouth	Devon v Cornwall (2)
North Mymms	Hertfordshire v Berkshire (2)
Didsbury	Cheshire v Suffolk (3)
Manor Park	Norfolk v Shropshire (3)
Gerrards Cross	Buckinghamshire v Staffordshire (4)
Wimborne	Dorset v Wales NC (4)

Sun 3 – Tue 5 July   CHAMPIONSHIP

Dunstable Town	Bedfordshire v Staffordshire (E1)
Bury St Edmunds	Suffolk v Lincolnshire (E1)
March	Cambridgeshire v Hertfordshire (E2)
Tynemouth	Northumberland v Cumbria (E2)
Alderley Edge	Cheshire v Oxfordshire (W1)
Eastnor	Herefordshire v Dorset (W1)
Abergavenny	Wales NC v Devon (W2)
Corsham	Wiltshire v Shropshire (W2)

Sun 10 – Tue 12 July   CHAMPIONSHIP

Cleethorpes	Lincolnshire v Staffordshire (E1)
Woolpit	Suffolk v Norfolk (E1)
Barrow	Cumbria v Cambridgeshire (E2)
Bishop's Stortford	Hertfordshire v Buckinghamshire (E2)
Wimborne	Dorset v Berkshire (W1)
Thame	Oxfordshire v Herefordshire (W1)
Sandford	Devon v Cornwall (W2)

Oswestry	Shropshire v Wales NC (W2)
Sun 17 July	**NCCA TROPHY**
	Quarter-finals Day
Sun 24 – Tue 26 July	**CHAMPIONSHIP**
Grantham	Lincolnshire v Bedfordshire (E1)
Longton	Staffordshire v Norfolk (E1)
Chesham	Buckinghamshire v Cumbria (E2)
Peterborough	Cambridgeshire v Northumberland (E2)
Finchampstead	Berkshire v Oxfordshire (W1)
Brockhampton	Herefordshire v Cheshire (W1)
St Austell	Cornwall v Shropshire (W2)
Usk	Wales NC v Wiltshire (W2)
Sun 31 July	**SHOWCASE GAMES**
tbc	Bedfordshire v Northamptonshire
tbc	Berkshire v Middlesex
High Wycombe	Buckinghamshire v Surrey
Saffron Walden	Cambridgeshire v Essex
Chester Boughton	Cheshire v Warwickshire
Truro	Cornwall v Somerset
Sedbergh School	Cumbria v Lancashire
tbc	Dorset v Hampshire
Eastnor	Herefordshire v Worcestershire
Grantham	Lincolnshire v Durham
Manor Park	Norfolk v Nottinghamshire
S.Northumberland	Northumberland v Yorkshire
tbc	Oxfordshire v Sussex
tbc	Shropshire v Derbyshire
tbc	Staffordshire v Leicestershire
Woolpit	Suffolk v Kent
Cardiff	Wales NC v Glamorgan
tbc	Wiltshire v Gloucestershire
Tue 2 August	**SHOWCASE GAMES**
Bovey Tracey	Devon v Somerset
tbc	Hertfordshire v Middlesex
Sun 7 August	**NCCA TROPHY**
	Semi-finals Day (Reserve day 8 August)
Sun 14 – Tue 16 August	**CHAMPIONSHIP**
Manor Park	Norfolk v Bedfordshire (E1)
Checkley	Staffordshire v Suffolk (E1)
Furness	Cumbria v Hertfordshire (E2)
Jesmond	Northumberland v Buckinghamshire (E2)
Nantwich	Cheshire v Berkshire (W1)
Banbury	Oxfordshire v Dorset (W1)
Bridgnorth	Shropshire v Devon (W2)
South Wilts	Wiltshire v Cornwall (W2)
Sun 21 – Tue 23 August	**CHAMPIONSHIP**
Flitwick	Bedfordshire v Suffolk (E1)
Manor Park	Norfolk v Lincolnshire (E1)
Tring Park	Buckinghamshire v Cambridgeshire (E2)
Hertford	Hertfordshire v Northumberland (E2)
Falkland	Berkshire v Herefordshire (W1)
Wimborne	Dorset v Cheshire (W1)
Truro	Cornwall v Wales NC (W2)
Sidmouth	Devon v Wiltshire (W2)
Sun 28 August	**NCCA TROPHY**
Wormsley	Trophy Final Day (Reserve day 29 August)
Sun 4 – Wed 7 September	**CHAMPIONSHIP**
Dartmouth, West Brom	Final

SECOND XI CHAMPIONSHIP FIXTURES 2023

FOUR-DAY MATCHES

APRIL

Mon 10	Billericay	Essex v Warwicks
	Radlett	Middlesex v Derbyshire
	Taunton Vale	Somerset v Glos
	Bradford PA	Yorkshire v Worcs
Tue 11	Southport	Lancashire v Leics
	Blackstone	Sussex v Kent
Mon 17	Billericay	Essex v Durham
	Newport	Glamorgan v Northants
	Southampton	Hampshire v Sussex
	Beckenham	Kent v Surrey
	Kibworth	Leics v Yorkshire
	Notts SC	Notts v Derbyshire
	Birm EFSG	Warwicks v Somerset
	Kidderminster	Worcs v Lancashire
Mon 24	Polo Farm, Cant	Kent v Essex
	Crosby	Lancashire v Glamorgan
	Radlett	Middlesex v Sussex
Tue 25	Guildford	Surrey v Warwicks
	Leeds (tbc)	Yorkshire v Notts

MAY

Mon 1	Repton S	Derbyshire v Worcs
	Kibworth	Leics v Durham
	tbc	Northants v Somerset
	York	Yorkshire v Lancashire
Tue 2	Polo Farm, Cant	Kent v Hampshire
Mon 8	Chesterfield	Derbyshire v Lancashire
	Horsham	Sussex v Essex
	Kidderminster	Worcs v Warwicks
Tue 9	Bristol	Glos v Surrey
	Southampton	Hampshire v Middlesex
	Notts SC	Notts v Leics
	Taunton Vale	Somerset v Glamorgan

JUNE

Mon 12	Rockhampton	Glos v Northants
Mon 19	Durham	Durham v Notts
	Polo Farm, Cant	Kent v Leics
	Chester BH	Lancashire v Essex
	Radlett	Middlesex v Somerset
	tbc	Northants v Yorkshire
	Stourport	Worcs v Glos
	tbc	Yorkshire v Northants
Tue 20	Abergavenny	Glamorgan v Sussex
	New Malden	Surrey v Hampshire
Mon 26	Billericay	Essex v Middlesex
	Notts SC	Notts v Lancashire
	Leeds, Weet (tbc)	Yorkshire v Derbyshire

JULY

Mon 3	tbc	Durham v Lancashire
	Colchester	Essex v Hampshire
	Newport	Glamorgan v Warwicks
	Rockhampton	Glos v Kent
	Kibworth	Leics v Notts
	tbc	Northants v Worcs
	Taunton Vale	Somerset v Sussex
Tue 4	New Malden	Surrey v Middlesex
Mon 10	Belper Mead	Derbyshire v Notts
	Crosby	Lancashire v Worcs
	Horsham	Sussex v Surrey
Tue 11	Scarborough	Yorkshire v Durham
Mon 17	Billericay	Essex v Surrey
	Bristol	Glos v Yorkshire
	Birm EFSG	Warwicks v Northants
	Worcester	Worcs v Glamorgan
Tue 18	Southampton	Hampshire v Somerset
	Teddington	Middlesex v Kent
Mon 24	Northampton	Northants v Leics

AUGUST

Mon 21	Milton Keynes	Northants v Glamorgan
Mon 28	Panteg	Glamorgan v Hampshire
	Bristol CC	Glos v Warwicks
	Loughborough T	Leics v Derbyshire

SEPTEMBER

Mon 4	Billericay	Essex v Kent
	Rockhampton	Glos v Glamorgan
	Southport	Lancashire v Yorkshire
	Peterborough	Northants v Sussex
	Taunton Vale	Somerset v Surrey
	Birm EFSG	Warwicks v Durham
	tbc	Worcs v Notts
Mon 11	S N'humberland	Durham v Derbyshire
	Northwood	Middlesex v Essex
	Notts SC	Notts v Northants
	Taunton Vale	Somerset v Worcs
	Blackstone	Sussex v Glamorgan
	Birm EFSG	Warwicks v Lancashire
	Guildford	Surrey v Yorkshire
Tue 12	Southampton	Hampshire v Leics
Mon 18	Blackpool	Lancashire v Kent
	Birm EFSG	Warwicks v Notts

SECOND XI TWENTY20 CUP FIXTURES 2023

MAY

Mon 15	Chester-le-St	Durham v Leics (x 2)
	Hove	Sussex v Surrey
Tue 16	Derby	Derbyshire v Notts (x 2)
	Polo Farm, Cant	Kent v Sussex (x 2)
	Birm EFSG	Warwicks v Glos
Wed 17	New Malden	Surrey v Essex
	Birm EFSG	Warwicks v Northants (x 2)
	Leeds, Weet (tbc)	Yorkshire v Leics (x 2)
Thu 18	Newport	Glamorgan v Glos
	Polo Farm, Cant	Kent v Essex
	Manchester	Lancashire v Derbyshire (x 2)
	tbc	Notts v Durham (x 2)
Fri 19	Taunton Vale	Somerset v Glos
	New Malden	Surrey v Sussex
Mon 22	Chester-le-St	Durham v Yorkshire (x 2)
	Southampton	Hampshire v Kent (x 2)
	Leicester	Leics v Derbyshire
	Richmond	Middlesex v Surrey
	Taunton Vale	Somerset v Warwicks
	Kidderminster	Worcs v Northants (x 2)
Tue 23	Chelmsford	Essex v Kent
	Newport	Glamorgan v Northants
	Bristol	Glos v Warwicks
	Westhoughton	Lancashire v Notts (x 2)
	Richmond	Middlesex v Sussex
Wed 24	Derby	Derbyshire v Leics
	Newport	Glamorgan v Somerset
	Southampton	Hampshire v Surrey
	Horsham	Sussex v Essex
	Barnt Green	Worcs v Warwicks
Thu 25	Southampton	Hampshire v Middlesex
	Barnt Green	Worcs v Somerset
	tbc	Yorkshire v Lancashire
Fri 26	Southend	Essex v Surrey
	Polo Farm, Cant	Kent v Middlesex
	Birm EFSG	Warwicks v Glamorgan
Mon 29	Southampton	Hampshire v Essex
	Taunton Vale	Somerset v Worcs
Tue 30	Cardiff	Glamorgan v Worcs
	Leicester	Leics v Notts
	Horsham	Sussex v Middlesex
	Taunton Vale	Somerset v Northants (x 2)
	New Malden	Surrey v Kent
	Sheffield ASC	Yorkshire v Derbyshire
Wed 31	Chester-le-St	Durham v Lancashire (x 2)
	Southend	Essex v Sussex
	Newport	Glamorgan v Warwicks
	Cheltenham	Glos v Worcs (x 2)
	Enfield	Middlesex v Kent

JUNE

Tue 1	Southend	Essex v Middlesex
	Cheltenham	Glos v Northants (x 2)
	Polo Farm, Cant	Kent v Surrey
	Mansfield	Notts v Leics
	Taunton Vale	Somerset v Glamorgan
Fri 2	Southampton	Hampshire v Sussex
	Worksop C	Notts v Yorkshire (x 2)
Mon 5	Southend	Essex v Hampshire
	Stowe S	Northants v Glamorgan
	New Malden	Surrey v Middlesex
Tue 6	Belper Mead	Derbyshire v Durham (x 2)
	Rockhampton	Glos v Somerset
	Ramsbottom	Lancashire v Yorkshire
	Horsham	Sussex v Hampshire
	Worcester	Worcs v Glamorgan
Wed 7	Birm EFSG	Warwicks v Worcs
Thu 8	Duffield	Derbyshire v Yorkshire
	Rockhampton	Glos v Glamorgan
	tbc	Lancashire v Leics (x 2)
	Hornsey	Middlesex v Essex
	New Malden	Surrey v Hampshire
	Birm EFSG	Warwicks v Somerset
Fri 9	Hornsey	Middlesex v Hampshire
Thu 15	Wormsley	Semi-finals and FINAL

THE HUNDRED FIXTURES 2023

Tue 1 August
100^F Nottingham   Rockets v Brave

Wed 2 August
100^F Lord's   Spirit v Invincibles
100   Cardiff   Fire v Originals

Thu 3 August
100^F Leeds   Superchargers v Phoenix

Fri 4 August
100^F Southampton   Brave v Fire

Sat 5 August
100^F Birmingham   Phoenix v Rockets
100   Manchester   Originals v Spirit

Sun 6 August
100^F The Oval   Invincibles v Fire
100   Southampton   Brave v Superchargers

Mon 7 August
100^F Manchester   Originals v Phoenix

Tue 8 August
100^F Lord's   Spirit v Brave

Wed 9 August
100^F The Oval   Invincibles v Originals
100   Nottingham   Rockets v Superchargers

Thu 10 August
100^F Birmingham   Phoenix v Fire

Fri 11 August
100^F Leeds   Superchargers v Invincibles

Sat 12 August
100   Lord's   Spirit v Rockets
100^F Cardiff   Fire v Brave

Sun 13 August
100^F Birmingham   Phoenix v Invincibles
100   Leeds   Superchargers v Originals

Mon 14 August
100^F Cardiff   Fire v Rockets

Tue 15 August
100^F The Oval   Invincibles v Spirit

Wed 16 August
100^F Southampton   Brave v Phoenix

Thu 17 August
100^F Nottingham   Rockets v Originals

Fri 18 August
100^F Lord's   Spirit v Superchargers

Sat 19 August
100^F Southampton   Brave v Invincibles
100   Nottingham   Rockets v Phoenix

Sun 20 August
100   Manchester   Originals v Superchargers
100^F Cardiff   Fire v Spirit

Mon 21 August
100^F The Oval   Invincibles v Rockets

Tue 22 August
100^F Leeds   Superchargers v Fire

Wed 23 August
100^F Manchester   Originals v Brave

Thu 24 August
100^F Birmingham   Phoenix v Spirit

Sat 26 August
100^F The Oval   Eliminator

Sun 27 August
100^F Lord's   FINAL

PRINCIPAL FIXTURES 2023

CC1	LV= Insurance County Championship Division 1
CC2	LV= Insurance County Championship Division 2
F	Floodlit
FCF	First-Class Friendly

LOI	Limited-Overs International
ODC	One-Day Cup
T20	Vitality Blast
[T20]	Friendly Twenty20 Match
IT20	Vitality Twenty20 International
TM	LV= Insurance Test Match

Thu 6 – Sun 9 April

CC1	Southampton	Hampshire v Notts
CC1	Canterbury	Kent v Northants
CC1	Manchester	Lancashire v Surrey
CC1	Lord's	Middlesex v Essex
CC1	Taunton	Somerset v Warwicks
CC2	Derby	Derbyshire v Worcs
CC2	Cardiff	Glamorgan v Glos
CC2	Hove	Sussex v Durham
CC2	Leeds	Yorkshire v Leics

Thu 13 – Sun 16 April

CC1	Chelmsford	Essex v Lancashire
CC1	Northampton	Northants v Middlesex
CC1	Nottingham	Notts v Somerset
CC1	The Oval	Surrey v Hampshire
CC1	Birmingham	Warwicks v Kent
CC2	Chester-le-St	Durham v Worcs
CC2	Bristol	Glos v Yorkshire
CC2	Leicester	Leics v Derbyshire

Thu 20 – Sun 23 April

CC1	Canterbury	Kent v Essex
CC1	Lord's	Middlesex v Notts
CC1	Northampton	Northants v Hampshire
CC1	Taunton	Somerset v Lancashire
CC2	Cardiff	Glamorgan v Durham
CC2	Hove	Sussex v Yorkshire
CC2	Worcester	Worcs v Glos

Thu 27 – Sun 30 April

CC1	Lord's	Middlesex v Kent
CC1	Birmingham	Warwicks v Surrey
CC2	Chester-le-St	Durham v Derbyshire
CC2	Bristol	Glos v Sussex
CC2	Leicester	Leics v Glamorgan

Thu 4 – Sun 7 May

CC1	Chelmsford	Essex v Surrey
CC1	Southampton	Hampshire v Warwicks
CC1	Nottingham	Notts v Lancashire
CC1	Taunton	Somerset v Northants
CC2	Derby	Derbyshire v Leics
CC2	Worcester	Worcs v Sussex
CC2	Leeds	Yorkshire v Glamorgan

Thu 11 – Sun 14 May

CC1	Canterbury	Kent v Hampshire
CC1	Manchester	Lancashire v Somerset
CC1	Northampton	Northants v Notts
CC1	The Oval	Surrey v Middlesex
CC1	Birmingham	Warwicks v Essex
CC2	Derby	Derbyshire v Glos
CC2	Chester-le-St	Durham v Yorkshire
CC2	Cardiff	Glamorgan v Worcs
CC2	Leicester	Leics v Sussex

Thu 18 – Sun 21 May

CC1	Southampton	Hampshire v Northants
CC1	Lord's	Middlesex v Somerset
CC1	Nottingham	Notts v Essex
CC1	The Oval	Surrey v Kent
CC2	Bristol	Glos v Durham
CC2	Hove	Sussex v Glamorgan
CC2	Worcester	Worcs v Leics

Sat 20 May

T20	Birmingham	Derbyshire v Lancashire
T20F	Birmingham	Warwicks v Yorkshire

Wed 24 May

T20F	Canterbury	Kent v Glos
T20F	Northampton	Northants v Worcs
T20F	Taunton	Somerset v Hampshire

Thu 25 May

T20	Manchester	Lancashire v Leics
T20F	Lord's	Middlesex v Surrey

Fri 26 – Sun 28 May

FCF	Chelmsford	Essex v Ireland

Fri 26 May

T20F	Bristol	Glos v Glamorgan
T20F	Southampton	Hampshire v Middlesex
T20F	Leicester	Leics v Warwicks
T20F	Northampton	Northants v Durham
T20F	Nottingham	Notts v Derbyshire
T20F	The Oval	Surrey v Kent
T20F	Hove	Sussex v Somerset
T20	Worcester	Worcs v Yorkshire

Sat 27 May

T20^F	Manchester	Lancashire v Notts

Sun 28 May

T20	Taunton	Somerset v Glamorgan
T20	The Oval	Surrey v Sussex
T20	Leeds	Yorkshire v Durham

Mon 29 May

T20	Derby	Derbyshire v Northants
T20	Chester-le-St	Durham v Notts
T20	Northwood	Middlesex v Glos
T20	Birmingham	Warwicks v Lancashire
T20	Worcester	Worcs v Leics

Tue 30 May

T20^F	Chelmsford	Essex v Glos
T20^F	Canterbury	Kent v Somerset
T20^F	Nottingham	Notts v Yorkshire

Wed 31 May

T20^F	Southampton	Hampshire v Surrey
T20	Northwood	Middlesex v Glamorgan
T20^F	Northampton	Northants v Warwicks

Thu 1 – Sun 4 June

TM	Lord's	ENGLAND v IRELAND

Thu 1 June

T20^F	Leicester	Leics v Derbyshire
T20^F	Hove	Sussex v Essex
T20^F	Leeds	Yorkshire v Lancashire

Fri 2 June

T20^F	Derby	Derbyshire v Warwicks
T20^F	Chester-le-St	Durham v Lancashire
T20^F	Chelmsford	Essex v Hampshire
T20^F	Cardiff	Glamorgan v Kent
T20^F	Bristol	Glos v Surrey
T20^F	Northampton	Northants v Leics
T20^F	Nottingham	Notts v Worcs
T20^F	Taunton	Somerset v Middlesex

Sat 3 June

T20^F	Southampton	Hampshire v Sussex
T20	Birmingham	Warwicks v Notts

Sun 4 June

T20	Chester-le-St	Durham v Leics
T20	Bristol	Glos v Middlesex
T20	Canterbury	Kent v Surrey
T20	Nottingham	Notts v Lancashire
T20	Taunton	Somerset v Essex
T20	Hove	Sussex v Glamorgan
T20	Worcester	Worcs v Northants
T20	Leeds	Yorkshire v Derbyshire

Tue 6 June

T20^F	Chester-le-St	Durham v Northants

Wed 7 – Sun 11 June

TM	The Oval	AUSTRALIA v INDIA

Reserve day on Monday 12 June.

Wed 7 June

T20^F	Cardiff	Glamorgan v Surrey
T20^F	Southampton	Hampshire v Somerset
T20^F	Canterbury	Kent v Essex
T20	Blackpool	Lancashire v Worcs
T20^F	Birmingham	Warwicks v Derbyshire

Thu 8 June

T20^F	Lord's	Middlesex v Sussex
T20^F	Nottingham	Notts v Durham

Fri 9 June

T20^F	Derby	Derbyshire v Notts
T20^F	Cardiff	Glamorgan v Essex
T20^F	Bristol	Glos v Somerset
T20^F	Canterbury	Kent v Hampshire
T20^F	Leicester	Leics v Durham
T20^F	Hove	Sussex v Surrey
T20^F	Birmingham	Warwicks v Northants
T20^F	Leeds	Yorkshire v Worcs

Sun 11 – Wed 14 June

CC1	Chelmsford	Essex v Somerset
CC1	Canterbury	Kent v Surrey
CC1	Southport	Lancashire v Hampshire
CC1	Nottingham	Notts v Warwicks
CC2	Chesterfield	Derbyshire v Yorkshire
CC2	Chester-le-St	Durham v Glamorgan
CC2	Bristol	Glos v Leics
CC2	Hove	Sussex v Worcs

Fri 16 – Tue 20 June

TM1	Birmingham	ENGLAND v AUSTRALIA

Fri 16 June

T20^F	Chester-le-St	Durham v Derbyshire
T20^F	Chelmsford	Essex v Glamorgan
T20^F	Lord's	Middlesex v Kent
T20^F	Northampton	Northants v Lancashire
T20^F	Taunton	Somerset v Surrey
T20^F	Hove	Sussex v Hampshire
T20	Worcester	Worcs v Warwicks
T20^F	Leeds	Yorkshire v Leics

Sat 17 June

T20^F	Bristol	Glos v Kent

Sun 18 June

T20	Chesterfield	Derbyshire v Yorkshire
T20	Cardiff	Glamorgan v Glos

T20	Manchester	Lancashire v Durham
T20	Leicester	Leics v Worcs
T20	Lord's	Middlesex v Essex
T20	Northampton	Northants v Notts
T20	The Oval	Surrey v Hampshire

Mon 19 June

| T20^F | Chelmsford | Essex v Somerset |

Tue 20 June

T20^F	Chester-le-St	Durham v Warwicks
T20^F	Bristol	Glos v Hampshire
T20^F	Leicester	Leics v Notts
T20^F	The Oval	Surrey v Glamorgan
T20^F	Hove	Sussex v Kent
T20^F	Worcester	Worcs v Lancashire
T20^F	Leeds	Yorkshire v Northants

Wed 21 June

| T20^F | Cardiff | Glamorgan v Somerset |
| T20^F | Northampton | Northants v Derbyshire |

Thu 22 June

T20^F	Chelmsford	Essex v Kent
T20^F	Bristol	Glos v Sussex
T20^F	The Oval	Surrey v Middlesex
T20	Worcester	Worcs v Notts
T20^F	Leeds	Yorkshire v Warwicks

Fri 23 June

T20^F	Chester-le-St	Durham v Yorkshire
T20^F	Cardiff	Glamorgan v Sussex
T20^F	Southampton	Hampshire v Essex
T20^F	Canterbury	Kent v Middlesex
T20^F	Manchester	Lancashire v Derbyshire
T20^F	Leicester	Leics v Northants
T20^F	Taunton	Somerset v Glos
T20^F	Birmingham	Warwicks v Worcs

Sun 25 – Wed 28 June

CC1	Chelmsford	Essex v Warwicks
CC1	Southampton	Hampshire v Middlesex
CC1	Northampton	Northants v Kent
CC1	Taunton	Somerset v Notts
CC1	The Oval	Surrey v Lancashire
CC2	Cardiff	Glamorgan v Sussex
CC2	Leicester	Leics v Durham
CC2	Worcester	Worcs v Derbyshire
CC2	Leeds	Yorkshire v Glos

Wed 28 June – Sun 2 July

| TM2 | Lord's | ENGLAND v AUSTRALIA |

Fri 30 June

T20^F	Derby	Derbyshire v Leics
T20^F	Chelmsford	Essex v Middlesex
T20^F	Southampton	Hampshire v Glamorgan
T20^F	Canterbury	Kent v Sussex

T20^F	Manchester	Lancashire v Yorkshire
T20^F	Nottingham	Notts v Warwicks
T20^F	The Oval	Surrey v Somerset
T20	Worcester	Worcs v Durham

Sat 1 July

| T20 | Hove | Sussex v Glos |

Sun 2 July

T20^F	Derby	Derbyshire v Worcs
T20^F	Cardiff	Glamorgan v Middlesex
T20^F	Southampton	Hampshire v Glos
T20^F	Manchester	Lancashire v Northants
T20^F	Nottingham	Notts v Leics
T20^F	Taunton	Somerset v Kent
T20^F	The Oval	Surrey v Essex
T20^F	Birmingham	Warwicks v Durham

Thu 6 – Mon 10 July

| TM3 | Leeds | ENGLAND v AUSTRALIA |

Thu 6 July

| T20^F | tbc | Quarter-finals 1 & 2 |

Fri 7 July

| T20^F | tbc | Quarter-finals 3 & 4 |

Mon 10 – Thu 13 July

CC1	Canterbury	Kent v Warwicks
CC1	Blackpool	Lancashire v Essex
CC1	Northwood	Middlesex v Northants
CC1	Taunton	Somerset v Hampshire
CC1	The Oval	Surrey v Notts
CC2	Chester-le-St	Durham v Glos
CC2	Cardiff (tbc)	Glamorgan v Leics
CC2	Hove	Sussex v Derbyshire
CC2	Worcester	Worcs v Yorkshire

Sat 15 July

| T20^F | Birmingham | Semi-finals and FINAL |

Wed 19 – Sun 23 July

| TM4 | Manchester | ENGLAND v AUSTRALIA |

Wed 19 – Sat 22 July

CC1	Chelmsford	Essex v Kent
CC1	Lord's	Middlesex v Surrey
CC1	Northampton	Northants v Somerset
CC1	Nottingham	Notts v Hampshire
CC1	Birmingham	Warwicks v Lancashire
CC2	Derby	Derbyshire v Durham
CC2	Oakham S	Leics v Worcs
CC2	Leeds	Yorkshire v Sussex

Thu 20 – Sun 23 July

| CC2 | Cheltenham | Glos v Glamorgan |

Tue 25 – Fri 28 July

| CC1 | Southampton | Hampshire v Essex |

CC1	Manchester	Lancashire v Northants
CC1	Nottingham	Notts v Kent
CC1	Taunton	Somerset v Surrey
CC1	Birmingham	Warwicks v Middlesex
CC2	Derby	Derbyshire v Glamorgan
CC2	Scarborough	Yorkshire v Durham

Wed 26 – Sat 29 July

| CC2 | Cheltenham | Glos v Worcs |

Thu 27 – Mon 31 July

| TM5 | The Oval | ENGLAND v AUSTRALIA |

Tue 1 August

ODC	Chester-le-St	Durham v Worcs
ODC	Cheltenham	Glos v Derbyshire
ODC	Southampton	Hampshire v Middlesex
ODC	Sedbergh	Lancashire v Essex
ODC	Scarborough	Yorkshire v Kent

Thu 3 August

ODC	Chelmsford	Essex v Notts
ODC	The Oval	Surrey v Leics
ODC	Scarborough	Yorkshire v Lancashire

Fri 4 August

ODC	Cheltenham	Glos v Northants
ODCᶠ	Taunton	Somerset v Warwicks
ODC	Hove	Sussex v Durham
ODC	Worcester	Worcs v Glamorgan

Sat 5 August

| ODC | Radlett | Middlesex v Surrey |
| ODC | Nottingham | Notts v Yorkshire |

Sun 6 August

ODC	Derby	Derbyshire v Glamorgan
ODC	Beckenham	Kent v Leics
ODC	Northampton	Northants v Sussex
ODC	Taunton	Somerset v Worcs

Mon 7 August

| ODC | Birmingham | Warwicks v Glos |

Tue 8 August

ODC	tbc	Glamorgan v Durham
ODC	Southampton	Hampshire v Essex
ODC	Leicester	Leics v Notts

Wed 9 August

ODC	Derby	Derbyshire v Sussex
ODC	Blackpool	Lancashire v Kent
ODC	Northampton	Northants v Somerset

Thu 10 August

| ODC | tbc | Glamorgan v Warwicks |
| ODC | Worcester | Worcs v Glos |

Fri 11 August

ODC	Chester-le-St	Durham v Derbyshire
ODCᶠ	Chelmsford	Essex v Middlesex
ODCᶠ	Manchester	Lancashire v Leics
ODC	Mansfield	Notts v Hampshire
ODC	Taunton	Somerset v Sussex
ODC	The Oval	Surrey v Kent

Sun 13 August

ODC	Chester-le-St	Durham v Northants
ODC	Chelmsford	Essex v Yorkshire
ODC	Bristol	Glos v Somerset
ODC	Southampton	Hampshire v Leics
ODC	Beckenham	Kent v Middlesex
ODC	Mansfield	Notts v Surrey
ODC	Hove	Sussex v Glamorgan
ODC	Worcester	Worcs v Warwicks

Tue 15 August

ODC	Manchester	Lancashire v Hampshire
ODC	Leicester	Leics v Essex
ODC	Radlett	Middlesex v Notts
ODC	Birmingham	Warwicks v Derbyshire
ODC	York	Yorkshire v Surrey

Wed 16 August

| ODC | Cardiff | Glamorgan v Glos |
| ODC | Northampton | Northants v Worcs |

Thu 17 August

ODC	Gosforth	Durham v Somerset
ODC	Canterbury	Kent v Notts
ODC	Guildford	Surrey v Lancashire
ODC	York	Yorkshire v Hampshire

Fri 18 August

ODC	Derby	Derbyshire v Worcs
ODC	Leicester	Leics v Middlesex
ODC	Hove	Sussex v Glos
ODC	Birmingham	Warwicks v Northants

Sun 20 August

ODC	Canterbury	Kent v Essex
ODC	Leicester	Leics v Yorkshire
ODC	Lord's	Middlesex v Lancashire
ODC	Northampton	Northants v Derbyshire
ODC	Taunton	Somerset v Glamorgan
ODC	Guildford	Surrey v Hampshire
ODC	Birmingham	Warwicks v Durham
ODC	Worcester	Worcs v Sussex

Tue 22 August

ODC	Derby	Derbyshire v Somerset
ODC	Chelmsford	Essex v Surrey
ODC	Cardiff	Glamorgan v Northants
ODC	Bristol	Glos v Durham
ODC	Newclose, IoW	Hampshire v Kent

ODC	Radlett	Middlesex v Yorkshire
ODC	Mansfield	Notts v Lancashire
ODC	Hove	Sussex v Warwicks

Fri 25 August

| ODC | tbc | Quarter-finals 1 & 2 |
| [T20] | Worcester | Worcs v New Zealanders |

Sun 27 August

| [T20]F | Bristol | Glos v New Zealanders |

Tue 29 August

| ODC | tbc | Semi-finals 1 & 2 |

Wed 30 August

| IT20F | Chester-le-St | England v New Zealand |

Fri 1 September

| IT20F | Manchester | England v New Zealand |

Sun 3 – Wed 6 September

CC1	Southampton	Hampshire v Somerset
CC1	Northampton	Northants v Lancashire
CC1	The Oval	Surrey v Warwicks
CC2	Chester-le-St	Durham v Sussex
CC2	Leicester	Leics v Glos
CC2	Worcester	Worcs v Glamorgan
CC2	Scarborough	Yorkshire v Derbyshire

Sun 3 September

| IT20 | Birmingham | England v New Zealand |

Mon 4 – Thu 7 September

| CC1 | Chelmsford | Essex v Middlesex |

Tue 5 September

| IT20F | Nottingham | England v New Zealand |

Fri 8 September

| LOIF | Cardiff | England v New Zealand |

Sun 10 – Wed 13 September

CC1	Canterbury	Kent v Notts
CC1	Manchester	Lancashire v Middlesex
CC1	Birmingham	Warwicks v Northants
CC2	Cardiff	Glamorgan v Yorkshire

| CC2 | Bristol | Glos v Derbyshire |
| CC2 | Hove | Sussex v Leics |

Sun 10 September

| LOI | Southampton | England v New Zealand |

Wed 13 September

| LOIF | The Oval | England v New Zealand |

Fri 15 September

| LOIF | Lord's | England v New Zealand |

Sat 16 September

| ODC | Nottingham | FINAL |

Tue 19 – Fri 22 September

CC1	Chelmsford	Essex v Hampshire
CC1	Manchester	Lancashire v Notts
CC1	Lord's	Middlesex v Warwicks
CC1	Taunton	Somerset v Kent
CC1	The Oval	Surrey v Northants
CC2	Derby	Derbyshire v Sussex
CC2	Leicester	Leics v Yorkshire
CC2	Worcester	Worcs v Durham

Wed 20 September

| LOIF | Leeds | England v Ireland |

Sat 23 September

| LOI | Nottingham | England v Ireland |

Tue 26 – Fri 29 September

CC1	Southampton	Hampshire v Surrey
CC1	Canterbury	Kent v Lancashire
CC1	Northampton	Northants v Essex
CC1	Nottingham	Notts v Middlesex
CC1	Birmingham	Warwicks v Somerset
CC2	Chester-le-St	Durham v Leics
CC2	Cardiff	Glamorgan v Derbyshire
CC2	Hove	Sussex v Glos
CC2	Leeds	Yorkshire v Worcs

Tue 26 September

| LOIF | Bristol | England v Ireland |

First published in 2023

by HEADLINE PUBLISHING GROUP

Front cover photograph ©Albert Perez/Getty Images

Back cover photo © Matthew Lewis/Getty Images

Spine image © Peter Dazeley/Alamy Stock Photo

1

Cataloguing in Publication Data is available from the British Library

ISBN: 978 1 4722 9088 5

Typeset in Times by
Letterpart Limited, Caterham on the Hill, Surrey

Printed and bound in Great Britain by
Clays Ltd St Ives plc

HEADLINE PUBLISHING GROUP

An Hachette UK Company
Carmelite House
50 Victoria Embankment
London EC4Y ODZ

www.headline.co.uk
www.hachette.co.uk